CHILDREN

DEVELOPMENT AND SOCIAL ISSUES

CHILDREN

DEVELOPMENT AND SOCIAL ISSUES

EDWARD F. ZIGLER
Yale University

MATIA FINN-STEVENSON
Yale University

D. C. HEATH AND COMPANY
Lexington, Massachusetts Toronto

for
Beatrice
and for
Ima

Acquisitions Editor   James Miller
Cover and Text Design   Sally Thompson Steele
Developmental and Production Editor   John A. Servideo
Photograph Research   Mary Stuart Lang

Cover illustration   Edward Henry Potthast, *A Holiday,*
30½″ × 40½″, oil on canvas, c.1915, Friends of American Art
Collection, Courtesy the Art Institute of Chicago.
Frontispiece   © Ray Ellis, 1986

Published simultaneously in Canada.

Printed in the United States of America.

International Standard Book Number: 0-669-07754-2

Library of Congress Catalog Card Number: 86-82189

BRIEF CONTENTS

PREFACE

In writing this book, our aim has been to provide a scientific and up-to-date picture of child development from the prenatal period through adolescence. At the same time, we examine how children and adults actually live, we study the current social conditions that influence their lives, and we demonstrate the practical applications of child development research and its relevance to the lives of children and their families.

We have sought to write clearly and thus enable the reader to acquire an appreciation for and a sensitivity to the developmental capabilities and needs of children at different ages. We try to communicate the sense of excitement that exists among child development researchers and specialists in the field by presenting what has been learned from the research and also by noting the questions now being asked and explaining some of the research techniques being used in the quest for answers. As well as conveying the new knowledge and viewpoints, we also emphasize the continuing importance of some of the classic studies that have been conducted, and we describe them so that readers can gain insight into the history of the discipline and how it has evolved over the years.

As we wrote each chapter, we faced the challenge of combining presentations of both the basic research in child development and its applications, without emphasizing one at the expense of the other. We believe that we achieved a balance by providing a comprehensive and rigorous view of the theoretical framework and research on physical, cognitive, social, and emotional development.

The study of child development has reached an exciting period in its relatively short existence. New discoveries and new controversies are emerging, providing us with yet more insights into the development of children. The discipline has undergone major transformations in the last decade. Many common assumptions about the developmental capabilities of children are being challenged, and new questions and issues that were not previously considered are now under investigation. For example, one of the most significant aspects of this new direction is the increased recognition among child development specialists that human existence, at any period of life, occurs not in isolation, but within a social context. Accordingly, researchers now emphasize that the study of children must include an appreciation of the family setting within which children live and knowledge of the dynamics that govern family relationships.

In each chapter we have integrated discussions of social issues with the scientific information provided. We focus on a number of questions that reflect the realities governing the lives of children and adults today. What are the effects of out-of-home day care on children? What are some of the possible causes of and solutions to teenage pregnancy and suicide? Can anything be done about the high rate of infant mortality in the United States? What are the benefits and disadvantages of new medical techniques that enable physicians to screen and prevent genetic diseases? By integrating these discussions with a reporting of the research, we hope to encourage readers to think critically about the conditions of children's lives and about policies that have been and can be developed for their benefit.

Many of the topics we cover are not value-free. However, we believe that as authors of a textbook, we have a special obligation to remain objective and refrain from advocating one or another point of view. Although we may not have succeeded in remaining neutral in all instances, we have tried to describe all sides of an issue and to discuss the studies that support them.

To the Student

Each of you has enrolled in a course on child development for a different reason, but you share an interest in—or perhaps even a fascination for—children. An understanding of children may not be new to you. No doubt you have vivid memories of your own childhood. You may have lived or worked with children at one time or another, and you may have had the opportunity to observe children and arrive at some understanding of their competencies and limitations at different ages. Eventually, many of you will be parents. In this book, we build upon your personal knowledge of children. We explain to you how children change as they develop and we examine some of the internal and external forces that influence their growth and development.

In presenting the material, we have kept your interests in mind by providing you with an understanding of the research and its implications, by clearly explaining the scientific terms, and by avoiding jargon whenever possible. As you read the text, you will find that we have attempted to provide a realistic picture of children. We highlight not only the many exciting aspects of working with, being near, or having children, but also some of the difficulties and concerns you may face as a citizen and as a parent.

We hope that you will find the text useful now and will keep it as a reference. Most of all we hope you will be left with enthusiasm for the study of human development and with the ability to think about ways you can help make changes that will improve your lives and the lives of children.

To the Instructor

In attempting to explain how children change as they develop, all authors of child development texts face the choice of whether to present the material chronologically or topically. There is no one best method, and there are benefits and limitations to each approach. In the topical approach, students acquire an understanding of the process of development, but they lack an understanding of the competencies of children at different ages that a chronological approach offers. On the other hand, a chronological approach can be limited because it often fails to provide an integrated and continuous presentation of a process that can be traced through the entire course of development—for example, cognition.

In order to overcome some of these limitations, we combine the two approaches—the material within each chapter is organized topically, but the general course of the text is chronological. Following the two introductory units on the history and biological foundations of child development, there are four chronological units: infancy, early childhood, middle childhood, and adolescence. Each unit includes chapters on physical, cognitive, and social-emotional development. Each chapter is written in such a way as to integrate developmental themes from one section to the next. In addition, we convey to the students the relatedness of development in a concrete manner by pointing out in several chapters the implications of increasing skills in one area of development to another. For example, in the chapters on physical development we discuss the implications of physical growth for social and cognitive development.

We begin each of the chronological units with an overview of the developmental highlights of the age group so that students develop a sense of what children are like at different periods of their development. We end each of these units with a discussion of atypical development so that students can appreciate the range of development and some of the ways it can deviate from the normal course. The Conclusion deals with child development and the life cycle. This chapter places the study of child development within a life-span perspective, showing that development does not end at age eighteen and encouraging the student to consider children in the context of a social environment that includes adults of different ages who influence children and are influenced by them.

For instructors who wish to teach a topical course, the following sequence of chapters will work well:

Introduction The Study of Child Development

Chapter 1 New Directions in Child Development: A Social Issues Approach
Chapter 2 Our Biological Heritage
Chapter 3 Prenatal Development and Birth

Physical Development
Chapter 4 Physical Development During Infancy
Chapter 7 Physical Development During the Preschool Years
Chapter 10 Physical Development During Middle Childhood
Chapter 13 Physical Development During Adolescence

Cognitive and Language Development
Chapter 5 Cognitive and Language Development During Infancy
Chapter 8 Cognitive and Language Development During the Preschool Years
Chapter 11 Cognitive Development During Middle Childhood
Chapter 14 Cognitive Development During Adolescence

Social and Emotional Development
Chapter 6 Social and Emotional Development During Infancy
Chapter 9 Social and Emotional Development During the Preschool Years
Chapter 12 Social and Emotional Development During Middle Childhood
Chapter 15 Social and Emotional Development During Adolescence
Conclusion Child Development and the Life Cycle

Special Features of the Text

We have devised several features that will facilitate use of the book and understanding of its contents. In every chapter we use photographs and drawings to highlight important ideas; we also include charts and graphs in order to clarify difficult concepts or to describe findings of specific research studies. There are a number of other features that will aid student mastery and review of the material.

- **Chapter Introductions and Outlines.** At the beginning of each chapter, we outline all the topics that will be covered, and we introduce the various questions that will be addressed.

- **Margin Heads.** We highlight important concepts and terms in the margins, thus enabling students to locate them quickly and easily within each chapter.

- **"A Closer Look" Sections.** These sections contain detailed discussions about a particular topic or issue, enabling the student to gain an in-depth understanding.

- **Chapter Summaries and Review Points.** At the end of each chapter, we provide a conceptual summary of the main topics covered and we also include review points that can serve as study aids for students.

- **Glossary and References.** Definitions of terms are provided in the Glossary, and a bibliographic listing provides complete information for references cited in the text.

- **Separate Name and Subject Indexes.**

Supplementary Materials

Besides these pedagogical aids, the following supplementary materials accompany the text:

- **Student Study Guide.** The *Study Guide* is available to help students understand and review the material. Each chapter in the guide includes a list of study goals; summaries of topics presented in the text; a review of important terms, concepts, and people; and a set of multiple-choice and true-false questions that will help students prepare for examinations.

- **Instructor's Guide and Test Item File.** The *Instructor's Guide* includes learning objectives for students; lists of important terms, people, and concepts; summaries of important topics; teaching tips; and a listing of audiovisual aids and other resources for supplementary lectures. The *Test Item File* contains more than four hundred multiple-choice and true-false questions that can be used for examinations.

- **Computerized Test Generating Program.** An easy-to-use, computerized test generating program is available for use with either an Apple or an IBM computer. The program contains all the test items in the *Test Item File* and is accompanied by a booklet giving complete instructions.

Acknowledgments

Several people have helped us write this book. We wish to extend special thanks to Carol Buell for her clerical and editorial assistance throughout all phases of manuscript preparation; to Barbara Poissonnier for helping us meet deadlines by typing drafts of several of the chapters and helping prepare the list of references; to Susan Shays Gilfillan for preparing the Glossary; and to Betty Ward and Kathryn Young for their work on the *Study Guide,* the *Instructor's Guide,* and the *Test Item File.*

We gratefully acknowledge the work of the editorial staff of D. C. Heath whose assistance greatly facilitated our work. Our thanks to John Servideo for his editing and coordinating of the project and for ensuring that the book is both instructive and visually appealing; to James Miller for his support in the final stages of manuscript preparation; to Mary Stuart Lang for the photograph research; and to Sally Steele for the design. We extend special thanks to Nancy Osman for the encouragement she gave us to write a child development book and for her support during the initial phases of the work. Throughout all phases of the writing, a number of scholars graciously responded to requests for detailed reviews of the chapters. We thank Dale Johnson, University of Houston; Danuta Bukatko, Holy Cross College; Joseph Cunningham, Brandeis University; Katherine Stannard, Framingham State College (Massachusetts); Deborah Switchenko, Hofstra University; Glaston Walker, Tarrant County Junior College (Texas); Billy Seay, Louisiana State University, Baton Rouge; Gary Allen, Old Dominion University; Barbara Rogoff, University of Utah; Patricia Wordin, California State University, Fullerton; Patricia Miller, University of Florida; Edward Riley, State University of New York at Albany; Richard Hanson, North Dakota State University; and Richard LaBarba, University of South Florida for their constructive comments and suggestions which helped us improve the book.

Finally, and most importantly, we extend our thanks and appreciation to our families for their help and encouragement during those difficult moments when it seemed that the book might never get off the ground. For their love and support during this and our other professional activities, we are grateful.

Edward F. Zigler
Matia Finn-Stevenson

CONTENTS

UNIT V   The Middle Childhood Years 451

THE AUTHORS

NATIONALLY RECOGNIZED LEADERS IN CHILD DEVELOPMENT

Edward F. Zigler earned his Ph.D. from the University of Texas at Austin. A former chairman of the Department of Psychology at Yale University, he is currently Sterling Professor of Psychology at Yale, head of the psychology section at Yale's Child Study Center, and director of the Bush Center in Child Development and Social Policy at Yale University. He is the author, co-author, or editor of numerous publications and has conducted extensive investigations on topics related to the development of normal and disadvantaged children, as well as psychopathology and mental retardation. Dr. Zigler is also well known for his role in the shaping of national policies for children and families. He testifies as an expert witness before congressional committees, and he served as special consultant to four Secretaries of the Department of Health and Human Services. He was one of the organizers of Project Head Start. Between 1970 and 1972, Dr. Zigler served as the first director of the Office of Child Development (now Administration for Children, Youth, and Families) and as chief of the U.S. Children's Bureau. He was named by President Ford to chair the Vietnamese Children's Resettlement Advisory Group. In 1980, President Carter named him chair of the Fifteenth Anniversary Head Start Committee, a body charged with charting the future course of the Head Start program. He is the recipient of many awards, including the American Academy of Pediatrics' C. Anderson Aldrich Award, the APA's G. Stanley Hall Award, the Award for Distinguished Contribution to Psychology in the Public Interest, and, most recently, the Award for Distinguished Professional Contributions to Knowledge.

Matia Finn-Stevenson obtained her Ph.D. at the Ohio State University. She is a research scientist at the Department of Psychology at Yale University, a member of the faculty of the Bush Center in Child Development and Social Policy at Yale, and director of the Bush Center's Humane Family Video Project. Dr. Finn-Stevenson has done extensive research on topics related to children's development and education and the evaluation and management of children's services. She is the author and coauthor of several publications on child and family welfare and policy and the editor of the *Networker,* a national newsletter on child and family policy issues published by the Bush programs. She has served as consultant to several state organizations and state government officials. Having developed and coordinated model programs for at-risk populations, Dr. Finn-Stevenson is currently working on the productions of video programs which will serve as a catalyst for a health and mental health intervention effort she is developing for children ages 3–18 and their parents and teachers.

UNIT I

THE STUDY OF CHILDREN:

HISTORICAL PERSPECTIVES AND CURRENT TRENDS

In this unit we present an overview of the goals and content of child development research, the history of the field, various theories of development, as well as the nature of research knowledge and the methods used to study children. Many of the topics we introduce will be discussed in greater detail in the units that follow.

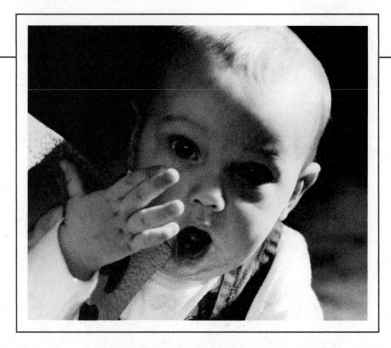

INTRODUCTION

THE STUDY OF CHILD DEVELOPMENT

WHY STUDY CHILDREN?

Before we begin to discuss the theories and research in child development, it is important to consider the question: Why study children? At one time the study of child development was considered important because it furthered our understanding of the nature of the adult. Popular sayings such as "The child is the father of the man," and "As the twig is bent, so grows the tree" attest to people's belief that the experiences of infancy and the childhood years contribute to the personality and behavior of the adult. Researchers still recognize that an understanding of the child can give us a better understanding of the characteristics of the adult. However, today researchers emphasize that the study of child development is important not because it can enhance our understanding of adults, but because every stage in childhood is important. Moreover, they have come to recognize that the process of development does not end in childhood, but is continuous throughout life.

Knowledge from child development research gives us a rich background of information about children's behavior and psychological growth under different environmental conditions. The study of the development of children involves an understanding of such processes as perceiving, feeling, thinking, and interacting with others. Knowledge of these processes aids us in our efforts to understand what we can expect of children at different ages, and it facilitates our ability to critically evaluate the conditions under which children live and the social trends that affect their lives.

The Goal and Content of Child Development Research

The goal of child development research is to acquire an understanding of the process of development by studying the changes that occur in children as they mature. The work of child development researchers includes devising scientific methods for the study of children, compiling information about children of different ages and backgrounds, and developing different theoretical frameworks that can explain children's behavior and the changes they undergo in the course of their development.

As researchers strive to accumulate an organized and systematic body of knowledge about child development and behavior, they focus on such broad questions as, How do children acquire the capacity to think? or, How do children feel, perceive, and interact with others, or acquire language skills? Beyond questions about specific developmental processes, however, child development researchers are also concerned with influences upon these developmental processes, and they engage in research that will help clarify the role that genes play in determining differences among individuals, for example, or the extent that variations among individuals may be related to observable differences in their experiences or environment.

Researchers have come to appreciate that the growth and development of children does not occur in a vacuum. In the real world, children grow up among many people and they influence and are influenced by many of these people.

These are broad areas of investigation. Researchers do not engage in a single study that attempts to answer such broad and complex questions. Rather, they synthesize the findings of many studies which look at related behaviors that are more circumscribed. For instance, in order to arrive at a closer understanding of how the child grows as a social being, able to benefit from and contribute to his interactions with other people, child development researchers would study the relationship between the newborn infant and his mother; they would look at differences between infants and young children whose mothers work and those whose mothers stay home; and they would investigate different childrearing practices to determine their effect on development. Or, in another example, in order to better understand why some children grow up to become happy and productive members of society and others grow up to become unhappy or disturbed adults, researchers analyze family relationships of mentally ill children; they examine the characteristics of children in families where child abuse occurs; or they assess the impact of stress or poverty on a child's development.

You can see from even these few examples that child development research concerns the study of the child in the context of the environment, not just the child alone. More and more, researchers are acknowledging that the growth and development of children does not occur in a vacuum. In the real world, a child grows up among many people and is likely to be influenced not only by these people but by the various institutions (such as the school) that he comes in contact with. So, while the goal of child development researchers is to gain greater understanding of the development of children, their subjects are not only children, but children and their families, as well as others who interact with and influence the child or family.

A BRIEF HISTORY OF CHILD DEVELOPMENT

The history of developmental psychology dates back to the 1880s. Since that time, the field has gone through periods of rapid growth, and progress has been made in the ability of researchers to describe and explain the development of the child. In their choice of areas of study, developmental psychologists have sometimes been influenced by prevailing theoretical viewpoints, but at other times they have been motivated by a concern with pressing social problems of their day. In this unit, we present a brief overview of the history of developmental psychology, and we look at various theoretical approaches that have guided the research as well as some of the research methods that have been developed and refined over the years. We also describe current trends in child development research and the attempts of some researchers to direct their research toward the resolution of contemporary social problems affecting children and families. These new trends in the research are reflected in the approach we take in this book wherein we discuss not only changes in the growth and development of children, but also relevant social issues and indicators that help us ascertain the changes and constancies in the lives of children.

Early Interest in Children

Interest in the nature of the child has deep roots extending far into the past. Plato, for example, who lived some 400 years before the beginning of the Christian era, was one of many ancient philosophers who devoted considerable thought to the topic of childhood training and education. Plato expressed some thought-provoking generalizations about child development, noting that children are born with different types of abilities and suggesting that each child should be guided into that type of service for which his particular aptitudes best apply.

John Locke. Other, more recent philosophers also wrote about the nature of the child. Their views are still studied and continue to exert a great deal of influence in the fields of child psychology and education. One of these more recent philosophers is John Locke (1632–1704). Locke, who wrote in the 17th century, believed that the child was an incomplete adult who was governed by strong urges and desires. He felt that these urges should be controlled and that the best way for teaching a child to control them was for adults, aided by their ability to reason, to create a carefully controlled environment for the child.

tabula rasa

Locke asserted that education and experience are fundamental determinants of child development. It was his belief that the child's mind, at birth, is a *tabula rasa,* or blank slate, which is therefore receptive to all types of learning. Locke believed that since the child comes into the world with a wholly unformed or blank mind, education and guidance are essential during the childhood years. He believed also that the goal of education should be to enhance the child's self-discipline and self-control. He advised parents and educators to begin as early as possible in the life of the child to teach him to discipline himself so that he would be able to deny himself the satisfaction of his own desires.

Jean-Jacques Rousseau. Locke thus advocated structured and constant supervision of the child so that his development could be appropriately molded. Another philosopher, Jean-Jacques Rousseau (1712–1778), writing almost a century later, believed that the child did not need strict supervision or structured education. In his book *Emile* (Rousseau, 1962), in which a tutor describes the growth and development of a boy named Emile, Rousseau put forth his view of the child as a "noble savage" who possesses an intuitive knowledge of what is right and wrong but encoun-

John Locke, 1632–1704.   *Jean-Jacques Rousseau, 1712–1778.*

ters pitfalls because of the restrictions imposed on him by society. Not unlike many progressive educators of the 1960s, Rousseau advised that the child be allowed to explore the world and to use the environment to suit his needs and interests.

During Rousseau's time young children were considered to be as-yet-unformed adults with few, if any, thoughts, feelings, or abilities. It was the task of parents and educators to teach children to become active and contributing members of society. Rousseau, however, saw the child as actively responding to the world around him and as an interested explorer who fits his abilities to the world as he plays and attempts to solve problems he encounters. Much to the dismay of his contemporaries (the book was banned in France at the time), Rousseau believed that the tasks of adults in the child's life were not to teach and train the child (as Locke advocated) but to provide the child with the opportunities to explore and to learn. Rather than lead the child, Rousseau advised that adults follow the child's lead as he explores his world.

You can see that Locke and Rousseau held strongly contrasting views about the nature of the child. These contrasting views were precursors of a fundamental division among researchers in child development, referred to as the *nature-nurture controversy*, that is, the debate about whether intelligence, for instance, is an endowed trait or wholly shaped by experience. Both Locke and Rousseau contributed to our understanding of children,

nature-nurture controversy

and they also encouraged others to study the childhood years. Their writings, however, were based merely upon speculations, because during their times the scientific study of children had not yet begun.

The Emergence of a Scientific Approach

Charles Darwin.   A scientific approach to the study of children did not emerge until the 19th century. During that time, the work of Charles Darwin on the principles of natural evolution focused scientists' interest on development in human beings. In fact, the publication of Darwin's book *On the Origin of Species* in 1859 is considered to be the most important force in the establishment of child study as a scientific endeavor.

Prior to Darwin's time, the different plant and animal species had been seen either as God's creation or as mutations, and each of the species was considered to be distinct. Darwin, however, put forth the notion of an evolutionary process, arguing that human beings are not set apart from others. Rather, he emphasized the fact that there is continuity among species and within species, and that the transmission of traits occurs through genetic heredity. Although Darwin was considered to be a revolutionary in his time, he sparked an avid interest in the study of any possible link between human beings and other species such as apes, and between the biological makeup of adults and that of their children.

A result of Darwin's work was that scientists embarked on the intensive study of the child in the hope that it would throw additional light on the psychological makeup of man. In fact, as we shall see in the following pages, Darwin himself was interested in the study of children, which lent credibility to child development as a field of scientific study. After the publication of *On the Origin of Species,* "Man was not to be understood by the analysis of his adult function," writes William Kessen (1965), " . . . rather, man was to be understood by the study of his origins—in nature and in the child." Such questions as, When does consciousness begin? How can we know the world of the infant? were derived from Darwin's views on the origins of man and were, according to Kessen, to dominate the field of child psychology for many years.

Early Observational and Empirical Studies: Baby Biographies

baby biography

The use of observations of children as the basis for theoretical formulations, and the careful recording of these observations in what became known as the *baby biography*—a day-to-day account of an individual child's development—are considered to be the next major step in the emergence of child study as a scientific endeavor. Baby biographies gained extensively in popularity in large measure because Darwin, who was an eminent scientist and theorist, published a biographical sketch of the development of his own son. That baby biography, written by Dar-

Charles Darwin, 1809–1882. Darwin's publication of the book On the Origin of the Species *in 1859 launched the study of children as a scientific endeavor. Before that time, numerous philosophers wrote about children's development and behaviors. However, their writings were based upon speculations rather than upon scientific evidence.*

win in 1840–41 and published in 1877, was a good example of an objective recording of the observation of such behaviors as the reflexes and sensory abilities of the newborn infant.

Several other biographies of infants were published in the latter part of the 19th and early part of the 20th centuries (Dennis, 1936). These baby biographies pointed to many significant aspects of psychological development and paved the way for later researchers' discovery of normal and universal patterns of development through the systematic observation of children's behavior.

Early Experimental Studies

As interest in children as objects of scientific study became more widespread, the study of child development became more and more systematic and methodologically sophisticated. It became more objective and was based on the study of large groups of children rather than on the study of a single child. Many researchers contributed to making child study an increasingly more scientific endeavor. The most notable of these is G. Stanley Hall (1846–1924), who was one of the founders of the American Psychological Association and the founder of child and adolescent psychology as subareas of general psychology.

Not only is G. Stanley Hall one of the founders of the study of the psychology of children, he is also regarded as a giant in early experimental research on child development. Like Darwin and other earlier scientists,

Granville Stanley Hall, 1846–1924.

Hall was interested in investigating the child's mind because he believed that an understanding of child development was crucial to the understanding of man. However, unlike those who preceded him, whose ideas were based largely on speculations, or who based their theories on the observations of one child, Hall's approach was to make generalizations about development and then to attempt to support these generalizations by collecting information from a large number of subjects in order to obtain representative data. Hall, for example, is credited with the development of the questionnaire as a method by which to collect information from a large group of subjects. Primarily through the use of questionnaires, Hall was able to obtain from children their views on numerous topics. He then collated the responses and interpreted the overall significance of his findings. The questionnaire has since become an important tool for researchers. You should note, however, that it is limited to studies of children who are old enough to have acquired language skills.

The Testing Movement

One of the first major achievements of early researchers in child development was the formulation of the intelligence test by Alfred Binet and Theodore Simon (1905) in France, and its extension and adaptation to America by one of Hall's students, Lewis Terman (Berndt & Zigler, 1985).

Binet and Simon set out to develop a method by which to distinguish normal and subnormal intelligence so that children could be placed in regular public schools or in special schools. Such methods were not then available, so decisions about the educational placement of children were often based upon subjective and biased information. To correct the problem and to secure a more objective measurement, Binet and Simon devised a series of short and simple tests. In these tests, children were asked for the definition of words, or they were asked to complete a sentence with the appropriate word (e.g., "The weather is clear, the sky is *blue*."). Binet and Simon first gave each test to a large number of normal children. The age at which roughly 75% of normal children passed a test defined the mental age required by the test. Children were considered subnormal if their mental age, as determined from the entire series of tests, was markedly below their chronological (actual) age.

Terman (1916) translated the Binet-Simon tests, adapted them for use in America, and added to them other questions. Eventually researchers suggested that the most meaningful measure of intelligence was the *intelligence quotient,* or *IQ,* which is the ratio of mental age to chronological age, a point that will be addressed in Chapter 14. Since Terman worked at Stanford University, his new test was labeled the Stanford–Binet. This test was quick and easy to administer, and it provided an indication of children's ability to succeed in school. That is, children who did well on the tests also did well in school, suggesting that the tests did measure intellectual ability. As we shall read in Chapter 14, intelligence tests are still being administered to children. However, during the past few decades there have been numerous criticisms of the tests (Cronbach, 1975), and now researchers understand that although these tests can predict children's school performance, they are not measures of how intelligent children are. That is, a child may do poorly on the test and also in school, perhaps because he is not motivated to succeed, but that does not mean that he does not have the intellectual potential to succeed.

intelligence quotient (IQ)

Increased Popularity of Child Study

Interest in child study consumed not only scientists but parents as well (Siegel & White, 1982). Another of Hall's students, Arnold Gesell (1880–1961), is well known both for his contributions to the field and for his influence on parents and educators who relied on his theory of maturation as an explanation of child development.

Gesell was a skilled observer who used controlled observational techniques, including photography, to document the development and behavior of full-term, preterm, and impaired infants. He believed that such documentation would help show the course of children's growth and provide a framework for a standardized diagnostic tool. On the basis of his observations Gesell developed standards for development in motor, visual, language, and social behavior.

From his observations of a large number of infants, Gesell concluded that there were certain *orderly* stages of development that formed a *universal* and *invariant sequence* (Gesell & Thompson, 1934). The stages were universal in that, within a given range, they occurred in all children observed. And they were invariant in that each stage set the conditions for the emergence of the next stage. That is, the child first crawls and then learns to walk; no child ever follows the reverse pattern. Gesell set out to determine which kinds of changes formed orderly patterns of growth and which appeared less regular and subject to greater degrees of individual variations. If development is orderly, he reasoned, it must follow a well-defined path. Understanding how this developmental path unfolds gives meaning to children's behavior at different ages.

maturational readiness

Thus Gesell considered development to be dependent on a naturally unfolding process. His theory of *maturational readiness* states that when a child is sufficiently mature he will benefit from training, whereas the child who is not ready requires far more effort and time for learning. This concept was very attractive to both parents and educators for it provided them with some guidance on such issues as toilet training and discipline. Parents in particular also relied on Gesell's idea of behavioral stages, which was derived from his belief that development was the result of forces of growth, some of which were dominant at one age, others at another. He labeled each age: "the terrible twos"; "the conforming threes"; the "lively fours" (Gesell & Ilg, 1942), which helped parents to understand as well as predict the behaviors of children of different ages. Thus the mother of a two-year-old who continuously disobeys her orders can take some comfort in the realization that this stage in development will pass.

The emphasis in child study during Gesell's time, which was the early 1900s, was on collecting large amounts of data on children and on providing direction and guidance for parents and educators. Gesell established one of the first child development research centers at Yale University in 1911 and another in Iowa in 1917. During the 1920s, many such centers and "laboratory schools" were established in numerous universities across the country, with the dual purpose of acquiring an understanding of how children develop and of using this understanding to facilitate childrearing and education. The existence of so many child development centers stimulated many interested individuals to concentrate on child development research, and it also enabled these individuals to study large groups of children, thus lending more scientific credibility to the research (Berndt & Zigler, 1985).

The interest in the study of children became so great that research dealing with children's development and behavior appeared with increasing frequency in psychological journals. By the 1930s, reports on research with children constituted a significant percentage of all published research in psychology. In the 1930s the study of child development became firmly established in America as a science. Because of the widespread interest in studying children, and the establishment of centers for that purpose, a great deal of descriptive information on children had been accumulated. With so much information on children already available, the research in child development assumed a different focus as researchers became less concerned with generating more data and more interested in testing the theories of development that had emerged on the basis of the data already accumulated. Thus the movement toward establishing child study as an increasingly more scientific endeavor included the building of theories that explained child development and behavior.

THEORIES IN CHILD DEVELOPMENT

What Is a Theory?

A theory may be defined as a statement or set of statements offered to explain a phenomenon. It is a way of organizing data, ideas, and hypotheses to provide a more complete understanding of what the data have been indicating in a more piecemeal fashion. A theory is important to the scientist primarily because it provides the scientist with direction for further research, not because it may be a correct explanation.

> The value of theories does not lie in the comfort that they provide the user, but rather in the things that the user can now do which he would not be able to do in absence of a theory. What is of major importance is not the validation of a prediction but rather the implication that such validation has for human action. Thus, a good theory directs us to appropriate actions as opposed to inappropriate actions. This is true whether our goals are navigating between celestial spheres or raising children. Thus theories must be evaluated not in terms of their inherent "trueness" but rather in terms of their usefulness as described above. (Zigler, 1963)

In science and in everyday life we rely on the use of theories to give us direction for action. In everyday life we use the word theory to mean a "hunch." On television you may see a detective who, on the basis of the available facts or clues, says he has a "theory." That is, he has what he thinks may be an explanation for the mystery under investigation. Likewise, a mechanic, upon being given a car that does not operate, listens to the engine noise and, based upon an initial examination of the car as well as his experience as a mechanic, offers his "theory" of what may be wrong with the car. On the basis of their "theories," both the detective and the mechanic can pursue a course of action that may either prove or disprove their explanations, but that at any rate will bring them one step closer to a solution. Without a theory, neither the detective nor the mechanic would be able to set the goal of what to do next. Scientific theories are similar to theories used in everyday life, except that they differ in the phenomena they explain. Also, scientific theories are governed by a set of rules.

Testability

testability

Among this set of rules is the rule of *testability*, which means that a theory must be able to be subjected to proof or disproof. That is, a theory must be stated in such a way that it can be tested by observable events. If a theory appears to explain a phenomenon but can never be put to a test, then its value to the scientist is limited.

hypothesis

In the process of theory testing, the scientist proceeds by setting out to test a *hypothesis,* which is a specific prediction derived from the theory. It is not assumed that the hypothesis, or prediction, is true or that it can be proved. Rather, there are different *levels of certainty* so at best the scientist hopes that the findings from the research will *support* the hypothesis. Vasta (1979) provides an example in which researchers set out to test the hypothesis that infants smile less when they are in the presence of strangers than when they are with those to whom they are accustomed. Even if the researchers find that all the infants tested do smile less in the presence of strangers, as scientists, they cannot claim that the hypothesis is absolutely correct. Rather, they can say only that their findings *support* the hypothesis. The only way absolute proof could ever be established would be to test all infants under the same circumstances. This requirement for absolute proof may seem absurd to you. After all, all the infants in the study did in fact smile less in the presence of a stranger. Bear in mind, however, that the example involved not *all* infants, but only a sample of infants. You should also keep in mind that usually experiments do not yield such clear-cut results as we have presented here. In such a study as we described only some of the infants would have smiled less, in which case the scientist must make some decision, on the basis of rules of statistics, as to whether the evidence is adequate to accept or to reject the hypothesis.

The Uses of Theories

As we mentioned earlier, this century has witnessed the emergence of numerous theories on the phenomenon of human and child development. In contrast to current theories, which are small in scope and attempt to explain limited aspects of behavior such as smiling and grasping in an infant, many of the earlier theories were ambitious attempts to explain everything related to developmental phenomena. Unfortunately, many such theories, for example, the psychoanalytic theory, do not meet the requirement of testability, so from the scientific perspective they are not really theories but rather they provide a "frame of reference" (Zigler, 1963) that is an aspect of theory building. Despite their being pretheoretical in nature, however, they have had a significant influence on child development research. Indeed, scientists welcome theories and conjectures, for in science one attempts to test such propositions with the measuring instruments and methods available.

Major Theories in Child Development

Theories of development can be divided into several general categories. For example, there are *epigenetic theories,* which explain development and behavior on the basis of the interaction between the environment and a person's genetic inheritance. There are also theories that explain behavior and development on the basis of the individual's past experience and learning. These are called *environmental theories.* Both epigenetic and environmental theories can be divided according to what aspect of development they focus on—thinking and learning or personality and social behavior. The variations in perspective of these theories can lead to markedly different interpretations of development. To date, no one theory has been found to be the only single, correct explanation, but all theories are useful in helping psychologists construct a picture of development.

epigenetic theories

environmental theories

To highlight the varied and rich resource of knowledge that theories in child development provide, we have chosen to present here several of the major theoretical approaches. These and many other theories are discussed throughout the book. By way of introduction, we will discuss only some of their major points, the theorists behind them, and some of the factors that led to their emergence.

The Psychoanalytic Theory

Sigmund Freud (1856–1939) developed the psychoanalytic theory. The impact of Freud's theory has been so widespread that few people are unfamiliar with his name. The psychoanalytic theory is generally referred to as a *biological theory of personality* because it focuses on biological drives as these are manifested within the social context. Freud, who was a physician and neurologist by training, was influenced in this thinking by the work of a fellow physician, Joseph Breuer. One of Breuer's female patients was severely disabled by a variety of symptoms such as paralysis and hallucinations for which Breuer could find no organic basis or cure. Breuer hypnotized his patient, who was eventually able, through the hypnosis, to remember and recount events in her past that had caused her psychic anguish and which she had apparently forgotten or repressed. Through her recounting of these psychologically painful events, the patient was eventually able to come to terms with them. Her physical symptoms also diminished.

biological theory of personality

Freud was extremely impressed by what he later called the "talking cure." He began to treat his own patients in a similar way, but he replaced the use of hypnosis with free association—he encouraged his patients to talk freely about whatever came to their minds. He compiled careful notes on the traumatic experiences and events that had been repressed into the unconscious memory of his patients, and, on the basis of this information,

Sigmund Freud, 1856–1939.

he developed not only his theory but also psychoanalysis as a method of treatment.

id

ego

superego

Freud's theory states that the id, the ego, and the superego all play a part in the development and structure of an individual's personality. The *id,* present at birth, is a force of energy guided by instincts and directed toward satisfying basic needs and desires, inevitably causing the newborn infant unresolved tensions as he struggles to deal with experiences in reality. In order to cope with reality, the *ego* emerges and functions essentially to regulate desires, modulate frustrations, and guide the individual's thought and behavior. During early childhood, the *superego* emerges. The superego is viewed as the internal representation of social and traditional values. The superego is not inherited, nor is it present at birth; rather, it develops as a result of learning and social interactions. The id, the ego, and the superego are concepts developed by Freud to explain the biological (id), psychological (ego), and social (superego) components of development.

oral zone

According to Freud, the emergence of the ego and superego parallel stages of psychosexual development during which what is gratifying to the id changes. At birth, and through the first year of life, the focus of the id is on the *oral zone,* and the infant seeks gratification through stimulation of the mouth by sucking or chewing. During the second and third year, the focus of the id is on the anal zone, and the id derives gratification from the anal musculature. Freud believed that this stage is complete once toilet training is successful.

phallic zone

From age 3 to 5 years, the *phallic zone,* or genital region, is the focus of id gratification, whereas during the next stage, in the latency period (6 years to puberty), there is reduced focus on the genital area, and sexual drives become dormant. Thus during this stage the child can expend efforts on learning and acquiring social skills. Finally, in the *genital* period, which occurs during adolescence, sexual desires awaken.

Freud's stages of psychosexual development

The Oral Stage

During this stage, which encompasses the first year of life, the focus of the id is on sensual pleasure. Thus the baby sucks not only the breast or a bottle, from which she derives food, but also her thumb or a pacifier, and she tends to pick up objects and mouth them just for the sheer pleasure that such oral stimulation brings her.

The Anal Stage

During this stage, which starts at about one year of age and lasts until the child is about three years of age, pleasure is derived not from oral stimulation but from the rectum. Hence the child at this age enjoys either retaining or expelling feces, and toilet training becomes a matter over which the parent and child battle, each one wanting to exert control. The parent feels obligated to toilet train the child and to remind her to expel her feces, whereas the child often wants to control her own bodily functions. Eventually the child minds her parents because she wants to please them.

The Phallic Stage

This stage, which lasts from age three to about age six, is considered by Freud to be a critical period during which pleasure is derived from the genitals. Hence children at this age are seen fondling their sexual organs, and they are curious about their peers' and parents' genitals as well. During this stage boys experience sexual desires for their mothers as they undergo the Oedipus conflict, but because they admire and fear their father, they eventually repress their feelings for their mother and identify with their father. Girls experience the Electra conflict, which involves sexual feelings toward their father, and they eventually resolve it by identifying with their mother.

The Latency Stage

This stage occurs from age six and lasts until puberty is reached. It is characterized by latent sexual feelings. During this period the child is no longer distracted by any sexual desires, so she spends time mastering a variety of tasks and acquiring different interests.

The Genital Stage

During this last period of psychosexual development, the focus is once again on pleasure derived from the genital area. This period begins at the same time as puberty and lasts through adulthood, and it is characterized by efforts toward sexual maturity as the individual seeks to find someone of the opposite sex with whom to share sexual pleasures.

Freud saw each of these five stages of development as critical to the developing child. His assertion was that any crisis or conflict that occurred in any of these stages would, if it remained unresolved, give rise to personality problems that might persist throughout life. Thus Freud argued that it was possible for the personality to become fixated at any given

negative fixation

positive fixation

anal retentive personality

psychosexual stage. For example, if the id doesn't receive sufficient satisfaction during the oral stage, it may be reluctant to leave that stage until satisfaction has been obtained. Freud referred to this as *negative fixation* and claimed that it can result in manifestations of oral-stage processes in adult life. On the other hand, the id may receive too much satisfaction during the oral stage and may want to retain oral-stage satisfaction later in life, beyond the time when it is appropriate. Freud referred to this as *positive fixation*. Freud believed that such fixations, whether negative or positive, could lead to problems. For example, he stated that a child who was not satisfied in his instinctual needs during toilet training because of overly strict demands made by his parents might be forced to seek satisfaction later in life through undue retention as a mode of personality functioning. Freud believed that such *anal retentive* personalities show signs of selfishness during adulthood. Similarly, an individual who during adulthood derives oral gratification by chewing tobacco, or eating, may be manifesting fixations which occurred during the oral stage.

Freud has had a significant influence on theories and methods of childrearing as well as on the clinical treatment of emotional problems. His theory forced many researchers in child development to examine such issues as guilt and sexuality and their relationship to the development and behavior of the child. However, his theory is no longer relied upon to the extent that it was in the past. In fact, there is considerable controversy surrounding Freud's theory and many who discount it. This is in large part because his theory is difficult to prove or disprove. Freud is also criticized for promoting an overly pessimistic and negative view of human development, with little recognition of rational thinking and intellectual growth. Moreover, critics point out that although much of his theory focuses on infancy and childhood years as the basis for personality development later in life, Freud never actually studied children. His theory is based on his adult patients' recollections of their past.

The Psychosocial Theory

Freud's theory paved the way for other theoretical formulations as a number of Freud's contemporaries, some of whom were his own students, broke with him to develop theories on the basis of their observations of their own patients. *Erik Erikson* (1903–   ) is one such example. Erikson, who had at one time intended to pursue a career in art, was impressed with psychoanalysis. He studied under Anna Freud, who was Freud's daughter, and after graduating from the Vienna Psychoanalytic Institute, he became a child analyst. He worked in an American school in Vienna, and during the 1930s when Hitler came to power, Erikson emigrated to the United States where he held a series of positions in child guidance clinics and major universities.

Erik Erikson, 1903–, with his wife.

Erikson's *psychosocial theory* is important for its emphasis on emotional development throughout the lifespan as well as for the expansion of its focus on the individual's instinctive drives to include the individual in society. According to Erikson, personality develops according to steps that are predetermined by the individual's readiness to be driven toward and to interact with the social environment. His theory is similar to Freud's in its focus on the individual's need to resolve conflicts. However, unlike Freud who regarded these conflicts as occurring only during the childhood years, Erikson states that conflicts can develop at any stage of life, including adulthood and old age, and that they are not necessarily the result of problems in infancy or early childhood (Erikson, 1963).

The crux of Erikson's theory is that human development consists of the progressive resolution of conflicts between needs and social demands. He theorizes that an individual progresses through a series of eight stages,

Erikson's psychosocial theory

STAGE 1 Trust versus Mistrust, First Year of Life

The infant's relationship with his mother is crucial during this stage, as the infant acquires a sense of trust and the knowledge that he is loved when he is cared for in a predictable, warm, and sensitive manner. If the infant's world is chaotic and unpredictable, and his parent's affection cannot be counted on, he develops a sense of mistrust and feels anxious and insecure in his interactions with others in his life. These basic attitudes of trust or mistrust are not established all at once, but are acquired over a period of about a year in the course of the infant's experiences with his primary caregiver.

STAGE 2 Autonomy versus Shame and Doubt, Age 2 to 3

Once the child is able to walk, run, climb, and talk, he begins to explore his world, and he acquires a sense of his own independence, at times becoming adamant when he wants to do things for himself. If parents nurture the child's attempts at becoming an independent individual, and allow him to freely explore his world, while at the same time monitoring him so he does not hurt himself, the child develops a sense of autonomy and a feeling that he is competent. If, on the other hand, parents overprotect the child, stifle his attempts to explore his surroundings, or criticize his efforts, he develops shame, doubt, and uncertainty about himself and his capabilities.

STAGE 3 Initiative versus Guilt, Age 3 to 6

After the child has gained a relatively secure sense of autonomy, he moves into the third stage of development and is ready to take initiative in his activities. He explores, plans, and works for goals, thus acquiring a sense of purpose and direction. Parents must encourage the child's initiatives. If they do not allow the child to take initiative or if they downgrade his activities, he develops a sense of guilt for his attempts at independence.

STAGE 4 Industry versus Inferiority, Age 6 to 12

During this stage the child becomes responsible for homework and other assignments, and he develops an awareness that tasks can be accomplished through industry, or that they can be failed. If parents reinforce the child's efforts with praise and reward, the child develops a sense of industry and curiosity, and he is eager to learn. If the child's work is downgraded, he develops low self-esteem and a sense of inferiority and inadequacy, often withdrawing from attempts to learn new skills. At this stage, parents are only one source of influence on the child's development. The child is also influenced by peers, by teachers, and by other adults he comes in contact with.

or crises. During each of these stages, the individual confronts and must deal with specific crises before progress can be made to the next set of problems. Failure to resolve problems at any stage can result in psychological disorders.

These eight stages, which are described in more detail in the chapters on social development, begin with the stage of *trust vs. mistrust* during infancy. For ego identity to emerge, Erikson believes, the infant must develop a sense of trust in himself and in the world. Such trust is predicated upon the sense that there are people in the infant's world who can be counted on to provide comfort and care. However, the amount of care

STAGE 5 Identity versus Role Confusion, Age 12 to 18

During this stage the individual is in a transition phase of his life. No longer a child, and preparing for life as an adult, the adolescent undergoes what Erikson calls a "physiological revolution," and he has to come to grips with an identity crisis. In the process of trying to form an identity, the adolescent experiments with different options open to him. The danger during this stage is role confusion, as the adolescent may not be able to piece together from the many possible roles a coherent sense of self.

STAGE 6 Intimacy versus Isolation, Young Adulthood

Once he develops a sense of personal identity and is comfortable with it, the individual can begin to establish intimate relationships with other people. Forming close relationships and committing himself to another person, the individual feels gratified. However, intimate relationships are also fraught with dangers. The individual can be rejected, or the relationship may fail through disagreement, disappointment, or hostility. Individuals who focus on the negative possibilities of intimate relationships may be tempted not to take a chance on becoming close to another person and instead withdraw from social contact, thereby becoming isolated, or establishing only superficial relationships.

STAGE 7 Generativity versus Stagnation, Middle Age

Erikson regards generativity as emanating from marriage, parenthood, and a sense of working productively and creatively. Having a sense of accomplishment in adult life means giving loving care to others and regarding one's contributions to society as valuable. Working, getting married, and bearing and rearing children in and of themselves are not sufficient to give an individual a sense of generativity. The individual must also enjoy his work and his family. An individual who does not enjoy his work and who cares little for other people acquires a sense of stagnation, a sense that he is going nowhere and is doing nothing important.

STAGE 8 Integrity versus Despair, Old Age

Toward the end of life, the individual reflects on his past accomplishments and the kind of person he has been. He looks back on life either with a sense of integrity and satisfaction or with despair. If earlier crises have been successfully met, the individual realizes that his life has had meaning, and he is ready to face death. If earlier crises have not been resolved successfully, the individual has a feeling of despair as he realizes that he has no time now to start another life and try out alternative roads to integrity. Individuals who have a sense of despair are not ready to face death, and they feel bitter about their lives.

given is not as important as the overall quality of the relationship between the infant and the caretaker and the feeling transmitted to the infant that his actions do indeed have meaning. If the infant is deprived of this close relationship in the course of his care, he will not develop a sense of trust and the feeling that the world is a safe place to be in. The subsequent psychosocial stages of development are *autonomy vs. shame, initiative vs. guilt, industry vs. inferiority,* and *identity vs. role confusion,* which occur during childhood and adolescence. *Intimacy vs. isolation, generativity vs. stagnation,* and *ego identity vs. despair* occur during young adulthood, adulthood, and old age.

Cognitive-Developmental Theory

cognition

In contrast to the psychoanalytic and psychosocial theories, which focus on personality and on social development, the cognitive-developmental theory emphasizes the ability of the individual to think. *Cognition* refers to the way in which we gain knowledge through perception, memory, and thought processing. The cognitive approach regards the child as a spontaneously active individual who constructs his own knowledge of the world. Such an approach holds the view that development is not a series of cumulative changes, but rather that as the child develops, the mind undergoes a series of reorganizations. With each reorganization, the child moves to a higher level of psychological functioning.

One of the most influential of cognitive-developmental theorists is *Jean Piaget* (1896–1980). Piaget was born and lived in Switzerland where he studied philosophy and logic as well as the biological sciences. For a time he worked in the laboratory of Alfred Binet in France where he helped develop the intelligence tests to measure the reasoning abilities of children. As he asked children questions, he was amazed to find out that children of different ages used different reasoning to produce answers. This led to his realization that how people understand the world changes with their development. In 1929 Piaget began to systematically observe his own three children and he kept detailed records of their activities. On the basis of his observations he developed his theory of cognitive development.

epistemology

Piaget referred to his work as genetic epistemology. *Epistemology* is the study of the nature of knowledge. He argued that all knowledge comes from action and that the individual is active in the acquisition of knowledge. That is, from the moment of birth the individual explores the environment with whatever level of capability he has, and through these explorations he learns, so that his views of the environment change.

Piaget is considered to have revolutionized developmental psychology in large part because he asserted that children not only know less than adults do, but also that their ability to reason differs according to their developmental stage. According to Piaget (1952) there exists an underlying organization of thought in the individual, referred to as *cognitive structures,* which is tied to stages in intellectual development. These stages are

cognitive structures

> *sensorimotor* (birth to age 2);
> *preoperational* (2–7 years);
> *concrete operational* (7–12 years); and
> *formal operational thinking* (12 years and over).

These stages, which are elaborated on in the chapters on cognitive development, emerge in a constant order of succession and neither heredity nor the environment alone explains their progressive development. Rather, cognitive development is based upon an interaction between individual

Jean Piaget, 1896–1980.

genetic potential (an inherited trait) and the kinds of experiences he encounters (environmental factors).

Another theorist, *Heinz Werner* (1890–1964), also emphasized the interaction of the individual with the environment. The major theme of Werner's theory is the *orthogenetic principle* (Werner, 1948), which stipulates that in physical as well as psychological development an individual moves from a global, undifferentiated state to one of higher differentiation and integration. He made an analogy between the development of the embryo and psychological development and saw behavioral responses and skills as being increasingly organized into hierarchies in a process he termed *hierarchic integration.*

orthogenetic principle

hierarchic integration

Like Piaget, Werner believed that all children pass through the same milestones of development in the same way. He stressed that the development of the human being reveals both change and stability. That is, people go through an ordered sequence of stages which are characterized by

adaptive change

organizational stability

different ways of understanding the environment. During each stage there is adaptive change and organizational stability. By *adaptive change,* Werner meant that with progressive development, the child acquires different ways of perceiving things, changing in the way he behaves. By *organizational stability,* Werner meant that even though changes occur, the child retains a basic inborn organization. Werner noted that throughout life people are organized and have some degree of competence and that their inborn organization and competence are the basis for changes in behavior.

Learning Theory

The theoretical approaches described thus far emphasize stages in development. The learning theory, on the other hand, emphasizes the relationship between stimuli in the environment and behavior. There are a number of learning theorists who have emphasized different aspects of learning. Despite their diversity, however, learning theorists agree that all behavior, with the exception of basic reflexes, is learned. One extreme view of this approach is that of John B. Watson (1878–1958). Watson accepted John Locke's view that the infant's mind was a *tabula rasa* to be entirely shaped by learning. He described the newborn baby as a "lively squirming bit of flesh, capable of making few simple responses," and he noted that parents take this "raw material and begin to fashion it to suit themselves" (Watson, 1928). Given his notion that the child is a blank slate waiting to be programmed and trained, Watson argued that if he were given any group of infants, he could turn each one of them into any kind of an adult—lawyer, doctor, artist, or beggar. Watson was convinced that not only thought but emotions, too, were acquired through learning. He designed and executed a number of experiments to show that

conditioning

many fears could be acquired and then eliminated through *conditioning,* the process of learning a particular response to particular stimuli.

On the basis of his views, Watson suggested to parents that there is a "sensible" way of treating children. Unlike researchers of today, Watson advocated discouraging emotional dependency between parents and children: "Treat them as though they were young adults. Let your behavior always be objective and kindly and firm. Never hug and kiss them, never let them sit on your lap. If you must, kiss them once on the forehead when you say goodnight. Shake hands with them in the morning. Give them a pat on the head if they have made an extraordinarily good job of a difficult task" (Watson, 1928).

classical conditioning

Learning theorists distinguish between several kinds of learning. The power of one kind of learning, *classical conditioning,* was demonstrated earlier this century by the Russian physiologist Ivan Pavlov. Classical conditioning is a kind of learning in which responses that are under involuntary control, such as glandular secretions and muscle reflexes, can become learned reactions to environmental events. This learning happens by a process of association. If an individual is frightened by an experience, for example, events associated with the original experience will tend to arouse fear later, even though those events are harmless in themselves. For example, a baby who experienced the painful prick of injection by a doctor wearing white later may associate someone else wearing white with the painful experience he has had in the past.

A second kind of learning is *operant conditioning*. Much of our understanding of this kind of learning comes from the work of B. F. Skinner (Skinner, 1953; 1957). Operant conditioning is based upon the tendency of the individual to repeat a behavior if it is rewarded or reinforced and to discontinue the behavior if it is punished or fails to be reinforced. Learning theorists who employ operant conditioning are called *behavior modifiers* because they use principles of reward and punishment to shape or modify an individual's behavior.

operant conditioning

behavior modifiers

Social learning theorists such as Albert Bandura (1977) employ the principles of both classical and operant conditioning to explain how children learn social behaviors. Social learning theorists emphasize that rewards for learning do not have to be concrete, as in a piece of candy. Rather, they may be social responses such as attention, affection, and praise. That is, a child who is smiled at and praised for his work or good conduct learns that behaving in certain ways brings rewards.

There is considerable controversy surrounding learning theories, and there is the question of how much of human behavior is learned and how much is not learned but is innate. Learning theorists have disagreed with maturational theorists such as Gesell who postulated that there is a genetically predetermined timetable for development so that important events such as walking and talking generally appear on schedule for most children regardless of their learning experiences. We note in Chapter 2 that researchers have learned over the years that genetic factors alone do not determine development. However, are people controlled by rewards and punishments to the extent that learning theorists such as Skinner suggest? As you will see in the chapters that follow, both genetic predispositions and environmental experiences are now known to influence behavior. Nevertheless, the work of learning theorists should not be discounted, for they have made important contributions to the field of child development, and they continue to do so and to encourage a scientific approach to the study of development.

SOURCES OF IDEAS AND EVIDENCE

Theories provide researchers with the opportunity to test hypotheses and ideas so that our knowledge and understanding of child development can be refined. Theories are often developed within various approaches from which researchers can draw ideas about the development of children.

The study of children from different cultures helps refine our understanding of how children learn to behave in ways that are acceptable to their particular culture.

The Cross-Cultural Approach

One such approach is referred to as cross-cultural because it permits researchers to apply knowledge gained about cultures other than theirs to the overall understanding of human behavior. The cross-cultural approach is based on the studies conducted by psychologists who study children in different societies and on the studies of anthropologists who have had a significant influence on the field of psychology and in particular have helped refine our understanding of how children learn to behave in ways that are acceptable to their particular culture.

The anthropologist Margaret Mead, for example, contributed a great deal to our understanding of the effects of culture on development. Her work has recently been discounted (Freeman, 1983), but it is worth noting, for whether it is correct or not is not as important as is the fact that she encouraged researchers to adopt the view that there are multiple considerations in the study of child development. In a classical example, Mead (1928), who was intrigued by the traditional Western view of adolescence as a time of extreme emotional stress due to the physical changes of puberty, visited the island of Samoa where she found adolescence to be uneventful. She concluded that for the Samoans, "adolescence represented no period of crisis or stress but was instead an orderly developing of a set of slowly maturing interests and activities." She discerned from her findings that our Western culture harbors many stresses which contribute to emotional difficulties during adolescence and that the physical changes of puberty alone do not account for these difficulties.

Cross-cultural studies have also been used to verify some theories of development. Piaget's theory of cognition, for example, has been subjected to the scrutiny of cross-cultural researchers who ask: Do children all over the world experience the same stages of cognitive growth described by Piaget and in the same sequence? (e.g., Cole et al., 1971; Scribner, 1976; Rogoff et al., 1984). This question is important, for Piaget, recall, based his theory in large part on observations of his own three children and of other children from Western European backgrounds. From cross-cultural studies we have found that while Piaget's stages of cognitive growth are universal, children progress through these stages at different rates, depending on their experiences.

Besides being used to verify theories of development and provide direction for the research, cross-cultural studies are also important as a method for studying certain issues. For example, in studying language development in children, we can see that initial speech in children progresses from the use of one or two words to increasingly longer and more grammatically complex sentences. One theory suggests that an innate process guides the acquisition of language in all humans. Another explanation is that common speech patterns of children are the result of characteristics of their native language. Using a cross-cultural approach, the researcher can examine speech patterns of children from different countries to determine whether there is a similar progression in the acquisition of different languages and can thus determine whether an innate process is at work in language development or whether it may be in fact a function of the characteristics of a particular language.

The Genetic Approach

Whereas the cross-cultural approach enhances our appreciation of external cultural and experiential factors in development, the genetic approach focuses on biological characteristics of the individual as significant factors in determining psychological development.

The genetic approach provides one side of the nature-nurture controversy, the extreme views being that development is wholly determined by the environment or that it is wholly determined by genetic makeup. Learning theorists, for example, believe that only the environment is at work, whereas maturational theorists such as Gesell believe that development is predetermined by genetic factors. Most psychologists now believe that development and behavior are the product of an interaction between these forces. However, there is recognition among an increasing number of researchers that this interaction is very complex, so that the relationship between genetic and environmental factors remains baffling.

Some researchers note that behavior tendencies such as aggression are transmitted genetically through family lines. Thus, according to the genetic viewpoint, an aggressive child may have had that trait transmitted to him genetically. Aggression *may* have a genetic link. However, researchers point out that besides the genes, a host of other factors related to the child, the family, and the community also influence aggression (Parke and Slaby, 1983). It is known too that aggression can be learned and that some children elicit anger and aggression in their parents. Infants have been found to have different temperaments. Some cry more than others, or sleep less, thus eliciting very different responses from their caretakers, creating, in effect, different environments and encountering and learning aggression. You can see, then, that although development results from an interaction between genetic traits and experiential factors, that interaction is very complex and subject to a great deal of debate.

The Comparative Approach

In the comparative approach the researcher gains an understanding of human development by examining an aspect of human behavior in relation to similar behaviors in other species, for example, monkeys or dogs. An example of the comparative approach is provided by the research of Harry Harlow and his colleagues who raised rhesus monkeys in the laboratory as orphans (Harlow 1961, 1963). This research was full of surprising findings, as we shall see later on when we consider in more detail (Chapter 6) how these monkeys came to regard robots covered with terrycloth as the mothers they never knew and how they grew up to be cruel and abusive parents to their own offspring. The key question is: Can we draw any conclusions between these studies on monkeys and children who grow up with no opportunities for interactions with adults? Many times the comparison between animal and children's behavior is only theoretical. However, it does provide direction for further research in child development as well as some possible explanations. For example, Harlow's studies with monkeys have helped researchers who study the characteristics of parents and children in families where child abuse occurs (Ainsworth, 1980). In many cases, young children who are abused also have difficulty relating to other people.

The Ethological Approach

The ethological approach is closely related to the comparative approach in that ethologists study behavior in many species. The focus of the ethological approach is on the evolutionary origins of behavior with emphasis on

By studying the behavior of other species, ethologists have contributed to our understanding of human development. For example, they have found that there is a critical period, almost immediately after birth, during which newborn chicks will follow the first prominent object near them, usually their mother. This photograph shows Konrad Lorenz, 1903–, followed by ducklings that were imprinted by him. Although a similar phenomenon has not been found in human infants, researchers did investigate the possibility of a critical period during which mothers and infants become attached.

behaviors that occur in the natural environment. Ethologists are generally concerned with identifying the determinants of development in an individual and finding out the evolutionary influences involved. That is, why the behavior has evolved in such a manner and how it is adaptive for the particular species under study.

The ethological approach provides a perspective as well as observational methods that enhance our knowledge about human development and is used in studies related to social signals, play behavior, and the mother-infant relationship. The research on imprinting is an example of the ethological approach. *Imprinting* is the process that is apparently responsible for attachment in some bird species. Ethologists have determined that there is a critical period, almost immediately after birth, during which newborn chicks will follow the first prominent object near them, which is usually their mother. A period of such following results in a unique attachment to that object. It has been suggested that there is a critical period for attachment in humans, too. The idea of a critical period for mother-infant attachment, or bonding (Klaus & Kennell, 1976), has been criticized for methodological and theoretical reasons. However, it

imprinting

has resulted in positive changes in hospital practices, which now allow mothers to have immediate and continuous contact with their newborn babies.

A researcher who is famous for his application of the ethological approach to child development research is *John Bowlby*. On the basis of his ethological and other studies, Bowlby noted that infants of different species exhibit several *species-typical behaviors* that help them stay close to the mother. Crying is an example of such behavior. When the infant cries, his mother attends to his needs. Such behaviors, according to Bowlby, have an evolutionary survival value in that they tend to keep the mother close and thereby help avoid accidents and attacks from predators. Besides noting that there are species-typical behaviors that promote proximity to the mother, Bowlby also described the phases of the mother-infant attachment process and the importance of attachment to later development. His ideas are supported by the research on rhesus monkeys as well as human infants (Ainsworth, 1973) and also by case studies Bowlby himself conducted on hospitalized and orphaned children (Bowlby, 1969). We describe Bowlby's research in more detail in Chapter 6.

species-typical behaviors

The Ecological Approach

Another source of knowledge for child development researchers is the ecological approach. The ecological approach refers to the study of the organism in its natural environment. The roots of the concept of ecology are in biology. Specifically, it concerns that branch of biology which deals with the relations of living organisms to their surroundings, habits, and modes of life. Extending this definition to child development, the ecological approach involves the study of the child in the context of his natural environment: the home, the school, and the community.

The ecological approach is not entirely new to child development research. Some years ago Barker and Wright (1951, 1955) attempted to describe in concrete detail the conditions of life and behavior of a single boy, in *One Boy's Day,* and of all children of a community, in *Midwest and Its Children.* This approach is enjoying a resurgence, in part because of the argument that laboratory-based research has not produced sufficient gains in our understanding of human behavior (Bronfenbrenner, 1977). Studying children in their natural setting is not a simple matter, however. This will become clearer in the section on research methods. Currently researchers are working to refine research techniques so that these can be utilized to study the process of development as it naturally occurs in children growing up in actual life circumstances. Furthermore, researchers are suggesting that psychologists should not rely on any one type of research, be that laboratory-based, ecological, or other. They suggest, rather, that they should integrate findings from different studies in order to acquire an understanding of development (Weisz, 1978).

DIMENSIONS OF CHILD DEVELOPMENT RESEARCH

The Difference Between Research Evidence and Personal Knowledge

Hypotheses derived from theories of development or from investigations in other disciplines are tested through research. Although in this book we rely primarily on research evidence, research is only one way by which we come to learn about and understand children. It is also possible to acquire an understanding of children through personal observations and experiences with them. Through these observations and experiences we can draw some conclusions about children's behavior and development. However, these conclusions are necessarily personal ones and cannot be generalized, for each one of us defines behaviors differently. For example, upon seeing a child take a toy from another child, you may define such behavior as assertiveness while another person may define it as aggressiveness. In other words, we cannot always agree with one another on a particular aspect of children's behavior, and we may not be able to ascertain why we disagree (Moore & Cooper, 1982).

Knowledge that we derive from formal research, however, is explicit and open to examination by others. Every aspect of the information-gathering process in each research study is described in detail and on the basis of definitions and rules so that scientists may verify whether the research methods employed are valid.

Types of Research

Applied and Basic Research.   There are various ways that one can classify the research in child development. For example, classification of the research may be made on the basis of the purpose of the research or on the ultimate use of the research findings. Or, the research may be classified on the basis of the type of methodology employed. When we categorize the research as being applied or basic, we base our categorization on the purpose or use of the research. The term *applied research* is used to define any   *applied research* research that is designed to meet society's needs or to provide information that could be put to immediate use. The research on child day care, for example, is applied because it is motivated by the need to know what the effect of being in day care is on the young child, since more and more families are sending their children for care outside the home.

Basic research, on the other hand, is defined as any research that is   *basic research* motivated not out of any specific social need or in order to solve a problem but simply by the desire to expand human knowledge and our understanding of ourselves and our environment. The knowledge that we derive from basic research is added to our store of information and may not become relevant to a real problem until later on.

Many researchers refer to applied and basic research as two separate and distinct categories. Although they may be somewhat different, they are at the two ends of the same continuum and thus may be considered to overlap and contribute to each other to the benefit of both. This reciprocity between applied and basic research is especially evident in child development research. Let us take for example studies on child abuse. These studies are applied in nature because they are conducted in response to the problem of widespread child abuse in the United States (Gerbner, Ross, & Zigler, 1980). The research on child abuse seeks explanations of the development of inappropriate interaction patterns between abusive parents and their children, and is therefore of immediate social relevance. Despite the clearly applied nature of child abuse research, however, Ainsworth (1973), in studying the development of attachment in families where abuse occurs, has drawn upon the basic research work of Harlow (1961, 1963). Harlow's research provided evidence that rhesus monkeys will cling to their surrogate (made out of terrycloth) mothers which emit frightening noises and to their real mothers who physically abuse them. Harlow's findings have been shown to have important implications for child abuse research and to support Ainsworth's (1980) applied research and findings that abused children seek to be with their abusive parents.

In this example we can see how the basic research of Harlow, although done for no specific or immediate social use, overlapped and contributed to the applied research on the social problem of child abuse. In the same way that basic research contributes to applied research, so there are numerous other examples where applied research has added to our store of basic knowledge.

Descriptive and Manipulative Research. Researchers also categorize studies according to whether they are descriptive or manipulative. *Descriptive research* is characterized by observational techniques and involves the collection of data, usually in large amounts, in non-laboratory settings. In this method, used extensively by Gesell and other researchers earlier this century, the researcher observes and records behavior or any other event but does not interfere with the "natural" situation.

descriptive research

In contrast, *manipulative research* involves an experimental approach wherein the researcher manipulates a variable and observes any consequent changes in the behavior under examination. In manipulative research, researchers do not wait for variations to occur, but rather they produce such variations so that they can examine the effects.

manipulative research

In descriptive research on childrearing practices, the researcher may go to the home and observe and record the interactions between the child and the parent. Using manipulative research on the same phenomenon, the researcher may bring the mother and child to the laboratory and systematically change aspects of the situation and observe the interaction between the child and parent under different conditions. The distinction between these two types of research is that whereas descriptive research focuses on what functional relationships typically *do exist,* manipulative research emphasizes the functional relationships that *can exist* if specific variables are manipulated (Vasta, 1979). To put it another way, descriptive research provides a description, whereas manipulative research can offer an explanation of the event or behavior under investigation.

Methods for Research with Children

Within each of the broad categories of possible types of research studies, researchers employ different methods. The use of different methods depends on the kind of information that is being sought, the ultimate intent of the research, and the researchers' orientations.

The Normative Method.   *Normative studies* provide information related to the sequence and "average" age of the appearance of behaviors. On the basis of normative studies researchers have established norms for gross motor development, fine motor development, language skills, mental development, and social and personal aspects of behavior. The focus of normative studies is not on how and why developmental processes occur, but rather on when and to what extent they occur. In normative studies researchers ask: When during development does a behavior typically appear? How much of a given behavior occurs in a given population? From normative studies we know, for example, that on the average, a baby will sit by the age of 6 months and begin to walk without assistance at around 12 months. It is important to realize, however, that there are extensive individual differences associated with each behavior, so that it is quite normal for a baby to begin to walk at 9 months, or perhaps 15 months. Normative studies supply researchers simply with an average age so it is important to recognize that some children will fall below the average and others above the average. This understanding of normative research findings is especially important for parents who tend to judge the behavior and progress of their infants and children according to the established norm without realizing that individual differences exist.

normative studies

The Observational Method.   Observational research techniques are not new to the research in child development. However, there is currently a revival in the interest in and use of such techniques because of the concern that the research focus on the study of children in the context of the natural settings in which they are reared, what is referred to as *ecological validity.*

The observational method relies on the observation and recording of behavior, and it requires that researchers collect information as they watch

ecological validity

the children. The use of videotape recordings can facilitate observation and also allows for repeated viewing of the behavior being studied.

Imperative to observational studies is the accuracy of the facts (behaviors, events) that are gathered, compiled, and analyzed. Two factors that are built into the research to ensure accuracy are reliability and validity. *Reliability* ensures objectivity about what is observed or measured and entails defining the behavior to be studied, specifying what counts and does not count, and training the observers to record all their observations accurately so that they always agree. *Validity* is related to the sample of subjects studied. The conclusions derived from the studies are valid only if the subjects studied, for example, a group of children, are *representative* of the larger population. That is, the sample of subjects must include boys and girls, children of various ethnic backgrounds, and other background characteristics that are found in children in the general population to whom the findings of the study are said to apply, or, to use the terminology used in the research, to whom the findings are *generalized*.

research reliability

research validity

generalized findings

The Experimental Method.   Experimental studies are used to answer questions about the causes of behavior. Consider an example provided by Moore and Cooper (1982) in which a researcher wished to test the hypothesis that viewing TV shows that portray violence causes high levels of aggression in the play of 4-year-old children. To test this hypothesis, a sample of children would be randomly assigned to one of two viewing conditions, a violent TV show and a nonviolent TV show. *Random assignment* is important, because it can be relied upon to ensure that both aggressive and nonaggressive children will be included in the two viewing conditions. The two groups of children would then view the TV shows for perhaps two or three 15-minute segments, after which they would be observed playing. Instances of aggressive and nonaggressive play among the children would then be recorded and compared, and later researchers would determine if the children who watched the violent TV show did indeed display more aggressive play behavior than the children who watched the nonviolent show.

random assignment

In designing a study of this kind, researchers seek to have control over as many aspects of the study as possible. Thus, since boys are generally more aggressive than girls in their play, researchers would ensure that there are equal numbers of boys in each of the two groups. The selection of toys and materials available to the two groups when they are observed playing is also important. The same toys should be available to both groups, since toys may vary in the extent to which they elicit aggressive behavior. You can see from this example that it would be hard to establish the comparability of the groups in a natural environment. Thus, experimental studies are often conducted in laboratory settings where the researcher has control over the environment. Variables under control in research studies are referred to as independent and dependent variables. *Independent variables* are the stimuli that the researcher selects in order to determine their effect on the *dependent variable,* which is the behavior under study. So in our example, the independent variable is TV violence and the dependent variable is play behavior of 4-year-old children.

    Conducting studies in laboratory settings enables the researcher to consider all the variables that exist. In our example we noted that care should be taken to select toys appropriately and to distribute the same toys to both groups under study. When a researcher fails to acknowledge a variable (referred to as the *extraneous variable*), or to control it, then the researcher cannot be absolutely sure that it was the independent variable that caused the effects on the dependent variable being measured. In a well-designed experimental study that minimizes the influence of the extraneous variable, any change in the dependent variable may be attributed to the independent variable, in which case the experiment is said to have *internal validity*. However, if sources of invalidity are present, for example, if there is a possibility that the extraneous variable causes the changes in the dependent variable, then the experiment is said to be *confounded,* meaning that it may not be valid.

independent variable

dependent variable

extraneous variable

internal validity

confounded experiment

Experiments Outside the Laboratory. While experiments conducted in the laboratory are important, as we have seen, they do have their limitations, especially in child development research. They are carried out in artificial settings, thus making any generalizations (that is, general statements that are based on the findings) highly questionable. In fact, the use of laboratory research has led some critics to claim that the field of child development constitutes a "science of the strange behavior of a child in a strange situation with a strange adult" (Bronfenbrenner, 1977). To overcome these limitations, researchers often use either the field experiment or the natural experiment. In the *field experiment,* the research is conducted in a natural setting. However, the researcher exercises control over the environment by deliberately introducing a change. Field experiments in child development research are conducted in settings that are natural to children, for example, in nursery schools, day care centers, or schools. The advantage of field experiments over laboratory experiments is that while the researcher still maintains control over the independent variable by creating a *deliberate* change in the environment, the findings are more readily applied to other children because the child was studied in natural rather than artificial circumstances.

field experiment

    In some instances there can occur a change in a child's life that was not due to research intervention. In these instances, referred to as *natural experiments,* the researcher may capitalize upon the natural change to draw conclusions. An example of a natural experiment is one conducted in a town in Canada. That town had just been introduced to television, so

natural experiment

children who had previously not watched television now began to watch it. This provided a naturally occurring experiment so that researchers could determine the effects of TV on children. By measuring the children's aggressive play behavior before as well as after children were exposed to television, these researchers demonstrated that aggression increased after television was introduced into the town. In this study, although the research can be seen as more applicable to all children because children were introduced to the independent variable in their natural setting, we cannot be absolutely sure of the findings because the researcher had no control over what the children were viewing on television, how long they were watching television, and so on.

positive and negative correlations

The Correlational Method. In correlational studies, the researcher assesses the extent to which variables appear to be related in some way. Although there are several kinds of correlational relationships, the two most common ones are known as *positive relationships* and *negative relationships*. For example, there is a positive correlation between children's height and weight. That is, as children's height increases so does their weight. There is a negative correlation between children's age and the amount of time they spend with an adult caretaker. That is, as children's age increases, the number of hours they spend with a caretaker decreases.

Correlations range from -1.00 to $+1.00$, with $+1.00$ being a perfectly positive correlation and -1.00 a perfectly negative correlation. Thus a correlation of $+0.25$ indicates a weak positive relationship and a correlation of -0.80 indicates a strongly negative correlation. It is important to realize that perfect correlations are relatively rare. Even in the instance of children's height and weight, rarely will a group of children who are ordered on the basis of their height fall into exactly the same order on the basis of their weight. Thus, the correlation must be determined using statistics. A correlation is determined to be *statistically significant* by the researcher if the relationship between the variables is greater than would occur by chance, even though it might not be a perfect correlation.

statistically significant

It is also important to note, and to bear in mind throughout the reading of this book, that correlations do not establish causes, they simply describe patterns of variations. Thus, even though there is a positive correlation between height and weight, this does not tell us that one variable caused the other. For example, consider the fact that there is a positive correlation between the number of churches and the number of crimes. That is, as the number of churches increases so does the number of crimes. But that does not mean that one variable caused the other. It may simply be the case that a third variable, say an increase in population, is at play in both the increase in the number of churches and the increase in the number of crimes.

Longitudinal Research.   Another important, although difficult to implement, tool in developmental research is the longitudinal study. Longitudinal research is not really a methodology in the sense that we have been discussing methods. Rather, it is a research perspective, for it may involve an experimental or a correlational study.

The major advantage of longitudinal studies is that they enable researchers to study changes in an individual's behavior over time, thus gaining valuable information regarding the stability or instability of behavior. An example of longitudinal research would be a study on the question: Do children who have good language skills at an early age continue to show high competence in linguistic skills as they grow older? Another advantage of longitudinal studies is their usefulness in evaluating environmental effects on development, since they enable researchers to address such questions as: Do different childrearing practices have long-term influences on children's behavior? What are the effects of day care on children's development?

Although valuable in those respects, longitudinal studies that are conducted over long periods of time also have several major disadvantages. One, they are expensive to undertake, both economically and in the amount of time required to find answers to problems that may require a more immediate solution or understanding. Research on day care is a case in point. Longitudinal studies on day care are important if we are to establish the effects on infants and children of spending a large portion of their day away from parents and home. However, day care is being used by an increasing number of families with young children, so that more immediate information on its effects is imperative, especially for the planning of social policies that can help families.

Another disadvantage of longitudinal research is the difficulty of finding people who are willing to commit themselves or their children to long-term participation in the study. When people are willing to make a commitment, the question arises whether they may be, in fact, representative of a larger population or whether they are better educated, more curious, or perhaps more cooperative than most people. There is an additional problem of *subject attrition,* meaning that some subjects invariably will drop out of the study. For example, one or more subjects may move out of town. While this is a possibility in any research study, it is more of a problem in a longitudinal study simply because of the long period of time involved.

subject attrition

A further disadvantage of longitudinal research is the phenomenon of *repeat testing.* Because of the need to administer numerous tests and measures at regular intervals, subjects in a longitudinal study may become "test-wise" and may improve in their ability to answer questions correctly. The problem for the researcher is that any improvement in scores on tests may be simply the result of practice in taking tests rather than any change in the individual.

repeat testing

historical events

Finally, a major disadvantage of longitudinal studies is the problem of *historical events*. During the period of any longitudinal study a variety of events and circumstances may take place over which control by the researcher is difficult or impossible. Political events, changes in social values and attitudes, economic conditions, and so on are likely to occur during the study and to affect the subjects. For example, in a longitudinal study that examines the relationship between discipline techniques and later social behavior of the child, very different effects might result from strict parental control if it occurs in the context of a very permissive social climate rather than during a period of rigid moral values (Vasta, 1979).

cross-sectional studies

cohort effect

Cross-Sectional Studies.   To overcome the disadvantages of the longitudinal approach, some researchers rely on the use of *cross-sectional* studies. Cross-sectional studies examine developmental questions by comparing groups of subjects at different age levels rather than by following the same individual for many years (Vasta, 1979). This design is useful in that it produces information in less amount of time than longitudinal studies can. A major disadvantage of this method, however, is what is known as *cohort effect*. Cohort effects arise when a researcher, wishing to investigate changes in a behavior over time, chooses the cross-sectional approach and studies a group of individuals at different ages at the same time. If differences among the individuals were observed, a conclusion might be drawn that these differences are a function of age. However, the individuals under study differ not only in age but in another important characteristic—generation. For example, individuals under study who are 60 years old and have lived through the Depression era and World War II are likely to have had very different experiences, and they would also have very different values from those in the study who are 20 years old and who had not experienced economic difficulties or war. Thus cross-sectional studies do not allow for the examination of behavioral changes as they occur in one individual over time but rather they focus on differences among individuals.

combined longitudinal and cross-sectional approach

Researchers often use a *combined longitudinal and cross-sectional approach*. In this combined approach, several groups of subjects of different ages are studied over a period of several years. The research might begin with groups at ages 1, 3, and 5. Initial assessment of the dependent measures would demonstrate any developmental differences in performance in these three age levels. In other words, it is a cross-sectional approach. If we continue to study these subjects over a longer period (a longitudinal approach) we would also have several years of data on each of the subjects, thus permitting an in-depth examination of the behavior in an individual, so that we would have comparison data at different age levels. In many ways, therefore, the combined longitudinal and cross-sectional approach is an excellent tool for addressing a wide range of questions concerning development (Vasta, 1979).

Retrospective Research.   The *retrospective approach* also is used as an alternative to the longitudinal study. It is defined as an attempt to link an individual's current behavior with events that occurred earlier in his life. In the retrospective approach, a questionnaire or a structured interview is used to uncover various aspects of the individual's life. Correlations between earlier events and current behaviors and developmental problems are examined to try to identify possible relationships (Vasta, 1979). Naturally, these hypothetical relationships can never be tested directly with these subjects. However, the retrospective approach can serve as the basis for further research with other individuals, and it also helps researchers understand determinants of behavior. For example, in attempting to find out some of the causes of learning disabilities researchers may use a retrospective study which examines events prior to or surrounding the birth of the children. They may find that a significant percentage of the mothers studied indicated that they underwent prolonged labor and difficulties during birth. This finding might encourage further investigation of developmental delays in infants to see how these affect learning and may lead to earlier identification of learning disabilities.

retrospective approach

Case Histories.   A retrospective research study may involve a case history, which is an account of the development of a particular child. The case history was not originally designed as a scientific tool. Rather, it was devised as a method of assessing a child so that scientific principles could be adequately applied for that child's training and care. The case history is typically prepared for a child who is having some psychological or other problem. It involves the attempt to collate all of the relevant facts about the child and his environment so that those who work with the child may gain a better perspective on possible problems in that child's life and ways that he can be helped. Data for the case history are obtained from as many sources as possible and include observations of the child, interviews with parents, caretakers, teachers, physicians, and other adults the child interacts with, as well as results of psychological tests given to the child.

As a scientific method, the case history has disadvantages. It is often subjective and may include a reporting of only those events in the life of the child the recorder regards as pertinent. Also, children for whom case histories are available cannot be considered to be representative of a population of children as a whole, since they are likely to be children who are receiving or are in need of psychological treatment. Nonetheless, the case history is very meaningful, for it provides researchers with a rich source of data from which to draw hypotheses for further investigation.

Ethical Considerations

Any research study that involves human subjects is generally reviewed by an independent review board. The approval of the review board is necessary before the study can begin. The review board examines the proposed research procedures involved in the study so that these may not in any way harm the subjects, and it ensures that the researcher will take steps to involve only those subjects who are informed of the research and are willing to participate.

The difficulty in applying these standards to children who participate in research is obvious. The Society for Research in Child Development developed ethical standards for research with children which include the following:

- Each child must be fully informed about the purposes of the study and the procedures to be employed.

- In cases where children are too young to understand the aims and purposes of the research, parental consent should be secured.

- Each child may withdraw from participation at any time during the study.

- Each child has a right to be compensated for his or her time as a research subject.

- Children will not be subjected to any harmful treatment during the course of the research.

- All information about individual participants obtained in the course of the research will be kept confidential.

- No matter how young the child, he or she has rights that supercede the rights of the investigator.

Today researchers as a matter of course employ these standards for the protection of children's rights. However, this was not necessarily true in the past, and the review procedure is in fact mandated by law. You should also be aware of the fact that an ethical course of action is not always clear. Consider an investigation of the hypothesis that premature infants may become abused children because they are difficult to soothe and may frustrate and anger their parents. Should the investigator fully inform the parents of the hypothesis and thus sensitize them to the fact that there could be something wrong with their relationship with their newborn baby? Or should the investigator proceed by masking the central question of the study, thereby deceiving the parents? Will there be any long-term harm or benefits to the parents and children by pursuing either action—providing full information about the research or withholding information? If you were the researcher, what would you do?

Consider another dilemma which arises in studies that examine the potential benefits of a new treatment or program. To evaluate the effectiveness of the treatment or program, researchers need to study subjects who receive the treatment and those who do not, often referred to as the control group. If the treatment proves effective, the question arises: Is the researcher obliged to provide the treatment to the control group after the study is completed? Would it be fair not to?

These are sensitive issues for which there is no single answer. While most researchers strive to uphold children's rights in the research and are in fact required to do so by law, there is the argument that since the fruits of the research potentially benefit us all, some amount of risk may be worth the eventual progress we achieve. This argument on the costs and benefits of the research is seldom easy to settle. Therefore, researchers rely on the independent review board procedure so that other scientists can have input on such difficult ethical questions as the ones presented in our two examples. Combining the judgments of several researchers may not necessarily lead to more ethical decisions, but it serves at least to keep researchers continually aware of the ethical implications of their work.

The Application of Research to Practice

Research findings are useful for they enhance our understanding of children and they have application to everyday life. However, several issues need to be kept in mind as you reflect upon the research you will be reading about in this book.

Multiple Causes of Behavior.   First, when a research study identifies a phenomenon as a causal factor, it is tempting to think of it as the *only* cause for the behavior being studied. A child's behavior and development are not that simple, however. We need to keep in mind that most of the behaviors of interest to child development professionals have multiple causes. It is the task of the researcher to isolate causes in order to study each one independently of the others, but it is generally understood that causes rarely function in isolation in a child's natural environment.

Norms of Behavior.   Second, most researchers emphasize, as we do throughout the book, the importance of recognizing individual differences among children. However, most research is directed at establishing norms of behavior; that is, what is generally true for *most* children *most* of the time, or what can we expect of children at a given age, or how children may react in certain situations. Such generalizations from the research are not necessarily applicable to all children under all circumstances. This raises the question: Are research studies useful? Admittedly, we usually get to know children as individuals, in which case generalizations from the research may not always be appropriate.

However, there are many other instances when children are considered collectively. For example, the decision of what to include in an elementary or secondary school curriculum is made on the basis of what we know from the research about the cognitive capabilities of children of different ages and about how children function in a group setting such as a classroom. Thus, knowledge from the research is useful, for it complements our understanding of children's development and it enhances the validity of the decisions we make about and for children.

The Uses of Research.   Finally, you should be aware that there are many professionals who rely on the evidence from research on child development. Besides the children's parents, some obvious examples are teachers, nurses, pediatricians, and child psychologists.

The chapters that follow include discussions of social issues that affect children's behavior and development. These include changes in family life such as divorce and factors in the social environment, for example, television. Even government policies have an indirect effect on a child's growth and behavior. Government officials, for example, have to decide what is an optimal number of children that can safely be cared for by one day care worker. Or, they make decisions about intervention programs for handicapped children and set standards for the health and nutrition of children. Such decisions, however, will not benefit children unless they are made on the basis of the knowledge of child development research. In the matter of child day care, for example, a policymaker may make an arbitrary decision that 15 preschool children can be safely cared for by one child care worker. It may be reasonably safe in the physical sense for one caregiver to look after a group of 15 children (the policymaker may assume that preschool children can run out of the building if there is a fire). But, what about the psychological ramifications of such a decision? As we shall see in subsequent chapters in this book, the single most important determinant in development is the interaction the young child has with the adults in his life. Can one child care worker give sufficient attention and warmth to all 15 children? You can see from this one example how the research in child development is important and necessary in decisions made by government.

SUMMARY

As you can see from the discussion so far, child development is a multifaceted field of complementary approaches to the understanding of young children. In this chapter we have introduced you to the field of child development by examining its relatively brief history and the theories and research methods that are used to explain development.

The field of child development did not gain the status of a science until this century. For centuries, however, there was interest in the nature of the child, and concrete questions were asked about how to best train and educate children. Directions and guidance on these matters were provided by philosophers. However, their speculations were yet to be tested by scientific inquiry. It was not until the 19th century, with the maturing discipline of biology which came to be explicitly concerned with the evolution of the organism, that there began to be a more objective and systematic study of the child.

Two principal questions concern current research in child development: How do children change as they grow and develop, and what factors serve to influence the changes? To come closer to an answer to these questions, researchers rely on information from other disciplines and on different theories of development from which to draw hypotheses for research. Such theories of development, several of which were described in this chapter, are based on different assumptions and focus on different aspects of development. Not any one theory provides an adequate explanation of development, but taken together these theories are useful in helping us construct a picture of development and in providing direction for research.

In their attempt to discover facts and confirm hypotheses and ideas derived from theories or the research in other disciplines, child development researchers employ a variety of research methods. Several research strategies used by contemporary investigators were described to convey the spirit and current status of the research and the scientific safeguards required for specific types of research if studies are to have results that are useful to others as well as to oneself.

Not any one research method is perfect. Each method has its advantages and its limitations. This is an important point to keep in mind as you read this book, which is based on the vast amount of information currently being produced in child development research. It is for this reason that scientists have to rely on several studies and the use of multiple research methods. Also, studies are not planned or interpreted as isolated pieces of work. Plans for research are influenced in many ways by previous studies. One interprets results in the framework of an ongoing program and a field of work to which many are contributing. By extending or challenging existing findings, one can contribute to the advance of knowledge.

Advancing knowledge is one purpose of the research in child development. Another is to apply the findings from the research to practical situations in ways which are beneficial to children and to their parents and others who help raise and educate them. The applied nature of the research and the relevance of studies in child development are especially evident in the next chapter where we look at the conditions under which most children live and at how child development research now focuses on the consequences for development of social changes that affect children.

REVIEW POINTS

1. The study of child development is relatively recent and did not emerge as a field of scientific inquiry until the late 19th century. However, interest in children dates to ancient times, as philosophers through the ages expressed some thought-provoking ideas about children's development and education.

2. Two of the more recent philosophers are John Locke and Jean-Jacques Rousseau, who held widely contrasting views on children's development. Locke maintained that the child's mind is a *tabula rasa,* or blank slate, and that the child needs education and guidance. Rousseau believed that the child is born with innate abilities and interests and should be allowed to explore the world freely and to learn from these explorations. The views of these philosophers were based on speculations and can be seen as the precursors of a fundamental division among researchers (referred to as the nature-nurture controversy), the debate about whether intelligence, for example, is an endowed trait or wholly shaped by experience.

3. The scientific approach to the study of children owes much to the work of Charles Darwin, who led researchers to the idea that the study of children could help shed more light on the psychological makeup of adults. Also contributing to child study as a scientific endeavor was G. Stanley Hall, the founder of child and adolescent psychology as subareas of general psychology.

4. One of the first major achievements of the scientific study of children was the development of the intelligence test by Binet and Simon, and its adaptation in America by one of Hall's students, Terman. Another of Hall's students, Gessell, also contributed to the child study movement, paving the way for the accumulation of vast stores of data on children's development.

5. Once researchers accumulated data on children, they began to focus their attention, in the 1930s, on the building of theories to explain children's development. Theories are important not because they are true or not, but because they serve as direction for further research. Theories may be divided into several general categories. Some explain behavior in terms of an interaction between genetic potential and environmental experiences. Others explain behavior in terms of experience and learning, not taking into account genetic inheritance.

6. Theories serve as one source of ideas for the direction of research. Researchers also acquire ideas from cross-cultural studies and from studies conducted in other disciplines such as genetics and ethology. The hypotheses derived from the theories and other sources of ideas are tested by research studies.

7. Research studies may be categorized as basic (motivated by the desire to expand knowledge) or as applied (designed to meet society's needs and provide information that could be put to use in the social setting). Within these two categories there are different methods for studying children.

8. Any one research study, however, is not expected to yield information on a particular question concerning children's growth and development. Rather, since different methods for study have advantages as well as limitations, researchers synthesize the findings of many studies.

CHAPTER 1

NEW DIRECTIONS IN
CHILD DEVELOPMENT:
A SOCIAL ISSUES APPROACH

Researchers in a number of different disciplines are accepting the view that research should not only be conducted for the sake of generating knowledge, but that it should also be directed toward the solution of contemporary social problems (Bevan, 1982; Takanishi, 1981; Lindblom & Cohen, 1979). In developmental psychology in particular, researchers are becoming increasingly aware that their work, which involves the study of children and families, by its very nature has social applications and relevance. These same researchers are concerned about the welfare and development of American children, and they seek to resolve social problems related to children in several different ways.

Some researchers, for example, become involved in the development of social policies and programs or in the evaluation of these to ensure that they address the needs of children (Travers & Light, 1982). This involvement is primarily to bring child development knowledge to bear on how federal and state governments respond to the problems of children and also on how business and industry can help facilitate family life. The increased participation of child development researchers in the policy process (Zigler & Finn, 1984; Zigler et al., 1983; Masters, 1983) has evolved over recent years as it became evident that the child is influenced by many factors. Examples of such factors are the people in his immediate social setting (the family), the larger or more remote social systems such as the school, the community, the government, and even the mass media, most notably television, over which the child and often the family have little, if any, control. Also, beginning in the mid-1960s, the implementation of a wide range of social programs for children (Zigler & Berman, 1983; Salkind, 1983) provided the opportunities for psychologists to participate in the policy process and to design and evaluate programs aimed at improving the lives of children. Through their participation in the development of social programs, researchers not only helped many children, they also refined their research methodologies and increased their understanding of children and the factors that can enhance or hinder their development. Thus several social programs (for example, Head Start, which we describe later in this book), were "natural laboratories" that facilitated the study of children.

CHILDHOOD SOCIAL INDICATORS

childhood social indicators

Another important factor that precipitated researchers' involvement in the policy process is the concern with the rapid pace of the changes our society is experiencing. Researchers note that the effects of such changes on children should be monitored through the compilation of *childhood social indicators*. Childhood social indicators are measures of changes or constancies in the conditions of the lives of children, and in the health, achievement, behavior, and well-being of children themselves (Zill et al., 1983;

Parke & Peterson, 1981; Sheldon & Parke, 1975). Social indicators may include such statistics as how many children are born each year; how many children are born into poverty; how many live in single-parent households; and information about how children spend their time (for example, how many children report that their parents let them watch television whenever they want to). The systematic compilation of childhood indicators as a knowledge base provides a powerful tool for understanding the influence of social changes on the development and well-being of children and can help us devise ways to help children. The users of such information, however, are not only child development researchers. Parents and professionals who deal with children and families—teachers, social workers, physicians, lawyers, judges, policymakers, and business executives—also need to be aware of the status of children.

Several disturbing social indicators documented in numerous sources (for example, Keniston, 1977) attest to the problems faced by children and their parents in the areas of health and psychological well-being. One of the most recent sources is the *Report of the Select Committee on Children, Youth, and Families* (1983). These problems include inadequate health care, poverty, child abuse and neglect, as well as an increase in youth unemployment and in the incidence of depression and suicide among youth. Other problems are the high divorce rate, the trends toward single-parent families, and the care and socialization of infants and young children outside of the home.

In addition to these problems, the nation's economic troubles and current political climate have resulted in the government's retreat from its commitment to social programs and from its responsibility for providing children's services. As a result, families suffer additional difficulties due to lost benefits (Finn, 1981; Miller, 1983). There are questions regarding the political motivations behind the cuts in social programs. Some argue, for example, that children's services are easy for policymakers to eliminate because children have no voice in Congress. They have no political power; they do not lobby; they do not make campaign contributions; and they do not vote (Miller, 1983). Yet their lives are profoundly affected by social conditions they did not create and by decisions beyond their control. Some researchers, therefore, become involved in advocacy (Ross, 1983; Hoffman, 1983), which entails bringing social issues that affect children to the attention of policymakers and others through the provision of expert testimony based on child development research and the publication of research findings in the popular media (McCall et al., 1981). We should point out that although many researchers believe that the application of child development knowledge is an important endeavor, other researchers question such activities and see their mission as working toward the refinement of theory rather than its application. Admittedly, complex ethical issues arise when researchers attempt to become involved in various aspects of the policy process (MacRae, 1981; Weiss, 1978). However, as well as contributing their expertise about children in the policy arena, many researchers are finding that their work benefits from the contact and stimulus of direct experience and the application of research (DeLone, 1982; Bronfenbrenner, 1974).

Our discussions in this book reflect these new directions in child development research and the changes in the role of researchers. We combine our presentation of developmental processes from the prenatal period through adolescence with highlights of childhood social indicators. In each unit, we focus on social issues that are relevant to the topic under discussion. For example, in Unit II, which treats development before birth, we discuss malnutrition and poor health care among pregnant women and the effects these have on the developing child. In the unit on infancy, we discuss placing infants in day care.

By way of an introduction to our social issues approach, in this chapter we describe some of the social changes that profoundly affect the development of children. More specifically, we outline childrearing issues and concerns that are relevant to this decade and beyond. From our perspective, little is more important than the nurturance of our children, who are the nation's future. As we shall see in this chapter, the scope and rate of recent social changes in demography, the economy, and technology have contributed to pressures and stresses on family life and have made the nurturance of children difficult. American families are increasingly unable to cope with their problems, and the effects on children may be significant.

Our goal in this chapter is twofold. One, we present an up-to-date although not necessarily comprehensive profile of social trends and the consequences these may have for children. Many of the topics we look at are discussed in more depth in other sections of the book. Two, we then discuss possible solutions to the problems of children. What can we do to counteract the negative effects of social changes? We believe that many of the solutions to the problem can be grouped under the broad heading of facilitating child and family life—making sure that we have programs and policies that maintain and support rather than undermine the family. Such programs and policies need not always be government-sponsored. Policies instituted by industry can affect families, and grass-roots self-help groups are also an important aspect of the solution. Again, our intent in this chapter is not to list all possible solutions, but rather, to focus on some of them and the means by which they can be achieved.

BACKGROUND: THE CONCEPT OF CHILDHOOD

Ideas about the nature of the child and concepts about what childhood entails are reflected in the way children are treated, in the concerns that we have for them, and in the policies that are created for their benefit. Every age has had its perceptions of the meaning and place of childhood in the

THE WICKET OF THE FOUNDLING HOSPITAL AT FLORENCE, ITALY.

FIGURE 1.1   The condition of children varies depending on society's concept of childhood and the value adults attach to children. Before about 1750, emotional attachment to children was difficult to establish because they were likely to die at an early age. Often they were placed in foundling homes or simply abandoned.

social order. In fact, the concept of childhood as we know it today is peculiar to the technological societies of this century and was virtually nonexistent at other times (Ariès, 1962). There were always children, of course, but they were not always viewed as such. In the Middle Ages there was a period of "infancy" which lasted until the age of 6 or 7. After that, the people we now refer to as children were simply assimilated into the adult world. In contrast, the 20th century has been characterized by the definition of childhood as a special period of the life cycle (Larrabee, 1960). The student should recognize that although the conditions of the lives of children today need to be improved, children have lived under worse conditions in the past. Conditions varied depending on the concept of childhood and the value adults attached to children.

A Brief History of Childhood

Not much is known about children in Europe before the 18th century; writings about them are relatively skimpy. Phillippe Ariès (1962), in his book *Centuries of Childhood,* offers a well-known account of the lives of European children in the Middle Ages. Because there were few, if any, documentary records of the time, Ariès, using fragmentary data, speculatively reconstructed the life of the medieval child.

However, more documentation is available for the years after 1700, and from it we know that prior to certain social reforms that resulted in improvements in their lives, young children suffered a great deal. First, there appears to have been no special emotional attachment to children. In fact, most children were not wanted. Before 1750 children in Europe were being born in great numbers. Women could be expected to give birth to as many as ten or twelve infants, most of whom died at birth or in their early childhood years. About two thirds of infants and children died before they reached the age of five (Kessen, 1965). With the chances of survival for children so slim, emotional attachment to them was difficult to establish and those who did survive birth were often abandoned in the streets and simply neglected. So rampant was the abandonment and neglect of children that the authorities in France and England instituted increasingly stricter penalties for infanticide. But even with these penalties, parents continued to abandon their children, except that they left them not in the streets, but in orphanages or foundling homes. It is difficult to imagine today how enormous the problem of unwanted children had been. Consider the fact that for every three births recorded in Paris, one baby was left in a foundling home (Kessen, 1965). Moreover, the children in the orphanages did not fare that well. According to records, 90% of all children left in orphanages in several large cities in Europe died (Kessen, 1965).

Children suffered problems of a different nature in the 19th century. During that period there were conflicting views of childhood that were nonetheless rooted in the self-interest of adults. Religious leaders and middle-class parents were concerned with the moral redemption of the child, and they resorted to several methods by which to "break the will" of children, an essential aspect of moral salvation. Letters of mothers from that period reveal that mothers felt they had to resort to severe punishment in order to "keep the children in line" and, although parents were at times kind and rational in their interactions with children, they generally believed that firm discipline would produce an upright citizen (Scarr, 1984).

Children of the poor, on the other hand, were regarded as economic assets and were exploited by their parents and by employers. They worked for long hours in dreadful working conditions, and they often died young.

FIGURE 1.2   During the Depression, many children worked to supplement family incomes. The children depicted in this photograph are working on a cotton plantation.

It must be borne in mind that it is in this district [of England] that the regular hours of a full day's labour are 14 and occasionally 16; and the children have to walk a mile or two at night without changing their clothes . . . there are very few [mines] . . . where the main roadways exceed a yard in height . . . so that in such places the youngest child cannot work without the most constrained posture. The ventilation, besides, in general is very bad, and the drainage worse . . . The ways are so low that only little boys can work in them, which they do naked and often in mud and water, dragging sledge-tubs by the girdle and chain. (From a speech by the Earl of Shaftesbury, June 7, 1842, as quoted in Kessen, 1965).

The exploitation of children was not as rampant in America as it was in Europe. In the United States, only some children under age 13 (less than 20%) living in urban areas were employed during the latter part of the 19th century. Their working conditions were also horrendous, but not as grim as those in England and Wales, where the children and often pregnant women worked in mines and factories for six days a week. The number of employed children in America decreased steadily during the early part of the 20th century, and by the 1940s, only 1% of young children were employed. In many rural areas, however, children either assumed a great deal of work around the house or farm, or they were apprenticed or rented out to another farm for labor (see Figure 1.2).

FIGURE 1.3   When they are not in school, many children spend most of their time watching television.

The decrease in the number of young children who were put to work in the late 19th and early 20th centuries reflects changes in public attitudes toward children. With improvements in health care and medicine, the chances of children surviving improved, as did general interest in them. Child labor laws here and in Europe ensured that young children did not work in factories and mines. Another milestone that signaled the changing attitudes toward children was the introduction of compulsory schooling. A 1933 report of the United States Office of Education indicates that between 1870 and 1915 the total number of American pupils aged 5 to 17 increased from 7 to 20 million (White, 1982). Thus childhood became a period protected for learning. For a time early in this century, young adolescents from poor homes still had to work, and many of them could not read or write. Nevertheless, children were starting to be recognized as needing education and protection. The uniqueness and separation of childhood as a special period is an unmistakable feature of our society (Larrabee, 1960), which has become increasingly more child-centered since the early 1900s.

The two decades that followed the end of World War II were perhaps the greatest period of child-centeredness in our society. During that time there was a very high birth rate, a phenomenon which is referred to as the postwar baby boom. A strong child and family orientation was fueled in part by the persuasive arguments of researchers and childrearing experts such as Bowlby (1951) and Spock (1968) who wrote of the importance of the mother in the child's life and of the pleasures of childrearing. Also, the affluence of that time allowed the majority of families to be supported by the husband's income so the mother was able to stay home and devote her time to caring for the children.

Since the early 1970s, however, our society has moved away from its focus on the child and the family. There is ample evidence that children are no longer adequately cared for, and there are strong indications of a general devaluation of children and childrearing. For example, the number of reported cases of child abuse in this country is increasing each year (Gerbner, Ross, & Zigler, 1980; see also Chapter 9). We shall see, too, in the social issues sections of subsequent chapters that there are many other indicators that point to the general neglect of children (see Figure 1.3).

Several social commentators and researchers who have studied the lives of children in the past 15 to 20 years contend that childhood, as we have come to regard it, is diminishing, meaning that children are once again living under conditions that threaten their well-being. What are these conditions? In his book *Our Endangered Children: Growing Up in a Changing World,* Packard (1983) examines the actual setting in which a child is likely to grow up today and its impact on the child. He writes that for the majority of today's children being young may mean, among other things

- wondering if your parents are going to split up;

- living in a single-parent family;

- having to adjust to newcomers in your home in case of the remarriage of one or both of your parents;

- for the very young, the possibility of being taken care of by a caregiver, usually outside the home;

- for older children, being left alone in an empty house;

- having relatively little contact with adults;

- sitting in front of the television set most of the time when you are not in school;

- being lonely a lot of the time;

- having parents who are likely to be self-absorbed, uncertain about their role in life or about the future, or who are experiencing a great deal of stress.

Obviously, these are different kinds of problems from the ones encountered by children in the past. Today's problems represent a new kind of adversity for children, and, as Packard writes, the new ways children are growing up today "promote a sense of insecurity that may lie behind a seemingly cheerful countenance. They often add [up] to a poor foundation for adult life."

GROWING UP IN THE 1980s

demography

What has brought on these changes in the way children are growing up today? As we shall see, the recent years have, indisputably, been ones of deep and far-reaching change in American society. The makeup and balance of our population (what we refer to as *demography*) is undergoing major changes. Our society is having to adjust to continued economic problems, and there has been a revolution in how women and men perceive their roles in their work and in their family life. In addition, there have been vast technological changes such as the introduction of television that profoundly affect our lives. In many ways we are still continuing to experience these changes, so we are in a period of transition. Even though these changes are transitional, it is instructive and important to consider how they are influencing the development of children and what the consequences may be for their future.

Demographic Changes

Let us look first at the changes that are occurring in demography. Because of the unusually high birth rates of the two decades after World War II, followed by the very low birth rates of the last 15 years, as well as increased longevity, the composition of our population has changed considerably. Ours has become, in fact, an aging society, with few children, a plethora of young adults, and mounting numbers of older individuals.

Let us paint a more graphic picture of the situation. In 1970, children under the age of 18 made up 34% of the population, which means that between 1970 and 1980, the number of children decreased by about 5%. During that same period, moreover, the number of individuals between the ages of 25 and 34 years has increased by 32%, and the number of individuals over 65 has increased by 17% (U.S. Bureau of the Census, 1981a). The significance here is not only that there are fewer children now than there were in the 1970s, but also that at the same time there are *more* young adults and older individuals.

How can we explain this change in demographic trends? The increase in the number of young adults is explained by the fact that these are the postwar baby boom children who have reached the stage of young adulthood. The increase in the number of older individuals is attributable to medical advances that enable people to live to an older age (Richmond, 1980). But why the decline in the number of births? This is explained by an overwhelming trend today for later marriage and childbearing. Two decades ago 28% of women in the 20- to 24-year-old age group were single, in contrast to 45% today (U.S. Bureau of the Census, 1981b). In the same period, the average age at which a woman has her first child has risen. Moreover, an increasing number of couples are choosing to have fewer or no children. For a variety of reasons, among them the fact that they have delayed childbearing, many couples cannot have children (Hendershot & Placek, 1981). The startling fact is that less than 38% of American families have any children living with them (see Table 1.1). Families that do have children tend to have one or two. We can see in Table 1.2 that in 1960, 21% of families had three or four children. In 1981, only 8% of families had three children, and 4% had four or more children.

Many factors account for the decrease in the birth rate and the fewer number of children per household. The women's movement of the 1960s made an increasing number of women aware of their career potential. Thus many women are choosing a career first and marriage and motherhood later (Dowd, 1983). Another researcher (Hoffman, 1975) suggests also that Americans may want fewer children because of the increasingly high cost of raising children today (estimated at between $50,000 and

TABLE 1.1   The total number of households in 1970 and 1982 with proportions of households that include children.

	Total Households and Percent Distribution by Type of Household		
	1970		1982
Total Number of Households	63.4 mil.		83.5 mil.
Percent of households			
Family households	81.2%		73.1%
Married couple, no children	30.3		30.1
Married couple, children 0–17	45.3% { 40.3		37.1% { 29.3
Male householder, children 0–17	0.5		0.8
Female householder, children 0–17	4.5		7.0
Other families, without children	5.6		5.8
Non-family households	18.8		26.9

Note: The Bureau of the Census defines a *family* as a group of two or more persons residing together and related by birth, marriage, or adoption. A *household* consists of all those persons who occupy a housing unit. It includes related family members, and all unrelated persons, if any. A person living alone in a housing unit or a group of unrelated persons sharing a housing unit is counted as a household. A *householder* is usually the person, or one of the persons, in whose name the home is owned or rented. If there is no such person in the household, the householder can be any adult household member.

Source: U.S. Bureau of the Census. "Household and Family Characteristics: March 1981," *Current Population Reports,* Series P20, No. 371, Table A; unpublished data from the March, 1982 Current Population Survey.

TABLE 1.2   The number of children per family. The proportion of families with 3 or more children has fallen sharply for all families. There has been a corresponding rise in the proportion of families with no children or only one child.

	Percent Distribution of Families by Number of Own Children Under 18 Years Old						
	1960	1965	1970	1975	1979	1980	1981
All families							
No children	43%	43%	44%	46%	47%	48%	48%
1 child	18	18	18	20	21	21	21
2 children	18	17	17	18	19	19	19
3 children	} 21	11	11	9	9	8	8
4 or more children		11	10	7	4	4	4
Black families							
No children	44%	40%	39%	37%	37%	38%	39%
1 child	16	17	18	22	23	23	23
2 children	13	14	15	17	20	20	20
3 children	} 28	10	10	11	11	10	10
4 or more children		19	18	14	9	8	8

Note: "Own children" includes biological, adopted, and stepchildren. The figures represent a cross-section of families at a given point in time, and as such do not reflect the distribution of families by the number of children they will ultimately have. For example, while 48% of families had no children in 1981, many of these families previously had or subsequently will have one or more children. Because the vast majority of U.S. families are white, the percent distributions for white families are very close to those for all families and so are not shown separately.

Source: U.S. Bureau of the Census, *Statistical Abstract of the United States, 1982–83,* Table 70.

$100,000 for each child) and the prevailing pessimism about economic conditions. In addition, perhaps the desire to have fewer children could be a reflection of public concern with overpopulation.

Whatever the reasons for the decrease in the number of children, there are likely to be some consequences for children and for society itself. We can learn about some of the consequences of demographic changes from what is happening in China where we have what may be termed a *natural experiment*. In order to contain the population growth, the government of the People's Republic of China has taken a number of steps to persuade families to have only one child. Billboards in major cities proclaim, "It is better to have one child only." There is also a vigorous government program that combines persuasion with economic incentives and penalties aimed at achieving one-child families. One-child families receive extra health care and school subsidies, as well as extra grain rations and a larger plot of land for growing produce for private sale. Families that have more than one child have privileges taken away from them, thus severely curtailing their financial and social status.

China has succeeded in slowing its population growth. Studies reveal that an increasingly larger portion of children in China have no siblings, and there are studies currently being conducted by Chinese and Western researchers to determine the effect of this trend on the child, the family,

FIGURE 1.4   In an effort to contain its population growth, the People's Republic of China has taken steps to ensure that families have only one child. This billboard advertises the benefits of a single-child family. With a generation of Chinese children growing up with no siblings, researchers question the effects this could have.

and society. For researchers the question is not whether the number of children should be limited, but how best to identify and combat the negative aspects of such a policy on the development of the next generation. Researchers point out that if for the next 30 years families have only one child, the next generation will grow up with no brothers or sisters, and their children will have no aunts or uncles.

The studies on Chinese children that have been done so far suggest that single children demonstrate superior intellectual abilities, but also that they display a higher incidence of many negative social behaviors. In one study that compared children with siblings and only children, the only children displayed a higher incidence of all negative social behaviors tested and were rated as disrespectful to elders, less cooperative, and lacking in self-care skills (Ching, 1982). According to the researcher, as well as others (e.g., Bronfenbrenner, 1970), interactions with older children are a major way children develop social traits. In families with more than one child, the siblings form the child's first play group. The more extensively children are involved in play situations with children of various ages, the greater the training they receive in mutual cooperation.

In China, the ramifications of a large number of single-child families are extensive and concern not only children but adults as well (see Figure 1.4). Although retired workers receive pensions, the Chinese constitution gives primary responsibility for the care of aged parents to their children. So there may be financial problems associated with having only one child. Also, the traditional emphasis in China is on having a son to carry on the family name, which poses a potential obstacle to the one-child family. What if the child is a girl? Reports have filtered to the West of abortions in families which already have a child and are afraid of the economic consequences of another. A recent report on 100 pregnant women in China who were screened to determine the sex of their unborn child stated that over 60% of women carrying girls chose to abort, whereas only 2% of women carrying a boy chose to abort (China Medical Journal, 1975).

Changes in the law have been made to help families make a better transition from what tradition dictates to what current policies require. It is now possible for a young couple to live with the maternal in-laws rather than the paternal in-laws, for a woman to retain her family name, and even for the parents to give their child the maternal surname, thereby giving families with a daughter a sense of continuity. But even with such changes, if the mother and the father both have no siblings, each would want their only child to have their family name, so you can see that the changes in the law, although helpful in intent, may have little practical effect.

What are consequences for *our* society of having fewer children? What will be the role of children in a society where there will be many more older individuals than children? Will children, particularly those most in need, receive better or worse schooling and other kinds of essential services as their numbers decrease? Will parents and taxpayers be more caring toward and interested in the fewer children there are or will the needs of the young be seen as conflicting with the goals of adults?

It is not easy to answer these questions or to be certain what the lives of these children as adults will be like. It is no doubt possible that the demographic transition we are now experiencing will produce at least some favorable results. Some contend that as the smaller cohorts of children today start entering the job market in the late 1980s, the reduced competition among them for entry-level jobs will increase their market value, employment, and earnings, which in turn will give them a sense of confidence about the future. With improved earnings and prospects, they may marry earlier and produce more children. One could argue further that, in due course, the rise in fertility will produce an improved climate of opinion toward children, and a bettering of their condition, just as was true of the 1950s and early 1960s.

This prediction is not very convincing because it assumes that young women, influenced by improved economic conditions, will revert to early marriage and childbearing. However, these assumptions ignore the nature of the revolution that has taken place in the aspirations and education of women. All evidence seems to point to the continued desire, as well as the

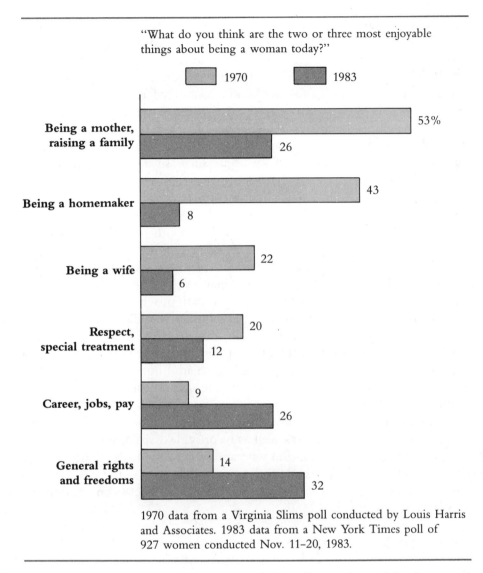

"What do you think are the two or three most enjoyable things about being a woman today?"

☐ 1970   ☐ 1983

Being a mother, raising a family
53%
26

Being a homemaker
43
8

Being a wife
22
6

Respect, special treatment
20
12

Career, jobs, pay
9
26

General rights and freedoms
14
32

1970 data from a Virginia Slims poll conducted by Louis Harris and Associates. 1983 data from a New York Times poll of 927 women conducted Nov. 11–20, 1983.

FIGURE 1.5 Women today are concerned about their rights and freedoms, and they indicate that one of the most enjoyable aspects of being a woman is having a career. In contrast, most women in 1970 indicated that being a mother and a homemaker were the two most enjoyable aspects of being a woman. "Women on Womanhood" December 4, 1983. Copyright © 1983 by The New York Times Company. Reprinted by permission.

need, of women to combine careers or jobs with marriage, and to defer childbearing until they have gained a secure foothold in the world of work (Dowd, 1983; Hoffman, 1975). This pattern of behavior favors not having more than one or two children, if any at all. To illustrate our point, you can see in Figure 1.5 that whereas in 1970 many women said they most valued being a mother, and only 9% said they most valued having a career or job, in 1983, the percentage of women who indicated that they most valued a career or job has increased substantially.

In addition, recent analyses of fertility trends reveal that the postwar baby boom has been an unusual phenomenon (Ryder, 1978). The United States now fits the general reproductive pattern prevailing throughout modern developed countries, which is characterized by few large families. It would appear, therefore, that a sharp upturn in childbearing is highly unlikely. Of course, there will be some increase in actual numbers of children being born as the baby boom generation starts having families, but this will be a temporary phenomenon in the long-term decline in childbearing.

On the basis of these predictions, we can see that a likely outlook for the near future is that young workers, after they have successfully obtained entry-level jobs, will be frustrated by the lack of promotional opportunities. Jobs on a higher occupational level will be occupied by the numerous members of the baby boom generation, who will not approach retirement age until after the turn of the century. So today's children, who will be young adults in a decade or so, can probably look forward to a static income (since there will be few opportunities for promotions) and a rivalry with older workers. Once they reach adulthood, they will be taking on a very heavy burden. It will be the task of their relatively small group not only to produce the nation's cadre of professional, administrative, technical, skilled, and unskilled workers, but to ensure the well-being of their own children as well as to provide assistance to an increasing percentage of the population who are older individuals (Bane, 1976a). Thus it is clear that every child today, or a child born in the years that lie just ahead, will be a scarce resource and a precious asset as an adult living in the next century.

Changes in Family Life

The recent changes in family life present additional possible consequences for children. The family's influence on children's development has been the focus of research studies for several decades. Until recently, researchers were usually concerned with investigating traditional family styles and traditional parental roles and their effects on children. They have looked at child development in the context of the two-parent family in which the mother remains at home to look after the children and the father is the primary breadwinner who has minimal direct involvement in childrearing. "The exclusive focus on families of this type has become increasingly anachronistic, however, in the face of demographic changes that have made traditional families less and less characteristic of the home environments in which most children are raised" (Lamb, 1982). Today, there are families in which both parents are employed outside the home; there are families in which fathers share childrearing responsibilities with their wives more equitably than parents in traditional families do; and there are stepfamilies and single-parent families which are the outcome of divorce or the mother's deliberate choice to avoid marriage. Researchers are beginning to look at child development in the context of these family forms and to examine the effects of nontraditional families on parental behavior and child development.

Still, the traditional family is regarded by some as the ideal family, and its decline is sometimes viewed as the cause of contemporary social problems. However, many researchers contend that the traditional family is of relatively recent origin, having emerged less than a century ago (Lamb, 1982), and they note that no family form is best at meeting all of parents' and children's needs and problems at all times. Just as does any other family form, the traditional family has its assets and liabilities. In traditional families, for example, mothers thrive on their children's dependence. The mother's role is to serve the family, and her primary task is childcare. Of course, babies and young children need adults who are attentive and caring, so in this setting the needs of children are well met. However, many women today are not comfortable with such a role. What used to be an expected and rewarded devotion to full-time motherhood has now become less and less respected, and many women feel embarrassed at being just a housewife (Scarr, 1984). From our perspective, it is unfortunate that the social climate is such that women feel this way, for it limits their options, assuming they could afford financially to stay at home. Additional difficulties are encountered by traditional mothers once children grow up and become independent. For some mothers who devote their lives to serving their children, the transition of not being needed may be painful.

It is also important to recognize that all cultural groups have their own standards of what is a proper family (Scarr, 1984). Whether a certain family form is regarded as good or bad for either parents or children often varies with the approval or disapproval afforded it by the community, and also with the support the community is willing to give the family. "In fact, much of what families can do for children depends on the meaning that the community gives to their family form, not what they can actually do for children. If the community undercuts and criticizes single-parent families, for example, both the parents and their children may feel disadvantaged, even if they are functioning quite well" (Scarr, 1984). This point should be kept in mind as we look at several current trends and changes affecting family life and resulting in the rearing of children in nontraditional family settings.

Divorce

One of the major changes affecting children is divorce. The number of divorces per year seems to have reached its peak, but still, close to a million divorces, involving approximately 3 million people, including children, are reported each year. In over 60% of these divorces, there are children under 18 involved (Select Committee on Children, Youth & Families, 1983). It has been established that between 32% and 46% of the children who have grown up in the 1970s will experience either the separation or the divorce of their parents (Bane, 1976b). Despite the large number of children involved in divorce, thus far there have been relatively few studies that examine the impact of divorce on children. As a result, too little is known about a child's experience during divorce, the extent to which children of divorced parents are at risk for developing emotional and psychological problems, and whether there are effects of divorce that are not immediately noticeable in children but are likely to appear at a later age.

However, several researchers have examined these questions. Two very influential research projects on the impact of divorce on children began in the early 1970s. One is headed by Mavis Hetherington and the other by Judith Wallerstein. To summarize their research findings to date, it appears that for children the divorce of their parents is not a single event, but a sequence of experiences, each one a transition in itself and each requiring adjustments (Wallerstein & Kelly, 1979). The transitions noted are (1) the shift from the family life prior to the divorce; (2) the disequilibrium and disorganization immediately following the divorce; (3) the experimentation with a variety of coping mechanisms, living arrangements, and relationships; and (4) the eventual reorganization and attainment of equilibrium. The households in which divorce has occurred recently are characterized by greatly increased disorganization and by marked changes in the management of children, including inconsistency of discipline and diminished communication and nurturance (Hetherington, Cox, & Cox, 1978). The overall meaning is that the parents pay less attention to the children.

Almost all children are found to experience divorce and the transition periods that follow it as painful experiences (Levitin, 1979; Wallerstein & Kelly, 1979). Even children who eventually recognize the divorce of their parents as constructive initially undergo considerable stress with the breakup of the family. The fact that so many children are involved in divorce and that it has become socially acceptable have not been found to alleviate the pain (Rofes, 1980).

Research evidence suggests that the most critical period for the entire family is the first year after divorce. The evidence also points to children's capacity to cope with the crisis. That is, they eventually adjust to their new living arrangements. The degree of their ability to cope, however, and the intensity of their distress, have been found to be related to

1. their age—the preschool child has been found to be more vulnerable and susceptible to emotional and psychological problems associated with the divorce and the period of a few years after the divorce than is the older child;

2. their sex and birth order—boys have been found to suffer for longer periods than girls and to exhibit more behavioral problems and difficulties in their relationships with their mothers and other adults and with peers;

3. whether or not they have siblings—only children experience more distress and psychological problems during the early stages of post-divorce than do children who have siblings;

4. the psychological status of the custodial parent and the availability and involvement of the non-custodial parent. (Hetherington, Cox & Cox, 1982; Wallerstein & Kelly, 1980).

Parents also undergo emotional, psychological, and economic stresses following the divorce. Often the parents' distress is so acute that they neglect to give their children sufficient attention and to recognize their children's painful experiences. Many parents also confide in their children, especially in the older ones, and burden them with information and problems that children have difficulty understanding. In addition, both parents are likely to be depressed for about a year after the divorce and to have difficulties adjusting to their new lives. Hetherington and her colleagues found that often mothers are depressed in part because the children of divorced mothers become especially disobedient and disturbed, especially once the mother has found a job. The divorced father, even though he does not have custody of the children, appears to be even more depressed than the mother during the first year after divorce (Hetherington, Cox & Cox, 1982).

Legal Battles for the Child. The most tragic and vulnerable children of divorce are those who are involved in legal battles between their parents regarding custody issues and visitation rights. Legal battles can continue indefinitely because any decision on any of the issues is modifiable by the courts. A parent's rage against an ex-spouse can also continue for many years and is often expressed in continued litigation over the child. Clinicians note that the fight for the child serves a psychological need in a parent and often wards off a severe depression (Bodenheimer, 1974–75).

The courts are directed to make custody decisions on the basis of the best interests of the child. However, putting this principle into practice is not always easy. Judges and lawyers are often unable to determine what the best interests of the child might be, and they have little help in this regard, since few psychologists or other mental health professionals look on the court as an arena of their interest. When the courts do have psychological services attached to them, they are often understaffed by people who are not trained to work with children (Wallerstein & Kelly, 1979). Goldstein, Freud, and Solnit (1973, 1979) have written books that provide some guidance for decisions on custody issues. The authors recommend, for example, that decisions regarding child custody be resolved in accelerated proceedings instead of long, drawn-out procedures; that they have

FIGURE 1.6 Demographic changes have made traditional families less and less characteristic of the home environment in which children grow up. Today there are several types of families, including single-parent families usually headed by the mother, as well as blended or reconstituted families which are the result of divorce and remarriage of the parents. Researchers are beginning to examine children's development in the context of these family forms and to study the effects of nontraditional families on parental behavior and child development.

psychological parent

final effect and not be reversible; and that they award full control of the children to the one *psychological parent*. However, not all psychologists are in agreement with these recommendations. Some researchers argue that a child needs both the father and the mother (Benedek & Benedek, 1977). In fact, studies point out that children can actually gain some stability and protection from the inevitable parental upsets that arise from divorce if they have contacts with several adults and if their relationship with one or the other parent is not stressed (Santrock, Warshak & Elliott, 1982).

Stepfamilies. Another source of potential problems and anxiety for children of divorce is the remarriage of one or both of their parents. Divorce and subsequent remarriage is so prevalent that 10% of American children under 18 live in stepfamilies (Cherlin, 1981), which are also referred to as *blended families, reconstituted families,* and *new extended families* (see Figure 1.6).

blended family

reconstituted family

new, extended family

Children and adults in stepfamilies experience a great deal of frustration and stress (Fishman & Hamel, 1981). Depending on whether one or both of their parents remarry, and the extent of their relationship with either parent, children may find themselves with new stepparents, siblings, and other kin with whom they have to form and maintain relationships. For children, the stress of living in stepfamilies can become acute. Not only are they affected by the tensions that may be experienced by the different sets of parents and other kin, they also have to accept and adjust to new family members. When they are able to adjust to the new family structure and develop meaningful relationships with new family members, however, they sometimes risk invoking anger and resentment from the original family members over what a parent may consider to be issues of loyalty. Take, for example, the case of a 10-year-old girl whose parents had been divorced since she was 2 years old. Both her parents remarried soon after the divorce, and she developed a close relationship with the father and stepmother, whom she visited every two weeks. She considered her stepmother's parents to be her grandparents. Her mother became very upset and angry whenever the girl mentioned that she visited her "grandparents" and insisted that the girl refrain from addressing them in such a way. Imagine the conflict this child must have experienced, being pulled one way by her feelings toward her father's family and another way by her feelings for her own mother.

Besides the question of loyalty that may arise, children in stepfamilies are also often confused about values and discipline. Children in stepfamilies have to know what is expected of them in two different homes, and they have to adapt to modes of discipline that may be different in the two homes (Jacobson, 1979). The same is true, of course, of children of divorce in general, whether or not their parents remarry.

The Single-Parent Family

More children than ever before are living in a home with only one parent. Currently, 1 in every 5 children and 1 in every 2 black children lives in a single-parent family (Select Committee on Children, Youth and Families, 1983). As we emphasize in Chapter 12, not all single-parent families are alike. However, the majority of single-parent families are headed by women who have low incomes and who are likely to have children under 5 years of age. Young children raised without a father and in poverty are the most at risk of any in the nation. That so many children are growing up in such a way is disturbing. Divorce is one reason cited for the increase in the number of single-parent families. After divorce the most rapidly growing category of single parenthood involves women who have never been married (Select Committee on Children, Youth, and Families, 1983).

Growing up in a single-parent family is not, in and of itself, necessarily harmful. The problems arise out of the difficulties associated with divorce and with poverty, which characterize many single-parent families. Ross and Sawhill (1975) propose that a family headed by a single parent is in a time of transition, since most single parents are divorced and often remarry later. One out of every five divorced adults remarries within a year after the divorce, and the average interval between divorce

cathy®   **by Cathy Guisewite**

and remarriage is five to six years. Most transitions are stressful not only for children but also for adults. The transitions involved in divorce, single parenting, and remarriage are especially stressful, as we have shown, since they involve losing a family member, restructuring the family, and adjusting to new ways of family functioning.

How does the lifestyle of the adults and children in some single-parent families differ from that of traditional families? Both adults and children in some single-parent homes suffer from the effects of stress that stem not only from the change in family structure, but from other sources as well. Single parents may experience task overload since by themselves they have to work full time, manage the household, and look after the children. Single-parent families usually are economically deprived. Over half the number of children under 18 living in single-parent families are in families with incomes below the poverty level (Select Committee on Children, Youth, and Families, 1983). Single parents who are women (and most single parents are) may also have difficulty disciplining their children. Hetherington and her colleagues (1978) found that even in traditional families children tend to exhibit less non-compliant and deviant behavior toward their father than toward their mother, and that when undesirable behaviors occur, the father can terminate these more readily than can the mother.

The stresses that single parents undergo affect children. For children, the parent is a protector, a source of nurturance, and a teacher. A parent provides structure and a sense of security for the child, as well as guidance. The child forms a primary relationship with the parent. Usually, this relationship exerts a positive influence on the child. However, when the parent is under stress, depressed, or unhappy, what stays with the child living in such a situation is depression or anger, and a negative definition of the self. We can see some of the consequences for children of growing up in single-parent families. In a recent study it was found that

TABLE 1.3 Poverty status in 1980 of U.S. families with children by type of family and age of children (in millions)

	Below Poverty Level		Percent of All Poor Families
	N	%	
All families with children under 18 (32.8)	4.8	14.7	100.0
Female-headed families with children (6.3)	2.7	42.9	56.3
With children under age 6 (2.4)......................	1.5	60.6	31.3

SOURCE:–U.S. Bureau of the Census, *Current Population Reports*, Ser. P-60, no. 133, "Characteristics of the Population Below the Poverty Level: 1980" (Washington, D.C.: Government Printing Office, 1982).

elementary school children who are learning disabled or who exhibit behavior problems in the schools are likely to be children from single-parent families (NAESP Report, 1980). In another study with secondary school students, it was found that those from single-parent families were more often tardy or absent, suspended or expelled from school than were children from two-parent families (Brown, 1980). The behavior and learning problems of children from single-parent homes identified in these studies may be manifestations of the emotional disturbances, confusion, and stress that these children are experiencing.

Studies also document that children in single-parent households may be growing up faster than children in two-parent families. On the basis of interviews with parents and children living in single-parent homes, Weiss (1979) noted that in such households children tend to share with the parent the responsibility for family decision-making and for managing the household and that the consequences for the children may be the fostering of an early maturity. He cites one woman, a mother of two girls age 7 and 5, as saying, "We all make decisions together as far as making plans on where we are going, what we are going to eat . . . and they help make decisions as far as things that I buy for the house. They make decisions on their own clothes, of course." In some cases the sharing of responsibilities may be advantageous for children who can learn at an early age to make decisions. However, some of the responsibilities that are placed on children may be too complex for them to grasp and can only result in confusion and frustration (Winn, 1983; Elkind, 1981).

Working Mothers

Even in families where the two parents are present there are difficulties. One source of difficulty is the continued economic crisis we are facing as a nation. Between 1950 and 1980, the average family income, adjusted for inflation, almost doubled. However, it only increased by less than 1%

from 1970 to 1980 (U.S. Bureau of the Census, 1983). Many families express a feeling of despondency about their economic well-being in the future (The General Mills American Family Report, 1981), noting that of the problems that worry them the most, money is number one.

Obviously the economic status of the family affects the children. It is indicated, for example, that parents who abuse their children are frequently unemployed or financially deprived (Garbarino & Sherman, 1980). In families where unemployment of one or both parents occurs, there may also be consequences for the children's health. Margolin and Farran (1983) found that the incidence of illness appears to be increased in the children of recently unemployed workers.

But by far the most widespread consequences for children of the economic problems affecting the family involve working mothers. There are many women who value their careers, and who choose to work. However, a large portion of mothers who work full time do so because they are the sole supporter of the family, or because the family depends on their income (Lamb, 1982). More than half of the children in this country have mothers who are working. Over 50% of mothers with children under 6 years of age are working full time. The most rapidly growing category of working mothers is those who have children under 3 years of age (U.S. Dept. of Labor, 1984).

Reviews of the research on the consequences for children who have mothers who work point out that there is no body of research evidence to indicate that women working outside the home is of itself harmful to children (Scarr, 1984; Hoffman, 1974). In fact, some of the research indicates that there are positive consequences associated with maternal employment. The research points to the fact that the mother's employment can help families keep up with inflation or stay out of poverty. Furthermore, employment outside the home can broaden the horizons of women, making their lives more interesting, giving them additional self-confidence and a new sense of efficacy about themselves. In so doing, working mothers enable children to play a useful role in family life as well as provide them with new perceptions about the roles of men and women in our society (Crosby, 1984).

On the other hand, the fact that parents need to or choose to work outside the home can be an emotional strain on family life. Much of this strain is because of the lack of adequate care that is available for children while their parents are working. In an intensive case study of American families (Lein et al., 1974), it was revealed that many families are experiencing a great deal of stress in trying to coordinate their work and child care arrangements. Many of these parents also expressed considerable anxiety about the kind of job they are doing as parents.

Part of the problem here is that, in the transition from an agrarian to an industrial and increasingly more technological society, and in the process of multiple moves from one job to another, many families no longer live near their kin, and they often do not have the experience, counsel, and

FIGURE 1.7 Latchkey children, who spend several hours a day alone at home, are particularly vulnerable to accidents and victimization by burglars.

support for child care they could once count on from grandparents, aunts, and uncles. There is no relative to count on for babysitting. What is more, the next-door neighbor who was once home all day and could be counted on for this task is likely to be working herself.

In some European countries the government assumes the obligation of facilitating family life and provides for liberal maternity and paternity leave policies and day care facilities that enable parents either to stay at home to look after their children while the children are very young or to go to work assured that their children are well cared for (Kamerman & Kahn, 1986; Allen, 1985). The United States, however, has no such policy (Zigler & Muenchow, 1983), nor are there sufficient day care facilities in the United States for infants, preschool (Select Committee on Children, Youth and Families, 1983), and school-age children (Levine, 1982). Thus American children are being cared for in a variety of settings that may not be adequate. In fact, many of them are left alone or with an older brother or sister. Reports indicate that an estimated two to seven million children between 7 and 12 years of age come home each day to an empty house (Families and Child Care: Improving the Options, 1984). These children have come to be called *latchkey children* because they carry their housekey on a chain around their necks (see Figure 1.7). Reports of these children encountering burglars or being victimized are not uncommon. In a recent study, an investigator discovered that one sixth of all fires in a particular city involved an unattended child (Smock, 1977).

latchkey children

Children who are left alone in their homes too long or too often grow up scared. Researchers suggest that a lifetime of fear may be the legacy of latchkey children. Long and Long (1983) studied 1,000 current and former latchkey children and their parents. When the former latchkey children discussed their experiences, over one third of them said, "I am still afraid to be alone." The Longs suspect that these adults are still carrying with them fears they suffered as children—fears that, never confronted, have never gone away. The children in the study who are currently left alone said that their biggest fear is that someone will break into their home. Their second biggest fear is that they will be hurt by accident or fire.

When considering latchkey children we have to realize that the problems and extent of fear of a latchkey child varies with the age of the child and the location of the home. One hour of being left alone has a very different impact on a 6-year-old child than on a 12-year-old. Being left alone in a safe, small town where people are fairly well acquainted with one another is different from being left alone in a rural setting where houses are sparse and far between, or in a city house or apartment where few adults in the neighborhood are home during the day and where most people are relative strangers to one another.

Child Nurturing and Television

Another major social force that profoundly affects the nurturance and development of children is television. Thirty years ago television did not dominate our lives as much as it does today. Whereas in the past only some families owned a television set, today, most families have more than one set to accommodate the different viewing preferences of parents and children. There is evidence that infants are already attentive to television by the age of 6 or 7 months (Hollenbeck & Slaby, 1979) and that the average elementary school child watches television 15 to 25 hours a week (Murray, 1980). We can see that children are growing up in a world in which they must learn to organize their experiences not only in relation to the social environment of the home, school, and neighborhood, but also in relation to the ever-present TV screen (see Figure 1.8). Let's consider the effects television has on our lives and the lives of children.

TV Violence.   Parents, educators, psychologists, and others who deal professionally with children have long been concerned about the possible effects of television on the child. Public concern about children's television viewing is generally focused on the content of programs, most of which portray a great deal of violence. Numerous studies provide evidence that heavy viewing of television programs is consistently associated with aggressive behavior in children and adults. This has been determined by both correlational and experimental studies, many of which are com-

FIGURE 1.8   By the age of 6 to 7 months, a baby is already attentive to the ever-present TV set. By the time this baby reaches elementary school age, he will spend 15 to 20 hours a week watching television.

piled in *Television and Behavior: Ten Years of Scientific Progress and Implications for the 1980s* (Pearl et al., 1982), which is a report submitted to the United States Surgeon General. Of course, there may be other explanations for aggressive behavior in children as well. For example, it is possible that aggressive children simply prefer more violent shows and thus tend to view these more often, or that aggressive children imitate parents who are themselves prone to violent or aggressive behavior and who may also prefer violent TV shows. In studies conducted by Jerome and Dorothy Singer (1980a,b), however, it was consistently found that children who are heavy viewers of aggressive action adventures or cartoons that depict violence are more likely to exhibit aggressive behavior than children who are not heavy viewers of such programs. Furthermore, neither of the two alternative explanations (the preferential viewing explanation and the parental aggression pattern explanation) could account for such behavior.

There are suggestions, too, that it may be only the *realistic* (as opposed to cartoons) violent or aggressive shows that are more easily imitated by children. However, the Singers' (1980a,b) studies indicate that cartoons that are violent also stimulate aggressive behavior. Other researchers point out that children who watch fantasy heroes such as "The Bionic Woman" or "The Incredible Hulk" are likely to show either overt aggressive behavior or dissatisfaction, unhappiness, and distress in school (Zuckerman et al., 1980).

TV Commercials.   Parents in particular have been concerned with advertising on television, partly because children are captive television viewers and partly because commercials shown during the time when children are most likely to watch television tend to be ones that promote unhealthy eating habits—advertising for sugar-filled cereals, candy, and soft drinks (Finn, 1977).

In America, television producers attempt to build up the viewers' anticipation by portraying fast-paced and action-packed adventures (Singer, 1981) so that the viewers become so engrossed in what is shown that they look forward to the next event or the outcome of an action or comedy sequence. Once the viewers' anticipation is built to a peak, a series of commercials appear on the set. Those who advertise on television presuppose that viewers will be so interested in the program that they will remain "glued" to the set and that they will not be able to avoid the commercials. This is not necessarily so, however, as many adults tend to get up to get food during a commercial, or they avert their gaze, read, or mentally tune out the commercials (Singer, 1981). However, children, especially those in preschool and elementary school, usually do not have such discriminating strategies. They respond with equal attention to commercial interruptions and to the shows. Young children do not have the ability to judge the relative worth of what is being advertised. Through commercials, children are encouraged to develop an attitude of *"continuous consumption"* (Baecher, 1983). Commercials usually depict "new and improved" versions of just about everything, leading to the feeling that everything new is an improvement on older things and that anything new is worth having; the old is only worth replacing. New toys, designer jeans, name-brand athletic shoes are bought and soon discarded in favor of yet different kinds of toys, another designer's jeans, and the latest name in sports shoes. So effective are the commercials in encouraging children's buying that *Action for Children's Television* [ACT]—a group of parents who monitor and try to change television's impact on children— considers television commercials a far greater problem than TV violence. According to ACT officials, up to three times as many commercials are aired during the time, particularly Saturday mornings, when shows are targeted to a young audience than when they are geared to an adult audience (Holden, 1972).

continuous consumption

The Effects of Television on Family Interaction.   The impact of television extends into life. When televisions were first purchased, a major reason given was that TV would bring the family together in the home (Maccoby, 1964). Television may increase the time that family members spend together watching programs. However, television viewing is essentially a non-interactive activity because very little conversation can occur during viewing. There is the potential for television to increase the interaction among family members. For example, it can stimulate discussions about programs. But most often television is used in ways that intentionally reduce family interactions. Parents, especially those of young children, rely on television as a babysitter and they note that having children watch television takes from them some of the burden of having to interact with the children and to provide them with entertainment or specific educational experiences (Parke, 1978). As Bronfenbrenner (1970) observes:

> The primary danger of the television screen lies not so much in the behavior it produces—although there is danger there—as in the behavior that it prevents: the talks, the games, the family festivities and arguments through which the child's learning takes place and through which his character is formed. Turning on the television set can turn off the process that transforms children into people.

Television vs. Reading.   We do not want to leave you with the impression that there are no advantages to watching television. If television is used appropriately, it can be a learning tool. Young children can learn a great deal from slow-action television shows that encourage viewer involvement (Singer & Singer, 1979). You will see in Chapter 9 that just as some television shows promote aggression in children, there are other shows that can enhance children's prosocial behavior. Also, through the introduction of television we have made great progress in mass communication. A little more than a century ago, most people were illiterate and had to rely on getting information by word of mouth. Only a small percentage of the population could read and write and could enjoy the possibilities that these skills offered. Today, through increased literacy and the almost universal access to radio and television, the average citizen is exposed to more information than ever before. More people read more books, magazines, and newspapers than ever before, and they hear and see actual and fictional events on radio and television. This tremendous acceleration in the availability of information for any individual is an important asset of the popular media in general and television in particular.

Television is only one aspect of the popular media that affect the development of children. Reading books and comics is also known to influence children (Maccoby, 1964). Books in particular are important in childrens' lives not only because they promote the skill of reading and writing, but also because they can enhance knowledge, imagination, and thought. In a few printed words the reader can become privy to memorable moments—moments of joy and agony, or heroism and bewilderment—that often become fixed in memory. Through books, children can share the experiences of heroes and heroines; they can learn about adventures, societal pressures and customs, religion, economics, and love. A story has been likened to the flare of a match: it brings human faces out of darkness.

This is also true of television. But television as a medium of communication is fundamentally different from other media because as we watch television we remain essentially passive. Words and images are presented to us on the screen. So rapidly does the material on television come to us that there is not time to talk or to reflect on what we have just witnessed. Only in sports programs do we get the "instant replay" that allows us to go over the event and think about it for a moment, perhaps seeing some aspect of the event our eye did not focus on before.

In contrast, reading allows a person to read a sentence or a paragraph, pause and perhaps turn back to an earlier page, and take time to think and piece together the combination of words and images. Also, while reading, one has to translate words into images in the brain (in radio, too, we have to listen to words out of which we create pictures in our mind). Reading, therefore, is much harder work than viewing television. It requires the active participation of the reader. However, it is also very rewarding for it enhances one's imagination. Because television viewing is a passive activity, researchers suggest that excessive viewing may alter children's capacity for sustained attention and deliberate thought. Teachers, for example, report that students are impatient with long presentations, and if we compare textbooks published two decades ago with those published today we can see that there is a dramatic decrease in the number of words used to convey information and an increase in the use of illustrations and pictures (Tower et al., 1979).

FROM PROBLEM TO SOLUTION: ADDRESSING THE NEEDS OF CHILDREN

Because of the societal changes we have described, it appears that children are spending less and less time with adults and that they are mostly alone, or with their peers, watching television. This is especially discernible when we compare the findings of studies conducted on the lives of children three decades ago (Barker & Wright, 1955) with similar studies conducted in recent years. The earlier studies found that children spent time with a number of adults over the course of a day, and in the diaries the children kept, they reported spending their time in youth-oriented and adult-directed activities such as scouting and family outings. In contrast, many children studied by Boocock (1977) in the late 1970s reported spending most of their time when not in school alone or with other children, mainly watching television, eating snacks, or "fooling around." Boocock found that most children spend less than two hours a day with an adult other than a teacher and that meals are rarely eaten together as a family. Similar findings are reported in studies of children in the 1980s (Medrich et al., 1982).

Other researchers found that children today have a greater dependency on their peers than they did a decade ago (Condry & Siman, 1974). They note also that the extreme attachment to age-mates is influenced more by a lack of attention and concern at home than by any positive attraction of the peer group (Condry & Siman, 1976). A child development specialist, asked to identify the greatest hazard facing children in our society replied in one word—*loneliness* (Roby, 1973).

Besides growing up lonely, children are also experiencing a great deal of stress. This is especially evident in single-parent households and in families where divorce and remarriage occurs or where both parents have to work. What are the effects of stress on a child? A recent study on the children of an entire community (Martha's Vineyard) is providing some knowledge about the effects of stress. The study, the *Martha's Vineyard Child Health Survey* (Garrison & Earls, 1982), is unusual in that it looked at an entire community of seemingly "normal" families, that is, families who were not seen by a psychiatrist or social worker and who were not previously identified as having problems. Included in the study were 400 preschool children, a significant number of whom were found by the researchers to exhibit psychiatric and behavioral disorders that stemmed, according to the researchers, from chronic, continual stress. The study also found that boys are more vulnerable to the effects of stress, but that in boys the effects of stress may not be manifested until they reach school age. Among the families reporting stress-producing difficulties that affect children, the most prevalent worry was financial security, followed by housing, work, marriage, and health problems.

Family Support Programs

In light of the contemporary problems facing children and families, many programs have been developed around the country. These programs may be grouped under the general heading of *family support programs*. They are different from previous efforts to help children because they regard child development as occurring in the context of the family. Any attempts to help children thus include helping strengthen families. Many of these programs, which range from information and referral services for day care to parent education (Weiss, 1983), are often grass-roots, self-help programs (Whittaker & Garbarino, 1983). Such programs are initiated and supported by the people they serve. The family support program movement is still in its infancy. However, many researchers acknowledge that it may be the wave of the future and that it is likely to have a major impact on the health, development, and well-being of American families because the programs represent the solutions of families to their own problems (Zigler & Weiss, 1985).

The Role of Government

Taking a lead from the family support movement, more changes that would facilitate the nurturing of children in this decade and beyond may be instituted through government policies. Most people regard government social policies as assistance aimed at the poor. Indeed, public assistance originated in the Social Security Act of 1935, which aimed to alleviate economic insecurity by providing publicly supported sources of income to economically deprived groups. Because of the overwhelming need for assistance at that time (the Depression), the Act began by singling out particular groups of people to be aided first: the aged, the blind, and children in fatherless homes. Currently, many children in families with an income below the poverty level, many of which are single-parent families, receive support from the government program known as Aid to Families with Dependent Children (AFDC). This support includes food stamps and health care. Adequate nutrition and health care are imperative to children's growth and development. Without these two forms of government support, the lives of the children who receive such support would be substantially different.

The importance of government support to children and families in need was recently documented. In 1981, the president and the U. S. Congress made a drastic reduction in the amount of money the federal government provides for social services. This reduction has meant that many services for children had to be severely curtailed. For example, Aid to Families with Dependent Children was slashed by $1 billion, and the cut, along with the enactment of more stringent eligibility requirements, removed hundreds of thousands of children from the program and reduced benefits for thousands more. What are the results? According to reports from Catholic Charities (one of the largest private agencies serving families in need) requests for emergency shelter for families and children nearly tripled between 1981 and 1983 (Harvey, 1983). This means that there are many more families without homes. The same reports indicate that requests for emergency food also tripled between 1981 and 1983. So enormous was the demand for food assistance that Catholic Charities was forced to limit each family to three days of food per week. So you can see that because of the $1-billion cut in the AFDC program, many families with children are homeless and hungry.

The Integration of Child Development Research and Social Policy

The many ways government can help families may be grouped under the heading of *facilitating family life*. Some of these ways involve ensuring that policies and other government activities support and maintain family life rather than undermine and weaken it. For example, the government's economic policies should not foster unemployment and thereby weaken the ability of families to support themselves (Mondale, in Zigler et al., 1983). Before any government activity is initiated, we should ask the simple question: How will it affect families?

Government policies that facilitate family life should be based on social indicators, many of which we discussed, and also on principles drawn from child development research. Emanating from the research are several basic conceptions about children's development. Admittedly, these are not free from debate. However, they are ideas that are shared and generally accepted by researchers and scholars in the field and as such they can guide policy development. Let us look at one such idea, *the principle of integrity and continuity*. This principle states that children and families benefit if integrity and continuity of the family is maintained. This principle is not new. As researchers, we have known that young children need the presence of a loving adult who takes care of them *over time*. In other words, children need not only loving care, but also continuity of care.

the principle of integrity and continuity

Despite our knowledge of this principle, until very recently government policies fostered not continuity of care but the breakup of the family. One such policy is related to the foster care program. Due to poor conditions in some families, such as a severely depressed mother or parents who physically abuse and neglect the children, children are taken out of their homes and placed in the care of foster parents. The intent of the program is that children will be removed from the family and taken care of *temporarily* until the family situation improves. Foster care parents are encouraged therefore not to develop long-term attachments for children in their care. In fact, foster parents become eligible to participate in the program only after authorities are convinced that the foster parents would have no intention of adopting any of the children. Oftentimes, the children are moved from one home to another to discourage any emotional attachments. Although the foster care program is supposed to be a temporary solution, studies have shown that children spend as much as five years and often their entire childhood moving from one foster care home to another (Lash et al., 1980; Keniston, 1977). Not only is this approach detrimental to children, it is also costly. Would it not be better to spend some of the money in ways that would ensure that the well-being of the family does not deteriorate? For example, home visitors could be sent routinely to homes to see if the parents and children need any help *before* conditions in the home deteriorate (Zigler & Finn, 1982). If the family situation is so bad, after a period of time, children should be given the opportunity to be adopted so that they can begin life anew (Cranston, 1979).

These solutions may seem simple and straightforward. Unfortunately, it was not until 1980 that modifications in the foster care program were made in the Adoption Assistance and Child Welfare Act. Why is it that the government would allow children to be hurt emotionally and psychologically? Part of the program arises not because policymakers do not care, but simply because the individuals who create government policies have expertise in the policy process and in fiscal matters but not in child development. In fact, they may not be aware that the policies they formulate can at times actually harm children. For this reason, many child development researchers realize that they have a dual role: to generate knowledge about psychological processes and development of children and to integrate that knowledge with social policy by helping policymakers formulate policies on the basis of principles drawn from child development research (Masters, 1983). In fact, it was the involvement of many child development researchers and practitioners that led to the recent modifications of the foster care system.

The Role of Business and Industry

Although the role of the government in facilitating family life is clear, in reality, government is constrained in the extent that it can provide for the nation's children. There is just so much money to go around. The reality of dwindling government funds means that we must look beyond the public sector for support for children and families. Perhaps we need to form an alliance with executives in business and industry who have the ability to institute changes that could have a positive effect on families.

One of the many ways in which the private sector can exert its influence to benefit children and families is in the area of work and family life. With working mothers now the norm rather than the exception, and with the increase in single-parent families, the impact of the workplace on family life has become a relevant issue. The relationship between these two institutions—the family and the workplace—has been the subject of several recent studies which emphasize an important point: Work and family life are not separate worlds, but are interdependent and overlapping (Brim & Abeles, 1975; Kanter, 1977). The interplay between work and family life and its effects on the child are within the concerns of developmental psychologists.

As we have said earlier, life for dual-career and single-parent families can be very stressful. Day care arrangements must be made for the infant and preschool child, and after-school facilities must be found for the older child. School vacations and days when the child is sick bring with them the need for still other solutions. As worker satisfaction and productivity

FIGURE 1.9   The on-site day care facility provided by Stride-Rite allows this employee to have lunch with her child.

have been found to be functions of family stability and other processes within the family system (Kanter, 1977), it behooves the private sector to offer services and benefits that can help families.

Although the role of the private sector in this regard has been slow to develop, several attempts have been made to accommodate to the needs of families. These include changes in the work structure to allow flexible work arrangements (Kuhne & Blair, 1978), part-time job opportunities (Schwartz, 1974), and job-sharing (Olmsted, 1979). Companies are required by law to offer maternity leaves (Bureau of Business Practice, 1979). At best, these are for three months, although school teachers, for example, may take up to one year's leave of absence without pay in order to stay with a newborn infant. As a nation, however, we lag far behind other countries because we lack policies that encourage the nurturing of infants and young children. According to several researchers, European nations make provisions for 6 to 12 months of maternity or paternity leave with pay in order to facilitate childrearing. In addition, facilities for child care are available for those parents who choose to return to work (Kamerman et al., 1976, 1986; Allen, 1985).

Some companies in the United States have on-site day care centers for employees' children, or they subsidize the cost of child care. Company-based day care centers have been successful for some corporations such as Stride-Rite in Boston (see Figure 1.9). Often, however, parents prefer to leave their children in day care facilities that are near the home. Also, not all corporations can afford to operate such facilities. Therefore, another, less expensive solution would be for several businesses to cooperate in the support of a day care center.

There are many other possible ways that industry can help facilitate family life (Zigler & Finn, 1982; Economic Policy Council, 1986), and the task of some researchers in child development is to help business and industry executives to plan and implement these. Moreover, researchers are also concerned with investigating whether the changes that are implemented in the workplace actually benefit children. Do parents who take advantage of flexible working arrangements actually spend more time with their children? Do such changes facilitate the reduction of stress in parents? Given the option of maternity leaves, do parents use them? These are some of the questions that developmental psychologists are asking.

The Role of Advocates

What Is Child Advocacy?   Many of the changes we describe cannot occur in the absence of advocacy. Some individual or group must see to it that there is an awareness of the problem and that change will take place. Advocacy is not a new idea. It has been practiced as long as people have displayed care and protection toward each other. Although the concept of *advocacy* has come to have negative connotations, advocacy actually has positive, caring aspects. It is defined as acting in behalf of one's own interests, pleading the cause of others, and defending or maintaining a cause (Blom et al., 1984).

advocacy

The need for others to assume the role of advocates for children has been stated in the introduction of this chapter, as children are, obviously, unable to act in behalf of their own interests. Child advocacy may take different directions, all of which fall under a general aim—to change the conditions that are harmful or undesirable to children and families and to prevent such conditions from occurring and developing.

In contrast to advocates who represent business concerns, child advocates are not well organized and there is often competition among groups representing different issues related to children. However, child advocates are finding that if they work in greater numbers and join forces to form coalitions (Zigler & Finn, 1981), they can better achieve their goals. Any interested individual may be an advocate for children. In increasing numbers, researchers and other professionals who deal with children are finding that they have to advocate for those they serve and that they cannot remain aloof from seeking solutions to children's problems. Parents, too, form an important element of child advocacy.

What do child advocates do? Essentially, the role of advocates is to monitor the conditions of children's lives and to see to it that changes are made to improve these conditions. Such changes often require government intervention. Part of the advocacy process involves educating the general public as well as policymakers about the needs of children. This aspect of the advocacy process is important because we seldom act unless we have a sense of the immediacy of the problem (Zigler & Finn, 1981). It is in this aspect of advocacy that the role of researchers is especially important. They can provide expert testimonies to government officials, and they can disseminate their findings from the research in child development not only in scholarly journals, but also in newspapers and magazines that are read by the majority of the people (Muenchow & Gilfillan, 1983).

Action for Children's Television.   Child advocates have focused on a number of important issues such as child abuse and neglect, day care, physical punishment, health care, and the needs of handicapped children. In their attempts to better the lives of children, advocates have directed their efforts not only to Congress and state and federal governments, but also to the courts, the public schools, and various social service agencies.

The importance of the activities of child advocates is exemplified in the advocacy group *Action for Children's Television* (ACT). For over 30 years ACT has struggled with the television industry as well as policymakers (who have the power to regulate the industry) concerning types of television programs, their scheduling, and the amount and type of advertising viewed by children. One result of the struggle has been the Surgeon General's report on the effects of television violence as well as deliberations by the Federal Communications Commission and the Federal Trade Commission of several issues related to children and television. It has been a long, difficult struggle for ACT, in part because the television industry has powerful people and groups advocating in its behalf and it also has substantially more resources than do child advocates. Nonetheless, in their persistence, ACT members convey their concerns to the public which increasingly sees the television industry as unresponsive to the needs of the audience but acquiescent to its sources of profit. Members of ACT and other child advocates hope that eventually the federal government will intervene with legislation that would help reduce the amount of advertising aimed at children and also ensure that the television industry allocates more time to educational programs for children.

SUMMARY

In this chapter we introduced the reader to the new directions in child development research and the approach we take in this book. We looked at childrearing issues and concerns that are relevant to the 1980s and beyond by focusing on social changes and trends that influence child and family life. We noted that ideas about the nature of the child and the concept of childhood are reflected in the way children are treated and in the policies that are created for them. Although the conditions of children today need to be improved, children have fared much worse in the past. Since the 1970s, however, children have faced a different set of problems that threaten to undermine their development. These problems stem from the high incidence of divorce, the increase in single-parent families, and the fact that most mothers today are working and cannot find suitable day care facilities for their children. Additional problems have surfaced from technological changes such as the introduction of television. Recent research findings indicate that violence depicted on television can lead to aggressive and violent behavior in children; that advertising on television is directed more at children than at any other group; and that we should be concerned with the intellectual and social development of children who are exposed to television for a substantial part of their lives.

The solutions to many of these problems lie in our ability to support and facilitate family life. This can be achieved in several ways. We described the role of government in facilitating family life, and we noted that government policies and programs should be based not only on social indicators, but also on principles drawn from the research in child development. We also described the role of the private sector in facilitating family life through the introduction of changes in the workplace. Researchers have the responsibility to help business executives plan and implement such changes. Also, they should investigate whether these changes actually benefit children. Finally, we discussed the role of advocates in actualizing the changes that can occur through public or private initiatives and in monitoring the conditions of children.

REVIEW POINTS

1. Child development professionals note that the study of children and families has social applications and relevance. Thus many researchers have recently become involved not only in the study of child development but also in the development of social programs and policies that can enhance family life.

2. The need for the development of such programs is paramount given indicators which reveal that many children growing up today face numerous problems, including inadequate health care, poverty, abuse, and neglect. Additional problems are an increase in youth unemployment and the incidence of depression and suicide among the young.

3. Although many children today face these severe problems, children in the past lived under worse conditions. Not much information is available on children before 1700. However, for the years after 1700, researchers know that young children suffered a great deal; they had to work for long hours under horrendous conditions, and many were abandoned by their parents.

4. Children in the 1980s face different problems brought on by major social changes, including demographic changes, changes in family life (such as the increase in the divorce rate and in single-parent households) and the changes involved in the introduction of television.

5. By studying the effects of these social changes on children's development, researchers can contribute to the knowledge of human development, and they can also play a role in enhancing the lives of children and their families.

6. There are several ways in which researchers can help enhance the lives of children and families. One way is to work with policymakers and make available to them information regarding the problems and the needs of children and what we know from the research about conditions that facilitate development. The integration of child development research and social policy can help ensure that policies and programs are designed to benefit children rather than harm their development.

7. Such policies and programs may be developed by federal and state governments. However, since government funds are limited, the role of industry should be considered as well. Industry can help facilitate family life by implementing changes in the work structure (flexible work schedules, job sharing, etc.) that allow parents to spend more time with their children. Child development researchers can work with the private sector in developing such alternatives, or they can study whether such alternatives are feasible and beneficial.

8. Researchers can work with advocates or they can assume the role of advocates on behalf of children. Child advocacy is important because children are unable to act on their own behalf. By monitoring the conditions of children's lives and by making changes that better these conditions, advocates can enhance the lives of children. Providing expert testimony to government officials on the needs of children is one area in which child development researchers can become involved.

UNIT II

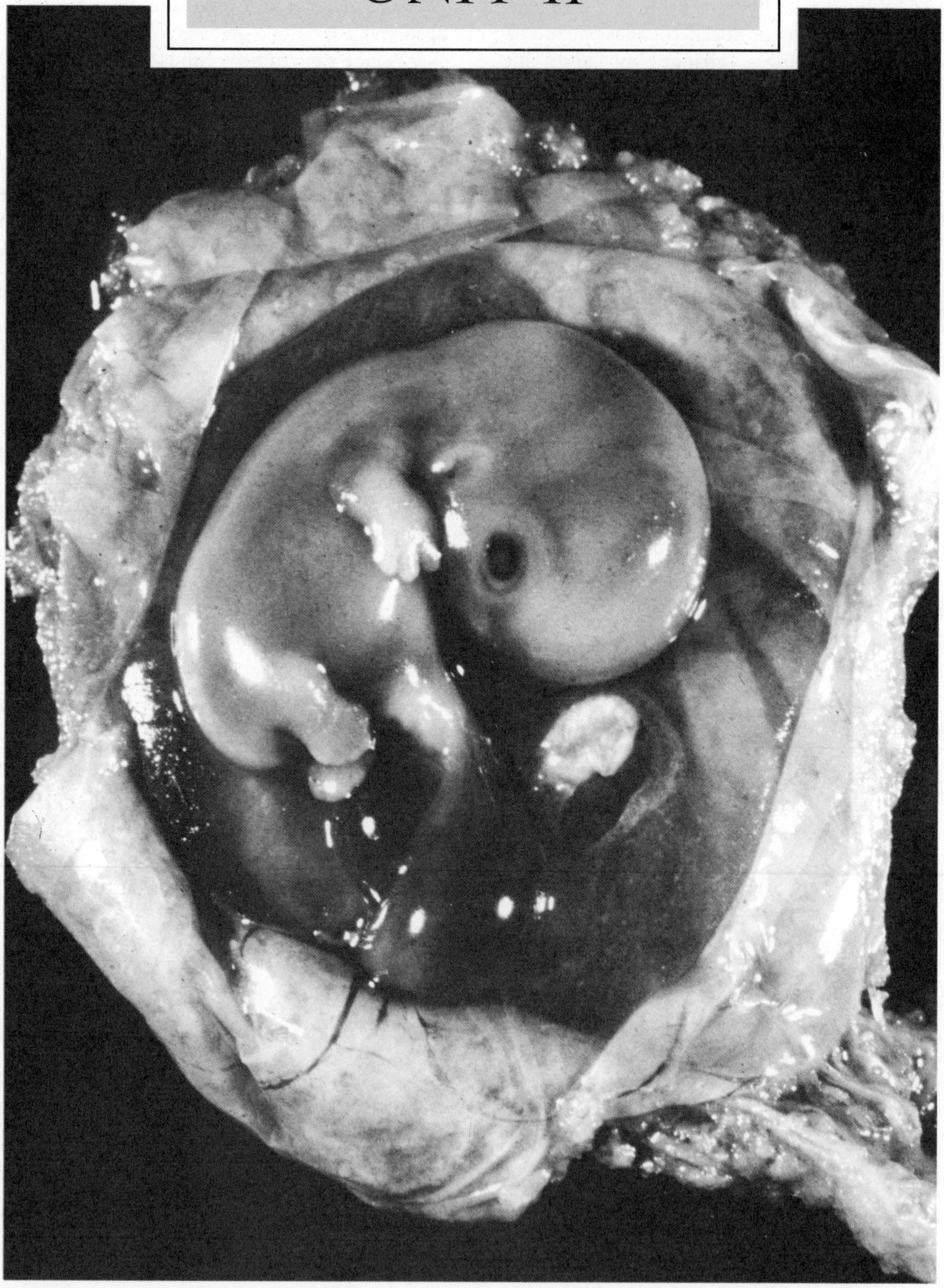

THE
BEGINNING
OF LIFE

In this unit we discuss the remarkable process of the beginning of life as we study the human organism before birth. There are no breaks in nature, so human development is continuous. Yet, the examination of certain aspects of the prenatal period will aid us in understanding development as a whole. In Chapter 2 we will examine the genetic factors that control the process of development, and we will consider the interaction between genetic and environmental factors that influence the emergence of physical and behavioral characteristics. In Chapter 3 we will describe the stages of prenatal development and the process of birth. Then we will discuss the manner in which external factors can affect normal growth processes and permanently alter the appearance and functioning of the child.

CHAPTER 2

OUR
BIOLOGICAL HERITAGE

Many of the developmental characteristics that unfold from the time the child is born until she reaches maturity are predictable. We expect an infant to attempt to sit up during the first few months of life, and later to take her first step, and eventually to walk. Despite the predictability of development and the similarities we can point to in the way children grow and develop, each child is unique in physical appearance and in every other characteristic as well. Even children in the same family rarely look or behave exactly alike. In some families one child may combine the features of both parents whereas another may resemble either the mother or the father. And then there is the child who may bear no resemblance to either parent. What accounts for variations such as these?

Obviously parents transmit hereditary material to their children, so why are not all children born to the same parents exactly the same? The answer lies in the complex process by which hereditary information is passed on from parent to offspring through the genes. There are so many possible combinations of genes that it is inevitable that children in the same family will inherit quite different characteristics.

The genes control or influence the emergence and nature of every human trait from eye color to intelligence. They account for our susceptibility to many inherited and other diseases and, in part, whether or not our offspring will be born with physical or mental abnormalities. So much of human development and activity is based upon genetic heritage that an understanding of the principles of genetics is an important aspect of the study of child development. As one researcher explains, to understand genetic factors in development is to understand how individual variation develops (Scarr-Salapatek, 1975). In this chapter, then, we present the precise mechanisms by which hereditary transmission is accomplished, and we examine some of what can go wrong in the process. We shall see also that although a vast amount of physical growth and development, and also some aspects of psychological development, are mapped out in a child's unique genetic makeup, environmental factors before and after birth also play an important role in development. The point we make throughout the chapter is: Neither heredity nor the environment alone determine development. Rather, human development is the result of complex transactions between genetic and environmental factors. Before we go on to some of the principles of genetics, let us examine several concepts that may help explain the relationship between genetic and environmental factors because these interact to have an effect on the child.

GENE-ENVIRONMENT TRANSACTIONS

Each individual's development is explained as the process by which a genotype is expressed as one or another phenotype (Scarr-Salapatek, 1975). A *genotype* is the genetic makeup of the individual, and it is what   *genotype*

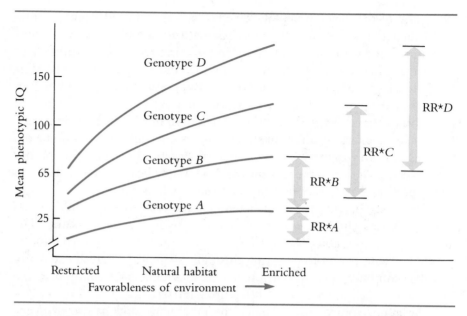

FIGURE 2.1   The intellectual reaction ranges of several genotypes in favorable and unfavorable environments. RR indicates the reaction range of phenotypic IQ. Genotype *A* is not part of the normal reaction range. By Irving I. Gottesman from *The Handbook of Mental Deficiency: Psychological Theory and Research,* ed. by Norman R. Ellis, New York: McGraw-Hill, 1963.

phenotype

makes each individual unique. The *phenotype* is the individual's observable and/or measurable characteristic. A given genotype—what the individual inherits—can give rise to many different phenotypes, or observable characteristics. Some genotypes, such as hair texture or eye color, are directly expressed as phenotypes. Others, such as intelligence or personality traits, are influenced by the genes but they are subject to environmental influence as well. Thus different phenotypes can develop from the same genotype, depending on the environment. This can happen because the genotype, or heredity, does not fix development. Rather, the genotype sets the limits within which an individual's abilities can vary. The limits may be viewed as the individual's potential. Whether or not the individual will realize his or her potential depends on environmental circumstances and the way the particular person responds to them. Psychologists refer to this

range of reaction

notion as the *range of reaction* (Gottesman, 1963). They note that the individual's genotype establishes a range within which the potential for certain characteristics will be realized.

Children vary in the way that they respond to conditions in the environment and to different life experiences. For example, if we put four children with different genotypes A, B, C, and D in an unstimulating, restricted environment or in a stimulating environment, we will see, as Figure 2.1 shows, that under a similar condition (the stimulating environment), a child with genotype D always performs better on intellectual tasks than the children with genotypes C, B, and A. This is because that child has the widest range of reaction for intelligence among the four children. Child A, on the other hand, has the most limited range of reaction, and thus she scores below average in intelligence, no matter what environment she is in, and even in the most favorable and stimulating environment, she does not perform well on intellectual tasks.

Each genotype has a unique range of reaction. However, this should not be interpreted to mean that the genotype (heredity) sets the limits on the development of a characteristic while the environment determines the extent that the characteristic will be developed to its full potential. Rather, during the course of development there is a constant and complex transaction between the genotype, or genetic factors, and factors in the environment (Hebb, 1980).

Nor is it entirely true that although the environment acts on the genotype that the genotype does not influence the environment. At one time the genotype was conceived of as a passive agent and environmental factors were seen as active agents which operate on the genotype to determine which phenotype will ultimately emerge. However, we now know that with respect to behavioral development this is not true. Rather, researchers portray a *transactional model of development* (Sameroff & Chandler, 1975), noting that each individual with a given genotype influences other people, thereby exerting some control over the environmental factors that she will experience. Even newborn infants are known to exert an influence over their environment. For example, infants with certain characteristics such as irritability and frequent and long crying spells can irritate their parents to the point where physical abuse of the infant results.

transactional model of development

In addition, there is the concept of *critical periods* which refers to the fact that the extent to which an individual's genotype is expressed in her phenotype depends on the timing of environmental influences. This means that different environmental factors or experiences at different points in the course of development can have differing effects on the development of the child (Gottlieb, 1976). This is especially true early in the prenatal period when certain drugs taken by the mother (an environmental factor) can result in severe abnormalities in physical and mental development.

critical periods

Canalization

Although some genotypes are subject to environmental influence, other genotypes follow a prescribed genetic course so their expression as phenotypes is not likely to differ much on the basis of differences in the environment. That is to say, some behaviors are inevitable, regardless of environmental influence. The term *canalization* (or *preparedness,* as some researchers prefer) is used to describe such behaviors. A behavior is said to be canalized not necessarily if it is innate, but rather if it is very easily learned.

canalization or *preparedness*

> What is inherited is ease of learning rather than fixed instinctive patterns. The species early, almost intuitively, learns the essential behaviors for its survival. . . . Human beings learn to talk, but they inherit structures that make this inevitable, except under the most peculiar circumstances. (Washburn & Hamburg, 1965)

A characteristic which is highly canalized is difficult to modify whereas less canalized characteristics can be modified and thus are vulnerable to environmental influence. For example, walking is a highly canalized behavior since all normal infants learn to walk. Certain personality and mental characteristics are less highly canalized since they are subject to environmental conditions the child experiences.

To summarize, then, the genetic endowment a child is born with should be viewed as the individual's potential. The extent that this genetic potential will be realized depends on environmental factors. Thus both a sound genetic makeup and a favorable environment are necessary for healthy development. Both affect the individual in so many ways that it is impossible to estimate which factor has the greater influence (Lewontin, 1982). With these points in mind, let us examine the process by which genetic information is transmitted from parent to child.

Transmission of Genetic Information

Mendel's Work.   Our understanding of how genetic information is transmitted has been facilitated by the work of Gregor Mendel (1822–1884), who is called the father of modern genetics. During Mendel's time scientists attempted to understand the process of inheritance by studying complex animal species. Inheritance was conceived of as the blending of a fluid, possibly blood, which was passed down by the parents to the child. Even today this idea persists among some people who have no knowledge of genetics, and the expression "blood relative," still in use today, is rooted in this premise. Mendel did not work with complex animal species. Rather, he obtained significant results by studying the simple traits of the garden pea plant. He demonstrated that in hereditary transmission there is no mixing or blending of blood or any other fluid but, rather, that *gene*   hereditary material is attached to an entity later referred to as the *gene*.

Homozygotes and Heterozygotes.   From principles derived from Mendel's work, referred to as Mendel's laws of inheritance, scientists have *alleles*   learned that for any given gene there are two *alleles*. A child receives one allele from the mother and one from the father. If both alleles give the same hereditary direction for the determination of a trait, the child is said *homozygous*   to be *homozygous* for that trait. If the alleles are different, the child is said *heterozygous*   to be *heterozygous* for that trait. These alleles do not blend. Rather, they *dominance*   behave in a pattern of *dominance* and *recessiveness,* meaning that in a hetero- *recessiveness*   zygous condition where the two alleles are different, one allele will dominate over the other. It is the dominant allele that determines the phenotype, or observable characteristic associated with a particular trait. The recessive allele, present but not observable, may reappear in successive generations. The dominant allele is usually symbolized by a capital letter, say H, whereas the recessive allele is symbolized by a lowercase letter, in this case h. The homozygous child for that trait will be HH or hh, whereas the heterozygous child will be Hh.

Let us assume that H is the dominant allele for hair texture and signifies curly hair and that h signifies straight hair. A child who inherits two dominant alleles from her parents will thus be HH. That is, she will have curly hair. A child who inherits a dominant allele from one parent and a recessive allele from the other will be Hh. But, since curly hair (H) is the dominant trait, she will also have curly hair. In the case of a child who has either one or both parents with curly hair, the hereditary transmission of that trait appears obvious. However, there may be a child who has straight hair even though both her parents have curly hair. Is something other than heredity at work here? Not at all. In this case, it simply means that both of the child's parents are heterozygous for hair texture, or Hh, thus their phenotypes are curly hair since that is the dominant allele. However, they each contributed a recessive allele h to their child. Since there are a number of combinations of alleles possible, even children in the same family do not always share the same characteristics.

Applying Mendel's Laws. Mendel's laws of inheritance have helped scientists understand not only how some physical traits such as hair texture are inherited, but also how certain abnormal conditions and diseases are passed on from parent to offspring. Let us look at how a condition known as *albinism* is passed on through the genes. The albino individual is born *albinism* with almost white hair, no skin pigmentation, and pink retinas. For our example, let us use (A) to represent the allele for normal skin pigmentation and (a) to represent the allele for albinism. Albinism is caused by a *recessive allele*. An albino child would be (aa). The parents of an albino *recessive allele* individual may also be albino (aa). Or, they may both be heterozygous (Aa) for albinism, meaning that they have a normal skin pigmentation but are carriers of the recessive (a) allele for albinism. Thus they each passed one recessive allele to the child. However, because the parents have one dominant allele for skin pigmentation, their phenotype, or what we observe, is normal skin pigmentation. As shown in Figure 2.2 (page 92), in the case where both parents carry a recessive gene for albinism, there is one chance in four of their having an albino child. There is also a chance that two of their children will carry the recessive gene. If two albino adults have children, all their children will be albinos, since the only possible allele the children can receive from either parent is (a).

Many other disorders, which are often life threatening, are passed on to the offspring by parents who both have the recessive allele for a particular

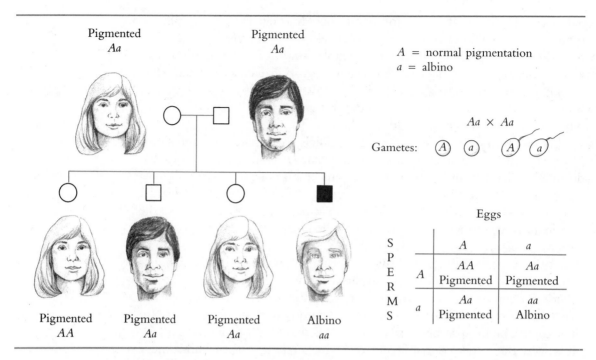

FIGURE 2.2 Monohybrid cross in the human. A common form of albinism is inherited as a simple Mendelian recessive. At left is a representation of a simple mating and pedigree in which the parents are both heterozygotes. At right is a Punnett square illustrating the same cross. It must be appreciated that in such a cross the *chance* is 3 to 1 for a normal offspring at any one birth. By no means does the figure mean that 1 out of 4 offspring *must* be albino in such a family. Norman V. Rothwell, *Human Genetics,* © 1977, p. 16. Reprinted by permission of Prentice-Hall, Inc. Englewood Cliffs, New Jersey.

phenylketonuria or PKU

condition. *Phenylketonuria,* or PKU, is caused by a recessive gene (p) which leads to the absence of a certain enzyme needed to convert the protein phenylalanine, found in milk, into tyrosine. Since milk is the basic diet of infants, the result is that phenylpyruvic acid accumulates in the PKU infant's body, causing damage to the central nervous system and resulting in mental retardation. An infant with phenylketonuria will appear normal at birth, but with the gradual build-up of the acid it will become increasingly evident that she is mentally retarded.

Approximately 1 out of 20 individuals is a carrier of the recessive allele for phenylketonuria. Fortunately, hospitals routinely check newborns for PKU. Once detected, infants can begin dietary therapy to prevent the damaging effects of the disease. The PKU test, when conducted during the first week of life, often gives inaccurate results, so many states also require that it be performed again about six weeks after birth.

Our ability to prevent PKU demonstrates the importance of environmental factors in gene expression. If PKU is detected shortly after birth, a

PKU infant can be given a special diet that will prevent the accumulation of the toxic substances which hinder the normal development of cells in the central nervous system. Here time is of critical importance. Placing an affected PKU child on a proper diet will be to no avail once the brain has been damaged, hence the need for early detection of the condition. An infant with PKU who receives a proper diet at the crucial period may appear no different than a person who has the normal allele for PKU. It is important to bear in mind, however, that while an environmental factor (dietary therapy) has prevented full expression of the genotype, the environment has not altered the individual's genes in any way, meaning that the genotype of the infant remains homozygous (pp) for the recessive gene even though the infant escaped the dire effects of the disease. An individual like this is referred to as a *phenocopy,* one whose phenotype (gene expression) has been environmentally altered so that it mimics the phenotype that is usually associated with another specific genotype. A phenocopy individual would still be able to transmit the defective recessive gene, but would appear and function normally.

phenocopy

There is also a reverse side to the phenocopy phenomenon. Using our PKU example, a woman with PKU who has escaped brain damage due to early detection and treatment, is likely, if she marries a person with the dominant allele in a homozygous condition (PP), to have a child who also has the dominant trait, although in a heterozygous condition (Pp). This child's genotype is such that he will be a carrier of the defective allele (p), but he will not be afflicted with the symptoms of PKU. However, one side effect of the PKU will remain in that the PKU woman when she is pregnant will have a high concentration of toxic substances in her uterus due to the fact that even though she has been treated for PKU, she still has abnormal metabolism. These toxic substances will not be harmful to her, but they will affect the unborn child and cause brain damage. This child, although not genetically programmed to suffer from PKU, will nonetheless suffer mental retardation (Lenke & Levy, 1980). However, there is some evidence which suggests that proper dietary care of the phenocopy woman while she is pregnant or before pregnancy may alleviate the detrimental effects to the offspring (Lenke & Levy, 1982).

The example of the PKU phenocopy demonstrates the relationship between genetic endowment and the environment. There are many other such examples, since rarely, if ever, is either heredity or the environment the sole determining factor in the expression of a trait or a characteristic. An important point to remember is that a child with a hereditary defect and her parents may be spared suffering if the environment is altered in time so that the expression of the defective gene is prevented. Conversely, given our present knowledge, even in the most favorable environment the expression of certain defective genes cannot be prevented. This is true, for instance, of albinism, which we discussed earlier.

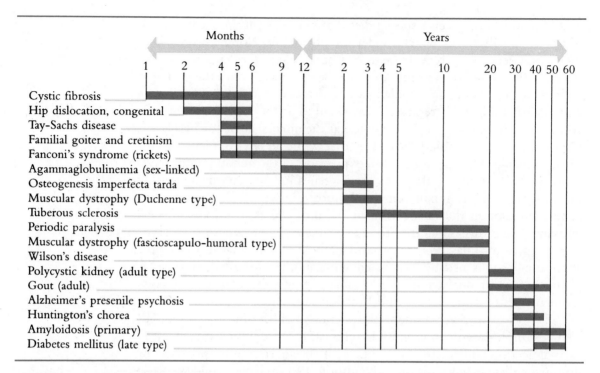

FIGURE 2.3   "Age ranges during which various genetic defects appear" from *Perspectives in Biology and Medicine* by Vasken H. Aposhian, p. 100. Copyright © 1970 by The Society for Research in Child Development, Inc.

Complex Gene Activity

Not all gene activity follows the simple, straightforward Mendelian model of inheritance. Many traits and diseases are acquired through this classic single-gene heredity pattern. In most cases, however, the transmission of hereditary information follows a multifactorial model of inheritance which is characterized by a complex gene activity that involves the action of many genes in the transmission of a trait, the influence of some genes over others, and the influence of environmental factors (Novitski, 1977).

polygenetic inheritance

When a number of genes act together in the transmission of a trait, the phenomenon is known as *polygenetic inheritance, poly* meaning many. None of the individual genes by itself would be sufficient to produce the trait in question. But acting in concert, they give the affected individual a genetic predisposition which, when activated by some conditions in the environment, manifests as an inherited trait. In yet another phenomenon, *pleitropy,* single genes can influence more than one trait.

pleitropy
modifier genes

There are some genes, known as *modifier genes,* which influence the actions or observable characteristics of other genes. For example, children with phenylketonuria have differing levels of phenylalanine in spite of the

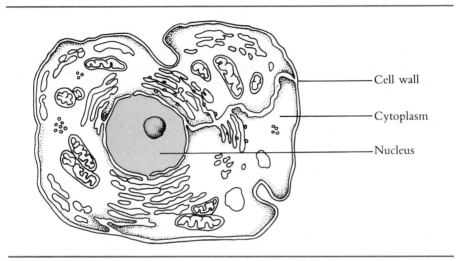

FIGURE 2.4 A human cell divided into its basic parts: the cell wall, the nucleus, and the cytoplasm.

fact that they have identical genes for phenylketonuria. This is a result of modifier genes which determine variations in the amounts of phenylalanine produced. You can see how complicated gene activity can be. In addition to the complex nature of genes, the effects of many genes do not manifest until later in life, as is the case with baldness and certain genetically inherited diseases (see Figure 2.3).

Genes and Chromosomes

Chemical Nature of Genes.   Having described basic principles involved in hereditary transmission, let us now examine more specifically the chemical nature of genes and their relationship to cells in the human body. The human body is made up of billions of cells, which are packets of life substances. Most cells have specialized functions: brain cells for intelligence and memory, heart cells for rhythmic contraction, and so on. Despite their specialized functions, all cells have similar, basic component parts. Each is made up of an outer membrane known as the *cell wall* which contains fluid called the *cytoplasm* (see Figure 2.4). Floating in the center of each cell is a special compact structure known as the *nucleus*. Within the nucleus we find the genes as well as other structures that direct the manufacture and traffic of substances within the cell.

cell wall
cytoplasm
nucleus

There are several types of genes, each type having a different function. For example, *structural genes* guide the manufacture of material (protein) that goes into the structural organization of the cell. *Operator genes* turn protein synthesis on and off in the adjacent structural genes. *Regulator genes* function to produce molecules that tell all genes when to turn on and

structural genes
operator genes
regulator genes

off. The differences among individuals are largely due to the regulatory genes which modify the basic biochemical processes of the genes (Novitski, 1977). The genetic material of the cell is the basis for an amazingly complex, self-regulating system which produces effects in the body, interprets feedback and reacts with new effects, and so on throughout the life cycle of the organism. It is important to note here that when even one gene is defective, the child will be affected with physical or developmental deviations.

chromatin

The genes are found within the nucleus on long tiny fibers called *chromatin.* When a cell is preparing for its division into two cells, the chromatin fibers contract into short, tightly coiled threads. When a cell at this point is stained in a laboratory procedure, these threads become highly visible under a microscope. For this reason, the threads have been given the name *chromosomes,* from the Greek words *chromo* and *soma,* meaning "color-body." As recently as 1956, it was thought that human beings, like chimpanzees, had 48 chromosomes in each cell. However, with improvements in staining techniques, the number of chromosomes in a normal human cell has been established to be 46. Each chromosome holds hundreds of thousands of genes. These genes are not scattered haphazardly along the chromosome. Rather, each gene has a specific place, called the *gene locus,* where it appears on every chromosome of that type. Thus if we look at another cell which contains a duplicate chromosome, we would find the same genes on the same loci. Every chromosome will have different gene loci, bearing genes which influence a different set of traits.

chromosomes

gene locus

DNA

DNA.   The most important component of the chromosome is *deoxyribonucleic acid,* or DNA, which controls the biological inheritance of all living things. DNA is often referred to as the alphabet of life. It contains a genetic code that is used to direct the operational functioning of *ribonucleic acid,* or RNA. Taking its instructions from DNA, RNA serves as a messenger to carry these instructions from the nucleus of a cell to its *cytoplasm,* where the instructions are carried out. The instructions that are being relayed concern how the organism is to develop. Since our bodies are made of protein, the DNA contains instructions for a specific type of protein chain.

RNA

The organism grows and develops as cells duplicate themselves. Let us see what happens to DNA during the process. DNA consists of a pair of intertwined coils of indefinite length composed of sugar phosphate molecules (see Figure 2.5). The two chains are linked together by chemical bonds which come off of one of four bases. These bases are *adenine, thymine, cytosine,* and *guanine.* They may be arranged in any order along one or two coils, but the guanine can link only with cytosine, and adenine can link only with thymine. Thus the sequence on one chain determines the sequence on the other.

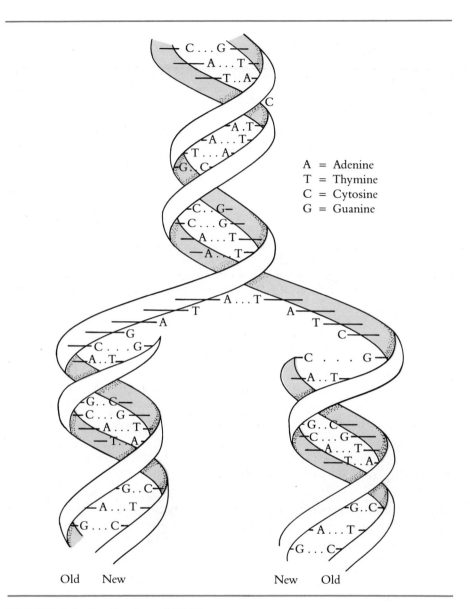

A = Adenine
T = Thymine
C = Cytosine
G = Guanine

Old   New   New   Old

FIGURE 2.5   Replication of DNA.

These four bases are important. They serve as units of information, the letters of the alphabet, if you will, which direct the synthesis of proteins vital to the cell's metabolism and development. Each protein consists of a specific combination of amino acids arranged in a particular order. Three letters in a code, that is, a series of three bases, spell a single amino acid. A series of such three-letter codes, arranged in a specific order on part of the DNA coil, makes up a sentence which translates into a complete protein, or a complete chain of a multiple protein. A section of code,

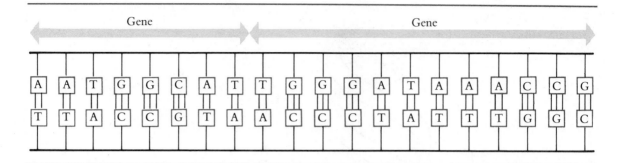

FIGURE 2.6   A gene segment of DNA. While the DNA exists in the form of a double helix, it is basically a linear molecule. When viewed as "untwisted," one nucleotide pair follows another in a linear order. A gene is a segment of a DNA molecule, and the difference between any two genes resides in the sequence of the base pairs contained in each. There is no set way in which the base pairs must occur in a gene. This fact makes possible an endless variety of genes which may be of different lengths. This figure is greatly simplified; in actuality, no gene would be composed of so few nucleotide pairs. From Norman V. Rothwell, *Human Genetics,* © 1977, p. 214. Reprinted by permission of Prentice-Hall, Inc. Englewood Cliffs, New Jersey.

from a start signal to a stop signal, is what we call a *gene* (see Figure 2.6). Thus you can see that genetic information is coded by the ordering, or arrangement, of the chemical steps at different locations on the chromosome. The particular order of these steps is what gives each gene its special character.

Beginning of Life and Cell Division

ovum

zygote

Life begins when a sperm cell from the father penetrates and fuses with the *ovum* cell (the egg) from the mother. Once penetration occurs, the ovum, now fertilized, becomes known as the *zygote*. From the moment of fertilization, the cells of the zygote multiply rapidly by cell division and develop eventually into the embryo, the fetus, and, at birth, the child.

gametes

somatic cells **or** *body cells*

The sperm and ovum are cells, but they are different from the other cells in the body. They are germ cells, or *gametes*. In reference to their function, gametes are also known as reproductive cells. All other cells are *somatic,* or *body cells* which make up the muscles, bones, and various body systems. These two types of cells differ in the number of chromosomes they contain and in the process by which they divide. Gametes have 23 chromosomes each. Somatic cells have 23 *pairs* of chromosomes, or 46 chromosomes in all.

mitosis

The process by which somatic cells divide is known as *mitosis*. In this process, each of the 46 chromosomes in the nucleus of the cell duplicates itself. The resulting two sets of 46 chromosomes move to opposite sides of the cell—one set to each side. The cell separates, and two new cells

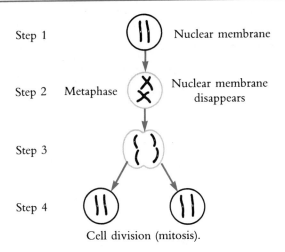

Step 1   Nuclear membrane

Step 2   Metaphase   Nuclear membrane
disappears

Step 3

Step 4

Cell division (mitosis).

Step 1: Shows the single cell with the pair of chromosomes we are following.
Step 2: The chromosomes split longitudinally, making a total of two pairs.
Step 3: The chromosome pairs separate; the cell nucleus and the cell itself
begin to divide.
Step 4: One chromosome member of each pair is now found in a new cell.
We note that there are two cells from the original single cell. This
whole process of cell division continues an infinite number of times
to constitute finally all the cells in the human body.

FIGURE 2.7   Cell division by mitosis. From p. 19 of *Know Your Genes* by Aubrey Milunski, M.D. Copyright © 1977 by Aubrey Milunski, M.D. Reprinted
by permission of Houghton Mifflin Company.

result (see Figure 2.7). In the process of human development, somatic cells
are formed by mitosis, each containing 46 chromosomes which are identical to those found in the zygote. The zygote has a complete set of chromosomes by virtue of the fact that both the egg and the sperm which formed
it, being gametes, contained exactly half as many chromosomes as somatic cells.

How did the egg and sperm develop only half the number of chromo-
somes? By a process known as *meiosis*. Meiosis is slightly different in the   *meiosis*
case of sperm cells than in egg cells, but to illustrate the process, let us use
the production of sperm cells as an example. The premeiotic sperm cell
has 46 chromosomes, as do somatic cells. These chromosomes duplicate
themselves as the cell divides once, producing two new cells, both of
which also divide, producing four cells in all, each of which will become a
mature sperm cell (Figure 2.8).

After the first division, the new cells divide again, but this time the
chromosomes do not duplicate themselves as they did prior to the first

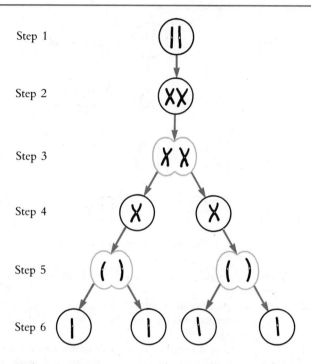

Step 1
Step 2
Step 3
Step 4
Step 5
Step 6

Step 1: Shows one cell with a pair of chromosomes.
Step 2: The chromosomes split longitudinally and begin to pair off.
Step 3: The cell nucleus begins to divide.
Step 4: The cell nucleus (and the cell that it occupies) has divided into two new nuclei, each containing a pair of chromosomes.
Step 5: The two chromosomes in each new nucleus now begin to move apart as the cell and its nucleus divide.
Step 6: A new cell and nucleus are formed, each with only one chromosome from the preceding cell. We can see that, from the original cell with a pair of chromosomes, there are four cells each with a single chromosome. These are the sperm cells (or eggs, if in the ovary) and they obviously contain 23 chromosomes, which is half of the original number. When a sperm with 23 chromosomes and an egg with 23 chromosomes meet in fertilization, a single cell is constituted with 46 chromosomes. We have therefore received half our chromosomes (and therefore genes) from our father and half from our mother.

FIGURE 2.8 Cell division by meiosis. From p. 18 of *Know Your Genes* by Aubrey Milunski, M.D. Copyright © 1977 by Aubrey Milunski, M.D. Reprinted by permission of Houghton Mifflin Company.

division. Instead, as the nucleus in each cell divides, each *part* of the chromosome pair migrates to opposite sides of the dividing nucleus. When cell division is complete, four cells stand where originally there was only one, and each cell contains not pairs, but 23 *single* chromosomes.

In the female, meiosis is the same, but the final result is not four eggs, but one. Three of the egg cells are stunted and have very little cytoplasm, and they do not survive long. The egg that does survive, however, retains a great deal of cytoplasm, making it one of the largest cells in the human body.

Genetic Variability

During the first division in meiosis, each of the 46 pairs of chromosomes line up with their lengths resembling parallel pairs. While the pairs are lined up, some of the sections of each chromosome may break away and attach themselves to adjacent chromosomes. This phenomenon is known as *crossing over,* and it entails essentially the reshuffling of genes. As a result of crossing over, the chromosomes are altered because genes are exchanged between pairs of chromosomes, and the characteristics of these genes are now carried on different chromosomes. This random reshuffling of genes can occur any time a sperm or egg cell is produced, and it is generally regarded as an important factor in genetic variability. Stern (1975) estimates that if a man produces one trillion sperm cells in his lifetime, this number represents about one sixty-million-trillion-trillionth of the total number of possible combinations of genes in a cell containing 23 chromosome pairs! And you wondered why you are so different from your brothers and sisters!

crossing over

Sex Chromosomes

In each cell nucleus 22 chromosomes from the sperm and 22 chromosomes from the ovum are known as *autosomes*. They are possessed equally by the male and female, and each pair of autosomes determines the same trait. But the twenty-third chromosome differs in the sperm and the ovum. In the sperm, or in males, the twenty-third chromosome is XY; in the ovum, or in females, the twenty-third chromosome is XX. An X chromosome is five times as long as the Y and therefore carries more genes on it. Since the mother is XX, then the twenty-third chromosome she can contribute to the offspring is always X. However, the father can contribute either X or Y; thus the zygote has a chance of being XY or XX, that is, male or female. So it is always the father that determines the sex of the child.

autosomes

Because some genes on the X chromosome have no equivalent genes on the shorter Y chromosome, sex-linked (or X-linked) recessive disorders can result. Since the male has only one X chromosome, if the recessive allele for a particular defect is present on it, the sex-linked defect will always be manifested because there is no equivalent allele on the Y chromosome to counteract its effect. In women, however, the defect will be expressed only if the matching allele on the other X chromosome is also defective.

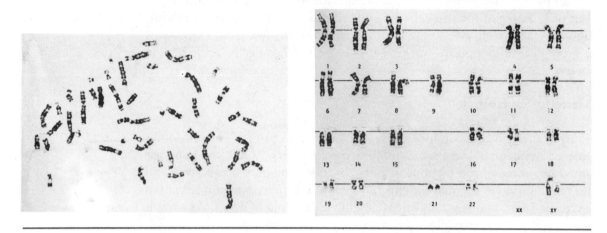

FIGURE 2.9   Chromosomes as they appear when photographed in their original positions (left) and arranged according to size and shape on a standard karyotype (right).

Sex-linked recessive disorders follow a pattern of transmission that makes them skip generations before they recur. One classic example of a sex-linked recessive disease is *hemophilia*, which is often referred to as the bleeding disease. Its victims lack the factor necessary for blood clotting and thus bleed excessively, either spontaneously or from cuts and bruises. Hemophilia appears to skip generations because a female who inherits the recessive gene from either her mother or her father usually possesses a dominant allele on her X chromosome to counteract the effects of the defective gene. Thus she becomes a carrier, but her own health is not impaired. When she bears children, however, as a carrier she is likely to pass the defective gene to some of her sons and her daughters. The daughters who receive the defective gene from the mother will, in all likelihood, be unaffected carriers like their mother. But any son who inherits the gene will definitely have the disease, since his Y chromosome does not contain a locus for that gene, and therefore the action of that gene cannot be counteracted. A father who has hemophilia will not pass the defective gene to his son, since from him, the son will receive only the Y chromosome. But all of his daughters are likely to be unaffected carriers of the defective gene and therefore they will pass it on to their children, so the man's grandson will have the disease. There is only a remote chance that the man's daughters will receive the recessive gene from him and from the mother and thus will be homozygous for that gene and affected by hemophilia.

Sex Chromosome Abnormalities.   Chromosomes may be photographed and then cut out of photographic enlargements and arranged into pairs *karyotype* according to length. This pictorial arrangement is referred to as a *karyotype*, and from it geneticists can detect such abnormalities as missing, broken, or additional chromosomes (see Figure 2.9). The importance of

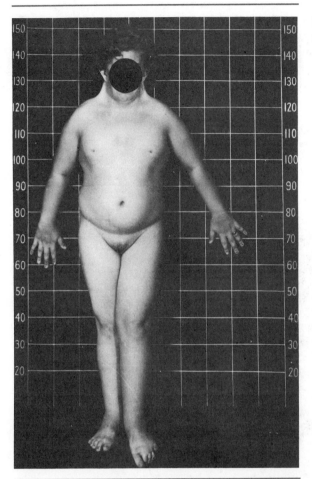

FIGURE 2.10 A young female with manifestations of Turner's syndrome.

the karyotype technique should not escape you for it has advanced our ability to identify genetic diseases. A quick glance at the karyotype enables the geneticist to see any abnormalities that may be present.

Ordinarily, the formation of sperm and ovum cells is a smooth process with the genes on the chromosomes properly segregated and distributed. On rare occasions, however, cells form that do not have a normal number of sex chromosomes. That is, there may be no sex chromosome at all, or there may be an extra chromosome. When an abnormal cell joins with a normal cell or with an abnormal cell, the resulting zygote will have either too few or too many sex chromosomes. If a child is born as a result of this union, he or she will have certain atypical physical and mental characteristics.

One such abnormality is absence of the sex chromosome X (XO instead of XX), known as *Turner's syndrome*. Women having Turner's syndrome are intellectually normal, but they evidence several physical abnormalities. They remain short in stature; they often have short fingers and unusually shaped mouths and ears (Figure 2.10). In addition, their bodies

Turner's syndrome

FIGURE 2.11   A young male with XYY syndrome, showing increased height associated with the extra Y chromosome.

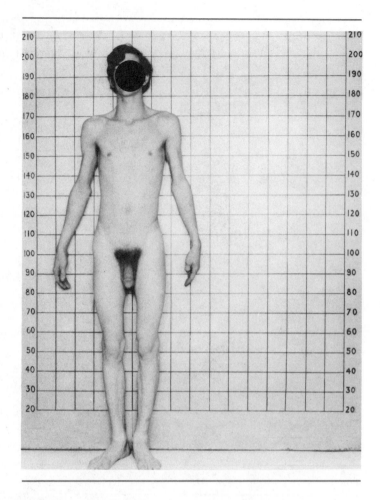

do not produce female hormones so that they are sterile and have incompletely developed breasts. However, treatment with estrogen can help women with Turner's syndrome to look more normal (Baer, 1977).

Sex chromosome abnormalities in males also occur. An example is the *Klinefelter syndrome* in which the afflicted individual has an extra X chromosome. These XXY (rather than XY) men are sterile and they have other physical abnormalities. They have many female characteristics such as developed breasts and they tend to be extremely tall (see Figure 2.11). In yet another sex chromosome abnormality, some men have an extra Y chromosome, so they are XYY rather than XY. They, too, are sterile and have a tendency to be tall.

In addition to the physical abnormalities of XXY and XYY males, it has been reported that they tend to be impulsive, antisocial, and even violent. Furthermore, they are likely to be in mental institutions or in prison (Jacobs, 1968; Hook, 1973). These findings are very controversial, however. Some researchers note that the prevalence of XXY and XYY males among criminals is no higher than in the general population

Klinefelter syndrome

(Baroankar & Shah, 1974). Until now the data in support of either view are limited and, therefore, no definitive conclusions can be drawn (Beckwith & King, 1974).

Mutations. Genetic variability can also result from mutations, which are changes in a gene, in the arrangements of the genes, or in the quantity of chromosomal material. There are *somatic mutations,* which affect body cells after cell division has begun. *Germinal mutations* affect the gametes. As a result of germinal mutation a child may have an allele that neither of his parents carried. Through complex calculations of mutation rates per gamete, we know that a newborn child stands a chance of 1 in 25 of carrying a mutation that was not passed to her by either parent. In this case, the departure from the normal is genetic in the sense that hereditary material is definitely associated with the change, but it is not necessarily inherited. While the abnormality may arise in the gamete of a parent and be transmitted to the offspring, it often stops there and goes no farther.

    Among the mutations present in a population, a large number will be recessives with lethal effects on the developing embryo and fetus. If mutations do not result in death before or at birth, they may be responsible for the death of the child at an early age, or for gross maldevelopment. Although geneticists do not yet completely understand the reasons for mutations, they note that some mutations occur through *mutant genes,* which are genes that increase the rate of mutations in individuals who carry them. There are also several environmental factors such as high temperatures, chemicals, and radiation which can lead to gene mutation. Radiation, for example, can occur naturally, or it can be produced by man, as is the case with X-rays or radiation from nuclear accidents or atomic fallout. In these cases the exposure to radiation during pregnancy is associated with high rates of abnormalities in the offspring, including mental retardation and leukemia (Milunsky, 1977).

somatic mutations

mutant genes

Down's Syndrome. An example of a mutation that involves chromosome anomalies is Down's syndrome which occurs in approximately 1 out of 500 births. Victims of this condition have a characteristic appearance which includes a folding of the skin of the upper eyelid, flattened face, small ears, and decrease in stature (see Figure 2.12, page 106). An assortment of abnormalities affecting internal organs such as the heart, lungs and thyroid is common, and in many cases mental retardation that varies in severity from case to case accompanies the condition.

    Down's syndrome is related to a deviation in the twenty-first chromosome. This was discovered in 1959 and it was the first time that a specific chromosome had been identified as being linked to a disease. It has been established since then that Down's syndrome individuals may have one of their twenty-first chromosomes translocated to another chromosome. In *translocation,* part of the chromosome attaches itself to another

translocation

FIGURE 2.12   A Down's syndrome child.

nondisjunction

chromosome, usually number 13, 14, 15, or 22. Then, although the right number of chromosomes (46) are present, the chromosomes are not arranged in the correct order. In other cases of Down's syndrome there is *nondisjunction* of a chromosome, so the Down's syndrome individuals will have an extra chromosome, or part of another chromosome, on chromosome 21. This may be the result of the failure of the chromosomes to separate during meiosis in the egg, so that the individual will have 47 instead of the normal 46 chromosomes.

The incidence of Down's syndrome is related to the age of the mother and it rises with maternal age at the time of conception. The older the mother, the greater the risk of having a Down's syndrome child. The incidence of Down's syndrome rises from 1 in 3,000 for mothers in their 20s, to 1 in 280 for mothers 35–40 years or older, and to 1 in 40 for mothers who are 40 to 45 years. This may be because at birth the human female carries all the potential egg cells that she will ever produce. It is known that these egg cells are especially vulnerable to such environmental agents such as viruses, radiation, and chemicals that can damage the chromosomes or interfere with the process of meiosis. The older a fertile woman is, the longer the time for such environmental factors to operate to the detriment of the cells. The incidence of other anomalies, for example, the XXY Klinefelter anomaly, is also known to increase with maternal age (Novitski, 1977).

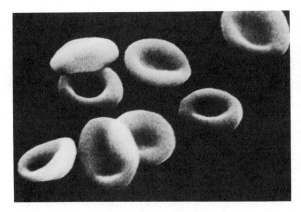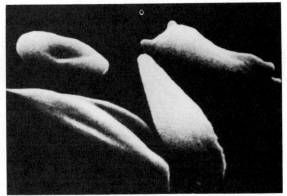

FIGURE 2.13 Normal red blood cells and sickled red blood cells.

The Gene Advantage and Natural Selection. All forms of life change in a process referred to as *evolution*. When we say man has evolved, we mean that the human species has changed over time. Evolution is a constant process of natural selection and the survival of the organisms whose genetic characteristics help them adapt to the environment. The more adaptive the organism is to the environment, the more likely it is to reproduce and survive. The less adaptive organisms will eventually be wiped out. Thus in different parts of the world there are people with similar genetic characteristics, a phenomenon referred to as *population gene pools*. Their genes have persisted because they help the individuals adapt to and survive in the particular environment.

evolution

population gene pools

Certain genetic diseases associated with gene mutations are also known to occur with greater frequencies among certain populations or ethnic groups. Often this is the case because the gene mutation, although detrimental, has some advantage in a particular environment. The best example is the genetic mutation that causes *sickle-cell anemia*. Sickle-cell anemia is a hereditary and ultimately fatal disease which attacks mostly blacks but also some Greeks, Italians, and to a lesser extent other peoples who live near the Mediterranean Sea, causing 100,000 deaths yearly. An individual who is homozygous for this gene produces abnormal hemoglobin which results in the distortion of the blood cells upon their exposure to low oxygen levels, as occurs in some blood vessels of the body (see Figure 2.13). This condition usually results in the early death of the individual, thus it is typically kept at a very low level in any population by the force of natural selection. However, among certain African populations, as many as 30% of the people may be carrying this harmful gene in a recessive allele, along with a normal allele. It was suspected, therefore, that some environmental factor was responsible for the high incidence of the detrimental gene. It was discovered that the frequency of this harmful

sickle-cell anemia

gene parallels the incidence of malaria. The greater the incidence of malaria in a particular geographical region, the greater the incidence of the sickle-cell gene. Further investigations revealed another interesting fact. The infant who is heterozygous for the gene and who thus produces both normal and sickle-cell hemoglobin in the red blood cells has a much better chance of resisting malaria than does a child of a normal genotype who produces only normal hemoglobin. For some reason not yet fully understood, the malarial parasite has greater difficulty in invading a red blood cell which contains both kinds of hemoglobin.

The sickle-cell trait does not protect adults from malaria. However, a small child with the trait has a greater chance of surviving the first malaria attack, and he will then develop antibodies against future attacks of malaria. Thus in malarial regions, the heterozygous presence of the sickle-cell gene actually has a selective advantage. Individuals who carry the defective gene have a higher rate of survival in these regions than those who do not carry the defective gene and hence die of malaria. In this way, the high frequency of the gene in the population is maintained. This would not be the case in areas where there is no malaria and where there is no adaptive function served by the sickle-cell gene.

This advantage explains why certain black populations were able to live in malaria-laden regions of Africa whereas these environments proved to be fatal to many Europeans who tried to settle there. The sickle-cell example also provides a dramatic illustration of the interaction between the genes and the environment.

Do You Know Your Genes?

We now know that many serious and often fatal disorders are either genetically transmitted or they occur because of mutations in the gene. The detection of many such disorders is now possible even before the birth of the child, as we shall see, so that parents can terminate the pregnancy in the case of a fetal defect. Ideally, however, each individual should be aware, before pregnancy occurs, of his or her genotype and the chances of passing a defective gene to the offspring. Unfortunately, most of us do not know which harmful genes we carry. If we have a child with a hereditary disease, then we know, at least about that one gene. This first clue, however, may be known too late to avert tragedy. There are, nonetheless, steps that can be taken by couples who wish to have children to determine their risk of bearing a child with a genetic disease.

Hereditary Disease and Ethnic Groups

The chances that a child will suffer from or carry a hereditary disorder may in large part be related to the parents' ethnic origin. As can be seen in Table 2.1, some diseases are found more frequently among some ethnic groups than among others. We have already discussed sickle-cell anemia,

TABLE 2.1 Selected genetic disorders in some ethnic groups.

If You Are	The Chance Is About	That
black	1 in 10	you are a carrier of sickle-cell anemia.
	7 in 10	you have an intolerance to milk (e.g., develop diarrhea).
black and male	1 in 10	⎧you have a hereditary
black and female	1 in 50	⎨predisposition to develop hemolytic anemia after taking ⎩sulfa or other drugs.
	1 in 4	you have or will develop high blood pressure.
white	1 in 25	you are a carrier of cystic fibrosis.
	1 in 80	you are a carrier of phenylketonuria.
Jewish (Ashkenazic)	1 in 30	you are a carrier of Tay-Sachs disease.
	1 in 100	you are a carrier of familial dysautonomia, a central nervous system disorder characterized by mental retardation, motor inco-ordination, and frequent convulsions.
Italian-American or Greek-American	1 in 10	you are a carrier of thalas-semia, a form of anemia.
Armenian or Jewish (Sephardic)	1 in 45	you are a carrier of familial Mediterranean fever, a dis-order characterized by fre-quent spells of fever and arthritis.
Afrikaners (white South African)	1 in 330	you may have porphyria, a metabolism disorder.
Oriental	close to 100%	you will have milk intolerance as an adult.

Source: Table from p. 63 of *Know Your Genes* by Aubrey Milunski, M.D. Copyright © 1977 by Aubrey Milunski, M.D. Reprinted by permission of Houghton Mifflin Company.

which tends to strike blacks. PKU, on the other hand, is found mostly in whites and is rare among blacks and Orientals.

Tay-Sachs disease, a disorder which causes brain destruction, blindness, and eventually death in early childhood, is found almost exclusively among Ashkenazi Jews (who are of Eastern European descent) but not among Jews of Sephardic (Spanish) origin. It should be clear, however, that any of these diseases could occur, through intermarriage or mutation, in any ethnic group. Tay-Sachs disease, for example, is found in children who are not Jewish, although for them it is at least 100 times less frequent. Knowledge about an individual's country of origin or ethnic group is crucial, therefore, for establishing the potential risk of carrying the genes

Tay-Sachs disease

for certain diseases. In the case where two individuals of the same ethnic group marry, the likelihood that their offspring will be affected by a genetic disease peculiar to that ethnic group increases, as they may both be carriers of a recessive gene for that disease.

Genetic Counseling

When a couple is faced with a problem they have reason to believe is genetic in origin, their best course is to obtain more information before having a child. Such information may be obtained through genetic counseling programs which help family members understand the genetic and medical implications of disorders so they are better able to make the decision of whether or not to pursue pregnancy.

Unfortunately, those individuals who seek genetic counseling are most often those who have already had one child with a genetic disorder, although other people who know of such a disorder in their families also at times seek counseling. According to one study, approximately half the people who seek genetic counseling do so for genetic defects determined by a single gene (for example, PKU); another 20% of the people do so for chromosome anomalies, mostly Down's syndrome; and another 20% for congenital defects with polygenetic or unknown genetic cause. Only on rare occasions do families seek genetic advice because of problems anticipated from exposure to environmental factors that are known to mutate genes (Novitski, 1977).

The genetic counseling procedure involves making a detailed pedigree which includes all known relatives, with their ages, their reproductive history, including any instances of stillbirths, abortions, and deaths, and their countries of origin (Milunsky, 1977). Sometimes the pedigree may show the course of inheritance of a specific disorder. Even in these cases, however, those receiving counseling must be educated in the *principles of probability,* which refer to the likelihood of having a child with the disorder. For example, a couple may be told that, since they are both heterozygous for a special trait, there is 1 chance in 4 that they will have a child with that disorder. If the couple has already given birth to a child with the disease, they will often assume that their next three children will be born normal. However, this is not the case. For *each* pregnancy there is a 1-to-4 chance that the offspring will be born with a defect, and thus there is risk each time a pregnancy is planned no matter how many normal or genetically abnormal children have been born.

principles of probability

Genetic Screening

Screening for genetic diseases has expanded at a rapid rate during the past two decades and promises to expand even more so in the future. Currently, there are several genetic disorders for which screening tests are available. One such disorder is PKU. Unlike PKU, however, there are

many disorders which can be detected but not treated. *Cystic fibrosis* for   *cystic fibrosis*
example, is the most frequent severe genetic disease of childhood in the
United States, yet no successful treatment for the disease has been found.
The incidence of affected children is in the range of 1 to 1200, and 1 out of
20 or 30 individuals are carriers of the disease. The disorder is a malfunc-
tion of the exodrine glands, and it is inherited as a recessive trait.

Screening is only the first step in the detection of a genetic disease and
should not be interpreted as diagnosis. Although screening tests are designed to detect infants with specific disorders, these tests actually detect
only a primary finding in a disorder (Novitski, 1977). The finding may
also be present in other disorders, or may be unrelated to any genetic
disorders. The PKU test, for example, detects high levels of phenylalanine (hyperphenylalaninemia), not specifically PKU, and although some
infants with hyperphenylalaninemia have PKU, others may have it in
association with another condition, or it may be an isolated, transient
finding of no clinical significance (Baer, 1977). Only with additional tests
can the specific genetic disorder be determined. Thus genetic screening
should be followed by more specific diagnostic tests and treatments.

PKU was the first genetic disease for which large populations were
screened. Sickle-cell anemia was the second such disease. Now Tay-Sachs
disease and other even rarer genetic diseases have been added to the list.
There are, as yet, several problems associated with genetic screening. One
problem arises, ironically, from the simplicity of screening tests, which
has resulted in screening for rare disorders in geographic areas that have
lacked the medical capacity for follow-up diagnostic testing. For example,
shortly after PKU screening began, reports appeared describing infants
without PKU who were put on low-phenylalanine diets because of aber-
rations detected in a single screening test. These infants frequently had no
evaluation after the initial screening test to determine whether or not they
truly had PKU.

DISCUSSION OF SOCIAL ISSUES: DETECTING GENETIC DISORDERS AND GENETIC ENGINEERING

In addition to screening tests that detect genetic abnormalities after birth,
there are tests that detect genetic abnormalities during pregnancy. The
latest such test, still in the experimental stage, is the *chorion biopsy*. This   *chorion biopsy*
test can be conducted during the first month of pregnancy. It involves
taking a sample of the chorion which, since it is made up from the cells
outside the fertilized egg, contains the same genetic material as the embryo. The examination and biopsy of the chorion can reveal the sex of the
unborn baby as well as such genetic abnormalities as Down's syndrome,
within one day. The chorion biopsy promises to be a significant medical
advance. In the cases where the parents would elect to abort the abnormal
embryo, this can be done with relatively little risk to the mother, as the

abortion can take place early in the pregnancy. Also, finding out the results of the test within one day relieves parents-to-be of undue stress and anxiety.

amniocentesis

In another test for abnormalities, a sample of the amniotic fluid is taken by inserting a needle through the abdomen into the amniotic sac in the uterus. This procedure is called *amniocentesis* (see Figure 2.14). The amniotic fluid, which also contains genetic information about the unborn child, is examined to detect any genetic abnormalities and also the sex of the child. This test, however, can be done only during the 4th month of pregnancy, and the results take approximately three weeks to become known. If the parents do elect to have an abortion, considerably more risk to the health of the mother is entailed with this procedure than with a chorion biopsy, as it would mean aborting the fetus during the fifth month of pregnancy.

The increased use during recent years of prenatal detection of genetic diseases and the abortion of abnormal fetuses has produced major controversies that are medical, moral, religious, and legal in nature. One argument against the widespread use of amniocentesis focuses on the risks to the mother and the unborn child that this procedure entails. Some researchers, however, contend that the benefits of the procedure far outweigh the risks (Fuchs, 1980). There is also the important moral question of denying life to the fetus because of its physical or mental defects. Parents who are informed that their child will be defective may decide to abort the fetus. It could be argued that an abortion is warranted in cases where severe mental and physical abnormalities would otherwise result. But the question is, how severe must a defect be in order to warrant the use of abortion? While amniocentesis can detect a genetic abnormality, it cannot tell us anything about its severity. Down's syndrome, for example, is associated with varying levels of mental retardation. Some Down's syndrome children, if given appropriate, stimulating experiences after birth as well as adequate medical attention have been shown to function relatively well once they reach school age. Should, then, all Down's syndrome fetuses be aborted?

Even if the abortion issue is resolved, there are other problems associated with late abortions because a live birth after an abortion is a possibility. When an abortion becomes a birth, it is unclear who must decide what procedures are in the infant's best interest and who is financially responsible for the infant. These questions arise because infants born of abortion are injured in the abortion process, so legal scholars are asking whether it would be possible for such a seriously injured infant to make a claim of "wrongful life" against the hospital. Also, medical technology has advanced to the point where the life of a child may be continued outside the womb by artificial life-supporting systems even if that baby is born extremely premature. When an abortion results in the live birth of a child with genetic abnormalities, should doctors withhold any life-prolonging

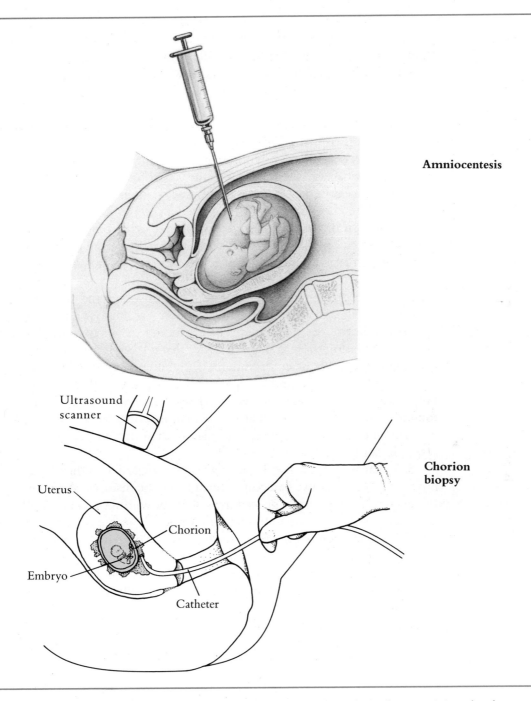

Amniocentesis

Chorion biopsy

Ultrasound scanner

Uterus

Chorion

Embryo

Catheter

FIGURE 2.14   Amniocentesis and the chorion biopsy are procedures for examining the chromosomal makeup of the embryo and fetus when some abnormality is suspected. In amniocentesis (top), a large needle is inserted into the woman's abdomen until it penetrates the uterus. A small amount of the amniotic fluid is removed and examined for the presence of abnormalities. In the chorion biopsy (bottom), a small piece of the chorion is removed and its cells are examined. In both procedures, ultrasound waves help determine the position of the fetus in the uterus.

intervention? What do you think? These are not easy issues to resolve, and some physicians now refuse to perform amniocentesis because of the possibility that an abortion would be called for.

genetic engineering

Other ethical problems are associated with advances in *genetic engineering,* which is a research activity that entails the manipulation of genes. Given the progress made in this area, researchers project that in the future we may be able to restore to normalcy the genes that are responsible for many of the diseases we described in this chapter. Perhaps we will be able to prevent PKU, either by synthesizing the genetic code for the missing enzyme in the disease and adding it to the cell or by transplanting a normal gene from a healthy cell. This is as yet speculative, but you can see that there could be enormous benefits to such a technique.

cloning

Although numerous benefits are associated with genetic engineering, there are some potential dangers as well. This is illustrated in the matter of *cloning,* which is an asexual form of reproduction in which all progeny are identical. There are many potential benefits to this type of research, too, for it leads to greater understanding of chromosomes and their relationship to growth and disease. However, there are many people who are opposed to both gene manipulation and cloning. They contend that with gene manipulation there is the possibility that a laboratory-created organism might escape to the environment, with potentially dire consequences. Also, they fear that cloning will result in some individuals and their "carbon copies" taking over the world. These fears are not altogether unfounded, so it is necessary that genetic engineering be conducted under government guidelines and regulations. With sufficient safeguards, such research can be useful.

Safeguards should also be in place with regard to other techniques now available, notably, detecting prenatal genetic diseases. Although useful, even relatively simple procedures can be powerful tools for tampering with the genetic pool of a population. A good example is amniocentesis, which not only reveals the presence or absence of genetic abnormalities, but also the sex of the fetus. It is improbable that most parents would choose to abort a fetus on the basis of its sex, but it could happen. You can imagine the drastic social changes that would result, not to mention the decrease in genetic variability. All these factors must be considered as we forge ahead with advances in genetic engineering and the detection of genetic disorders (Etzioni, 1977).

HEREDITY AND BEHAVIOR

As we have seen, the study of genetics provides us with valuable information concerning physical growth and development and the etiology and nature of some abnormalities. It is also important in the understanding of variations in human behavior. For many years, developmental psychologists were preoccupied with determining the relative amounts contributed by genetic or environmental factors to different behavioral characteristics as they asked: Is human behavior determined by a person's genetic heredity (nature) or is it determined by upbringing (nurture)? The concern with this question resulted in what is called the nature-nurture controversy, briefly mentioned in the Introduction. Many researchers assumed extreme positions on the issue. Some researchers emphasized the exclusive role of genetic heredity whereas others took an equally extreme position by denying any biological contributions to behavior and emphasizing the role of learning and experience. We know now, however, that when posed in this either-or manner, the question is meaningless (Anastasi, 1958). The point is, there are no genes for behavior. However, genes act at a molecular level on the development and maintenance of structures that do have consequences for behavior (Scarr-Salapatek, 1975). The inheritance of behavioral traits follows a multifactorial pattern which involves the action of many genes and an interaction between heredity and the environment. Since, as it is now known, development is the outcome of both hereditary and environmental factors, researchers are now attempting to ascertain in what way and to what extent genetic and environmental factors interact to affect development, and how this interaction differs for specific behavioral traits.

Methods of Studying Heredity and Behavior

To find this out, researchers employ different kinds of studies, some using children and families, others using animals.

Animal Studies. The environment of animals can be controlled more easily and their behavior is not nearly as complex as that of humans, so the genetic contributions to behavior can be more easily understood using animal studies. The results of such studies cannot be directly applied to humans, but nonetheless, animal studies are important and deserving of a brief discussion here because they demonstrate the different ways in which genetic inheritance may be expressed in various environmental settings.

One of the techniques used in animal studies is *selective breeding*. In this technique animals which evidence similarity on a particular trait are mated with each other. Studies using this technique have been conducted to assess whether emotionality or learning ability are inherited traits. In one such classic study on learning ability, Tyron (1942) selected 142 rats who were given 19 trials in a complex maze. Some rats learned the maze quickly and made few errors. Others learned slowly and made many errors. The "bright" rats were then mated with each other, as were the "dull" rats, and their offspring were tested in the maze. The experiment was repeated for 8 generations. The researcher found that the differences

selective breeding

between the two groups in errors made while running the maze became greater with each generation. Since each new generation had no prior experience in running the maze, the difference between the bright and the dull groups was considered to be due to genetic inheritance.

Tyron's experiment demonstrates that heredity and learning ability are related. However, in a subsequent study, Searle (1949) took rats from the 22nd generation of Tyron's rats and tested them for about thirty different traits such as emotionality, activity levels, discrimination learning, as well as performance on Tyron's maze. Searle confirmed Tyron's findings on the original maze but when he tested the rats using other mazes, he found that in some cases, the bright and dull rats differed not only in their performance on the maze, but also in other traits such as emotionality. It could well be that this emotional difference (or any other difference) in the rats may have affected their ability to perform on the maze.

Other animal studies demonstrate not the effects of heredity on such behavioral traits as learning ability and emotionality, as the above studies do, but the effects of the environment. Fuller (1967), for example, studied the learning ability of two breeds of dogs who were reared in different environments. Some pups from each breed were raised normally; others were reared in isolation and were deprived of any environmental stimulation. Fuller found that although the effects of isolation differed according to breed, the dogs reared in isolation generally demonstrated a poorer learning ability. Fuller, however, found that the dogs were hindered *emotionally* by the experience of isolation, not intellectually, and thus were unable to perform. When these dogs became emotionally stronger, their maze performance improved.

In another study on the effects of the environment, Cooper and Zubek (1958) used strains of bright and dull rats reared in one of two different environments: an enriched environment which included considerable sensory stimulation through the use of balls and tunnels, and a restricted environment which contained only a food box and water pan. When the researchers tested the rats for maze learning they found that the enriched environment helped the dull rats but not the bright ones, and that the restricted environment had no effect on the dull rats, but it hurt the performance of the bright. Thus this study clearly demonstrates that behavioral traits can be altered by environmental circumstances and that developmental characteristics are the result of an interaction between genetic and environmental factors.

Many other animal studies have been conducted which, along with ones like the examples cited, have helped demonstrate a point made earlier in the chapter: the organism inherits a range of modifiability, or a range of reaction. Each genotype specifies a range of phenotypes which are possible under certain environmental circumstances. If the range of reaction is narrow for a particular trait, environmental factors will have little or no influence on its development. But if the range of reaction is broad, environmental influence will be significant.

FIGURE 2.15   Concordance in identical twins.

Twin Studies.   Studies using twins and adopted children are also used to determine the extent that genetic and environmental factors contribute to human traits. The idea behind twin studies is that two people with identical genes would be expected to have identical traits if those traits are largely genetically determined. Pairs of people with identical genes are known as *identical,* or *monozygotic, twins* since they develop from a single (*mono*) fertilized egg (*zygote*) and thus share the exact genotype. If one twin possesses a genetic trait, the identical partner will possess it too. The similarity between the twins is called *intrapair concordance* (see Figure 2.15).

 Besides monozygotic twins, there is a second type of twins, known as *fraternal,* or *dizygotic, twins,* who develop simultaneously in the womb but from two separate eggs. Dizygotic twins have only half their genes in common. Twin studies capitalize on the innate difference between monozygotic and dizygotic twin types by investigating whether for a given trait the concordance rate for monozygotic twins will be significantly higher than the concordance rate for dizygotic twins. A higher monozygotic concordance rate is taken as strong evidence that the trait has a significant genetic influence.

 In twin studies, the assumption is made that environmental factors are the same for twins of each type as long as they grow in the same home and experience the same family life. If identical twins show more of a resemblance on some traits than fraternal twins do, it is assumed that the trait is

monozygotic twins

intrapair concordance
dizygotic twins

influenced by genetic factors. Some researchers, however, have questioned these assumptions and ask, is it not possible that parents, in reacting to the similarities of identical twins, treat them exactly alike? If this is the case, then how can we be sure that it is the genes and not the environmental circumstances that determine a particular trait under investigation? To determine how parents actually relate to twins, Lytton (1976) observed mothers of identical and fraternal twins. The researcher found that indeed mothers of identical twins responded to them in a similar way, whereas mothers of fraternal twins did not. However, the mothers' responses were found to be related to the behaviors of the children. Since identical twins behave in a similar way, then it is not surprising that they elicit similar responses from their mothers. Similar findings were obtained from other studies which found that even in cases where mothers mistook the zygosity of their twins, they nonetheless responded in relation to the behavior of the twins (Scarr, 1968).

There are also studies of monozygotic twins reared apart and, therefore, under different environmental circumstances. These studies are harder to execute since it is not always possible to find a large sample of identical twins who have been separated from birth. Any similarities found in such twins would be due largely to genetic factors since these twins did not share similar environments. You should note, however, that researchers find that in cases of twins reared apart, their environments are often similar, so that even though they do not grow up together, they nonetheless share similar backgrounds. The most useful studies include monozygotic twins who grew up in widely different environments.

Adoption Studies.   Adoption studies help us understand genetic and environmental influences on behavior. There are three groups suitable for study: the adopted children themselves when they are grown, the biological parents, and the adoptive parents. This three-way comparison is very instructive because the biological parents are related to the adopted child genetically, without sharing the same environment, whereas the adoptive parents share the same environment with the adopted child without being genetically related. Significant similarities between the adopted child and the biological parents indicate hereditary influence, whereas similarities between the adopted child and the adoptive parents can be due only to chance or to the influence of a shared environment.

A problem arises with adoption studies, however. Adoption agencies attempt to place children with adoptive parents who are similar in physical and other characteristics to the biological parents. This may dilute any findings on the relative influence of genes and the environment.

Heredity and Intelligence

The study of the extent that heredity influences intelligence is both complex and controversial, in part because there is no agreement about how to

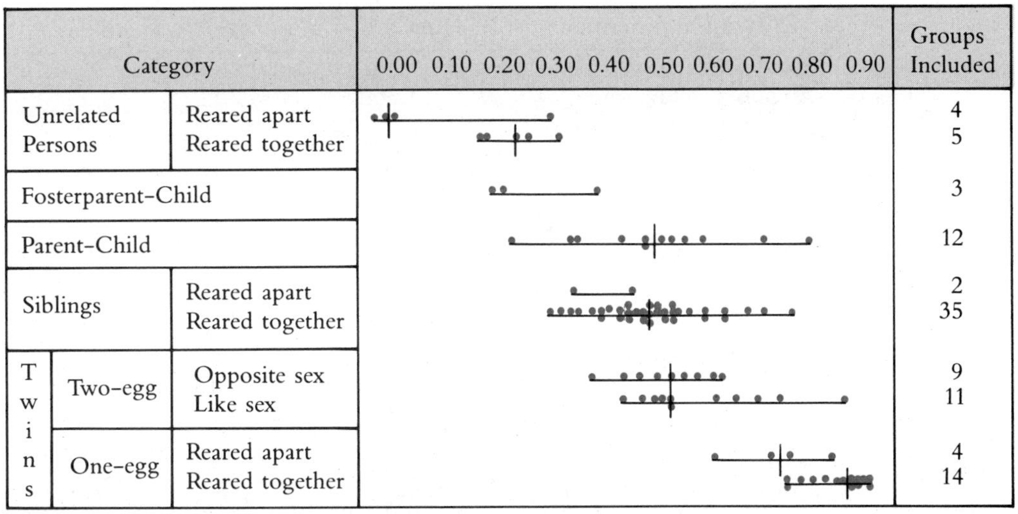

Category		0.00 0.10 0.20 0.30 0.40 0.50 0.60 0.70 0.80 0.90	Groups Included
Unrelated Persons	Reared apart		4
	Reared together		5
Fosterparent–Child			3
Parent–Child			12
Siblings	Reared apart		2
	Reared together		35
Twins	Two-egg	Opposite sex		9
		Like sex		11
	One-egg	Reared apart		4
		Reared together		14

FIGURE 2.16   Correlation coefficients for "intelligence" test scores from 52 studies. Some studies reported data for more than one relationship category; some included more than one sample per category, giving a total of 99 groups. Over two-thirds of the correlation coefficients were derived from IQs, the remainder from special tests (for example, Primary Mental Abilities). Midparent-child correlation was used when available, otherwise mother-child correlation. Correlation coefficients obtained in each study are indicated by dark circles; medians are shown by vertical lines intersecting the horizontal lines which represent the ranges. From "Genetics and Intelligence: A Review," Erlenmeyer-Kimling, L. and Jarvik L. F., from *Science* Vol. 142, Fig. 1, p. 1478, 13 December 1963. Copyright © 1963 by the American Association for the Advancement of Science.

define intelligence or about what intelligence (IQ) tests actually measure (we discuss these issues in Chapter 14). However, the results of twin and adoption studies suggest that performance on intelligence tests is highly influenced by heredity. As you will see, intellectual characteristics are malleable, thus environmental factors also have a significant impact on intellectual performance.

The evidence that performance on intelligence tests has a genetic component comes from numerous studies that are based on the rationale that if heredity influences intellectual performance, there should be a greater similarity in intelligence (IQ) scores among individuals who have more genes in common. In a summary of over fifty different studies, which involved 30,000 correlations, Erlenmeyer-Kimling and Jarvik (1963) found that the greater the genetic similarity between individuals, the more likely they were to have similar IQ scores. Recall that correlation coefficients do not indicate causes; rather, they are estimates of how two measures (in this case, IQ scores and genetic similarity) vary together. As you can see in Figure 2.16, the correlation of IQ scores for unrelated persons is small. The correlation increases, however, as genetic similarity increases.

TABLE 2.2   Correlations in intelligence of monozygotic (MZ) and dizygotic (DZ) twins and heritabilities (H) found in a number of twin studies.

Author of Study	Date	Country	MZ	DZ	H
Von Verschuer	1930	Germany	*	*	.62
Day	1932	U.S.	.92	.61	.80
Stocks and Karn	1933	England	.84	.65	.54
Newman et al.	1937	U.S.	.90	.62	.74
Gottschaldt	1939	Germany	*	*	.82
Wictorin	1952	Sweden	.89	.72	.61
Husén	1953	Sweden	.90	.70	.67
Blewett	1954	England	.76	.44	.57
Thurstone et al.	1955	U.S.	*	*	.65
Burt	1958	England	.97	.55	.93
Zazzo	1960	France	.90	.60	.75
Vandenberg	1962	U.S.	.74	.56	.41
Nichols	1965	U.S.	.87	.63	.65
Huntley	1966	England	.83	.66	.50
Partanen et al.	1966	Finland	.69	.42	.51
Schoenfeldt	1969	U.S.	.80	.48	.62

Source: Reprinted with permission of Macmillan Publishing Company from *Encyclopedia of Education,* Lee C. Deighton, Editor in chief. Volume 5, page 125. Copyright © 1970 by Crowell Collier and Macmillan, Inc.

Thus, for dizygotic twins it is quite high but for monozygotic twins it is higher still. So we can see that genetic heredity is an important factor in intellectual performance.

The question of how important remains. One method of determining the relative importance of both heredity and the environment is use of the *heritability ratio,* which is a mathematical estimate of the proportion of trait variance having genetic causes. Researchers calculate the heritability ratio for a particular trait through the comparison of identical twins who have been separated early in life and who have lived under different environmental circumstances. Since such twins are genetically identical, if they are very similar in a trait, yet they have lived apart, this would provide evidence for the importance of environmental influences on the trait. Thus the heritability ratio will be low. If the identical twins are raised apart but nevertheless resemble each other in a trait, the evidence is strong that that trait is influenced by genetic heredity, and the heritability ratio will be high.

You can see in Table 2.2 that the heritability ratio for intelligence varies according to the different studies, but it is clear that for the population studied, variability in intelligence has a substantial genetic factor. If the genetic factor is important, then the correlation between the IQ scores of identical twins reared apart (and therefore in different environments) should remain high. Indeed, summaries of studies reveal that this is the case (Vandenberg, 1971).

heritability ratio

However, there are some limitations to these studies. The limitations come to light when researchers examine not the statistical evidence, but the raw data upon which the evidence is based. Consider a study which looked at IQ scores of different sets of identical twins reared apart since infancy (Newman, Freeman, & Holzinger, 1937). In one case of twin girls, the researchers found significant differences in IQ scores. They noted that one of the twins lived all of her life in an isolated, rural area where she received only a minimal education. The other twin lived in a more stimulating environment and she received a college education. In the same study, the researchers found a difference of only 1 IQ point between identical twin boys even though one of the twins was raised by a farmer of modest means, the other by a well-to-do physician. Depending on which set of twins we focus on, we could argue that environment makes a difference (as in the case of the first set of twins) or that heredity is the important factor in development (as in the case of the second set of twins).

Besides this limitation, different results may be obtained depending on the research method used. When studies are correlational in nature, the genetic influence on intelligence is highlighted. However, when studies use IQ scores as a measure of intelligence, they tend to illustrate the effects of the environment. Several studies of adopted children illustrate this point. Skodak and Skeels (1949) examined the IQ scores of 100 adopted children who were tested at repeated intervals for a 16-year period. Educational level, which is related to IQ score, was available for both the biological and adoptive parents. With increasing age, the adopted children's IQ scores became more highly correlated with the educational level of their biological parents than with that of their adoptive parents. In fact, in a later analysis of the data, Honzik (1957) showed that the correlation found for the adopted children and their biological parents was similar to that found for children (*not* adopted) and their parents who had reared them (see Figure 2.17). These findings provide support for the argument that the genetic influence on intelligence is significant. However, when researchers looked not at the correlations, but only at the IQ scores found in these same studies, they noted that the environment is a determinant. The mean IQs of 63 biological mothers of the adopted children was 86. The mean IQs of their children, tested at adolescence, was 106, or a 20-point difference. It is rare that a child will have exactly the same IQ as that of her biological parents, but a 20-point difference in IQ is substantial enough to warrant the argument that environment is a key determinant of intelligence.

In summary, although studies of twins and adoptive children document that genetic factors make a significant contribution to individual differences in performance on intelligence tests, it is clear that environmental factors also play a major role. You will see in Chapters 4, 5, and 8 that for some infants and children, stimulating environments can dramatically raise the IQ score, whereas restricted environments in which the children are deprived of tactile and verbal stimulation can lower it.

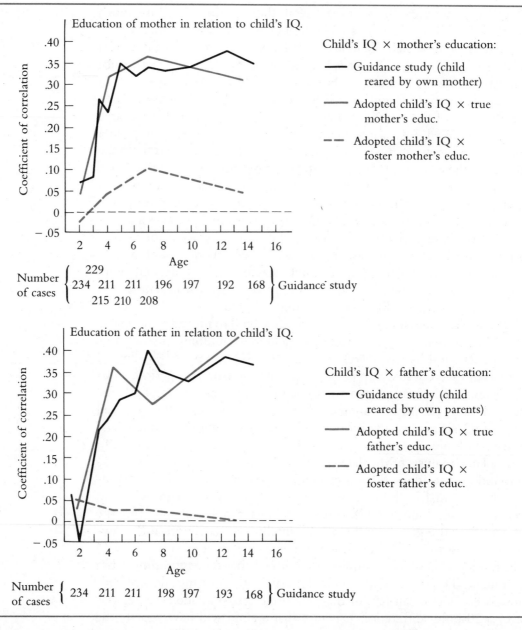

FIGURE 2.17   "Intellectual resemblance of adopted children to true and adopted parents and of children to their own parents" by Marjorie P. Honzik from *Child Development,* 28 (2) p. 219, Fig. 2 and p. 222, Fig. 4. Copyright © 1957 by The Society for Research in Child Development, Inc.

Inheritance of Personality Traits

Twin studies have also been used to determine whether there is a genetic influence on personality traits. However, because of problems in defining and measuring personality traits, it is difficult to ascertain a genetic influ-

© 1984 United Features Syndicate, Inc.

ence for all personality traits. Nevertheless, for some personality traits, for example, introversion/extroversion, which denotes the extent of a person's sociability, there does appear to be a genetic influence (Shields, 1962). (Introverted individuals are withdrawn and inhibited; extroverted individuals are outgoing and appear self-confident.)

The individual's temperament—whether he is calm or irritable, easy-going or difficult—also appears to be determined by the genes (Thomas, Chess, & Birch, 1971). Researchers point out that the individual does not inherit a specific personality trait, but rather, a general way of responding to the environment (Scarr, 1969). Researchers also note that although there is some evidence for a genetic component for some personality traits, personality seems to be influenced largely by environmental factors (Slater & Cowie, 1971). In a study of identical twins reared apart, researchers found that the twins showed some similarities in the way they interacted with other people, but they differed in their interests, ambitions, and other aspects of their personalities (Juel-Neilsen, 1965).

More recent studies of twins yield different findings which suggest that heredity has more of a bearing on personality development than is generally believed. In one such series of studies, researchers compared 23 pairs of twins reared apart since birth (Holden, 1980). Several pairs of twins grew up in different parts of the world and they had different cultural and religious upbringings, yet they had remarkably similar personality profiles. In one case study of identical twin males who were separated in infancy, one living in Trinidad, the other in Europe, researchers found that both men had similar interests and capabilities. Both had quick tempers and both liked the same foods (Chen, 1979). The twins also exhibited a number of idiosyncrasies, such as fidgeting with rubber bands and reading magazines back to front.

Several other pairs of twins involved in the study showed surprising similarities which were difficult to explain. For example, one pair of twin men had sons named James Alan and James Allan. Both men had married and divorced women by the name of Linda and remarried women named Betty. A pair of twin women had sons named Richard Andrew and Andrew Richard and daughters named Catherine Louise and Karen Louise!

In an extensive review of the research on twins reared apart, Farber (1981) notes also that twins who have had the least contact with one another are the most alike. Some researchers suggest that this could be due to the fact that when they are reared together, identical twins often want to assert their own individualities and may do so by downplaying their similarities. Identical twins raised apart do not have to assert their individualities in this way, so their similarities are more pronounced (Farber, 1981; Lewontin, Rose, & Kamin, 1984). Although this is a plausible explanation for some of the fascinating findings recently elicited from the research on twins, much more research needs to be conducted.

SUMMARY

A child's development is largely programmed by the genes. However, genetic factors by themselves do not determine the course of child development, for they do not operate in a vacuum. Rather, they interact with and are influenced by environmental factors. Genetic endowment can be seen as a potentiality. Whether or not the genetic potential will be realized depends on factors in the environment.

The genes are carried on 46 chromosomes, half of which come from the mother and the other half from the father. The mechanisms that underlie the functioning of genes are very complex. Each gene occurs in two alternative forms called alleles which behave in a pattern of dominance and recessiveness to determine the observable characteristic of a trait. Physical characteristics such as eye color and hair texture are established by this pattern of dominance and recessiveness, as are certain abnormal conditions and diseases such as albinism and PKU.

Although some characteristics and diseases are transmitted through a single gene, most human traits are determined by a complex interaction of many different genes. Gene activity is further complicated by biological and environmental factors such as the age of the mother and experiences after birth which modify the phenotypical expression of the genotype. In addition, gene mutations can lead to a variety of abnormalities. The survival of mutations depends on how adaptive that mutant characteristic is to the environment. Sickle-cell anemia, for example, when carried as a recessive trait, has proved adaptive in regions where there is a high incidence of malaria but destructive in other areas.

Because of the survival of mutations which have an adaptive advantage in certain geographic areas, some genetic diseases occur in greater frequencies among some ethnic groups. Genetic counseling and screening as well as prenatal detection of genetic diseases are some of the mechanisms available to prevent genetic deviations in development. However, several ethical problems are associated with these procedures. For example, should a child with a genetic disease be aborted? Also, these procedures can detect not only genetic diseases but the sex of the child as well. Will parents who want a boy choose to abort a female fetus, and, if so, what would be the consequences for society as a whole?

Although we know a great deal about hereditary transmission and the causes and detection of many genetic diseases, by comparison, we know very little about the genetic processes involved in behavioral traits. We do know that several genes on unrelated chromosomes converge to create specific patterns of behavior. The inheritance of behavioral traits follows a multifactorial pattern that involves not only the action of many genes, but also an interaction between heredity and the environment. This has been established through numerous animal studies, as well as other studies using twins and adopted children which investigated the genetic contributions to such traits as intelligence and personality.

REVIEW POINTS

1. Human development is explained as the process by which the genotype (the genetic makeup of the individual) is expressed as one or another phenotype. *Phenotype* refers to observable or measurable characteristics of the individual. Different phenotypes may develop from the same genotype, depending on environmental factors and also on the way children respond to their environment and to different life experiences. It is useful to think of the genotype as the potential the individual is born with. The extent that this potential will be realized depends on environmental experiences.

2. We owe much of our understanding of genetics to the work of Gregor Mendel who demonstrated that heredity is transmitted through the genes. Each gene has two alleles, which behave in a pattern of dominance or recessiveness. It is the dominant allele that determines the phenotype, or observable characteristic associated with the particular gene.

3. Mendel's work helped us understand how physical traits such as color and texture of hair are inherited, and also how some diseases are inherited. Some diseases, such as albinism and PKU, are inherited through a single-gene pattern. However, some traits and diseases are inherited through several genes acting in concert and under certain environmental conditions.

4. There are different types of genes, and these are found in the cells which make up the human body. The genes in the cells are found on long tiny threads. When stained in a laboratory procedure, these threads become visible under a microscope, and are therefore called chromosomes. There are 46 chromosomes in body cells, each of which holds thousands of genes. The most important component of the chromosome is DNA, which contains the genetic code that controls the biological inheritance of all living things.

5. Several physical and behavioral defects are associated with chromosome abnormalities. An example is Down's syndrome. However, many such defects can be prevented through genetic counseling and screening. There are also procedures which can detect genetic abnormalities during pregnancy. One such procedure is amniocentesis, which lets parents know if their unborn child has an abnormality. If so, an abortion may be considered. Although amniocentesis is regarded as beneficial, there are ethical and moral problems entailed in the practice.

6. The study of genetics not only provides us with valuable information regarding physical growth and the hereditary component of some abnormalities, it also helps explain individual differences in intelligence and personality. These traits are the outcome of both heredity and environmental experience, so researchers attempt to find out how and to what extent genetic and environmental factors interact to affect development.

7. In this regard, researchers employ animal studies and studies using twins and adopted children. Studies using adopted children, for example, can measure the intelligence of the biological parents, the adopted children, and the adoptive parents to determine if intelligence is largely an inherited trait or a trait influenced by environmental factors. However, these studies are not without problems, since researchers have found that adoption agencies attempt to place children with individuals who are similar to the biological parents of the children. Using numerous studies which attempt to overcome these and other methodological problems, researchers have found that genetic potential is a significant aspect of intelligence, but that environmental factors also play a role.

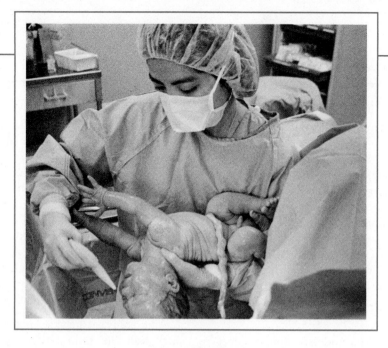

CHAPTER 3

PRENATAL DEVELOPMENT
AND BIRTH

The development of a human baby from a single cell that is formed when the ovum is fertilized by a sperm remains the greatest miracle of nature. The whole process takes an average of only 266 days. During this short time the single cell becomes a complex structure of many millions of cells, each of which is highly developed to perform a specialized function within the human body. By the time the baby is born it is 6 billion times heavier than the egg cell from which it came!

Growth during the prenatal period is remarkably regular and predictable. Changes in the organism occur in a fixed order at a fixed time. We have amassed a great deal of knowledge about what happens inside the uterus during the prenatal period, although we know little about why the baby develops as it does. How do some cells "know" that they are to become brain cells, or that they are to become the face or limbs? What we do know is that fetal development is controlled by the genes and chromosomes, explained in Chapter 2. As human beings, we are what our parents' genes have made us. But not entirely! The environment in which we live in the uterus before birth and in the world afterwards can modify the effects of heredity considerably. It is now known that during the prenatal period, the fetus is vulnerable to a variety of factors that can influence the course of development. Many of these factors are related to the mother's physical condition, her emotional well-being, her diet, or the drugs she takes during pregnancy.

In this chapter we take a look at the stages of prenatal development, and we examine the factors that are known to affect the course of embryonic and fetal growth and subsequent development of the newborn baby. We take a look, too, at some environmental and family factors at birth and after birth which can result in complications in the child. In addition, we discuss the social aspects of pregnancy and birth and the circumstances surrounding conception. Do pregnancy and childbirth have anything to do with love? Why do people have children? These are two of the questions we address. Finally, we take a look at the failure of some couples to conceive and some of the causes and treatments for infertility.

PRENATAL DEVELOPMENT

Conception

About once each month, on approximately the fourteenth day of a woman's 28-day menstrual cycle, a mature *ovum,* or egg cell, is released from the ovary and arrives in the fallopian tube. If a sperm from the male penetrates the ovum, their nuclei join together. At this point, the ovum is said to be fertilized, and pregnancy begins. Whereas this process appears simple, it is not. Before fertilization can occur, the sperm must be deposited in the female's vagina (see Figure 3.1) at the time of the male orgasm.

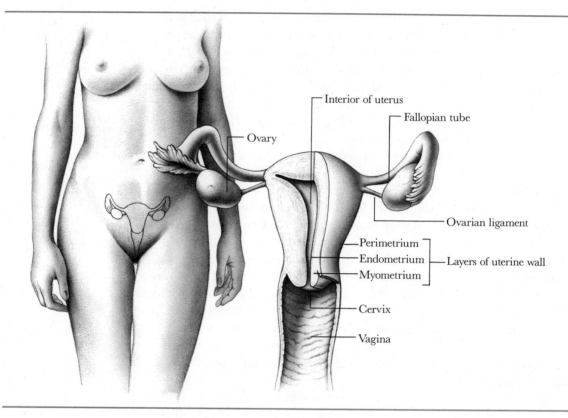

FIGURE 3.1   The female reproductive system.

Once deposited, the sperm face a difficult journey to reach the egg. Most of the semen, which contains the sperm, leaks out of the vagina soon after it has been deposited. What sperm are left have to make their way past the cervix to the outer part of the fallopian tube. Many sperm die before completing their journey, since the vagina and cervix are covered with an acidic secretion that is hostile to sperm. Some women worry that the acidity of the vaginal secretion may be the cause of their failure to conceive. This is not the case. The successful sperm escape the effects of the vaginal secretion by reaching the fallopian tube within a few minutes. However, for conception to occur, there need to be a sufficient number of sperm deposited in the vagina because many sperm do not make the journey. Thus, if the male is infertile, which occurs when his sperm is abnormal or of low count, conception will be difficult to achieve.

capacitation

Of the millions of sperm that are deposited in the vagina, only a few hundred reach the outer end of the fallopian tube. The sperm that do arrive there undergo a process called *capacitation*. As a result of this process, enzymes are produced which enable the sperm to dissolve the outer membrane surrounding the egg cell and penetrate into its center. The successful sperm is very highly selected; once the egg cell is penetrated by

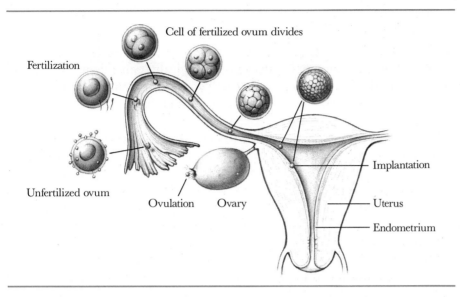

FIGURE 3.2   Fertilization and migration of the ovum, from the fallopian tube to implantation in the uterine wall.

the sperm, it changes its outer membrane so that no penetration by other sperm can occur. In this way, multiple fertilization by a number of sperm is avoided.

The timing of fertilization is very precise. The egg cell lives for up to about 24 hours after entering the fallopian tube, and the sperm, once deposited, can survive for only up to 48 hours. For conception to occur, intercourse must take place within two days of ovulation.

Immediately upon fertilization, the ovum, now known as the zygote, begins the process of cell division and also the journey from the fallopian tube to the uterus. It takes the zygote about 7 to 8 days to pass down the fallopian tube and to implant itself into the *decidua,* the thickened lining of the uterus wall (see Figure 3.2). Thereafter, rapid growth and development occur, so that by 8 weeks, a recognizable embryonic baby is present in a bag of fluid called the *amniotic sac.* This sac is formed by two membranes that develop from cells on the outside of the fertilized egg. The outer of the two membranes is called the *chorion,* and it encloses the inner membrane, the *amnion,* which contains the amniotic fluid.

decidua

amniotic sac

chorion
amnion

Stages of Prenatal Development

The nine months *in utero* are divided into three periods that correspond to the developmental stage of the organism: the period of the ovum, the period of the embryo, and the period of the fetus. During these periods, the organism undergoes a number of changes.

period of the
ovum

During the *period of the ovum,* which lasts approximately 2 weeks from the time of conception, the zygote establishes itself in the wall of the uterus. Tendrils from the zygote penetrate the blood vessels in the uterine wall, and thus the zygote begins a physiologically dependent relationship with the mother, a relationship that will continue throughout pregnancy.

period of the
embryo
ossification

The *period of the embryo* lasts from the time of the zygote's attachment to the uterine wall until the first occurrence of *ossification,* the formation of solid bone, in the embryo. This period lasts from 2 weeks following conception to the end of the eighth week. This period is a very hazardous one. Not all embryos are properly attached to the wall of the uterus, thus most miscarriages (spontaneous abortions) occur at this time, as the embryo can become detached from the wall of the uterus and be expelled. It has been estimated that close to 50% of embryos are aborted during this period, usually without the woman even knowing she is pregnant (Tanner, 1978). Such spontaneous abortions occur because of abnormalities in the embryo, in the uterine wall, or in other life-supporting structures of the uterine environment.

ectoderm

mesoderm
endoderm

During the embryo period, differentiation of important organs occurs (Annis, 1978). The inner mass of the zygote differentiates into three layers. From the *ectoderm,* hair, nails, part of the teeth, the outer layer of the skin and skin glands, as well as the nervous system and sensory cells develop. From the *mesoderm,* muscles, skeleton, excretory and circulatory systems, and inner skin layers develop. From the *endoderm,* the gastrointestinal tract, eustachian tubes, glands, and other organs such as the lungs, pancreas, and liver develop. By the end of the fourth week after conception, a small vessel, which is destined to become the heart, begins to pulse even though at this point the embryo is no larger than a human thumbnail. By the end of this period, at eight weeks after conception, the embryo is approximately one inch long and begins to resemble a human being. It is somewhat out of proportion, because its head is about as large as the rest of its body. Its face and features are recognizable, and its fingers, toes, and external genitalia are present (see Figure 3.3).

placenta

villi
intervillus space

Several structures which support the fetus also develop during the embryo period. One is the *placenta,* which is also referred to as the afterbirth. The placenta is a fleshy disc that grows on part of the chorion, which surrounds the developing embryo. It is made up of a large number of finger-like projections called *villi,* which burrow into the lining of the uterus and come to lie in a space called the *intervillus space.* The placenta, which allows for the passage of substances from the maternal bloodstream to that of the fetus, is the vital link between the mother and the unborn baby on which the life of the fetus depends. If, for example, the blood supply from the mother is reduced (high blood pressure in the mother may be one cause for this), then the fetus will literally starve and will be born smaller than it otherwise would have been. If a serious reduction in the blood flow occurs, the fetus may die from lack of oxygen.

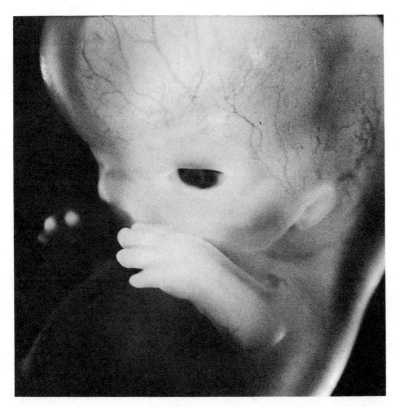

FIGURE 3.3   At 8 weeks, the embryo is already recognizable as a "baby." The umbilical cord has formed and some of the facial features are visible.

Substances that are made up of large molecules cannot pass through the placenta, which is why it is sometimes referred to as the *placental barrier*. However, along with the important nutrients that the fetus needs, some hazardous substances such as drugs that the mother ingests may pass through the placental barrier and harm the fetus. It is important to mention that there is no mixing of maternal and fetal bloodstreams. Each bloodstream is separate, and substances that pass from the mother to the baby, or vice versa, have to come out of one bloodstream, cross the villi, and only then enter the other bloodstream.

placental barrier

The embryo is joined at the abdomen (at the place of its future navel) to the placenta by the umbilical cord, which also develops during the embryo period. The umbilical cord is relatively long. In fact, at birth, it is actually longer than the newborn baby. This allows the growing embryo flexibility of movement. The umbilical cord is made up of arteries and veins that carry the blood to and from the placenta. The fetal heart can pump blood through the umbilical arteries to the placenta and receive blood back from it in the umbilical vein.

amniotic fluid

Also developing during the embryo period is the *amniotic sac,* which, as we explained earlier, contains a liquid substance known as the *amniotic fluid* which protects the embryo against physical shock and temperature change.

period of the fetus

The next period, the *period of the fetus,* lasts from the beginning of the third month until birth. During this period muscular development occurs at a rapid rate and various body parts become more differentiated. The central nervous system also develops very rapidly. However, the development of the central nervous system is not complete at birth but continues for six months thereafter (Tanner, 1978).

By the end of 16 weeks after conception, the mother usually can feel the movement of the fetus. At this point the fetus is about 4½ inches long, its lips are well formed and can be moved, and its mouth can open and close. By the end of 24 weeks, the eyes are fully developed and can open and close, and the fetus develops nails, sweat glands, a coarser skin, and hair (much of which is shed *in utero* although at times hair shedding continues after birth). After that time, there is gradual improvement and organization of the nervous and sensory systems.

age of viability

At the end of 26 to 28 weeks after conception, a time known as the *age of viability,* fetal development is sufficiently advanced that if birth occurs the child will survive. If birth occurs before that time, the nervous and respiratory systems are usually not mature enough so the baby's survival outside the uterine environment is less likely (see Figure 3.4). However, because of medical advances in the care of premature babies, the age of viability is periodically revised. For example, some babies born as early as 24 weeks after conception are now able to survive. Thus the age of viability may be changed to 24 weeks. As we shall see toward the end of this chapter, extremely premature infants may survive, but they will have poorly developed motor skills and difficulties in feeding and sleeping for at least several months after birth.

Environmental Influences on Prenatal Development

Development during the prenatal period is completely normal for most babies. However, there are many things that can go wrong during this period. In fact, the prenatal period is referred to as a *critical period.* A

critical period

critical period is a time in the process of development during which the organism is especially sensitive to a particular influence. The same influence before or after the critical period has less impact on development, or no impact at all.

For many years it was thought that the baby in the uterus was insulated from all external influences. However, now we know that this is not true as a number of environmental factors such as drugs, chemicals, and viruses can cross the placental barrier and cause damage to the developing

FIGURE 3.4 The fetus at 20 weeks.

fetus. In addition, such factors as the mother's age and her diet during pregnancy contribute to atypical development (see Table 3.1, page 134).

The scientific study of abnormalities caused by environmental influences during the prenatal period is called *teratology,* from the Greek word *teras,* which means "monster." The environmental agents which can produce abnormalities and malformations in the developing fetus are called *teratogens.* The study of the effects of teratogens and of other factors that influence human development is important as it may lead to the elimination of some congenital defects (Wilson & Fraser, 1977). It is also relevant in this text for two reasons. First, knowledge of some of the causes of atypical development is necessary for the understanding of children's growth and development. Second, there are important social implications associated with the study of what can go wrong during prenatal development because poor pregnant women are more likely than affluent pregnant women to be exposed to the effects of teratogens and other adverse influences. For example, some women of low socioeconomic status do not receive adequate nutrition during pregnancy. Must we simply accept

teratology

teratogens

TABLE 3.1 Factors that may affect the fetus.

Factors	Effect
Drugs	
Alcohol	Small head size, defective joints, congenital heart defects, mental retardation
Nicotine	Low birth weight, prematurity, stillbirth, spontaneous abortion, nicotine dependency at birth; associated with sudden infant death syndrome, hyperactivity, and increased respiratory infections during first year of life
Aspirin—moderate use	Relatively safe until third trimester, use then may prolong labor and lengthen clotting time for both mother and baby, increasing the risk of hemorrhage
Tetracycline	Liver, bone, and teeth damage, discolored teeth, abnormally short arms or legs, webbed hands
Thalidomide	Stunted limb growth
Tranquilizers	In first trimester, cleft palate and other birth defects, neonatal jaundice
Heroin	Low birth weight, maternal toxemia, postpartum maternal hemorrhaging (including risk of neonatal death), altered neonatal sleep patterns, fetal addiction/withdrawal, respiratory depression
Methadone	Low birth weight, hyperirritability, respiratory depression
Caffeine	Low birth weight
Marijuana	In animals: reduced growth rate, spontaneous abortion, low birth weight
LSD	Poorly understood; stillbirth, spontaneous abortion (animals: neonatal death, temporary chromosomal damage)
Diseases or medical conditions	
Rubella virus	First-trimester miscarriage, deafness, blindness, cataracts, heart malformations, various other defects
Diabetes	Maternal toxemia, abnormally large fetus, stillbirths, spontaneous abortion
Syphilis	Malformations, mental retardation, syphilitic infant, deafness, blindness, spontaneous abortion, stillbirth
Influenza	In first trimester—malformations
Gonorrhea	Blindness, gonococcal arthritis, increased risk of ectopic pregnancy
Anemia	Neonatal anemia
Herpes, type II	Neonatal death
Hormones	
Androgens	Females—masculinization of internal and/or external genitals
Estrogens	Males—less aggression and athletic skill compared to age-matched controls
Progesterone	Masculinization of female fetus
DES	In males—semen and testicular abnormalities, reduced fertility; in females—abnormal vaginal or cervical growth or cancer, miscarriage later in life.
Other	
Oral contraceptives	Congenital abnormalities

FIGURE 3.5 Many chemicals and drugs are known to influence the development of the fetus. Pregnant women are advised to refrain from using them.

this as a fact or should we try to correct the problem? The more we know about the possible environmental factors that can affect the course of fetal growth, the more able we will be to prevent problems through timely medical care, changes in living conditions, and specific social programs.

Before we go on to discuss the effects of teratogens and other possible sources of influence on development, we need to clarify why some fetuses may be affected by adverse environmental factors while other fetuses are not. A pregnant woman who is told to stop smoking, for example, because it will harm her unborn child, will sometimes answer, "I smoked during pregnancy with my first child and she is alright." Or, "My mother smoked for the nine months she was pregnant with me, and I certainly turned out normal." (See Figure 3.5.) This may be so because the effects of teratogens vary according to the genotypes of both the mother and the fetus. Thus some mothers and/or some unborn children are genetically predisposed to adverse influences on development. Additionally, environmental influences such as inadequate nutrition and other factors, such as the mother's age, can interact with a teratogen to influence development.

You should also note that the effects of teratogens and other adverse influences vary depending on the developmental stage of the embryo or fetus. Teratogens cause damage to developing but not yet fully formed organs. Since different organs begin and end their development at different times during the prenatal period, their vulnerability to the influence of teratogens will vary. From the research that has been done thus far, we know that the vulnerable period for the eyes, for example, is 20 to 50 days after conception. For the heart it is 20 to 40 days after conception. In general, the first three months of pregnancy are particularly vulnerable to adverse influences. Teratogens encountered during this time will affect the basic structure and form of the body and have serious effects on the nervous system.

continuum of reproductive casualty

Thus there are variations in the degree to which the influence of specific teratogens will culminate in abnormalities in the child. These variations occur on what is called a *continuum of reproductive casualty,* and they range from relatively minor problems such as slightly retarded growth and learning difficulties to such major ones as severe mental retardation and physical deformity. However, it is not only what happens before birth that matters. Researchers are suggesting that the extent to which the effects of a teratogen or any other adverse influence will be manifest is often determined by experiences after birth. Sameroff and Chandler (1975) refer to this notion as the *continuum of caretaking casualty,* which

continuum of caretaking casualty

ranges from a stable family situation in which there are few adverse environmental factors to a poor or unstable family situation in which there may be several factors which may harm the baby. They note that it is the interaction between the reproductive casualty continuum and the caretaking casualty continuum that often determines developmental outcome. That is, although 10 percent of all children are born with some kind of handicap, many of these handicaps decrease with age, or disappear entirely, because of a strong innate self-righting mechanism in the human organism toward normal development. However, if a child who has been exposed to harmful influences before or during birth is also subjected to massive influences of negative factors in the home after birth, these will contribute to the retention, and possibly even the increase, of the severity of the handicap. Researchers are particularly concerned with children who are poor, as they may not only suffer from prenatal neglect, but also they may continue to be subjected after birth to the harmful conditions associated with poverty, such as poor sanitation and inadequate shelter, lack of adequate health care, and malnutrition (Birch & Gussow, 1970).

Even if a child is born with a handicap, it is important for us to realize that whether or not the handicap will limit the child's development often depends on the reaction of the adults, namely the parents, to the handicapped child (McGillicuddy & Sigel, 1982). Are the parents of a congenitally blind infant caring toward him or do they reject him? Will the parents of a lethargic, unresponsive baby become anxious and frustrated and perhaps even abusive of a child who fails to meet their expectations? It is such possible reactions of adults to the handicapped child that are ultimately the most important factors in how the handicap will affect the child's development. With these points in mind, let us now examine some of the specific influences on the course of fetal growth and also some conditions during birth that can affect development.

Influence of Teratogens

Radiation and Chemicals.   Many of the adverse influences on development are related to the condition of the mother, but other adverse influences are teratogens such as radiation or chemicals, which are known to cause damage to the fetus. X-rays and other forms of radiation are examples of teratogens which can cause damage to genetic material in the parent even before conception occurs.

The effects of radiation are cumulative as radiation builds up in the body over the years. Low dosages of radiation, such as those involved in routine x-ray examinations, may not be harmful to adults, but they could cause serious harm to the fetus. Pregnant women are advised not to subject themselves to x-rays; women of childbearing age should wear a protective shield to guard against radiation. There are instances, however, where women are unable to protect themselves and their unborn children. The nuclear accident at Three Mile Island is one example. Radiation spill from this accident did not result in any congenital problems in the babies born to women in the immediate area surrounding the site (Upton, 1981). It remains to be seen whether those children were impaired in any other ways.

Studies conducted on the victims of the atomic bombing of Hiroshima have shown that high levels of radiation can cause miscarriages and stillbirths as well as numerous deformities related to the central nervous system (Murphy, 1947).

Some chemicals are also known to cause damage to genetic material, and some may have a more direct influence on fetal development. Many such chemicals are added to commonly used items such as hair dyes and household cleaning fluids. Overexposure to such chemicals is known to cause birth defects. In many instances, physicians advise pregnant women to limit exposure to chemicals and to avoid excessive use of household compounds such as oven cleaners during the first three months of pregnancy.

Drugs Taken by the Mother.   Various drugs are also known to have deleterious effects on the developing fetus and thus are referred to as teratogens. The thalidomide disaster in Europe during the late 1950s and early 1960s has increased our awareness of the often unknown effects of some drugs. *Thalidomide* was prescribed to pregnant women as a sedative or

FIGURE 3.6   Thalidomide children.

anti-nausea drug to be taken in early pregnancy. Many mothers who took this drug produced babies with gross anatomical defects in their limbs (see Figure 3.6) or missing limbs, with the feet and hands attached to the torso (a deformity known as *phocomelia*). Besides thalidomide, there are other drugs which can influence fetal growth. Some such drugs are iodine and acne medications which are particularly dangerous because they are in such common use that women in the first stages of pregnancy may use them not knowing that they are pregnant (O'Brien & McManus, 1978). Any woman who is not actively trying to prevent pregnancy should refrain from using such drugs for the first two weeks after ovulation until she is certain she is not pregnant.

phocomelia

Another drug that is known to have an effect on the unborn child is *diethylstibestrol,* also known as *DES*. Unlike other drugs, however, DES has delayed effects which are not manifest until the child reaches maturity. DES is a synthetic hormone that was prescribed between the late 1940s and early 1960s to an estimated 2 million women in the United States who were at risk of miscarrying. Although the children of these women appeared normal, in the late 1960s it was found that their mature daughters were developing vaginal deformities and cancer of the cervix.

DES

In addition to the drugs taken during pregnancy, medication administered during labor and delivery to ease the pain and sedate the mother is also known to affect the newborn baby (Brackbill, 1979). The use of such medication is controversial, in part because it is sometimes administered unnecessarily. Some researchers question the need to place the baby at risk for complications that may arise as a consequence of the medication. In babies born to mothers who receive such medication, several short-term effects on the infant have been documented, including disruptions in feeding for several days after birth and decreased neonatal responsivity (Brazelton, 1961; Conway & Brackbill, 1970), which can last up to one month after birth. Although these effects may not appear serious, psychologists are concerned with the reaction of mothers to babies who are unresponsive as this can be a very frustrating experience for the mother (Parke et al., 1972). This can lead to problems in the relationship between the mother and baby. In addition, babies whose mothers received medication during delivery have more difficulties than other babies adjusting to the postnatal environment. For example, some cannot tolerate loud noises and others seem irritable and do not respond easily to attempts to comfort them (Stadley et al., 1974).

Drug addiction. In addition to prescribed medications, there is concern that other drugs taken by some pregnant women will affect the unborn child. For example, hallucinogens such as LSD have been implicated as causal agents of physical birth defects and behavioral disorders (Ostrea & Chavez, 1979), although the evidence here is not as yet conclusive. There is clear evidence, however, that maternal addiction to morphine, methadone, and heroin causes dependence on these drugs in the infant. Withdrawal symptoms such as vomiting, trembling, and even death within the first few days after birth of infants born to addicted mothers have been reported (Strauss et al., 1975). The severity of the symptoms is related to how long-term the mother's addiction has been (Burnham, 1972). If the mother refrains from drug use for several months before birth, generally the baby will not suffer withdrawal symptoms.

Caffeine, nicotine, and alcohol. Other commonly used drugs such as caffeine contained in coffee and some soft drinks, nicotine, and alcohol are also known to influence the course of fetal growth and result in spontaneous abortions, prematurity, and low-birth-weight babies (Streissguth et al., 1980a).

Researchers are not entirely sure how these commonly consumed drugs affect the fetus. In the case of smoking, however, researchers have established that when she smokes, the pregnant woman creates a dangerous environment for the unborn child because smoking increases carbon monoxide levels in her blood, thus depriving the fetus of vital oxygen (National Research Council, 1982). Studies have demonstrated that the fetal heart rate increases when the mother smokes, apparently because of oxygen deprivation (Quigly et al., 1979). In addition to this danger, there is the threat that nicotine and other chemicals contained in the smoke will

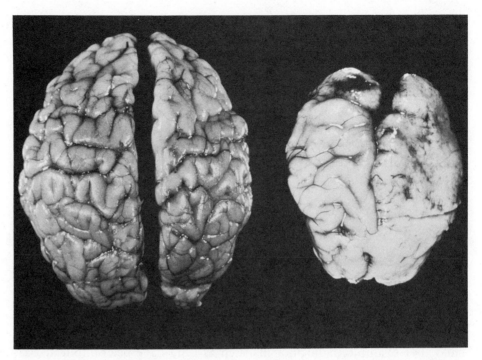

FIGURE 3.7   A normal brain (left) and the brain of an infant afflicted with fetal alcohol syndrome (right).

pass through the placental barrier (U.S. Department of Health, Education and Welfare, 1979). Frazier et al. (1961) note that pregnant women who are smokers are twice as likely as nonsmokers to have premature babies. Other researchers have found that the rate of prematurity is directly related to the amount of maternal smoking (Butler, Goldstein & Ross, 1972). Mothers who smoke are also more likely than those who do not smoke to have full-term low-birth-weight babies. This condition is related at times to neurological problems in the development of the child.

Fetal Alcohol Syndrome.   FAS is a condition related to the consumption of alcohol during pregnancy (Jones & Smith, 1973). About 1 to 2 live births per 1000 suffer the symptoms of fetal alcohol syndrome, which include impaired functioning of the central nervous system (involving retarded mental and motor development, hyperactivity, poor attention spans, and small brain size; see Figure 3.7); deficiencies in height, weight, and head circumference; and a cluster of facial characteristics including short eye slits, a low nasal bridge, and narrow upper lip (Streissguth et al., 1980a). About 3 to 5 live births per 1000 show some but not all of these symptoms (Abel, 1980).

The risks of FAS and the severity of symptoms increase the more a pregnant woman drinks (Rosett & Weiner, 1985). Drinking one or two ounces of alcohol per day, the risk of FAS is about 10 percent; drinking two or more ounces each day increases the risk to 19 percent (Abel, 1980). The fact that alcohol abuse is associated with other factors that also can affect the developing fetus (such as smoking and using drugs, poor nutrition, ill health, poverty, and stress) raises the question of whether one or all of these other factors may be primarily responsible for the observed effects of the disorder. However, the ill effects of drinking can be seen even when these factors are controlled, which makes alcohol appear to be a particularly harmful substance during the prenatal period even when it is consumed in moderate amounts (Streissguth et al., 1980b).

Diseases of the Mother

Besides the teratogenic effects of some drugs, the fetus may be affected also by diseases the mother contracts. The placenta is an effective barrier against most maternal diseases. However, certain infectious diseases can be transmitted from the mother to the fetus. Infants have been born with smallpox, measles, chicken pox, mumps, scarlet fever, tuberculosis, malaria, and Acquired Immune Deficiency Syndrome (AIDS) which they contracted through the mother. The transmission of syphilis is also a possibility. The spirochetes of syphilitic mothers often produce such severe damage that spontaneous abortion or stillbirth occurs. If a child survives, he is often born with physical or mental deformities. In some cases, the infant may appear normal at birth only to manifest a deformity several years later. Unlike many other diseases, syphilis does not affect fetuses under 18 weeks of age, so the syphilitic transmission from the mother to the child can be prevented if the mother is treated with antibiotics early in pregnancy (Pritchard & McDonald, 1976).

Depending on the time when the pregnant woman contracts a disease, its effects on the fetus will vary. Mumps, for example, results in a higher incidence of malformation if contracted in the first three months of pregnancy than later in pregnancy. In rubella (German measles), the occurrence of developmental deviations in the fetus decreases from 50 percent if the mother contracts the disease in the first month to 17 percent if she contracts it in the third month. There are almost no abnormalities occurring if the mother contracts rubella after the third month of pregnancy (Annis, 1978). The rubella virus can cause deafness, blindness, cataracts, heart abnormalities, and various other disorders. Some children who contracted the rubella virus during the prenatal period also appear to be mentally retarded, possibly because the blindness or deafness caused by the virus interferes with their intellectual growth.

Disorders that are not transmissible from the mother during pregnancy can also affect the fetus. Diabetes in the mother causes babies to be large and mature-looking at birth, although they are immature in their functioning. If the diabetes in the mother is not well controlled, it can

toxemia

result in miscarriage or stillbirth and can cause respiratory distress in the newborn baby, which can be fatal (Gellis & Hsia, 1959).

Another common maternal disorder is *toxemia,* a condition which we suspect is caused by toxic substances in the blood. Toxemia results in the swelling of the mother's limbs and may also result in dysfunction of her kidneys and circulatory system. Although its cause is unknown, because it is prevalent among the poor, it is suggested that malnutrition may play a role. Increased rates of cerebral palsy, epilepsy, mental retardation, reading disability, and hyperactivity have been found among children whose mothers had toxemia during pregnancy. Researchers hypothesize that toxemia leads to brain damage by depriving the fetus of oxygen (DeMyer, 1975).

The Mother's Age

Another factor that appears to influence pregnancy is the age of the mother. Mortality rates and incidences of retardation are higher in children born to mothers under 20 or over 35 years of age. With teenage mothers, however, the problems are not necessarily related to the age of the mother. According to Baldwin and Cain (1980), the intellectual deficits suffered by children of teenage parents can be explained not by biology but by social and economic factors. Teenage mothers are more often from lower socioeconomic backgrounds, non-white, and unmarried. Their difficult life circumstances affect their children in negative ways. Furthermore, the birth of a baby makes it difficult for the mother to complete school, hindering later job prospects and contributing to further economic problems. Education and support systems for a teenage mother may help the child's intellectual development a great deal. In at least one study, how well the babies developed was related to their young mothers' personal development in education, employment, and family planning matters (Badger, 1980).

Birgitte Mednick and her colleagues (1979) suggest that inadequate medical care and not age may be responsible for the higher incidence of mortality among infants of teenage mothers. Statistics regarding infant mortality are usually based on studies of representative samples of the general population. Mednick compared the results of this type of study with studies of women who received prenatal care from university hospitals and found that in the university hospital samples, the incidence of infant mortality was the same or lower for mothers ages 14 to 19 as for mothers in their twenties. This study demonstrated, therefore, that it is lack of prenatal care that contributes to the mortality of infants of young mothers.

However, the higher risk to infants of mothers who are over age 35 is the result of biological factors related to age. In Mednick's study, older age of the mother was related to progressively higher incidences of infant mortality in both university hospital and representative sample study types. The older mother is also more likely than a mother below age 35 to give birth to an infant who suffers from specific genetic diseases. Fortunately, scientific technology (the chorion biopsy and amniocentesis) is becoming increasingly able to detect the more likely problems such as Down's syndrome. In any case, the risk is not so great that any woman over 35 should be dissuaded from having a baby. Another factor related to the age of the mother is *parity,* or the number of births she has had. Women who give birth to their first baby after age 35 are more likely to have difficulties during pregnancy and birth.

parity

Genetic Problems

Rh Factor.   In addition to the genetic problems discussed in Chapter 2, there is the genetic problem that arises from incompatibility between the blood of the mother and that of the infant. If the mother has Rh negative blood and the baby has inherited Rh positive blood, this difference in blood characteristic will cause a reaction in the mother and eventually the fetus, culminating in possible miscarriage. If the baby is not miscarried, he may be born mentally retarded.

The problem here involves a build-up of antibodies in the mother's bloodstream which in turn have a toxic effect on the fetus. Usually, the first-born baby is not affected, but by the second pregnancy, antibodies in the mother's bloodstream build up to the extent that damage to the fetus is inevitable. However, if the mother receives regular prenatal examinations, her Rh negative blood characteristic will be detected and any subsequent problem can be prevented through appropriate treatment which may entail blood transfusions.

The Mother's Emotions

The notion of the influence of a pregnant woman's emotions on the fetus has been regarded with skepticism in the past (Ferreira, 1969). However, there is ample evidence to indicate that the pregnant woman's emotions do have an impact upon the fetus and can result in prematurity (Blau, 1963), prolonged pregnancy (Cerutti, 1969; Ritson, 1966), physiological malformations (Strean & Peer, 1956), and syndromes of restlessness and fussiness in the newborn (Turner, 1956). The mechanism by which the mother's disturbed emotions affect the fetus is scientifically explained. Emotional reactions in the mother result in the increase in the levels of cortisone, adrenaline, and other hormones in the maternal bloodstream (Whol, 1963). These substances pass through the placental barrier and affect the fetus. Hyperventilation, usually associated with anxiety, is also shown to have adverse effects upon fetal development (Motoyama, 1966). In addition, the mother's negative emotions may indirectly damage the fetus through her use of tranquilizers or excessive smoking. The mother's emotional state during pregnancy can also affect the birth process. It has been found that women who scored high on anxiety measures during pregnancy had more complications during delivery and more children with congenital abnormalities than women who scored low on anxiety (Davies et al., 1971).

The Mother's Diet

Some of the most significant factors that influence fetal growth and development are the mother's diet and nutrition. During the rapid growth of the prenatal period, there is a major need for the mother to have an adequate diet. Research findings have shown that infants of poorly nourished mothers are more likely to be born prematurely than infants of well-nourished mothers. Also, they are more likely to die at birth or shortly after, or to suffer from low birth weight (Brozek & Schurch, 1984). Research also documents an association between poor nutrition during pregnancy and impaired mental development in the child (Pollitt & Thomson, 1977). In one study it was found that even mild nutritional deficiencies in the diet of pregnant women and infants can disrupt a child's emotional stability in later childhood (Barrett, 1982; Barrett, Radke-Yarrow, & Klein, 1982). Children who were malnourished prenatally were found to be generally more withdrawn, sadder, more dependent, and unfriendly than children whose mothers had adequate diets during pregnancy. While a good maternal diet is imperative during pregnancy, the need for adequate nutrition predates pregnancy because certain dietary deficiencies in the mother can lead to disorders in the offspring. For example, maternal vitamin D deficiency can cause congenital rickets in the offspring and iodine deficiency can lead to *cretinism,* a syndrome that is characterized by mental retardation and dwarfing (Montague, 1962).

cretinism

Malnutrition and Brain Growth

Malnutrition during the prenatal period is also known to affect the development of the brain. Several approaches are used to study the effects of maternal malnutrition on brain development. One approach is to perform autopsies and examine the brains of animals or infants who died at birth or shortly after. Another approach is to compare newborns having well-nourished mothers with those whose mothers are poorly nourished. (The weight of the placenta at birth sometimes helps determine the extent of dietary deprivation during pregnancy.) These types of studies have shown that malnutrition during the prenatal period interferes with the development of the nervous system and that the specific damage often depends on the stage during which the malnutrition occurs. There are periods during which the brain undergoes accelerated growth, referred to as growth spurts. If malnutrition occurs then, damage will be more deleterious than if it occurs at a time of slower brain growth. For the human organism, accelerated brain growth occurs from the latter part of the prenatal period through the first two years of life. At birth, the infant's brain is about one-quarter of its adult weight. It increases in weight substantially during the first two years of life, and, although it continues to grow, the growth rate is markedly decreased between the ages of 2 and 10 years. When the child reaches the age of 10, his brain has attained about 96 percent of its adult size (Dobbin, 1974).

During the prenatal period the brain grows mainly by cell division. Cell division continues after birth, but at a somewhat decreased rate. Between 6 months and 2 years, brain growth is characterized not so much by the formation of new cells through cell division as by the increase in the size of the brain through a process called *myelination,* which involves the development of a fatty protective covering on nerve fibers. Studies which involve autopsies of malnourished animals and children suggest that malnutrition during the prenatal period leads to deficits in brain weight at birth and to a decrease in the number of brain cells (Winick, Brasel & Rosso, 1972).

myelination

DISCUSSION OF SOCIAL ISSUES: POVERTY, PREGNANCY, AND CHILD DEVELOPMENT

In the United States, poverty is often related to ethnic origin. Pregnant women who are both poor and black are more likely than others to suffer from the deleterious effects of malnutrition and lack of adequate health care, (Children's Defense Fund, 1985). A team from the Field Foundation (Kotz, 1979) declared that Americans had virtually eliminated the problem of severe malnutrition in certain areas in the United States. Recently, however, because of economic setbacks that affect government spending on social programs for the poor, as well as unemployment and increases in the price of food, serious hunger has once again become a problem for many Americans. Reports from all over the country (FRAC, 1983) have documented that thousands of people depend on soup kitchens, breadlines, food banks, and community food distribution centers because they have no other means of obtaining food. Many of these people are young, and the hardest hit are those most at risk—unborn infants and young children (see Figure 3.8).

Associated with these developments are reports documenting an increase in infant mortality in the United States (Select Panel for the Promotion of Child Health, 1981). Traditionally used as an indicator of the overall health and well-being of the population, the U.S. infant mortality rate has been decreasing over the past few years. Nonetheless, the United States still ranks only nineteenth in infant mortality rates worldwide,

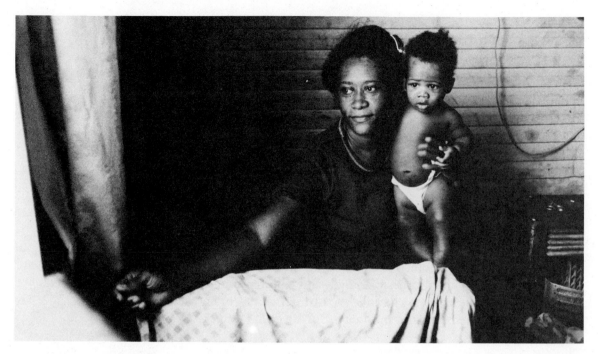

FIGURE 3.8   Although we have improved the infant mortality rate, in some parts of the country the infant mortality rate is very high. What is even more alarming is that the infant mortality rate is twice as high for blacks as it is for whites. Lack of prenatal care and poor nutrition during pregnancy are cited as major causes of infant mortality.

meaning that despite our relative wealth and technological advancement, the health care of some segments of our population is much like that of the population of impoverished countries. Although we have improved the infant mortality rate in this country, in some parts of the United States, where unemployment is very high and where there were severe cutbacks in government spending for programs for the poor, as many as 33 out of 1,000 babies die during their first year of life. What is even more alarming is that the infant mortality rate is twice as high for blacks as it is for whites (Children's Defense Fund, 1985). Approximately two-thirds of all infant deaths are associated with low birth weight (Chase & Byrnes, 1983), which in turn is associated with poor nutrition during the prenatal period and lack of prenatal medical care (Cravioto et al., 1966). The link between infant deaths, poverty, and ethnic origin is painfully clear.

The WIC Program

Several years ago, a government-sponsored preventive health and nutrition program for pregnant women and young children was developed. Known as the *Supplemental Food Program for Women, Infants, and Children,* and popularly referred to as *WIC,* this program ensures the supply of high-protein and iron-fortified foods to low-income pregnant women, infants, and young children up to age five. WIC also includes nutrition education and counseling to encourage good eating habits as well as prenatal care. All participating women and children receive medical evaluations.

WIC has been hailed as one of the most successful government health programs for several reasons (Hill, 1984), including the fact that when the program was legislated, lawmakers included the appropriation of sufficient funds with which to evaluate the effectiveness of the program. The role of research and evaluation is very critical in social programs (Travers & Light, 1982). Such programs are often at the mercy of changing economic and political trends and they are likely to be eliminated in favor of spending money for other types of programs. Having research findings that document the success of a program often helps ensure that the program continues.

Several research studies on the effectiveness of WIC have been done. In a series of studies (Kotelchuck et al., 1981, 1984) for the Massachusetts Department of Public Health, 4000 WIC mothers were compared with 4000 non-WIC mothers on health, nutrition, and the incidence of infant mortality. Results indicate that mothers participating in WIC had a 21 percent decrease in the incidence of low birth weight in infants as compared with non-WIC mothers. There was also a decrease of about one-third in infant mortality rates. Furthermore, the researchers note that the longer a mother participates in the program, the more improved are the outcomes of pregnancy. Those mothers who participated in WIC for 7 to 9 months during pregnancy showed the most positive results. According to the researchers, "birth weight [of offspring] increased . . . , length of gestation [time in uterus] increased . . . , and neonatal mortality was decreased" (Kotelchuck et al., 1981).

In addition to the improved health benefits, other studies have demonstrated that children who receive nutritional supplements during the prenatal period through the WIC program have higher cognitive functioning and behavioral adaptation 5 to 7 years later (Hick et al., 1982). In these studies, researchers compared two groups of children, siblings who had received nutritional supplements at least 3 months prenatally and up to 12 months postnatally, and those who did not receive the WIC supplement until after the first year of life. Thus the former group received vital nutrition during that stage in development that corresponds to an increase in the rate of brain growth. The results of the study revealed that the early supplementation of nutrition was associated with higher levels of intellectual functioning as well as significantly better behavioral adjustment in the home, longer attention span, and higher grades in school. So you can see how through one social program such as WIC we can prevent some of the effects of poverty on pregnancy and child development.

TABLE 3.2 The Apgar scoring system.

Sign	Score		
	0	1	2
Heart rate	absent	slow (<100)	>100
Respiratory effort	absent	weak cry; hyperventilation	good; strong cry
Muscle tone	limp	some flexion of extremities	good flexion
Reflex irritability (response to skin stimulation to feet)	no response	grimace	coughing, sneezing, crying
Color	entire body blue or pale	body pink, extremities blue	entire body pink

BIRTH

Apgar scoring system

As with prenatal development, the birth process for most infants and mothers is normal. The mother's labor proceeds without complications, the infant's heartbeat remains strong, and the infant is born vaginally rather than by Caesarean section. A normal delivery means that there is no need to sedate the mother or operate on her in order to facilitate the birth. Immediately after birth the condition of the newborn is assessed using the *Apgar scoring system* which was developed by the physician Virginia Apgar (see Table 3.2). At 1 minute and 5 minutes after birth, the infant is rated for heart rate, respiratory effort, reflex irritability, muscle tone, and body color. For each of these five factors, a score of 0, 1, or 2 is given. The higher score indicates a favorable condition. A total Apgar score of between 7 and 10 is taken to mean that the infant is in good condition; a score below 5 indicates that the infant may suffer from developmental disabilities; and a score of 3 or lower indicates that the infant's survival may be at stake and that emergency procedures must be instituted.

Birth is a traumatic event for the infant, involving a relatively sudden change from a state of dependency to one of a separate existence. At one time, complications during childbirth were a major cause of death for infant and mother alike. Today, however, childbirth is relatively safe, although it still carries some risks. Let us examine some of the risks.

Anxiety During Childbirth

Evidence has been collected which suggests that maternal anxiety during birth affects the birth process and the newborn. It has been found that women who have high anxiety scores have a greater likelihood than women with low anxiety scores of experiencing difficulties during labor and of giving birth to children with abnormalities (Davies et al., 1971). Although these findings are controversial, we do know that strongly negative emotions affect the autonomic nervous system, which in turn controls the smooth functioning of the muscles of the uterus that are of key importance during birth. These findings indicate that consideration should be given to the psychological as well as the physiological well-being of the mother.

Natural Childbirth and Gentle Birthing

Several practices—natural childbirth, Lamaze, and rooming in—have arisen out of concern for the psychological needs of the mother. The major tenet of natural childbirth, a process described in the book *Childbirth without Fear* (Dick-Read, 1972), is that much of the pain experienced by the mother during birth is due to the anxieties about the experience rather than to the physiological process itself. In *natural childbirth* the mother takes no medication during labor, or takes it sparingly only at the final phase of delivery. The need for medication is eliminated because the mother is taught to counteract her fears about the pain of childbirth. Also, she is taught various physical exercises which help prepare her body for relaxation during the birth. *natural childbirth*

In yet another technique—the Lamaze method—the mother is taught how to breathe in response to uterine contractions. Preparation for the Lamaze method involves an educational process in which the expectant parents read relevant material, meet with medical staff and other expectant couples in group discussions, and practice exercises for proper breathing and strengthening the uterine muscles. During labor, although a physician is in constant attendance, the mother herself decides if she should be sedated.

Most pregnant women and their husbands are introduced to the natural childbirth or the Lamaze method by trained nurses or other specialists in hospitals or private clinics. Many of the would-be parents opt for these birthing procedures even though in some cases they may find out that a Caesarean will be necessary. Another increasingly popular birthing method is *gentle birthing,* developed by the French obstetrician Frederick Leboyer. Leboyer (1975) argues that the birth process is an unnecessarily traumatic experience for the baby. Having survived and grown for 9 months within the warm, dark, and relatively noise-free uterine environment, at birth the baby enters a cold, noisy world, full of bright lights—conditions that some physicians say are necessary in hospital labor and delivery rooms. Not only does the baby enter such a seemingly harsh environment, he is also held upside down by his feet and slapped on the back until doctors are sure that he is alive and can breathe! *gentle birthing*

Many of these "rituals" of birth, adhered to until a few years ago, are unnecessary, according to Leboyer. He advocated a gentler method of delivery in which the baby would be born in a dimly lit delivery room and then gently held in warm water so that he would feel as if he were still surrounded by the amniotic fluid in the uterus. This latter aspect of the Leboyer method is controversial. However, many physicians as well as parents have been influenced by other aspects of the Leboyer method. These days babies are rarely held upside down and slapped on the back. Rather, in many cases, the baby is placed on the mother's abdomen for a few moments and gently wiped and covered with a blanket, and then the umbilical cord is cut.

Birthing Rooms and Rooming In

Many hospitals are changing routine medical practices that can cause undue stress to both mother and infant during birth. For example, some medical staff, aware of the possible psychological impact of the birth on both the mother and newborn, have birthing rooms, which are comfortable, home-like rooms where both labor and delivery take place, often to the sound of soothing music and in dim lighting. Most hospitals have replaced the practice of removing the infant from the mother immediately and instead allow the mother and baby to stay together in one room—a practice called rooming in. This practice was initiated in part as a response to the growing number of couples who seem to prefer to give birth at home or in birthing centers rather than in impersonal hospitals. (See Figure 3.9.) Even those couples who value the medical care available in a hospital have insisted in recent years that they be allowed to remain with their baby immediately after birth because of some studies that have alluded to the importance of the first few hours after birth to the development of an affectionate bond between the mother and infant (Klaus & Kennel, 1976). While it has not been established that there is in fact a critical period for mother-infant bonding, the fact that these studies contributed to changes in hospital practices is significant. For example, rooming in often helps reduce many of the common anxieties mothers have if the baby is taken from them immediately. Not only do the anxieties disappear with rooming in, but the mother also has a better opportunity to get to know and learn to care for the baby. Probably the greatest result of rooming in is the more immediate closeness that develops among mother, father, and the new child. However, not all mothers are at ease with rooming in. Many would like their entry into parenthood to be more gradual. Some need a few days to recover from stress and fatigue and to adjust to their new role in life. In these cases, the hospital should make provisions to assume primary caretaking responsibility during the first day or two of the baby's life.

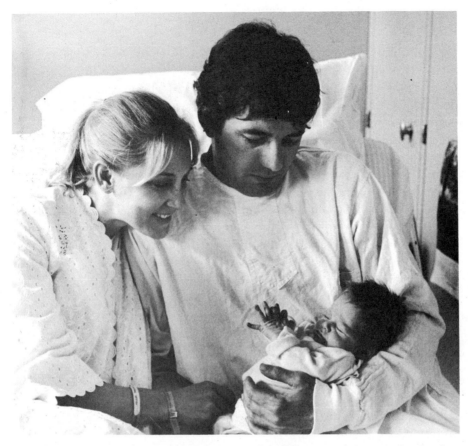

FIGURE 3.9 Birth is a far more pleasant experience for the entire family than was true several decades ago. Most hospitals have replaced the practice of removing the infant from the mother immediately after birth and instead allow the entire family to enjoy their first few hours together.

Risks to Infants During Delivery

In the delivery process, the two major dangers to the infants are (1) pressures on the head, which may cause some blood vessels in the brain to break, resulting in hemorrhaging, and (2) a lack of sufficient oxygen once the infant is separated from the mother. Both hemorrhaging and failure to begin breathing early enough influence the supply of oxygen to the nerve cells of the brain.

Lack of Oxygen

During labor and delivery all infants undergo some deprivation of oxygen and retention of carbon dioxide. In some cases, infants may be deprived of so much oxygen that they suffer dire consequences. This can occur in breech birth (where the infant is in the wrong position for delivery) or if

anoxia
cerebral palsy

the umbilical cord is squeezed or becomes tangled, thus depriving the infant of oxygen. The neurons in the brain have an especially strong requirement for oxygen, and if deprived of it, some brain cells may die. The deleterious effects that result may range from slight brain damage to death. Children who suffer a severe lack of oxygen at birth, a condition called *anoxia,* often develop *cerebral palsy,* a condition related to a variety of motor defects such as paralysis of the legs or arms, tremors of the face or fingers, or an inability to use the vocal muscles. Some children who suffer from anoxia also evidence developmental delays and have been found to be irritable and to have difficulty directing their attention. They also tend to have a low IQ at age 3, although there is some evidence that IQ scores tend to increase by the time the children are seven years of age, especially if the anoxia was mild (Corah, et al., 1965).

Prematurity and Low Birth Weight

About 7 percent of all infants in the United States are born prematurely, but they account for 50 percent of all deaths among newborns. This fact alerts us to the vulnerability of the premature infant. Preterm babies are babies born too soon. They are called preterm or premature babies because they have not had their full term of 38 to 42 weeks in the uterus. Babies born before the end of the 37th week of pregnancy are considered preterm. (See Figure 3.10.)

At one time, all low-weight babies were thought to be preterm. Now doctors know that it is not weight but time in the uterus that defines preterm. Some preterm babies weigh as much as 5 pounds 8 ounces. Some full-term babies, on the other hand, weigh as little as 5 pounds, but they are physically mature enough to breathe and suck normally after birth, whereas preterm babies are not. However, low birth weight in a full-term infant is considered much more serious. In a full-term baby, low weight suggests that fetal development has been impaired and that there may be a permanently slower rate of development, perhaps due to maternal illness, smoking, poor nutrition, or any other of the factors known to influence prenatal growth. The preterm infant, on the other hand, is of low weight primarily because of the premature birth. Surprisingly, the maturation of the infant's nervous system seems to be unaffected by time of birth. That is, an infant born prematurely at 28 weeks will, 10 weeks later, be like one born at 38 weeks (Tanner, 1970). It appears that a variety of reflexes make their appearance on schedule whether the baby is in or out of the uterus.

Because they are born too soon, the preterm babies' biological systems are not developed enough to work on their own. This can result in jaundice or breathing difficulties and may mean that the preterm baby will be retarded in sensory and motor development. Despite their biological immaturity, many preterm babies will catch up in their development

FIGURE 3.10 Medical technology is saving increasingly smaller babies. There is concern that while these babies are saved, they will suffer developmental delays and learning disabilities. Whether this is true is not yet known; more longitudinal studies are needed. Researchers do know that if these babies receive appropriate care and stimulation, they will less likely evidence neurological or other defects.

(Kopp & Parmelee, 1979). However, the smaller the baby, the greater the risks involved and the more intensive the care needed. No matter how small they are, all preterm babies need to be cared for and kept warm in an incubator while they catch up with normal infants. After several weeks in the incubator, most preterm babies are ready to go home.

Preterm and low-birth-weight babies almost always suffer from deviations in neurological functioning during the first few months of life.

minimal brain dysfunction

They often appear lethargic, and they are slow to respond to environmental stimuli. In their behavior, they are similar to infants who have been diagnosed as having known organic brain damage. Consequently, some researchers suggest that preterm babies are suffering from *minimal brain dysfunction* (also referred to as attentional deficit disorders), meaning that they have organic abnormalities which we do not yet know how to detect. Although the neurological problems characteristic of preterm and low-birth-weight infants may disappear with age, researchers contend that the dysfunction remains and is manifest in the lack of attentional abilities these children exhibit in later childhood and in the retardation of perceptual, language, and other learning skills (Parkinson et al., 1981).

However, many psychologists object to the label "minimal brain dysfunction" because there are no tests that can establish that such a problem exists. Also, some researchers point out that the characteristics and behaviors of premature infants may be the outcome of several other related factors such as delivery complications, inability to withstand the stresses of birth and postnatal life, and their isolation in the incubator which deprives them of sensory and social stimulation. The importance of this last factor is illustrated by the results of a study by Scarr-Salapatek and Williams (1973). Premature infants who were held, fondled, and talked to more often gained weight faster and were more advanced developmentally than their isolated counterparts. Other studies also established that stimulated preterm infants are more advanced in mental development, neurological development, and sensorimotor and motor skills than unstimulated preterm infants (Rice, 1977). In addition, fewer incidences of *apnea,* or temporary cessation of breathing, are found among stimulated premature infants (Korner et al., 1975).

apnea

Mothers of Premature Infants

Another important factor in the developmental outcome of preterm infants is the parents' reaction to them. Some researchers suggest that there may be a disruption in the affectionate bond between the mother and the premature infant, due perhaps to separation of the infant from the mother immediately after birth and for several weeks thereafter, or due to the characteristics of the infant and the stresses the parents experience (Brown & Bakeman, 1978). Mothers of premature babies often experience strong conflicting emotions after the birth of the child. Feelings of fear about the baby's condition or about their ability to care for the child alternate with feelings of hope and pride. Disappointment may occur when the anticipation of a chubby, cuddly baby is dashed by the reality of the small, skinny premature baby whose head may appear too big and whose body is covered with fine hair and very delicate skin. Mothers sometimes feel angry, wondering why their baby was born prematurely, or they may blame themselves and experience intense guilt. Then there are moments of gratitude that wash away such feelings. Such erratic mood changes can last for months after delivery (Quinn et al., 1978). Leaving her baby in the hospital adds to the mother's concern, and regular visits to the hospital are often difficult for mothers who have other children at home or who have to return to work.

Fathers of Premature Infants

The father of the preterm infant has problems, too. Aside from dealing with his own worries about the infant, he has to remain the prime source of comfort and support for his wife who is often emotionally and physically drained. During the first few days after birth, the father's initial concern is for the medical condition of the baby, and he may have extensive contact with medical staff. As a result, the wife tends to feel left out, jealous, and neglected, although in time, and as she becomes more routinely involved with visiting or partially caring for the infant, these feelings change. You can see, however, that both parents of a preterm infant are subjected to a lot of stress and that they need emotional support.

The need for emotional support continues after the baby is brought home. While there is joy and relief, there are also ongoing pressures and worries. Because preterm babies are biologically immature, they require more attention and more feedings, and their sleep is often disrupted. Later in their lives, preterm babies may be no different from other babies. For the first several months, however, they are sluggish and unresponsive in their behavior; they are late to smile; and their heads are floppy because their muscles are not yet developed. Even though these characteristics tend to diminish, if parents compare their infants with the development of full-term babies, they become worried, frustrated, and disappointed. In addition to these stresses, research indicates that parents find the cry of the preterm baby more irritating than that of a full-term baby (Thoden et al., 1985). Preterm babies are also more irritable and less easy to soothe than full-term newborns (Friedman et al., 1978). Their irritability often strains the relationship between parents and infant and between the mother and father (Liederman, 1983). These problems may make preterm babies vulnerable to child abuse. Studies show that a fairly high proportion of abused children were born prematurely (Egeland & Brunquette, 1979).

Due to the stresses involved in having and caring for a preterm infant, parents often seek help. Hospital-based programs are available to help parents cope with stress and to arrange for other services such as financial aid or home visits from a public health nurse or a foster grandparent. There are also mutual support groups in which parents of preterm infants meet regularly to share experiences and knowledge. Researchers report that when parents participate in such groups they tend to provide better care and to feel more at ease with their preterm babies than parents who do not participate in such groups (Friedman & Sigman, 1980; Quinn et al., 1978).

In addition to emotional support as a mediating factor in the relationship between the infant and the parents, Sameroff (1975) and Belsky (1978) note that when disruptions in such a relationship persist, they are often attributable not only to individual differences in the responsivity of the child and the general competence of the mother, but also to other factors in the family. These researchers note that disruptions tend to be more marked and more enduring for economically deprived families than for middle-class families because of all the additional stresses (unemployment, lack of adequate shelter, etc.) these families face each day.

There are indications that if the preterm babies are in middle-class rather than poor homes, and if they are exposed to sufficient stimulation and are encouraged to be independent, the physical and mental problems associated with prematurity may be overcome. Even babies born extremely prematurely may do well by the time they reach school age. Medical advances have been too recent to determine the long-term outcomes of children born extremely prematurely. However, recent findings indicate that the majority of the children studied, who are now between 2 and 9 years old, are free of serious developmental problems (Friedman & Sigman, 1980). We should point out that developmental predictions for preterm infants are difficult to make, in part because of individual differences in the way all children, preterm and full-term, develop. However, from the research we know that parents can make a difference, because appropriate stimulation can enhance the psychological and physical development of the preterm infant. When parents persistently try to make eye contact with the baby, talk to it during feeding, and hold and rock the baby in spite of the fact that the baby will remain, for a time, unresponsive and late to smile, the baby's future development is enhanced (Wertmann, 1980).

SOCIAL ASPECTS OF PREGNANCY AND BIRTH

Although pregnancy and birth are biological phenomena, they nonetheless occur within a social context which includes factors that can influence the life of the child. Is the child born to a family where there is love? Is the child wanted by his parents? These are some questions that arise out of the social aspects of pregnancy and birth.

Love and Marriage: Traditions and New Directions

Love, which is one of the basic forces in behavior, has its roots in our biological makeup. It is one of the most intense and sought-after of all human emotions. We all want to form bonds or close relationships with others. The need and desire for the company of others is also found in animals. Love is not a prerequisite to conception, but it deserves mention here.

Generally love is associated with romance and is described as including an understanding of one another, the sharing of ideas and feelings, the receipt and provision of emotional support and help, and the giving and receiving of affection (Sternberg & Grajek, 1983). Love is considered as a bond between two mates, or between parent and child. In developmental psychology, the bond between parent and child is the most often discussed aspect of love. Curiously, the bond between two individuals which may have led to the birth of a child is rarely discussed. This may be, in part, because sexual intercourse which culminates in conception is not necessarily an act of love. Nevertheless, most people have access to contraceptives which allow them to engage in sexual activity without conceiving a child. Also, in most cases marriage precedes the birth of a child and the family is the setting to which most newborns are introduced, thus love and marriage are important facets of pregnancy and birth. However, changing social attitudes toward the concept of the family are making it acceptable for single women to give birth to and raise a child without being married or otherwise emotionally involved with the child's father. Some single women choose to be clinically inseminated with sperm without ever knowing who the donor is. In addition, an unprecedented number of teenage girls become pregnant and give birth without being married (U.S. Department of Health and Human Services, 1983). Even in these cases, it could well be that the desire to become pregnant is motivated by the woman's need to love, or to have somebody to love. This love is not necessarily the love of or for a mate, but the love of and caring for a child. Consider the fact that 94 percent of teenage girls who give birth each year choose to keep their babies (Zelnick & Kantner, 1978) despite the obvious hardship this entails. Usually they are not married or yet out of school, and they are likely to be poor and unemployed. Keeping the baby despite these difficulties could be an indication of their desire to have someone to love.

Attitudes Toward Pregnancy and Childrearing

Since giving birth to a child represents a major milestone in a woman's life, pregnancy and birth inevitably precipitate a variety of emotions. These emotions, of course, vary a great deal from woman to woman. Some may feel that giving birth to a child represents an essential self-fulfillment as a woman. Few, however, do not feel at least some apprehension. The first-time mother is often genuinely concerned about whether she will be competent to care for her child. Mothers may feel that their own dependency needs should have primacy and that it is unfair to be required to be the giver of affection and care rather than the recipient.

Infertility

About one out of five couples who want to have children cannot conceive, and there is concern that the number of infertile couples is increasing (Hendershot & Placek, 1981). Infertility can be related to problems in the man or the woman, and in 10 to 20 percent of the cases, no cause for infertility can be determined. In the man, some of the causes of infertility may be too few sperm, abnormally shaped sperm, or low sperm motility, which means that the sperm have difficulty in moving up the vaginal tract to meet the egg cell. In the woman, infertility may be caused by the failure of the ovary to produce egg cells, the secretion of a mucus that is hostile to sperm, or blocked fallopian tubes which prevent the egg from passing down to the uterus.

Infertility can be emotionally traumatic for both the man and the woman, especially now that there are fewer babies being given up for adoption. Treatment of the causes of infertility is not always possible. However, it seems that every day a new "miracle" method is developed which enables infertile couples to have children. These methods soon become routinely employed in hospitals and fertility clinics. Still, they are not problem-free, so they should be considered from a realistic perspective.

Donor Sperm

One of the easiest ways to deal with male infertility is to inseminate the wife with sperm collected from an anonymous donor. At times, the husband's sperm is mixed with the donor sperm so that there is always the possibility that the child is fathered by the husband. The parents are advised to keep the procedure a secret, even from their own gynecologist, so that, in time, they come to believe that the father as well as the mother are biologically related to the baby. Although this method has

been successfully employed for a number of years, there remains the possibility that the father would reject a child to whom he is not biologically related. Also, Acquired Immune Deficiency Syndrome (AIDS) has become a problem. For this often fatal disease there is, as yet, no cure. It is ordinarily transmitted during sexual contact. However, it can also be acquired by a woman who has been artificially inseminated with the semen of a donor who

About 1 out of 5 couples who want children cannot conceive, and the number of infertile couples may be increasing. Several solutions to infertility have been developed, but they are associated with various problems.

has AIDS. The unfortunate aspect of this problem is that current screening techniques for AIDS are inadequate. Therefore it is hard to identify, with any precision, which sperm donors have been exposed to the AIDS virus. Artificial insemination, which has provided hope for many couples, has turned to tragedy for some who now have to face the possibility of their contracting AIDS.

Test-Tube Babies

This procedure is used in women whose fallopian tubes are blocked. In the procedure, an egg is retrieved from the woman, using a relatively simple surgical technique for which total anesthesia is required. The egg is then placed in a petri dish (not in a test tube as the popular name denotes) along with the husband's sperm. When the sperm has penetrated the egg and fertilization has occurred, the fertilized egg is then carefully implanted in the uterus and pregnancy begins. The success of this procedure is dependent on a very elaborate process by which the lining of the uterus is prepared for the egg. Although this procedure is used mostly for women with blocked tubes, it can be used also in cases of low sperm count, since only a few sperm are needed for fertilization in this way.

Egg Transplant

Recently, a healthy infant was born to an infertile woman in Los Angeles County. She was able to give birth to the infant through yet another "miracle" of modern-day medicine and genetic engineering: egg transplant. In this procedure, a fertile female donor is inseminated with sperm from the would-be mother's husband. Five days later, the fertilized egg is retrieved from the donor and implanted into the infertile woman's uterus where pregnancy resumes. This process is praised not only for the hope it offers infertile women who fail to ovulate, but also as a means by which to stem genetic diseases. Researchers note that a woman with a known genetic disease may opt for this procedure in order to prevent passing her genes on to her offspring (Buster, 1984).

Plans are underway to open ovum-transfer centers in hospitals and fertility clinics despite objections from critics who oppose the procedure because they feel it poses a fundamental challenge to the concept of parenthood.

Surrogate Womb

In yet another procedure, a fertile woman "donates" the use of her uterus. The donor is clinically inseminated with sperm from the husband and she carries the baby throughout the pregnancy. After birth, the baby is adopted legally by the infertile couple. This procedure involves legal help and is quite expensive. It requires that the donor sign a contract in which she agrees to give up the baby. The problems that are associated with this procedure include breach of contract by the woman who refuses to give up the baby once it is born. Or, the baby may not be biologically related to the husband. A woman who signs a contract for a surrogate pregnancy also agrees to abstain from sexual intercourse for a number of days in order to ensure that the right sperm penetrates the egg. But does the woman abstain? This is a potential problem.

Another problem arises when we consider the question: Must the couple who choose to have a child through a surrogate womb procedure accept the child as their own? In one case where a handicapped baby was born through the surrogate womb procedure, the husband rejected it, contending that it was not his child. The surrogate mother also rejected the child, noting that she had signed a contract with the couple agreeing only to carry the baby through pregnancy. The welfare department ordered that blood tests be made to determine paternity. The blood tests revealed that it was the surrogate mother's husband who actually fathered the child, which meant that the woman had breached her contract by having intercourse with her husband at a time she had agreed not to. Had it been the other man's child, he would have been held legally responsible for the child, but not without consequences for the child, who would have to live in a home where he was not wanted.

TABLE 3.3   The value of children.

1. Adult status and social identity (included here is the concept that motherhood is woman's major role)
2. Expansion of the self, tie to larger entity, "immortality"
3. Morality: religion, altruism, good of the group, regarding sexuality, impulsivity, virtue, character norms building
4. Primary group ties, affection
5. Stimulation, novelty, fun
6. Achievement, competence, creativity
7. Power, influence, effectance
8. Social comparison, competition
9. Economic utility

Source: "The Value of Children to Parents" by Lois Wladis Hoffman from *Proceedings of the American Philosophical Society,* 119, (6) Table 1, p. 431. Reprinted with the permission of the American Philosophical Society.

Still others may wonder how they will work out the conflicting demands of employment and a family.

Fathers, too, have mixed emotions. Many men take at least an initial pride in the fact that they are to become fathers. However, they may also worry about the possibility of being displaced by their wife's affection for the new baby and may view the infant as a competitor. As is true for women, the birth of a baby may have significance for the fathers' feelings of adequacy in their sex role. In many societies, including ours, a baby is an overt symbol of the father's masculinity and virility. Many fathers may feel a sense of fulfillment at the birth of the baby, but at the same time they may feel apprehensive about their new responsibilities in life.

Despite these conflicting feelings, many couples are overjoyed at the birth of their baby. They also find that being mutually responsible for a new human being adds dimension to their earlier relationship. Since so many couples seem to be genuinely delighted and happy when they first have a baby, those with troubled marriages sometimes have children in the hope that the newborn child will improve the relationship. Any individual contemplating such a decision, however, should realize that while a baby may enhance a marriage, it also may present many problems and stresses and put the marriage to a severe test.

The Desire to Have Children

Why do people have children? In an attempt to answer this question, researchers have examined the many motivations for having children as these are expressed in different societies (Hoffman & Hoffman, 1976; Hoffman, 1975). The researchers organized the responses they collected according to a set of psychological needs which they refer to as values (see Table 3.3). The value of children to their parents lies in their capacity to satisfy one or more of these needs.

TABLE 3.4   Advantages of having children. Reported by married women under 40 with at least one child; national sample of the United States.

Values	% persons who gave such a response	% persons who did not give response	Total %
Adult status and social identity	21.9	78.1	100
Expansion of the self	35.2	64.8	100
Morality	6.8	93.2	100
Primary group ties and affection	66.2	33.8	100
Stimulation and fun	60.1	39.9	100
Achievement and competence	11.0	89.0	100
Power	2.2	97.8	100
Social comparison	0.1	99.9	100
Economic utility	7.9	92.1	100
N = 1258			

Source: "The Value of Children to Parents" by Lois Wladis Hoffman from *Proceedings of the American Philosophical Society*, 119, (6) Table 2, p. 433. Reprinted with the permission of the American Philosophical Society.

The values or reasons for having children were accumulated on the basis of answers to the question: What would you say are the advantages or good things about having children compared with not having children? The question was asked of people in different countries. Obviously, the reasons for having children differed according to culture and were often dependent on the social climate of the time as well as the economy of the particular society. In an Indian village, for example, most respondents considered the advantages of having children to be related to their economic utility and value (Value 9 in Table 3.3). The most common reason given for having children, mostly sons, is to have someone take care of one in old age. The villagers report that if they do not have a son to take care of them, they will starve since the government does not provide for old-age security. In the United States over half of women (Table 3.4) and men (Table 3.5) responded that the value of children was for the affection (Value 4 in Table 3.3) they provide, and the fact that children provide stimulation and fun (Value 5 in Table 3.3). Some respondents noted their reasons for having children: "They bring liveliness to your life"; "We love playing with them"; "They're so funny"; and "They bring you happiness and joy."

Learning to Be Parents

There is some concern about the reasons American parents have for having children especially since some parents neglect to think realistically

TABLE 3.5 Advantages of having children. Reported by men with wives under 40 with at least one child (Hoffman, 1975).

Values	% persons who gave such a response	% persons who did not give response	Total %
Adult status and social identity	19.8	80.2	100
Expansion of the self	32.4	67.6	100
Morality	6.4	93.6	100
Primary group ties and affection	60.1	39.9	100
Stimulation and fun	55.3	44.7	100
Achievement and competence	9.5	90.5	100
Power	2.2	97.8	100
Social comparison	.3	99.7	100
Economic utility	10.1	89.9	100
N = 358			

Source: "The Value of Children to Parents" by Lois Wladis Hoffman from *Proceedings of the American Philosophical Society*, 119, (6) Table 1, p. 434. Reprinted with the permission of the American Philosophical Society.

about the difficulties and constraints of childrearing. They regard the coming child simply as a pleasurable plaything and anticipate the fun of dressing the baby in cute clothes and showing it off to friends and family. Needless to say, after a few late-night feedings, messy diaper changes, and difficulties in soothing a baby who may cry more often than they had anticipated, these parents become tired, angry and disenchanted, and they may vent their frustrations upon the child.

Due to the immature expectations of some parents regarding what parenting entails, some hospitals teach new parents how to be a parent. In some elementary and high schools, courses on parenting are also offered (Harman & Brim, 1980; Fitzgerald, 1974, 1981; see Figure 3.11). These courses used to involve merely teaching the parents to take physical care of the newborn. However, some health practitioners and educators are going beyond this and now include teaching about the capabilities of the newborn and about basic principles of psychological development in infancy and early childhood. Why? First, because now we have amassed a great deal of knowledge about the capabilities of the newborn. For example, immediately after birth the newborn can hear and see somewhat and is able to follow objects with his eyes. This knowledge is helpful to new parents who, without this information, would think the baby only sleeps and cries for the first 3 months of life. The second reason for giving parents information about psychological development is because of the increase in the incidence of child abuse and neglect. Some parents expect

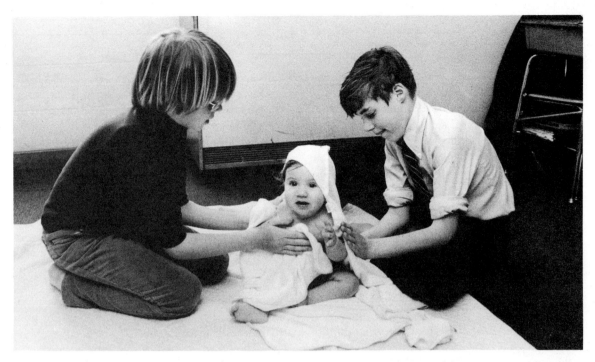

FIGURE 3.11   In some elementary and secondary schools, parenthood courses are offered in which children learn firsthand about some of the realities of having a baby. Education for parenthood programs were first developed in the early 1970s by the federal government in response to the fact that many parents have naive expectations of the growth and development of children.

too much from an infant too early in life and they become angry and often abusive if these expectations are not met. Some parents mistake normal developmental behaviors, such as the baby throwing an object to the floor over and over again, as actions deliberately aimed against them. Parents often retort, "He is just doing this to test me," or "He really tries to get me angry," when what the baby is doing is actually part of a repertoire of developmental activities to be expected at a certain stage in life. When parents are made aware of the developmental characteristics of children at different stages of development, they are more patient and understanding with their children.

SUMMARY

At the moment of conception, when the sperm cell penetrates the egg cell, the fertilized egg becomes known as a zygote. From that moment, cells begin to multiply rapidly and to differentiate their functions, developing eventually the several membranes that protect the infant. Cell division and differentiation occur during the three developmental stages of the prenatal period: the periods of the ovum, the embryo, and the fetus.

The infant is most vulnerable to the effects of teratogens during the embryo period. Some teratogens are chemicals and drugs that cross the placenta and enter the fetal bloodstream. There are other factors that influence development. These factors are related to the age of the mother, her health, her nutritional status, and her diet during pregnancy. The effects of teratogens and other influences vary according to the stage of development of the unborn child and the organs that are developing at the time of exposure, as these affect developing but not yet fully formed organs.

The effects also vary depending on the genotype of the mother and child. The effects of teratogens and other influences range from mild mental retardation and developmental delays to gross physical and mental abnormalities. Except for extreme instances, whether or not the child's abnormalities will be maintained often depends on factors after birth and on the parents' reaction to the child. Children who are poor are more likely than affluent children to suffer from the effects of teratogens, and they are also less likely to overcome these effects after birth. Infant mortality, for example, which is a consequence of the effects of teratogens, is more likely to occur among poor blacks despite prevention possibilities that include adequate prenatal nutrition and medical care.

The birth process poses additional risks to the infant, although in most cases it is a normal event. The risks include lack of oxygen and prematurity. Premature infants suffer from neurological deviations during the first few months of life, but these can be overcome if stimulating experiences are provided. The risk that the developmental deviations associated with prematurity will last is, again, greater among the poor than among the affluent.

The social context within which the child is conceived and reared is also important to developmental outcome. There are many reasons for having children. Researchers note that many American parents desire to have children because children are fun to be with. Often parents may have unrealistic expectations of children's development and become angry and frustrated. For this reason, schools and hospitals are beginning to offer courses in parenting.

Infertility is affecting an increasing number of couples. Although there are different methods for overcoming the failure of some couples to conceive, these are associated with ethical and legal problems for both the parents and the children.

REVIEW POINTS

1. The nine months of pregnancy are divided into three periods: the period of the ovum (conception–first 2 weeks); the period of the embryo (2–8 weeks); and the period of the fetus (8 weeks–birth). During each of these periods, the organism undergoes a number of changes.

2. During the initial stages of pregnancy the fetus is particularly vulnerable to the effects of teratogens, which are environmental factors such as drugs, chemicals, caffeine, nicotine, and alcohol that can cause physical and mental malformations. Whether the organism will be affected by these teratogens, and the extent of the influence, is dependent on the genetic predisposition and the time during prenatal development that such adverse influences were encountered.

3. Besides being vulnerable to the influence of teratogens during prenatal development, the organism is subject to the influence of the mother's emotions and age. Diseases the mother contracts during pregnancy may also result in physical and mental malformations in the child. Additionally, the mother's nutritional status and diet during pregnancy influence prenatal and postnatal development.

4. The mother's diet during pregnancy is especially important because during this period the fetus experiences rapid brain growth. Infants whose mothers were malnourished during pregnancy generally are found to be withdrawn, more dependent, and more unfriendly than other children. Inadequate diet during pregnancy is also associated with infant mortality and premature births.

5. In the United States, pregnant women who are poor and black are more likely than others to suffer from malnutrition and the lack of adequate health care during pregnancy. Thus infant mortality for blacks is twice as high as it is for whites.

6. To help improve prenatal and postnatal care for those from low-income backgrounds, the U.S. government sponsors the Supplemental Food Program for Women, Infants, and Children. Known as WIC, this program ensures that pregnant women and their young children receive an adequate diet.

7. Besides the adverse influences during the prenatal period, complications can also occur during birth, although for most infants and mothers, the birth process is normal. However, medical advancements now ensure that risks associated with birth are minimized. In addition, the birth process is now a more comfortable experience for the parents and the baby due to natural childbirth and gentle birthing techniques and the practice that permits the baby to room in with the mother for a few days after birth.

8. Those babies who are born prematurely or who are of low birth weight, however, may have to be taken care of in intensive care units. It is now known that if these babies are fondled and talked to while they are in intensive care, they gain weight faster and are less likely to suffer from delays in development. The birth of a premature baby is difficult for parents. However, support programs in which the parents can share their experiences with other parents of premature infants can be helpful.

9. Reasons for having children vary according to different cultures and the economic climate of the times. In the U.S. today, most parents say they want children because they are fun to play with. To encourage a more realistic perspective on parenthood, child development experts and educators have developed parenting classes.

10. About one out of every five couples is unable to have children. New treatments for infertility are being developed and are becoming routine in hospitals and fertility clinics. These methods, which now include the use of donor sperm, egg transplants, surrogate wombs, and in vitro fertilization offer hope to many couples. However, these methods are not without problems.

UNIT III

INFANCY

The development of the newborn baby from a tiny, apparently helpless human being into an organism with well-integrated and differentiated responses in the space of relatively few months is a never-ending source of wonder for parents and researchers alike. During infancy, the period between birth and age two, physical growth is so rapid that changes in the size of the baby, his shape, and his body proportions occur almost daily. There are also changes in the baby's ability to master certain skills and in his responses to the environment. Not only does the baby rapidly master a variety of skills, he is born with sensory and perceptual abilities that enable him to interact with the environment from the first day of life.

CHAPTER 4

PHYSICAL DEVELOPMENT DURING INFANCY

The changes in physical development and the acquisition of skills during infancy follow a predictable and orderly sequence that is governed by the genes and by the interaction between genetic and environmental factors. The course of physical development and the physical characteristics of the infant have a direct and indirect influence on psychological development. The emergence and development of intellectual skills, for example, cannot take place until certain levels of physical and neurological maturation are reached. We have seen, too, in discussing preterm and low-birth-weight babies, that the physiological characteristics of the newborn influence caregiving styles and parental responses to and interaction with the child. At a later age, a child's physical attributes, such as obesity, for example, which may elicit teasing and ridicule, or attractive features, which often elicit admiration, inevitably affect the child's self-image and emotional well-being.

Since physical development has important implications for psychological development, in the chapters on physical development we discuss the progress of physical growth and the changes in the physical characteristics of the child at that stage, how these correspond to other aspects of development, and how they influence the child's interactions with other children and adults. In this chapter, we look at physical growth during infancy and at the infant's repertoire of sensory, perceptual, and motor skills. Before we begin our discussion of physical development, however, let us describe the characteristics of the newborn baby during the first month of life. The newborn baby is so different from the infant he becomes even a few weeks later, and our understanding of the capabilities of the newborn is so new, that the first few weeks of life deserve special emphasis.

THE NEWBORN BABY

No matter how carefully a birth is prepared for, the arrival of the baby is overwhelming for the parents as well as for the baby. Having suddenly become responsible for a tiny and dependent human being, parents face a total upheaval in their lives, and a period of adjustment. The baby is brand new and seems so vulnerable. Most parents, particularly those who have no other children, may not know how to care for the baby. Furthermore, during the first few hours or days after birth, parents have no idea how the baby looks when he is content, therefore they do not know when he is discontent. They do not know how much he ordinarily cries, so they cannot tell whether or not his cries signal what could be a serious medical problem. The parents lack a baseline for the appearance and behavior of the newborn (Leach, 1983).

The baby himself, who has yet to adapt to life outside the womb, has to establish this baseline. During the first month or so after birth, the baby

TABLE 4.1   Contrasting characteristics of prenatal and postnatal life.

	Prenatal Life	Postnatal Life
Physical environment	Fluid (amniotic fluid)	Gaseous (air)
External temperature	Roughly constant temperature	Temperature fluctuates with atmospheric conditions
Sensory stimulation	Sensory stimulation other than kinesthetic or vibratory stimuli at a minimum	All sense modalities stimulated by a variety of stimuli
Nutrition	Hematotropic, dependent on nutrients in mother's blood	Dependent on availability of food and functioning of the digestive tract
Oxygen supply	Oxygen passes from maternal to fetal bloodstream at the placental surface	Oxygen passes from lung surface to newborn's pulmonary blood vessels
Elimination of products of metabolism	Discharged into mother's bloodstream	Eliminated by lung, skin, kidneys, and gastrointestinal tract

Source: "Contrasting characteristics of prenatal and post natal life" p. 174. Reprinted with permission of Macmillan Publishing Company from *Developmental Physiology and Aging* by Paola S. Timiras. Copyright © 1972 by Paola S. Timiras.

will establish a predictable pattern of sleeping, crying, eating, looking, and listening. Only after he establishes such a routine, however, do parents feel that here is a person they can understand and whose behavior they can, to an extent, predict. Some babies take longer than others to reach this stage. On the whole, mothers report that they begin to feel comfortable caring for their babies sometime between two and six weeks after birth (Leach, 1983).

In the meantime, whether or not they are comfortable in caring for the newborn, parents must look after him. The baby's physiological needs are few. Essentially, he needs to be fed and kept warm, comfortable, and clean. However, to fulfill each of these needs is a new experience not only for the parents but also for the baby, who has to contend with a myriad of sensations he never encountered before: the experience of light, changes in temperature, feelings of fullness and emptiness, the sensations of being held and put down, and so on. In the womb, when the mechanisms for the baby's functions were being developed, existence was relatively effortless. At birth, however, the heart, circulatory system, respiratory system, and nervous system, among other functions (see Table 4.1) are adapting to life outside the womb. The baby is very busy these first few days, just being alive and staying that way.

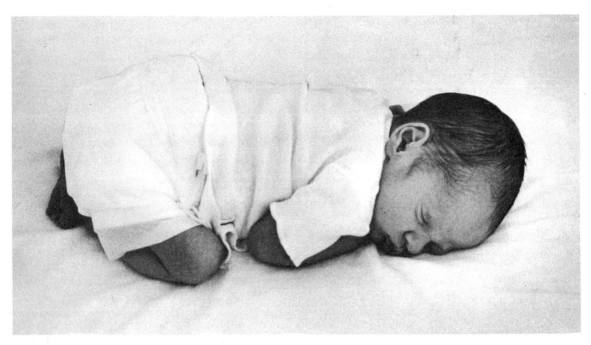

FIGURE 4.1   For the first few days after birth the newborn baby's appearance is hardly beautiful. Nevertheless, adults are naturally attracted to him.

Characteristics of the Newborn Baby

If you have ever seen a newborn baby, you have no doubt marveled at how perfect his hands, toes, and fingernails are, how tiny he is, and how a whole, perfectly formed human being could be so little. Beyond being perfectly formed and tiny, however, there are other characteristics of the newborn baby that are amazing, including his appearance and his individuality. In addition, researchers are finding that although the newborn is dependent on adult care, he is actually a competent human being who is capable of survival and who demonstrates the ability to respond to environmental stimuli.

Appearance

Adults are naturally attracted to the newborn baby, but his appearance right after birth often surprises them and contributes to parents' hesitancy and insecurity in caring for him. Not only is the newborn baby very fragile, other aspects of his appearance seem odd, and, as you can see in Figure 4.1, he is hardly beautiful. He has a short neck, if any at all; a growth of fine-textured hair, called *lanugo*, all over his body; a bulging   *lanugo* abdomen; a broad, flat face; disproportionately small arms, legs, and trunk; and a disproportionately large head that in some babies is misshapen. He also has flexible bones, soft, dry skin that may be speckled with blotches, and he is prone to all sorts of other conditions and appearances that, although they appear odd, are perfectly normal for newborns. Examples of such conditions include swollen breasts in both male and female newborns and swollen genitals, which result from the secretion of high levels of hormones during the prenatal period. So odd is the newborn's appearance for the first few days after birth that adults' attraction to him is indeed surprising.

Individuality

Although all newborns have an unusual appearance relative to what they look like a few weeks after birth, newborn infants vary greatly in their size, shape, degree of physical maturity, and even in their personality traits.

> It is quite wrong to think of newborns as identical buds, from which in the fullness of time flower the variegated colors of the preschool assembly. The newborn already has had a long and very eventful history. . . . Just like 6-year-olds or the 14-year-olds—although perhaps not so obviously—[newborns] represent a wide variety of degrees of physiological maturity.   (Tanner, 1974)

Whereas some of the differences among newborns are related to their prenatal experiences, as Tanner (1974) so eloquently emphasizes in the preceding quotation, there are also many differences among newborns that appear to be genetically determined. Freedman and Freedman (1969) found differences between newborns of Chinese-American background and European-American background in the extent that they cried and in their ability to be calmed. They found that Chinese-American newborns tend to be more easily calmed when crying than are European-American newborns. Other researchers have found differences depending on the sex of newborns. Moss (1967), for example, notes that boys are more difficult to pacify than are girls. Phillips et al. (1978), who had set out to prove that there was no difference in activity level between the two sexes at birth, found instead that boys are awake for longer periods than girls and that they move their heads, hands, bodies, and faces more frequently than do girls. The newborns in Phillips' study had normal deliveries and were matched for birth weight and birth order. They were also wrapped in blankets of the same color to reduce the possibility of observer bias during the rating of newborn behavior.

Since there are differences among newborns in their activity level, the extent to which they cry, and in their ability to be calmed, researchers wonder if a newborn has a personality. Determining whether the newborn exhibits personality traits right from birth would help clarify the nature-nurture question of whether personality is formed by experience or whether it is a genetically endowed trait. You recall from previous discussions that on the basis of research with twins, researchers note that personality is likely to be the result of a combination of experience and genes. This same conclusion is arrived at on the basis of research with newborns. For example, researchers note that newborns exhibit different temperament traits right from birth. *Temperament* is a broad term which refers to the individual's pattern of responding to the environment, and it is said to be the foundation upon which later personality is developed. Thus, there are individuals who are quiet and calm when they encounter new situations, whereas there are others who are emotional or tense.

temperament

In one of the most extensive longitudinal studies on temperament, Thomas et al. (1970, 1977) studied 140 individuals from infancy through adolescence, and they also studied more groups of infants and children for shorter periods of time. They found that immediately after birth newborns evidence different ways of responding to the environment and of expressing themselves, and that these differences sometimes persisted through the childhood years. These researchers found also that the temperamental traits among newborns, and later, children, tended to occur in clusters so they were able to categorize the individuals in their study as "easy" infants, "difficult" infants, "slow-to-warm-up" infants, or infants who exhibit a mixture of traits that do not add up to a general characterization. The findings from their research are given in Table 4.2, which shows that early in life the child has a distinct temperament. As the child grows, the temperament tends to remain constant in quality. The shaded areas of Table 4.2 represent the characteristics of temperament that most clearly classify a child as easy, slow to warm up, or difficult. Easy infants adapt easily to most situations, they exhibit a positive mood, they enjoy being handled, and so on.

Difficult infants, on the other hand, seem to be in a continual state of distress, they are easily frustrated, and they may tense up when they are picked up or hugged. Thomas and Chess contend not only that these temperament differences are genetically endowed, since they are apparent right from birth, but also that they are stable over time. That is, easy infants tend to continue to exhibit positive personality traits throughout their life, whereas difficult infants continue to be difficult. In fact, these researchers found that 70% of the difficult infants in their study entered psychiatric counseling or treatment in later life, whereas only 18% of the easy infants did.

However, some researchers contend that the stability of the traits noted by Thomas and Chess is a function not only of genetic factors, but of the different caregiving approaches the infants elicit from birth. For example, deVries and Sameroff (1984) present data on infant temperament

TABLE 4.2 Stability of selected temperament traits over time.

Temperamental Quality	Rating	2 Months	6 Months
Activity Level	High	Moves often in sleep. Wriggles when diaper is changed.	Tries to stand in tub and splashes. Bounces in crib. Crawls after dog.
	Low	Does not move when being dressed or during sleep.	Passive in bath. Plays quietly in crib and falls asleep.
Rhythmicity	Regular	Has been on four-hour feeding schedule since birth. Regular bowel movement.	Is asleep at 6:30 every night. Awakes at 7:00 A.M. Food intake is constant.
	Irregular	Awakes at a different time each morning. Size of feedings varies.	Length of nap varies; so does food intake.
Distractibility	Distractible	Will stop crying for food if rocked. Stops fussing if given pacifier when diaper is being changed.	Stops crying when mother sings. Will remain still while clothing is changed if given a toy.
	Not distractible	Will not stop crying when diaper is changed. Fusses after eating, even if rocked.	Stops crying only after dressing is finished. Cries until given bottle.
Approach/Withdrawal	Positive	Smiles and licks washcloth. Has always liked bottle.	Likes new foods. Enjoyed first bath in a large tub. Smiles and gurgles.
	Negative	Rejected cereal the first time. Cries when strangers appear.	Smiles and babbles at strangers. Plays with new toys immediately.
Adaptability	Adaptive	Was passive during first bath; now enjoys bathing. Smiles at nurse.	Used to dislike new foods; now accepts them well.
	Not adaptive	Still startled by sudden, sharp noise. Resists diapering.	Does not cooperate with dressing. Fusses and cries when left with sitter.
Attention Span and Persistence	Long	If soiled, continues to cry until changed. Repeatedly rejects water if he wants milk.	Watches toy mobile over crib intently. "Coos" frequently.
	Short	Cries when awakened but stops almost immediately. Objects only mildly if cereal precedes bottle.	Sucks pacifier for only a few minutes and spits it out.
Intensity of Reaction	Intense	Cries when diapers are wet. Rejects food vigorously when satisfied.	Cries loudly at the sound of thunder. Makes sucking movements when vitamins are administered.
	Mild	Does not cry when diapers are wet. Whimpers instead of crying when hungry.	Does not kick often in tub. Does not smile. Screams and kicks when temperature is taken.

continues on page 176

1 Year	2 Years	5 Years	10 Years
Walks rapidly. Eats eagerly. Climbs into everything.	Climbs furniture. Explores. Gets in and out of bed while being put to sleep.	Leaves table often during meals. Always runs.	Plays ball and engages in other sports. Cannot sit still long enough to do homework.
Finishes bottle slowly. Goes to sleep easily. Allows nail-cutting without fussing.	Enjoys quiet play with puzzles. Can listen to records for hours.	Takes a long time to dress. Sits quietly on long automobile rides.	Likes chess and reading. Eats very slowly.
Naps after lunch each day. Always drinks bottle before bed.	Eats a big lunch each day. Always has a snack before bedtime.	Falls asleep when put to bed. Bowel movement regular.	Eats only at mealtimes. Sleeps the same amount of time each night.
Will not fall asleep for an hour or more. Moves bowels at a different time each day.	Nap time changes from day to day. Toilet training is difficult because bowel movement is unpredictable.	Food intake varies; so does time of bowel movement.	Food intake varies. Falls alseep at a different time each night.
Cries when face is washed unless it is made into a game.	Will stop tantrum if another activity is suggested.	Can be coaxed out of forbidden activity by being led into something else.	Needs absolute silence for homework. Has a hard time choosing a shirt in a store because they all appeal to him.
Cries when toy is taken away and rejects substitute.	Screams if refused some desired object. Ignores mother's calling.	Seems not to hear if involved in favorite activity. Cries for a long time when hurt.	Can read a book while television set is at high volume. Does chores on schedule.
Approaches strangers readily. Sleeps well in new surroundings.	Slept well the first time he stayed overnight at grandparents' house.	Entered school building unhesitatingly. Tries new foods.	Went to camp happily. Loved to ski the first time.
Stiffened when placed on sled. Will not sleep in strange beds.	Avoids strange children in the playground. Whimpers first time at beach. Will not go into water.	Hid behind mother when entering school.	Severely homesick at camp during first days. Does not like new activities.
Was afraid of toy animals at first; now plays with them happily.	Obeys quickly. Stayed contentedly with grandparents for a week.	Hesitated to go to nursery school at first; now goes eagerly. Slept well on camping trip.	Likes camp, although homesick during first days. Learns enthusiastically.
Continues to reject new foods each time they are offered.	Cries and screams each time hair is cut. Disobeys persistently.	Has to be hand led into classroom each day. Bounces on bed in spite of spankings.	Does not adjust well to new school or new teacher; comes home late for dinner even when punished.
Plays by self in playpen for more than an hour. Listens to singing for long periods.	Works on a puzzle until it is completed. Watches when shown how to do something.	Practiced riding a two-wheeled bicycle for hours until he mastered it. Spent over an hour reading a book.	Reads for two hours before sleeping. Does homework carefully.
Loses interest in a toy after a few minutes. Gives up easily if she falls while attempting to walk.	Gives up easily if a toy is hard to use. Asks for help immediately if undressing becomes difficult.	Still cannot tie his shoes because he gives up when he is not successful. Fidgets when parents read to him.	Gets up frequently from homework for a snack. Never finishes a book.
Laughs hard when father plays roughly. Screamed and kicked when temperature was taken.	Yells if he feels excitement or delight. Cries loudly if a toy is taken away.	Rushes to greet father. Gets hiccups from laughing hard.	Tears up an entire page of homework if one mistake is made. Slams door of room when teased by younger brother.
Does not fuss much when clothing is pulled on over head.	When another child hit her, she looked surprised, did not hit back.	Drops eyes and remains silent when given a firm parental "No." Does not laugh much.	When a mistake is made in a model airplane, corrects it quietly. Does not comment when reprimanded.

continues on page 177

Table 4.2 continued.

Temperamental Quality	Rating	2 Months	6 Months
Threshold of Responsiveness	Low	Stops sucking on bottle when approached.	Refuses fruit he likes when vitamins are added. Hides head from bright light.
	High	Is not startled by loud noises. Takes bottle and breast equally well.	Eats everything. Does not object to diapers being wet or soiled.
Quality of Mood	Positive	Smacks lips when first tasting new food. Smiles at parents.	Plays and splashes in bath. Smiles at everyone.
	Negative	Fusses after nursing. Cries when carriage is rocked.	Cries when taken from tub. Cries when given food she does not like.

in three African societies which suggest that each culture's childrearing patterns and maternal orientation, in addition to the infant's characteristics, contribute to temperament, meaning that temperament is sensitive to environmental influences. This is not too difficult to understand. As a parent, you would no doubt enjoy looking after a good baby, and the baby's positive response to you would encourage you to play with him more and hold him more. But if you have a baby who is likely to tense up every time you hug him, this would very likely discourage you from handling the baby too often, so you might resort to avoiding physical contact with the baby (Wolff, 1971). As long as the baby continues to be difficult, your reactions to the baby would continue to be the same, so you can see how babies elicit different responses from adults and how these responses eventually change the type of care the infant receives, which, in turn, could influence the infant's personality.

Dependence and Competence

Of all newborn organisms, the human newborn is the most dependent on adult care. He must be fed, pacified, cleansed, and protected. What is more, the period of dependency for the human newborn is longer than that for any other species. Not only is the newborn dependent on adult care, he also looks helpless. Appearing helpless serves an adaptive function, for it elicits a protective and nurturant response from adults. Despite the prolonged dependency of the newborn infant, he is not totally unprepared for life outside the womb. On the contrary, at birth the baby has remarkable capacities for dealing with the world and surviving. He is able to eat, to eliminate body waste, and he is also able to regulate his body temperature, which is subject to frequent variation.

Table 4.2 continued.

1 Year	2 Years	5 Years	10 Years
Spits out food he does not like. Giggles when tickled.	Runs to door when father comes home. Must always be tucked tightly into bed.	Always notices when mother puts new dress on for first time. Refuses milk if it is not ice-cold.	Rejects fatty foods. Adjusts shower until water is at exactly the right temperature.
Eats food he likes even if mixed with disliked food. Can be left easily with strangers.	Can be left with anyone. Falls to sleep easily on either back or stomach.	Does not hear loud, sudden noises when reading. Does not object to injections.	Never complains when sick. Eats all foods.
Likes bottle; reaches for it and smiles. Laughs loudly when playing peekaboo.	Plays with sister; laughs and giggles. Smiles when he succeeds in putting shoes on.	Laughs loudly while watching television cartoons. Smiles at everyone.	Enjoys new accomplishments. Laughs when reading a funny passage aloud.
Cries when given injections. Cries when left alone.	Cries and squirms when given haircut. Cries when mother leaves.	Objects to putting boots on. Cries when frustrated.	Cries when he cannot solve a homework problem. Very "weepy" if he does not get enough sleep.

Source: Table from pages 108–9 of "The Origin of Personality," by Thomas A. Chess and H. C. Birch, *Scientific American,* August 1970. Copyright © 1970 by Scientific American, Inc. All rights reserved.

Infant Reflexes.   The competency of the newborn is further evidenced in the fact that nature ensures the survival and adaptability of the newborn by equipping him with certain *reflexes,* which are specific, involuntary responses to stimuli. The baby is born with a host of reflexes (see Table 4.3, page 178), many of which disappear after the first two or three months of life. Some reflexes are adaptive in that they help infants secure food or they protect them from harm. Coughing, sucking, blinking, and crying are examples of built in adaptive reflexes. They are termed "built in" because they are available to the infant immediately after birth and thereby help to ensure his survival. There is no need for the infant to learn to suck, for example; if he did have to learn, he would be in danger of dying of starvation.

reflexes

Another adaptive reflex is the *rooting reflex*. It is most readily elicited in infants who are one or two weeks old by gently touching a finger to the corner of the baby's mouth (see Figure 4.2c) and moving it slowly toward the cheek. Usually the infant will move his tongue, his mouth, or his entire head in an attempt to suck the finger. This reflex is obviously important in feeding as it is more easily elicited when the baby is hungry. Babies who breastfeed release the nipple for a brief period, only to regain it later. It is easier for the baby to retrieve the nipple if it rubs against his mouth and cheek and the rooting reflex takes over.

The infant possesses other reflexes, but these have no obvious value to survival so researchers think they are relics, left over from our evolutionary past. One such reflex is the *Moro reflex,* named after Ernst Moro, the German pediatrician who first described the reflex in 1918. This reflex appears if the newborn infant is held in mid-air and suddenly released for a moment so that he almost drops, or drops about six inches (see Figure

TABLE 4.3   Selected newborn reflexes.

Reflex	Description	Age of Disappearance
Blink	When a light is flashed on the infant's eyes, both his eyelids close in response.	remains
Babinski	When the sole of the infant's foot is stroked, the toes spread out in response.	around the end of the first year of life
Grasping	When a finger or any other graspable object is placed in the palm of the infant's hand, the infant grasps it tightly.	very strong during the first 2-3 months, then disappears around 3 or 4 months; becomes voluntary around 5 months
Moro	When the infant is held upside down as if he is almost going to be dropped, he throws his arms out and clenches his hands.	after the first 4 or 5 months
Stepping	When the infant is held upright with his feet against a flat surface, he moves his feet as if walking.	after 2 or 3 months
Swimming	When the infant is placed horizontally in water, he makes paddle-like movements.	after 2 or 3 months
Rooting	When the infant is lightly touched on the cheek with a finger, he turns his head toward the finger and opens his mouth in an attempt to suck the finger.	after 2 or 3 months
Sucking	When the infant encounters something suckable that he can put in his mouth, he sucks it.	after 3 or 4 months

4.2a), at which point he will throw his arms upward and clench his fingers, as if in a fist. Although of no apparent value to the human infant, the Moro reflex is very adaptive for the infant monkey, who is held by the mother next to her chest (Prechtl and Beintema, 1977). When the mother moves, the monkey's sense of sudden loss of support automatically produces the Moro reflex, that is, the monkey will grasp and cling to its mother. Researchers are not positive that the Moro reflex is related to our evolutionary past, but it does indeed appear to be likely. The instinctive clinging, exemplified by the Moro reflex, may explain the discomfort which many infants display when they are held in positions that prevent them from making full contact with the caretaker. Most infants are happy when they are carried in a cradled position in the mother's arm, held against her chest, or held with their backs touching her chest.

Other reflexes reveal neurological apparatus present in the newborn that is later used for important abilities such as walking. Even though the newborn is incapable of balancing on those tiny, bent legs, he actually knows how to stand before he is physically able to do so. Although infants cannot walk until they are about a year old, the newborn baby, when held upright on a hard surface will step forward as if walking (see Figure 4.2b). This stepping reflex, like many others, disappears by the time the infant is two months old, as higher brain functions and learning later provide the baby with the responses needed for these activities (Touwen, 1976). However, recent studies reveal that newborn infants who are given active exercise of the stepping reflex show an increase in their response and also walk earlier than do infants who do not receive the exercise (Zelazo, Zelazo, and Kolb, 1972). In our opinion, exercising the newborn's stepping reflex so he will eventually walk at an earlier age is of little value. However, studies such as the one by Zelazo and colleagues help researchers formulate and test hypotheses about infant growth and development (Thelen & Fisher, 1982). Our knowledge of infant reflexes also provides a framework for the neurological assessment of newborns, as the absence of any of the reflexes may be indicative of serious disturbance in development (Self & Horowitz, 1979). In addition, knowing about infant reflexes enables parents to play with the newborn baby through attempts to elicit reflex responses. The ability of the newborn to respond with reflex action is dependent on his state of arousal, as we see in the following section. Thus, researchers have studied the pattern of sleep and wakefulness that the newborn displays.

Infant States. Infant *state* refers to the extent to which the baby is asleep or aroused. Newborns spend most of their time asleep, but their sleep is not regulated as it is in adults. Rather, they sleep approximately 3½ hours out of every 4-hour period, and over the course of the day, they undergo cycles of wakefulness and sleepiness and varying degrees of activity and sleep (see Table 4.4). Infant states are not random, but are predictable and organized, alerting us to the physiological competence of the newborn and to the fact that he has internal mechanisms (an inner clock, one might say) which regulates much of his behavior (Schaffer, 1977). There are individual variations in how much time infants spend in each state, as some babies require more sleep, others less, and some babies are more irritable than others so they cry more. There are also developmental changes in states. According to some researchers, the newborn baby typically sleeps a total of 16 to 20 hours a day (Hutt, Lenard, & Prechtl, 1969). As the baby matures, he sleeps less but for longer periods of time. By the time he is approximately six months to a year old, the baby will sleep through the night.

a

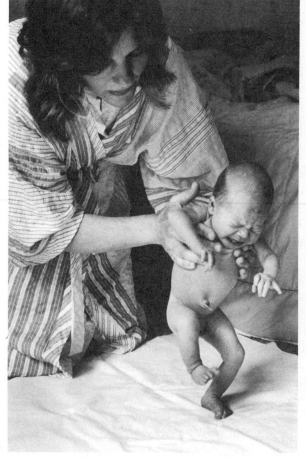

b

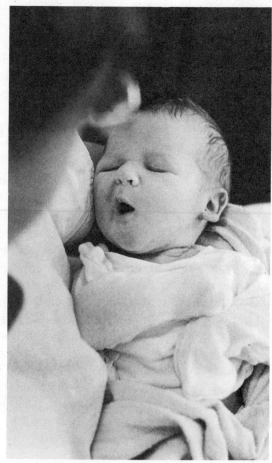

c

FIGURE 4.2 Six reflexes seen in newborn infants: (a) the Moro reflex; (b) the stepping reflex; (c) the rooting reflex; (d) the sucking reflex; (e) the grasping reflex; and (f) the Babinski reflex.

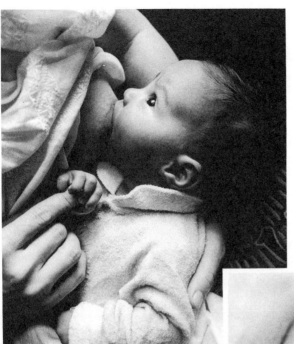

d

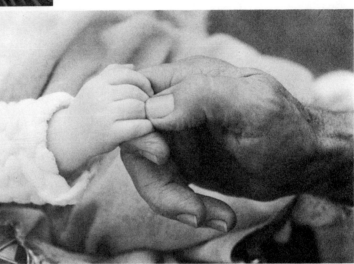

e

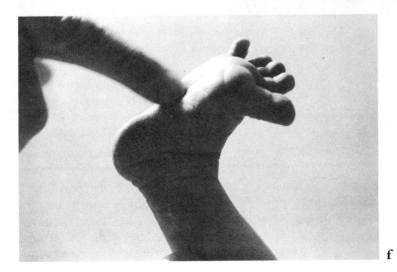

f

TABLE 4.4 Infant states.

State	Description
Regular sleep	The newborn's eyes are closed, he is breathing regularly, and he makes no movements except for sudden, generalized starts. A newborn in this state cannot be aroused by mild stimuli.
Irregular sleep	The newborn's eyes are closed, breathing is irregular, and muscles twitch from time to time. Although in this state the newborn still makes no major movements, external stimulation such as a bright light or noise can elicit smiles or pouts.
Drowsiness	This state is experienced either before or after sleep. The newborn's eyes may be open or closed and breathing is irregular. However, the baby in this state is highly sensitive to external stimuli.
Alert inactivity	The baby is free from distressing internal and external stimuli. He is awake, his eyes are open, and he is looking at the immediate environment.
Waking activity	The baby is awake with his eyes open but is not alert. However, the infant in this state seems to engage in frequent motor activity, with his whole body moving.
Crying	The baby is awake and crying intensely, often kicking his feet and thrashing his arms.

Source: Adapted from Wolff, 1966.

It is important to understand infant states because they influence the extent to which the infant benefits from environmental stimuli. In order to benefit from the environment, the infant must be in an alert, quiet state. In this state, sensory pathways are open and the infant can see, hear, and respond to touch. Obviously, when the infant is in a sleep state, or when he is in a state that is characterized by intense crying, his attention is not directed toward outside stimuli. Often, sleep and crying are ways in which infants regulate the amount of stimulation they receive, for they cannot cope with a lot of stimulation when they are very young.

Brazelton (1976) notes that whereas some infants change from one state to another when they are subjected to too much stimulation, that is, they fall asleep or they begin to cry, other infants avert their gaze, thus signaling that they can no longer cope with stimulation, which may be, for example, a playing situation with the parents. The Brazelton Neonatal Behavioral Assessment Scale (Brazelton, 1973; Brazelton, Als, Tronick, & Lester, 1979) assesses the behavior of infants in relation to the states they

TABLE 4.5   The Brazelton Neonatal Behavioral Assessment Scale.

		Scoring
Neurological Items		
Elicited reflexes and movements	plantar grasp hand grasp ankle clonus Babinski standing automatic walking crawling tonic neck reflex Moro rooting sucking passive movements of both legs and both arms	These neurological items are rated on a 3-point scale for low, medium, and high intensity of response; asymmetry and absence are also noted.
Behavioral Items		
Specific behaviors observed or elicited	focusing and following an object reaction to an auditory stimulus reaction to persons reaction to a voice reaction to a person's face and voice	These behavioral items are rated on a 9-point scale; the midpoint of the scale denotes the expected behavior of a 3-day-old normal baby.
General behaviors observed	degree of alertness motor maturity cuddliness consolability with intervention peak of excitement irritability amount of startles self-quieting activity hand-to-mouth facility number of smiles	

Source: Adapted from Brazelton, 1973.

are in. It is a test that examines the capacity for interaction. Using this test, the examiner attempts to elicit the best performance of which the infant is capable. The examiner is trained to make efforts to influence the infant to an optimal state and to modify the techniques used to elicit a response until the best response is produced (see Table 4.5).

Most of the scoring of the infant's behavior is done after the test items are administered at least once. Also included in the test findings are a description of the examiner's overall impressions of the baby, a discussion of the conditions under which the test was done, and a notation of the infant's state at the time of testing.

Breastfeeding

The question of whether a baby should be breastfed or whether he should be bottle fed has been a point of dispute for some time, with experts changing the advice they give parents. At times mothers have been admonished for breastfeeding their babies and at other times encouraged to do so (Kessen, 1965).

Breastfeeding was a common practice for centuries. Even those babies whose mothers were wealthy enough to choose to abstain from the practice were breastfed—not by their mothers but by a wet nurse. However, the pasteurization of milk helped initiate sanitation practices which paved the way for the substitution of cow's milk for breastfeeding. Eventually, bottle feeding became the preferred practice, with many mothers believing that this method is not only more convenient, it is also a nutritionally more sound practice for the baby, especially if infant formula is used.

Bottle feeding may be more convenient, especially for mothers who are working. However, physicians and psychologists are now noting that, for several reasons, mothers should attempt to breastfeed their babies, especially during the first few months after birth. At birth the baby is suddenly transferred from a regulated environment to one in which adaptation is required for survival. He must receive adequate nourishment and quickly develop immunologic mechanisms that enable him to survive.

Increasing evidence has shown that newborn babies can acquire these immunologic mechanisms from breast milk (Garrard, 1974; American Academy of Pediatrics, 1978). Besides the advantage of breast milk in terms of immunity, it is known that breast milk contains a blend of nutrients needed by the human infant and that the practice of breastfeeding facilitates the development of a close psychological bond.

Despite the obvious advantages of breastfeeding, there are many mothers who are either unable to or do not want to breastfeed their infant, in part because they have to work full time and leave the baby in some form of substitute care. Some mothers manage to collect breast milk and leave it with the caretaker to feed to the infant, but this is not possible in all cases.

Some mothers do not breastfeed their babies because they simply do not know how to. When breastfeeding was a common practice, mothers received encouragement and instructions from relatives who lived nearby. Many mothers today are isolated from their relatives, and may not even have seen anyone else breastfeed before.

The American Academy of Pediatrics believes that breastfeeding is so important for the development of the baby that policies should be implemented to encourage the practice. In its report, the American Academy of Pediatrics recommends that parenting education classes in schools include instruction on the importance of breastfeeding and that the nation should adopt legislation to enable mothers to take a three-month leave of absence from work so they can care for and

breastfeed their babies, at least for the first few months of life (American Academy of Pediatrics, 1978).

Support for breastfeeding is also available from *La Leche*. This international organization encourages and provides information about breastfeeding. Local chapters of *La Leche* exist in numerous communities across the United States. At regular meetings, breastfeeding mothers can exchange information and offer and receive support.

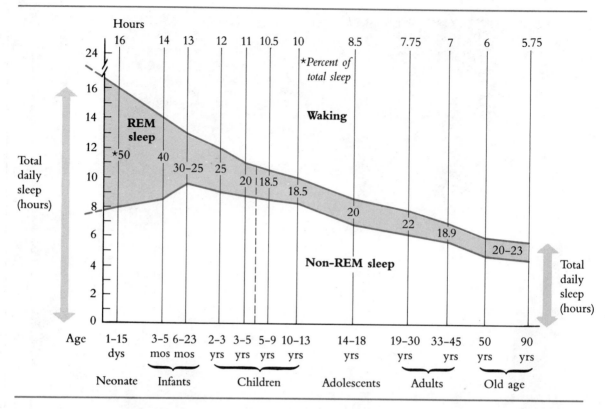

FIGURE 4.3 Changes in sleep organization. With increasing age, sleep patterns change considerably. Note the substantial decrease in REM sleep over the life span. However, non-REM sleep remains constant for many years. Adapted from "Ontogenetic Development of the Human Sleep-Dream Cycle," Roffwarg, H. P. et al., Vol 152, Fig. 1, p. 608, 29 April 1966. Copyright © 1966 by the American Association for the Advancement of Science.

Do Babies Dream While They Sleep?

REM sleep

Since the newborn spends so much time sleeping, does he dream? Obviously, the answer to this question eludes us since the newborn cannot tell us what he experiences during sleep. By recording the brain activity of newborn infants, however, researchers have established that the newborn spends as much as half of his sleeping hours in rapid eye movement (REM) sleep. Premature infants spend even more time in REM sleep. *REM sleep* is characterized by rapid eye movements and fluctuations in the heart rate, blood pressure, and brain waves. In adults, dreaming occurs during this period, and REM sleep is often called simply dream sleep. A certain amount of REM sleep is essential for optimal functioning in adults. The reason for this is not entirely understood, but researchers know that adults who obtain little REM sleep or who are awakened during REM sleep are irritable and disorganized the next day (Dement, 1960). However, in contrast to the amount of time infants spend in REM sleep, adults spend much less time in REM sleep. The percentage of REM sleep drops from 50 percent in the newborn period to only 25 percent in the 2- to 3-year-old child, to less than 20 percent in adults between the ages of 33 and 45 (Roffwarg, Muzio, & Dement, 1966). The distribution of different phases of sleep also changes with maturity (see Figure 4.3). Adults usually spend an hour in non-REM sleep before they drift into REM sleep. Newborn infants, however, can enter REM sleep from any waking or sleeping state (Korner, 1968).

Experts in sleep research propose that autostimulation accounts for the increased time infants spend in REM sleep (Roffwarg, Muzio, and Dement, 1966). According to the *autostimulation theory*, REM sleep is a spontaneous neurological firing in the brain which provides stimulation to higher brain centers. The high degree of REM sleep during the newborn period thus stimulates the development of the central nervous system. As the infant matures and becomes increasingly more alert, this type of internal stimulation is less necessary because the nervous system is more mature, and the infant is more capable of processing external stimuli. Emde and his colleagues have proposed that the more external stimulation the infant experiences when awake, the less time he spends in REM sleep (Emde et al., 1971). These researchers found, for example, that circumcised infants (circumcision being an extreme impact on the baby) spend less time in REM sleep. The autostimulation theory may also explain why premature infants, whose nervous system is less mature than that of full-term infants, spend more time in REM sleep. You should be aware, however, that the principle of autostimulation is as yet only a theoretical explanation of the sleep patterns of babies and it has not been confirmed as fact.

autostimulation theory

Influencing Infant State. Parents often try to influence the newborn's state. Naturally, the state they most want to change is the state in which the infant is crying. It is important to quiet the unhappy baby, not only because a baby who cries continually can be unnerving for the parents, but also because the quieter and calmer the baby is, the more he is able to become acquainted with the environment (Korner, 1972) and also to increase his body weight and adjust to life (Stuart and Prugh, 1960).

There are various ways to soothe the baby. Feeding the baby is one way. Another is swaddling the baby with a blanket, a practice more common in Russia and China than it is in the United States. Researchers find that swaddling often reduces crying and muscular activity and that it lowers the baby's heart and respiratory rates (Lipton, Steinschneider, & Richmond, 1965). Other researchers note that stimulating the restless baby, for example, walking with the baby, rocking him, introducing rhythmic sound, or clothing or unclothing him, also results in lowered heart and respiratory rates and in the cessation of crying (Brackbill, 1971). These findings from the research can be utilized by parents and caregivers, especially for premature infants, who are often irritable and who spend more time in a crying state than do full-term infants.

Knowledge of ways to soothe the infant can also help reduce the incidence of physical abuse of the infant, which often occurs when adults find themselves unable to pacify him (Frodi, 1985). Crying is the young baby's only method of communicating with adults. Researchers note that babies cry differently depending on whether they are hungry, in pain, or simply irritable. However, parents cannot always distinguish between these cries (Muller, Hollien, and Murray, 1974; Donovan and Leavitt, 1985). This is especially true during the first few days of the baby's life when facial expressions, physical movements, and non-crying noises are unfocused and difficult for the parents to interpret. As they become more attuned to the baby, parents also increase in their ability to distinguish among the different infant cries and are able to tell, for example, when the baby is crying because he wants attention or because he is in some way uncomfortable or in pain (Boukydis, 1985).

Obviously, parents would prefer that the baby never cried. At the same time, they must understand that a baby must cry. It is his only reliable signal for his need for assistance or care. What parents have to ascertain is what type of assistance the baby requires. In other words, why is the baby crying? Researchers have studied the causes of crying from birth through the first several months of life. One such researcher (Wolff, 1969) lists the causes of crying as hunger, cold, wet or soiled diapers, and pain, which are relatively obvious since they indicate some discomfort the baby is experiencing. However, Wolff also lists other causes of crying that are less obvious, including spontaneous jerks or twitches which awaken the baby, overstimulation or stimulation of the infant when he is not in an alert state, and being undressed. Apparently, some babies object to being undressed. This is not a reaction to cold or to the caretaker's handling. It appears, rather, to reflect loss of restraint and skin contact. Such babies can be pacified during undressing if a blanket is placed over them.

SENSORY AND PERCEPTUAL CAPABILITIES OF THE NEWBORN

Until the 1950s, a newborn baby was considered to be an essentially passive, incompetent creature who simply cried, ate, slept, and who possessed a few simple reflexes. With the surge of infancy research beginning in the 1960s, researchers have come to realize that the newborn baby comes into the world equipped with acute senses and capable of making immediate responses to the environment. In fact, we now know that all the senses function at birth or shortly after, as the newborn baby can hear, see, smell, taste, and respond to touch. Most of these sensory abilities, although present, are immature and become more refined and acute as the infant grows (Lowery, 1978). Limited perceptual ability is also present at birth, as newborn infants are known to pay selective attention to aspects of their environment. For example, they pay attention to bright lights and loud noises. There is a difference between sensory abilities and perceptual

Sudden Infant Death Syndrome

*E*ach year approximately 8,000 infants in the United States die, apparently the victims of Sudden Infant Death Syndrome (SIDS), or crib death (so-called because it often occurs during sleep). SIDS is the most common cause of death for infants between 1 week and 1 year of age. More infants die of SIDS than of cystic fibrosis, leukemia, cancer, heart disease, and child abuse combined. Not only in the United States but worldwide, statistics reveal that 1 out of 350 infants dies of this condition.

SIDS has probably occurred since biblical times, although our awareness and understanding of the extent of this fatal condition is only recent. Researchers now know that the peak incidence is among infants 2 to 3 months of age and that SIDS is more likely to occur during the winter months. Nearly all SIDS deaths occur while the infant is quietly asleep. No crying or noisy struggle precedes the death, which can happen unnoticed even if the parents are sleeping in the same room.

Male infants are at greater risk for crib death than females. And, although crib death can strike any child, and most victims are well-cared-for and well-nourished infants, the incidence of SIDS is higher among poor families. It is also higher among babies born prematurely or who are of low birth weight and among babies born to women who smoked heavily or were seriously anemic during pregnancy. In addition, SIDS is more likely to occur in infants who have a cold or a runny nose and to infants who are bottle fed rather than breastfed. These characteristics, which have been found to be common among infants who succumbed to SIDS, enable us to identify infants who are at high risk for SIDS so that special attention can be given to them for its prevention.

The prevention of SIDS, while not yet entirely possible, is dependent on researchers' attempts to isolate its causes. Numerous theories have been advanced to explain the condition. For example, botulism (acute food poisoning) appears to be the cause of some cases of SIDS, and there may also be a genetic explanation, as a baby born in a family where an infant has died of SIDS may wake up from sleep less often than do most other babies, suggesting that he may be vulnerable to SIDS.

Some researchers also note that SIDS could be related to a subtle damage to the body's respiratory control center, which is located in the brainstem. This damage usually occurs during the prenatal period due to a drop in maternal blood pressure, maternal anemia, or cigarette smoking by the mother during pregnancy, and it is suspected to be a problem in babies who are born prematurely.

Researchers are also investigating the possibility that *apnea,* the temporary cessation of breathing common in premature infants, is the cause of SIDS. Researchers believe that brief apneic pauses during sleep are predictive of longer, potentially fatal pauses. An apnea monitor is used to prevent SIDS in infants with apnea. The monitor is attached to the infant's thorax during sleep and records respiratory activity. If no respiration occurs for 20 seconds, an alarm is set off, and the person responding must initiate respiration, usually by gently shaking the infant. (Based on research by Black, 1979; Steinschneider, 1975; Marx, 1978; Harper, Leake, Hoffman, Walker, Hodgman, & Sternman, 1981; and Naeye, 1982.)

sensation
perception

abilities. *Sensation* refers to the ability to detect a certain stimulus in the environment. *Perception* refers to the ability to process or interpret these sensations. The newborn infant's capabilities in both these areas are indeed amazing and alert us to the extent and significance of physiological development before birth.

When you consider the amazing newborn (Pines, 1982) and his repertoire of sensory and perceptual skills, however, you must realize that this is not a new breed of baby. Babies have always had those skills. What is new is researchers' ability to study the newborn's behavior. It is difficult to study infants, and especially newborns, since many of the methods developed to study children and adults are dependent on motor and verbal responses and therefore are useless when studying young infants. The newborn baby cannot tell us what he sees, and he cannot point to an object or otherwise specify a response. However, research methods have been developed that are based on the responses that the newborn and infant *can* make. The heart rate, rate and change of respiration, muscle contraction, and other physiological functions are measured to probe the newborn's capabilities. For example, if a researcher detects a change in the baby's respiration upon hearing his mother's voice but not upon hearing other sounds, this would suggest that the newborn recognizes or is sensitive to his mother's voice. Some researchers also monitor the newborn baby's eye movement and sucking pattern as a means of establishing an index of the effects of sensory stimuli.

habituation

In much of the research, researchers rely on habituation and dishabituation to interpret the findings. *Habituation* is a type of learning which indicates that a particular stimulus has become familiar, or learned, and thus no longer elicits interest. For example, a newborn is shown an object and if he has not seen it before, he will evidence his interest by getting somewhat excited. His heart rate may increase, perhaps. After repeated exposure to the object, the baby will no longer be interested and thus will evidence no response. If at the same time that the baby is shown the familiar object he is also shown a new object, one that is similar but slightly different from the familiar object, he may notice the difference, in which case he may evidence his interest once more and will respond to the

dishabituation

new object. This is known as *dishabituation;* it reveals that the baby can discriminate between objects and remembers what he has seen in the past.

Many of the findings on newborn capabilities are in many cases preliminary and therefore will undergo many different interpretations as researchers' understanding becomes clearer. In addition, at this time there is no overall theory that guides the research, in part because researchers are primarily concerned with finding appropriate methods of study (Banks & Salapatek, 1983). But, the discovery of effective techniques for assessing sensory and perceptual capacities of very young infants is leading researchers toward the time when such theories will be forthcoming. As Acredolo and Hake (1982) note, now that the "methodological barriers holding back the curious" have been breached, there is an "exhilarating rush toward the solution of the nature-nurture question so long at the heart of psychological and philosophical debate."

Hearing

At birth, the newborn's auditory canals are filled with fluid, so for the first day or two after birth, his hearing may be impaired. However, as soon as the fluid obstruction disappears, the newborn baby hears remarkably well. He can localize sounds and discriminate among sounds of different loudness, duration (Bartoshuk, 1964), and pitch (Leventhal and Lipsitt, 1964). Low-pitched sounds tend to elicit more consistent responses among newborns than do high-pitched sounds (Eisenberg, Coursin, Griffin, and Hunter, 1964). Continuous sound seems to have a soothing effect on the young infant (Brackbill, 1970). Not only can the infant hear shortly after birth, there is some indication that unborn babies respond to loud noises (Bench, 1978), because the *cochlea,* the main hearing organ, is func-   *cochlea* tional about four months before birth.

One of the most remarkable aspects of newborn hearing is the selective responsivity of the newborn to adult speech. Freedman (1971) found that newborns respond to the sound of a female voice more often than to the sound of a bell. The selective responsivity of the newborn to human speech may have an important survival value, according to some researchers, for it plays a vital part in the development of an affectionate bond between the parent and the child (Hutt, Hutt, Lenard, Bernuth, and Muntjewerff, 1968). Researchers also suggest that the newborn does not have to learn to respond to the adult voice, but rather, that his auditory system is prewired for these sounds. In a study on young rhesus monkeys who were reared for their first month of life without hearing the vocalizations of adult monkeys, Sackett and Tripp (1968) found that the young monkeys' response to pitch was selective and that they reacted more frequently to pitch ranges of frequencies similar to those of adult monkeys' vocalizations. Of significance in this study is the fact that young monkeys do not themselves have voice pitches of these frequency ranges, which suggests that the vocalizations of adult monkeys are unique to the adults of that species and that the ability of the young monkeys to respond to these is innate.

Dancing to Human Speech

Newborns are not only born with a sensitivity to human vocalization. From the first few days after birth, they are able to tune into the syllabic content of the speech they hear. During a conversation adults usually move in synchrony with the speech being made. That is, just when the speaker changes from one syllable to the next the listeners will flex an arm, tap a finger, shift the weight of their legs, etc. (Condon and Sander, 1974). In an intriguing study, researchers found that the newborn baby synchronizes his movements precisely to the patterns of adult speech. To illustrate this amazing phenomenon, the researchers (Condon and Sander, 1974) filmed and analyzed the newborn's movements. Their subjects, infants ranging in age from 12 hours to 2 weeks, were filmed while listening to natural speech in English and in Chinese, to disconnected vowel sounds, and to tapping sounds. Analysis of the films shows that infants who were already moving when the speech began synchronized their movements to the acoustic structure of the speech. The infants' movements were found to start and stop in concert with the speech they were hearing. Watching the film, one has the impression that here is a subtle sequence of ballet, so precise and definite is the interaction. The synchrony of movement to speech was observed when both English and Chinese speech was used even though all the infants were of English-speaking parents. However, no synchrony was observed when the infants heard either disconnected vowel sounds or the tapping sound. This study provides a dramatic example that the newborn is predisposed to listen selectively to human speech.

Other studies provide additional evidence of the infant's responsivity to human vocalization. For example, babies aged approximately 1 or 2 months can hear the difference between such similar sounds as "pa" and "ba" (Eimas & Tartter, 1979). Moreover, researchers are finding that with a little practice, the infant soon comes to recognize and prefer his own mother's voice, provided, however, that the mother speaks normally. Mehler, Bertoncini, Barrière, and Jassik-Gerschenfeld (1978) found, by measuring the sucking responses of 1-month-old infants, that they distinguished their mother's voice from a stranger's voice. This finding held as long as the mother spoke in her usual fashion and addressed herself to the infant. When the mother simply read from a book in such a way that there was no intonation in her voice, the infants did not show a discriminating response to her voice. Miles and Meluish (1974) also found that infants at 20 and 30 days of age would suck on a nipple more when they heard a tape recording of their own mother's voice than they did when they heard a tape recording of the voice of another woman.

Seeing

Besides studying the newborn baby's ability to hear, researchers have also studied the newborn's ability to see. In fact, vision in infancy is perhaps the most widely investigated topic, with researchers acquiring increasing amounts of information about the visual world of newborn babies.

Researchers have found that at birth, the eyes of the human newborn are physiologically and anatomically ready to respond to many aspects of the visual field (Reese & Lipsitt, 1970). Researchers also know that babies can see objects, as long as the objects are close by (Lewis, Maurer, & Kay, 1978) and that they can distinguish between some colors (Warner & Wooten, 1979), although researchers are not entirely sure which these colors are.

It is also known that newborn babies are able to regulate the amount of light entering into the eye, and that they are sensitive to bright light, much more so than are adults. Thus a baby who is moved into the sunlight will squint, tighten his eyelids, or fuss until he is moved back into the shade. With age, the baby's sensitivity to bright light lessens.

Although newborn infants are physiologically ready to respond to aspects of the environment, they have poor *visual acuity,* which is the ability to detect the separate parts of an object (Banks & Salapatek, 1983), and they are not able to focus well at a distance (Haynes, White, & Held, 1965). A newborn baby, for example, cannot see objects that are, say, 40 yards away. However, up close he can see quite clearly. So when the baby is held approximately 7 to 15 inches away from an adult's face, he can see the face well. The ability to focus improves with age as neural development becomes more advanced. While research in this area is not as yet conclusive, researchers note that by 6 months to 1 year of age, the baby sees as clearly as adults do (Acredolo & Hake, 1982).

visual acuity

Strategies for Looking

It is known also that newborn infants have strategies for scanning the environment, and some parts of objects seem more interesting to them than others. In order to find out what parts of the visual target the newborn attends to, Salapatek and Kessen (1966) used an infrared camera that enabled them to see precisely on what parts of the object the newborn's eyes were focused. When they showed the newborn a triangle form, they found that he looked only at the edges, not the whole form. Later research by Salapatek (1969) suggests that by 2 months of age, infants focus on the center or internal area of the visual target, as well as on both its edges.

On the basis of such studies as the one just described, Haith (1980) has found that the baby has visual scanning rules. Let us look at what the newborn sees when his mother bends over him. The movement of the mother's face will elicit scanning by the baby. In the course of his searching, what the baby will focus on is subject to developmental changes. At 1 month of age the infant will focus on the edge of the face, that is, the hairline at the top or side of the face. Some parents become frustrated by this phenomenon for they feel that they fail to maintain eye-to-eye contact with their baby and must chase the infant's eyes before being able to look directly into them. By 2 months of age, however, the infant, now more skillful visually, will concentrate his focus on high-contrast areas within the general outline (see Figure 4.4). That is, he will look at the eyes, rather than at the hairline. By 3 months of age, the infant is capable of finding and focusing on the mother's eyes rather quickly even while the mother

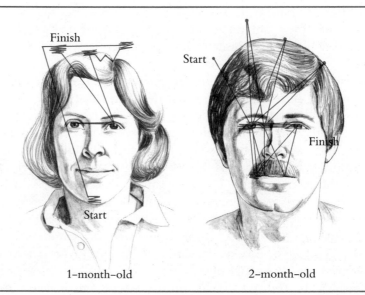

FIGURE 4.4   Scanning patterns of the newborn. Adapted from "Visual scanning of triangles by the human newborn" by P. Salapatek and W. Kessen (1966) from *Journal of Experimental Child Psychology,* 3.

talks (Haith, Bergman, & Moore, 1977). This latest feat may not seem remarkable, but for the 3-month-old infant it is. The infant of this age usually looks at objects that make a sound, so one would think that when the mother talks to the baby, the baby would look at her mouth. But this is not so. The baby focuses on the eyes. Researchers do not yet understand why the infant has different rules when it comes to face-to-face speech with adults, but it is important that he does, for eye-to-eye contact is an important aspect of the development of social ties (McCall, 1980).

With age, infants also improve in their ability to perceive different patterns and shapes. To establish the development of pattern perception in infants and to find out if infants can discriminate among patterns, Fantz (1961) measured the amount of time infants gazed at a visual target. If the infant looked longer at one form, it was assumed that the infant preferred that form. In this classic study, which was of infants at 2 months of age, Fantz found that infants looked longest at a pattern of a face, then at a pattern of newsprint, and then at concentric circles (bullseye) than they did at non-patterned objects. In a related study (Fantz, 1963), Fantz found that at 48 hours of age infants looked longer at a colored pattern than at a plain block of color, and longer still at a circle with eyes, nose, and mouth sketched in than at a plain piece of paper (see Figure 4.5). But of most interest to the infants in this study was a face pattern which also moved. Therefore, these very young infants were selecting for visual inspection objects which had the qualities of a human face.

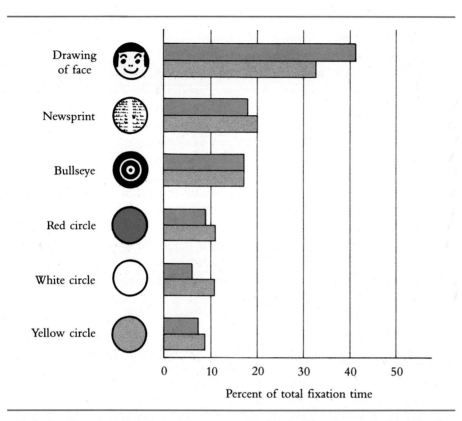

FIGURE 4.5 Infants prefer to look at a pattern rather than at color, and they prefer to look at a human face rather than at a pattern such as a bullseye or newsprint. The black bars represent preferences of infants 2 to 3 months old, and the color bars show preferences of infants older than 3 months. Adapted from "The Origin of Form Perception," by R. L. Fantz, *Scientific American,* May 1961, p. 72, bottom. Copyright © 1961 by Scientific American, Inc. All rights reserved.

In another study, Fantz (1966) showed newborns and 3-month-old infants a drawing of a normal face and a drawing of a scrambled pattern. He found that newborns showed no preference for either drawing. By three months of age, however, they clearly preferred the pattern of a normal face, which means that by that age, the face had become a meaningful visual object. Although they prefer a face over other patterns, infants at this age still do not have the ability to recognize their parents' faces and react the same to the face of their mothers and that of another woman (Haith, Bergman, & Moore, 1977).

Depth Perception

Young babies also have some idea of depth. Depth perception may be an innate mechanism, as it protects the young of any species from falling. In one experiment, Gibson and Walk (1960) constructed a visual "cliff" which consisted of a glass-covered board divided into two sections. On one section a checkered pattern was set up, and on the other side a clear glass surface with a checkerboard pattern several feet below it was put, so that on one side an illusion of depth was created. The babies in the experiment were 6 months old or older. They crawled readily on the nondeep side of the "cliff," but they refused to crawl to the side of the cliff that looked deep even though their mothers were on that side. Obviously, by six months of age the infants might have learned about depth perception, so we cannot be sure that depth perception is innate. However, Campos, Langer, and Krowitz (1970) studied 2- and 3-month-old infants to see if at that age they had any depth perception. Since the infants could not crawl, the researchers placed the infants on their stomachs on both sides of the cliff and recorded their heart rates on the deep and nondeep sides. They found that the babies had a faster heartbeat when placed on the deep side, suggesting that perhaps the babies were distinguishing and responding to the deep side as a new experience.

Touch, Smell, and Taste

Researchers' knowledge of the newborn's sensory capabilities extends beyond infant hearing and seeing. We know for example, that the newborn is responsive to touch, as exemplified by his reflex responses and the fact that a crying baby can usually be soothed by being held or picked up. We also know that the newborn's sense of smell is developed at birth. Lipsitt, Engen, and Kaye (1963) observed that newborn infants can distinguish between smells such as anise, garlic, vinegar, and phenyl alcohol. With repeated exposure to a smell, the infants will eventually take no notice of it. Researchers refer to this as habituation, which is a process whereby a particular stimulus (in this case, a particular smell) becomes so familiar to babies that they no longer react to it. But when a new smell is introduced, the babies detect the difference. So it is clear that not only can infants smell some odors, they also remember that they have previously encountered an odor, and they can distinguish a difference between one odor and another. Other researchers found that newborns also turn away from an unpleasant odor more frequently than they turn toward it (Rieser, Yonas, & Wilkner, 1976). But the substances used in these experiments were strong-smelling. The question remains, can the infant recognize other odors, say, his own mother's? In one study, MacFarlane (1975) asked nursing mothers to wear pads inside their bras in between feedings. Then the mother's pad was placed on one side of the infant, and a clean pad was placed on his other side. Even infants as young as 5 days of age turned their heads more often toward their mother's pad than toward the clean pad. In a follow-up experiment, MacFarlane compared pads worn by the newborn's mother with pads worn by another nursing mother. At

2 days of age, the infants did not discriminate between the two pads, but at 6 days of age they spent more time facing their mother's pad than that of another mother, and at 10 days of age they spent even more time facing their mother's pad.

Much of the sense of taste is based upon smell, so it should follow from the preceding studies that the newborn has the ability to detect differences in flavor. That this is indeed the case has been confirmed by studies (Crook and Lipsitt, 1976) which show that infants' sucking responses differ depending on whether they are given sweet or salty solutions. In addition, Lipsitt (1977) determined that newborns would suck two different-tasting liquids at different speeds even though both these liquids had the same smell.

Interconnectedness Among the Senses

We have described the senses one by one for the sake of simplicity. You should note, however, that the sensory systems do not necessarily operate in isolation from one another. We expect to be able to see something we hear, which is the reason we turn toward the source of sound. Thus the information gained from one sense is used to "inform" other senses, a process referred to as *cross-modal transfer of information*. How the infant develops cross-modal transfer of information is the subject of some debate. Piaget (1971) contends that the infant learns this process through gradual associations. That is, the infant learns to link vision with touch through repeated visual observation of hand movements and that he learns to link vision with hearing through his efforts to locate the source of sound. Piaget also contends that there is a developmental progression in this process, in which the infant gradually moves from use of the senses in isolation to their eventual interconnectedness. Current research, however, suggests that coordination of the senses may be present at birth and that during infancy the baby learns not interconnectedness, as Piaget stated, but rather, differentiation of the senses one from another (Bower, 1974; Spelke, 1976). Much of the evidence for this comes from such studies as the ones discussed earlier. For example, the fact that the infant turns his head and his eyes toward the source of sound evidences the fact that the infant uses the two senses in a perceptual event.

cross-modal transfer of information

DISCUSSION OF SOCIAL ISSUES: THE QUEST FOR SUPERBABIES

We have shown that newborn babies can discriminate among various sensory stimuli. Their sensory and perceptual capabilities are well developed, so they are ready to profit from the physical environment and from their interactions with caretakers. Our understanding of sensory and perceptual development is important because during infancy the child's major mode of interaction with the environment is through touch and the use of his eyes, ears, nose, and tongue.

Based on the new knowledge of the newborn's capabilities, and on research that sufficient, early stimulation is necessary before children reach school age lest they be permanently disadvantaged, there are those who advocate programs of infant education. They suggest giving the infant a large variety of stimulating experiences—mobiles, toys, musical items, colored beads, mirrors, and so on. In addition, there are baby gym classes to which parents are encouraged to take their infants so that the babies will learn to capitalize on their innate reflexes. There are also infant programs that are said to promote the ability to read and learn during infancy. Educators who promote early reading suggest that this can be accomplished by age 2 by accommodating to the infant's capabilities, for example, using very large letters (Doman, 1975). These and other activities popular with many parents today are promoted on the basis that they can help parents bring up children who are much smarter and better than average, in other words, *superbabies* (see Figure 4.6).

Superbaby programs are quite expensive. For example, an infant reading "kit" costs about $80.00 and a two- or three-day workshop on teaching infants to read can cost parents upwards of $300.00. The programs are said to be based on notions derived from studies that show that severely deprived environments can delay development, which, in turn, can be overcome by extra perceptual and sensory stimulation (White, 1967; White & Held, 1966). With the influx of knowledge on the newborn's sensory and perceptual abilities, a topic which is currently enjoying extensive coverage in popular magazines and newspapers, many parents are feeling pressured to continually stimulate their baby's senses and provide him with as many experiences as possible and as early in life as possible. One question that arises is, can infants actually develop at a faster rate if they are "taught" to master skills. The answer to this question becomes evident in the next section, for it is shown there that while extreme deprivation can indeed deter the infant's growth and development, beyond the amount of environmental stimulation needed for normal development, no amount of learning will speed up the maturation process.

Even assuming that some infants can be encouraged to develop faster, is that so important that parents should spend money and change their caretaking patterns to accommodate to claims that babies can and should develop faster? Certainly, the infant should not be deprived of stimulation. Thus, the question is not whether stimulation is or is not important. Instead, the question is, in what amounts and in what ways should stimulation be provided? Most parents who care about their infants are likely to play with them, and to give them toys and also periods of undivided attention during the day. Beyond the stimulating experiences that the infant receives naturally, some researchers contend that overstimulation is

FIGURE 4.6   Can infants develop at a faster rate if they are "taught" to master skills? Beyond the amount of environmental stimulation needed for normal development, no amount of learning will speed up the maturation process.

not only of no value, but it may actually harm the infant. Bower (1977) contends that overstimulation could cause the baby to become temporarily withdrawn, even though the infant himself has the capacity to regulate the amount of stimulation he can cope with. In studies by other researchers (e.g., White & Held, 1966), it was also found that whereas some babies, notably those who had been deprived of an enriched environment,

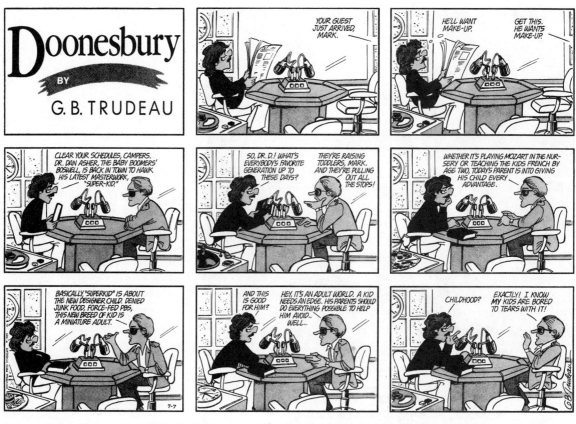

Doonesbury, Copyright 1985, G. B. Trudeau. Reprinted with permission of Universal Press Syndicate. All rights reserved.

can benefit from stimulation, an overly stimulating surrounding is unnecessary for most infants who may become confused and irritated if they receive too much stimulation. So the best guide for parents and infants is simply to have a good time together (McCall, 1980) and for parents not to worry about exercising their baby's reflexes or stimulating his senses, as physical development will usually take care of itself.

An additional point to note is that not all activities are equally stimulating to all infants. In a study on individual differences at birth, Korner (1971) found that infants differed in how much they cried, how soothable they were, and how capable they were of self-comforting behavior. She also found that infants differed in their capacity to take in and synthesize sensory stimuli. Some infants have a low sensory threshold. Such infants are likely to cry excessively during the first few months of life. They tend to become overwhelmed and overstimulated unless the caretaker can act as a shield and tension-reducing agent. In contrast, there are infants who have high sensory thresholds to all sensory stimuli. They are infants who, for optimal development, require a great deal of stimulation. On the basis

Learning in the Womb

Having established that babies are capable of responding to their environment immediately after birth, and that they can even recognize and show preference for their mother's voice, researchers have been intrigued with the questions: Why do infants come into the world so skilled? and Do they learn in the womb? A relatively new body of research suggests that indeed learning may begin even before birth.

Among those who are studying fetal learning are Anthony DeCasper and his associates. They hypothesize that since the fetus in the womb hears the mother's stomach noises, her heartbeat, and her voice, the newborn baby would have a preference for these sounds right after birth. To test this hypothesis, they have devised a study in which babies were given a nipple to suck. The nipple was attached to a tape recorder, so that by sucking in one pattern of longer and shorter sucks the babies would hear their mother's voice. By sucking in a different way, they would hear some other recording, say another woman's voice or their father's voice. In a series of such studies (described by Kolata, 1984), researchers found that babies sucked so as to hear their mother's voice.

In a follow-up study, the researchers had 16 pregnant women read part of the children's book *The Cat in the Hat*. The women, who were in the last 6½ weeks of their pregnancy, read to their fetus the same part of the book twice a day for a total of 5 hours. When the babies were born, the researchers used their sucking test and found that the babies sucked so as to hear a recording of their mother's reading of *The Cat in the Hat* as opposed to hearing a recording of the mother's reading of the book *The King, the Mice and the Cheese,* which is quite different in tone. This type of study suggests that babies may be influenced by their prenatal experiences.

Of course, no conclusions may be drawn on the basis of the research done so far. However, these types of studies, along with studies using animals, will eventually help in our understanding of how early in life infants can be conditioned. Such studies on fetal learning offer researchers the opportunity to understand the functional organization of the brain prior to birth and may eventually help psychologists and neurologists to assess and facilitate the development of some babies, especially those who are born prematurely and whose brains may be underdeveloped.

of her studies as well as other research, Korner proposes that the low-high sensory threshold is a personality characteristic that persists beyond infancy. For example, Honzik (1964) describes children who differ in their reactions to the environment. They are, in her terms, *reactive-expressive* to new situations, or they are *retractive-inhibitive*. Honzik notes that this personality characteristic is persistent throughout childhood and adolescence. Thomas and his colleagues (1963) also found a strong persistence in children's tendency to seek out new stimuli or to withdraw from new situations. Kagan (1965) notes that some children respond quickly and impulsively to problems or situations that arise, whereas others respond reflectively and with caution.

These studies suggest that there are clear-cut and extreme differences in how individuals deal with stimulation and excitement. Differences in responsivity to and synthesis of external stimuli are, in all likelihood, an expression of neurophysiological makeup (Korner, 1971). This means that there is no one way of providing a good environment for the infant. In fact, the only good way to provide an environment that will promote optimal development is to respond to the individual requirements of each infant.

PHYSICAL GROWTH AND MOTOR DEVELOPMENT

Physical Growth

Another amazing aspect of the growth and development of infants is their rapid rate of physical development. Physical growth occurs so rapidly during infancy that by the time the infant approaches his second birthday, parents wonder if he really ever was as small and dependent as the tiny baby they brought home from the hospital. You should keep in mind that although all infants grow rapidly, there are individual differences among infants in their rates of growth. Some babies evidence steady growth whereas others seem to grow in spurts (Lampl & Emde, 1983).

Immediately after birth infants lose weight, but after the first few days of life they start to gain weight, and weight gain during the first few months of life is substantial (Eichorn, 1979). On the average, infants double their birth weight by the time they reach the age of four months, and by the time they are two years of age, they have quadrupled their birth weight. Substantial gains also occur in length (height); infants more than double their length by the time they are two years old.

Growth during infancy is not merely a matter of gain in weight and height. Because different parts of the body grow at different rates, the baby's body proportions change as he grows older. Changes in proportion are most evident in the size of the head in relation to the total body (see Figure 4.7). The newborn has a disproportionately large head which is about one quarter of his overall length. As the baby grows, the head

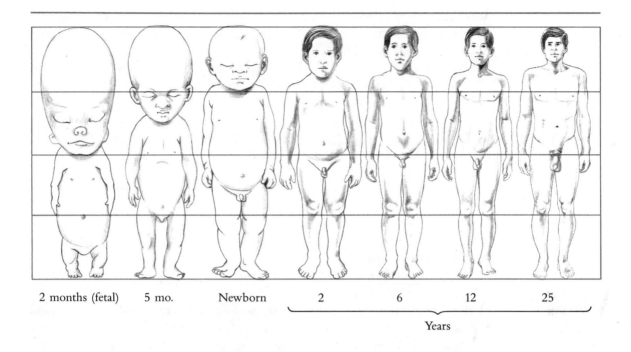

2 months (fetal)   5 mo.   Newborn   2   6   12   25

Years

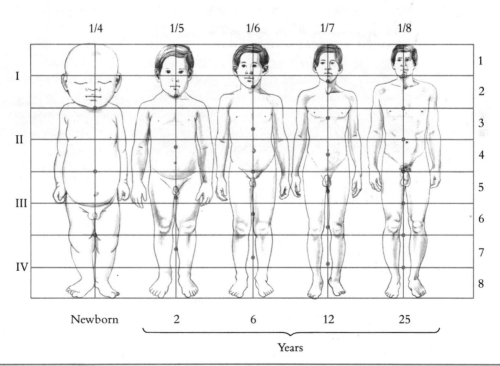

FIGURE 4.7   Changes in body proportions. In the newborn, the length of the head is approximately one fourth of the total length of the body. In the adult, it is only one eighth. Conversely, the legs are comparatively shorter in the baby than in the adult. Adapted from "Contrasting characteristics of prenatal and post natal life," p. 283. Reprinted with permission of Macmillan Publishing Company from *Developmental Physiology and Aging* by Paola S. Timiras. Copyright © 1972 by Paola S. Timiras.

becomes proportionately smaller. By the end of the first year of life, the head is one fifth of the infant's height, and during adulthood it is one eighth of the adult's height. Similar proportional changes can be seen in legs. Newborns have short legs which account for only a small part of their overall height, whereas adults' legs account for about half their height.

ossification

Other aspects of physical growth during infancy include the continuation of *ossification* (hardening of the bones, a process that began during the prenatal period) and skeletal growth. The infant's legs and arms grow stronger and also longer, enabling him to acquire new skills. For example, the newborn's legs are bent and fragile, and they are not strong enough to support the body in an upright position. However, toward the end of the first year of life the infant's legs straighten and become increasingly stronger, so that by the age of 15 months, most infants are able not only to stand, but also to walk unassisted.

cephalocaudal sequence

Two principles govern physical growth. The first is that growth occurs in what is referred to as a *cephalocaudal sequence,* that is, from head to toe. Thus the head develops first, and then the rest of the body. This pattern of growth is followed even before birth; in the fetus, the head forms first, then arm buds appear, then the leg buds. Similarly, facial muscles are present before other muscles in the body. During infancy, the cephalocaudal pattern of growth is evident in the fact that the head is much larger than the rest of the body. Growth also occurs on the basis of

proximodistal direction

a *proximodistal direction,* that is, development first occurs at the center of the body, and then at the extremities. For this reason, the baby's arms are small in proportion to the trunk of the body, which develops faster than the arms. The baby's hands and fingers are also small in proportion to his arms, again, because the arms, being closer to the center of the body than the fingers, develop first (see Figure 4.8).

The Brain

One of the most important aspects of physical development during infancy is the changes in the brain. Although brain development is an important aspect of physical growth, it has far-reaching implications for psychological development, for the brain is the basis of intellectual functioning. The more mature the brain is, the more capable is the infant of understanding and acting upon the environment and of communicating with others.

Our understanding of the human brain has increased substantially in recent years as researchers have systematically mapped out the structure and growth of the brain, relating this to changes in human behavior. You recall that considerable brain growth occurs while the fetus is still in the uterus. Thus, the baby is born with neural apparatus which permits a great deal of behavior. Brain growth is not complete at birth, but contin-

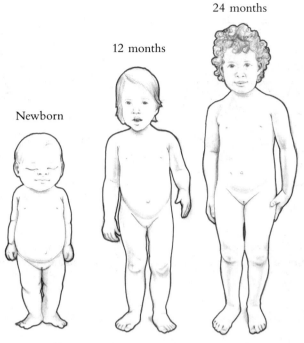

24 months

12 months

Newborn

Cephalocaudal growth

Proximodistal growth

FIGURE 4.8 Cephalocaudal (head to toe) and proximodistal (from the center to the extremities) growth patterns.

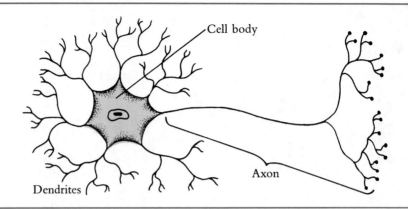

FIGURE 4.9   The nerve cell. Unlike other cells in the body, the cytoplasm in neurons, or nerve cells, is drawn out into dendrites and axons, which receive and send impulses.

ues for six months thereafter at a very rapid rate, which accounts for the rapid behavioral development of the infant (Tanner, 1978). Brain growth continues after that age, although at a slower rate, and by the time the infant is 2 years old, the brain attains 75 percent of its adult weight.

neurons

neuralgia or glial cells

The human brain, when exposed, looks rather like a walnut (refer to Figure 3.8). Like other organs, it is made up of cells. Two kinds of cells make up the brain. *Neurons,* or nerve cells, receive and send impulses, or signals. *Neuralgia,* also called *glial cells,* feed and support the nerve cells. During the prenatal period, and until the baby is six months old, brain cells increase in number at a very rapid rate. After that period, there occur other changes that account for brain maturation.

dendrites
axons

Each nerve cell, or neuron, consists of a cell body, a nucleus, and a cytoplasm, much as other cells in the body are constructed. However, in neurons, the cytoplasm is drawn out into very large numbers of fine, wire-like processes called *dendrites* and *axons* (see Figure 4.9). Dendrites and axons themselves have many branches which connect with other branches that come off of other cells. The function of dendrites is to receive the impulses, whereas the function of axons is to send impulses. These impulses, or messages, are transmitted through the axons and dendrites by tiny chemicals. The "connectivity" of the neurons, that is, the number of connections the axons and dendrites make with other cells, account for the functional maturity of the brain, governing even the most basic and simple of all actions. Any of our actions, even those such as a baby's picking up a toy or your picking up a pencil, may take only a fraction of a second, but they can occur only on the basis of numerous messages that travel from the eyes, to the brain, to the hand.

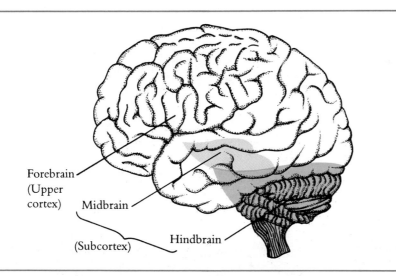

Forebrain (Upper cortex)

Midbrain

(Subcortex)   Hindbrain

FIGURE 4.10   The hierarchy of the brain. The brainstem, which is made up of the hindbrain and the midbrain, matures earlier than the forebrain, which is associated with higher mental functions.

Different parts of the brain mature at different times. Think of the brain as having three layers: the forebrain, the midbrain, and the hindbrain (see Figure 4.10). The forebrain is known as the *upper cortex* and the midbrain and hindbrain, often referred to as the *subcortex,* make up the brainstem. Connecting the brainstem to the rest of the body is the spinal cord which carries fibers from the brain to connect with muscles or sense organs in other parts of the body. This entire system is the *central nervous system.*

First to develop and achieve maturity are the hindbrain and midbrain. Thus, for the first few months of the baby's life, behavior is controlled by the subcortical centers of the brain. The hindbrain, which controls vegetative functions such as breathing, is mature at birth. The midbrain, which controls emotions, state of arousal, reflexes, and vision, is somewhat mature at birth, but does not achieve full maturity for several months thereafter. The forebrain, or upper cortex, however, which is responsible for much of our intellectual behavior, speech, and motor coordination, is immature and hardly functional at birth. During the first six months of life, however, the upper cortex undergoes rapid development. Its neurons increase in number, size, and in their connectedness. After the newborn period, behavior becomes not a function of the subcortical brain, as was the case in the infant's initial repertoire of reflexes when movement was involuntary, but rather, of the upper cortex. The baby's developing capacity to control movement, as described in the next section, is evidence of the fact that after the first few months of life, behavior comes to be a function of the maturing cortex.

upper cortex
subcortex

central nervous system

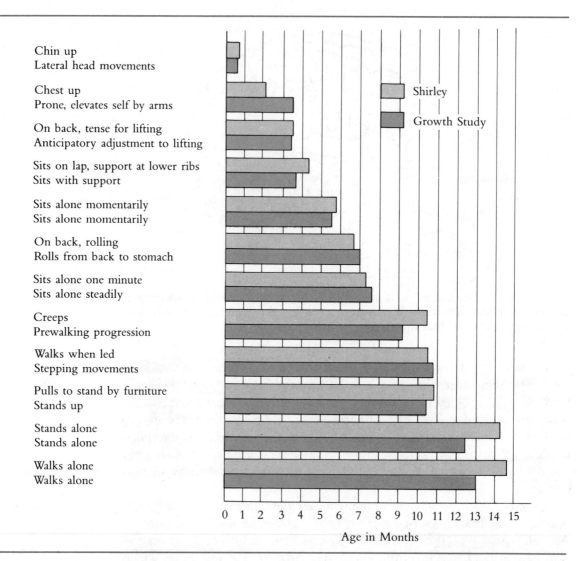

FIGURE 4.11 Milestones in motor development during infancy. Adapted from "The development of motor abilities during the first three years," by N. Bayley (1936). *Monographs of the Society for Research in Child Development,* vol. 1, no. 1. Washington, D.C.: Society for Research in Child Development, National Research Council, p. 16, Fig. 4.

Motor Development

Infants not only experience rapid changes in physical growth during the first two years of life, they also acquire greater use of their muscular movement. *Motor* is the term that is used to denote muscular movement, and motor development is the process through which the child acquires movement patterns and skills.

There is a definite order in the acquisition of motor skills, proceeding from the simple to the complex (see Figure 4.11). Initially, movement in the newborn baby is involuntary reflex action, and the newborn has an impressive number of reflexes, many of which disappear as the cortex matures. Brain maturation, and also increases in strength that occur during infancy, eventually allow the baby to exhibit more control over a variety of differentiated movements. These new abilities are then integrated into more complex behavior patterns. For example, the baby's control over the separate movements of legs, feet, and arms is eventually integrated into walking. This integration of individual abilities into a complex behavior has been termed by Werner (1948) *hierarchic integration*.

hierarchic integration   X

Walking

Motor development also follows a cephalocaudal and proximodistal pattern. Thus a baby will first learn to lift his head, and sometime later to sit up and eventually, to stand. To illustrate the sequential order of motor development, we will examine two skills, walking and grasping. Independent walking is a major motor accomplishment during infancy. For the infant the ability to walk is important, for walking is the foundation upon which other motor skills develop or are learned (Malina, 1982). The ability to walk allows the child to develop new and more rapid means of locomotion (e.g., running), and it also frees the hands from their role as supports, so the infant can experiment with a variety of manipulative skills.

The developmental changes that lead to walking are essentially a series of postural changes through which the infant gains the control necessary for maintaining an upright posture. The general sequence of developmental changes that lead to walking are described in detail by Shirley (1933) among others, and can be seen in Figure 4.12 on page 210. The sequence begins with head and trunk control, which eventually lead to the ability of the infant to roll over, sit up with support and without support, crawl, stand, climb stairs, and walk.

It is important to note that this sequence of motor development is universal. However, the age during which a particular skill emerges will vary from child to child. Thus, some infants can walk at one year of age and others at fifteen months. Of course, walking is a milestone in the development of the baby, and many parents are anxious for the infant to begin to walk. In fact, so much importance is attached to walking that many parents equate early walking with superior intelligence. However, the age at which walking begins is of no importance developmentally, and it is not an indication of how intelligent an infant is.

Grasping

Another important motor sequence that develops during infancy is grasping. Grasping begins as a reflex, but in the newborn period, it is not a true grasp, because only the fingers and not the thumb are involved. In fact, one of the most exciting events that adults experience in the proximity of

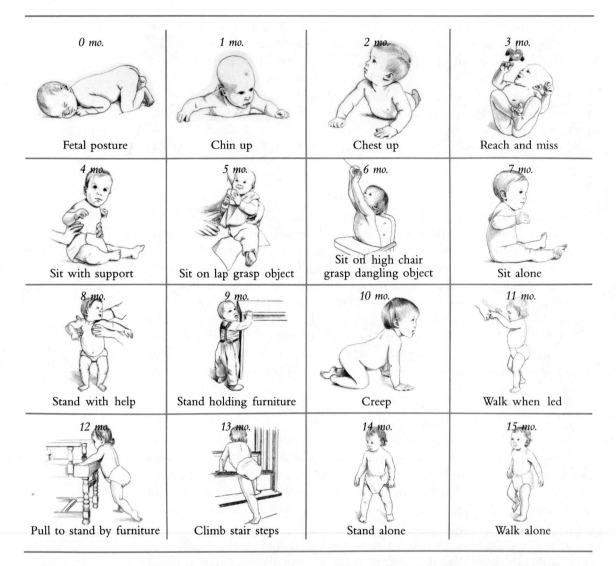

FIGURE 4.12 Postural changes that lead to walking. Adapted from *The First Two Years: A Study of Twenty-Five Babies,* by Mary M. Shirley, vol. 2, Fig. 1, frontispiece. University of Minnesota Press, Minneapolis. Copyright © 1933 by the University of Minnesota.

the newborn baby is his grasp. When an adult touches the newborn's fingers, the newborn will grasp the adult's finger and hold onto that finger with amazing strength. Even though it is just a reflex action, many adults are very touched by the experience.

As the baby grows, he is able to extend his arms, and he often extends his arms toward objects, although at first he cannot coordinate between sight and touch. Eventually, at about three months of age, the infant reaches and attempts to grasp any object nearby, hence infants that age reach for the face, mouth, or glasses of adults around them. At first, however, the infant does not have as much control over his movements,

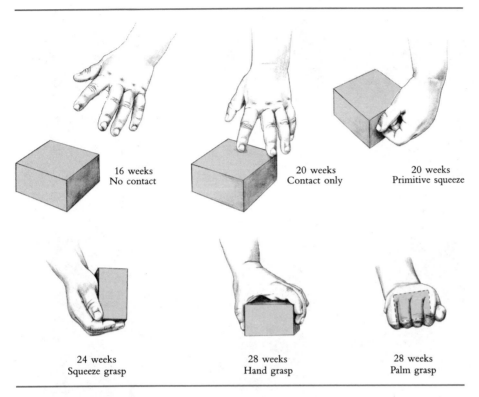

16 weeks
No contact

20 weeks
Contact only

20 weeks
Primitive squeeze

24 weeks
Squeeze grasp

28 weeks
Hand grasp

28 weeks
Palm grasp

FIGURE 4.13 The sequence of motor abilities that leads to grasping. Adapted from Halverson, H. M. (1931). "An experimental study of prehension in infants by means of systematic cinema records." *Genetic Psychology Monographs,* Vol. X, Nos. 2–3, pp. 212–213.

so he often misses objects. Eventually, however, he can reach for and grasp an object, first with the palm of the hand, as shown in Figures 4.13 and 4.14, then with fingers. In the final stage, grasping occurs with fingers and thumb surrounding the object, and the infant can pick up the object.

Both walking and grasping enable the child to achieve active locomotion and manipulation of objects so that over the course of the first two years of life, the infant becomes increasingly more able to manipulate his environment in a variety of different ways.

Maturation

You can see that there are orderly and stable changes that occur in physical growth, in neural development, and in motor ability. Thus, physical development is said to be a function of maturation. Maturation refers to the

FIGURE 4.14 Grasping enables the infant to manipulate objects and, therefore, to manipulate his environment in a variety of ways.

orderly physiological changes in the organism over time. The sequentiality and universality of the maturational process is impressive. It characterizes all species and appears to be the result of the genetic blueprint.

Since maturation follows such an orderly sequence, it is sometimes defined as a series of changes that occur independent of learning. This brings us again to the nature-nurture question. Is development a matter of maturation, or is it influenced by environmental factors? In many respects, physical development is a function of maturation as bodily growth and the development of motor skills are biologically determined. However, it is important to keep in mind two points. One, some environmental input is necessary to stimulate normal physiological and neural development. For example, when chimpanzees are raised in the dark, the neural cells in their retinas fail to develop normally and the animals' vision is permanently impaired (Riesen, 1947, 1958). Two, provided that the environmental stimulation is at least the minimum needed, the rate of physiological development cannot be altered much. No amount of training will ever enable a three-month-old infant to walk or a one-year-old child to talk in complete sentences, a fact which parents should keep in mind in their desire for superbabies (Gottlieb, 1983).

Influences on Motor Development

Several classic studies related to the acquisition of motor skills illustrate the two points just presented. Dennis and Dennis (1940) studied infants of the Hopi Indians. Some of these infants were reared in the traditional Hopi manner, that is, they were placed on cradleboards and swaddled so that they could not move their hands and legs. Other Hopi infants were not placed on cradleboards, rather they were allowed the freedom to move their arms and legs. There were no differences in the age during which both groups of infants began to walk, and the average age at which infants in both groups walked was 15 months. This study alerts us to the fact that maturation, for the most part, governs the acquisition of motor skills.

However, other studies illustrate that whereas maturation is important, environmental stimulation is also necessary for the acquisition of motor skills, even though this stimulation does not necessarily have to be related to motor development. In a description of the development of infants in several Iranian orphanages, Dennis (1960) notes that in two of those orphanages the infants were extremely retarded in their motor development. In these orphanages, there was not a sufficient number of caretakers, so the infants spent most of their time lying on their backs in a crib. They drank from propped bottles; they were never placed in different positions, taken out of their cribs, or played with. At age 2, or later, the infants were taken out of their cribs and placed on the floor, usually in a sitting position, but, again, they were not given any toys, and caretakers did not spend time with them. Because the ratio of caretakers to infants was about 1 to 8, there was not enough time for each caretaker to care for as well as play with each infant. In contrast to these children, infants in another institution showed normal levels of motor development. In that institution there were more caretakers and they were given training in child development. The infants in these institutions were held more frequently by adult caretakers; they were held while they were fed; and they were placed in different positions. At 4 months, these infants were occasionally placed in playpens, and they had access to a variety of toys.

Dennis obtained similar findings when he studied infants in Lebanese orphanages. He notes that in some orphanages in Lebanon, infants were not receiving sufficient attention from their caretakers and were retarded in the acquisition of motor and other skills (Dennis, 1973).

The extreme levels of environmental deprivation experienced by the infants in the orphanages are rare, but they provide a dramatic example of the vital role played by the environment in the emergence and development of motor skills. The experientially deprived infants did eventually develop motor skills but at a much later age than the other infants.

FIGURE 4.15   An African baby in a dashiki and an American baby being carried on his father's back. Carried in an erect position, babies learn to keep their heads steady and they have ample opportunities for experiential stimulation.

Additional evidence on the importance of environmental factors in the acquisition of motor skills is provided by studies on blind infants and by cross-cultural studies that point to cultural differences in motor development. Fraiberg (1977) notes that when blind infants, whose motor development is generally severely slowed, were exposed to sound as a means by which they could identify objects and people (e.g., they were given toys that made sound; their mothers talked to them when approaching or while dressing them), they acquired motor skills earlier than did blind infants in a control group who did not receive the intervention.

Researchers note, too, that the acquisition of motor skills varies in different cultures. Newborn African infants, for example, are more precocious in motor development. Geber and Dean (1957), in a study of Ugandan, European, and Indian infants, all of whom were born in Africa, found that the Ugandan infants had superior muscle tone and could turn their heads from side to side and raise their heads before the other infants could. They were also more advanced in other motor skills such as sitting without support, standing upright, and walking. However, as Geber (1962) notes, this precocity lasts only until the age of 18 to 20 months at which time the level of motor development of Ugandan infants is the same as that of the other infants.

Some genetic differences may be responsible for the precocity in motor development found among the Ugandan infants (Bayley, 1965), but the differences may also be attributable to differences in child care methods. African mothers, for example, carry their newborn babies on their backs in a *dashiki,* which provides support for the infant's head so that the baby is in an erect position and learns to keep his head steady (see Figure 4.15). In addition, the babies are carried everywhere in this erect position; thus they have ample opportunities for experiential stimulation. They can see different things, they are able to hear their parents and others talk, and so forth. These examples illustrate the interplay among sensory and motor systems. You will see in the next chapter that these aspects of development also have implications for cognitive development.

SUMMARY

Physical growth and motor development occur at a very rapid rate during infancy, as the infant quadruples his birth weight by the time he reaches the age of two years, and he more than doubles his height. The infant also acquires a number of motor skills during the first two years of life and)also more control over his motor movement due to brain maturation. Thus he is able to have greater locomotion, and he is also able to manipulate the environment in a number of different ways. Physical growth and development follow a predictable and orderly sequence that is largely governed by maturation. However, environmental stimulation is necessary for optimal development. This becomes especially evident in the acquisition of motor skills during infancy. As studies of infants in orphanages show, infants who are left alone in their cribs and who do not receive even minimal adult contact are extremely retarded in their motor development. The same is true of blind infants, who are delayed in their acquisition of motor skills unless they receive stimulating experiences that enable them to identify objects and persons by sound.

While the infant makes tremendous progress in physical growth and the acquisition of motor skills, we have seen that he is born with an impressive number of skills. The surge of infancy research over the past few years has enabled researchers to document the facts that the infant can hear, see, touch, taste, and smell, beginning at the first day of life. The "new" capabilities of the newborn infant are highlighted in the popular media, thus parents are pressured to provide stimulating and enriching experiences to the baby at a younger and younger age, in their quest for a superbaby. The notion behind the baby gym classes and infant reading programs—both part of the superbaby trend—is based on the research which attests to the importance of early experience. However, while a certain amount of environmental stimulation is indeed important, beyond the amount needed for optimal development, the genetic blueprint for growth probably cannot be altered much.

REVIEW POINTS

1. The arrival of the newborn baby is an overwhelming event for the parents as well as the baby. Parents have to get to know the baby and ascertain when and whether he is content or discontent, and the baby has to adjust to life outside the womb.

2. The human baby is dependent on adult care and must be fed, pacified, cleaned, and protected. Although the period of dependency for the human newborn is longer than that for any other species, the infant is competent in a number of ways. He has available to him a number of reflexes which ensure his survival. Some of these reflexes remain, but others disappear by the time the infant is 2–3 months old as higher brain functioning and learning provide the baby with new responses needed for interaction with the environment.

3. The baby's ability to respond with reflex action is dependent upon his state, a term which refers to whether the baby is asleep or awake. Infant states are predictable and organized. However, there are individual differences among infants in general, and also variations in how much time infants spend in each state, some babies requiring more sleep than others. Infant state is also related to the extent that the infant is in an alert, quiet state that is conducive to learning, or in a crying state.

4. At one time it was thought that the newborn infant exists in a world that is confusing and overwhelming. Researchers now know that the baby has amazing sensory and perceptual skills. From the moment of birth the infant can hear, see, smell, and taste, and he responds to touch. The research on infant sensory and perceptual development is as yet new, so researchers are not guided by an overall theory on the infant's capabilities. However, having developed research techniques that facilitate the study of infants, researchers are nearing the time when such theory will be forthcoming.

5. Parents are as intrigued as researchers are with the capabilities of newborn infants and they have been pressured by books and news reports to teach their babies such skills as reading. Parents are encouraged by the erroneous notion that the faster a skill is mastered, the more intelligent the individual must be. However, each infant has an optimal level of environmental stimulation necessary for normal development. Beyond this optimal level of stimulation, infants will not necessarily benefit from extra stimulation. Indeed, some infants may find an overly stimulating environment confusing and may become irritated by it. Parents are advised simply to have a good time with their baby, playing together when he seems to enjoy doing so and letting him rest when he seems to want to rest.

6. Another amazing aspect of infant development is the rapid physical and motor growth that occurs during the first two years of life. Physical and motor development occur in a predictable and orderly sequence, although the rate of development varies from infant to infant, with some infants learning to walk earlier than others.

7. Motor development occurs as a function of brain growth. As the brain cells increase in number, size, and in their connectedness, the infant's motor activities become less a matter of involuntary reflex movement, as is true of the first two or three months of life. Gradually the infant acquires more control over his actions.

8. Several classic studies on the acquisition of motor skills reveal that whereas maturation is important, some environmental stimulation is also necessary. Infants who are severely deprived of experiences and who are not picked up, held, and talked to frequently are more retarded in their development than are other infants. However, as with other aspects of development, beyond the amount of stimulation needed for optimal development, the genetic blueprint for growth and for the acquisition of motor skills probably cannot be altered much.

CHAPTER 5

COGNITIVE AND LANGUAGE DEVELOPMENT IN INFANCY

As researchers are finding out, infants are more complex and responsive organisms than was realized previously. Even at birth they have sensory and perceptual skills through which they gather information about their world, which in turn enables them to develop still more complex skills. Not only do infants possess the ability to gather information about their environment, they are also capable of organized intellectual behavior and, over the relatively short period of the first two years of life, they accumulate a vast amount of knowledge, including the ability to understand and speak the language they hear.

In this chapter we examine what infants understand about the world they are born into, and how that understanding develops. You will see that researchers have made significant strides in their ability to study cognitive and language development and in their understanding of the mental and linguistic skills of infants. Nevertheless, there exists a great deal of controversy surrounding these topics. Most of the controversy stems from the nature-nurture issue regarding the role of heredity and the environment in development. The question is, how do babies acquire the ability to think, or to talk, through maturation or through experience?

Most child development professionals agree now that both heredity and the environment are important and that maturation and experience work together in the process of growth and development. Some disagree, however, over the relative importance of each. Specifically, researchers are at odds over the answers to such questions as: will infants learn on their own as long as there is a sufficiently stimulating environment for them or do they need to be taught? What is a good environment that is conducive to the infant's cognitive development? The answers to these questions are not only of theoretical interest, they are of practical concern as well. Many infants whose parents work spend a large portion of their day in day care centers or family day care homes. Are the experiences infants receive in such settings, where they are taken care of not individually but in groups, conducive to their mental growth? What are the effects on cognitive development of being raised in group care? Additional concerns arise from recent claims that have been made that parents should take advantage of the infant's powerful desire to learn and that they should teach their infant to read or accomplish other academic tasks, thereby not only giving her a head start in life, but also increasing her intellectual potential. Is there any scientific evidence to support the claim that infants can and indeed that they should be taught academic skills? Is there any evidence that points to the fact that an individual's intellectual potential can be increased? Before we try to sort out the facts and myths surrounding the various claims that have been made regarding these questions, we will take a look at some of the research that has been done which demonstrates the infant's interest in the environment and her amazing ability to learn from her experiences.

COGNITIVE DEVELOPMENT

Perceiving the World

No matter which position they take on the relative importance of heredity or the environment in development, researchers are impressed with the infant's ability to learn and with her delight in learning. Recall from the previous chapter that even as a newborn, the infant utilizes her motor, sensory, and perceptual skills to gather information about the world. The infant is no longer viewed as a helpless entity incapable of anything except crying, feeding, and sleeping. She is seen, rather, as a competent and interested individual who actively attends to various aspects of the environment, learning and remembering as she does so about people, objects, and events—how they look, how they feel, and how they react to her.

The research on the sensory and perceptual skills of the infant comes under the heading of infant perceptual development which is, in the words of one cognitive development expert, "one of the 'hottest' areas in developmental psychology, thanks largely to the invention of research methods that made it possible to assess the perceptual abilities and dispositions of even very young infants" (Flavell, 1985). Of course, babies cannot tell us what they perceive. However, researchers have been able to make inferences about infants' perceptions from such nonverbal behaviors as sucking, head turning, and looking and from physiological responses such as the heart rate.

Flavell (1985) notes that there have been two major movements in the relatively short history of infant perceptual development research. The first, which received its impetus from the pioneering work of Robert Fantz (1961) has generated the studies described in the previous chapter which have shown that at birth, infants are capable of seeing, hearing, smelling, tasting, and that they have a sense of touch. Some of these senses are immature at birth when compared with the same senses slightly later in infancy, but they evidence the fact that babies are born ready to interact with the environment.

The second movement was initiated by Eleanor and James Gibson (1969) who study higher-order perceptual processes, that is, infants' ability to perceive objects, people, events, and places they encounter. These researchers are interested in what infants perceive from the information the senses provide them. For example, infants can hear and they are known to prefer the sound of the human voice, but do they also know that the voice they hear is part of a configuration of eyes, mouth, and nose that make up the face of the individual talking to them? If they reach for objects, do they know anything at all about the objects? Answers to these questions are important not only because they alert us to the abilities of babies, but also because they enhance our understanding about the nature of knowledge.

Object Perception

Some studies on perceptual development have been designed to find out whether the ways in which the human infant structures her world are innate or learned. One such series of studies is related to the perception of objects. The world of the infant is full of different objects of different shapes, sizes, colors, and textures. Do infants notice these differences and are they aware that an object is a distinct, bounded entity separate from other aspects of the environment? What do infants know about objects? In a review of studies on object perception, Spelke (1982) suggests that over the course of the first two years of life and as they have experience touching and exploring objects, infants acquire knowledge about the characteristics and properties of objects, and the fact that objects exist as separate entities. However, even at three months of age, infants have the knowledge that an object exists as a unitary, bounded entity, separate and distinct from other objects and surfaces around it. By four months of age, infants evidence the fact that they may perceive certain properties of objects. They adjust their reaching according to the spatial properties of objects and they are more likely to reach for an object that is suspended close to them than one that is suspended farther away (see Figure 5.1). Also, they attempt to reach for a large object in a different way than they attempt to reach for a small object. Given findings from numerous such studies, Spelke (1982) suggests that infants may be born with organizing principles which enable them to perceive objects, and that these unlearned principles are subsequently used to acquire more information about objects.

Memory

As we noted in the previous chapter, the studies on perceptual development are not as yet integrated into a consistent theory and they are, as yet, subject to various interpretations. However, the studies clearly demonstrate that the infant is able to attend to various aspects of the environment, and also to learn from it.

The studies on perception in infancy also demonstrate that the infant can remember her experiences. This point is implicit in the previous chapter where it is shown that infants are not only capable of smelling or hearing, for example, they can also remember the smell of their mother's breast and the sound of her voice.

The study of memory in infancy is very recent, so at present, there are more questions than answers as researchers attempt to ascertain how and when memory develops and how infant memory is similar to or different from the memory of older children and adults. Nevertheless, numerous recent studies have yielded exciting findings which serve to unravel some of the mystery that has surrounded the topic in the past. Researchers have

FIGURE 5.1 During the course of the first two years of life, the baby looks at, touches, or otherwise explores the objects around her. She acquires knowledge of the characteristics and properties of different objects, learning that objects are bounded entities, separate from other aspects of the environment.

found, for instance, that even babies as young as 2 to 4 weeks retain the knowledge about a stimulus they have learned. This was demonstrated by Ungerer, Brody, and Zelazo (1978) who had the mothers of babies that age repeat (in front of the babies) the same word 60 times a day for 13 days. By the end of this period, the babies evidenced their recognition of the word by widening and moving their eyes when they heard the word.

The researchers point out that familiarity is a key aspect of the memory of young infants. That is, the infants were able to remember only highly familiar words, such as those repeated 60 times a day. They did not remember other words such as their own names, that were not subjected to such intensive repetition. Other researchers concur that familiarity is important. Rose (1981) and Fagan (1973) found that babies are more likely to remember photographs of human faces than they remember photographs of abstract patterns, perhaps because they are more familiar with human faces than they are with patterns. Researchers note further that babies are more likely to remember some aspects of a stimulus than they are others. In testing the memory of 5-month-old infants, Strauss and Cohen (1980) found that when the babies were given the opportunity to study a stimulus with multiple aspects, they remembered the shape of the stimulus for 24 hours, but its color for only 15 minutes. The researchers suggest that the shape of the stimulus is a more important cue to its identity than is its color—at least to a 5-month-old infant.

productive memory

Are infants capable of productive memory? *Productive memory* involves remembering an event or stimulus experienced previously, without the reappearance of that event or stimulus. In the studies that have been cited so far, researchers ascertained that infants can remember something they have seen or heard after they were reintroduced to it. It is difficult to ascertain if infants can remember in absence of the event or stimulus being reintroduced, since productive memory is usually tested on the basis of verbal recall. Ashmead and Perlmutter (1984) asked parents to keep a record of instances which revealed memory behaviors in infants aged 7 to 11 months. The parents did record instances of productive memory, especially in the case of the older infants. For example, one baby kept looking at the side of her changing table one day and looked puzzled, as if searching for something she couldn't find. Usually, a bottle of baby lotion was placed there and she may have remembered that fact because her eyes brightened when her mother showed her the baby lotion which was apparently placed elsewhere on that one occasion.

Learning

That babies perceive their world and can remember their experiences is one aspect of the research on the amazing mental capabilities of the infant. Another aspect of the research is related to infant learning in which researchers study infants in experimental conditions to discover how early in life and under what conditions learning occurs.

Classical and Operant Conditioning.   Two types of learning have been investigated with infants: classical conditioning and operant conditioning. In *classical conditioning,* which was demonstrated by Ivan Pavlov's experiments with dogs early this century, an individual can be taught, or conditioned, to make a response. Noting that at the sight of food dogs began to salivate, Pavlov conditioned his dogs to salivate under other circumstances such as at the ringing of a bell. To achieve this, he fed his dogs, and at the same time he also rang a bell. After several such feedings, with the bell ringing each time, the dogs came to associate the bell-ringing with food. Eventually they salivated upon hearing the bell even when no food was given to them. Apparently, the dogs' reflexes had been conditioned to respond to the bell in the same way that they responded to food. In *operant conditioning,* the subject makes a response because she is rewarded for it in some way. This requires that the subject first initiate an action and then experience a consequence for having initiated it. In this way pigeons, rats, and chimpanzees have been trained either to peck at a certain bar or to press or push a certain button in order to get food. In both operant and classical conditioning learning occurs through a series of trials and errors, and learning is more durable after the conditioning itself has ended, depending on the number of trials—the more trials, the more long-lasting the learning.

classical conditioning

operant conditioning

Conditioning the Infant.   Researchers have demonstrated that classical and operant conditioning both are means of learning not only in animals but also in children (learning also occurs through observation and imitation, to be discussed later). How early in life can children be conditioned? In an attempt to answer this question, researchers have studied conditioning to see if it occurs before birth. Although such studies are far from conclusive, there are indications that even before birth the infant can be conditioned. Can newborns be conditioned? Studies on classical conditioning with newborns and young infants provide us with evidence that in some cases newborns and infants can be classically conditioned (Fitzgerald & Brackbill, 1976). However, there are certain prerequisites to successful classical conditioning in infancy: the infant needs to be in an awake-alert state (Clifton, Sigueland, & Lipsitt, 1972) and the interstimulus interval, that is, the time lapse between the conditioned stimulus (in Pavlov's example, the bell) and the unconditioned stimulus (the food) needs to be long enough to allow the infant to process the information. Apparently, the younger the infant, the longer time she needs to process information (Fitzgerald & Brackbill, 1976). The studies that demonstrate classical conditioning in infants are rather controversial, however. Sameroff and Cavanaugh (1979) point out that often these studies cannot be replicated. That is, whenever a study has reported that infants can be conditioned, a second study has failed to yield the same results.

Whereas the results of studies on classical conditioning in early infancy are open to argument, the studies on operant conditioning in early infancy present more clear-cut results that support the view that the young infant's behavior can be changed by experience. These studies show that with a pleasant reinforcement, for instance, a taste they like, infants can be taught to change the way they suck or to turn their heads in a certain sequence. Sameroff (1968) demonstrates that the infant's sucking response (that is, whether she sucks by squeezing the nipple between her tongue and palate or by employing a suction technique) can be modified by giving and withholding milk (the reinforcer).

In yet another classic study, Papousek (1967) employed both classical and operant conditioning to change infants' behavior. This study is significant, for it emphasizes an important principle: learning and maturation are interdependent processes. That is, as the individual gets older, she is more capable of learning than she is earlier in life, a concept we refer to as *learning readiness*. Papousek's study includes infants in a range of ages: newborns, 3-month-old infants, and 5-month-old infants. Using a bell (as a conditioned stimulus) and milk (as the reinforcer), every time the infants turned their heads to one side or another Papousek was able to condition the infants to turn their head to a certain side. He demonstrated not only that learning occurs during early infancy but also that the younger the infant, the more trials are required before the infant can be conditioned. For newborns, an average of 177 trials was needed before they could be said to be conditioned, whereas for the 3-month-old infants, an average of only 42 trials was needed and for the 5-month-old infants, an average of 28 trials.

learning readiness

Observation and Imitation.

Young infants have been found to imitate certain facial expressions. Imitation is an important aspect of learning, especially social learning, as by observing the behaviors of others and imitating them, children acquire many skills. This will become apparent in later chapters especially those that focus on how young children learn to behave in ways that are acceptable in a particular culture.

Through imitation the infant and young child acquire new behaviors. Recall that in operant conditioning the behavior must occur *before* it can be reinforced. In imitation, adults can serve as models which the children imitate so that children add to their repertoire of behaviors. Thus, imitation is considered a means by which an infant and child can be shown and then induced to behave in one way or another.

As with other behaviors in infancy, much of the research on imitation focuses on how early in life babies can imitate. To this end, researchers have been surprised in recent years to find that babies 2 to 3 weeks of age

FIGURES 5.2 and 5.3   Imitation in young infants.

can imitate lip and tongue protrusions (Meltzoff & Moore, 1977; see Figure 5.2) and such facial expressions as those denoting happiness, sadness and surprise (Field, Woodson, Greenberg & Cohen, 1982; see Figure 5.3). However, the topic of how early in life imitation begins is a controversial one. The controversy is not related to whether or not babies have been seen to imitate. Rather, the controversy centers on whether what is being observed by researchers is true imitation. It is not easy to determine whether infants' responses indicate true imitative behaviors because pseudo-imitation can occur. For example, when the examiner says "Ahh" and the infant responds by saying "Ehh," this vocalization is similar to the one the examiner made and may be considered to be in the same class of behaviors, but it is still not an exact imitation. Thus, researchers must be careful to note only instances of exact imitation.

Pseudo-imitation may also occur in the case when the examiner may reinforce a desired behavior, say tongue protrusion, by smiling or hugging the infant. It is difficult for parents in particular to abstain from rewarding the infant in this way. Any time an infant appears to be imitating a behavior, adults seem to be elated (Stern, 1977) and may reinforce the baby who, in fact, may have stumbled on the behavior by chance and was not necessarily imitating the parent.

The topic of early imitation is controversial also because thus far, researchers have only demonstrated that newborns can imitate only those behaviors which they can spontaneously emit. In other words, it has not been established that young infants can actually learn a new behavior or action through imitation. This leads some researchers to note that it is not true imitation. Researchers disagree on this point depending on their theoretical bias. Those who believe that babies are born with well-developed cognitive structures which enable them to acquire more and more information from the environment tend to argue that even though young babies have only been found to imitate actions within their behavioral repertoire, they are indeed exhibiting true imitation. Those researchers who believe that the ability to imitate is not innate, but rather, gradually acquired over the infancy period, tend to argue that these young babies are not imitating because they are not demonstrating their ability to learn new behaviors through imitation.

The Theory of Jean Piaget

The theorist Jean Piaget is one who would adhere to this latter argument. Piaget's thoughts on imitation are discussed later in the chapter. To understand these, it is important to have some background on Piaget's theory and his contributions to our understanding of cognition.

cognition

Cognition is defined as the act of knowing. It includes not only learning and the acquisition of knowledge, but also thinking, imagining, creating, problem solving, and other skills associated with intellectual behavior (Flavell, 1985). Piaget, who was a trained observer, spent countless hours patiently watching, recording, and analyzing the activities and behaviors of his own three children and later other children. From these observations he built what researchers describe as the most comprehensive theory of cognitive development to date (Flavell, 1985; Sternberg, 1984).

Piaget's work has dominated the field of developmental psychology for the past two decades and has given impetus to a large body of the research done on cognition. In recent years, however, researchers have found that Piaget has underestimated the cognitive capabilities of infants and young children, for two major reasons. One, Piaget did not have available to him the innovative experimental techniques which are used to generate the studies (described earlier) on the perceptual capabilities of the infant. Two, Piaget may have underestimated the importance of perceptual learning and its role in cognitive growth (Flavell, 1985). Despite these apparent limitations in his work, however, Piaget's theory continues to be regarded as an important contribution.

In particular, Piaget is noted for his exploration of cognitive growth as a continuous process that begins at birth and continues over four major stages: the sensorimotor, preoperational, concrete operations, and formal operations periods. Each stage is associated with a specific age period: infancy, the preschool years, the school-age years, and adolescence (see Table 5.1).

Each individual, according to Piaget, progresses from one period to the next at her own rate so the age at which a child reaches any of the periods is relatively unimportant. What is important, however, is that

TABLE 5.1   Piaget's stages of cognitive development.

Stage 1: **Sensorimotor** **Period** **(Birth to Age 2)**	During this stage, the infant's interactions with the environment are governed by overt sensory and motor abilities. Thus the infant learns about the world around her by looking at, reaching for, grasping, and sucking objects, gradually acquiring an understanding of them. The infant at this stage does not have the capacity for representational thought—the ability to maintain a mental picture of objects; it is not until age 2 that she is able to do so. Once she acquires this ability, she is able to solve simple problems mentally rather than by trial and error, and she realizes that objects continue to exist even if she cannot see or touch them.
Stage 2: **Preoperational** **Period** **(Age 2 to 7)**	During this stage the child makes significant improvements in her ability for representational thought, and she acquires a symbolic mode of functioning. That is, she is able to understand, create, and use symbols or signs to represent something which is not present. Symbolic functioning is evident in the child's rapid acquisition of language, which is a system of signs used to represent objects and ideas; in her ability to imitate behaviors some time after she has seen them performed; and also in her make-believe play in which she may imaginatively use a variety of toys to represent real objects. Although the preoperational child makes significant advances in these ways, her thinking is still limited. She believes that everyone thinks as she does; she is unable to think of another person's point of view; and she is often swayed by appearances rather than by logic. For example, if she sees a half glass of milk being poured into a short, wide container, and the same amount poured into a large, narrow container, she will assume that one of these containers has more milk, because the containers do not appear to hold an equal volume.
Stage 3: **Concrete** **Operations** **Period** **(Age 7 to 12)**	During this stage, the child is no longer swayed by perceptual appearances, and her thinking becomes increasingly logical. Seeing a half glass of milk being poured into a short, wide container, and into a tall, narrow one, the child knows that the amount of milk has not changed, in part because she is now able to reverse the process to think back to the original half glass of milk. This ability for reversibility of thought enables the child to figure out arithmetic problems and ascertain that if 2 + 2 = 4, then 4 − 2 must equal 2. During this stage the child also acquires the ability to classify objects into groups. She knows, for example, that German shepherds and poodles belong to a class of dogs and also to a higher order class of animals. Furthermore, the child evidences systematic thinking, and she is able to make deductions: if shown Stick A, which is longer than Stick B, and then Stick C, which is shorter than Stick B, she can deduce that A must logically be longer than C without having to compare the two. However, the concrete operational child can think logically only about concrete things.
Stage 4: **Formal** **Operations** **Period** **(Age 12 to 18)**	During the final period of cognitive development, the child acquires the ability to think logically about abstract propositions and things that she has never experienced. She is able to think about hypothetical problems, and she acquires the ability to systematically think about all possible solutions to a particular problem, much as a scientist does. This last stage of cognitive development is not attained by all individuals. Moreover, some individuals evidence the capacity for formal operational thought in some areas but not in other areas, depending on their interest and knowledge. For example, an adolescent who has just purchased a car and is intensely interested in it attempts to find out as much as he can about how the car works, and when the car breaks down he evidences his ability for formal operational thinking by trying to think about all the possible reasons for why the car doesn't work. That same youth, however, may not evidence the same kind of thinking in another area, say school work, which is of no interest to him.

*cognitive
structures*

these periods of mental growth occur in an invariant order; no period is ever skipped and each lays the groundwork for the next. In addition, each of the periods of cognitive development is characterized by different *cognitive structures*. These structures of the mind, according to Piaget, provide the framework of understanding within which the individual can make sense out of the world. The way of understanding the world for a nine-month-old infant, for example, is physical and involves the many ways she explores and manipulates objects—grasping them, mouthing them, and so on. An eight-year-old child's understanding of the world is different and entails, in part, the ability to classify objects. A nine-year-old child, for example, understands that an object may belong to two classes of things simultaneously. That is, a wooden object with four legs and a top may be classified as a table and also as a piece of furniture. The cognitive structures are the means by which information from the environment becomes understood, coded, and remembered.

The significance of Piaget's work lies in the revelation that infants and children not only acquire more knowledge as they grow older, but the way they understand the world and the way that they think actually changes with age. In addition, Piaget is noted for his contribution to our understanding of how infants and children learn about the different aspects of their environment and how they progress in their cognitive growth. A major tenet of Piaget's theory is related to the nature of the human organism, the fact that the individual—an infant, child, or adult—is not a passive recipient of information, but rather, an active organism engaged in the task of acquiring knowledge, constantly exploring the environment in her attempt to understand it. It is through the interaction between the individual and the environment that advances in cognitive ability occur.

To explain the individual's interactions with the environment, Piaget uses the term scheme (in some texts, the word schema, or its plural, schemata, is used instead). Schemes are the strategies by which the infant interacts with the environment. They include sucking, grasping, reaching, and so on. Initially, these schemes are the innate reflexes such as the sucking and grasping reflex. As she grows, the infant uses these schemes in an increasingly more organized way and the schemes eventually become based not on reflex or motor activity, but rather, upon mental representations.

Two inherent tendencies govern the individual's interaction with the environment, which in turn results in the modification of schemes. These two innate tendencies are *organization* and *adaptation*. It is the nature of the individual, explains Piaget, to organize her experiences and to adapt herself to what she has experienced.

organization

adaptation

In organizing her experiences, the individual integrates two or more schemes into a more complex, higher-order scheme. This can be illustrated with the newborn baby whose schemes function separately at first.

About Piaget

Jean Piaget was a prolific thinker who has written numerous books and articles. From an early age, he displayed signs of being a genius and acute observer. When he was only 10 years old, he published an article on a rare, part-albino sparrow he had observed. Although his impact on the field of developmental psychology is widely recognized, Piaget was not a psychologist but was trained in the biological sciences. He was also interested in epistemology (a theory of knowledge) and considered himself a genetic epistemologist—one who studies the basis of knowledge by investigating its development.

Piaget was born in Switzerland where he spent most of his life. However, for several years he worked in Paris as an assistant to Theophile Simon, one of the developers of the intelligence tests that were the basis for some of the IQ tests now in use. In the course of his work for Simon, Piaget became intrigued by the answers children gave to questions on the tests. Piaget was not interested in the right answers, however. Rather, he found the wrong answers to be of special interest. In his analysis of these wrong answers, Piaget came to the realization that children do not necessarily think the same way adults do. " . . . [I]t was much more interesting to try to find the reasons for the failures," he wrote as an explanation of his work. "Thus I engaged [the children] in questions . . . with the aim of discovering something about their reasoning process underlying the right, but especially their wrong answers. I noticed with amazement that the simplest reasoning task . . . presented for normal children . . . difficulties unsuspected by the adult" (Piaget, 1952).

So intrigued was Piaget by what he had observed that he returned to Switzerland where he set out to do what became his life's work: to chart the course of children's thinking as the means by which to ascertain the development of knowledge. He did this by meticulously observing his own three children, Laurent, Lucienne, and Jacqueline from the moment of their birth, writing down what they did and what they said and later analyzing and interpreting their behaviors. He did not simply adhere to one explanation or interpretation of the behaviors he observed, however. Rather, he examined various possible explanations before formulating his theory.

Although Piaget began to write about his ideas and theories of cognitive development in 1921, his work did not begin to have an impact on researchers in the United States until the 1950s. Initially, his ideas were rejected as unscientific. Noting that he relied upon the naturalistic method of data collection, which focuses on direct observations, researchers argued that his findings were invalid because of the possibility of observer bias in recording and interpreting of data. In addition, Piaget's writing tends to be obscure and inconsistent in parts, rendering his already complex ideas difficult to understand. He wrote in French, so the translation of his work required not only knowledge of two languages, but also firsthand knowledge of his ideas.

It was not until several American cognitive psychologists studied with Piaget in Geneva that his work became better understood in this country. Of these psychologists, the most notable is Flavell (1963, 1985), who translated and analyzed Piaget's writings, paving the way for literally thousands of other researchers to investigate his formulations.

Some of Piaget's notions have recently been questioned. Nonetheless, his theory of cognitive development and the research spawned by that theory have spurred so much scientific inquiry that Piaget's contribution to the study of children's thinking is said to be "nothing short of stupendous, both qualitatively and quantitatively" (Flavell, 1977).

Thus, if you place a rattle in front of the baby's eyes, she will look at it; if you place it in the palm of her hand, she will grasp it. As she grows older, the infant becomes capable of integrating these schemes, so if you place the rattle in front of her eyes, she will not only look at it, she will also reach for it and then grasp it. Eventually the infant will look at the rattle if it is placed within her visual field, she will grasp it, and put it in her mouth to suck, incorporating several schemes; looking, reaching, grasping, and sucking. But at first, the newborn infant can perform only one of these schemes at a time.

The second principle of functioning is *adaptation* which, simply defined, refers to the process of adjusting to the environment. Adaptation is accomplished by means of two other complementary processes: assimilation and accommodation. These are usually referred to as separate cognitive activities for the sake of clarity, but Piaget noted that they are, in fact, inseparable aspects of the process of adaptation.

assimilation

Assimilation means interpreting external objects, places, people and events in terms of one's presently available way of thinking. Thus a two-year-old may be observed playing with a large cooking pot as if it were a car, or pretending that a chip of wood floating on a shallow stream is a boat. In Piaget's terms, this sort of "pretend play" is the child's way of "assimilating" the pot or the piece of wood to her mental concepts of what a car or boat is. What the child is doing, in fact, is taking in new information and interpreting it (in this case even distorting it) to make it agree with what she already knows.

accommodation

Accommodation entails changing and expanding upon what one already knows. For example, a two-year-old child who for the first time sees a Great Dane may wonder why the animal is referred to as a dog, since it does not look like the small dogs she has seen before. However, once she hears the Great Dane bark, she begins to understand that although it is slightly different than most other dogs she has seen before, this animal is actually part of a class of dogs because it behaves in the same way that dogs generally do. Accordingly, the child's concept of dogs is expanded.

Assimilation and accommodation are equally important in any cognitive encounter with the environment, and they occur in mutually dependent ways. They result in the gradual transformation of the mind in the course of the child's adaptation to the environment. Piaget believed that the individual adapts to the environment because, like all biological systems, she seeks equilibrium. When her existing knowledge does not match what she encounters in the environment, this creates a cognitive tension or disequilibrium and also a sense of not understanding. To restore equilibrium, the infant or child must change and expand upon (accommodate) her view of the world. Thus, equilibration is, according to Piaget, a fundamental aspect of cognitive growth as it motivates the individual to maintain a balance between assimilation and accommodation. It

equilibrium

is primarily this need for *equilibrium,* or the process of restoring harmony between reality and one's view of the environment, that is the principal motive responsible for cognitive growth (Flavell, 1977).

The Sensorimotor Period

According to Piaget, the first period in cognitive development is the sensorimotor period, which lasts from birth to age 2. During this period, the infant's interactions with the environment are governed by overt sensory and motor abilities such as seeing, touching, grasping, reaching, and sucking. Thus, during infancy, thinking occurs as part of the infant's explorations of her environment. The infant learns by acting on the objects and people around her.

To understand thinking in infancy, consider that as an adult, when you think of people, objects, or events, you have a mental picture of these. You remember objects, and you can mentally compare one object with another. You carry this information "in your head," so to speak. The infant, however, does not have this capability, so her way of representing objects is not through mental images, but through actions that she performs on them. A toy is to the infant something to hold, put in the mouth, or look at.

Gradually, the infant develops the ability to maintain a mental image of the toy and other objects and also the capacity for *object permanence* which is defined as the comprehension that objects continue to exist even when one cannot see, touch, or smell them directly. Object permanence is one of the most important accomplishments of the sensorimotor period. Whereas we as adults know that a particular object we encounter, say a doll, does not exhaust the class of dolls and that dolls exist whether we are able to see or touch them, the infant does not have this knowledge. However, over the course of the sensorimotor period, and through her active exploration of objects—touching them, mouthing them, dropping or otherwise manipulating them—the infant becomes capable of constructing concepts of objects such that she understands that these objects are examples of other similar objects and they are distinct entities that continue to exist even when she cannot see them. To describe this gradual progress in cognitive development that occurs during infancy, Piaget divided the sensorimotor period into six stages, each of which builds on the preceding one.

object permanence

Stage 1: Reflex Activity (Approximately Birth–1 Month of Age). During Stage 1 the infant possesses a number of innate reflexes. Although many of these reflexes disappear after a few weeks due to neurological maturation of the brain, other reflexes such as sucking and grasping remain, but they undergo significant functional changes. Piaget regards these reflexes as the building blocks of cognitive growth. According to Piaget, these reflexes are the infant's first sensorimotor schemes, and they become gradually more efficient and more voluntary. Piaget emphasized that a child at any age practices the kinds of activities that she is capable of doing. Thus, during the first month of life the infant is sucking, looking, and grasping, and through these activities she is learning.

Stage 2: Primary Circular Reactions (Approximately 1–4 Months of Age).

During Stage 2, progress occurs on several major fronts. First, through repeated actions that involve her own body and the modification of these actions, the infant's initial sensorimotor schemes become more refined, and the infant attempts to repeat actions she may have stumbled on by chance or from which she derives pleasure. That is, if the infant by chance turned herself over, she will repeat this activity over and over again, each time deriving pleasure from doing so. Sucking, which during Stage 1 was a reflex that was related to hunger and food, now occurs for the sheer pleasure of it. The infant sucks just about anything, not only her bottle or a nipple, but her fingers, toys, and other objects. These repeated (hence the word *circular*) actions are focused on the body (hence the word *primary*).

Second, there now appears some rudimentary coordination between the schemes. Whereas in the previous stage the infant either grasped an object or looked at it, at this stage the baby will stop and look at an object before she grasps it, indicating the development of coordination between the two schemes of looking and grasping, or, in other words, the beginning of eye–hand coordination.

Object Permanence. Another significant change that occurs in this stage is related to object permanence. In the first month of life (Stage 1), the infant was not aware of any boundary between herself and objects in the environment. In the second stage, however, she acquires the notion that objects are separate entities. Hence at this stage, when the infant drops a rattle, she will stare at the place where it last was, her hand. But after a few seconds she gives up and quickly forgets that she even held the rattle. For the infant at this stage, out of sight is out of mind!

Stage 3: Secondary Circular Reactions (Approximately 4–8 Months of Age).

Whereas the infant's actions were focused on her body in Stage 2, the infant's attention is now centered on objects (hence the word *secondary*). The infant continues to repeat her actions over and over again, but this time it is not so much for the sheer pleasure of it as for the results the actions bring about. Again, this behavior begins by chance as the infant, in her manipulation of an object, brings about an unanticipated outcome. For example, the infant grasps and shakes a rattle, and the rattle unexpectedly responds with a sound. At first, the infant is likely to pause in wonderment, but she shakes the rattle again, and even more confidently and quickly the third time, and she continues to repeat this action for a considerable period of time, in much the same way each time.

Object Permanence.   At this stage further progress is also made in object permanence. For example, when a rattle the infant is holding drops and is then partially covered with a cloth, the infant will recognize the rattle and will attempt to uncover it. However, when the rattle is completely hidden by the cloth, the infant's reactions will be the same as they were in Stage 2. That is, out of sight, out of mind; she will not look for the rattle even if she watched the cloth being put over it.

Stage 4: Coordination of Secondary Schemes (Approximately 8–12 Months of Age).

A significant cognitive change occurs during Stage 4 as the infant at this stage shows clear intention to solve a problem. Piaget gave an example of how he held a matchbox in one hand to show his infant son, Laurent, but before Laurent could reach for and grasp the matchbox, Piaget held a pillow in front of it as an obstacle. Laurent hit the pillow in an attempt to move it out of his way so he could attain his goal—grasping the matchbox. In this way, the infant intentionally exercised one scheme (hitting) as the means by which to exercise another scheme (grasping) in order to obtain a goal (getting the matchbox). This major accomplishment, the appearance of intentional means-ends behavior, would not have occurred in a previous stage, as a younger infant might have been distracted by striking the pillow repeatedly, or he might have simply given up his attempts to grasp the matchbox once an obstacle was placed in his way.

Object Permanence.   The infant at this stage is also capable of retrieving her rattle even if it is completely hidden from her view. However, object permanence is still not fully developed; the infant will attempt to remove a cloth that is completely covering the rattle, but if the rattle is covered with one cloth and then removed from under that cloth and put under a different cloth, the infant will look only under the original cloth even if the rattle was displaced as she was watching. She is not capable at this stage of figuring out displacements.

Stage 5: Tertiary Circular Reactions (Approximately 12–18 Months of Age).

This is the highest level of purely sensorimotor activity. As the word *circular* implies, the infant's actions are still repetitive. However, the infant is now actively searching for novel experiences. For this reason, this stage is sometimes referred to as the stage of active experimentation. Recall, too, that at this age, the infant is likely to be walking, so she has greater opportunity to explore the environment.

The infant's actions during this stage are no longer repeated in exactly the same way each time as in previous stages. Rather, they are repeated in a way that alerts us to the fact that the infant is learning something about the consequences her actions have on objects. She purposely varies her movements to observe the results. For example, the infant drops her rattle. When she is given back the rattle, she will drop it again and again.

In Stage 3, dropping the rattle would have been done in the same way each time. In this stage, however, the infant varies how she drops objects, and she watches what happens. For example, instead of eating her pudding or cereal, the infant may drop a spoonful on the floor, first with some force, later with less force, each time watching what happens as she changes her actions. Parents often think that the baby is doing this to annoy them. In reality, the baby is simply learning how objects behave when she acts on them. Most babies not only learn how objects behave when they act on them, they also learn some of the consequences their actions have on their parents' behavior for, in deference to parents' patience, there is nothing more frustrating than continually picking up objects or cleaning up the food the infant drops! Understanding that this is part of the infant's cognitive development may help parents cope, however.

Object Permanence. At this stage the infant will search for an object that has been hidden under two different cloths but only if she sees the object being placed under the cloths. If she cannot see the object being placed, she does not search for it. For example, if you take the rattle and close your hand about it so that it is no longer visible and then put your hand under one cover and then under another and finally hide the rattle under a third cover, the infant will search for the toy by looking at your hand, or she will remove one of the covers, but she will not search any further because she cannot, at this stage, figure out invisible displacements. It is not until the infant is about 18 months, when object permanence is fully developed, that she is capable of searching for a toy that has been invisibly displaced (see Figure 5.4).

Stage 6: Beginning of Representational Thought (Approximately 18–24 Months of Age).

Finally, the infant reaches the stage of what we normally call thought. She has a fully developed notion of object permanence, and becomes capable of retaining a mental image of objects or events. In Piaget's terms, she becomes capable of representational thought. This new ability of the infant has important real-life implications for the infant and her parents. Now that the infant can maintain an image of an object in her head, she experiences a keen sense of loss when that object is missing. An infant at this stage is likely to make many demands and to cry either when her mother leaves the room or when she cannot find a toy. The infant's capability for representational thought also enables her to progress in her ability to solve problems.

Prior to this stage, the infant solved problems mainly by trial and error, always using action. For example, in her attempt to get something out of a small box the infant might try sticking her finger in the box, shaking the box, and so on until eventually one of these methods worked. During this final stage, however, the infant does not need to try out all these activities manually; she can go over them mentally before she acts.

FIGURE 5.4   Stages of object permanence.

In other words, she has become capable of reasoning and also of imagining and inventing solutions to problems that confront her.

Imitation

Representational thought is also exemplified in another activity, imitation. The ability to imitate is important, for through observation and imitation, the infant learns about aspects of her social world and she adds to her repertoire of behaviors. The fact that the young infant can imitate is another indication of her ability to learn. Piaget, in charting the course of the infant's increased ability to imitate, noted that the younger infant, in Stage 2 or 3, is capable of repeating the actions she herself initiates. It may not be true imitation since the infant herself starts the process, but nonetheless, if she sticks her tongue out, a scheme obviously within her repertoire, and her mother imitates her by sticking her tongue out, the infant

FIGURE 5.5   In an example of deferred imitation, this child, imitating the actions of her mother, pretends to "discipline" her stuffed animal.

will again stick her tongue out, and so on. Later, in Stage 4, the infant becomes capable of imitating an action initiated by an adult because she is able at this point to modify her schemes somewhat. When her mother waves "bye bye" and closes and opens her hand, the baby attempts to imitate her by opening and closing her hand, which is a modification of the grasping scheme.

In Stage 6, a significant advancement occurs as the infant can imitate even when the person she is imitating is no longer present, or when the activity she is imitating is no longer seen by her. Known as *deferred imitation,* this form of imitation can occur because the infant is capable of retaining and retrieving a mental representation of the activity. A two-year-old may be seen alone reenacting some activity she had observed earlier, say her mother pointing a finger at her; she will point her finger in much the same way at, perhaps, a doll (see Figure 5.5).

Although, as Piaget maintained, the infant's ability to imitate improves as she grows older, recent studies indicate that the infant may be able to imitate earlier in life than Piaget suggested. Recall that Meltzoff and Moore (1977) found that at 2 weeks of age infants can imitate facial gestures modeled for them such as sticking out their tongues and making lip protrusions. This suggests that they have an inborn capability to match their own movements to those of another. In fact, researchers are finding out that in other aspects of cognition besides imitation, Piaget may have underestimated the abilities of infants. T. G. R. Bower (1971) has shown

*deferred
imitation*

that the infant may have object permanence very early in life but that she does not search for objects because of her limited memory span. In other words, she forgets about the objects. You will see later that in numerous other studies researchers, devising new ways to study children's cognitive skills, are pointing out some of the shortcomings of Piaget's work and the fact that in a number of ways, Piaget's theory fails to address certain aspects of cognitive growth. However, this should not be taken to mean that Piaget's theory is not significant. Indeed, one of the most important aspects of Piaget's work is the fact that it has advanced researchers' understanding about children's thinking and allowed them to further refine his original assertions.

LANGUAGE DEVELOPMENT

Indeed, an important aspect of Piaget's theory is its description of the gradual process by which the infant acquires the ability for mental representation. This ability is significant not only because it enables the infant to think about objects that are not actually present, but also because it heralds advances in the most remarkable of human abilities—language. Having the capacity for mental representation, the infant can use a word to refer to an object and she learns to respond to words and use words as a way of organizing her experiences and perceptions (Halliday, 1975).

Theories of Language Acquisition

The infant's ability to learn language is a marvelous achievement. Anyone who has ever learned a second language, especially its grammar, can attest to the fact that this is no easy task. Nevertheless, most young children learn language, and, by age 2, once they acquire the ability of mental representation, language development progresses at a phenomenally fast pace. The 18-month-old infant generally has a small vocabulary that is limited to about 20 words, and she may use only one word at a time. By the time she enters first grade, she will not only have an extensive vocabulary, she will also be able to speak in complete, well-formed sentences and she will acquire the ability to understand and appropriately use the basic rules of grammar.

How do children acquire the ability to speak? Do they need to be taught language or are they innately disposed to acquire it? Although researchers agree that language acquisition follows a predictable course and that each child progresses through several distinct milestones of language development, there are some disagreements as to how language is acquired. Some researchers emphasize environmental influences; others point to the genetic bases of language development. Most current thinkers, however, take a middle-of-the-road approach to this nature-nurture question and see language development as being influenced by both environmental and biological factors. They note that the human organism is equipped to learn language, but that experience with language is necessary for language development.

The Learning Theory Approach

B. F. Skinner (1957) has claimed that adults, through their systematic reinforcement of the behavior of children, cause children to acquire any new skill, including language. Thus when a baby babbles or a child utters a new word, parents, in their delight, respond by clapping their hands, smiling, or otherwise getting excited. The baby, so rewarded and happy at the reaction she has managed to produce, makes the same sound or utters the same word again. The adults' reactions to the vocalizations of the infant serve as reinforcement, thereby increasing the frequency of the infant's vocalization. As she grows older, the child continues to be reinforced each time she attempts to speak correctly and eventually, through her attempts to repeat words and sentences in the correct form and order, the child acquires the ability to speak the same way as adults do.

Studies have shown that reinforcement does indeed play an important role in the acquisition of language. For example, infants babble more when their parents reinforce their babbling by touching them or smiling at them right after they babble (Rheingold, Gewirtz, & Ross, 1959). In addition, preschool children whose parents talk to them a great deal (we refer to these children as having a linguistically enriched environment) and, equally important, whose parents listen to them, are more verbal than children whose parents ignore them. Yet, the learning theory explanation fails to account for the fact that infants and children, when they first learn the language, have a unique way of speaking. They may say "no sleepy," when they mean "I am not sleepy yet." Or, they might refer to "mouses" or "feets" instead of mice and feet. Adults do not speak that way, so obviously the child is not simply imitating them and repeating what she hears; rather, she is creating her own language. The learning theory approach also fails to account for the fact that language develops slowly during the first two years of life and phenomenally fast during the preschool years. There also appears to be a sensitive period, namely, between age 2 and puberty, for language acquisition during which children acquire language skills more easily than they would at an older age. Evidence for this critical period is available from studies which show that children acquire a second language more readily than adults do. In addition, individuals who suffer brain damage during this sensitive period are able to compensate for this damage and still learn to speak, whereas brain damage suffered as an adult can result in the loss of speech (Lenneberg, 1967). Does this mean that there is some biological explanation to language development?

Biological Orientation

The linguist Noam Chomsky (1968) believes that there is indeed a biological explanation for language development. He notes that despite differences in languages, cultures, and families, infants and children all over the world acquire very similar language skills at about the same age. He explains this phenomenon by proposing that human beings have an innate ability to learn language. He suggests that the central nervous system contains a mental structure which he calls the *language acquisition device.* This enables infants to listen carefully to speech sounds and patterns from birth and throughout infancy, and to process these sounds. This mental structure, according to Chomsky, also triggers various milestones of speech so that infants begin to babble at about 6 months, they are able to produce single words at about one year of age, and they can speak in short sentences at about two years of age.

language acquisition device

The language acquisition device further helps explain the innate capacity of the human brain not only to process words, but to understand the structure of language and the fundamental relationship between words. According to Chomsky, there are two levels of structure to language: *surface structure,* which refers to the grammatical rules of language, an example being the order of words in a sentence, and *deep structure,* which refers to the basic syntactical relationship between words. For example, the sentences "Marie picked up the crayon." and "The crayon was picked up by Marie." have a different surface structure. However, they have the same deep structure and they convey the same message. Children have the ability to recognize that even though the two sentences differ in terms of surface structure, they have the same meaning.

surface structure
deep structure

Eric Lenneberg (1967) is another theorist who adhered to the biological explanation of language development. He proposed that the human being's ability to produce and understand language is an inherited species-specific characteristic. He argued that language is based on highly specialized biological mechanisms which predispose humans toward learning language and also shape its development. These biological mechanisms include the articulatory system which produces speech sounds. Whereas humans have these mechanisms, animals do not. It is suggested that for this reason, although apes can be taught sign language (Patterson, 1980), they cannot be taught to speak. They lack the anatomical apparatus necessary to produce speech sounds (Gardner & Gardner, 1980).

Milestones in Language Development

Lenneberg further pointed out that since infants go through similar milestones of language development, these milestones are related to brain maturation, in much the same way as is true of the development of motor skills. The milestones which infants go through during the first two years

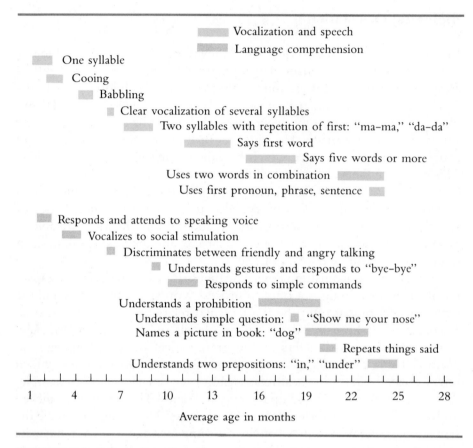

FIGURE 5.6 Some of the language milestones that occur during the first two years of life. The average ages indicated are approximations, and the lengths of the lines show the range of ages resulting from a compilation of several studies. Adapted from McCall (1980).

of life are listed in Figure 5.6. These reveal the fact that language development proceeds along a regular and predictable course and that although the infant does not begin to speak until some time between the ages of 12 and 18 months, language development actually begins at birth, as from that time on, the infant applies herself to the task of listening and responding to language.

expressive language receptive language

To understand the notion that language development begins at birth, it is important to distinguish the two aspects of language, which are *expressive* (or productive) language and *receptive* language. Expressive language refers to the ability to talk. Receptive language refers to other conditions necessary for language development, such as listening attentively, discriminating among sounds, and understanding what is being said. Recall that newborns are disposed to listening selectively to sounds and that they are especially attentive to the sound of the human voice (Condon & Sander, 1974). Not only can infants as young as 2 months old respond differentially to the voice of their mother and the voice of another woman (Mehler et al., 1978), they also synchronize their body movements to adult speech patterns (Condon & Sander, 1974). In the next chapter you will read that even though infants cannot engage in conversation in the same way that older children and adults do (using language) they are quite adept at communicating their needs and they learn how to take turns, a necessary aspect of any conversational exchange (Stern, 1977). Equally impressive, even very young infants have been found to be capable of discriminating among speech sounds. Eimas et al. (1971) found, for example, that infants raised in an English-speaking environment can distinguish the difference between such speech sounds as "pa" and "ba." This remarkable ability seems to be related to social experience, as infants raised in a non-English-speaking environment are unable to distinguish these subtle differences in speech (Eimas, 1982).

Early Sounds

Besides having the ability to perceive speech sounds and discriminate among these, the infant is also producing sounds from the moment of birth. These early sounds are not simply random noises. Rather, regardless of the language of their parents, the sounds infants make during their first year of life follow a highly ordered sequence: crying, which begins at birth, followed by cooing (described as nonsyllabic, partially repetitive vowel sounds), which starts at the end of the first month, then babbling, which begins at around six months (Oller, 1980).

Babbling is an important milestone in language development. Initially it involves uttering simple consonant-vowel syllables and repeating these in succession, as in "ba ba ba ba," "ma, ma, ma, ma" or "da, da, da, da." Eventually, "variegated babbling" (Oller, 1980) appears, and this involves variations in the consonants and vowels repeated, as in "ba di" and "ba da." Researchers do not yet know why infants babble, but they suggest that babbling helps develop the muscles of the sound producing apparatus, and that the infant, once she comes to associate certain movements of the throat, tongue and lips with certain sounds, goes on to repeatedly practice this newly acquired skill (Menyuk, 1972). Recent evidence also suggests that there may be a relationship between babbling and later speech. Oller, Weinman, Doyle, and Ross (1976) found that the phonetic content of babbling varies from language to language, resembling the speech children make later in life. Weir (1966) found that the pitch of babbling of infants from different countries varies, reflecting the pitch of the language the infants hear around them.

Researchers further note that all infants babble, even those who are deaf and cannot hear others or themselves. Babbling in deaf infants diminishes after a while because the infants cannot hear so they are not reinforced to continue to babble or to progress in the acquisition of more sophisticated language skills. In fact, studies have shown that deaf children and hard of hearing children are not only unable to acquire the ability to speak, they also have trouble when they are older, with written vocabulary and grammar (Meadow, 1975). However, if the hearing difficulty is diagnosed early in life, and if deaf infants are communicated with using sign language, they develop the ability to sign as fast as hearing infants develop the ability to speak (Schlesinger and Meadow, 1972).

Unfortunately, deafness in infancy often goes unnoticed in part because deaf infants babble so parents assume they can hear and thus they deprive the infants of appropriate experiences that would enable them to compensate for the handicap. Child development professionals suggest therefore that even when infants babble, parents should look out for indications that there may be a hearing problem and note how the infant responds to loud noises. Even hearing infants at times ignore loud noises, but they do turn their heads toward the source of sound and occasionally they would startle at a sound, evidencing the fact that they can hear. Deaf infants never do so, thus an alert parent or caretaker can spot the problem.

Communicating by Sound and Gesture.   After the babbling period, the infant progresses to the use of a variety of short speech sounds, coupled with gestures, to express a variety of emotions and needs. Anyone who has spent any length of time with an infant about 10 months to a year old is familiar with this phenomenon and knows that infants at this age may not have the use of words, but nonetheless can be extremely expressive. They can whine or shriek and point to an object to indicate that they want it. Or, they can scream to indicate that they are angry or that they do not want to comply with a demand (for instance, that they yield a toy) expressed to them (Dore, 1978). Although in some of their communicative expressions infants can be frustrating, in other of their expressions they can be delightful. They become adept at conveying a surprise expression, raising their eyebrows and saying "oooh!" They can indicate, by shaking their heads back and forth and saying "uh uh" or "oh oh" that they know that they, or someone else, may have done something wrong such as drop and break a glass. At this point in their lives infants may not have the ability to speak, but they can communicate! Parents of infants at this age also note that even though their children cannot speak, they can understand everything that is said to them.

The First Words

True linguistic utterances, the first words, do not appear until some time around the end of the first year of life or the beginning of the second year. So eagerly anticipated is this milestone that parents often read meanings into the infant's babbling, assuming that these are actual words. It is difficult to establish exactly when words have meaning. When is "dada" a word designating father rather than just babbling, "da da da da"? Whereas some researchers note that first words appear in the range of 10 to 13 months (McCarthy, 1954), Nelson (1973) suggests that the age when the vocabulary reaches 10 words (around 15 months) should be used as a formal indicator that this milestone has been reached.

When the infant acquires first words, she uses them, as Bloom (1973) notes, one at a time. First words are further distinctive in their pronunciation and meanings (Dale, 1976). Typically, they consist of one or two syllables, and often, words such as "bottle" or "lamb" are likely to have different versions, such as "baba" for bottle, in which one syllable is simply duplicated, or "nam" for lamb, in which consonants are replaced.

Nelson (1973) studied early vocabularies, noting that infants usually acquire 50 words before they begin to combine them instead of using them just one at a time. She also found that there is considerable uniformity in these early vocabularies. She classified these early vocabularies into six categories. The most common category was of general nominals: *doggie, milk, ball.* Next most common was the category of specific nominals: *mommy,* names of pets. Almost as common was the category of action words such as *give* or *byebye.* Less common were the modifiers such as *dirty,* or *mine,* and the personal-social words such as *no, yes,* and *please.* Function words, such as *what* or *for,* were least common. Nelson counted the number of words within each category that the infants possessed rather than the frequency with which they used these words. Some infants no doubt used some words in the less common categories over and over again. Her study demonstrates that the vocabulary of the infant is highly selective and that those items, such as mommy, milk, and ball, that play an important role in the infant's life are more likely than others to be incorporated into the early vocabulary. Nelson also points out that we can learn more about the selectivity of the infant's vocabulary by looking not only at what is included, but also at what is omitted from each category. *Shoe* and *sock,* for example, are common. But *pants, sweater, diaper* are missing, even though a baby is just as likely to wear these as she is shoes and socks, perhaps even more so. The difference is, however, that shoes and socks are items that the infant can act on easily, whereas pants, sweaters, and diapers are not. That is, the infant can easily take off her shoe or sock, but it is harder for her to take off a sweater. Thus a crucial factor in what words are included in early vocabularies is whether the infant can act on an object (Dale, 1976). Other researchers also point out that besides words for objects or people that play an important part in her life, or upon which she can act, the infant's early vocabulary is likely to include words which refer to specific categories rather than to higher level generalities. For example, the infant is likely to include *flower* in her vocabulary rather than *plant* which is more general, and *doggie* rather than the more general term *animal* (Rosch et al., 1976).

Researchers note further that although there is considerable uniformity in early vocabularies, there are individual differences among infants as some use more words in one category than do other infants. Nelson

(1981) contends that the individual differences in early vocabularies may reflect the temperament and disposition of particular infants. An infant who is active may use such words as "go" or "sit" extensively, whereas an infant who is sociable and interested in people may use such words as "nice" and "byebye" often. Despite these individual differences, each infant's vocabulary includes all the types of words discussed earlier.

The Meaning of Words.   The fact that an infant uses a word is no indication that it means the same to her as it does to an adult, as many parents often find out, much to their chagrin. A father may be excited that his year-old infant finally says "dada," but how disappointed he becomes when any strange adult is greeted with "dada" as well! This occurs with other words, too. First the infant learns to point to a dog and say "doggie." Later, she overgeneralizes and calls any four-legged animal doggie, be it a cow, a horse, or a lamb. The infant is not making mistakes however. Rather, she is reasoning on the basis of her previous experience. As Bloom (1975) notes, it is reasonable for the infant to use the same word for objects that are related: "It is as though he were reasoning, 'I know about dogs, that thing is not a dog. I don't know what it's called, but it's like a dog'." This overextension of the use of a word is a phenomenon found in the language of children all over the world.

In addition, the way the infant uses overextensions is very similar to the way adults use them in that they are based on perceptual properties of an object or action. For example, adults may use the word "ball" or "ball-shaped" to indicate anything that is round (Clark, 1973), just as the infant uses the word "doggie" to describe any four-legged animal or the word "dance" to refer to any kind of turning around or jumping up and down type of action (Rosch, 1975; Clark & Clark, 1977).

Holophrasic Speech.   Finally, although the infant uses her first words one at a time, Dale (1976) points out that she uses these first words not simply as single words, but rather as sentences. First words, according to Dale, "appear to be attempts to express complex ideas, ideas that would be expressed in sentences by an adult. The term 'holophrasic speech' is often used to capture this idea of 'words that are sentences'." For example, the infant may take a spoon and say "me," meaning "I want to feed myself." Or, the infant whose mother is about to wash her face may push her away, saying "self," meaning "I want to do it myself." The infant is using one word, but means something adults would use a sentence to express. In addition to using single words, the infant may also use some action such as pointing or pushing to make her intentions and desires clear.

Combining Words

At around 18 to 20 months of age, the infant, who now has a slightly larger vocabulary, begins to combine words. Although at this point the

language of the infant is a little more elaborate than it was, it is still somewhat limited to concrete aspects of the environment. That is, the infant
will comment on an action ("cookie all gone" or "doggie bark") or she
will refer to objects that she sees or objects that she possesses or that others
possess: "my doggie," "mommy room." Not only among English-
speaking children but among children from other countries whose language is quite different, there are similarities in the two-word sentences
that children use (see Table 5.2, Slobin, 1970) and evidence of the fact that
at this age the language of the child is creative rather than an imitation of
adult language. In addition, the language of the two-year-old is more

TABLE 5.2   Semantic similarities in infant speech from several languages.[1]

Function of Utterance	Language					
	English	German	Russian	Finnish	Luo	Samoan
Locate, name	there book that car see doggie	buch da (book there) gukuk wauwau (see doggie)	Tosya tam (Tosya there)	tuossa Rina (there Rina) vettä siinä (water there)	en saa (it clock) ma wendo (this visitor)	Keith lea (Keith there)
Demand, desire	more milk give candy want gum	mehr milch (more milk) bitte apfel (please apple)	yeshche moloko (more milk) day chasy (give watch)	anna Rina (give Rina)	miya tamtam (give-me candy) adway cham (I-want food)	mai pepe (give doll) fia moe (want sleep)
Negate[2]	no wet no wash not hungry allgone milk	nicht blasen (not blow) kaffee nein (coffee no)	vody net (water no) gus' tyu-tyu (goose allgone)	ei susi (not wolf) enää pipi (anymore sore)	beda onge (my-slasher absent)	le 'ai (not eat) uma mea (allgone thing)
Describe event or situation[3]	Bambi go mail come hit ball block fall baby highchair	puppe kommt (doll comes) tiktak hängt (clock hangs) sofa sitzen (sofa sit) messer schneiden (cut knife)	mama prua (mama walk) papa bay-bay (papa sleep) korka upala (crust fell) nashla yaichko (found egg) baba kreslo (grandma armchair)	takki pois (cat away) Seppo putoo (Seppo fall) talli 'bm bm' (garage 'car')	chungu biro (European comes) odhi skul (he-went school) omoyo oduma (she-dries maize)	pa'u pepe (fall doll) tapale 'oe (hit you) tu'u lalo (put down)
Indicate possession	my shoe mama dress	mein ball (my ball) mamas hut (mama's hat)	mami chashka (mama's cup) pup moya (navel my)	täti auto (aunt car)	kom baba (chair father)	lole a'u (candy my) polo 'oe (ball your) paluni mama (baloon mama)
Modify, qualify	pretty dress big boat	milch heiss (milk hot) armer wauwau (poor doggie)	mama khoroshaya (mama good) papa bol'shoy (papa big)	rikki auto (broken car) torni iso (tower big)	piypiy kech (pepper hot) gwen madichol (chicken black)	fa'ali'i pepe (headstrong baby)
Question[4]	where ball	wo ball (where ball)	gde papa (where papa)	missä pallo (where ball)		fea Punafu (where Punafu)

[1]The examples come from a variety of studies, published and unpublished. Data from the three non-Indo-European languages are drawn from the recent doctoral dissertations of Melissa Bowerman (Harvard, in progress: Finnish), Ben Blount (Berkeley, 1969: Luo), Keith Kernan (Berkeley, 1969: Samoan). The examples given here are representative of many more utterances of the same type in each language. The order of the two words in the utterance is generally fixed in all of the languages except Finnish, where both orders can be used freely for some utterance types by some children.

[2]BLOOM (Columbia dissert., 1968) has noted three different sorts of negation: (1) non-existence (e.g. *no wet*, meaning "dry"), (2) rejection (e.g. *no wash*, meaning "don't wash me"), and (3) denial (e.g. *no girl*, denying a preceding assertion that a boy was a girl).

[3]Descriptions are of several types: (1) agent + action (e.g. *Bambi go*), (2) action + object (e.g. *hit ball*), (3) agent + object (e.g. *mama bread*, meaning "mama is cutting bread"), (4) locative (e.g. *baby highchair*, meaning "baby is in the highchair"), (5) instrumental (e.g. *cut knife*), (6) dative (e.g. *throw daddy*, meaning "throw it to daddy"). (The use of the terminology of grammatical case is suggestive here; cf. Fillmore's discussion of deep cases as underlying linguistic universals.)

[4]In addition to wh-questions, yes-no questions can be made by pronouncing any two-word utterance with rising intonation, with the exception of Finnish. (Melissa Bowerman reports that the emergence of yes-no questions is, accordingly, exceptionally late in Finnish child language.)

Source: Adapted from Slobin, D. I. "Universals of grammatical style in children." G. B. Flores & W. J. M. Levelt (eds.), *Advances in Psycholinguistics*, pp. 178–179, table 1. Amsterdam: North-Holland Pub. Co., 1970.

Listening and Talking to Infants

Language facilitates the infant's ability to convey information and to influence the behavior of others around her. She has already been able to make her needs known in the absence of language, through crying, for example. So, in what ways does language "work" for her that crying does not? In other words, why should she bother learning it?

Researchers suggest that in her early use of language the infant is not only talking, she is also hoping that she will be listened to, and being listened to serves as a reward. When the infant says, "See doggie?" she looks to see if she has had any effect on the adult. Is the mother looking at the dog? After all, that's what language is for, to communicate a message. One of the most important ways of facilitating language development, therefore, is to listen to the infant and to indicate to her that her communication did have an effect: "Yes, big doggie" or some similar response would provide such a cue to the infant and convey to her whether or not she was right in the statement she made. If the "doggie" the child points to is a horse, an appropriate reply such as, "No, it's a horse," would serve to correct the child and expand her vocabulary.

Talking to the baby is also important as studies have shown that by talking to their infants, parents provide a model of how to speak (Moerck, 1980). For example, when a child is pointing at a ball, the father might say "Yes, that's a *ball*," or "You want to play *ball?*" By emphasizing the word ball and touching or bringing the ball over, the baby learns that this object is called a ball.

In responding to or otherwise verbally interacting with infants, parents and other adults use simplified speech. That is, they use short and simple sentences that are repeated (Phillips, 1973). In addition, adult speech (and especially maternal speech) to infants is slower and has a higher pitch (Newport, 1976; Stern, 1977) than the speech adults use with other adults or older children. Not only do adults change their speech in the presence of infants, infants and young children seem to prefer simplified speech.

Spring (1974) recorded a mother talking to her 12-month-old child and to an adult. Tape recorders containing both recordings were given to a group of 12-month-old infants. When these infants pushed one panel on the recorder, they heard the simplified speech; when they pushed the other, they heard the adult speech. Most infants in the study pushed the panel for simplified speech, thus indicating their preference. Similar findings were obtained in another study (Snow, 1972) using 2-year-olds. These children preferred to listen to a recording told in simplified speech as opposed to one in regular speech.

Speaking to the infant in simplified speech may be important. Some aspects of such speech, for example, the repetitions or the slower speed of speaking, may have a functional value in that the message being conveyed in the speech is more likely to be understood by the infant. However, should parents continue to use simplified speech to children beyond the infancy stage? Dale (1976) wisely suggests, on the basis of a number of studies, that "talking baby talk to a child for the first 5 years of life would surely hinder learning, but so would speaking the language of an encyclo-pedia or a diplomatic treaty." There should be, according to Dale, an optimum level of language complexity that changes with the development of the child, challenging him, "but not impossibly so."

An important principle to emphasize here is that of readiness: children control the linguistic input available to them by selectively attending to the speech of others around them, so as the child grows, she will attend to more complex speech. The language spoken to her should reflect this ability (Dale, 1976), and most people do accommodate to the child's level of language development in this way.

Although language development is influenced by biological factors, experience is also important. Infants and young children whose parents talk to them, and equally important, listen to them, are more verbal than those children whose parents ignore them.

telegraphic speech

limited and simpler than the language of adults. Nouns, verbs, and adjectives are used, but auxiliary verbs, articles, and prepositions are omitted, much as you would omit them if you were sending a telegram. In fact, one term used to describe early speech is *telegraphic speech*. A two-year-old would say "see truck" rather than "Look at the truck." If your car broke down and you were sending a telegram to your parents, you would not say, "My car broke down so please send me money." Rather, since each word costs money, you would say instead, "Car broke send money," conveying the message as efficiently as possible by minimizing the number of words.

Once the infant acquires the ability to combine two words, she progresses, during the preschool years, to speaking in increasingly longer utterances, first combining three words, later speaking in sentences (Brown, 1973). You will see in Chapter 9 that there continues to be a regular and predictable progression in the child's language development and also that the language of the child is not a simple version of adult speech but a language that is unique to the child as she attempts to grasp the rules of structure and grammar and apply them to her speech.

NEW WAYS INFANTS ARE GROWING UP TODAY

Teaching Babies to Read

Despite the fact that a two-year-old has yet to master the ability to speak in complete, well-formed sentences, claims are made that infants can, and should, be taught to read and acquire other basic academic skills. These claims are receiving extensive media attention as a result of the research on cognitive and language development which has shown that the infant is not a helpless organism living in a world of "booming, buzzing confusion" (James, 1890) but rather, an individual who is interested in many aspects of her environment and who possesses the potential to learn from the moment of birth, or even before.

The idea that infants can be educated has tempted parents for centuries. Mozart, who learned to play the harpsichord by age 3, is said to have been taught music by his hard-driving father. Whereas in the past only some parents attempted to pressure their children to acquire specific skills early in life, today many parents are being challenged to teach their babies to read, do math, play musical instruments, or speak a foreign language. Indeed, parents are becoming concerned that if they do not engage in such activities, they will be depriving their child and inhibiting her intellectual potential. Parents, eager to give their babies a good start in life, resort to reading numerous "how to" books which promise a step-by-step approach to raising a clever child (e.g., Beck, 1975; Freeman, 1983) or they enroll in programs which offer them training on how to teach their babies. One Philadelphia-based organization known as the Better Baby Institute advertises that through intensive training or through the purchase of a "Better Baby Reading Kit" parents can be taught how to enhance their infant's cognitive ability and how to teach her to read beginning at a very early age. The Better Baby Reading Kit includes information about teaching babies to read, instructional guidelines for the parents to follow, as well as a set of flash cards printed with words of varying lengths to be used with the baby.

Besides the Better Baby Institute, other programs exist, some of which approach parents immediately after the birth of the baby offering to sell them books or a set of toys which are said to be specifically matched to the infant's different cognitive abilities at each stage of development (Badger, 1982). Many parents get the message that by purchasing the toys, and by being shown how and when the baby should use them, they can capitalize on the infant's desire to learn and thereby increase her intellectual potential. Since parents are literally bombarded with the idea that their role is to teach the infant and increase her intelligence, such programs must be considered as major intervention efforts and a change in the way infants are being raised, and must be evaluated accordingly. Should parents be advised that their baby can learn to read? Can it be shown that teaching the baby would not harm her development?

Should Parents Teach Their Babies?

In an analysis of such programs and of empirical studies on precocious reading, Zigler and Lang (1985) point out that there is no conclusive evidence that infants can be taught to read. This means that we cannot state, with any assurance, that a baby can actually learn to read. In addition, there is a substantial body of research on reading development which has shown that before the child acquires the ability to read, she first acquires, during the preschool years, pre-reading skills which are the building blocks upon which later reading fluency is based (Chall, 1983; Crowder, 1982).

Beyond the fact that there appears to be no scientific evidence to support the claim that babies can learn to read, developmental psychologists are concerned that programs that emphasize academic instruction in infancy may interfere with the infant's development. Several researchers point out that these programs encourage parents to focus on the intellectual development of the child to the extent that they may ignore her social and emotional development (Scarr, 1984). "The overemphasis on training the [child's] mind," as Zigler and Cascione (1980) point out, "has led to a distorted view of parental tasks. The parents' job has come to be viewed as little more than programming a computer."

These researchers point out that spending time teaching the baby may take time away from other activities infants and parents engage in naturally and through which they develop a close and loving relationship. You will see in the next chapter that in the course of her developing such a relationship with her caregivers, the infant learns that she is cared for and valued. Not only in infancy but later in life as well, the child is better able to learn when she feels secure in the knowledge that her parents value her efforts. One of the problems with teaching the baby to read in the absence of any evidence that she can learn to read is that both infant and parents may feel frustration and failure if the baby does not learn to read, and the infant may get the message that she is not pleasing her parents.

In the course of her developing a close relationship with her parents, the infant also learns that she has control over the environment and that her actions do make a difference. If she cries, her mother or father will pick her up, feed her, talk to her, or otherwise attempt to comfort her. When she turns over for the first time, takes her first step, or utters a word, her parents clap their hands and cheer in delight. This input is very important for it serves to reward the baby and inspires her to further efforts. Not only through her interactions with responsive caregivers, but also through her play and the manipulations of objects, especially objects that respond to her actions (for example, a rubber duck which squeaks each time the infant squeezes it or a mobile which plays music when the infant pulls its string), the infant learns that she is a competent individual who is capable of controlling aspects of her environment (Watson & Ramey, 1972; Finkelstein & Ramey, 1977). The infant gains competence and a sense of mastery because she realizes that every time she squeezes the rubber duck, it squeaks. She can make it do something! An infant who has the opportunity to feel competent in this way is motivated to interact with people and objects she encounters, thereby acquiring knowledge. An infant who is not given the opportunity to exert influence over the environment develops a sense of helplessness rather than a sense of competence, and the belief that she cannot do much to alter her circumstances. An infant who feels helpless withdraws in her attempts to interact with the environment, and she loses her motivation to learn (White, 1959; Turner, 1980).

Parents who are concerned that they have to teach their infant may be inhibiting her potential for learning rather than enhancing it because, as we have shown, cognitive development during infancy occurs in the context of play and exploration of the environment. Recall that through her manipulation of objects she encounters, grasping them, putting them in her mouth, dropping them, and so on, the infant learns about various aspects of her world and her place in it. Those infants who are required to engage in the pursuit of academic skills, looking at flashcards rather than touching them, mouthing them, or dropping them on the floor, may be deprived of the opportunity to explore their world. Elkind (1981) points out that parents who are concerned with spending time teaching their baby rather than lovingly playing with her or observing her as she freely roams about the house exploring its various aspects, destroy for the infant the atmosphere of open inquiry and curiosity which is important if she is to acquire a broad-based knowledge of the world. Admittedly, the books and programs that encourage parents to teach infants do not indicate that the parents are to spend all their free time doing so. However, considering that the infant spends a great deal of her time sleeping and that other necessary activities such as feeding, changing, and bathing the infant take up much of the time that the infant is in an awake-alert state that is conducive to learning, then even half an hour a day spent simply staring at flash cards may be considered too long and as time taken away from the opportunity for free play and spontaneous interactions with people.

The Nature-Nurture Issue

Parents who feel pressured to teach their baby academic skills and who are concerned that they should somehow enhance her intellectual potential do not mean to cause the baby harm. On the contrary, their intentions are well meant. However, they are drawn by the ideas that faster is always better and that the earlier in life the child acquires an academic skill, the more intelligent she is. In addition, parents have been encouraged to believe that the infant, at any age, can be taught any skill. However, programs that emphasize academic instruction in infancy appear to base their curricula on a set of assumptions about the nature of learning and the nature of the child that are contradictory to what we now know about development. Recall that earlier in this century, J. B. Watson (1926) made the claim that babies can be trained to achieve specific skills and he boasted: "Give me a dozen healthy infants, well-formed and my own specific world to bring them up in and I'll guarantee to take any one at random and train him to become any type of specialist I might select—a doctor, lawyer, artist, merchant-chief and, yes, even into beggar-man and thief . . ." In addition, programs that emphasize academic instruction in infancy give the impression that the human brain is like a vessel that can be filled with knowledge. Such analogies are based on the notion, described in the Introduction, that development is a product of environmental input only and that the child's mind is a blank slate, or *tabula rasa*. We have seen in this chapter, however, that the newborn baby is born with sensory and perceptual skills with which she gathers information about the environment and that cognitive growth is the result of an interaction between biological potential and environmental experiences.

Not only today, but in the past parents have been drawn to either side of this nature-nurture controversy as researchers over the years have themselves taken opposing sides on the question of how babies acquire the ability to think and learn, through maturation or through experience. During recent generations, the pendulum of thought has at times swung toward an emphasis on environmental stimulation as a significant aspect of intelligence and at times toward an emphasis on the child's own natural motivation for learning stemming from the maturational process. Rather than emphasize either nurture or nature as an influencing factor in development, parents need to understand that both natural ability and the environment are significant in the development of the child, and that child-rearing and educational practices must reflect a balance between the two.

The question that remains is: If environment and experience are part of the picture in cognitive development, how much can and should we intervene by shaping the environment and the child's experiences in order to optimize development? In what kinds of environments should we intervene, and with what kinds of experiences, and when? We hold the view that the infant is a natural learner. As long as the infant is in a nurturant environment wherein her caretakers respond to her needs and allow her to play, she will extract from the environment the information that she needs at any given stage.

It is important, however, to determine those conditions that may hinder the process of learning and to discover why it is that some infants do not learn at the same rate as their peers. To this end, researchers have conducted studies which have shown that normal infants who grow up in a perceptually and socially impoverished environment such as was at one time found in some orphanages are likely to suffer significant deficits in social, emotional, and intellectual development (Dennis, 1973). In such orphanages, there was rarely more than one adult caregiver for every eight or more infants, so infants did not get the opportunity for adult interaction and play; they simply lay alone in their cots with nothing to look at but the ceiling directly above them. Dennis (1973) notes that the longer infants stayed in such unstimulating and unresponsive settings, the lower was their IQ and the more retarded they were in their language development. The fact that the infants did not have anything to look at or to manipulate, nor the experience of being picked up, held, smiled at, and talked to was the reason given for their retardation in mental and language development.

The Role of Parents in Cognitive Development

Most infants, of course, do not grow up in an orphanage. They grow up within a family setting where they are often exposed to a great deal of environmental stimulation. In most homes, the television set is on, there are people coming in and out of the house, and the baby is taken out of her crib and played with at different times. Even within such settings, however, some infants do not develop to their full intellectual potential.

FIGURE 5.7   Children whose parents do not pay attention to them learn not to attempt to interact with their parents or to ask them questions.

In their attempts to ascertain possible influences on the intellectual development of infants who grow up in home surroundings, researchers focus on the mother, since it is the mother (or for that matter, the father, the day care provider, or any other person who is charged with the baby's care) who mediates the infant's experiences (see Figure 5.7). They have found that the amount of time the adult spends interacting with the baby and the quality of the interactions are important determinants of the infant's cognitive development (Clarke-Stewart, 1977). Studies have shown, for example, that mothers who hold, touch, smile at and talk to their infants a great deal are more likely to have infants who are more advanced cognitively than other infants who do not receive such parental attention, and further, that these cognitive advances persist beyond the first few years of life (Clarke-Stewart & Apfel, 1979; Yarrow, Rubenstein & Pedersen, 1975). However, it is not that holding the baby more often or talking to her causes the advanced cognitive skills to persist throughout the early childhood years. Rather, researchers explain that those parents who engage in positive caregiving practices that enhance the child's cognitive development during infancy are likely to engage in similar positive practices when their child is older (McCall, 1980). Hence, parents who talk and listen to their infant and play with her are likely to respond similarly to the child during the preschool and school-age years. In turn, their child will interact more frequently with them, asking them questions and involving them in her play and other activities. Infants whose parents do not pay attention to them soon learn not to attempt to interact with their parents or ask their parents questions. Therefore, parental influences on cognitive development are considered not only in terms of the parental behaviors toward the child over time, but also in the context of the complex reciprocal relationship between the parent and child. As Belsky, Lerner, and Spanier (1984) point out

> . . . it would probably not appear to be the case that the intellectual brightness fostered by parents during infancy directly determines subsequent intelligence, but rather that a bidirectional and transactional process of parent-to-infant-to-parent-to-toddler-to-parent-to-preschooler effects characterize the connections that link together various developmental periods. . . . Primarily through such complex reciprocal pathways of influence . . . parental effects identified during infancy are connected to developmental outcomes and processes beyond the opening years of life.

DISCUSSION OF SOCIAL ISSUES: INFANTS IN DAY CARE

The findings that cognitive development does not occur in a vacuum but that it is in some ways dependent on the active participation of adults who take care of the infants raise some concerns given the recent social phenomenon of placing infants in group care. Due to two trends—the increase in single-parent households and the need for both parents to work full time (see Chapter 1), more women than ever before are in the work force and therefore they must find suitable care for their babies. Studies indicate further that the fastest growing segment of women's participation in the labor force is among women with infants who are one year of age and younger. It is no longer uncommon for mothers to return to work as soon as their infant is born, or within a month or two of the birth. There are indications that by the year 2000, four out of every five infants under one will have a mother in the labor force (Ad Hoc Day Care Coalition, 1985).

Whether one sees this trend as good, bad, potentially reversible, or here to stay, it is a demographic reality of tremendous import, for the development of many of the nation's infants is at stake. There are concerns with the growth and development of infants who are raised in group care because compared to an older child, the infant is more dependent on her caretaker, more vulnerable to adversity, and less able to cope with internal or environmental discomfort or stress. In addition, cognitive, emotional, social, and physical aspects of development are more closely related in infancy than they are at an older age. Thus the routines of the infant's care—feeding, bathing, diapering, and comforting her—are of the utmost importance not only to the baby's physical well-being, but to her cognitive, social, and emotional development as well. Furthermore, infants need to form a satisfying, secure, and ongoing relationship with a few caretakers before they can benefit from or even cope with a larger number of children and adults in their world. It is important that they be taken care of individually or, at least, in a very small group of other children, and that they be cared for by one consistent caretaker whom they can get to know rather than by several successive caretakers, each one of whom may have a different approach to child care.

There is a great deal of debate and controversy about whether the infant should be raised by her own parents or by other caretakers. The chief question is whether spending time away from both parents and being raised in a group setting harms the baby's cognitive and socioemotional development. Although this area of research is expanding rapidly, the topic is too new for any firm conclusions to be drawn. Nevertheless, some child development experts point to the fact that studies have not shown that the day care experience actually harms the baby's development (Clarke-Stewart, 1982) or they point to the work of noted researchers such as Bettelheim (1969), Bronfenbrenner (1973), and Kessen (1975) who have shown that in other countries such as Israel, the Soviet Union, and China, children have been successfully raised in group settings with no detriment to their development.

The fact that infants are raised in group settings is not the issue. The issue is, rather, the conditions that exist in these settings. Do the infants have the opportunity to play with and interact with adults or are they left alone in a crib all day? Do they receive adequate nutrition and health care? Are there enough caretakers so that each infant receives individual attention? The answers to these questions are important for they would enable us to ascertain if infants who are raised in group settings are receiving adequate care that enhances rather than inhibits their development.

The Effects of Day Care on Cognitive Development

Unfortunately, we do not yet know the answers to these questions. The phenomenon of placing infants in day care is rather new in this country.

Child development experts do know, on the basis of studies cited earlier and other classic studies (e.g., Spitz, 1945; Yarrow, 1964), that some forms of infant care (prolonged residence in institutions, for example) are likely to influence development adversely. However, not enough information exists as yet to determine whether or not day care is associated with similar negative influences on infants' cognitive development.

You can appreciate the need for such information. The increasing numbers of parents who place their babies in day care deserve to know of any possible consequences of such an experience on the development of their children. Policymakers need to ascertain if day care for infants is a viable solution to the day care dilemma many parents face, or if there are alternative solutions that can be implemented. To this end researchers have attempted to study the effects of day care on infants. In a review of such studies, Douglas Frye (1982) notes that most of the studies have focused on the effects of day care on the infant's intellectual and social development and they found that no negative influences can be ascribed to the experience. Indeed, some studies have indicated that for some infants, particularly those from economically disadvantaged homes, the day care experience is positive as it enhances their cognitive development (Kagan, Kearsley, & Zelazo, 1978; Ramey & Campbell, 1977). Perhaps this is so in day care in which the infants receive environmental stimulation that may be lacking in their own homes.

Yet, the research on infant day care is associated with a number of shortcomings. Most of the studies take a narrow approach to cognitive development and measure the effects of day care on cognition only in terms of IQ scores (Belsky & Steinberg, 1978). There are other methodological flaws associated with the studies (Frye, 1982) and most have been conducted in high quality day care centers, usually those on a university campus or nearby. The only conclusion that can be arrived at on the basis of such studies is that as long as infants are in high quality day care centers where they receive appropriate and nurturant care, they will not suffer from any cognitive or other deficits.

However, in a 1982 Census Bureau Survey of child care arrangements, it was revealed that most (75%) of infants one year old or under in out-of-home care are not taken care of in a day care center, but rather, in someone's home, most commonly, a family day care home wherein a woman, sometimes a mother herself, takes care of several infants and young children in her own home (U.S. Department of Commerce, Bureau of the Census, 1982).

Parents choose to place their baby in a family day care home because often, this is the most affordable type of care they can locate. In addition, the homelike atmosphere appeals to parents who feel that in such settings, the infant is getting the attention she would in her own home.

This is not an unreasonable assumption. However, in a national survey of family day care homes, it was found that some of these were of

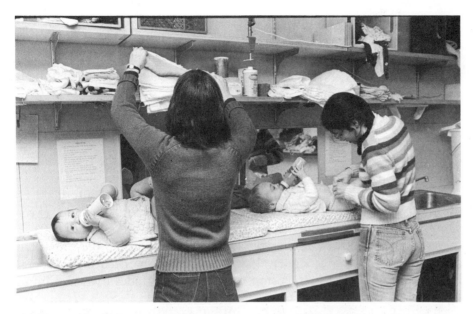

FIGURE 5.8 Today it is not unusual for mothers to return to work when their infants are as young as 4 to 6 weeks of age. Often the babies are placed in an out-of-home day care setting. The quality of the care given in such settings and the training of the caretakers can vary tremendously.

poor quality in terms of the number of infants per caretaker and the food and health care provided to infants (Fosburg, 1980). In addition, researchers point out that the quality of care in family day care homes is likely to range from excellent to extremely inadequate, but at present "there are no means to assess where homes lie along that spectrum" since only 25% of such settings are licensed and therefore subject to some sort of evaluation (Ad Hoc Day Care Coalition, 1985).

The quality of care may be poor not only in family day care homes, but in some day care centers as well (see Figure 5.8). In one of the first studies to document conditions that characterize day care facilities in America (Keyserling, 1972), investigators reported that only 9% of the places could be said to offer "superior" care; about 50% of the settings offered care that was "fair or custodial in nature, providing no . . . services beyond the meeting of physical needs", and 11% were rated as providing poor quality care. In some cases, infants were in cardboard cribs or in a room with open gas heaters. In other cases, investigators found "babies in a dark room strapped into an infant seat inside a crib and crying."

Implications for Child Development Professionals

Our discussion of infant day care as a social issue should not be interpreted to mean that we oppose group care for infants. Rather, we are presenting this discussion as an example of the interaction between child development research and social policy. Since an increasing number of infants are being raised in group care, are there any ways that researchers can help ensure that these infants receive appropriate care that is conducive to their development?

Regulating Day Care.   Indeed, several possibilities exist in which child development experts can work together with policymakers in the matter of infant day care. One of these possibilities is related to the regulation of day care centers and family day care homes.

The regulation of day care facilities is important for it entails the identification of standards for the appropriate care of infants in groups (Provence, 1982). Although regulations governing day care facilities exist in some states, they vary considerably from state to state and they are often not enforced (Young & Zigler, 1986). What may be needed are federal regulations which can help ensure that each state abides by a minimum standard for the care of infants.

The federal government has vacillated since 1968 in its involvement with day care regulations (Nelson, 1982; Beck, 1982). Since that time, child development experts and policymakers have proposed, revised, and reproposed federal regulations which suggest not necessarily optimal care, but at least minimal standards for day care, standards below which the infant's development could be impaired. Included would be the requirement, for example, for a staff-to-infant ratio that would ensure that one adult would not look after more than three infants. Currently, because the salaries of the caretakers is the biggest expense item for day care centers, one caretaker is required to take care of as many as 8 or 10 infants. In family day care homes, caretakers also attempt to take care of too many babies, as each additional baby means more income. In such situations there is no time for the caretaker to attend to each infant's individual needs and respond to her appropriately. These situations are also very dangerous. In the case of a fire, how could one caretaker carry 8 infants to safety? Common sense alone dictates that such a staff-to-infant ratio is inappropriate and dangerous. Nevertheless, in an analysis of the licensing requirements in the various states, Young and Zigler (1986) found that whereas some states license day care centers and homes only if they adhere to a 1-to-3 or 1-to-4 staff-to-infant ratio, eight states have no such requirement, and other states allow one caretaker to take care of as many as 8 infants. They also found that most of the states have licensing requirements that apply to day care centers but not to family day care homes, which are the most common type of group care for infants.

Getting all states to establish appropriate standards for the care of infants is only part of the problem. In many cases, these standards would apply only to those centers and homes which are licensed. The fact remains, most family day care homes are unlicensed and operate without the knowledge of any state official because in this way they do not have to report their income to the Internal Revenue Service. Among the tasks facing those who are concerned with the welfare of children are (1) to find a way to ensure that the federal government establishes a minimum standard for the care of infants which the states can then adopt and enforce; and (2) to find the means which would ensure that parents who have to work feel secure knowing that their babies are growing up in a safe and nurturant environment. These are by no means easy tasks, but they are not insurmountable either—models exist in many other countries (Advisory Committee on Infant Care Leave, 1985) which, with some modification, may be applied to the United States.

SUMMARY

In recent years researchers have shown that the infant has the capacity for organized intellectual behavior and that she uses her sensory and perceptual skills to gather information and knowledge about the environment.

Evidence of the infant's ability to learn is available from studies on conditioning in infancy which have shown that through reinforcement and reward the infant can be taught to change the way she is sucking or to move her head in a certain way. Additional evidence is provided from the theory of Jean Piaget. Piaget was the first theorist to alert us to the fact that infants and children do not simply acquire more knowledge as they grow older, the way they think changes with age.

According to Piaget, the individual undergoes four periods of cognitive development, each of which is characterized by different cognitive structures. These structures are not physical entities that fit somewhere in the brain. Rather, they are an interrelated group of actions, thoughts, and memories which the individual uses to make sense out of the environment. A cognitive structure or way of understanding the world for a 9-month-old baby involves the many strategies or, in Piaget's word, schemes, by which she explores the environment and manipulates objects. A cognitive structure for a 9-year-old involves her ability to classify objects.

Piaget has shown also that the individual is not passive but, rather, an active organism who constantly explores her environment, attempting to organize her experiences and adapt to her world. Adaptation is accomplished by means of two complementary processes: assimilation and accommodation. Assimilation means interpreting external objects and events in terms of one's presently available way of thinking, whereas accommodation entails changing or expanding upon what one already knows.

During the first period of cognitive development, the sensorimotor period which lasts from birth to age 2, the infant undergoes 6 stages during which she gradually acquires the understanding of object permanence, the notion that objects continue to exist even though one cannot see, feel, or smell them. During the final stage of this period, the infant acquires the ability of mental representation, meaning that she can retain an image of an object in her mind. Having this ability, the infant can also begin to use a word to refer to an object or an event, so tremendous progress begins to be made in her ability to acquire language.

Language development progresses through a regular and predictable course from birth as the infant cries, coos, babbles, and then utters her first word. After that point, the infant's vocabulary increases, and by age 2, she begins to combine words and speak in two-word sentences. How do infants acquire the ability to talk and understand language? Although there are two different schools of thought on the issue, one emphasizing biological factors, the other experiential ones, most researchers note that both heredity and the environment play a role in language development. The human organism is biologically equipped to learn language, but experience is necessary for language development.

The same is also true of cognitive development which is governed by both maturation and the environment. However, over the years there have been disagreements as to the relative importance of each. Sometimes psychologists emphasized the fact that learning occurs naturally through the forces of maturation. At other times they emphasized that through environmental stimulation the baby's intelligence can be increased. Often, parents are swayed by either school of thought, and they change in the way they raise their children.

Currently, parents are feeling pressured to teach their babies to read and thereby increase their intellectual potential and school achievement. However, there is no evidence that a baby can be taught to read, nor is there proof that precocious reading results in increased intelligence or later success in school. In fact, psychologists are concerned that by focusing on the infant's intellectual growth parents may neglect her social and emotional needs. Parents should realize that both maturation and experience are important in development and that the fact that the infant can and does learn does not mean that she should be vigorously or intensively taught.

The fact that experience has an important role in cognitive development is shown in studies which reveal that infants who grow up in the deprived setting of certain types of orphanages grow up with significant mental and socioemotional deficits. In such settings, one person takes care of as many as 8 infants, so there is no opportunity for each of the infants to get the attention and stimulation she needs.

Although orphanages no longer exist in our country, many infants are growing up in group settings where one caretaker takes care of as many as 8 or 10 infants. Psychologists are concerned that infants who grow up in such settings may suffer psychological harm. However, the issue of infant day care is a controversial one.

REVIEW POINTS

1. Infants are more complex and responsive organisms than was once realized. They are capable of organized intellectual behavior, and they are continuously using their sensory and perceptual skills to gather information about their surroundings.

2. The research on perceptual development in infancy is providing researchers with information on the perceptual abilities of even very young infants. These infants cannot tell us what they see or hear, but by measuring infants' nonverbal behaviors such as sucking and head turning, investigators have been able to make inferences about infants' perceptions.

3. Researchers have also found that young infants have some capacity for memory and that

they are capable of learning. Two types of learning, classical conditioning and operant conditioning, have been investigated experimentally. Learning also occurs through observation and imitation, and researchers have found that infants as young as 2 or 3 weeks of age can imitate such behaviors as lip and tongue protrusions that are within their behavioral repertoire. The area of infant imitation is a controversial one. Researchers disagree on whether the ability to imitate is innate or gradually acquired over the infancy period.

4. Jean Piaget adhered to the latter argument. Piaget is a notable theorist whose theory of cognitive development has dominated the field of developmental psychology for the past two decades. In recent years researchers have found that in some ways Piaget may have underestimated the cognitive capabilities of infants and young children. Nevertheless, his theory continues to be regarded as an important contribution to the field.

5. Piaget is noted for his revelation that as children grow, their understanding of the world changes. He described cognitive growth as beginning at birth and continuing over four major periods: the sensorimotor, preoperational, concrete operations, and formal operations periods. Each child progresses through these periods at her own rate and is an active organism, acquiring knowledge through her explorations of the environment in her attempt to understand it. It is through the interaction between the individual and the environment that advances in cognitive ability occur.

6. During infancy the child is in what Piaget termed the sensorimotor period of cognitive development. During this period the infant's interactions with the environment are governed by overt sensory and motor abilities such as seeing, touching, reaching, grasping, and sucking, so that the infant learns by acting on the objects around her, touching, feeling, mouthing, and dropping these. It is not until the end of the period, at the age of 18–24 months, that the infant becomes capable of mental representation—the ability to maintain a mental image of objects.

7. Mental representation enhances language development, which progresses at a phenomenal rate once the child has become capable of it. However, language development begins at birth and includes at first receptive language skills such as listening attentively to and discriminating among sounds and understanding what is being said. There is an orderly progression to language development, as infants undergo a period of babbling, and at about the first year of life, they utter first words, using these one at a time. Later they combine words, and during the preschool years they learn to speak in increasingly longer utterances.

8. Even though at age 1 or 2 infants cannot speak in complete sentences, many parents feel pressured to teach their babies to read and master other academic skills. Researchers emphasize, however, that there is not evidence to substantiate claims that babies can be taught to read. Indeed, parental emphasis on academic instruction during infancy may hamper the child's development because during infancy the child needs to engage in warm and loving interactions with adults around her so she can come to feel secure in the knowledge that she has the ability to act and change her environment.

9. Infants acquire such security gradually as they play with and receive individual attention from their parents. Infants whose parents are working, however, are often placed in group care. Although group care is in and of itself not harmful to the baby as long as the baby receives quality care, researchers and policymakers have to monitor the kind of care these infants receive.

CHAPTER 6

SOCIAL AND EMOTIONAL DEVELOPMENT IN INFANCY

F ar from being a helpless organism, even at birth the infant is endowed with an impressive array of capabilities. Not only does the infant possess far greater physiological and intellectual capacities than we suspected previously, he is also a social being, born with the desire to be close to the people around him and exquisitely well prepared to interact with and even influence his environment. Through his interactions with his caregivers, the infant grows in his capability to establish emotional ties with the people in his social world, and he derives from these relationships a sense of security and the knowledge that he is loved. Researchers emphasize the importance of emotional security during infancy, noting not only that sound emotional growth proceeds from the relationships the infant establishes with those around him, but also that it influences all aspects of development. The infant who is developing well emotionally displays a zest for life, enjoys people, and is curious about his surroundings, continuously striving to encounter new experiences and learn from these. An infant whose emotional health is weak or in jeopardy evidences disinterest in his surroundings and tends to retreat from affective contact with the environment.

In this chapter we discuss the infant's capacities for developing into a feeling and loving individual and what may hinder this development; the unique role of parents in offering the infant not only physical but also emotional nurturance; and the course of establishing an enduring and loving relationship—what researchers refer to as *attachment*—between the infant and another person. What is the significance of this first relationship? Does an infant relate to his father in the same way that he relates to his mother? What are the essentials for emotional security and optimal social development in infancy? Before we answer these questions, we will discuss the social predisposition of the infant and the course of social and emotional development during the first few months of life. It is during this period that the infant and those around him form their first mutual ties and begin to learn about and from one another.

EARLY SOCIAL DEVELOPMENT: BECOMING ACQUAINTED

Few areas of developmental psychology have expanded as rapidly in recent years or have captured the interest of psychologists and other professionals as much as the topic of early social development. Recognizing that the newborn infant possesses an array of sensory and perceptual skills and that shortly after birth he shows his interest in the human face and seems to respond to his mother's voice and even to prefer his mother's smell, researchers have sought to study the infant as a social being and to document the emergence and development of his interactions with his mother and others who are important in his daily life.

You will see that much of the emphasis of the research on early social development is on the role of the mother in the infant's social world. The mother-infant relationship has been studied extensively in part because in the past, the mother has been seen as the primary caretaker. You should note, however, that many of the same findings on the research on the mother-infant relationship may apply to the relationships between infants and others who are important in their lives. This will become clear later in this chapter.

Although the mother-infant dyad is not the sole interpersonal interaction in early infancy, it is an important relationship. The research has produced a number of interesting findings about this relationship. For example, whereas in the past mother-infant interaction has been characterized as unidirectional in terms of the mother's effect on the infant, researchers have found that the infant and the parent are in fact partners in the social interaction. Both contribute to it and both are capable of influencing each other's behavior in a process of mutual adaptation. Their interactions have been likened to a carefully choreographed dance in which both partners synchronize their steps, each taking turns and each modifying his or her behavior in accordance with that of the other. In the course of their interactions, the mother and infant become increasingly attuned to each other's characteristics and needs. The infant learns the basic cues and conventions that govern human social behavior, and he evidences his ability to engage his mother in social interaction by inviting her to play and by maintaining and modulating the flow of a social exchange. The mother, for her part, learns about her baby, what his behavioral cues mean, and what seems to comfort or distress him. She becomes increasingly confident of her ability to care for the baby and experiences pleasure and satisfaction when the baby appears happy and content and is responsive to her social overtures. By relating to and interacting with one another in mutually satisfying ways, the mother and infant lay the foundation for a strong and enduring attachment to one another.

Research on Mother–Infant Interactions

synchrony

The loving relationship between the mother and infant, and the *synchrony* (also referred to as "reciprocity" and "mutual modification of behavior") that comes to characterize their interactions, are especially evident in the playful activities mothers and infants engage in. This synchrony is dependent on the infant's ability to signal his needs and his capacity to respond to his mother's behavior and upon the mother's ability to perceive the infant's signals and respond appropriately.

Tuning-in to One Another.   Daniel Stern (1977) spent many hours observing mothers and infants as they interacted, videotaping many of these interactions and later painstakingly analyzing the tapes. He explains the

nature of positive mother-infant interaction as he describes a few moments in the lives of a mother and her three-and-a-half-month-old son.
The baby, working seriously at feeding from a bottle, is sucking away,
occasionally glancing up at his mother and the mother from time to time
looking at him. At one point the infant notices his mother glance at him.
He stops sucking, lets go of the nipple, and his face eases into a faint
suggestion of a smile. The mother, reacting to what she perceives may be
an overture for play, opens her eyes wider and raises her eyebrows a bit.
They look at each other. With their eyes locked in mutual gaze, the
mother and infant remain motionless for an instant until the mother
breaks the silence by saying "Hey," and at the same time opening her eyes
wider and throwing her head in an upward motion. Stern writes

> Almost simultaneously the baby's eyes widened, his eyes tilted up and,
> as his smile broadened . . . the mother said: "Well, Hello . . . heello . . .
> heeellooo" so that her pitch rose and the hellos became longer and more
> stressed on each successive repetition. With each phrase the baby ex-
> pressed more pleasure and his body resonated almost like a balloon being
> pumped up, filling a little more with each breath.

Stern goes on to describe how, after some easy social exchange between them, each one gazing at the other and each taking turns to smile,
vocalize, or otherwise make his or her delight known, the pace and excitement of the interaction between the mother and the infant increased to an
even higher level. After a short while, the infant, apparently not able to
withstand quite so much excitement and stimulation, and having satisfied
his need for a few moments of play, broke his gaze, turned away, face
averted and frowning, indicating his desire to terminate the interaction.
The mother, sensitive to the baby's cue, ceased playing.

The synchrony in mother-infant interaction, the ability of the infant to
initiate a social exchange, and the sensitivity of the mother in responding
to the infant's social overtures and apparent desire to terminate the interaction, are documented by other researchers (e.g., Brazelton et al., 1974).
They note that such animated and exciting face-to-face play sessions last
only a few minutes and are interspersed with periods of quiet and rest and
the daily routines of care (see Figure 6.1). You should also be aware that
although we highlight here the positive aspect of the mother-infant interaction in order to convey to you the current findings from the research,
we do not mean to idealize the relationship. During the first few months
of the baby's life, there are many moments of joy for both the mother and
the infant, but also many moments of stress, tension and frustration, as
every parent who has been wakened up for 2 a.m. feedings can attest to.
Although the episodes of synchrony, when discussed in the research or
observed on video, are very exciting, in the daily life of the mother and
infant they may account for a total of no more than 30 minutes out of each
day (Thoman, 1978; Clarke-Stewart, 1973). In families which are experiencing problems or in families where there are several children demanding

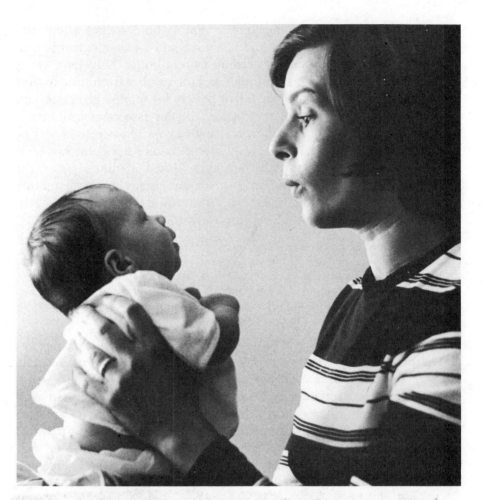

FIGURE 6.1   One of the ways in which adults communicate with infants is through their exaggerated facial expressions. Using a mock surprise expression, this woman is communicating to the baby that she is interested in playing with him.

the mother's attention, these moments may add up to even less time (Zahn-Waxler et al., 1984). However, when the mother and baby do have the opportunity to take some time out from routine activity and engage in face-to-face play, the interaction between them proceeds along the pattern we have described unless there are some disorders in their relationship.

Barriers to Positive Social Interactions.   Disorders can arise when the mother has difficulty taking care of the baby. Recall from Chapter 4 that frail, hypersensitive, and premature babies and babies who are unresponsive or who are difficult to calm experience difficulty adjusting to the environment and may influence the mother negatively right from the beginning. It is very frustrating to take care of, and almost impossible to

FIGURE 6.2   Many babies are responsive to their parents' care, but some are difficult to soothe and they may influence their parents in a negative way right from the beginning.

enjoy, a baby who is continuously crying and who does not seem to respond to any of the attempts to calm him. Also, there are some babies who may not be alert enough to be responsive to their mothers (Thoman, Korner, & Beason-Williams, 1977), or who are sensitive to touch and thus resist being held, making their mothers feel rejected and helpless in their ability to effectively care for their infants (see Figure 6.2).

Just as the characteristics of the infant can present barriers to positive social interaction, so too can the characteristics of the mother. Researchers point out that the mother's sensitivity is a crucial aspect of the pattern of interaction. They note that the mother must be responsive to the infant when he communicates his desire to play. She must recognize the fact that when the infant grimaces, yawns, or averts his gaze, he is signaling his desire to end the play session. Not all mothers, however, respond to the infant's signals appropriately. Mothers who are depressed or preoccupied with responsibilities and problems either at home or in the workplace may not have the ability or the energy to respond to their baby and may not engage in these precious episodes of play. There can also be a mismatch in the mother–infant pair. For example, the baby may have a high threshold for stimulation and may want to engage in longer or more frequent play sessions than his mother is capable of. In such a case, the mother may become exhausted and ultimately exasperated by the baby and angered by the demands the baby places on her (Tronick & Gianino, 1986).

intrusive mothers

Some mothers seem to have more energy than their babies, and they do not allow the baby to break eye contact and stop the interaction (Hodapp & Mueller, 1982). Such mothers, referred to by researchers as *intrusive mothers,* do not ease off when the babies avert their gaze. Instead, they try to continue to play with them. An intrusive mother would thus "chase" after her baby's eyes in an effort to reestablish eye contact, or she might increase the number and intensity of her vocalizations and other behaviors in order to get her baby's attention. These attempts on the part of the mother are usually futile. Brazelton and his colleagues (1974) and Fafouti-Milenkovic and Uzgiris (1979) note that increasing the intensity of behaviors toward an already uninterested infant does not elicit eye contact and may serve to distress the baby. They also point out that by being intrusive, the mother deprives the infant of the opportunity to learn that through his actions and facial expressions he can communicate his needs and desires and thus regulate his world. A baby whose mother is continually intrusive eventually learns that he is not able to make his feelings known, so he stops trying.

Trust vs. Mistrust. The sensitivity of the mother extends beyond her ability to respond to the social overtures of the baby and the baby's need to play. The mother must also be able to respond lovingly and sensitively to the infant's physical needs. When the mother is able to do so, the infant develops a sense of basic trust, a sense that the world is a good and safe place.

Erik Erikson (1963), whose theory is presented in the Introduction, suggests that this basic sense of trust is a vital aspect of personality development. He proposes that there are eight stages between birth and old age. Each one is defined by what he calls a "crisis," which takes place in the context of the encounters between the individual and others in the social setting. This crisis is not some one-time tragic event, but rather, a period in life when the individual attains a certain stage in development. Erikson describes each crisis in terms of an opposition between two characteristics, and in infancy these are *trust* and *mistrust.* The infant develops a pervading sense of trust over a period of time during which his physical as well as his social and emotional needs are met in a loving, caring, and supportive manner and when he is given an opportunity to become accustomed to the caretaking routines of one or two special people in his life. Erikson's notions are only theoretical and have not been supported by empirical research. Nevertheless, they provide a framework for our understanding of the importance of the sensitivity of the mother, or any other caretaker. Researchers note that a sensitive and loving mother conveys to her baby that she enjoys him; she holds the baby close to her and gazes affectionately at him before and after leisurely feedings, evidencing her reluctance to part from him. An insensitive mother, or one who is unable or resents having to care for her baby, expresses her resentment in the abruptness and coldness with which she handles the baby; she tends to hold the baby away from her and does not linger over feedings but terminates them as quickly as possible. Mothers, or any other caretakers, are not always sensitive and loving, nor always insensitive and cold in their interactions with their infants. Rather, most mothers, even if they are usually sensitive, may at times be abrupt with their babies, perhaps when they are in a hurry or when they themselves are depressed or frustrated. Similarly, mothers who are insensitive may at times display warmth in their interactions with their babies.

To the extent that the mother evidences more sensitive or more insensitive care, the infant, over a period of time, will learn what to expect from his world, whether love, relaxation, and warmth or anger and coldness. On the basis of such experiences, the infant may learn either that he can trust others to respond sensitively to his needs and to care for him, or he may come to feel that he is not worthy of such care and thus he may develop mistrust.

The Social Predisposition of the Baby

The mother must be able to change her behavior to accommodate the changes in the infant's behavior that occur as the baby matures. The mother-infant relationship does not remain constant but changes as the baby acquires more refined motor, cognitive, and social skills, alerting us to the fact that there is an interrelationship among the various aspects of development. For example, the synchronous pattern of mother-infant interaction during episodes of face-to-face play described previously does not develop until the infant is about three or four months of age. Not until that time has the infant established a repertoire of vocalizations and facial expressions that permit him to engage in play sessions with another person.

Communicating with the Baby. Although the baby's ability to express himself in the social setting becomes increasingly more elaborate, from birth the infant attracts and is attracted to the people in his environment, and he begins very early in life to establish the skills he needs for successful social interactions. The mother and others in the infant's social circle help the infant in this regard by communicating with him.

One way in which adults communicate with an infant is through their exaggerated facial expressions (Papousek & Papousek, 1979; Stern, 1977). They raise their eyebrows and open their mouths in an expression of mock surprise or they knit and lower their eyebrows in an expression of a frown. Other expressions include smiles and a blank face. The exaggeration of the facial expressions helps the infant attend to them, and the "faces" themselves communicate something to the infant. For example, the mock surprise expression serves as a greeting and is used to invite the infant to join in social interaction. Indeed, frequently this expression does get the infant's attention. The smile serves to maintain an interaction, and it lets the infant know that the adult is interested in playing, whereas the frown and the expressionless face signal to the infant that the adult is not interested in interacting (Stern, 1977).

In addition to making faces, adults also vocalize to infants in an exaggerated manner (Kaye, 1980). They often do not use actual words when they are addressing themselves to a baby but use instead nonsense words or squeals and squeaks (Stern, 1977). They also speak in a higher pitch and volume, and they punctuate with greater variations in sound level than is *baby talk* usual when they speak to other people. Often referred to as "baby talk," this way of speaking to a baby is utilized by adults in all cultures (Ruke-Dravina, 1977) and appears to be geared to the sensory capacities of infants (Sachs, 1977). Apparently babies prefer to listen to this way of talking and have been observed to respond by increasing the pitch of their own vocalizations when they hear a high-pitched voice (Webster, Steinhardt, & Senter, 1972).

Adults also pause between utterances as if to give the infant time to understand and respond. Mothers in particular often vocalize to the infant as if they are both engaged in a conversation. That is, they speak, pause, and then respond to their own vocalizations as if they imagine a response.

Mother   Aren't you my cutie?
          [Pause]
Imagined response by the infant   Yes.
Mother   You sure are. . . .   (Stern, 1977).

By speaking and then pausing in this way, the mother gives the infant enough time to process the information, and she also introduces the baby to the time frame to which his later conversational skills must conform (Sachs, 1977). In other words, she is teaching the baby how to take turns in speaking, as normal conversational exchange requires.

The Baby Communicates.   For his part, the baby communicates with those around him through sound and facial expressions, and he gradually learns to distinguish between expressions and behaviors, such as crying, that prompt the caretaker's attention and produce some kind of relief and comfort and those, such as moving his arms and legs, which may go unnoticed. That is, he discovers by process of trial and error which of his expressions and behaviors are useful and which are not. Crying, of course, is one of the most potent ways by which the infant can communicate and engage adults' attention, because the infant's cry has an immediate effect on those around him. Wiesenfeld and Klorman (1978) found that mothers' heartbeats increased as they watched video recordings of an infant crying especially when they watched recordings of their own babies crying.

Although most mothers are physiologically aroused by the baby's cry, they differ in their ability to ascertain why the infant is crying and in their ability to comfort the baby (see Chapter 4). Some mothers also believe that they should not respond immediately to the baby's cry, contending that if they do, the baby will become spoiled and will use crying as a manipulative device. These mothers assume that to respond to crying is to reinforce it. According to the findings from the research, however, the reverse is true. Ainsworth and her colleagues (Ainsworth, Bell, & Stayton, 1972) observed babies and mothers from the time the babies were 3 weeks old until they were 54 weeks old. They found that mothers who waited to respond to crying had babies who cried more often than the babies whose mothers picked them up right away. They also found that the mother's responsiveness to the baby's crying during the first three months of life is related to the baby's crying at a later age. That is, babies who at 7 months were observed to cry more than other babies were likely to have mothers who had been unresponsive to their cries at 3 months of age. It could well be that those babies whose mothers respond to their cries soon learn that they do not need to cry a great deal to elicit their mother's attention.

Another expressive behavior by which the infant communicates and engages the parents' attention is the gaze. Even though infants cannot focus at birth, they are attracted to the human face and spend a great deal of time, when they are feeding, for example, looking at their mother's face. In fact, although at a distance newborns can see only fuzzily at first, they see objects that are very close quite well. During feeding the face of the caretaker is close to the baby. "This may be," as McCall (1980) writes, "a way nature helps [the] parent and child to become important to one another."

It is not only the baby who spends time looking at the mother. Mothers, too, look at their babies during feeding, but only occasionally, because they do not want to interrupt the baby's feeding (Peery & Stern, 1976). Although the baby and mother gaze at one another from the baby's birth, it is not until the baby is about 4 to 6 weeks old that the mother and baby are able to establish eye contact. At this age, the infant's visual motor system has developed to the extent that he is able to visually fixate his *mutual gaze*

mother's eyes (Wolff, 1963), and from that point on, the mother and infant can remain locked in *mutual gaze* for increasingly long periods of time (Schaffer, Collis, & Parsons, 1977).

The infant's ability to establish eye contact is an important milestone in his social development. It vastly increases the responsivity of the infant and makes the mother feel that it is a real person she is taking care of. In addition, once she is able to establish eye contact with the baby, the mother realizes for the first time that it is her the baby is looking at, and she becomes increasingly interactive with the baby as a result, and also more attached to him. This is evident in studies of blind infants. Fraiberg (1974) has shown that mothers of blind infants have trouble forming attachments to them. In fact, eye contact is so much a part of establishing an emotional bond that a sighted infant's failure to establish eye contact with the mother is usually interpreted by psychologists as one of the early signs of disturbed mother-infant relations or of some other problem in the infant's development.

The Emotional Life of the Infant

The baby is also adept at communicating his emotions, expressing his joy and delight by smiling and his distress and fear by crying. Before we describe the specific emotions of the infant, however, it is important to discuss briefly the study of emotional development.

Researchers have long been interested in the emotional life of babies and have attempted to ascertain the origins and course of such emotions as joy, fear, and anger. Psychologists' interest in the topic dates to Darwin's publication of the book *The Expression of Emotions in Man and Animals* in 1872. During the past few decades, researchers have concentrated more on cognitive development than on the baby's emotions. However, renewed interest in the topic of emotional development has emerged in recent years (Lewis & Michalson, 1983), and researchers have been able to document the stages of emotional development, beginning at birth (Greenspan & Greenspan, 1985; Sroufe, 1979). Several new directions to the research on emotional development are emerging (Campos & Barrett, 1984), with researchers offering different explanations for the development of emotions during infancy. Some of these explanations stem from the classic studies of Katharine Bridges (1932). Bridges observed a group of infants day after day for the first two years of life and from these observations theorized that babies are born with just one basic emotional reaction, a *generalized excitement*. As they mature, this excitement differentiates into general positive affect (delight) and general negative affect (distress). These emotions are then differentiated into more specific emotional states such as elation and affection, anger, disgust, and fear (see Figure 6.3).

generalized excitement

Sroufe (1979), having drawn on the work of Bridges and other researchers, also notes that the baby is born with only one basic emotion,

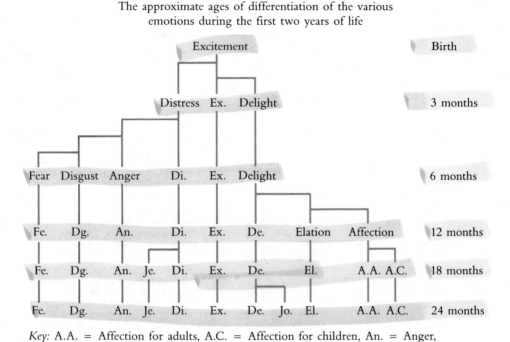

The approximate ages of differentiation of the various
emotions during the first two years of life

Key: A.A. = Affection for adults, A.C. = Affection for children, An. = Anger,
De. = Delight, Dg. = Disgust, Di. = Distress, El. = Elation, Ex. = Excitement,
Fe. = Fear, Je. = Jealousy, Jo. = Joy.

FIGURE 6.3 In her classic study, Katharine Bridges showed the differentiation of emotions—from general excitement to general positive emotions (delight) to general negative emotions (distress). These emotions were then differentiated into more specific emotional states. Reprinted from *Child Development*, 3 (4), 324–341, p. 340, fig. 1. Copyright © by The Society for Research in Child Development.

generalized excitement, and that as he matures, the full emotional panoply blossoms, one feeling at a time (see Table 6.1, page 274), and the baby becomes gradually capable of expressing his delight, by smiling, and his distress, by crying.

Smiling

Perhaps the most social and communicative of the infant's emotional expressions is the smile. Nothing entrances a parent or other adults more than the infant's smile. When parents see their baby smile, they often feel that it is a sign that the baby has come to know them and appreciate their loving care. However, immediately after birth and for the first few weeks of life, the baby is not necessarily smiling at his parents. Even blind infants smile during the first few months of life (Freedman, 1964), and young,

TABLE 6.1   Stages in emotional development. The age specified is neither the first appearance of the affect in question nor its peak occurrence; it is the age when the literature suggests that the reaction is common.

Month	Pleasure-Joy	Wariness-Fear	Rage-Anger	Periods of Emotional Development
0	Endogenous smile	Startle/pain ↑ Obligatory	Distress due to: covering the face, physical	Absolute stimulus barrier
1	Turning toward	attention	restraint, extreme discomfort	Turning toward
2				
3	Pleasure		Rage (disappointment)	Positive affect
4	Delight Active laughter	Wariness		
5				
6				Active participation
7	Joy		Anger	
8				
9		Fear (stranger aversion)		Attachment
10				
11				
12	Elation	Anxiety Immediate fear	Angry mood, petulance	Practicing
18	Positive valuation of self-affection	Shame	Defiance	Emergence of self
24			Intentional hurting	
36	Pride, love		Guilt	Play and fantasy

Source: *Handbook of Infant Development*, edited by Joy D. Osofsky, Table 13.2, p. 473. Copyright © 1979 by John Wiley & Sons. Reprinted by permission of John Wiley & Sons, Inc.

normal babies tend to smile most when they are not attentive to the parent, such as during states of irregular sleep and drowsiness, which suggests that there is a biological component to the smile. However, experience is also important; babies who are in socially stimulating environments smile more frequently than babies who are deprived of social interactions. Blind infants, who are unable to see others respond to their smiles, begin to smile later than do sighted infants (Freedman, 1964).

In the first year of life, there appear to be three stages of smiling. Soon after birth there is the spontaneous or *endogenous* (that is, internally triggered) smile. Such endogenous smiles appear during the first week of life when the baby is asleep. These smiles seem to be the result of a central nervous system activity (Wolff, 1963; Sroufe, 1979). If the baby is startled, perhaps by some sudden noise, his level of excitation or arousal is raised. When the baby later relaxes below his threshold of arousal, the smile muscles relax, too, which sometimes causes a tiny involuntary smile to appear (see Figures 6.4 and 6.5). Such a smile, although it is associated with a relaxed and pleasant state, does not signify conscious pleasure as do later smiles.

endogenous smile
0 - 3 weeks

Soon after this stage, the baby begins to smile at a nodding head, blinking lights, sounds, or anything else that has rhythm or repetition, and he does so when he is in an awake-alert state. This smile, called the *nonselective social smile,* is *exogenous,* meaning that it is triggered by something in the external world. The nonselective social smile occurs around

exogenous smile
3 - 4 weeks

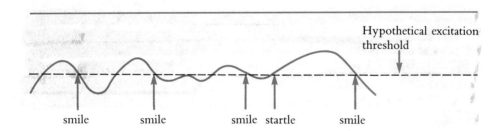

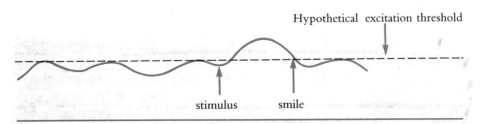

FIGURE 6.4 Schematic drawing of the excitement-relaxation cycle of the baby's behavior. When the baby is aroused above his threshold, tiny, involuntary smiles appear. Adapted from *Handbook of Infant Development,* edited by Joy D. Osofsky, figure from p. 482. Copyright © 1979 by John Wiley & Sons, Inc.

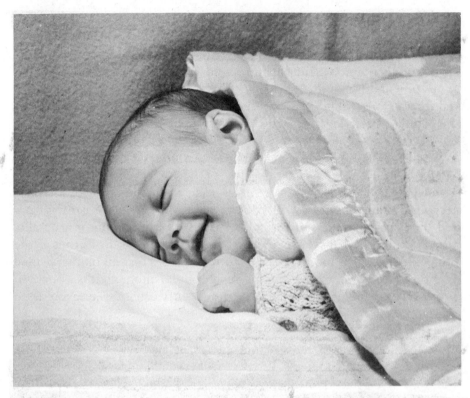

FIGURE 6.5   The endogenous or internally triggered smile does not signify conscious pleasure, but it is associated with a relaxed, pleasant state.

the third or fourth week of life and is elicited most readily when the baby is watching a human face or when he hears his mother's voice. As the infant grows, this smile becomes increasingly social and instrumental, and at about five to six months of age, the *selective social smile* emerges. During this stage, the infant smiles at those individuals he is familiar with, but unfamiliar faces elicit no smile from the infant and may at times elicit crying.

(selective social smile 6 months)

Theories of Smiling.   Not only parents but psychologists, too, are intrigued with the infant's smile. They ask: What makes the baby smile? Several theoretical answers to this question have been offered.

evolutionary theory of smiling

The *evolutionary theory of smiling* emphasizes the adaptive value of the smile. According to this theory, the baby is born with the ability to smile. His smiles serve to increase adults' interactions with him, thus ensuring that his need to establish human relationships will be met. Researchers who adhere to the evolutionary theory note the more attention that is bestowed upon the baby when he smiles, the more he will smile. There is some empirical evidence to support this contention. Brackbill (1958) found that infants smile more when adults coo, cuddle, or smile at them

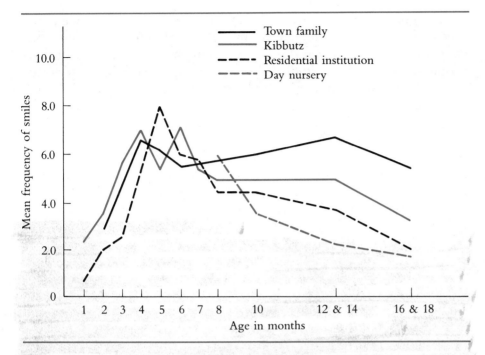

FIGURE 6.6   The amount of smiling by infants is dependent upon the amount of social interaction they experience. Infants reared in a family environment exhibit more smiling than infants reared either in a kibbutz, a residential institution, or a day nursery. Adapted from Gewirtz, J. L. (1965). "The course of infant smiling in four childrearing environments in Israel." In B. M. Foss (Ed.), *Determinants of Infant Behavior,* vol. 3, fig. 24. London: Methuen; New York: Wiley. (© 1965 by Tavistock Institute of Human Relations).

and that their smiles are extinguished when they are in the presence of an unresponsive adult. Jacob Gewirtz (1965) found that the development of smiling varies among infants depending on their childrearing setting. Those infants who grow up in a normal family setting where they are frequently picked up, played with, and talked to when they smile, smile earlier and more frequently than infants raised in institutions where they are deprived of frequent interactions with caretakers (see Figure 6.6).

Cognitive theorists emphasize the cognitive bases of the infant's social behavior and emotional expressions (Kagan, 1984, 1978). They contend that the smile is an innate expression of the pleasure and joy infants experience when they master a cognitive task. This theoretical explanation, derived from the work of Piaget (1952), predicts that the infant will take longer to smile at a more complex visual stimulus than a simpler one, because he cannot at once assimilate a complex stimulus into his cognitive framework. To test this hypothesis, Shultz and Zigler (1970) showed 3-month-old infants a doll (the stimulus) which was either stationary or swinging. The swinging doll was the more complex stimulus because the contours of the object are more difficult to define when it is moving than when it is stationary. Although the infants smiled in both situations, they smiled more readily when the doll was stationary. In addition, the very serious way the infants studied the more complex stimulus before they smiled appeared to reflect the hard cognitive work they were doing to scan and recognize the swinging doll.

Fear

Not only is the infant capable of feeling and expressing his joy and pleasure, as evidenced in his smiling, he is also capable of fear. Psychologists note that there is a developmental component to fear, as children evidence different fears depending on their age. For example, toddlers associate fear with pain and are afraid of people who remind them of a painful experience (a doctor, for instance, who reminds them of receiving an injection). Later, during the preschool years, children fear concrete objects such as lions and tigers, but they do not associate these with previous painful experiences, as obviously children have little or no first-hand contact with such animals. During the middle childhood years, children begin to be afraid that they will fail in school. This is because during the middle childhood period children are able to think in an increasingly more logical manner, suggesting that there is a link between children's fear and the child's cognitive status. This is true not only of older children but of infants as well.

To illustrate the cognitive bases of fear, Kagan (1984) describes a study in which infants aged 1 month and 7 months were shown a picture of a distorted human face. The 1-month-olds responded with interest to the bizarre face and rarely cried. The 7-month-olds reacted with crying and other signs of distress. The difference, according to Kagan, is that the older infants had a mental image of what a face should look like, to which they compared the distorted one and became distressed at the mismatch. The 1-month-olds did not yet have the cognitive abilities that would allow such comparisons and so were not disturbed.

stranger anxiety
separation anxiety

Fear of Strangers and Separation Anxiety. Two fears which are especially evident during the first year of life are *stranger anxiety* and *separation anxiety*. Fear of strangers refers to the infant's negative response to the approach of an unfamiliar adult. Separation anxiety refers to the crying, fretting, and other distressed behavior the infant exhibits when a parent or other adult to whom he is attached leaves.

Fear of strangers, or stranger anxiety, is thought to be the first real negative emotion of the baby. It is evident in a baby who will watch a stranger's face for a few seconds, then frown and breathe heavily, and finally turn away or start crying. In an early study on the topic, Morgan & Ricciuti (1969) observed infants 4 to 12 months of age. Each infant sat

Social Referencing

Researchers note that infants' and young children's emotions, and their understanding of other people's emotions and behaviors, are subject to social influences. Lewis and Feiring (1981) explain that when young children observe their parents interacting, they learn, among other things, about some of the emotions of the mother and the father, and about the nature of their relationship. Researchers note further that parents' and others' reactions to people or situations influence children's responses. Thus infants whose mothers greet strangers positively are likely to respond to the stranger in a positive way as well. In other words, the infants are capable of using another person's behavior to form an understanding of the social situation and how they can respond to it. This is known as *social referencing* and it was demonstrated in a study by Feinman & Lewis (1983). In the study infants' behavior was observed under two conditions: one, when their mother greeted an unfamiliar person positively and spoke to the infant about the person in a warm way, and two, when the mother greeted and spoke to or about the unfamiliar person in a neutral tone. When the mother spoke positively to and about the stranger, the infants smiled at that person and offered that person toys significantly more so than they did when the mother spoke to and about the stranger in a neutral tone.

Similar studies (Klinnert, Campos, Sorce, Emde, & Suejda, 1983) confirm these findings, with researchers noting not only that the emotional expressions of the mother help regulate infants' behavior, but also that the emotional expressions of other adults are influential as well. Klinnert, Emde, Butterfield, and Campos (1983) found that when an unfamiliar object is introduced into a room where the infant, the mother, and another adult are present, and when that adult poses a joyful face, the infant tends to approach and touch the unfamiliar object significantly more so than when the adult poses a fear expression.

Infants utilize social referencing to make sense out of potentially dangerous situations. In a study that demonstrates this fact, Sorce et al. (1981) used the visual cliff experiment. Recall from Chapter 4 that in this experiment, infants evidence their fear of the deep side of the cliff. In the Sorce et al. (1981) study, the researchers found that when the visual cliff is constructed so that the deep side appears to be very deep, infants do not attempt to cross it, nor do they seek to see how their mothers feel about the cliff. However, when the visual cliff is set up so that the deep side is not so deep as to clearly signal danger, the infants look at their mother. When the mothers, on the other side of the cliff, were instructed to put on a fear expression, none of the infants in the study crossed the cliff. When the mothers were instructed to pose a joyous expression, 15 out of the 19 infants crossed the cliff. It is clear that those who crossed utilized their mother's specific facial affective information to make sense of the ambiguous situation and to determine whether or not to cross the visual cliff.

These and similar other studies on social referencing are important not only because they yield valuable information on infant development, but also because they serve to emphasize the importance of the social context for understanding emotional reactions. According to Campos and Barrett (1984), this understanding serves to provide direction for future research on emotional development.

either on the mother's lap or several feet away from her when an unfamiliar adult approached them. Infants younger than 8 months old were generally positive toward the stranger whether they were sitting on their mother's lap or not. However, the older infants who were not sitting on their mother's lap showed a much more negative reaction toward the stranger than the same-age infants who sat on their mother's lap. In several other studies researchers have found that stranger anxiety does not necessarily occur with every 8- to 12-month-old infant or each time an infant that age sees a stranger. The phenomenon is influenced strongly by the infant's past experience with strangers (Rheingold & Eckerman, 1973; Brooks & Lewis, 1976; Sroufe, 1977) and the particular situation the baby is in, for example, whether or not the mother is present.

Researchers note also that the infant, who is able quite early in life to recognize the emotional states and moods of his parents (La Barbera, Izard, Vietze, & Parisi, 1976), typically observes his mother's face when he sees a stranger approaching. If his mother smiles at or speaks positively to an unfamiliar adult, the baby often responds with less fear and negativity than he does if his mother speaks to the stranger in a neutral tone

social referencing

(Feinman & Lewis, 1983). Known as *social referencing,* this ability of the infant to be influenced by other people's emotional expressions is considered an important factor in how infants, and older children, acquire the ability to manage their own emotional expressions and states (Lewis & Michalson, 1982).

An individual does not have to be a stranger to elicit wariness and distress in the infant. Often family members whom the infant does not see frequently are hurt and embarrassed by the infant's apparent rejection of their social overtures. They sometimes suspect that the parents taught the baby to reject or dislike them. These people would be comforted to know, however, that babies become distressed not only when they see an unfamiliar adult, but also when they see their mother made up or dressed up differently than usual or when they see their father disguised in some way, for example, when his face is covered with shaving cream or when he is dressed up as a clown or Santa Claus (see Figure 6.7).

Psychoanalysts suggest that fear of strangers is related to the baby's love for the mother and his fear of losing her (Spitz, 1965). Ethologists regard the phenomenon as a response to an intuitive appraisal of a potentially dangerous situation or as an instinctual flight reaction to any strange stimulus (Freedman, 1965). Cognitive theorists, however, interpret stranger anxiety differently, suggesting that it arises from the fact that it represents extreme discrepancy from the schema that the infant possesses for the familiar people in his environment. That is, the baby's distress at the sight of a stranger is due to his inability to assimilate the face of the stranger (Kagan, 1976, 1984), hence the fear he evidences when he does not recognize his mother or father in disguise.

FIGURE 6.7 Fear of strangers is the first real negative emotion of the baby, who becomes more afraid of strangers when he is about a year old. This child's fear of Santa Claus is heightened by Santa's unusual clothing.

Similarly, researchers interpret separation anxiety in cognitive terms. Separation anxiety (or separation distress) refers to the infant's response to being separated from the mother. Such responses may be reduced bodily activity, fussiness, and loud crying (Tennes & Lampl, 1964). Researchers note that stranger anxiety and separation anxiety are separate although interrelated phenomena and that separation anxiety begins to occur at about 5 months. It increases gradually until about age 13 months when it is at its peak. After that age, it declines and the infant does not demonstrate as much distress at being separated from the mother.

Separation anxiety begins at 5 months and peaks at 13 months.

Explaining separation anxiety in cognitive terms, researchers note that the phenomenon reflects the emergence of a new cognitive process, namely, object permanence. A baby whose mother leaves him can think about her even in her absence, but he cannot yet understand where she has gone or whether she will return, hence the anxiety. Before object permanence is attained, however, the infant has no memory of his mother, and therefore does not miss her. Separation anxiety declines with age, because the infant is able to comprehend that although his mother has gone, she will return.

ESTABLISHING RELATIONSHIPS

Attachment

Separation anxiety also indicates, in part, the infant's attachment to his mother. Attachment is considered to be one of the most important of the infant's emotional experiences. It is defined as the strong and enduring bond, the feeling of love, if you will, that develops between the infant and the person he most frequently interacts with. We will focus here on the infant's attachment to the mother, since much of the research on attachment focuses on the infant and the mother. Bear in mind, however, that infants have important relationships and attachments to other people as well. They interact with and grow to love their fathers, siblings, grandparents, and others who are important to them in their daily lives (Lamb, 1981).

In order to measure attachment scientifically, researchers have used the infant's behavior toward his parent as a gauge, studying the extent that the infant looks at his mother, orients his body toward her, smiles at her, clings to her, and becomes upset when she leaves him. They have found that attachment does not emerge suddenly but is acquired over a period of a few months. Before the infant becomes attached, he needs to have sufficient exposure to his caretaker and the opportunity not only to become acquainted and familiar with her but also to ascertain that she will respond to his needs.

Ainsworth (1973) has identified several phases in the attachment process. During the first or preattachment phase, which lasts for the first several weeks of life, the baby does not discriminate among people and is as likely to be delighted with or comforted by someone else as by the mother. By the time he is about three months old, the baby enters the second phase of the attachment process, at which point he discriminates between familiar and unfamiliar people and responds differently to them. During this phase the infant smiles more at people he is familiar with than those he is not familiar with. During the third phase, which begins at about six to eight months of age, the infant exhibits preference for his mother and is said to have established an emotional bond with her (see Figure 6.8). He seeks to be close to his mother and to maintain physical contact with her. He embraces her a great deal and will often hold his arms outstretched in request to be picked up. He sometimes cries or otherwise protests when the mother leaves his sight. In the presence of strangers, the infant will seem wary and uncomfortable, especially when in unfamiliar situations. This phase of the attachment process peaks at about one year of age. During the second year of life, the strong attachment to the mother begins to wane gradually, and the baby becomes increasingly sociable and at ease with others.

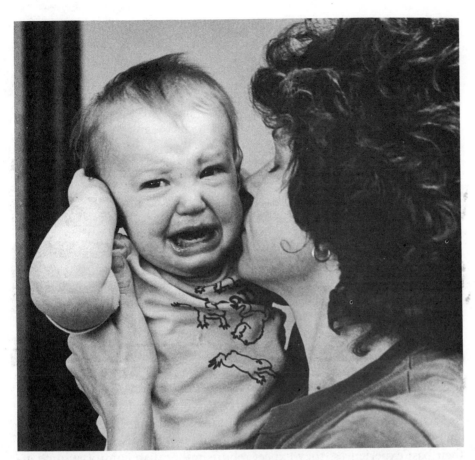

FIGURE 6.8 Sometime between 6 months to 1 year of age, the infant becomes increasingly attached to his mother. During this period, mothers find that leaving the baby for even a few moments can result in crying or other protests at the separation.

Individual Differences in Attachment

Attachment results in a feeling of emotional security in the infant, who grows up regarding his mother as a secure base or island of safety from which he can venture forth and freely explore his surroundings. Although all infants usually develop attachments to their mother and eventually to several other people as well, there are individual differences in the quality of the mother-infant relationship. Mary Ainsworth has developed a laboratory experiment to assess individual differences in attachment. In this experiment, called the *Strange Situation Procedure* (Ainsworth & Wittig, 1969), the infant and the parent are asked to stay in an unfamiliar room. Once they are in this unfamiliar place, a stranger enters. After introducing the child to the unfamiliar adult, the child is separated from his mother,

strange situation procedure

first by leaving him with the stranger and then by leaving him completely alone. The mother returns after each of these brief separations.

Observing the infant's behavior in each of these situations and, especially, the infant's behavior toward the mother during episodes of reunion, Ainsworth classified the infants in terms of the security of their attachment relationship. She found that infants who by 12 to 18 months use their mother as a secure base from which to explore their surroundings and who seem to be happy when she returns, positively greeting her following the separation, can be described as *securely attached* infants. Infants who fit this category, considered the healthiest pattern of attachment, are likely to be curious about the stranger in the room and perhaps even temporarily hesitant, but they would soon warm up to him or her.

securely attached infants

There are some infants, however, who are insecure in their attachments to the mother. Infants who have formed *anxious attachments* tend to be distressed in an unfamiliar situation even when their mother is with them. When their mother returns after brief episodes of separation, such infants are inclined to resist physical contact with their mother or to display their distress.

anxious attachment

Other insecurely attached infants form *avoidant attachments*. These infants do not explore their surroundings as much as the securely attached infants do. They tend to ignore their mother even when she is present, and they rarely show distress when they are separated from her briefly.

avoidant attachment

Michael Lamb (1984) notes that the way infants behave in the Strange Situation Procedure experiment is indicative of their prior social experiences. That is, some infants behave avoidantly because on the basis of their past experiences, they expect rebuffs rather than comfort. Some infants who form anxious attachments and who resist physical contact do so because they do not know what to expect of adults whose behavior has been unreliable and unpredictable in the past.

Theories of Attachment

This interpretation of the antecedents of attachment is, as yet, speculative (Lamb, 1984). Nevertheless, individual differences in attachment have been observed not only in the laboratory setting, but in the home as well (Ainsworth, Blehar, Waters, & Wall, 1978). Why do infants become attached to their mother, and what aspects of the infant-mother relationship influence attachment in infants and determine whether their attachment will be secure or insecure? Psychologists' answers to these questions have changed in recent years. An earlier learning theory view held that infants become emotionally attached to their mother because she is a source of relief from discomfort and pain. Operant learning theorists such as Jacob Gewirtz (1965) claimed that initially the mother is nothing special, merely a neutral stimulus for the infant. But, after repeatedly associating the mother with pleasurable events such as feedings, the mother takes on rewarding properties and becomes a desired object for the infant.

A more complete explanation of the nature and process of attachment is provided by John Bowlby (1969). Drawing upon ethology, psychoanalytic theory, and the cognitive-developmental theory of Piaget, Bowlby views attachment as a unique response which serves to protect the young from harm. He suggests that the infant's attachment to his caretaker is best described in terms of a *behavioral system*. According to him, the set goal of the attachment behavioral system is proximity of the infant to the caretaker. This goal of proximity is accomplished by the behavior of both the infant and the caretaker. Thus any behavior on the infant's part that initiates, maintains, or elicits proximity to the caretaker may be termed an attachment behavior. Such behavior includes, as we have seen, smiling, crying, clinging, and so on. Bowlby also believes that the infant's attachment behavior is innate and elicited by certain stimuli such as the mother herself or a frightening situation. In turn, the infant's behavior elicits protective responses from the mother.

behavioral system

Alan Sroufe and his colleagues have elaborated upon Bowlby's explanation of the development of attachment, emphasizing the affective component of the attachment relationship. They explain the relationship in terms of individual differences in the regulation of affect (Sroufe & Waters, 1977). They note that in the secure attachment relationship, the infant can use the caretaker as a ready source of comfort and security. Furthermore, they point out that from such a relationship the infant develops the capacity, in the early childhood years, to give and receive affection and enjoy social interactions with parents and others (Sroufe, Schork, Motti, Lawroski, & LaFreniere, 1984).

Influences on Attachment

Schaffer and Emerson (1964) also suggest that the infant has an innate need to be close to people. They offer an explanation of what might influence the attachment process. Having studied the development of attachment in a group of infants from the early weeks of life to age 18 months, they found that infants differed in the age during which they became attached to their caretaker and in the level of intensity of their attachment. They found also that some babies focused their attachment on one person and that others were attached to several people. Additionally, the caretaker's responsiveness to the infant's crying and the amount of his or her interaction with the infant were found to be related to the attachment. That is, the infants did not simply become attached to the person who fed and cared for them. Rather, the infants became attached to the person who, in the context of many interactions over a period of time, had responded to their needs.

Several other researchers, notably Ricks (1982), Clarke-Stewart (1973), and Ainsworth and her colleagues (1972), provide evidence in support of the fact that parent-infant interaction during the first few months of life, particularly in response to the infant's signals, is important in attachment. They note that if the mother, or any other primary caretaker, is sensitive and responsive to the infant's social overtures, needs, and temperament and adjusts her behavior accordingly, the infant will grow up feeling that his caretaker is accessible and responsive, and he will form a secure attachment to the caretaker. These researchers found that babies whose mothers were slow to respond, who were not affectionate toward them, or who were unskilled at handling them, developed anxious attachments. Infants whose mothers did not like or were indifferent to physical contact with their babies developed avoidant attachments.

We reiterate, however, that although the mother's sensitivity may be a factor in the development of attachment, the infant also plays an active role in developing the relationship. Remember that the infant's characteristics at times determine the ability of the mother or other caretaker to care for the baby. In one study (Waters, Vaughn, & Egeland, 1980), researchers found that babies classified as insecurely attached at 12 months of age had evidenced as newborns signs of unresponsiveness and motor immaturity. Thus it may have been more difficult to provide sensitive and responsive care to them than to other babies.

Belsky, Lerner, and Spanier (1984) emphasize that some mothers are able to overcome the barriers to social interaction imposed by their infant's characteristics and that factors other than personal characteristics also play a role in the interaction between the mother and the infant. Crockenberg (1981), for example, found that highly irritable newborns developed insecure attachment, but not in every case. Rather, the attachment was insecure only when their mothers had little support from friends and relatives. Under such conditions, the mothers are apparently under psychological strain caused by their having to care for the irritable and difficult baby and at the same time not having any assistance. It appears that much more research is needed to identify precisely which characteristics of the mother and infant contribute to the establishment of attachment and what other factors might play a role (Lamb, 1982).

Importance of Attachment

Although more research on the influences on attachment is needed, researchers do know that attachment is a crucial factor in many aspects of the infant's development.

Summarizing the research, Lamb (1978a; 1982) notes that through interactions with his mother, the infant acquires security and a sense of trust in the mother's reliability and predictability. This sense of security and trust, which becomes a fundamental aspect of the personality of the infant (Erikson, 1963), is important to the development of autonomy and independence later in the life of the child. It ensures that the infant will feel at ease exploring his surroundings and learning from them. Researchers note that securely attached infants are more willing than insecurely attached infants to venture forth and explore their world, thereby maximizing the likelihood that they will learn from their explorations of the environment. Securely attached infants are also more socially mature than insecurely attached infants, and they are more inclined to establish social interactions with their age-mates.

On the other hand, insecurely attached infants may be so concerned about ensuring the presence and proximity of their mother that they have less opportunity for exploration and establishing and maintaining close relationships with others. Stayton, Hogan, and Ainsworth (1971) found that securely attached infants are generally more competent in a variety of ways than the insecurely attached infants and that they are more capable of positively communicating their desires (using facial expressions, gestures, and vocalizations) than the insecurely attached infants.

In studies linking attachment in infancy with behavior during the preschool years, Pastor (1981) and Waters, Wippman, and Sroufe (1979) found also that preschoolers who as infants were classified as securely attached displayed the most competence. They were more self-directed in their activities, more interested in exploring their environment, and more likely to have good relations with their peers than the preschoolers who as infants were insecure in their attachments. In a study of the relationship between the quality of mother–infant attachment and infant competence in social relationships, Easterbrooks and Lamb (1979) found that infants who were rated as securely attached were more friendly and more likely than those who were rated as insecurely attached to initiate interactions with their peers.

Maternal Deprivation and Separation.   Additional insights into the importance of attachment and its implications for the later development of the infant are derived from studies which have looked into what happens when attachment does not occur, that is, when infants are deprived of the opportunity to interact with and form an attachment to their caretaker.

maternal deprivation

Harlow's Studies.   The consequences of maternal deprivation cannot be ethically studied using experiments with human infants. Nevertheless, data are available from research studies which have manipulated the rearing conditions of animals.

These animal studies, most notably a series of experiments by Harry Harlow and his colleagues, have illuminated for researchers the significance of the infant's interaction with his mother. In Harlow's initial experiments, infant monkeys were separated from their mothers at 6 to 12 hours after birth and were raised in laboratory settings. They were then

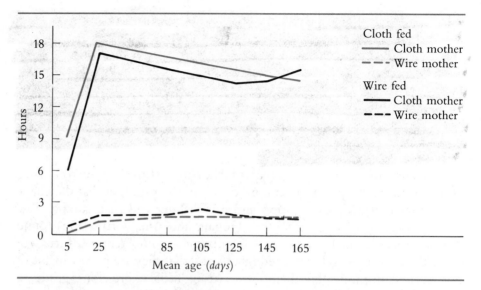

FIGURE 6.9 Contact time to cloth and wire surrogate. Adapted from *American Psychologist,* 25 (2) fig. 2, p. 162, by Harlow and Suomi. Copyright © 1970 by the American Psychological Association. Reprinted by permission of the publisher and authors.

provided with surrogate mothers. These substitute mothers were either made of heavy wire or of wood covered with terrycloth. In some of the experiments, both surrogates were present in the cage with the baby monkey, but only one was equipped with a nipple from which the baby could nurse. Some of the infant monkeys received nourishment from the wire surrogate, the others from the cloth surrogate (Harlow & Zimmerman, 1959). As you can see from Figure 6.9, even the infant monkeys who received their nourishment from the wire mothers spent the greatest amount of time clinging to the cloth mothers, suggesting that the contact comfort provided by the mother determines the monkey's degree of attachment. However, lactation can also be a factor in determining the infant monkey's degree of attachment. Monkeys who were raised with two cloth surrogates, only one of which provided them with nourishment, clearly preferred to stay close to that surrogate (see Figure 6.10).

Although the contact comfort provided by the cloth mothers seemed to result in normal behavior in infancy, the monkeys raised with these surrogates displayed bizarre behavior later in life (see Figure 6.11). They were not able to mate easily. They failed to learn to communicate, and they were not able to deal with fear. Those monkeys who eventually became mothers did not seem to know how to nurture their babies. They failed to nurse their babies, and they seemed to reject them (Harlow, 1971). Monkeys who were raised without any surrogate mother, cloth or wire, but only with other infant monkeys, also exhibited problems. They

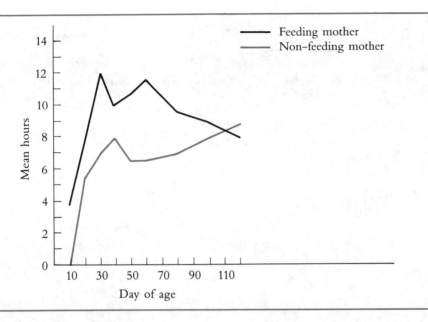

FIGURE 6.10 Infant preference for lactating cloth surrogate. Adapted from *American Psychologist,* 25 (2) fig. 7, p. 164, by Harlow and Suomi. Copyright © 1970 by the American Psychological Association. Reprinted by permission of the publisher and authors.

did not learn to explore or feel secure, and they spent most of the time clinging to each other (Harlow & Mears, 1979).

Evidence regarding the importance of the caretaker in the infant's life is also available from naturally occurring experiments as in cases of infants who are institutionalized or who, perhaps because of the cruelty of their parents, grow up in isolation without the benefit of warm human interaction. In a series of classic studies, Rene Spitz (1945, 1965) found that institutionalized infants became depressed because of a lack of nurturant care. He studied infants in two settings. One was a foundling home, where infants were kept in individual cubicles and were looked after by a nurse. These infants were kept clean and were fed, but they were not given any individual attention nor the opportunity to interact with and get to know their caretaker. In Spitz's words, they experienced very little "mothering." The second setting was a prison in which mothers who had been jailed cared for their own babies. In both the foundling home and the prison the infants received good medical and physical care. However, in the prison, the infants also received individual attention, and they grew up normally. Infants in the foundling home, on the other hand, did not receive individual attention and failed to grow up healthy. They were vulnerable to disease and were retarded in their psychological development.

FIGURE 6.11   Photograph of an infant monkey clinging to the cloth surrogate, from the original study by Harlow and Suomi.

Spitz's conclusion that the lack of mothering was the cause of the foundling home infants' failure to thrive has been criticized (Pinneau, 1955), because there were some methodological flaws in his studies. Nevertheless, later research clearly supported his contention that infants who are not given sufficient attention and affection are likely to suffer physical and emotional consequences (Rutter, 1979). The consequences need not be permanent, as long as the infants eventually receive nurturant care (Skeels, 1942, 1966).

However, when infants continue to be deprived of affection, they may grow up exhibiting delinquent and disturbed behavior later in life. This point is made by John Bowlby (1953, 1969, 1980), who was asked by the World Health Organization to report on the mental health status of homeless children. The assignment gave him the opportunity to study adolescents who spent their infancy and childhood years in institutions or foster homes. The adolescents had been repeatedly moved from one institution or foster home to another, never having the opportunity to establish close and loving relationships with adults. Having grown up without love, these adolescents were "affectionless" and unable to care for others and to love.

Thus, while the physical care and feeding of the baby are necessary, they are not sufficient for normal social and emotional development. The baby also needs to have the warmth and affection of a nurturant caretaker who will cuddle him, smile at him, and laugh and play with him and who, simply stated, is interested in him. Not only are these factors essential for normal social and emotional development, they are also crucial for normal physical and cognitive development. Infants who are deprived of love and affection are stunted in their growth and evidence deficits in language and mental skills (Dennis, 1973).

Consistency and Continuity of Care. Whether the infant receives such loving care from his biological mother or some other warm and sensitive adult is immaterial (Schaffer, 1977). However, there are two conditions which must be met if the infant is to develop normally. Care must be consistent and continuous. Consistency of care refers to the notion that the infant must be given the opportunity to interact with and become familiar with one caretaker. In institutions, an infant may have many caretakers. With the experience of many changes in caretakers and in the type of care he receives from each of them, an institutionalized infant fails to learn about and come to rely on the predictability and responsivity of any one caretaker. Often such an infant fails to form an attachment. The same can happen with an infant whose mother is working and who is placed in different types of caretaking arrangements or whose caretakers keep changing (Schaffer, 1977).

consistency and continuity of care

The infant must also have continuity of care—he must be given the opportunity to establish a long-term and unbroken relationship with the person he becomes attached to (Schaffer & Emerson, 1964; Schaffer, 1977). Although infants can withstand brief separations from the individual they become attached to, long-term separations are difficult for them to cope with. Initially they react to even short periods of separation by crying, screaming, or otherwise showing their distress. When the separations are long in duration, the infants eventually stop crying and become apathetic, which is a way of withdrawing from the environment emotionally.

DISCUSSION OF SOCIAL ISSUES: FOSTER CARE

The importance of continuity of care is especially apparent in infants placed in foster care after they have formed specific attachments to their mothers. Yarrow (1964) found that infants placed in foster care after age 7 months showed severe emotional disturbances because at that age they are

Reversibility of the Negative Effects of Early Deprivation

Although infants suffer when they are deprived of a warm and nurturant relationship with a parent or caregiver, the negative effects of early deprivation are not permanent and may be reversed once the infant is given appropriate care. This is demonstrated in one of the most remarkable and classic studies in the field of developmental psychology. In this study, conducted by Harold Skeels (1942, 1966), 25 infants were being raised in an orphanage where they received adequate physical care but no individual attention from the caretakers. Due to overcrowded conditions in the orphanage, 13 of the infants were transferred to an institution for mentally retarded adults where each of the infants was "adopted" and given individual attention by one of the mentally retarded women. Thus Skeels was able to compare these two groups of infants, one group which remained in the orphanage and the other group raised in a markedly more stimulating and socially responsive environment.

The two situations presented an opportunity for Skeels to assess the impact of an improved social setting on the infants' development. Using the infants who remained in the orphanage as the control group and the infants who were moved to the institution as the experimental group, Skeels assessed the mental status of the infants at the time when the transfer occurred. At that time the infants were an average age of 19 months. He found that the 12 infants in the control group had an average IQ of 86.7. The average IQ of the 13 infants in the experimental group was 64.3, which placed them in the category of mentally retarded. Tested a year and a half later, however, the two groups reversed their positions. The experimental group gained an average of 28.5 IQ points, evidencing an average IQ of 92.8. The control group lost 26.2 IQ points, evidencing an average IQ of 60.5.

Trying to ascertain if the IQ gains evidenced by the experimental group would last, Skeels followed up the subjects. He tested them again 2½ years after the study ended. Eleven of the 13 subjects had been adopted some time during this interim period, and two of them remained institutionalized. Skeels found that the adopted children had an average IQ of 101.4, but the IQs of the 2 institutionalized children dropped. Also assessing the mental status of the 12 children in the control group who remained institutionalized, Skeels found that their average IQ was 66.1.

Perhaps even more revealing, there continued to be marked differences between the institutionalized subjects and those who were adopted, and those differences were apparent in adulthood. Skeels tested the subjects after a 21-year interval from the time the original study was conducted. He found that 11 of the 13 subjects in the experimental group who were adopted were in no way retarded and functioned as normal adults. Several of them completed high school and attended college. Four of the control group subjects however, remained institutionalized. One had died. Only about half of them attained a third-grade education.

The implications that the detrimental effects of early experience can be altered have been reported in other studies described in previous chapters (Dennis, 1973) and in reviews of such studies (Clarke & Clarke, 1976). Such implications are also inherent in studies using animals. Recall that monkeys who are reared in isolation are socially inept, and they evidence disturbed behavior. In attempts to rehabilitate these monkeys, researchers have paired them with normal monkeys the same age. These attempts have failed, however, perhaps because the isolated monkeys became overwhelmed by the normal monkeys' social overtures. Trying to gradually ease the isolated monkeys' transition to living with other animals, Suomi, Harlow, and McKinney (1972) paired monkeys who had been isolated for the first 6 months of their lives with normal monkeys 3 months of age. Since the normal monkeys' social behavior is not as sophisticated as that of older monkeys, they would not overwhelm the isolated monkeys. The normal monkeys served as "therapists" to the isolated monkeys. An isolated and therapist monkey pair was placed together for two hours a day, three days a week. For two days a week, the isolated monkeys were subjected to "group therapy" in which two pairs of isolated and therapist monkeys were placed together. The researchers found that after six months of therapy, the isolated monkeys were rehabilitated to the extent that their behavior was similar to that of monkeys who had been reared under normal conditions. At 2 years of age, the monkeys who were previously isolated showed complete recovery and they were able to conduct themselves successfully in all social situations. Other therapy studies, with monkeys who had been isolated for 12 months (Harlow & Novak, 1973), have also been successful, attesting to the reversibility of the negative effects of early deprivation.

sufficiently mature to have become attached to their mother, but they are as yet unable to understand the breaking of the relationship that is the most important part of their world.

Observing that not only in infancy but in later childhood as well, children need to experience continuity in their interpersonal relationships, psychologists have made attempts to change policies that govern the foster care system. The foster care system was instituted to respond to the needs of children when the behavior of their parents constitutes a serious risk for the child (Cox & Cox, 1985). This can occur in family situations where a parent physically abuses the child or fails to meet the child's physical and emotional needs. In such cases, social agencies intervene, remove the child from the home, and place him in a foster home.

One of the problems with the foster care system is that it is crisis-oriented. That is, social agencies often intervene only at the point when the child's health and development are in imminent danger. Another problem with the system is that although it is supposed to provide temporary care for children until such time as decisions about permanent placements can be made, some children remain in foster care their entire childhood. What is even worse, they are moved from one foster home to another. In a survey conducted by the Children's Defense Fund (1978), it was found that 52% of the children in the foster care system had been out of their family homes for two or more years and that 18% of the children had been moved from one foster home to another two or three times.

During the last decade, researchers and advocates for children have brought the matter of the inadequacy of the foster care system to the attention of policymakers. According to the research, families whose children are in foster care have severe internal problems, too little access to resources they need, and inadequate skills to manage their children (Weisbrod, Casale, & Faber, 1981). Instead of spending money on a system for care that is inadequate and potentially harmful to the child, proposals have been made that would channel public funds toward preventive services which would eliminate the need to remove the child from the home (Zigler & Finn, 1982). For example, a home visitor could be sent to a family on a regular basis to assess the parent-child relationship, to find out what the parents need, and to offer them support and education *before* the family situation becomes a threat to the child.

There have also been suggestions for improvements of the foster care system when children must be removed from their homes. These suggestions have been incorporated into Public Law 96-272. This law, known as the Adoption Assistance and Child Welfare Act, not only ensures permanent families for such children, it also pulls together three elements: prevention of foster care placements, attempts to reunite foster children with their biological parents, and permanent adoptive families for children who cannot return home (the Edna McConnell Clark Foundation, 1985). As such, the law serves to increase federal adoption aid and requires that states not only tighten their control over the foster care program, but also that the states ensure that each child who is in foster care is assured consistency and continuity of care. Thus, a foster care arrangement is no longer regarded as adequate unless it is a permanent living situation (Watson, 1982). Although these basic changes in the foster care system and the focus on giving the child an opportunity to be adopted raise a number of unresolved issues regarding children's needs and parents' rights (Jones, 1985), they have resulted in a better living situation for many children. In a recent (1985) report to Congress, the Secretary of the U.S. Department of Health and Human Services noted that the number of children in foster care dropped from 500,000 in 1977 to 243,000 in 1982 and that the average time a child spent in the foster care system was reduced from 47 months in 1977 to 35 months in 1982. What has happened, in effect, is that the foster care program has moved away from being a receiving and holding system for children who cannot live with their parents to one in which an increasing number of children are eligible for adoption and thus have an opportunity to become permanent members of a family. Unfortunately, however, not all states have made equal progress in their approach to foster care. Several obstacles have slowed the implementation of the act, one of which is the failure of the federal government to appropriately monitor states' efforts in this regard (Edna McConnell Clark Foundation, 1985). Nevertheless, P.L. 96-272 is certainly an improvement over previous attempts to serve children and families in need.

FIGURE 6.12 By the year 2000, four out of every five infants younger than one year of age will have a mother in the work force.

Infants of Working Mothers

The importance of attachment for the infant's development and the need for consistency and continuity of care have also raised questions regarding the social and emotional development of infants whose mothers are working (see Figure 6.12). This is an important area of research given the fact that almost 4½ million mothers of children under three years of age are employed or actively seeking work (Ad Hoc Day Care Coalition, 1985). Perhaps even more importantly, the number of mothers returning to work while their babies are less than a year old has increased by 95% between 1970 and 1984. Researchers suggest that given these rates, by the year 2000 four out of every five infants under one will have a mother in the labor force (U.S. Department of Labor, 1984).

Researchers who have examined the effects of maternal employment on children note that the influence of maternal employment varies according to the age of the child, since the mother plays a different role in the child's life during infancy, childhood, and adolescence, and the child, too, makes different demands on the parent during these different developmental periods (Hoffman, 1979). It is during infancy, however, that the issue of maternal employment is a sensitive one for many parents. The fact that the infant is so dependent on adult care and the fear many parents have that their baby will grow to love someone else are at least two reasons why some mothers experience difficulties deciding to seek or return to employment while their children are very young (Belsky, Lerner, & Spanier, 1984). Many mothers who have to or who do decide to work feel guilty leaving the baby in the care of another person. The difficulty of finding suitable care for the baby and the high cost of quality care further exacerbate the problem for many families (Scarr, 1984).

Effects of Day Care on Attachment.   Psychologists who have investigated the effects of maternal employment on the social and emotional development of the infant have generally done so in the context of studies on the effects of day care on attachment. In general, several such studies have shown that day care is not associated with any disruption in the emotional bond between the infant and the parent. In a review of such studies, Rutter (1982) contends that "not only do day care children develop emotional bonds in much the same way and at much the same time as children reared at home, the main bonds are usually with the parents rather than with the child care staff." Infants who are reared in day care have been found to show more distress when they are separated from their mothers than from their day care provider, and they are also more likely to go to their mothers for comfort when they are upset than they are to approach their caretaker (Caldwell, 1970; Farran & Ramey, 1977). Researchers note further that studies of infants from stable, middle-class homes who are in high-quality day care centers reveal that while some infants with employed mothers do form attachments to their caretakers, the emotional bond between the infant and caretaker does not weaken the infant's emotional tie to the mother (Farran & Ramey, 1977; Kagan, Kearsley, & Zelazo, 1978).

Some of the more recent studies reveal, however, that infants from highly stressed families who are in out-of-home care arrangements of varying quality are vulnerable to the negative influence of the day care experience. In such situations, the infant may develop an insecure attachment to the mother (Vaughn et al., 1980). In a review of the literature on the research on infant day care, Gamble and Zigler (1986) further note that there are indications that (1) in families facing significant life stresses, substitute care during the first year of life increases the likelihood of insecure parent-infant attachment; and (2) that an insecure attachment in infancy makes the child more vulnerable to stresses encountered later in life.

There have also been a few studies which have looked beyond the possible effects of the day care experience on the infant and investigated the actual effects of maternal employment on the baby's development. The studies focus specifically on parent-infant interaction. In one such study, Cohen (1978) observed employed and nonemployed mothers and their infants as they interacted in a laboratory setting. No differences were found in the manner in which employed and nonemployed mothers of babies interacted with their infants during the first year of life, but when the same babies were 21 months old, more positive interactions were observed among the nonemployed mothers and their infants. The researcher notes, however, that a greater proportion of the employed mothers were single and thus likely to be under more stress generally. The stress may have accounted for the differences, rather than the mothers' employment status per se.

Other studies (Hock, 1980; Pistrang, 1984) indicate that some working mothers of young infants do indeed experience high levels of stress as they attempt to meet their obligations in the family and in the workplace. There is documentation that mothers who do experience high levels of stress, especially if their babies are premature or difficult to care for, are less able than other mothers to relate to the baby in a sensitive manner (Harwood, 1985; Crnic et al., 1983, 1984). Despite the difficulties these mothers encounter, and the possible negative effects on the babies, many mothers have to work for financial reasons (General Mills American Family Report, 1981). The only option for these parents is to place the infant in the care of someone else.

Infant Care Leave.   The fact that out-of-home care for infants is the sole option available to working couples and many single parents concerns a number of developmental psychologists and policymakers. They point out that in most industrialized countries, parents of young infants are eligible for paid leaves of absence which are provided by law expressly so that the parents who wish to can look after their babies themselves (Kamerman & Kahn, 1981). In a recent study of European parental leave policies, Allen (1985) found that in Sweden, West Germany, and France, parents have a choice between two kinds of arrangements for the care of the newborn infant. One of the parents can take advantage of a paid infant care leave supported by the employer or a social insurance fund (see Figure 6.13), or both parents can continue to work, in which case provisions for high-quality day care are made. Why are infant care leave policies available in European countries? Allen (1985) notes that this is due in part to demographic and economic circumstances which have forced these countries to take a collective responsibility for the children of working parents. In these countries, according to Allen, birth rates are substantially lower than in the United States, and over the past few decades, these countries have experienced labor force shortages. As a result there is a strong societal interest in the well-being of children. Allen suggests that with the declining birth rate in the United States, our nation may now be in a position similar to that of many European nations and we may be ready to institutionalize a parental leave policy that would ease the strain for parents who have to juggle work and family life.

infant care leave

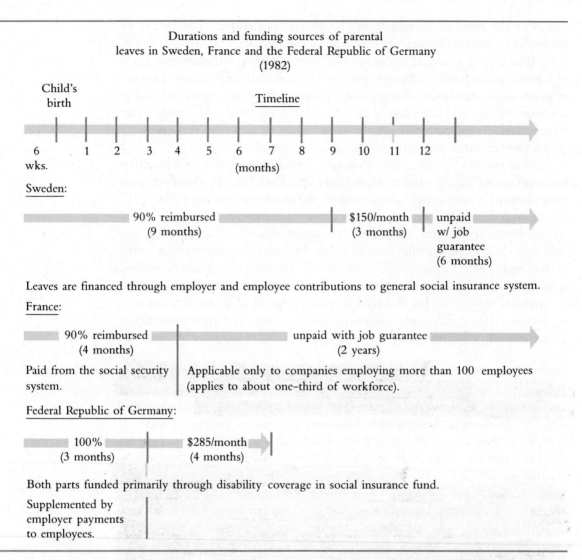

FIGURE 6.13 In Sweden, France, and the Federal Republic of Germany, parents are provided with a paid leave of absence to care for their young infants. Adapted from "Durations and Funding Sources of Parental Leaves in Sweden, France, and the Federal Republic of Germany," reprinted from *The Networker, 6,* (4) by permission of *The Networker* and Joseph P. Allen.

Relations with Others

The Father's Role. It would not be fitting to end a discussion on the infant's social and emotional development without first noting that the infant interacts not only with his mother but also with siblings, peers, other adults, and, of course, with his father. Although the father has been acknowledged by developmental psychologists as being physically present during infancy, his role in the infant's life has only recently begun to be investigated (Lamb, 1981; Parke, 1981).

Hodapp and Mueller (1982) suggest that there are at least three reasons for this general lack of research interest in the father. First, mothers have traditionally assumed the role of the primary caretakers of children. In accordance with sex-role stereotypes, this was considered appropriate. Second, researchers themselves have been influenced by the prevailing social climate and have concentrated on the study of the mother's relationship with the infant. They have focused on such topics as breastfeeding and the hormonal changes associated with nurturance. Finally, both psychoanalytic and behavioral theories, which no longer dominate the field of developmental psychology, highlight the role of the mother in the infant's life. Such theories have attributed a great deal of importance to the mother's relationship with the infant. However, societal changes, along with the current emphasis among researchers on the study of the child within his entire social network (Bronfenbrenner, 1977; Belsky, Lerner, & Spanier, 1984; Weinraub, Brooks, & Lewis, 1977), have resulted in a wave of studies on father-infant interactions. The studies have shown that babies not only interact with their fathers, they also form an attachment to them (Lamb, 1981).

With the new interest in the father-infant relationship, researchers are beginning to acquire specific data about how fathers care for and play with their children and how much time fathers and infants spend together. The research is admittedly new and therefore not yet entirely conclusive. It does appear, however, that although it is becoming increasingly acceptable in our society for fathers to take some, if not the primary responsibility for the care of their infants, the actual amount of time most fathers and infants spend together is still very limited. In a review of the research on the amount of time fathers spend with infants, Parke (1981) notes that fathers do not spend as much time caring for and playing with the infants as do mothers, and that in most families, it is the mother who is totally responsible for the care of the infant. Some fathers have never even had the experience of changing diapers!

Although fathers spend only a limited amount of time each day with their infants, when they do care for their infants they appear to be as competent as mothers are (Parke & O'Leary, 1976) and as sensitive to the babies' cues (Parke & Sawin, 1976). Also, the babies are found to be responsive to their father's care (see Figure 6.14). In comparing the amount of milk consumed by bottle-fed infants when fed by the father versus the mother, Parke and Sawin (1976) found that in each case, babies consumed nearly identical amounts of milk. In another comparison of father-infant and mother-infant interactions, researchers found that when fathers and infants played together, their interactions were regulated in the same attention/withdrawal pattern described in the discussion of mother-infant interaction (Yogman, Dixon, Tronick, Als, & Brazelton, 1977).

FIGURE 6.14 A father may not spend as much time in the routine care of the baby, but according to the research, he is as capable of performing the job as the mother!

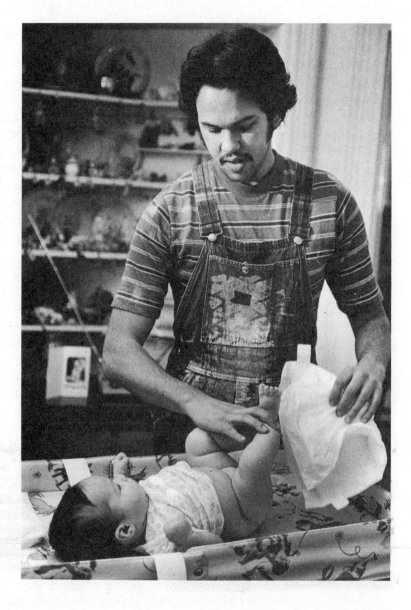

Whereas the father-infant interactions are similar in structure to mother-infant interactions, and fathers and infants do form attachments (Lamb, 1978b), there are important differences which seem to characterize the father-infant relationship in general. First, many of the interactions between the father and the infant occur in the context of play. Although most fathers interact less with their infants than do mothers, the average father spends a greater percentage of his time with the baby in playful, highly arousing interaction (Parke, 1978; Lamb, 1978b; Belsky, Gilstrap, & Rovine, 1984). Moreover, the father is less likely to interact with the infant for purposes of caregiving than is the mother, although, as we have said, he is as capable of providing care as is the mother. When fathers interact with their babies, it is usually for playing.

Second, there are differences between fathers and mothers in how they play with their infants. Yogman et al. (1977) found that fathers tend to be more physical in their interactions with their very young (2 to 3 months old) infants and that they tap the infants rhythmically or play poking games with them more than mothers do. On the other hand, mothers are more verbal in their interactions with their infants; they tend to speak to them often and to engage them in vocal games. The differences between the interactions of fathers and mothers persist as the infants grow older. In studies of infants 7 to 13 months old (Lamb, 1977) and 15 to 30 months old (Clarke-Stewart, 1978), researchers found that mothers are more likely to engage in games such as peek-a-boo and pat-a-cake with their babies. Fathers engage in more physical rough-and-tumble games, especially with sons. Tiffany Field (1978) further notes that even in cases of fathers who are the primary caretakers, fathers engage in more physical play with their infants than mothers do. Male monkeys are also more likely than female monkeys to engage in physical play with their offspring (Suomi, 1977), suggesting that men may be predisposed to physical play.

Beyond establishing that there are differences between the father-infant and mother-infant relationships, researchers recognize that including the father in the study of infancy does more than give researchers another interesting topic to study. Pedersen et al. (1980) and Belsky (1981) point out that the study of the father in the infant's life is important because it emphasizes the *family system* comprised of mother, father, and baby and thus paves the way for looking at joint parental influences on the infant. Alison Clarke-Stewart (1978) suggests that there are reciprocal parent-child influences that are complex and entail mother-to-child-to-father-to-mother influences. In her study, she found that the mother's stimulating involvement with the baby promoted secure emotional development and enhanced the intellectual status of the child. In turn, this increased the father's interest and involvement in parenting. The father's involvement in parenting then encouraged the mother to become still more involved with the infant.

Belsky (1981) further points out that the inclusion of the father in the study of infancy and the focus of the study of infant development within the context of family life pave the way for researchers to look into the effect of the infant on the husband-wife relationship. This should also yield important insights into how the marital relationship affects parenting and therefore, the infant's development. The insights obtained will be important for what they can tell us about early human development. Despite the enormous upheavals in family life of the last decade, the mother-father-child family is still the primary context for the infant's first relationships and initial stages of development.

FIGURE 6.15   The ever-increasing number of infants placed in group care has provided researchers with the opportunity to study peer interactions during infancy.

Peer Relations

The redirection in the study of infancy and the focus of researchers on the study of the infant within the broad social setting have resulted also in investigations of the relationships of infants to their age-mates. In the 1930s several studies focused on peer relations in infancy. Researchers noted the friendly behavior of infants toward one another and observed that infants touched, cooed at, and exchanged toys with one another when they were together (Shirley, 1933). However, from that time until the mid-1970s, no further attention was paid to the topic of peer relations in infancy. With the ever-increasing number of infants in some form of group care, infant-infant interaction has become a prevalent phenomenon that offers the opportunity for researchers to study peer relations.

The recent studies on peer relations suggest that infants are interested in and respond to other infants. In fact, even at birth they respond to other neonates' cries, more so than they respond to the cries of older children (Martin & Clark, 1982). At a slightly older age they also seem to accept unfamiliar peers readily and they are less fearful of them than they are of unfamiliar adults (Lewis & Brooks, 1974). How do infants who are the same age interact with one another? Mueller and Vandell (1979) suggest that peer interactions in infancy follow a developmental sequence. Initially, infants younger than three months of age simply look at other infants. At three to four months of age, they try to touch each other. By six months, they smile at one another. As the infants grow older and become more mobile, they approach and follow their age-mates (see Figure 6.15).

True social exchanges between infants begin around one year of age and also evidence a developmental sequence (Mueller & Lucas, 1975). First, object-focused interactions occur, and the infants seem to be more interested in an object they are playing with than they are with one another. In playing with a pull toy train, for example, one infant might pull and the other might toot, but no attempt is made by either infant to interact with the other. Slightly older infants evidence contingency games in which one infant might say "da," and the other might laugh, with this sequence being repeated several times. Contingency games are games in which one child acts and the other responds in some manner to the act. Finally, when infants are approximately 20 months of age, a stage of complementary interchanges occurs. The infants engage in run-and-chase and offer-and-receive games, with each of the infants able to take turns running and chasing each other and giving and receiving toys in a reciprocal and coordinated manner.

contingency games

You will see in Chapter 9 that as the child grows older, peer interactions become more complex and that peers assume an increasingly large role in the child's life.

SUMMARY

The infant possesses not only far greater physiological and intellectual capabilities than had previously been suspected; he is also a social being, born with the ability to attract people and the desire to be close to them. He is well prepared to interact with and influence his caregivers by gazing at them, smiling, and averting his gaze. This is documented in the research on mother-infant interaction which has shown that when mothers or other adults are communicating with the baby, they behave in such a way as to accommodate to his capabilities.

As the mother and baby communicate with and interact with one another, they become increasingly attuned to each other's characteristics and needs. The infant learns the basic cues and conventions that govern human social behavior. The mother, for her part, becomes increasingly confident in her ability to care for her baby and to interpret her behavioral cues. By relating to and interacting with each other in mutually satisfying ways, the infant acquires a sense of trust and the realization that the world is a warm and safe place to be in, and he is able to establish a strong and enduring attachment to the mother.

The infant's attachment to the mother occurs in phases and is strongest when the infant is about 8 months old. During that time, the infant experiences stranger anxiety and separation anxiety. Researchers have also found that there are individual differences in attachment. Some infants are securely attached; others evidence anxious and avoidant attachments which are indicative of disturbances in the mother-infant relationship that may be due either to the characteristics of the baby or to the characteristics of the mother. Such disturbances may also be due to life stresses the mother experiences and the unavailability of support systems such as family members, neighbors, and friends.

Researchers emphasize the importance of attachment, noting that it influences other aspects of development. They have found that monkeys who were not given an opportunity to become attached to an adult exhibited bizarre behaviors later in life. Human infants also need to have the opportunity to establish warm human relationships if they are to develop normally. Such a warm relationship need not be with their biological mother. What is important is that the infant experience consistency and continuity of care.

Infants placed in foster care situations often do not get the opportunity for continuity of care, especially if they are placed in several foster homes during their childhood years. Infants of mothers who are working are also vulnerable depending on the type of day care arrangements they are in and the ability of their mothers to care for them in a sensitive manner. Some psychologists have found that although employed and nonemployed mothers generally interact with their infants in similar ways, the mother's employment is often associated with high levels of stress which may interfere with the mother-infant relationship.

Although much of the research on social and emotional development involves the infants' relationship with their mothers, infants interact with others, most notably their fathers. Fathers, although as capable of providing nurturant and sensitive care as mothers, spend less time with their infants than mothers do. Most often they play with their babies rather than provide routine care. Babies also play with other babies when they have the opportunity to do so.

REVIEW POINTS

1. Recognizing that the newborn baby possesses an array of sensory and perceptual skills, researchers have sought to study the infant as a social being and to document the emergence and development of his interactions with those around him.

2. Much of the research focuses on the mother-infant relationship. Researchers point out, however, that other people are also important in the infant's life and that babies become emotionally attached not only to their mother but also to their father, grandparents, siblings, caretakers, and others with whom they have regular contact.

3. In the course of his interactions with his caretakers, the infant learns that he is cared for and loved. The caretakers also learn about the various needs and desires of the baby and how they can best meet these needs. As they interact with one another, the baby and caretaker take turns, each synchronizing his or her gestures and intonations to those of the other.

4. Babies communicate with their caretakers from the moment of birth through crying, gazing, and smiling. Smiling is one of the most social and communicative of the infants' emotional expressions, and it occurs in stages. Initially smiles are spontaneous and result from central nervous system activity. Later smiles are triggered by something in the external world, and they evidence pleasure.

5. Fear is another emotion that seems to occur in sequence. Two fears have been extensively studied by psychologists: stranger anxiety and separation anxiety.

6. Separation anxiety is one of the measures of the infant's attachment to the caretaker. Attachment, which is one of the most important of the infant's emotional experiences, is defined as the strong and enduring bond between the infant and the adult he most frequently interacts with.

7. There are individual differences in attachment. Some infants are securely attached to their caretaker, others form insecure attachments.

Those infants who form insecure attachments are less likely than the securely attached infants to explore their surroundings and learn from these. They are also less likely to establish meaningful social relationships with others.

8. Insecure attachments may be the result of insensitive caretaking and the failure of the adult caretaker to respond to the needs and social cues of the infant. However, infants may contribute to the disorder in the relationship, as often mothers or other caretakers find it difficult to take care of an unresponsive infant or an infant who cries a great deal and who is difficult to soothe.

9. Contingent care, that is, care that is responsive to the needs of the infant, is crucial to the establishment of secure attachment and to the emotional health of the baby. It does not matter whether the baby receives such care from his biological mother or from another adult. What does matter is that the infant receive the opportunity for consistency and continuity of care. During the first year of life, it is important that the infant be taken care of by one individual he can come to know and depend on and with whom he will be able to establish a long-term relationship.

10. When infants have to be removed from a disturbed family situation, they are placed in foster care. Until recently, foster care policies violated the principles of continuity and consistency of care. Infants were removed from one foster care home and placed in another so frequently that they were unable to establish meaningful relationships with their foster parents. Furthermore, they remained in foster care for most of their childhood years. Recent changes in foster care policies, incorporating findings from the research, have greatly improved the foster care system.

11. Although much of the research focuses on the relationship between the infant and his mother, researchers now focus on father-infant relationships as well. Also, they are investigating the infant's interaction with other infants.

Atypical Development

Now that we have discussed the course of growth and development from the prenatal period through the first two years of life, it is instructive to take a brief pause to introduce the topic of atypical development and consider some of the ways in which development may deviate from its normal course.

The topic of atypical development is broad. It includes research on the incidence, genesis, and nature of specific disorders in growth and development and the study of children who are born with physical or mental defects that are handicapping, such as blindness, deafness, brain damage, motor dysfunction, and/or a genetic disease. Also included in this topic is the study of children who are mentally retarded and of children who suffer from one or more of a variety of emotional and behavioral disorders, some of which may not become apparent until the early childhood or adolescent years. Discussions of some such abnormalities in development, and the research and social considerations associated with these, appear in various chapters throughout the book. In some chapters we discuss disturbances in behavior and personality that can result from family dysfunction and the abuse and neglect of children. In other chapters we highlight individual differences among infants and older children in temperament, activity level, and ability to learn, and we note how these differences contribute to variations in psychosocial development. In this and the other sections on atypical development, we elaborate on the topic. However, since this book is primarily about what we know from the research about normal children, these sections will be necessarily brief, but of sufficient length to enable you to appreciate the current understanding of the various disorders and some of the social issue considerations associated with them.

ATYPICAL DEVELOPMENT IN INFANCY

The Birth of Severely Handicapped Infants

The social issues related to the topic of atypical development are in many instances emotionally laden and painful to deal with, and they defy easy resolution. This is especially so in the case of infants who are born with severe and multiple handicaps. Until recently, nature determined the fate of most of these babies. However, now that the medical world has the skills to extend the lives of these infants, questions arise as to who has the right to determine the fate of the babies and whether they are to live or die.

Baby Doe. Consider the case of a baby boy known only as Baby Doe. This baby was born on April 9, 1982, in Bloomington, Indiana. He had an incomplete esophagus and Down's syndrome, which causes moderate to severe mental retardation. Advances in neonatal surgery would have enabled physicians to attach the esophagus to the stomach, thereby insuring the baby's survival. However, the baby would have remained mentally retarded. Baby Doe's parents were confronted with a difficult decision: to assent to the operation that would save the life of their child, who would remain retarded, or to allow the child to die of starvation. Even though physicians advised them to the contrary, and sought a court order to proceed with surgery, the parents chose to let the baby die and the courts upheld their decision. Baby Doe died on April 15, only one week after his birth (Wallis, 1983).

Baby Jane Doe. In yet another example, a baby girl, known as Baby Jane Doe, was born with *spina bifida,* failure of the spinal column to close, as well as with an abnormally small head and fluid in the brain. Physicians predicted that with conservative treatment and without a series of operations, the baby girl would die within the first two years of life. Surgery could allow the child to survive into her 20s, but she would remain paralyzed and would require repeated operations. Her parents agonized over the painful decision they had to make, in the end rejecting surgery and opting instead for conservative treatment. In this case, the physicians were in agreement with the parents, but the federal government sued for the release of the baby's health records so that federal lawyers could determine what course of action to take.

spina bifida

The lawsuit over Baby Jane Doe's health records and, ultimately, her fate, marks the first time the federal government has gone to court in defense of a handicapped infant, and it has generated a fierce controversy (Campbell, 1983; Sherlock, 1979). At issue are the questions: how should society protect the rights of severely handicapped infants, and who should make life and death decisions in their behalf? Involved in the controversy are not only the federal government and the health profession but also right-to-life organizations and several groups which advocate for handicapped citizens. These groups and the federal government contend that in every case of a handicapped infant, every effort should be made to provide treatment and prolong life. The federal government has issued regulations prohibiting discriminatory failure to feed and care for handicapped or seriously ill infants.

Physicians see the role of the federal government in this regard as intrusive. They argue that each handicapped infant deserves individual attention and that case-by-case decisions should be made depending on the severity of the handicap and ultimate prospects for recovery (Duff, 1979, 1981). Many physicians further argue that decisions regarding the fate of the baby should be made within the context of a "moral" community which includes physicians, nurses, social workers and clergy, if so desired by the family (Campbell & Duff, 1979). Their task is to support the family in its grief and to counsel the parents. However, it is the parents, with the advice and support of the baby's physicians, who should make the decisions about the care of the baby (Duff, 1981). Some parents who have given birth to a handicapped baby and have written about the agony they have experienced agree that as parents, they should have the right and responsibility to decide the fate of their babies (Stinson & Stinson, 1983). However, there could be cases where parents would refuse to approve treatment that would clearly benefit the child or where parents would make decisions that conflict with the advice of physicians, as in the Baby Doe case. Would parents make decisions simply because they do not want the emotional and financial burden of caring for a handicapped baby? To eliminate this possibility and ensure that any caretaking decision is made with the best interests of the baby in mind, it has been proposed that hospitals create "infant bioethical review committees" (Wallis, 1983). These committees, to be made up of medical experts, laypeople, clergy, and lawyers, would be consulted in any decision to forgo treatment and they would attempt to resolve conflicts between the parents and doctors over how to proceed in the care of the baby. However, even this compromise approach has some pitfalls. In many cases, severely handicapped babies have to be treated within a few hours or days if they are to survive. The question is, could the proposed bioethical review committees resolve conflicts in time to save the baby? Obviously, there is no easy resolution to the dilemma we face in the care and treatment of severely handicapped newborns. But it is a problem that as a society we have to confront and attempt to resolve, since each year advances in medicine are made that enable us to save yet more babies who only a few years ago would have died at birth or shortly after.

Beyond the question of who has the right to decide the fate of severely handicapped babies, there are concerns that improved medical technology enabling the survival of babies born with defects has contributed to a possible increase in the number of handicapped infants. This has brought on intense argument among physicians, policy makers, and even philosophers on the issues of whether, as a society, we should continue to work on techniques to enable the survival of handicapped infants and whether sustaining their lives is beneficial to society or potentially too costly. Since handicapped individuals require special care and education not only in infancy but throughout their childhood and adult years as well, any increase in the number of handicapped individuals is likely to result in a substantial burden on society.

The issue of whether, as a society, we should be sustaining life at any cost is not an easy one to settle. Moreover, there are those who question whether medical technology has in fact contributed to an increase in the number of handicapped infants, asking, are there more handicapped individuals now than there were in previous years? This question yields answers which are subject to dispute. There are some who contend that the number of handicapped infants born annually has doubled over the past 25 years. This contention is made on the basis of analyses of patterns of births in the United States which reveal that in the 1950s approximately 70,000 handicapped infants were born annually; currently about 140,000 handicapped infants are born each year (Lyons, 1983; Newaceck et al., 1986).

Improved medical technology is only one reason cited for the possible increase in the number of handicapped individuals. Other reasons are related to changes in life style. For example, during the past 25 years, cigarette smoking, which is known to have an adverse influence on the developing fetus, has doubled in popularity among women of childbearing age and thus is cited as one of several possible reasons for the increase in the number of infants born with a handicap. Another possible reason is related to toxic substances in the workplace. These are known to have teratogenic effects on the development of the unborn baby and are affecting an increasingly larger number of women of childbearing age, since many such women are now working. It is argued that with many women, in particular pregnant women, being subjected to or subjecting themselves and their unborn children to adverse environmental influences, it is not surprising that many more babies are now born handicapped than was true in previous years.

These factors provide a compelling argument in support of the view that the number of handicapped infants has doubled in recent years. However, this view is not adhered to by all professionals. Not disputing the fact that currently 140,000 handicapped infants are born annually, some medical and child development professionals point out that this does not mean that there are now more handicapped individuals than there were in previous years. Rather, it may mean that there are now more infants who are diagnosed at birth as handicapped. The point is that whereas many handicapping conditions are now diagnosed early in life, in the past they were not detected until children were older.

Identifying the Handicapped Infant

During the past 25 years enormous advances have been made in our ability to identify infants who may be handicapped. Also, child development professionals have come to appreciate the fact that the best chance for the optimal development of a handicapped child depends on the early identification of the defect and the prompt referral of the child to professionals who can evaluate the child's developmental status and make recommendations for follow-up services.

To this end, several screening tests have been developed to identify, as early in life as possible, those infants who may be atypical in their development. Often a handicap is not readily apparent at birth. Clinicians note that screening tests are not diagnostic and are useful only in identifying the infant who is suspected of having a disorder. The identified infant is tested again to verify the original testing and, if warranted, is sent for more formal developmental evaluations and diagnosis of the disorder (Frankenburg, 1981).

Several of the screening tests that have been developed are routinely administered to all newborn infants in order to identify those who may be suffering from a specific genetic disorder. Other tests are used to identify infants who may suffer from subtle abnormalities and assaults to the central nervous system. Examples of the latter type of tests are the Prenatal Risk Factor Scale (Hobbs et al., 1973) and the Parmelee Obstetric Complications Scale (Littman & Parmelee, 1978). These make use of medical records and interview data to determine the amount of risk the baby has been exposed to prenatally or at birth and whether, because of such risk, the baby should be further evaluated.

Some screening tests focus on the direct examination of the young infant in order to establish her neurological status. Some of these include an examination of a variety of reflexes, since the absence of an expected reflex, or the presence of a reflex for a longer period of time than is considered normal, could be an indication of some damage to the central nervous system (Prechtl, 1982). Besides being geared toward the detection of possible central nervous system damage, other tests are also oriented toward the detection of behavior problems in the baby which may interfere with her interactions with her caretakers. Such tests examine the sensory and perceptual skills of the baby, her ability to initiate an interaction with the environment and modulate the amount of environmental stimulation she is subjected to, as well as her capacity to cope with distressing situations (Als, 1981).

Infants at Risk

Such screening tests are useful in identifying infants who may be *at risk* for atypical development. These at-risk infants may not necessarily evidence a handicap, but they enter the world with certain vulnerabilities or with limited sensory and perceptual skills necessary for benefitting and learning from experiences in the environment (Gorski, 1984).

Some of the infants who are considered to be at developmental risk are those who have experienced prenatal and perinatal complications (Nelson & Ellenberg, 1979), and those who are born small for their gestational age. These full-term but underweight babies may be small for their gestational age for several reasons (discussed in Chapter 3), including prenatal malnutrition and smoking by the mother during pregnancy. In follow-up studies of such infants, researchers have found that compared to their full-weight peers, these infants evidence mild intellectual deficits (Parmelee & Schulte, 1970) as well as decreased reflex behavior, alertness, and responsivity, at least for the first year of their lives (Als, Tronick, Adamson, & Brazelton, 1976).

Postmaturity gestation (when the pregnancy lasts beyond 41 to 42 weeks) is another factor that places the infant at risk for developmental delays or disabilities. In explaining the risks faced by the postterm infant, researchers note that such an infant has to rely on an old placenta that is functioning beyond the time for which it is naturally programmed (Gorski, 1984). As a result, postterm infants are born with thickened, peeling skin, and they have a wizened facial expression (Clifford, 1954). They are more vulnerable than infants born on time, with their parents reporting that the babies have a high incidence of illness and trouble in establishing feeding and sleeping routines. In addition, during their first year of life, postterm infants score lower on scales of mental development than do infants born on time (Field, Dabiri, Hallock, & Shuman, 1977).

postmaturity gestation

Just as postterm infants are vulnerable and at risk for developmental delays, so are infants who are born prematurely. Recall from previous chapters that premature infants are vulnerable to illnesses during the first few months of life. They have trouble adjusting to the environment, often evidencing disturbances in sleep and in their ability to be soothed. However, as is the case with other at-risk infants, not all infants born prematurely are equally vulnerable. Some recover full health and function and behave like full-term infants as early as their first year of life (Kopp & Parmelee, 1979). Others, especially those infants who are subject to the stresses of poverty, may not evidence normal neurological and behavioral development (Francis-Williams & Davies, 1974), and they may be so irritating to their parents, or so unresponsive to their parents' care, that they may be subjected to physical and emotional abuse. By identifying these at-risk infants, and alerting parents to some of their baby's vulnerabilities and characteristics, many of the problems associated with prematurity or with other developmental risk factors may be prevented (Sameroff & Chandler, 1975; Yarrow, 1979).

Developmentally Disabled Infants

Screening tests are also used to identify infants who may suffer from a developmental disability. A developmental disability is defined as a chronic disorder which can be manifest in mental or physical impairment. It is likely to continue indefinitely and to result in substantial functional limitations in the individual's ability to learn and acquire the capacity for independent living. Among the major disorders that are grouped under the general term of developmental disabilities are mental retardation, cerebral palsy, language and learning disabilities, blindness, and deafness. Other disorders or diseases such as epilepsy or cystic fibrosis may also be considered in the category of developmental disabilities if they are so severe as to impose limitations on the child's ability to learn and on her eventual capacity for self-care (Golden, 1984; Gabel & Erickson, 1980).

Visual Impairments

A developmental disability may not always impose limitations on the infant's capacity for developmental progress if the infant is helped in her ability to compensate for the handicap. For example, consider infants who are born blind or with severe visual impairments. Many such infants have a genetic basis for the handicap, or they may be blind because of some assault to development experienced during the prenatal period (Roeske, 1980). When the blindness is not associated with any other defect, then, in their motor development blind infants seem to develop in much the same sequence as do sighted infants, and they achieve some motor milestones such as sitting or standing at about the same age as do sighted infants. However, blind infants are delayed in their mobility patterns so they reach for objects, crawl, or walk at a later age than do sighted infants. Researchers have found that whereas sighted babies begin to crawl at an average of 9 months of age, blind infants do not begin to crawl until sometime during the second year of life (Fraiberg, 1971, 1968; Adelson & Fraiberg, 1974). It is explained that mobility patterns require visual elicitation and that the ability to see is a powerful incentive for mobility, hence blind infants' delay in crawling and other mobility skills.

Although blind infants are delayed in their acquisition of mobility skills, they eventually acquire these so that blindness does not affect motor development to any great extent. The same is true of cognitive, language, and social development. Blind infants have been observed to acquire cognitive, language, and social skills in much the same sequence as do sighted infants, but they do evidence developmental delays. This is indicated in a series of studies by Selma Fraiberg (1977), who notes that the developmental delays evident in blind infants are probably due to the "experiential poverty" of such children. She suggests that parents who know that their baby is blind should attempt to help the baby compensate for the handicap by providing her with auditory cues. For example, parents of a blind infant should try to talk to their baby whenever they come close to her and provide the baby with toys and other objects that make a sound. Often, however, auditory cues alone are not sufficient. The blind infant may be attracted to a toy that makes a sound, but the sound does not give the infant any information about the toy's physical properties—whether it is round or square, or whether it is graspable. For this reason, parents need to be taught how to use auditory and other sensory cues to promote their babies' development (Fraiberg, 1977).

Hearing Impairments

The need to facilitate parents' ability to help a baby compensate for a handicap is also evident in the case of infants who are deaf. There are two major causes of congenital deafness: genetic deafness and rubella contracted by the mother during the first 3 months of pregnancy (Mindel, 1980). However, deafness can also occur in infants who are premature or who suffer from other developmental disabilities.

The research on deaf infants is limited, in large part because if these infants do not suffer from any other developmental problems, they babble and make other vocalizations in much the same way as do infants who can hear. During the first few months of life these infants appear normal, so a diagnosis of deafness is not made until they are older (Meadow, 1980). The research on deaf infants is further limited because most of the studies that have been done focus only on one aspect of development—language acquisition. For the most part, researchers attempt to ascertain the impact of the hearing impairment on the child's ability to learn to speak. Recall from these studies that during the first 9 months of life, language development in deaf infants progresses in much the same way as it does in hearing infants (Lenneberg, 1967). However, in the absence of corrective hearing aids, deaf infants older than 9 months of age begin to show increasingly significant deficits in language development and difficulty in their ability to learn language skills (Schlesinger & Meadow, 1972). If the hearing impairment is not detected, the child deteriorates not only in her ability to communicate, but also in her ability to learn other cognitive skills, and as a result her parents or teachers may consider her to be mentally retarded. However, if the hearing impairment is detected early in life and the infant is provided with corrective hearing aids or is introduced to sign language, the negative impact of the handicap on the child's development is minimized (Wolfson et al., 1980).

Cerebral Palsy

Blindness or deafness can occur as a single defect. Often, however, either one of these disorders is associated with other handicapping conditions.

This is especially the case with cerebral palsy. Cerebral palsy results from brain damage (due to oxygen deprivation, severe nutritional deficiency, radiation, or other problems) suffered during the prenatal or perinatal period. It is characterized by paralysis, muscle weakness, incoordination or some other aberration of motor dysfunction, and it is associated with other handicapping conditions. For example, mental retardation occurs frequently among children with cerebral palsy (Molnar, 1979), and speech and/or hearing problems occur in 70 to 80 percent of children with cerebral palsy (Love & Walthod, 1977). Besides these associated defects, cerebral palsied children may also suffer from severe visual impairments, learning disabilities, and frequent seizures (Huttenlocher, 1979). However, the cerebral palsied, like others who are developmentally disabled, vary greatly in the severity of their motor dysfunction and also in the extent that they suffer from other disabilities. Some cerebral palsied children are so severely handicapped by motor dysfunction and other disorders that they need help in the activities of daily living. Others are only mildly handicapped and can function independently.

Services for At-Risk and Disabled Infants

The developmental disabilities we have described represent only some of the disorders that are identifiable at birth or shortly thereafter. Several other disorders which are genetic in origin are discussed in Chapter 2. Still other handicapping conditions exist which, as you will see in later sections, do not become apparent until later in life. No matter what the disorder is, however, two points should be kept in mind:

1. Handicapped infants are, like normal infants, a heterogeneous group. They differ not only in the severity of the handicap but also in their temperament and ability to compensate for or overcome the disability.
2. All infants, even those who are disabled, are competent and active learners who should be given the opportunity to initiate an interaction with and respond to the environment (Lewis, 1984).

Early Intervention Programs

Many early intervention programs have been developed and implemented in recent years because empirical evidence has shown that without special and comprehensive intervention, disabled infants or those who are at risk for developing problems may not develop early skills and relationships needed in order to lead productive lives. The aim of early intervention programs is to prevent disorders that may arise from genetic and/or adverse influences to development and to remediate the effects of identified disorders (Hanson, 1984a).

Early intervention programs are available in most communities, providing the handicapped infant and the family with access to a broad variety of services that they may need. However, not all handicapped and at-risk infants are referred to such programs at an early age. Variations exist in the extent to which states and/or localities support early identification and intervention efforts. Furthermore, programs vary greatly from community to community in the quality and type of services they provide, and even in the location in which they provide the services. Some of the services are home-based wherein trained personnel go to the child's home. Others are both home- and center-based and they may be located in a variety of settings such as hospitals, private and public schools, and mental health and social service clinics.

In evaluating several early intervention programs, it has been found that whether the services are delivered in a home or at a center is not important. What is most important is that the program focus not only on the child but on the parents as well. This point is made clear in our discussions of blind and deaf infants whose parents have to be shown how to structure the infants' environment so that it is conducive to their development. Hanson (1984b) and Taft (1981) make a similar point. They note further that whereas the handicapped infant needs preventive or remedial therapy to overcome the handicap, the parents often need support in coping with the ramifications of the disability and of living with a handicapped child. When the parents are helped in this regard and when they are shown how to recognize the particular needs and characteristics of their child, both the handicapped infant and the parents benefit significantly. You can see that although as a society we have yet to resolve numerous considerations associated with the care and treatment of handicapped infants, we have at the same time made significant strides in the early identification of and services provided for the handicapped.

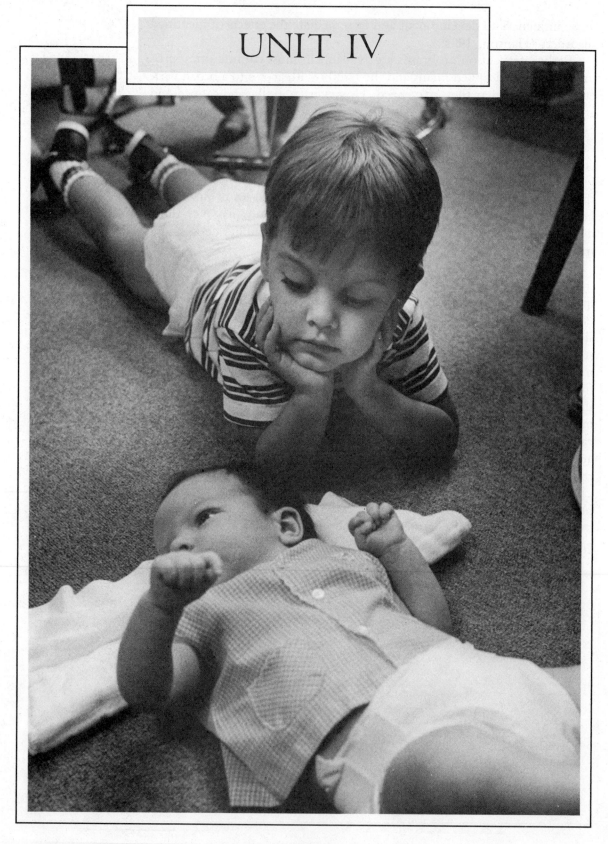

THE
PRESCHOOL
YEARS

During the past two decades, there has been a tremendous surge of interest in the study of preschool children. This is due in part to a growing realization that during the preschool period children experience many impressive psychological and physical changes which contribute to their later mental, emotional, and physical well-being. Prior to the 1960s, researchers attached little importance to the preschool period, and the early childhood years were looked upon as a time of frivolous play. Play, which characterizes the preschool period, was viewed as being of little or no value developmentally. Researchers now realize that play is of crucial importance. It is the medium through which children gain much of their knowledge, and play is actually the child's equivalent of the work of adults. Through play children are actively involved in enhancing their cognitive skills, and they also become increasingly more capable of understanding and dealing with the world around them.

CHAPTER 7

PHYSICAL DEVELOPMENT
IN THE PRESCHOOL PERIOD

PROGRESS IN PHYSICAL GROWTH
AND MOTOR DEVELOPMENT

In this chapter we will focus on the changes in physical growth and motor development that children undergo during the preschool years. These changes allow them to become involved in increasingly more complex play situations. Having acquired the ability to walk, preschoolers, through play, go on to develop a wide variety of fundamental motor skills. They engage in new experiences such as climbing, jumping, and throwing objects, for the sake of performing such activities and also for the sheer joy of knowing what they are capable of doing. Progress in physical development enables preschool children to become increasingly more independent, and they develop a sense of competence. They become more adept at feeding themselves, and they eventually acquire the muscular strength and coordination needed to undress and dress by themselves, control their bowel and bladder, and acquire such fine motor skills as writing and drawing. Not only do preschool children master these and other skills, they also begin to assert their individuality, and to think of themselves as more grown up. It is not unusual, for example, for a three-year-old girl to suddenly announce to her parents that she is no longer a baby, or to refuse any help in her attempts to perform routine tasks.

In part, preschoolers' increased awareness that they are no longer babies is related to the changes in their appearance and body proportions. During the preschool years, children not only increase in their strength and in their ability to execute motor tasks, they also lose some of the features that are characteristic of infants, such as bent legs and a protruding stomach. Their body proportions increasingly approach those of adults. Such changes in physical growth and development are governed by the genetic blueprint of each individual. Several environmental factors such as adequate nutrition and health care are also fundamental aspects of growth and development; yet, there are many preschool children in this country who do not enjoy them. Among the questions we address in this chapter are: Who are those children? and What are the barriers to good child health care? Before we go on to find out the answers to these questions, let us first examine the course of normal physical growth and the progress in motor development.

Physical Growth

During the preschool years, physical growth is not as rapid as it is during infancy, and some of the drama and excitement of seeing the individual acquire new skills almost daily is gone. Yet, if we compare the two-year-old child at the beginning of the preschool period with the six-year-old child he eventually becomes, we realize that the changes in physical development during the preschool years are striking indeed. These changes

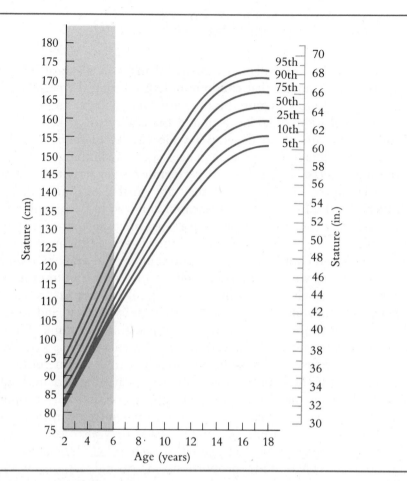

FIGURE 7.1 Girls' growth in height during the preschool years. Source: National Center for Health Statistics, 1976.

facilitate the transition of the individual from baby to child, and they include not only weight and height gains, but also skeletal maturation and brain growth.

Weight, Height, and Changes in Body Proportions

The fact that growth during the preschool years progresses at a much slower rate than it does during infancy is evidenced in the gains in weight and height. During the first two years of life, the baby as much as quadruples his birth weight and more than doubles his height. But between the ages of two to six, the average North American child gains only 4 to 5 pounds a year, and he grows about three inches a year. Thus, by the age of six, the child weighs, on the average, 45 pounds, and he measures about 43 inches. Of course, there are many variations in weight and height. Some six-year-olds can weigh as much as 50 pounds or as little as 35

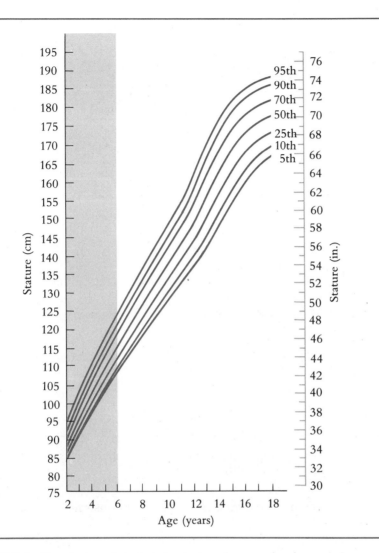

FIGURE 7.2   Boys' growth in height during the preschool years. Source: National Center for Health Statistics, 1976.

pounds. Some others are close to 50 inches tall or only slightly over 40 inches tall (National Center for Health Statistics, 1976; see Figures 7.1 to 7.4).

Because of this slower rate of growth, the child eats much less for his size during the preschool period than he did as an infant, a fact which often alarms parents and prompts them to seek medical advice. However, there is nothing abnormal about the change in the amount of food the child consumes. During the preschool period, and also during the middle childhood years when growth is also slow, the child does not need as many calories to sustain growth. Later, during the adolescent period when growth once again assumes a fast pace, changes in appetite also

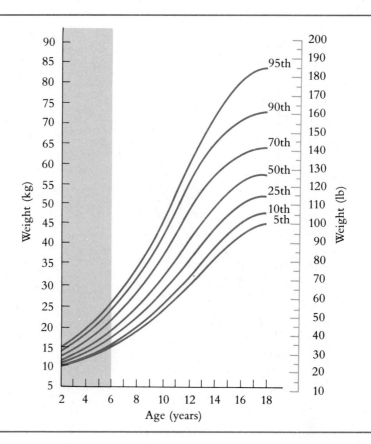

FIGURE 7.3 Girls' gain in weight during the preschool years. Source: National Center for Health Statistics, 1976.

occur, and, it seems to parents, the adolescent consumes enormous quantities of food.

For preschool children the gain in weight and especially in height is important, for they equate weighing more and growing taller with becoming older. However, the gain in weight and height is not as significant as the change in body proportions, which, in part, accounts for the individual's remarkable transformation from baby to child. Between the ages of two and three years, the child still has the protruding stomach, swayback, bent legs, and relatively large head characteristic of infancy. At that age, the individual, no longer a baby but not quite a child either, is often referred to as the toddler. Eventually, between the ages of three and six years, the child loses his baby fat, and he becomes taller and thinner. That is, his legs straighten and they account for a larger proportion of his body size. At the same time and because of the increase in height, the size of the child's head lessens in proportion to body size, so you can see that the child is not only growing, he is also becoming more adult-like in his body proportions.

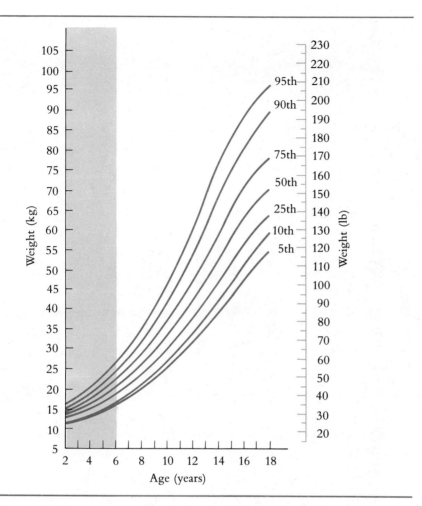

FIGURE 7.4   Boys' gain in weight during the preschool years. Source: National Center for Health Statistics, 1976.

Internal Changes

Skeletal Maturity.   At the same time that the child loses his baby look, several internal changes take place. One such change is related to skeletal maturity, which means that the child's bones become longer, thicker, and harder. During the prenatal period, skeletal development begins as a cartilage which is gradually replaced by bone. This process is referred to as *ossification*. Ossification, which continues after birth and is not complete until late adolescence, occurs at a rapid rate during the preschool period, enabling the child to become involved in activities which require strength.

ossification

In order to determine if physical development progresses normally, physicians use the child's *bone age* (or, skeletal age) as an assessment tool.

bone age

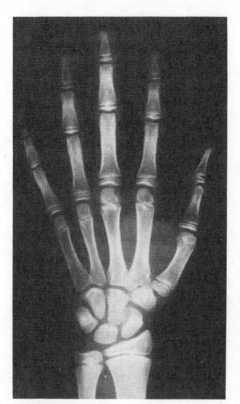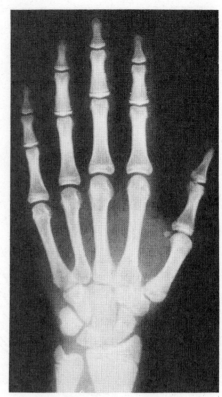

FIGURE 7.5   X-rays of the hands of two boys aged 14 years. The bone age of the boy whose hand is shown on the left is 12 years; the bone age of the boy whose hand is shown on the right is 16 years.

Bone age is determined by taking an x-ray of the child's hand and comparing the child's rate of ossification with ossification norms for his particular age (see Figure 7.5). Knowledge of the child's bone age is valuable for predicting the child's eventual height. This is especially important in cases of children who are either too tall or too short, because physicians need to determine if medical intervention is necessary. For example, a four-year-old girl who is much taller than her peers may have the bone age of a six- or seven-year-old, in which case her eventual height would be within the normal range, and no medical treatment is called for. A six-year-old boy who is very short may have a bone age of a four-year-old, in which case his eventual height would also be within the normal range. However, on the basis of their bone age, it can be determined that medical intervention is necessary for some children (Tanner, Whitehouse, Marshall, Healy, & Goldstein, 1975).

Brain Growth.   Another important internal change that occurs during the preschool years is the growth and maturation of the brain. This facilitates the acquisition of language skills during the preschool years, and also the child's ability to master increasingly more complex motor tasks.

You recall that during the prenatal period and infancy, brain growth is evident in the increase in brain weight. Much of the increase in brain weight occurs before the age of two years, at which time the brain weighs 75 percent of its adult weight. During the preschool years there is also a gain in brain weight, and by the time the child is five years old, the brain attains 90 percent of its adult weight. By age ten it reaches 95 percent of its adult weight. Increases in brain weight are the result of different changes, however. During the prenatal period and early infancy, when the brain cells are rapidly increasing in numbers, the weight gains are due to the increase in the number of neurons, the basic nerve cells of the brain. Weight gains during the preschool years and later reflect not a greater number of neurons, but rather, an increase in the size of neurons, due to *myelination,* and an increase in the size of *glial cells* which support the nerve cells.

myelination
glial cells

Myelinization occurs within several functional centers within the brain. The brain is organized into right and left hemispheres. The right hemisphere controls the left part of the body, giving directions to the left ear, eye, hand, and leg. The left hemisphere controls the right side of the body, giving directions to the right ear, eye, hand, and leg (Tyler, 1974). These two hemispheres are not mirror images of each other. Rather, within each are "centers" that control different abilities and functions (see Figure 7.6). The left hemisphere contains the brain centers that are responsible for receiving, processing, and producing language. The right hemisphere contains the centers that are responsible for spatial information, either visual or tactile, and visual imagery (Tyler, 1974). Thus, the left hemisphere codes input in terms of *linguistic descriptions* whereas the right hemisphere codes *images.* Both of these hemispheres are utilized most of the time, although there are some researchers who contend that some people are predominantly left-brained or right-brained. For example, an individual who is good at analyzing situations or problems may be left-brain dominant. This may be an oversimplified description of brain functioning as left-right distinctions are not absolute. The two hemispheres have differences, but each can sometimes fill in for the other. For example, some people with left-brain injuries who have lost their ability to speak (a left-brain function) still retain the ability to sing, a right-brain function. Taking advantage of this differentiation, scientists are trying to teach stroke victims to communicate by using the right brain's musical center.

The division of labor, so to speak, that is reflected in functioning of the brain according to different centers, allows the brain to work efficiently, since an individual can master more skills if each part of the brain is responsible for a specific function or type of knowledge. However, there are disadvantages to this mode of operation, the main one being the

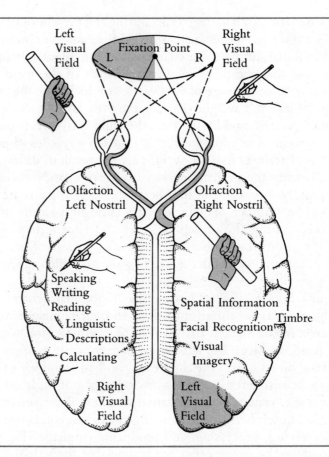

FIGURE 7.6 Lateralization of the brain. The right hemisphere controls the left side of the body and it contains the centers responsible for spatial information and visual imagery. The left hemisphere controls the right side of the body and it contains the centers responsible for receiving, processing, and producing language. Thus, the left hemisphere codes input of linguistic descriptions; the right hemisphere codes images.

inability of the brain to compensate for loss or damage to one of its parts. Thus a victim of brain damage due to injury or stroke may lose his ability to speak, depending on the part of the brain that is damaged. If such an injury occurs before early adolescence, when the speech center of the brain completes maturation, the right hemisphere might take over this function, permitting the individual to speak normally despite the injury (Lenneberg, 1967). The greater *plasticity of the brain* prior to early adolescence applies to other functional centers as well. During the childhood years, recovery from a variety of forms of damage to the brain is possible, provided that one functional center can take over or compensate for the loss of the functions of the damaged center.

plasticity of the brain

The functional centers for language skills begin their development early in life but their maturation takes several years to complete and is

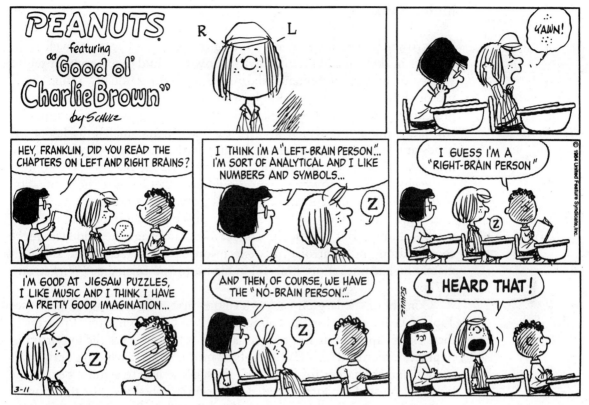

© 1984 United Features Syndicate.

associated with *myelogenetic cycles,* periods during which myelination occurs to particular functional centers within the brain. Recall from Chapter 4 that myelination is the process in which nerve fibers become coated with a protective myelin sheath so that their ability to perform their major duties (to send and receive impulses or signals) is enhanced. Lecours (1975) notes that there are three myelogenetic cycles that occur which seem to be associated with increased language ability of the child. The first cycle, involving the brainstem, starts before birth and is related to the ability of the infant to produce sounds. The second cycle starts around birth and continues to occur at a rapid rate until about age four. This cycle is related to the acquisition of language skills during the preschool period. The third myelogenetic cycle, which involves the upper cortex, is not complete until early adolescence.

Another change that contributes to brain maturation during the preschool years is the myelination of nerve fibers which are used in the control of voluntary movement. Myelination of these fibers is complete around the age of three or four (Tanner, 1978), hence the increased capability of the preschool child to master fine motor skills such as those required in holding a pencil or tying shoe laces.

myelogenetic cycles

Motor Skills

gross motor skills

fine motor skills

The growth in height that occurs during the preschool years, as well as the changes in skeletal and brain growth, allow the child to experiment with a variety of motor movements and to acquire and gradually refine many motor skills. There are two kinds of motor skills that develop during the preschool years, *gross motor skills,* which involve the use of large muscles, and *fine motor skills,* which involve the use of the small muscles of the hands and fingers. Acquiring proficiency in these skills is one of the most important tasks of the preschool child, and it usually occurs in the context of the child's play. However, you should note that because the acquisition of motor skills is dependent on physical growth and practice, the process occurs gradually. Thus, at the beginning of the preschool period, the child is quite clumsy. But, by the time he reaches school age, he evidences more coordination and control in his execution of motor activities, and ultimately he becomes more graceful in his motor performance (Wickstrom, 1977).

Control of the large muscles develops first, so gross motor skills (see Table 7.1) are easier for the young preschool child to master. Progress in these skills can be quite impressive as long as the child has the opportunity to practice them (NAEYC, 1980). Fine motor skills depend on brain maturation and are harder for the young preschool child to acquire because he lacks the muscular control needed to execute such skills. For this reason, two- and three-year-olds are rarely found sitting still at a table or a desk. Rather, they prefer to run wildly across the room, climb a chair, or push large objects, activities which require the use of large muscles. However, even though he does not have complete control over fine motor muscles, the young preschool child often enjoys painting or drawing. Also, he does make many attempts to master such tasks as cutting paper with a pair of scissors or putting together pieces of a puzzle, often giving his full concentration to the execution of the task (see Figure 7.7). Eventually, the child develops proficiency in many fine motor skills, and by the time he reaches school age, he has greater control over the manipulative tasks involved in dressing and undressing and he can draw and even write with greater ease.

Developing Motor Skills

Practice is an essential element of motor development, and practice of and experimentation with a variety of motor skills can be observed in the play behavior of the child, who is, it often seems, in perpetual motion. In infancy, the practice of motor skills is evident as the infant engages in repetitive play in order to develop motor coordination. This is true also of the younger preschool child. As he grows older, however, the preschool child's movements are not always directed at developing a specific motor skill. Having mastered some motor task, the child uses this skill to become proficient in other tasks. For example, having learned to hold a

TABLE 7.1 The sequence and emergence of selected motor abilities (left) and manipulative abilities (right).

Movement Pattern	Selected Abilities	Approximate Age of Onset
Walking Walking involves placing one foot in front of the other while maintaining contact with the supporting surface.	Rudimentary upright unaided gait	13 months
	Walks sideways	16 months
	Walks backwards	17 months
	Walks upstairs with help	20 months
	Walks upstairs alone—follow step	24 months
	Walks downstairs alone—follow step	25 months
Running Running involves a brief period of no contact with the supporting surface.	Hurried walk (maintains contact)	18 months
	First true run (nonsupport phase)	2–3 years
	Efficient and refined run	4–5 years
	Speed of run increases	5 years
Jumping Jumping takes three forms: (1) jumping for distance; (2) jumping for height; and (3) jumping from a height. It involves a one- or two-foot takeoff with a landing on both feet.	Steps down from low objects	18 months
	Jumps down from object with both feet	2 years
	Jumps off floor with both feet	28 months
	Jumps for distance (about 3 feet)	5 years
	Jumps for height (about 1 foot)	5 years
Hopping Hopping involves a one-foot takeoff with a landing on the same foot.	Hops up to three times on preferred foot	3 years
	Hops from four to six times on same foot	4 years
	Hops from eight to ten times on same foot	5 years
	Hops distance of 50 feet in about 11 seconds	5 years
	Hops skillfully with rhythmical alteration	6 years
Galloping The gallop combines a walk and a leap with the same foot leading throughout.	Basic but inefficient gallop	4 years
	Gallops skillfully	6 years
Skipping Skipping combines a step and a hop in rhythmic alteration.	One-footed skip	4 years
	Skillful skipping (about 20 percent)	5 years
	Skillful skipping for most	6 years

Movement Pattern	Selected Abilities	Approximate Age of Onset
Reach, Grasp, Release Reaching, grasping and releasing involve making successful contact with an object, retaining it in one's grasp, and releasing it at will.	Primitive reaching behaviors	2–4 months
	Corralling of objects	2–4 months
	Palmar grasp	
Throwing Throwing involves imparting force to an object in the general direction of intent.	Body faces target, feet remain stationary, ball thrown with forearm extension only	2–3 years
	Same as above but with body rotation added	3.6–5
	Steps forward with leg on same side as the throwing arm	5–6 years
	Mature throwing pattern	6.6 years
	Boys exhibit more mature pattern than girls	6 years and over
Catching Catching involves receiving force from an object with the hands, moving from large to progressively smaller balls.	Chases ball; does not respond to aerial ball; responds to aerial ball with delayed arm movements	2 years
		2–3 years
	Needs to be told how to position arms	2–3 years
	Fear reaction (turns head away)	3–4 years
	Basket catch using the body	3 years
	Catches using the hands only with a small ball	5 years
Kicking Kicking involves imparting force to an object with the foot.	Moves against ball; does not actually kick it	18 months
	Kicks with leg straight and little body movement (kicks at the ball)	2–3 years
	Flexes lower leg on backward lift	3–4 years
	Greater backward and forward swing with definite arm opposition	4–5 years
	Mature pattern (kicks through the ball)	5–6 years
Striking Striking involves imparting force to objects in an overarm, sidearm, or underhand pattern.	Faces object and swings in a vertical plane	2–3 years
	Swings in a horizontal plane and stands to the side of the object	4–5 years
	Rotates the trunk and hips and shifts body weight forward; mature horizontal patterns	5 years
		6–7 years

Source: *Motor Development and Movement Experiences for Young Children* by D. L. Gallahue, p. 65, Table 3.1 and p. 66, Table 3.2. Copyright © 1976, reprinted by permission of John Wiley & Sons, Inc.

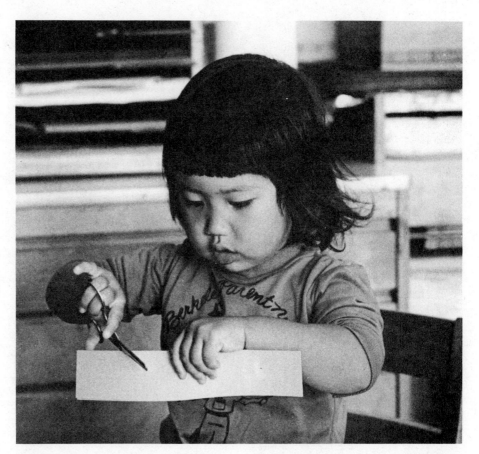

FIGURE 7.7   This preschool girl is concentrating on cutting paper with scissors.

pencil, the preschool child shows a consistent, age-related progression from scribbles to recognizable forms such as circles and lines to representational figures (Figure 7.8; Kellogg, 1967, 1969). In other words, the child begins by scribbling, but over the course of the preschool period, he begins to make pictures (see Figure 7.9). A similar change is evidenced in gross motor skills. Once the child learns to skip, he usually experiments with skipping on one foot, or skipping on alternate feet, and he often skips just for the sake of skipping. By school age, however, skipping becomes part of a variety of games the child plays with other children. Thus, in motor development, repetitive practice is an initial phase in the mastery of a skill. Once the skill is acquired, it is used for new purposes.

Sex Differences and Similarities

Although boys and girls follow similar patterns in motor development during childhood, there are some underlying physical differences between boys and girls that contribute to differences in performance of motor

Design Stage
Ages 3–4

Pictorial Stage
Ages 4–5

Combines   Aggregates   Early Pictorial   Later Pictorial

FIGURE 7.8 Sequential development in self-taught art. Note the development of the forms in these drawings of preschool children between the ages of 3 and 5 years. Adapted from Rhoda Kellogg (May 1967) "Understanding Children's Art" in *Psychology Today, 1,* (1) pp. 18–19. Copyright © 1967 American Psychological Association.

skills. For example, boys are slightly taller, on the average, and also more muscular than are girls. They tend to lose their baby fat sooner than girls do, and they continue to have less body fat not only during the childhood years but also later in life. On the other hand, girls mature more rapidly in bone ossification, and certain functional centers in their brains mature at an earlier age (Tanner, 1978).

Due to these differences, during the preschool years boys, having the advantage of height and strength, are usually better than girls in such motor skills as throwing, catching, and hitting. Girls, however, are better

FIGURE 7.9   During the preschool period, the child's drawing skills show consistent, age-related progression from scribbles to recognizable shapes and representational figures.

than boys at fine motor skills (Tanner, 1978), such as writing, drawing and skipping that require coordination and balance rather than strength. However, you should note that, as with all types of skills, the sex differences noted may be related not to underlying physical differences, but to differences in the amount of practice and encouragement children are provided to perform particular skills (Sinclair, 1973). While it is known that boys prefer to spend more time outdoors practicing gross motor skills by running, climbing, and riding bicycles, and girls prefer to spend more time indoors practicing such fine motor skills as drawing, it is not known whether these preferences are related to biological or cultural differences. It will become apparent in later chapters that in our society many people adhere to sex-role stereotyped behaviors and often they buy different types of toys for boys than they do for girls (Kacerguis & Adams, 1979). A parent may buy a ball for a 4-year-old boy and a doll for a 4-year-old girl, thus encouraging each to engage in different types of play. The point is that for whatever reason, boys and girls do spend more time practicing those skills that they are said to be better at (Harper & Sanders, 1975).

FIGURE 7.10   One of the great accomplishments of the 6-year-old child is learning to tie shoe laces.

Increased Competence in Self-Help Skills

The child's increasing capacity to perform gross and fine motor skills and his increasing muscular growth is evident in the accomplishment of self-help skills. The preschool child gains greater independence over feeding activities, and he also learns first to undress and later to dress himself. The young preschool child is not skilled at dressing himself because putting on a pair of pants or tying shoe laces requires fine motor skills. Undressing is accomplished earlier, because this entails simply removing shoes and grasping a sock and pulling it off. However, acquiring the ability to dress is very important for preschool children, and one of the hallmarks of the development of the 6-year-old is mastery of the task of tying shoe laces (see Figure 7.10).

Toilet training is accomplished during the early part of the preschool period, usually by the time the child is three. There are individual and sex differences in toilet training: girls are generally toilet trained at an earlier age than are boys, and boys are likely to wet their beds at night longer

THE FAMILY CIRCUS ®   By Bil Keane

Copyright 1984
The Register and Tribune
Syndicate, Inc.

"Seven years I've spent learning to tie my shoelaces
and NOW they give us Velcro."

Reprinted with special permission of King Features Syndicate, Inc.

than girls do (Oppel, Harper, & Rider, 1968). Individual differences in toilet training may be related to differences in the maturity of the muscles. Some researchers contend that no child can be toilet trained until he has matured to the point at which he is physically capable of controlling the muscles that allow him to retain his feces and urine (McGraw, 1940).

However, other researchers emphasize the cultural relativity of toilet training readiness, contending that in some societies toilet training is achieved during the first year of life. deVries and deVries (1977) note that with a conditioning approach employed by the East African Digo mother, the infant accomplishes night and day dryness by 5 to 6 months of age. In this conditioning approach, the mother gradually toilet trains the baby by taking him outside the house and placing him in a special position that facilitates elimination (see Figure 7.11). This procedure begins when the baby is 2 to 3 weeks of age, and it is followed day and night, each time the mother senses that the baby has to eliminate (for example, after feeding and before and after naps). While the baby is held in a position for elimination, the mother makes a "shuus" sound so that the infant eventually associates the sound with voiding. When the infant voids at the "shuus"

FIGURE 7.11   Toilet training the African baby. The Digo people
of East Africa have markedly different ideas about toilet training
readiness and they are successful at this undertaking when the child
is still very young.

sound, he is rewarded by being hugged, smiled at, or fed by the mother.
By 5 months of age, the infant learns to communicate his need to urinate
by attempting to squat in the appropriate elimination position.

A similar procedure is used by the Digo mother to teach the baby to
move his bowels. Obviously, the living conditions in East Africa may be
conducive to early toilet training because the infant is not required to use a
potty. In addition, the African baby's precocious motor development may
also be a factor. The deVries's study does alert us to the fact that toilet
training is influenced by parental attitudes and practices and also by societal expectations. The question is: When should children in our society
begin toilet training? On the basis of his clinical practice, Brazelton (1962)

recommends a child-oriented approach to toilet training, which he notes should begin at about 18 months because at that time the child is physiologically and psychologically ready. Thus the child lends himself to participate in a relatively trouble-free training process. Unfortunately, most parents begin toilet training at an earlier age, normally when the child is only a year old, despite the fact that the later the toilet training is begun, the faster the child learns (Sears, Maccoby, & Levin, 1957). Many parents also scold and punish the child for not mastering toilet training. Although those children who are scolded and punished do not become toilet trained any sooner or later than children whose parents are more understanding, it is unnecessary to upset the child or to make an issue out of the process. All children become toilet trained by the time they are three years of age. Parents should realize that toilet training is a gradual process, so even when a 4- or 5-year-old child has been toilet trained, he is likely to have accidents when he is tired or unduly stressed (Stuart & Prugh, 1960).

INFLUENCES ON GROWTH

Physical growth during the preschool years, and also the acquisition of motor skills, follow a predictable course in most children, because physical development is largely governed by the genes. However, there are variations in physical growth and development among children, in particular, differences in weight and height gain. It is not unusual for children to be taller or shorter than their peers. In most cases, these variations are a reflection of genetic differences in children. However, there are also differences in growth among children in different countries that are due not only to genetic factors, but also to differences in nutrition and health care (Meredith, 1963, 1978). This attests to the fact that environmental influence on growth is potentially significant.

Nutrition

There is a close relationship between nutrition and the child's growth and development; nutrients of the right kind and in adequate supply are critical for normal growth. It is known that malnutrition has deleterious effects on the central nervous system (Brozek & Schurch, 1984) and that it interferes with the development of adaptive and intellectual capacities in children, especially if it occurs during the critical periods for brain growth (Birch & Gussow, 1970). It is known also that malnourished children are susceptible to infectious diseases and that their ability to combat illness is impaired (Scrimshaw, Taylor, & Gordon, 1968).

Malnutrition, when it occurs during the preschool years, also limits skeletal development, resulting in the stunting of physical growth (Jackson, 1966). This is the reason for the short stature of many children in developing countries where malnutrition is rampant (Birch & Gussow, 1970). When preschool children experience only a moderate degree of malnutrition for only brief periods of time, temporary stunting of growth is usually overcome when the nutritional deficiencies are corrected. However, there are limits to the child's ability to recover from malnutrition (György, 1960).

Emotional Factors

While the recovery from malnutrition is dependent partly on physical factors (that is, the extent and duration of malnourishment and the institution of adequate nourishment), emotional factors are also at work and can be even more influential than the physical factors. This is illustrated by a classic study of children in two German orphanages (Widdowson, 1951). Children in the first orphanage were given food supplements to enrich their deficient diets and consumed 20 percent more calories than children in a similar orphanage. Yet the children in the second orphanage grew more and gained more weight. This outcome was explained by the fact that at the time the food supplement was introduced, a new administrator had taken charge of the first orphanage. He was a strict disciplinarian who often distressed the children with unjustified rebukes at mealtime. Interestingly, eight children who may have been the administrator's favorites were not subjected to this stress, and they did benefit from the food supplements. Possibly the stress agitated the other children and caused them to eat less, or the stress caused poor digestion. Tanner (1978) explains that in some children, stress causes a decrease in the brain's production of growth hormone, preventing the children from growing.

Other studies attest to the relationship between recovery from nutritional deficiencies and emotional disorders. As Pollitt and Gilmore (1977) note, the availability of nutrients, in and of itself, is not sufficient to meet the malnourished child's needs since, in malnourished infants and preschool children, the selective characteristics of both the child and the mother affect the caretaking and feeding activities of the mother, which, in turn, affect the child's growth. A study of Zeskind and Ramey (1978) underscores this point. In their study, malnourished children who were given food supplements and who also participated in a supportive day care program where they interacted with other children and adults improved more than the malnourished children who were given food supplements but who remained at home. The researchers suggest that because malnourished children are socially unresponsive, their mothers become less apt to interact with them, causing the children to continue to exhibit unresponsive behavior and the mothers to continue to withdraw from interacting with them. The group of children in the day care program did receive supportive interactions and their responsivity thereby increased, thus preventing the cycle from starting.

Failure to Thrive and Deprivation Dwarfism.   The effects of emotional factors on growth are further illustrated by the disorder known as deprivation dwarfism, in which a child receives adequate nutrition but fails to grow normally because he is subjected to emotional abuse and neglect (in other words, the child knows that he is not loved or wanted). This emotional situation inhibits the secretion of adequate amounts of growth hormone (Patton & Gardner, 1963). Often, the pattern of emotional abuse of these children begins in infancy. Infants who fail to grow as a result of emotional abuse are referred to as *failure-to-thrive babies.*

failure-to-thrive babies

In failure-to-thrive and deprivation dwarfism cases, there is often a complex and self-sustaining relationship between parental attitude and children's behavior. Women whose children exhibit the syndrome have often experienced stressful events during their own childhood years (Patton & Gardner, 1963) or they suffered from later disruptive life events such as a major illness, the death of another child, poverty, or marital breakup (Barbero, 1975). However, while failure-to-thrive and deprivation dwarfism are related to mothering disorders, certain characteristics of the child may be contributing factors. Researchers note that some children seem to be especially vulnerable: 20 to 40 percent of failure-to-thrive children were low birth weight infants (Parke & Collmer, 1975). Recall from previous discussions that such infants are difficult to care for. Brazelton (1961) also notes that a deficit in responsiveness among some newborns is a major factor in the establishment of an unhappy relationship between mother and infant.

It is hard to diagnose a child whose failure to grow is the result of emotional abuse. However, when a child fails to respond to hormone treatment, physicians suspect emotional maltreatment. Frasier and Rallison (1972) give the example of a preschool child who failed to grow even though she was given growth hormone. Suspecting that emotional factors might be responsible for the problem, the physicians suggested that the child leave the mother and stay with relatives. During the time the child stayed with her relatives, her growth rate was twice what it had been at home. When she returned home, however, her growth rate slowed again. Other researchers (Patton & Gardner, 1963; Gardner, 1972) note that most infants and children who suffer from retarded growth due to emotional neglect grow rapidly in the hospital but stop growing and even lose weight when they return home.

Obesity.   The problems associated with nutritional deprivation and failure-to-thrive are severe. At the opposite end of the spectrum is obesity, which also has physical and psychological problems associated with it, although they are less immediately life threatening. Obesity is an excess of body weight. It results from eating more food than the body uses for its basic energy needs and from expending less energy than is supplied by the diet. Obesity is associated with an increased risk of high blood pressure, gall bladder disease, and adult onset of diabetes. All of these conditions contribute to increased rates of heart disease and stroke. Social and psychological costs are incurred as well. Obese people are subjected to prejudice and often they may be teased or socially isolated.

Although obesity is not usually a problem associated with the preschool years (Stuart & Prugh, 1960), the incidence of obesity in young American children is increasingly high (Winick, 1975; Mayer, 1968). Among the reasons for the increase in overweight young children, researchers cite the increased reliance on highly processed foods (U.S. Department of Agriculture, 1980) and the higher prevalence of eating away from home and snacking. Both practices contribute significantly to the total calories consumed during the day. In addition, television advertising contributes to children's forming bad eating habits (Gallo, Connor, & Boehm, 1980). Researchers also note that American children as a group are exceedingly sedentary by world standards and even in comparison to the norms of past decades in this country (Bray, 1979). The fact that children are more sedentary may be related to educational policies. According to Janis & Bulow-Hube (1986), there have been significant reductions during the past ten years in the amount of government spending for such programs as physical education. Thus many schools have few or no physical fitness programs for children.

Obese children are likely to grow up to be obese adolescents and adults. Abraham, Collins, and Nordsieck (1971) found that 86 percent of overweight boys and 80 percent of overweight girls were overweight as adults in contrast to 42 percent of average weight boys and 18 percent of average weight girls being overweight as adults. The tendency to being overweight may run in families, according to Winick (1974), who notes that in families where both parents are fat, the children are likely to be fat. One explanation for this is hereditary influence. However, fat parents may also feed their children fattening foods or too much food. Mayer (1968) suggests that overfeeding babies at the critical period of infancy when fat cells develop may cause a permanent increase in the number of fat cells, making it harder to lose weight later in life. The evidence for this theory is not conclusive, however, as some researchers believe that fat cell formation is completed during the prenatal period so the number of cells cannot be affected by feeding habits after birth. Whenever they are formed, however, fat cells change in size depending on an individual's diet, but they never decrease or increase in numbers (Tanner, 1978). Thus, the more fat cells an individual has, the more likely he is to be fat, and the more difficult it is for him to maintain an average weight.

Health

Health is another factor which influences growth. Adequate health care is very important to normal growth, because illness can influence the child's growth and development. For example, a major illness which lasts several months may cause considerable slowing of growth. The mechanisms by which growth is slowed vary from one illness to another. In a number of illnesses, changes in endocrine balance are involved. In particular, a change in the secretion of hormones from the adrenal gland is known to slow growth (Tanner, 1978). However, as long as the child receives adequate medical care, once he recovers from the illness, he undergoes a "catch up" period during which growth takes place at twice its usual rate, so the child eventually attains his normal height and weight (Tanner, 1978).

The need for adequate health care is emphasized because during the preschool years, the child is vulnerable to respiratory infections and a number of illnesses, such as German measles and the mumps. These types of diseases do not cause any discernible retardation in growth as long as the child is well nourished (Miller, Court, Walton, & Know, 1960). However, if a child becomes ill, he needs to be adequately cared for if he is to recover without any complications. Even a seemingly minor problem such as an ear infection, when not properly treated, can lead to major and irreversible conditions, namely, deafness. In addition, many childhood illnesses can be prevented through immunization, which is a routine aspect of regular medical checkups. As long as the child receives adequate health care, complications which can arise from illness can be minimized or the illness prevented.

DISCUSSION OF SOCIAL ISSUES: CHILD HEALTH CARE

If you were asked if children in America are in good health, you would probably say that they are. Through medical advances and increased attention to health promotion and disease prevention, the health status of American children has improved drastically during the past two decades (Kotelchuck & Richmond, 1982). Janis (1983) notes also that another significant factor in the improvement of children's health is the increased public spending for children's health and welfare that occurred during the 1960s and 1970s. This resulted in an increase in the number of health services for children and in a substantial decline in the number of children who became ill (Davis & Schoen, 1978). In addition, many educational programs for children (for example, Project Head Start) include provisions for the medical care of children (North, 1979).

new morbidity   Despite these improvements, several health problems persist. One is related to the phenomenon referred to as the *new morbidity,* a term that encompasses a wide range of behavioral and psychosocial factors that threaten the health of children. Child abuse and childhood accidents, each of which cause a significant number of deaths during the childhood years, are well-known examples.

Another problem is that not all children have shared equally in the general improvement in health. Sharp disparities in both health status and access to and use of health services persist according to family income. As one physician notes, "Poverty is the single most influential factor affecting the health status of children" (Shirley, 1982). Not only do poor children suffer from inadequate health care, there are indications that their health status has actually become worse over the past few years. The Select Panel for the Promotion of Child Health (1981) documents this in its report *Better Health for Our Children: A National Strategy*. It reveals that over 30 percent of all black children suffer from nutritional deficits. This figure contrasts with 15 percent of white children. Also, it states that preschool children from poor families have almost twice as many bed disability days as preschool children from middle-class families, and that four times as many poor children report unmet medical needs as do more affluent children.

These indicators underscore the persistent gap in health status and access to health care services between rich and poor, white and minority children. These facts are relevant to students of developmental psychology, because good health is a fundamental prerequisite to psychological functioning and affects the motivation and achievement of the child. As Birch (1972) notes:

> The child who is apathetic because of malnutrition, whose experiences may have been modified by acute or chronic illness, whose learning abilities may have been affected by some "insult" to the central nervous system cannot be expected to respond to opportunities for learning in the same way as does a child who has not been exposed to such conditions. Increasing opportunity for learning, though entirely admirable in itself, will not overcome such biologic disadvantages.

In addition, research studies document that there is an unmistakable link between poor health and classroom failure, school absenteeism, and children's misconduct in the streets (Lewis & Balla, 1976). The combination often leads to a life of delinquency and crime.

Barriers to Good Child Health Care.   What factors account for the inadequate health status of poor children? Inequalities in access to health services and also inequalities in the quality of health care are two influential factors that affect the health status of children. According to Lefkowitz and Andrulis (1981), although the absolute number of primary care physicians has been increasing over the past ten years, rural and inner-city areas that are inhabited by the poor and by blacks suffer a severe shortage of health manpower. Thus, there are problems simply because there are not enough physicians who are available to care for poor children (see Figure 7.12).

There are other problems as well. In order to rectify the inequalities in access to health care, the government initiated Medicaid, a program that

Preventing Accidents

*H*aving acquired physical and motor skills that permit them a great deal of independent action, preschoolers evidence their insatiable curiosity to find out as much as they can about their world. An unlocked kitchen cabinet seems to them to be an invitation to explore and even taste some of its poisonous household cleaning agents. They see nothing dangerous about showing off their newly acquired ability to balance themselves on a bannister or on a second-story window ledge, making themselves vulnerable to all kinds of accidents.

Childhood accidents occur not only among preschoolers but among older children as well. Such accidents present cause for grave concern. In the United States, accidents constitute the leading cause of death and injury among children between the ages of one and fourteen, accounting for over 10,000 deaths annually (National Safety Council, 1981). Accidents claim more children's lives than do cancer, pneumonia, heart disease, and homicide combined. Furthermore, between 40,000 and 50,000 children are permanently disabled each year due to some type of accident (Select Panel for the Promotion of Child Health, 1981; Gratz, 1979). The most frequent severe accidents that involve young children are car injuries, falls, choking, drowning, and poisoning.

Many of these accidents are preventable. In the United States, some progress has been made. Since the installation of child-resistant bottle caps, children's deaths from aspirin poisoning have been reduced by 60%. Many handicaps caused by lead poisoning have been reduced after federal regulations banned the use of more than a trace of lead in household paints. Federal regulations that have required crib manufacturers to make narrower spaces between the slats of a crib are responsible for lessening the number of infants who are strangled by getting their heads caught between the slats. Similarly, federal laws requiring that pacifiers be made large enough so that they cannot be swallowed or drawn into the child's upper airways have virtually eliminated deaths caused in this way (Baker, 1981).

Despite this progress, however, the number of childhood deaths from accidents remains high. Statistics compiled for the World Health Organization reveal that there are more childhood accident fatalities in the United States than in many other industrialized and developing countries (Marcusson & Oehmish, 1977). Given the enormous advances we have made in our ability to prevent and treat numerous life-threatening diseases, why is our nation still unable to prevent childhood injuries?

In an analysis of childhood prevention policies in the United States, Margolis and Runyan (1983) suggest that, in part, the United States has been unsuccessful in preventing childhood accidents because those who are concerned about accident prevention usually emphasize only one dimension of the problem when in fact there are multiple causes and concerns that need to be addressed. Focusing on only one aspect of the problem limits the range of possible prevention options. For example, it has been suggested that parents have the primary responsibility for the care and supervision of young children and that accidents occur as a result of the parents' ignorance. In fact, many parents leave drugs and poisonous chemicals within easy reach of young children. Thus, some researchers have noted the need for educational efforts directed at the parents as a means of preventing childhood accidents.

Such educational awareness efforts are a necessary component of a childhood injury prevention policy. However, in and of themselves they are ineffective. This has been demonstrated by Dershewitz and Williamson (1977) and by Dershewitz (1979) who recently conducted a child safety campaign. In this campaign, parents were taught ways that they could childproof their homes. They were also given a booklet to help them implement the instructions. To ascertain if parents implemented the instructions as a result of the program, follow-up inspections were made in the homes of these parents as well as in the homes of families which did not participate in the program. The researchers found that parents who had participated in the program and who thought that they had made their homes safe as a result had as many household cleaning agents, prescription drugs, knives, and matches within reach of young children as did parents who did not participate in the program. Alerting parents to the potential dangers inherent in their homes and teaching them how to avoid childhood accidents do not guarantee that such accidents will be prevented.

The need to incorporate safety measures that go beyond parent education and awareness of the problem is further illustrated when we consider childhood automobile fatalities, which are the major cause of death for children ages 1 to 4 years. Child auto restraint laws which legally mandate that all young children wear seat belts and that infants be placed in a car seat and buckled have resulted in an increase of such practices. However, there are many states where there are no child auto restraint laws or where such laws are not enforced. In these states, despite widespread mass media campaigns to educate parents and persuade them to "buckle up" their children while traveling in a car, 93% of children under 10 years of age still travel unrestrained (Robertson, 1981).

The American Academy of Pediatrics and other organizations have placed high priority on educating parents about the use of car seats and seat buckles beginning with the infant's return from the hospital (Christopherson & Sullivan, 1982). Despite these efforts, many parents still do not realize the importance of the practice. At a relatively low speed of 15 to 30 miles per hour, an automobile crash can hurtle the child in the direction of the dashboard head first. Even parents who are aware of the risks frequently do not use child restraints because they find it inconvenient, uncomfortable, or costly or because at times, children are sleepy and may beg to be allowed to lie on their parent's lap (Margolin & Runyan, 1983). On such occasions parents who would otherwise insist that the children use the seat belt are tempted to let the children have the comfort they desire.

For these reasons, injury control specialists suggest that rather than rely on parent education as a means of accident prevention, manufacturers must be required to install some automatic safety measures such as seat belts that work automatically. Another suggestion is that manufacturers install air bags which inflate instantly in the event of a crash. It is estimated that such automatic devices would save 9,000 lives a year if all cars had them (Robertson, 1981).

However, policymakers are faced with a dilemma in that any policy that would promote the use of automatic safety devices is seen by some as an infringement on automakers and on the freedom of choice of drivers (Butler, Starfield, & Stenmark, 1984). As yet, such a policy is not politically feasible. The auto industry complains that automatic safety devices are costly. Many Americans regard them as an intrusion on their freedom. As parents and policymakers, how can we balance the competing goals of the safety of children and our freedom of choice? Can you think of an effective argument to present before a group of policymakers to convince them of the importance of the trade-off between individual freedoms and the lives of children? How do you feel about the trade-off?

provides medical care to the needy. Medicaid is especially important to children from poor families. Without Medicaid, eight out of every ten poor children would have no health coverage. This fact gains in significance when you consider the fact that one out of every five children lives in poverty (Bureau of the Census, 1982).

Medicaid was intended to remove the financial barriers to health care. Instead, it has perpetuated the inequalities in health care because it rewards doctors and health care institutions for delivering not necessarily good care, but the most costly care. Consider this example. Under the Medicaid system, if a child visits a doctor because of a stomach ache, Medicaid will pay a substantial amount of money for an exploratory examination that involves specialized instruments or hospitalization. Nothing is paid for a counseling session with the physician, which may be all the child needs. This example illustrates the fact that even in the case of well-intentioned policies, problems can arise in their implementation (Lasswell, 1971). This point alerts us to the fact that once policies are implemented, they must be evaluated to ensure that no unintended problems inhibit their proper implementation.

Another problem is that Medicaid is not administered under the same guidelines in all states. In some states, Medicaid covers only 10 percent of

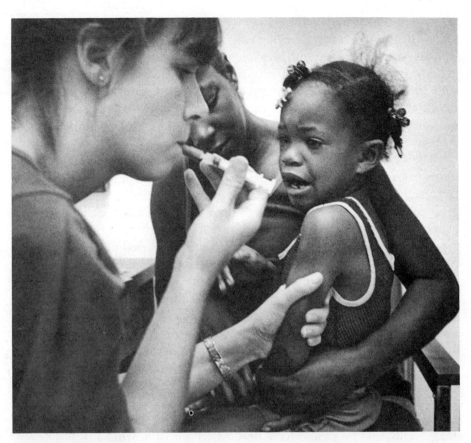

FIGURE 7.12 Poor and black children, who live mostly in rural and inner-city areas, suffer from inadequate health care because of the shortage of medical personnel. However, many programs for children, such as Project Head Start, include provisions for medical care.

all poor children, and even then it pays only a small part of their medical expenses. Nineteen states do not cover prenatal care for women despite the importance of such care in preventing immediate health problems and problems that appear later in children's lives (Dutton, 1981). In part, the problem is a financial one. The fact is that many states are currently hard pressed to make ends meet, and they are faced with other social problems, such as unemployment, which also require extensive expenditures. At the same time, federal appropriations for services are being cut, thus limiting even more the amount of money the states have.

Whenever the issues of costs and budget cuts arise, they are coupled with the need to decide priorities. How should the money in hand be spent, and for whom? Unfortunately, health services for children are frequently the first items to be cut in any budget squeeze (Lazarus, 1982). In New York City, the health department's budget was cut from $50 to $40 million between 1974 and 1978. The services that were trimmed most extensively or entirely eliminated were pediatric treatment centers and school health programs (Lash, Sigal, & Dudzinski, 1980). There was a similar, disproportionate impact on children's health services in the wake of federal cutbacks in social services by the Reagan Administration in 1981. Substantially less money was awarded to community health centers, which are where 50 percent of poor children receive health care and immunizations. Thus, fewer children are now served by community health centers (Schorr, 1982).

The decision to trim or eliminate those health services for children stems not from government officials' dislike of children, but from other factors. Janis (1983) cites lack of advocacy for children's health as one problem, and she notes that the existence of a number of government programs for children creates a paradox in which there is no single voice for children's health issues. There is also the belief that preventive health services such as regular medical checkups for children are unnecessary. According to some, these services add to the already high costs of caring for people who are actually sick (Foltz, 1980). Are preventive services such a regular checkups for children wasteful? You be the judge as you consider this actual example of a boy who, at eight years of age, had failed the first grade twice. His major problem was a hearing loss that developed as a result of an ear infection he suffered when he was two years old. The boy would have been spared such suffering had his parents taken him to a physician within a year after he had his ear infection. The hearing loss would have been identified before the boy suffered serious deficits in language skills, and he would have been fitted with a hearing aid. However, since his parents were on a tight family budget and had to pay all their own medical bills, they waited until their children became seriously ill before they saw a doctor. Their son's ear infection, although it resulted in irreparable harm, did not seem to be too serious at the time.

There are many similar examples. As many as 10 percent of all children in the United States have hearing problems. As many as 20 percent have visual problems (Select Panel for the Promotion of Child Health, 1981). As our example illustrates, severe hearing and visual deficits can stem from relatively minor health ailments. No matter what causes these deficits, however, detecting them during the preschool years is important, for it enables the child to be treated appropriately, and early detection and treatment can prevent serious problems in learning and language development. The fact that defects go undetected among so many preschool children is especially tragic considering that we do have the capability to provide early screening through medical checkups. The Early and Periodic Screening, Diagnosis, and Treatment (EPSDT) program under Medicaid is a preventive service which aims to detect and treat health problems during the preschool years. This type of program has been shown to save $8.00 in later medical and educational costs for each dollar spent! (Select Panel for the Promotion of Child Health, 1981)

Because preventive health services are not only successful but also cost-effective, our failure to provide all children with such services prompts some individuals to contend that in our society, children are not regarded as a priority. Perhaps the failure to respond to the health needs of our children is not deliberate but stems simply from ignorance of the fact that health care is not being adequately provided for a large segment of the population of children (Janis, 1983; Zigler & Finn, 1981).

SUMMARY

In contrast to the infancy period when growth occurs at a dramatically rapid rate, physical growth during the preschool years progresses at a slower, more gradual rate. However, significant changes occur in ossification, which is the process whereby the bones become longer, thicker and harder. This contributes to skeletal growth during the preschool years and to the ability of the child to become involved in activities which require strength.

There are environmental influences on growth, including malnutrition, emotional factors, and health. These can result in the stunting of growth and can lead to growth disorders such as deprivation dwarfism, or, at the other extreme, obesity. Despite the important influence of nutrition and health on physical growth and development, many American children, specifically those who are poor, do not receive adequate health care. Some of the barriers to child health care stem from problems in the administration of Medicaid, the government program that was set up to ensure payment for health services to the poor, and also from the erroneous belief that preventive services such as regular medical checkups for children are wasteful. However, such services are cost-effective and they are important in detecting and treating hearing, visual, and other defects during the preschool years, as well as preventing additional problems in learning and language development.

Finally, we have seen that one of the most significant aspects of physical development during the preschool years involves the brain. Aspects of brain maturity, along with increases in height, allow the child to acquire and refine many motor skills during the preschool years and also to achieve self-help skills. Another important aspect of brain maturation is related to brain specialization. The brain is divided into left and right hemispheres which control opposite sides of the body and which include different functional centers. The centers that facilitate language skills are in the left hemisphere, and during the preschool years, these undergo myelination and increases in their ability to function. Hence, the child is able to acquire language skills during the preschool period.

REVIEW POINTS

1. During the preschool years physical growth is not as rapid as it is during infancy. Nevertheless, significant changes occur in physical and motor development. These include not only weight and height gains and changes in body proportions, but also skeletal maturation and brain growth.

2. The growth and maturation of the brain is an important internal change that occurs during the early childhood years. This enables the child to acquire language skills at a rapid rate and also to master complex motor tasks.

3. The child becomes more competent in self-help skills such as feeding and dressing and also he becomes more independent. Additionally, the child is able to practice and thereby refine many gross motor skills such as running and skipping, and also many fine motor skills such as tying shoe laces and drawing. There are some sex differences in children's acquisition of such skills. These differences may be attributable to variation in the rate of brain maturation between boys and girls, but they may stem also from the fact that boys and girls are encouraged by adults to engage in different types of activities.

4. Physical and motor development is largely governed by the genes. However, environmental influences also play a major role. One of the most significant of such influences is nutrition.

Malnutrition limits skeletal development, resulting in the stunting of physical growth. Emotional factors are also known to be related to the stunting of physical growth. Children who are emotionally abused and who are not loved fail to grow despite the fact that they receive adequate nutrition.

5. Health is another factor that influences growth. During the preschool years the child is vulnerable to different kinds of respiratory and other childhood illnesses. The child usually overcomes these, but he needs to be medically checked on a regular basis to ensure that there are no complications arising from such illnesses. For example, a seemingly minor health problem such as an ear infection can result in deafness if not properly treated.

6. Although the health status of American children has improved drastically during the past two decades, there is a wide range of behavioral and psychosocial factors that threaten the lives of children. One of those is deaths from accidents.

7. There is a gap in health status and in access to health care services between rich and poor, white and minority children. Over 30% of all black children suffer from nutritional deficits compared to 15% of white children, and children from poor families are twice as likely to be sick as are children from middle-class families.

CHAPTER 8

COGNITIVE AND
LANGUAGE DEVELOPMENT
DURING THE PRESCHOOL YEARS

The change from baby to child evidenced in the preschool child's physical development is apparent in the child's cognitive development as well. Intellectual skills develop rapidly during the preschool years as the child explores his environment, thereby acquiring knowledge about the properties of objects in his world and an understanding of people and events he experiences. The child also acquires impressive language skills during the early childhood years, and he grows in his ability to effectively interact and communicate with others.

In this chapter we discuss the progress in cognitive and language development that occurs during the preschool years as well as some of the ways parents and educators can enhance the child's development. In our discussion of cognitive development we elaborate on the theory of Jean Piaget. His theory is especially relevant in a discussion of cognitive development during the preschool years, for Piaget has shown that the young child's mode of thinking is significantly different from that of older children and adults. Whereas Piaget set out only to *describe* children's cognitive development, many researchers in this country have elaborated on his work and have attempted to see whether some aspects of cognitive growth can be accelerated and how. One outcome of this has been the emphasis on early childhood education and the provision of nursery school experiences not only to middle-class children but to children from economically disadvantaged homes as well. Although these experiences serve to prepare the child for formal schooling, the child learns from all his experiences, and his intellectual growth is influenced by his interactions with his parents and day care providers as well as the types of television shows he watches. Before we examine the contexts in which the child learns, let us discuss cognitive growth during the early childhood years as it is described by Piaget.

COGNITIVE DEVELOPMENT

The Preoperational Period

During the preschool years the child is in what Piaget terms the preoperational period of cognitive development. This period, which begins in the latter part of the second year of life and continues until the child reaches the age of 6 or 7, represents a transition in the child's mode of thinking. The child has advanced beyond the restrictions imposed on him by a sensorimotor level of cognitive development, but he has still not attained the kinds of skills necessary for thinking logically. Piaget emphasized that, unlike other periods of cognitive development, the preoperational period is characterized by a number of changes but not by the attainment of abilities and that there are limitations inherent in the preoperational child's mode of thinking. From the answers they give to seemingly simple questions, we can see that the mental world of preschool children is one in which fantasy and reality are interchangeable. The ideas formed by the children are somewhat distorted and incomplete, so they are unable to reason logically. Additionally, preschool children tend to assume that everyone thinks as they do and that everyone shares their views, feelings, and desires, an assumption which clearly restricts their understanding of the people around them.

Recent studies have shown, however, that Piaget may have underestimated the cognitive capabilities of preschoolers. Whereas Piaget's description of the preoperational period leads one to focus on the limitations inherent in young children's mode of thinking (Flavell, 1985), there is cognitive growth during the preoperational period, especially in the refinement of representational thought. Recall that at the end of the sensorimotor period of cognitive development, the child has attained the ability to mentally represent objects and events. This new ability greatly expands the child's sphere of mental activities. No longer tied in his thinking to the present as was true during the sensorimotor period, the preoperational child can think about past events, dwell on the future, and wonder what is going on right now somewhere else.

However, mental representation is not fully attained all at once. The one-year-old baby who has taken his first few steps needs to practice walking before he can fully master the task. The young preschool child needs to devote his early years to the practice of his new ability to mentally manipulate his experiences with the environment, and he does so in the context of his play and interactions with adults and other children. First he becomes adept at using one representation at a time (Corrigan, 1983). He is able to pretend, for example, that he is a doctor; he will do so by pretending to represent one activity, say the doctor giving an injection. Later, he is able to use several representations at one time, and he can pretend to be a doctor doing several activities—giving an injection, taking someone's temperature, bandaging an ankle, and so on.

Symbolic Functioning

As the young child practices his ability for representational thought, he acquires a symbolic mode of thinking, or *symbolic functioning*. Symbolic functioning is regarded as one of the major distinctions between the child who is in the sensorimotor period of cognitive development and one who is in the preoperational period. It refers to the child's ability to understand, create, and use symbols to represent something which is not present.

Ault (1977) explains that the degree of correspondence between an actual object, say a hammer, and a symbolic representation of that object can vary from highly concrete to highly abstract. When one uses a plastic toy hammer to represent a metal hammer, the degree of correspondence between the symbolic representation (toy hammer) and the actual object is highly concrete. When one evokes a picture of a hammer in one's mind, the degree of correspondence between the symbolic representation (mental image of a hammer) and the actual object is slightly more abstract but is still somewhat concrete. The mental image of the hammer retains some of the features of the object it represents, such as the color and shape. However, a word made up of the letters *h-a-m-m-e-r* is a highly abstract symbolic representation of the object in that it is only an arbitrary representation of an object—the word bears absolutely no resemblance to the object it represents. Piaget called these abstract symbols signs, and he noted that at first, the child mediates his thinking through the use of concrete symbols, but eventually he acquires the ability to mediate his thinking through the use of highly abstract symbols (signs) such as words, and he learns to distinguish between a word and what that word represents. Clearly, the child must be able to call forth an image of a hammer and think about it as he uses or hears the word *hammer,* even though no actual hammer may be present.

Three behaviors emerge during the early part of the preoperational period which reflect the preschool child's use of symbols to mediate his thinking: deferred imitation, symbolic play, and the acquisition of language. Deferred imitation is an imitation of a behavior some time after that behavior was observed. When the preschool child observes the behavior of his parent, playmate, or an actor on television, he forms a mental representation of that behavior. Later, he recalls this mental representation, and he acts out the behavior. Piaget cites an example of how his daughter observed another child throw a temper tantrum, stamping her feet and crying. The next day, Piaget's daughter suddenly stood up, stamped her feet, and cried. She did so with such deliberateness in her actions, Piaget noted, that it was as if she were trying out the behavior to see what it was like. To be able to do this, his daughter had to have symbolic function, for without this ability to create a mental picture of the event, she would not have been able to imitate the behavior a day later. The same is true of a preschool child who, some time after watching Superman on television, jumps off the edge of a chair, with his arms outstretched, pretending he is the superhero.

The child's ability to imitate a behavior and to pretend to be someone or something else is important. It shows that the child has a stable mental image of what he is pretending to be and also that he is able to hold this image over time and recall it later. This ability signifies the fact that the child is capable of remembering what he has seen or heard. Of course, the child can never imitate all the attributes of a person or object he is pretending to be, so in his imitations he extracts only some of these attributes, and in this way he becomes a symbol of that person or object. The way the young child is symbolizing whatever he is pretending to be is usually individualized and not readily understood by others. For example, a three-year-old who is running around the room waving his arms may be

FIGURE 8.1 *(above)* Recalling what he has seen on television, this youngster is imitating the actions of his favorite superhero. *(left)* The preschool child's ability to play imaginatively is a precious characteristic which may be, in essence, the creativity and individuality we value in older children and adults.

pretending to be an airplane, but an adult observing the child may think that the child is pretending to be a bird, or Batman. As he grows older, however, the child's imitations become more closely related to what is being imitated. For example, in pretending to be an airplane, the child will not only hold his arms outstretched, he will hold them stiff as if they were the wings of a plane, and he will hum to indicate its engine noise.

Symbolic functioning is also evident in the child's symbolic (or pretend) play. Piaget (1962) describes many examples of symbolic play, noting that as children learn how objects are used, they engage in pretend activities that reflect these uses. Thus, a young preschool child may be seen drinking from an imaginary cup or brushing her hair with an imaginary hairbrush (Garvey, 1977). At first, such symbolic play is directed toward oneself, but eventually it is directed toward others as well. The child plays with her doll pretending that her doll is drinking from an imaginary cup, or she serves make-believe coffee to her mother, pretending that she is the hostess at a party (see Figure 8.1).

Not only is the child capable of playing imaginatively in these ways, he also becomes increasingly adept at using objects as if they were something else. The child uses sand to represent food, and he plays with a broomstick as if it were a horse or with a cardboard box as if it were a truck. If he does not have a toy train to play with, he makes believe that several blocks being pushed together along an imaginary track are a train, and he enhances the scene by whistling "toot toot" and stopping at an imaginary station.

Obviously, a broomstick is not a horse, and several blocks being pushed together do not make up a train. Nevertheless, symbolic play is significant in cognitive growth, for it allows the child to assimilate the objects he encounters in his experiences. For example, a real horse or a real train is transformed into his mental construction of the world, so he eventually acquires the meanings of objects. Piaget asserts, therefore, that the child must not be discouraged from indulging in a world of make-believe and should not be hurried through this stage, for, through her manipulations of representational thought in the course of her symbolic play, she gradually attains a more mature mode of cognitive functioning. The preschool child's ability to play imaginatively is a precious characteristic which may be, in essence, the creativity and individuality we value in older children and adults. As Flavell (1985) notes, the preschool child pretending that several blocks are a train knows that these do not make up a train. Yet, he is able to mentally transform the blocks in his play and consider them a train.

The symbolic mode of thinking is apparent not only in the child's play, but also in his acquisition of language, as language is a system of signs which are words used to represent objects, events, thoughts, and feelings in such a way as to allow for effective communication. In noting that language is a sign system, Piaget made a distinction between signs and symbols. According to Piaget, *signs* have public meanings which are shared and understood by society, and are thus used to communicate. On the other hand, *symbols* are private and personal and often understood only by the individual using them. Symbols may bear a resemblance to what they signify. A short stick may resemble a knife, a spoon, or a screwdriver, depending on what the individual pretends it to be. Signs (words) bear no resemblance to what they represent so that their meanings must be slowly assimilated by the child (Pulaski, 1980).

signs

symbols

Language skills are acquired very rapidly during the preschool years. However, the first words the child learns do not immediately serve as signs which represent objects. Initially, the word *cat* is no different for the child than other properties of what the child knows about a cat, such as its soft fur or its meows. It is only gradually that the child realizes that the word *cat* is not part of the thing he knows, but rather, a representation of it.

The Development of Concepts

Even when the child attains the notion that a word is actually an arbitrary representation of something, she still uses a word to refer only to a specific object or event rather than a class of similar objects or events. She uses the word *cat* to refer only to the family cat she knows, or the word *ball* to refer only to her own ball. She soon realizes, however, that other cats and balls exist and that they are similar to her own cat and ball. Once the child has this insight, her understanding of the environment is enhanced, and she is able to acquire knowledge at a much faster pace and to organize her knowledge into concepts. A *concept* is a way of organizing information so that it is applicable not only to a specific object or event, but to other similar objects and events as well. For example, the concept of dog identifies a particular animal and it refers also to all dogs. Once she acquires the concept of dog, the child can guess that when shown a tiny poodle that she has never seen before and is told that it is a dog, that this poodle must have similar characteristics to other dogs she knows. According to Piaget, the acquisition of concepts is a major step in cognitive growth, and it is significant because it greatly simplifies learning. As Bruner (1965) notes, if we had to "register" all the differences around us and had to respond to each object or event as unique, ". . . we would soon be overwhelmed by the complexity of the environment."

concept

Classification. Some of the more abstract concepts, such as the concept of number or of space, are acquired very slowly and are not fully attained by the child until the next period of cognitive development, which occurs during the school-age years. However, many other concepts of objects such as a car, a house, or an apple, are acquired early in the preoperational period. Having acquired such concepts, the preschool child evidences his appreciation of the differences among objects, and he can classify them into different categories. For example, he knows that although there are several types of apples, some of which are green, some red, and some both green and red, they are still all classified under one category, and they are different from bananas or oranges.

Although the child can tell the difference between two objects such as apples and bananas, and can place them in their appropriate class, his overall understanding of the notion of classification is still in the process of being acquired and it is not completely grasped until the end of the preoperational period. To demonstrate this, Piaget devised a simple experiment in which children were given paper cutouts of geometric shapes in various sizes and colors. They were asked to group together those cutouts that were alike. Younger and older preschool children performed differently on the task because, according to Piaget, they are at different levels of conceptual development.

Children between the ages of 2½ and 4½ who had no understanding of the concept of classification simply made interesting figured designs (see Figure 8.2a). That is, they used the paper cutouts to make a picture of a snowman or of a house, apparently ignoring all of the discriminable dimensions of the objects they were asked to classify (Inhelder & Piaget, 1959).

Older preschool children between the ages of 4½ and 6 or 7 demonstrated some understanding of the concept of classification, as they started to group together the cutouts according to a single dimension, making a pile of all square pieces, for example. However, they soon became distracted and began to group the cutouts along another dimension, such as color, so they added to the same pile of square pieces all the pieces that were yellow, regardless of their shape (see Figure 8.2b).

By the end of the preoperational period, the children, evidencing their understanding of the properties of classes, were able to sort the cutouts along several *different* dimensions, so that they grouped together all the small red triangles in one pile, all the large red triangles in another pile, and all the yellow circles in yet another pile (see Figure 8.2c).

In this experiment, Piaget demonstrated that by the end of the preoperational period the child acquires an understanding of two important principles: (1) that an object may be considered to have a single characteristic (such as a particular color, shape, or size) or multiple characteristics; and (2) that although an object may be classified along one of several characteristics (an object may be square, red, and small), it cannot be classified along different attributes of the same dimension simultaneously. That is, an object cannot be both square and round. This cognitive achievement extends to other aspects of development. For example, having acquired an understanding that objects have different characteristics, the child applies this knowledge to his social world, and he begins to appreciate the fact that people have multiple social roles. He may be con-

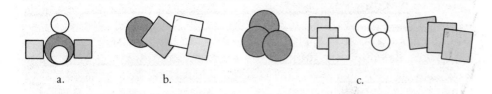

a.   b.   c.

FIGURE 8.2 Parts a and b illustrate two typical errors in sorting on a multiple classification task. Part c shows the sorting done correctly.

sidered a child by his parents, but he is also a boy, someone's friend, and his grandmother's grandson. Although this realization begins at the end of the preoperational period, it will take the child some time before he will fully grasp the implications of the complement of roles and the fact that each may require a different set of behaviors from him.

Prelogical Thinking

Not all researchers agree with Piaget that children acquire an understanding of the concept of classification as late in the preoperational period. Nancy Denney (1972) studied preschool children in Buffalo, New York. She found that many of them had an understanding of classification as early as the age of 4 and they were able to sort cardboard cutouts into different categories according to their color or shape when they were asked to put the things that are alike or the things that go together into groups. She believes that her findings may be accounted for by the fact that in the United States many children, through their experiences in nursery schools and exposure to such television programs as "Sesame Street" and "The Electric Company," are encouraged to attend to the various properties of objects, thereby becoming aware of classifications at an earlier age. You will see in a later section of this chapter that in other aspects of cognition researchers are finding that preschool children may be more advanced than Piaget gave them credit for. Nevertheless, Piaget's theory remains important, for it provides us with insight into the cognitive world of preschool children, and it also serves to explain some of children's apparently illogical answers to simple questions.

Class Inclusion.   Even after children can consistently classify objects, they have difficulty understanding the relationship between groups at different levels of the classification system. That is, they have difficulty understanding that one class is included in another and that an object may be classified into two classes simultaneously. For example, a child may be capable of classifying such objects as apples and bananas according to their differences, but he is unable to describe how apples and bananas are alike, because this requires the understanding that although apples and bananas belong to two different classes, they may also be combined into a higher-order class called fruit. Lacking this kind of understanding, the child predictably maintains that apples and bananas are not the same.

Piaget developed a number of experiments, often referred to as Piagetian tasks, which reveal the prelogical nature of the preschool child's mode of thinking. In one such task, the *part-whole problem,* the child is shown 7 blue beads and 3 white beads, all of which are made from wood, and he is asked whether there are more blue beads or more wooden beads. Ault (1977) describes the experiment.

part-whole problem

Adult You see all these beads I have. Some are white and some are blue. What do you think the blue beads are made of?

Child Wood.

Adult That's right. What do you think the white beads are made of?

Child Wood.

Adult Right again. Both the blue beads and the white beads are made of wood. Now, do you think there are more blue beads or wood beads?

Child Blue.

Adult Why?

Child Because there are more.

Adult More what?

Child More blue.

Adult More blue than what?

Child More blue than white.

Adult But I wanted to know about the wooden beads. Are the white beads made out of wood?

Child Yes.

Adult Are the blue beads made out of wood?

Child Yes.

Adult So all the beads are made out of wood?

Child Yes.

Adult So are there more wood beads or blue beads?

Child Blue.

You might think that the child is being stubborn, but in reality he has difficulty understanding that although the beads may be categorized into two different classes according to their color, they actually belong to a

FIGURE 8.3 Conservation of liquid.

higher-order class as well, since they are all wooden beads. The child also confuses *part* of the wood beads group (the blue beads) with the *whole* group of wooden beads, which includes both blue and white beads.

Conservation. In another classic series of experiments on conservation, Piaget demonstrates that the preschool child is limited in his mental abilities for he does not think logically, which inhibits his ability to reason. This is evidenced in the child's misunderstanding of seemingly simple concepts.

For example, to adults it is obvious that a given quantity of liquid remains the same no matter what the shape of the container. If you are shown two different containers, one tall and narrow, the other short and wide, and you see someone pour the same amount of water in each, you would know that despite the fact that the amount of water in one container may appear to be more or less than the amount of water in the other (see Figure 8.3), there is exactly the same amount of water in each container. The preschool child, however, is more easily fooled by appearances because he lacks an understanding of the concept of *conservation,* the

the concept of conservation

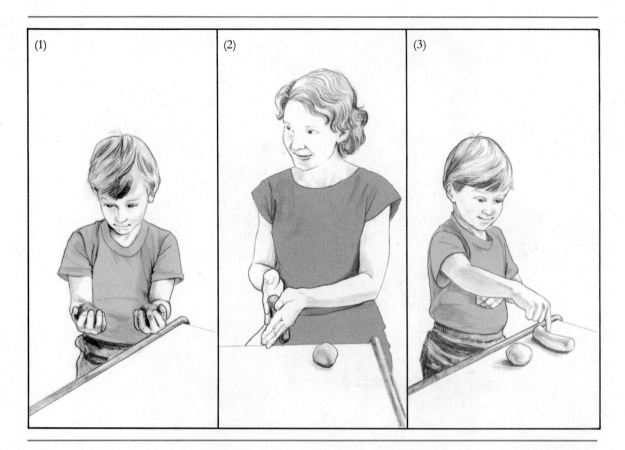

FIGURE 8.4   Conservation of substance.

notion that an amount is conserved (remains the same), even though the shape changes.

Preschool children also have problems with conservation of substance. If you show a child two balls of clay of equal size and ask him if both pieces have the same amount of clay, he will say that they do. Then, if you ask him to roll out one of the pieces of clay into a thin, sausage shape and then ask him if the two pieces have the same amount of clay, he may answer that one of the pieces is now bigger, stating that the sausage-shaped piece has more clay because it is longer than the other piece (see Figure 8.4).

Why does the preschool child have problems understanding change? The answer to this question may seem to be of no practical significance, for it makes little difference to the child or his parents if the child knows whether two pieces of clay are the same size even when the shape of one piece changes. However, the explanation is important, for it enables us to know not only that children think differently than adults do, but also in what ways. Also, it shows that the ideas that seem simple to adults are difficult for the child because they are beyond his cognitive capacity. Piaget (1952) noted that there are two principles that govern preoperational thinking and hinder the child's performance of tasks. The first is *irreversibility of thought,* which refers to the inability of the child to go forward and then backward in his thinking; hence he has trouble understanding change. For example, the child cannot understand that the ball of clay can be *transformed* in shape simply by rolling it and that by rolling it again, it can be transformed back to its original shape. In his thinking, the child moves forward only, so he reasons on the basis of what he visualizes for the moment rather than thinking back to the shape the piece of clay originally was. Irreversibility of thought is apparent in some of the answers to questions the child is asked. For example, if you ask a girl if she has a sister (and she does), she will say that she does have a sister. If you ask her if her sister has a sister, she will say no! About the age of 5 or 6 the child acquires the ability to reverse, and this is a major milestone in the development of logical thinking.

irreversibility of thought

In addition to irreversibility, the child tends to *center* his attention on one aspect of a problem or situation, and he neglects to focus on other aspects. For example, in the conservation task, the child is unable to focus on length and height simultaneously. He centers on either the length or the height and he is easily fooled by appearances into thinking that one piece of clay has more clay than the other.

centering

Practical Applications.   The preschool child's inability to apply the rules of logic to his thinking is evident not only in Piagetian experiments, but in the everyday experiences of the child as well, although this fact is not immediately apparent to parents and caretakers. Consider the child who feels shortchanged because he got a piece of pie that is shorter but wider than that of his brother. No amount of explanation can convince the child that both pieces are the same size, hence parents often come to realize that it is useless to reason with the preschool child.

Another consequence of prelogical thinking is seen in the child's understanding of relationships between events. When adults reason, they do so on the basis of deductive reasoning, in which aspects of the general are attributed to a particular situation, or they use inductive reasoning, in which aspects of a particular situation are applied to a more general context. The preschool child, able to center, or focus, only on an aspect of an event, uses neither type of reasoning. Rather, he uses *transductive reasoning.* That is, he goes from one particular to another particular, often ascribing cause-and-effect relationships to unrelated events. If he falls, he blames the sidewalk, or if he is hurt, he may blame a child who is not even near him at the time. Parents often think that the child is being silly or that he is lying. However, this is merely his understanding of what happened. Transductive reasoning is not limited to preschool children. Adults often attribute cause-and-effect relationships to unrelated events, so for this reason we always caution you not to interpret correlational studies which show that there is some relationship between two variables as meaning

transductive reasoning

that one variable caused a change in the other. However, whereas you are capable of understanding other possible, logical relationships, the preschool child is not.

Other Characteristics of Preoperational Thought

The limitations inherent in preoperational thought are evident not only in the child's understanding of the physical world, but also in his ideas and beliefs about what happens in his environment. As anyone who has spent any length of time with a 3- or 4-year-old child knows, children at that age are constantly asking Why? "Why is the grass green?" "Why is the ball rolling?" "Why are there waves only at the edge of the lake?" "Why do butterflies die so soon?" "Why is it raining?" "Why does the sun set?" Why? Why? Why? A scientific explanation of such phenomena rarely satisfies the preschool child. He is not as interested in hearing that the ball he dropped is rolling down the hill because "it is on an incline," as much as he is interested in hearing "The ball knows you are going down the hill, too."

According to Piaget, the preschool child spontaneously invents myths about his environment. By constantly asking why, he seeks to reaffirm these myths, hence mythical explanations have great attraction for him. One of the myths the child adheres to is known as *finalism,* which is the belief that everything has a purpose and as such, everything, including movement, is meant to accomplish some end: the ball is rolling so it can be down the hill; the sun sets at night so it can go to bed.

finalism

artificialism

Another childhood myth is *artificialism,* which is the belief that everything is made by someone (see Figure 8.5). For example, Piaget's daughter was used to seeing clouds of smoke rising from her father's pipe, and she assumed that her father was also responsible for making the clouds in the sky. Asking other children questions related to the origin of the sun, Piaget received such answers as: "Some men made it into a big ball . . . then afterwards they told it to go up in the air." How were stars made? "People took little stones and made them into little stars."

Artificialism is evident not only in children's thinking about natural phenomena such as the sun and stars but also in their understanding of where babies come from. Noting that his daughter constantly asked "Where did you find the little baby?" and "How are babies made?", Piaget (1952) stated that she did not appear to be entirely satisfied with any of his replies and that she would often ask a question and provide the answer herself, incorporating some of his previous explanations: "How do babies make themselves? They're bubbles of air. They're very tiny. They get bigger and bigger and when they're big enough they come out from inside the mother's tummy. . . . Babies are air first, aren't they? They're so small. So they must be air first. But there must be something in the air that babies are made of" (Piaget, 1952). Some children, perhaps

FIGURE 8.5   By asking the preschool child different questions, Piaget discovered that at this age, children make up mythical explanations for natural phenomena. For example, they believe that the sun is a manmade ball or that the stars are little stones that people have made into tiny lights and placed in the sky.

those who have been told about the father's role in conception, have said that babies come from their mother's tummy and that the father "puts his hand in the tummy. Then he puts [the baby] on the bottom . . . and the mommy then closes her tummy and the baby is born" (Formanek & Gurian, 1980).

Young preschool children also believe that all things are living and endowed with intentions and feelings. Known as *animism,* the belief that inanimate objects are alive is evident in the preschool child who thinks that the sun follows him wherever he goes, that the ocean is asleep at night, or that a flower is hurt when it is picked. According to Piaget (1952), when the child ascribes feelings and thoughts to all things, he is, in fact, assimilating these things (the sun or the ocean or the flower) into his schemes, and in so doing he distorts external reality. Gradually, as the child participates in activities and interactions with adults and older children, his view of the world becomes more realistic.

animism

Egocentrism.   Not only do preschool children believe that inanimate objects are alive and endowed with intentions and feelings, they also believe that these objects revolve around their lives. This is known as *egocentrism,* and it is defined as the belief that the world centers on one's own life. Because they are egocentric in their thinking, preschool children believe, for example, that it snows so *they* can make a snowman or that the grass grows so *they* can walk on it. They also understand life events in an egocentric way, so it is hard for them to accept death, illness, and divorce. Often, a preschool child blames himself for the death of a grandmother, or he explains that she is dead because she doesn't love him. The preschool child whose parents are separated or divorced also blames himself, and he tends to think that his parents divorced because he did something to upset them. For this reason, it is important that both parents reassure the child that they love him and will continue to do so despite the divorce.

The child's egocentric thought also prevents him from seeing another person's perspective, or putting himself in the place of others. It is not that the child is selfish or insensitive. Rather, his understanding of the world is an integral aspect of the cognitive process. As the child becomes increasingly capable of stepping away from himself and recognizing that other people have feelings and thoughts that differ from his own, he advances in his ability to think and understand. Although egocentrism dominates the preoperational child's thinking, it is present at every stage in development to some extent (Elkind, 1978).

Perspective-Taking.   To demonstrate the child's basic inability to adopt another person's perspective or point of view, Piaget and Inhelder (1963) conducted an experiment in which children aged 4 to 11 years were shown a three-dimensional exhibit of three mountains (see Figure 8.6). Children were asked to walk around the exhibit so they could see that the mountains looked different from various positions, and they were then asked to sit on a chair facing one side of the exhibit. A doll was placed on a chair so that it faced another side of the exhibit. Each child was asked to choose a picture that showed what the doll saw. Invariably, children under age 6 thought the doll saw the same scene as they; children between the ages of 6 and 7 knew that the doll saw a different scene, but they were not sure which one, whereas the older children between the ages of 9 and 11 selected the correct view from the doll's perspective. To choose the correct view for the doll, the children had to recognize that the doll, which was seated in a different position from theirs, had a different view of the mountains than they had, and they also had to have had the ability to mentally change the position of the mountains, to visualize the scene, and then to compare it with the pictures. This is quite a difficult task. For this reason, researchers suggest that Piaget may be wrong in his assertion that egocentrism lasts throughout the preoperational period. In variations of the three mountain experiment, researchers have shown that when the

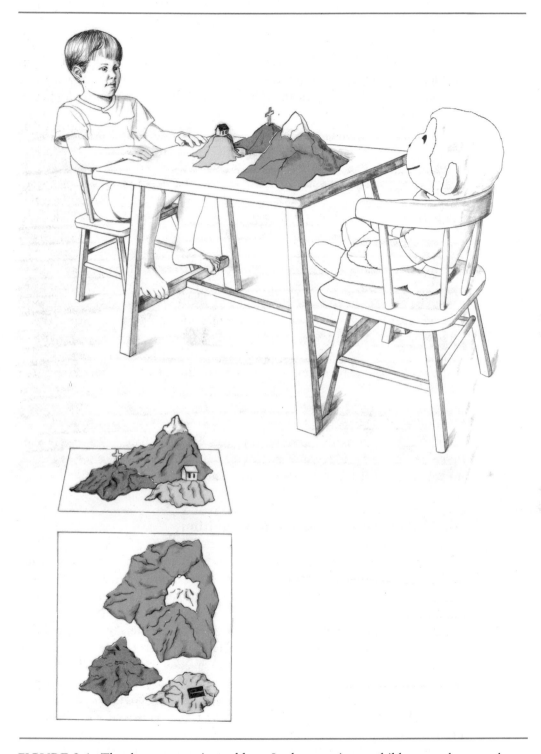

FIGURE 8.6 The three mountain problem. In the experiment children are shown a three-dimensional exhibit of three mountains that look different from various positions (see inserts). Children are then asked to tell the examiner what the mountains look like from the perspective of a doll (or, as in this illustration, a stuffed monkey), seated opposite them.

task is simplified, children at a younger age are able to give the right answer, indicating that they are not egocentric in their thinking. For example, it is easier for children to give the right answer when they are able to rotate the exhibit so as to indicate the doll's view (Huttenlocher & Presson, 1973).

In their attempts to identify the age during which egocentrism begins to decline, researchers recently devised a number of other ways to study perspective-taking in children. In one such study, the child sits on the floor with his mother and another adult. One of the adults is asked to close her eyes. While the adult's eyes are closed, the child chooses a toy that only he and the other adult who can see know about. It is their secret. When 2- and 3-year-olds are asked if the other adult also knows about their toy, they answer yes, evidencing their inability to recognize that another person's point of view may be different from their own. However, when 4-year-olds are asked the question, most of them say no because at this age they realize that only the adult who could see while they picked out the toy knows what was going on and therefore shares their secret (Marvin, Greenberg, & Mossler, 1976). In another study, Shatz and Gelman (1973) found that when 4-year-old children are speaking to infants, they modify their speech patterns so they can be better understood by the infants. They speak more clearly and slowly, and they repeat what they say, thus demonstrating that they are able to recognize as well as respond to the needs of their young listeners. In both these studies, researchers have shown that children are indeed capable of perspective-taking at an early age and that they are not quite as egocentric in their understanding of the world as Piaget suggests.

An Alternative Explanation to Cognition

These studies are important, for they underscore some of the shortcomings of Piaget's theory, leading researchers to argue that whereas Piaget has demonstrated certain cognitive limitations in the preschool child's mode of thinking, preschoolers are more capable than Piaget suggested. Now that we have a better understanding of preschoolers' cognitive skills, we should be careful not to overestimate how much young children understand. Nevertheless, you should be aware that generally developmental psychologists today are in agreement with Flavell (1985), who notes that "the developmental psychologists's portrait of cognition during the period of early childhood . . . used to be rather negative. For example, preschool children's thinking was characterized as 'preoperational' or even 'preconceptual.' However, recent research has shown that an impressive number of fragile but nonetheless genuine competencies have been acquired by the end of this period. It seems that we had underestimated the young child's abilities, just as we had underestimated the infant's."

You should also note that Piaget's theory, while useful in providing us with greater insight into the emergence and development of cognitive skills, is but one explanation of cognition. You will see in Chapter 11 that researchers are not only becoming increasingly appreciative of the cognitive abilities of preschool children, many of them are also adhering to a different theoretical explanation of cognition. Piaget described cognitive development as occurring over four distinct stages from infancy through adolescence. Each stage is characterized by different mental processes. Other researchers describe cognition in terms of *information processing*. They contend that some of the cognitive limitations Piaget observed among preschoolers are due not to different mental processes, but rather to their limited capacity for memory.

information processing

The study of memory in young children is an example of the research on information processing. Memory is a fundamental aspect of cognition. In the three mountain task which is used to measure perspective-taking, children need to be able to remember what the mountains looked like from different vantage points. Memory is also an important aspect of other cognitive abilities, and when we say that an infant or young child has learned something, we presuppose that he remembers it. Memory is present early in life. Recall that even infants have a rudimentary capacity for memory. With age, this capacity increases so that by age 2 children can remember single events. For example, they remember having received a specific toy from an aunt or an uncle, or a particular game they played with their relatives on a previous visit. By age 4 they are able to remember more complex details and also a sequence of events. If you attempt to skip a page or two in a story you read to a child that age, you will be reminded by that child that you are not adhering to the story as written! Studies have also shown that children ages 4 and 5 can remember the sequence of a series of pictures, or the way items are grouped on a supermarket shelf (Brown, Branford, Ferrara, & Campione, 1983).

Young children also remember the words that they hear. As you will see in the next section, language development occurs at such a rapid rate during the early childhood years that it often astonishes adults how easily children learn new words and grammatical rules. Keep in mind, however, that although preschoolers are budding linguists, some aspects of language are still difficult for them and will not be mastered until an older age.

LANGUAGE DEVELOPMENT

Language skills develop rapidly during the preschool years. Recall that toward the latter part of the second year of life, the child began to combine words rather than use one word at a time and that gradually his sentences became longer. However, the child's speech still had a "telegraphic" characteristic to it. That is, the child spoke in very short sentences, using words as efficiently as possible, and including only those words that are essential to convey the message.

Learning Words and Speaking in Sentences

During the preschool years the child acquires the ability to speak in longer sentences; he uses an average of 4 or 5 words per sentence at the age of 4 and an average of 6 or 8 words per sentence at the age of 5. In part, the increase in the length of the child's sentences reflects the child's knowledge of new words as well as his ability to learn new words rapidly. The growth of the preschool child's vocabulary is impressive. Recent studies estimate that the preschool child's vocabulary is quite large and that at age 6 the child knows between 8,000 and 14,000 words (Carey, 1977). Researchers suggest that preschoolers' knowledge of so many words may be the result of exposure to television.

Some preschool children seem to have the ability not only to know but also to use correctly difficult words such as *rivalry* or *decaffeinated* as long as these words are explained to them. In fact, they have a fascination with words, wanting to know the meaning of any new word, and often picking up and using not only difficult words but profanity as well. However, despite the young child's ability to acquire new words rapidly and even at times to use them in the appropriate context, she does not always know the meanings of words. In addition, her use of words is limited in several ways by her mental thought processes. For example, because she is egocentric in her thinking, the young child often makes up words, and she expects others to understand her. Some of the words the child makes up are quite creative. An example is *stocks,* which combines both socks and stockings, and the child may refer to either, depending on what she is thinking about at the moment (Thompson & Chapman, 1977). Or, when the preschool child is asked to explain a word, she explains it in terms of an action that she may perform, again, evidencing egocentric thinking. For example, she defines the word *stone* as "something I pick up" or she defines the word *hole* as "something I dig." In addition, some seemingly simple words are difficult for the child to understand fully. For example, words that convey comparison, such as *little, big, near,* and *far* are difficult for her to use appropriately at all times. Thus, a 4-year-old child may refer to her baby brother as little, but will get upset when she is referred to as little in comparison to an adult. As far as the child is concerned, babies are little, but she is big (de Villiers & de Villiers, 1978).

Learning the Rules of Grammar

Language growth is not simply the accumulation of words; knowledge and use of the grammatical rules of language is also an important accomplishment during the preschool years. Grammatical rules such as word order and word form lend meaning to words. Although the preschool child is not able to follow complex grammatical rules such as those entailed in forming the subjunctive or using *whomever* correctly, he does demonstrate the ability to learn and apply basic grammatical rules such as putting the subject before the verb.

Children's acquisition of grammatical rules takes place over the course of the preschool years, but even in young children who use only one- or two-word sentences, the understanding of the basic grammatical rules of language is evident, as they use gestures and intonation to give meaning to their thoughts (Brown, 1973). To illustrate our point, let us look at children's questioning. Young preschool children often speak in sentences that have a question mark attached to them, for example, "nice doggie?" Researchers are not sure why the child speaks in questions, but they speculate that he is looking for confirmation that he is being listened to (Brown & Hanlon, 1970). Initially, children's questions entail nothing more than raising their voices at the end of a sentence to indicate that they are asking a question, not making a statement. Then, they place a question word such as *where* or *why* at the beginning of a sentence without further modifying the sentence in any way: "Where my mommy?" It is only later on in the preschool period that children learn to apply a specific rule when asking a question, as in: "Where *is* my mommy?", placing the verb before the subject.

Gradual grammatical progress is also evident in children's use of negatives. In English, the negative sentence is constructed by transforming a declarative sentence. That is, the sentence "The girl is eating her sandwich" may be transformed into the negative by adding the word *not,* as in "The girl is not eating her sandwich." Initially, young children simply add the word *no* to an otherwise affirmative sentence, as in "No take this." Eventually, they learn the correct use of negation, as in "Don't take this." It is interesting to note that although different languages have vastly different rules of negation, children in other parts of the world form early negative sentences the same way as do English-speaking children, by simply placing the word *no* at the beginning of the sentence (Slobin, 1970). Bloom (1973) also found that as they grow, children use the word *no* differently; at first they use *no* to indicate absence or nonexistence as in "Daddy no here," indicating that their father is gone, and soon after that they begin to use *no* to indicate negation as in "no bed," meaning "I don't want to go to bed."

As you can see by this brief explanation of children's formation of questions and negations, the acquisition of grammar is a gradual process that progresses from the simple to the complex. Brown (1973), who conducted longitudinal studies on language development, further notes on the basis of these studies that the rules of grammar are acquired in a remarkably regular order. He illustrates this by children's use of *morphemes*   *morphemes* as the means by which they qualify and give more precise meanings to words. The -*ing* ending denoting the present progressive tense (as in "I am walk*ing*") is one example of a morpheme. Other morphemes are the suffix -*ed* which denotes the regular past tense and the -*s* ending which denotes the third person singular of a verb or the plural. Brown identified 14 such morphemes, or qualifiers. Although the rate at which children acquire these qualifiers differs from child to child, the order in which the qualifiers are acquired is the same for all children (see Table 8.1). Thus children begin with the present progressive tense, or -*ing* ending, and eventually they acquire other more complex qualifiers, such as those that designate the use of plurals or the past tense.

Once children learn a grammatical rule as it applies to one word, they generalize its use to other words, even words they are not familiar with. Jean Berko (1958) cites an experiment she had conducted in attempting to evaluate 4- to 7-year-old children's understanding of pluralization. The children were presented with a line drawing of a bird-like object and were told "This is a Wug. Here is another Wug. Now there are two _____?" Children were required to verbally fill in the blank. This experiment was repeated using several other nonsensical words such as *bix* or *zat,* all of which required different plural endings. Although all the children made some errors, even the youngest children often gave the correct plural endings to these words, thus demonstrating, (a) that they learn general rules for pluralization rather than individual words in their plural form, and (b) that they can apply these general rules of language to novel situations.

Overregularization. Children apply the general rules of language in their use of other qualifiers as well. However, when they first learn a rule, they tend to apply it to all words, thus rendering quite a bit of charm to their speech. For example, even children who have used the word *went* correctly, once they learn the -*ed* ending designating the past tense, they tend to switch and say "goed" rather than "went." In the same way, once they learn the plural ending -*s,* even though they already know and use the words *mice* and *feet,* they switch and say "mouses" and "foots." Some children go even further and say "footses" or "feets." In all of these cases, the children are ignoring the irregularities and exceptions that are inherent in language, and they *overregularize* by applying general rules to all words.

overregularize

A similar phenomenon is evident in children's articulation. Children's ability to articulate often lags behind their vocabulary. In other words, even after they acquire a large vocabulary, some young children have trouble pronouncing words correctly. They tend to drop the first consonants of some words such as spoon ('poon), and early in the preschool period they often substitute consonants, so "doggie" is pronounced as "goggie." In addition, they have difficulty articulating certain sounds

TABLE 8.1   A summary of the grammar of each of the 14 morphemes in the order that they are learned by the child. (Adapted from Brown, 1973).

Morpheme	Segment Structure Features	Example
1. Present progressive -ing	+ progressive	He is walk<u>ing</u>.
2., 3. Preposition on, in	+ on, + in	He is <u>in</u> the house.
4. Plural -s	+ singular, − singular	The boy<u>s</u> are in the house.
5. Irregular past e.g., went	+ present, − present	They <u>went</u> home.
6. Possessive 's		The boy<u>'s</u> book is here.
7. Uncontractible copula e.g., is, was	+ singular + present − singular − present	<u>Are</u> these your books?
8. Articles e.g., the	+ definite + singular − definite − singular	He has <u>the</u> book.
9. Regular past -ed	+ present, − present	He jump<u>ed</u> up and down.
10. Third person regular -s	+ singular + present − singular − present	He jump<u>s</u>.
11. Third person irregular e.g., does	+ singular − singular	<u>Does</u> he want the book?
12. Uncontractible auxiliary e.g., is	+ progressive + singular + present − singular − present	<u>Is</u> he jumping?
13. Contractible copula -'s	+ singular + present − singular − present	That<u>'s</u> mine.
14. Contractible auxiliary -'re	+ progressive + singular + present − singular − present	They<u>'re</u> jumping.

such as "th" so that "thick" is often pronounced as "fick." When they do learn to articulate a sound, they often apply it to many other words. A 3-year-old boy we know learned to pronounce the "th" sound correctly. For the first few days after he learned it, he pronounced such words as "think" and "thank you" correctly and clearly, but he also tended to say "thoday" for today and "Thommy" for "Tommy"!

Eventually, the child learns to speak clearly as well as grammatically correctly, although if by the age of 5 the child cannot speak well, then a speech therapist should be consulted. Parents and caregivers should refrain from teasing the child or from encouraging what they may consider to be cute baby talk. Speaking to an infant in a modified way, using simplified words, and speaking slowly with an emphasis on some words is important during infancy, but it can hinder language development if continued beyond the third year of life. Instead, preschool children can be encouraged to speak clearly by the adults' use of the correct speech patterns when speaking to preschool children.

Egocentric and Socialized Speech

Not only do children acquire increasingly complex language skills, the functions of language also change for children as they grow older. Piaget (1955) characterizes speech as either *egocentric* or *socialized*. In egocentric speech, children either carry on a monologue, apparently deriving pleasure from the repetition of words, or their speech largely focuses on what they want. Whereas many children engage in egocentric speech at the beginning of the preschool period, the older the child becomes, the more he needs to be able to communicate his thoughts, intentions, and desires to others, so speech comes to serve a more social function. In his socialized speech, the child demonstrates the ability to communicate effectively, for socialized speech includes an exchange of information between the speaker and the listener. Piaget stated that early socialized speech occurs when the child and his listener are both talking about the same subject in at least three sentences.

Learning to Communicate

As the child grows, his ability to communicate increases. In order to be able to communicate effectively, three skills are needed:

1. the ability to engage the listener's attention;
2. the ability to display sensitivity to the listener's characteristics and feedback, that is, to speak in such a way that the listener understands and to determine if the listener actually understood the message;
3. the ability to listen, since communication is a reciprocal process that includes not only effective speaking, but also effective listening.

As most parents and caretakers can attest, preschool children demonstrate at least one of these communication skills—the ability to get the listener's attention. Three- and four-year-old children want to be heard, and they attract attention to what they have to say by tugging at their mother's skirt, by prodding their father with a finger, or by literally placing their face directly in front of the face of their parent or another adult, so it becomes very difficult not to pay attention to them.

However, the young preschool child is still unable to communicate fully, for she lacks the sensitivity to the listener's characteristics and often she fails to pay attention to the listener's responses. Piaget noted that throughout the preoperational period, that is, until the age of 7, the child

FIGURE 8.7   When preschool children are asked to talk to an infant, they use simplified speech and short utterances, revealing their sensitivity to their young listeners' characteristics. Thus, preschoolers are not quite as egocentric as Piaget believed them to be.

engages primarily in egocentric speech since she does not consider the listener's perspective, and at times she does not make an attempt to determine whether she is being understood. Piaget also noted that early in the preschool period children are likely to engage in *collective monologue*. That is, they appear to be conversing with one another but they are not actually listening to one another or responding to what the other is saying.

collective monologue

Whereas many psychologists are in agreement with Piaget that the young preschool child engages primarily in egocentric speech without any apparent intention of communication, current research attests to the fact, mentioned earlier, that egocentric speech does not last as long as Piaget suggested. Indeed, most preschool children evidence an awareness of the people they converse with (see Figure 8.7). Recall from an earlier example

373

that by the age of four, children seem to be sensitive to their listener's characteristics, and they adjust their speech accordingly (Shatz & Gelman, 1973). When 4-year-olds are asked to tell a 2-year-old or other 4-year-olds about a toy, they are likely to talk differently to the 2-year-old than to the older children, using simplified speech and shorter utterances. Furthermore, recent studies suggest that when they are playing with one another, or simply talking to one another, preschoolers do listen and respond appropriately to each other's statements or questions (Wellman & Lempers, 1977), and they do not always engage in a collective monologue.

Language and Thought

Still, preschoolers are somewhat egocentric in their speech, often overestimating the clarity of the message they are conveying. They may say, "I want my toy," but they do not realize that they need to clarify which toy they want. They expect the listener to know what they are referring to (Beal & Flavell, 1983). Since egocentric speech and egocentric thinking occur at about the same time in the child's development, researchers have wondered if and how language development and cognitive development are related. Does the child think first and then express his thoughts in words either mentally or verbally, or does language enable him to think?

For adults, language and thought are so indistinguishable that thinking often seems like talking or communicating with oneself. Of course, when preschool children are acquiring and using language they are thinking. They remember words, and they associate a word with its meaning. They figure out grammatical rules about combining words and using sentences; and when they are speaking, they are in fact using words to express their feelings and thoughts. The question is, do children first have a thought and then try to express it in words, or does language shape their thoughts?

This is an important although controversial question, with researchers taking different views. Piaget (1955) viewed cognitive development as occurring first and language second. In fact, language, according to Piaget, is only possible given the development of cognition. Thus, language does not structure thought, it is the vehicle for expressing it. To underscore this point Piaget explained that even during infancy, before he has acquired language skills, the infant can solve problems, and he acquires basic concepts. As the preschool years pass and the child's linguistic ability increases, language begins to assume a greater role in the child's thoughts and behavior. To illustrate this, Piaget asked children to crawl and then to describe what they were doing when they crawled. At age 3, the children would crawl when he told them to, but they could not describe what they did, explaining erroneously that they moved both hands together and then both knees together. At age 5 or 6, however, the children could accurately describe what they did when they crawled. Hence Piaget pointed out that although young children have the necessary motor skills and vocabulary, it is not until later in the preschool years that they acquire the cognitive skills necessary to understand and explain their behavior.

Although Piaget noted that language development is an extension of the child's cognitive growth, other theorists see language as taking on a far more significant and distinct role. The Russian psychologist Lev Vygotzky (1962) contends that with the beginning of symbolic thinking at about age two, language comes to regulate the child's thoughts and behavior. Unlike Piaget, Vygotsky does not think that the child's egocentric speech implies a lack of awareness of other people's perspectives. Rather, Vygotzky believes that egocentric speech has a specific function, which is self-regulation and self-guidance. That is, the child uses egocentric speech to direct his behavior. At first this self-directing speech is external and audible to others, but over time, speech becomes internalized. Thus, whereas Piaget argues that egocentric speech declines and disappears, Vygotzky contends that it simply becomes internalized. However, Vygotzky emphasizes that inner speech is not merely talking to oneself, it is actually a rapid sequence of ideas fleeting across one's mind, some of which are translated into words, others into images. The important point to remember about Vygotsky's view is that inner speech, just like egocentric speech, functions to control the child's behavior.

Although many psychologists agree with Piaget that thinking occurs first and then is expressed in words, many others agree with Vygotzky that language facilitates thinking. In addition, some researchers contend that whereas initially the child learns language, eventually language facilitates his learning. As Lois Bloom (1975) puts it, during the preschool period, children first learn to talk and later, they talk in order to learn. This view is supported by Bruner (1964), who sees language as a tool provided by culture, noting that language actually expands the child's mind. He explains that although at first children understand the world only in terms of the actions they perform on it, by the age of three, when children start speaking fluently, they use language as the means by which to organize and reorganize their experiences. Language enables them to acquire more and more information about their environment.

GETTING READY FOR SCHOOL

As the child progresses during the early childhood years in his ability to think and talk, she becomes capable of organizing her knowledge into concepts, she becomes increasingly logical in her thinking, her egocentricity declines, and she also acquires impressive language skills which enhance her ability to learn. Piaget has contributed to our understanding of the preschool child, for he has shown the learning potential that exists even before the child enters school and that learning and cognitive growth occur as functions of an interaction between genetic potential and environmental experience. Whereas it has been known for many years before Piaget that children can and do learn at a young age, after Piaget's theory became accepted, researchers began to examine the possibility of accelerating cognitive growth through intensive training and by providing certain experiences during the preschool years.

Piaget himself noted that there are many things, such as social skills and cleanliness, that children should be taught during the preschool years, but he did not believe that preschool children need any intensive academic training or that such training would necessarily hasten their cognitive growth. Rather, he emphasized that the young child is an active participant in his own learning and that it is through his explorations of the environment and interactions with people that he progresses cognitively and acquires knowledge. Piaget emphasized that the child does not learn by being told and instructed; he learns by doing and experiencing. Through his experiences in handling objects and manipulating them in a variety of different ways, the child acquires an understanding of the properties of objects and the fundamental relationships between his own behavior and its effects on objects. Through hypothesizing and trying to figure out an answer, rather than being told the correct answer, the child gradually develops mental constructions that enable him to gather knowledge and become increasingly organized and objective so that by the end of the preschool period he is able to think more logically.

The Learning Environment of the Young Child

The Family.   The preschool child is naturally curious about his world, and he learns through his own discoveries about what people and objects are like and how they behave. Parents play an important role in the child's understanding of the world, teaching him why he needs to wash his hands before dinner, to be careful while crossing the street, and to be wary of strangers. There are many ways that parents can enhance their child's learning.

Between the ages of 2 and 6 the child spends most of his time at home with the family. Therefore, the home may be regarded as the child's first school and the parents as his first teachers. As such, they should stimulate the child's mind so the child is interested in learning. A home that makes the child feel secure enough to venture forth and explore his surroundings and parents who are responsive to the child and who interact with him facilitate the child's cognitive growth. By reading to the child, playing with him, and providing him with playthings as well as by taking him on special outings to the zoo, the library, the park, or simply to the grocery store or to play at a neighbor's house, parents help the child acquire the cognitive skills necessary for gathering and organizing new knowledge. By paying attention to the child and by sharing his daily discoveries, his successes, failures, and concerns, parents enhance the child's natural inclination to learn from his experiences (see Figure 8.8).

FIGURE 8.8 The preschool child is naturally curious about his world, often learning through his own discoveries about people, objects, and events. Parents play an important role in the child's understanding of the world. They facilitate the child's cognitive growth by reading to the child, talking to him, or otherwise interacting with him.

There are some elements in parents' behavior toward the child that seem to be particularly conducive to intellectual growth. Researchers note that parents who are sensitive and loving toward their preschool child promote the cognitive competence of the child. During the preschool period, being a sensitive and loving parent translates into providing the child the freedom to explore his surroundings and to express his feelings and thoughts. Intellectual competence is facilitated by supporting the child's tendency toward independence (Radin, 1971). Parents whose behavior enhances their child's cognitive development are doing more than recognizing the child's need for independence by allowing him to freely explore the environment, however. They also challenge and encourage him to master the developmental tasks that he confronts. At the same time they remain available to provide him with assistance as he needs it.

Radin (1971, 1982) found that such parental behavior toward the preschool child not only fosters cognitive development during the preschool years, it also enhances the child's academic success and his desire and motivation to learn once he is in school. Radin found that preschoolers whose mothers were sensitive to them and who used verbal or physical reinforcements to encourage them to complete tasks on their own scored higher on intelligence tests than those children whose mothers did not relate to them in these ways. They were also motivated to achieve academically, and they identified with the teacher once they entered school.

Day Care.   Although the parents' interaction with the child is an important aspect of the child's cognitive growth, many children do not have the opportunity to interact with their parents to a great extent. In many cases, children grow up in single-parent families or they grow up in families where both parents are working. In either case, parents are severely restricted in the time they are able to spend with the child and they often have insufficient time and energy to attend to the child's needs for intellectual stimulation. In fact, Nancy Rubin (1984) points out that parents, specifically mothers, do not become as involved in their children's activities as they once used to. Rather, they "manage" their children's time, coordinating but not participating in the various activities the children engage in during the day.

Since the number of preschool children who are in some form of day care has quadrupled over the past two decades—and is expected to increase even more during this decade (Select Committee on Children, Youth, and Families, 1983; Hofferth, 1979), the day care setting must be considered as another context within which the child receives intellectual stimulation and must be evaluated as such.

In general, the research suggests that children who attend a well-run day care center are not at a developmental disadvantage compared to those children who spend most of their time at home (Rutter, 1982). In fact, Clarke-Stewart (1982) points out that good day care centers are likely to provide more educational opportunities than some children would encounter at home. However, this is the case only if the children are attending a quality day care center.

The parents must ascertain whether the center their child attends is a good day care center that is conducive to proper development. In this regard, parents often focus on the curricular offerings of the center, feeling secure if they know that their child is receiving some training in academic tasks that will prepare her for school. A good day care center, however, is not determined by whether or not the child is exposed to academic training. It is determined by the behaviors and attitudes of the caretakers toward the child. According to the National Day Care Study (Ruopp, Travers, Glantz, & Coelen, 1979), caretakers with some training in early childhood education and child development spend more time with each child, comforting the child, praising her, and providing her with guidance than do caretakers without such training. The children in centers where such caretakers are employed do better on standardized IQ tests when they are tested, suggesting that just as parents can enhance the cognitive development of preschool children, the caregivers' behavior toward the child is important as well. Other studies suggest that frequent verbal interaction between the caretaker and child also seems to be a key determinant of quality day care because it facilitates the child's language development and her social and emotional development as well (McCartney, Scarr, Phillips, Grajek, & Schwartz, 1982). In addition, a good day care center

1. employs a sufficient number of caregivers so that all children are supervised at all times and each child has ample opportunity to interact with her caretaker;
2. ensures that the number of children per class does not exceed 12 for 3-year-olds and 16 for older preschoolers;
3. provides a safe surrounding as well as a considerable variety of play materials for the children—books, puzzles, paints, sandboxes, large-muscle equipment, and so on (Ruopp et al., 1979).

Researchers also point out that since the care and socialization of children who attend day care is in reality a joint effort between parents and caretakers, it is in the best interests of the child for the parents and caretakers to form a close relationship with each other and for the parents to become involved in the day care experiences of their children (Zigler & Turner, 1982).

You will see in the next section that studies on Head Start, a program for economically disadvantaged preschool children, have shown that parents' involvement and participation in the activities of their children in the program benefit both the children and parents in significant ways and also that the parents' involvement facilitates the caregivers' ability to relate appropriately to the children. You should note, however, that parents in general do not spend time forging a close relationship with their children's caregivers and that they are often unaware of the kinds of activities their child engages in while he is in the day care center. In fact, surveys indicate that parents on the average spend only 7.4 minutes per day in a day care facility (Zigler & Turner, 1982) and that they interact only occasionally with the caregivers, usually at the point of arrival or departure from the day care center (Powell, 1977). Parents are not uninterested in their child's day care experiences. Rather, they may feel that by becoming involved they are interfering in the role and responsibilities of the day care provider. Alerting parents to the importance of developing a close relationship with the caretaker, and suggesting to caretakers ways that they can encourage parents to participate in their children's experiences may alleviate the problem.

Television.   Children's learning environment includes not only the home and the day care center, but also television. Most homes have at least two

Training Day Care Providers

Child development professionals have long recognized the fact that the quality of care a young child receives from his adult caretakers is the most important factor in the child's life. Several studies, including the *National Day Care Study* (Ruopp et al., 1979), have found that caretakers play a central role in children's development and that young children in out-of-home care are likely to receive care that fosters their healthy development if: (a) the *staff-child ratio* in the caretaking situation is appropriate for the age of the children involved (1:3 infants, 1:4 toddlers, 1:8 preschoolers); (b) the *group size* is appropriate, depending on the age of the children (no larger than 6 for infants, 8 for toddlers, and 12 to 16 for preschoolers); and (c) the caretakers who are responsible for the children's care have training in child development.

Unfortunately, public attitudes regarding child caretakers do not reflect the central role caretakers have in children's lives, or the fact that the caretakers are actually substituting for the children's family for a large part of the day. All too often most caretakers are regarded simply as babysitters. They earn very low wages, have few fringe benefits, and are often not evaluated to ensure that they are capable of taking care of young children in groups. As a result, turnover rates in day care centers average 30% a year, compared to 10% in other helping professions (Select Committee on Children, Youth, and Families, 1984). Therefore, parents cannot feel confident that their children are being taken care of by competent adults who have demonstrated their knowledge of children's development and their ability to take care of children.

One way by which the poor public image of child caretakers may be improved and by which parents may be able to evaluate the quality of care their children receive is to provide training for caretakers and the means by which to assess their abilities. A model for the training and assessment of caretakers was developed as early as 1972 when, with the support of government funds, the *Child Development Associate,* or CDA, program was initiated. This program not only offers a model for the training and assessment of caretakers, it also accredits those who have been evaluated as capable of taking care of children in groups.

The CDA program emphasizes the importance of a reciprocal relationship between the child and the caretaker and the need of the caretakers to understand the basic principles of child development, for example, the function of play in the child's life. The program utilizes competency-based training and assessment, which means that the caretakers are trained and evaluated on the basis of their ability to work with young children and their ability to relate to each child individually, as opposed to their knowledge of facts. This approach is quite a departure from the academic trappings that are usually associated with an accreditation system. Individuals who have successfully completed the CDA training and assessment procedure are awarded the CDA Credential, which is not a license, but an award that signifies that the individual possesses certain knowledge and skills and can apply these in the care of children.

The CDA program is an example of the work of child development researchers in an applied setting and also an example of the ways in which research can contribute to the enhancement of the lives of children. Indeed, research is an important aspect of the CDA program because the program is based on knowledge from the research on child development and the delineation of skills, or competencies, that are desirable in an individual

who takes care of children. These skills are known as the CDA Competency Standards. They include the ability to establish and maintain a safe and healthy learning environment, the ability to enhance the physical and psychological development of children, and the ability to promote the positive functioning of children in a group setting. Each of these skills is defined further in terms of the functions that the caretakers perform. For example, in "promoting positive functioning of children in a group setting," the caretakers are expected to demonstrate that they can help children get along with others, that they are able to provide a routine for the children, and that they can establish simple rules that are understood by the children (Ward, 1976). The evaluation of the caretakers is made possible by and is directly relevant to the tasks they perform on the job, tasks which serve to ensure that chil-

dren receive care that is conducive to their development.

CDA is but one example of several efforts now underway to develop the means by which to train and evaluate the abilities and performance of caretakers in a variety of settings, including day care centers and family day care homes serving infants and young children. These efforts are important in at least two ways. They provide a standard by which parents can determine that their children are being taken care of by individuals who are sensitive to the needs and characteristics of children. And, they serve to advance the public image of caretakers. Once it is recognized that definite knowledge and skills are required of a child caretaker and that there are the means to train and accredit individuals, child care will come to be recognized as the important profession that it is.

television sets. The sets are typically on for 7 hours a day, and the preschool child watches television for an average of 3 to 4 hours a day (Liebert, 1980).

Television is often a focal point of parental concern. Parents may feel guilty, thinking that their child spends too much time watching television. There is also the anxiety that some kinds of content, notably violent and sex-oriented programming, are likely to induce unacceptable behaviors or dispositions in the child. In addition, the fact that children become engrossed in television-viewing to the point where they ignore playing with other children or with their toys is of concern to researchers, who note that children who watch television a great deal lag behind their peers in intellectual development (Liebert & Poulos, 1975). Overarching these issues is the growing realization that television may be spiraling out of parental control. Direct access to television, without parental intervention, is easier to obtain than it used to be. In many situations, children are in single-parent or dual-career families and parents have a difficult time monitoring the children's television viewing. All these concerns generate common questions parents often ask: How much TV should my child watch? What should he watch? Am I depriving my child by not permitting her to watch television?

On the other hand, parents often encourage their children to watch educational TV programs such as "Sesame Street," which began in 1969 in an attempt to provide educational experiences to the economically disadvantaged preschool child. Through fast-paced movements of shapes, letters, and numbers, children are given the opportunity to acquire important concepts and greater awareness of their environment, which, it was hoped, would prepare them for school. Some studies suggest that the fast pace of the program often induces inattentiveness in children once they enter school (Singer & Singer, 1982). Furthermore, although children are able to imitate what they see on television, they usually do not learn problem-solving strategies by watching "Sesame Street" (Hodapp, 1977). Many other researchers regard "Sesame Street" and other educational television shows such as "The Electric Company" as viable means of increasing children's knowledge (Salomon & Cohen, 1977). They have also found that by watching slow-paced programs such as "Mr. Rogers' Neighborhood," children increase their understanding of social skills (Gottman, 1977; see Figure 8.9).

However, researchers point out that if any benefits are to be accrued from watching television, the child must watch television with a parent or another caregiver who offers the child explanations about what he is watching (Singer & Singer, 1976). Mediating the child's television-watching in this way is important because young children have not developed what Greenfield (1984) terms *television literacy*. That is, they do not always know how to interpret the relationship between camera shots (a shot is a sequence in which the camera is continuously on), and they do not under-

television literacy

FIGURE 8.9   Children can learn valuable social skills from television programs such as "Mr. Rogers' Neighborhood."

stand many of the visual signals used on television. They can become confused about what they are seeing unless someone explains it.

Preschools.   Another aspect of the child's learning environment is the preschool. Children not enrolled in day care are usually enrolled in a preschool program for several mornings a week. The preschool program (or nursery school) is an important step toward preparing the child for school, because it provides the child with the opportunity to learn to get along with peers and an adult in a position of authority, as well as the opportunity to play with a variety of play materials and thereby to attain cognitive skills.

Many nursery schools have expanded to become day care centers, so a distinction between day care centers and nursery schools must be made. Day care centers, which incorporate some of the activities conducted in a nursery school, are utilized to care for the child for a large part of the day. Nursery schools, on the other hand, are not designed as caretaking facilities, but as a preschool setting where, over a 2- to 3-hour period each day or several times a week, the child can play with other children and become ready for formal schooling. Nursery schools typically include a short period of group activities such as story-telling in which children learn to pay attention to the teacher, and show-and-tell, in which children get the opportunity to talk about important happenings in their lives. Group activities are usually followed by a short break for juice and cookies, during which each child has the opportunity to develop such skills as pouring juice from the pitcher. In addition, children are often taken to different places of interest. They engage in free play, choosing from a number of different activity centers such as the art area, the dress-up corner, the housekeeping corner, or the reading section. Besides these activities, children also become familiar with following a routine similar to what they are likely to encounter once they enter kindergarten. They also engage in such basic academic tasks as learning how to write their names, recognizing the letters of the alphabet, and picking out and naming colors.

Of course, not all nursery schools are the same. Some encourage free play whereas others, such as those that follow the guidelines developed by Maria Montessori earlier this century, advocate the need for structure in the child's life. In many Montessori preschools, children and teachers refer to play as "work" and children are expected to be quiet as they busily select and engage in various activities.

The nursery school experience is beneficial to most children, for whom the nursery school functions as a transition from learning as it occurs in the context of the home to learning as it occurs within a more formal setting. By attending nursery school, the child learns to behave and interact with others in a group setting, and he also has access to a variety of playthings and opportunities for play he may not encounter in his home. All these factors further facilitate the development of his cognitive skills, readying him for school.

DISCUSSION OF SOCIAL ISSUES: PRESCHOOL INTERVENTION PROGRAMS

Many children are ready to start school and they benefit from formal instruction by the time they are 6 years old. Unfortunately, some children enter school without the skills to cope with the school environment. Such children, most often from poor homes, do not do well in school, and they fail to acquire the basic skills that would presumably give them equal opportunity to participate in and function within our society. Without an education, these children face a life of unemployment and hopelessness, and the cycle of poverty perpetuates itself.

In order to reverse this trend, educators, social scientists, and policy makers joined forces in the 1960s to mount a War on Poverty, which was a massive effort to eradicate social class inequities in the United States. The War on Poverty included job training programs and provisions for increasing welfare benefits. Particular emphasis was placed on providing preschool education for disadvantaged children. It was hoped that such preschool education would promote children's cognitive development, foster school achievement and thus break the cycle of poverty.

The decision to concentrate on the preschool child was based on scientific evidence regarding the influence of early experience on intelligence. First, on the basis of animal studies and other research, Hunt (1961), in his book *Intelligence and Experience,* argued that intelligence is in large measure an environmental product. He contended that it is possible to promote a faster rate of intellectual development and higher levels of adult intelligence by "governing the encounters that children have with their environments, especially during the early years of their development." Second, on the basis of longitudinal studies, Benjamin Bloom (1964) stated that intellectual development reaches its peak growth rate during the early childhood years and that by the time the child is 6 years old, approximately 75% of his intellectual capacity has been developed. The conclusion reached on the basis of the work of Hunt and Bloom was that economically disadvantaged children, as a result of their lack of appropriate experiences in the home, must suffer from deficits which can only become greater as they grow older (Horowitz & Paden, 1973). First grade was considered already too late to change the path of educational failure. Some intervention was needed during what was considered to be the critical period of development, the preschool years, in order to provide children with experiences that would stimulate their intellectual development and enhance their ability to succeed in school.

However, researchers have since realized that intellectual development results from an interaction between biological and environmental factors, so there must be a limit to the malleability of intelligence. They have also come to appreciate the fact that intelligence, as well as any other trait, might be influenced to a greater or lesser degree by biological or environmental factors not only during one specific period such as the preschool years, but at other points in life as well. The problem with the critical period hypothesis is that it limits intervention to a single period of life. However, there are other critical periods of life. The prenatal period is a critical period for physical development and the growth of the brain. While adolescence has long been considered an important period in development, recent studies by Feuerstein (1980) suggest that in attempts to modify some types of retardation (those that may be the result of lack of experiences in the environment), it is adolescence that is the most effective and critical time for intervention. Hence, while researchers and policy makers still believe in the importance of early intervention, intervention programs are no longer confined to the early childhood years. In addition, early intervention programs do not now focus only on intelligence but also on the child's health, his nutritional status, and his motivation to learn and succeed. All of these are important determinants of school achievement.

Project Head Start.   Numerous early intervention programs have been developed since the 1960s. A description of each one of these is beyond the scope of this chapter. But we will focus on one of the most notable of these—Project Head Start. Project Head Start began in the summer of 1965 as a summer program for 4- and 5-year-old children whose socioeconomic status predicted the likelihood that they would do very poorly in school. Eventually the program was extended to a full academic year, and it is now available not only to preschool children, but in some cases to parents and children from the prenatal period through age 8.

As is the case with other early intervention programs, Head Start has had a tremendous impact on the lives of economically disadvantaged children and their parents, and it set in motion a number of experiences which enhanced their success in school and in life generally. You should note, however, that although Head Start is often taken as synonymous with early childhood intervention (Richmond, Stipek, & Zigler, 1979), not all intervention programs are like Head Start. There are variations among programs in their goals, their methods of intervention, the duration of the services they provide, and the age of the children to whom they provide services. Nor is every Head Start program alike. Project Head Start, in fact, is not one program; it is actually a family of over 2,000 programs which vary in the type and quality of services they render. Some are center-based, others provide services in the home. Some are demonstration projects which provide a constellation of services to children and families beginning even before the birth of the child; others focus on providing services to parents and children only during the preschool years (*Head Start in the 1980s*). What all these efforts share is a commitment to enhancing the quality of life of children and families.

Project Head Start also differs from other early intervention efforts in that its planners did not focus on the deficits of economically disadvantaged children. Rather, appreciating the fact that these children came from different, but not necessarily inferior cultural backgrounds, they adopted an approach which respected children's varied backgrounds. This is reflected in the provision that parents be involved in all planning and administrative aspects of each program. Parent involvement has by now become a standard aspect of most intervention programs for children and infants. But at the time it was regarded as a significant breakthrough from past practices in which paid professionals dictated the operation of children's services. Involvement of parents in Head Start programs has proven to be successful for the parents as well as the children. Intellectual performance increased largely because the parents, who had been given responsibility, began to feel better about themselves, and their children, too, began to feel that they had more control over their lives, so they were more motivated to succeed in school (Coleman et al., 1966).

In addition, Head Start does not focus on promoting children's intellectual performance per se. Rather, from the beginning Head Start was guided by the knowledge that the extent that the child will succeed in school depends not only upon mental and verbal skills, but also upon how healthy he is, how he feels about himself and others, and how motivated he is to succeed (Zigler, 1973). Remember that a child who is ill or hungry is not likely to attend to academic tasks or benefit from any experiences provided, and a child who does not have the capacity to positively relate to other children and adults in a position of authority is not likely to behave in a way that is conducive to learning in school.

The importance of Project Head Start extends beyond its impact on the lives of children and their families. Since its inception, Head Start has provided the context in which researchers could become involved in the policy process, and as such it facilitated a turning point in the field of developmental psychology. Prior to the time when Project Head Start began, researchers regarded basic research and the accumulation of knowledge as their primary duties. Many researchers have since come to accept the view that, in part, their work should be directed toward the solution of social problems. These researchers now recognize that through their participation in the social policy process not only are they in the position to improve the lives of children, they also have the opportunity to learn more about children's development and the processes which can enhance and inhibit their development.

Evaluation of Early Intervention Programs.   Through their participation in Head Start and other early intervention efforts, researchers have significantly increased their understanding of how to evaluate such programs, and they refined the methodologies by which to evaluate the programs.

Much of what the researchers learned about the evaluation of programs they learned in the context of their evaluation of Project Head Start. Initially, evaluators focused on the general question: Have children benefited from their participation in the program? To answer this question, they used only IQ tests. If children's IQ scores increased, then, it was thought, the program could be considered successful; if the IQ scores remained the same, the program could be said to have no effect on the children.

There are problems with the question that was the focus of the evaluations, as well as with the use of IQ tests as the only evaluation tool. First, by focusing only on the benefits accrued by the child as the result of participation in the program, evaluators preempted the possibility of finding out if other members of the family benefited. Subsequent studies revealed, in fact, that the positive effects of early intervention are not restricted to the child, but extend to parents and siblings as well (Gordon, 1979). Second, the use of the IQ score as a measure of the benefits of the program yielded false optimism and later disenchantment with early intervention efforts (Zigler & Berman, 1983; Salkind, 1983; Bronfenbrenner, 1975) since they revealed that although initially children's IQ scores

FIGURE 8.10   Project Head Start began in 1965 as a summer program for socio-economically deprived children. Since that time, Head Start programs have been extended to a full academic year. These programs have had a tremendous impact not only on the lives of children who attend them, but on their parents' and siblings' lives as well.

increased because of their participation in the program, these gains later faded out. As a result, Head Start and other early intervention projects lost much of their initial popularity, and efforts to keep them alive until this day entailed a great deal of advocacy on the part of parents and professionals (Valentine & Zigler, 1983).

In part, problems with the evaluation of Head Start stemmed from the fact that the goals of the program were not stated clearly at the outset. For example, because of the failure to include parent participation as one of its goals, this aspect of the program was never evaluated. In addition, the use of the IQ test as a criterion by which to measure the success or failure of a preschool program is inadequate. The IQ test is useful, for it is a good predictor of success in school. However, it fails to measure how a child feels about himself, and how healthy he is. Since these are also aspects of intervention, and since they influence the child's school achievement, they should be incorporated into the evaluation (Zigler & Trickett, 1978).

Finally, an important component of any evaluation is cost-effectiveness: how much does the program cost, and how much would it have cost society if the children did not attend the program? This is an important question to address, for in their consideration of whether to continue to fund a program or discontinue it, policy makers make an ultimate decision on the basis of costs and benefits (Travers & Light, 1982).

Future Directions.   Having incorporated these principles into longitudinal evaluations of the effects of Project Head Start and other early intervention programs, researchers have been able to document the long-term benefits of preschool intervention programs (Lazar & Darlington, 1982; Lazar, Hubbell, Murray, Rosche, & Royce, 1977) and to demonstrate their impact on the lives of children. Studies document the fact that disadvantaged children who enrolled in preschool programs achieved markedly greater success in school and in their personal lives than comparable children who did not receive early childhood education (*Head Start in the 1980s*). Records show that at age 19 or older, the rates of employment and participation in college or vocational training after high school are far greater among individuals who as children attended preschool programs than among individuals who did not. Those individuals who attended preschool intervention programs are involved in fewer arrests, and fewer of them had dropped out of high school (Berrueta-Clement et al., 1984).

Preschool intervention has also proved to be cost-effective for society. Although quality preschool intervention is not cheap, it is cheaper than providing remedial education programs later in children's lives. Several studies have shown that for every $1.00 spent on preschool intervention programs, society saves $8.00 in potential remedial programs and other costs incurred in having the children retained in grade (Weikart, 1982).

In addition, evaluation studies give us some indication of the future directions for early intervention programs, because they indicate that those programs which are most effective are those similar to the Child and Family Resource Project (CFRP), which is a Head Start demonstration program. Such programs serve families and children from the prenatal period through age 8 by using existing community services. The rationale is that effective early intervention lies not in a single program designed to aid children alone or to remediate any one particular problem, but in a host of family support services (Report of the Comptroller General, 1979).

The results are impressive and may prompt the argument that we provide mandatory preschool programs to all children. Some caution must be exercised in this regard. Every child deserves a head start in life, but if the nation's financial status is such that it cannot afford to provide a quality preschool program for all children, advocating for mandatory preschool programs may well result in more programs, but low quality programs which may harm rather than benefit children.

Even in absence of a federal policy mandating preschool services, more and more preschoolers are receiving early education. In many states, local and state school districts are mandating that formal schooling begin at age 4 (Fiske, 1984). Although early schooling is supported not only because of the value of preschool education but also because many parents are now working and require care for their children during the day, it does provide the means through which more of the nation's children can benefit from preschool experiences.

SUMMARY

During the preschool years, significant advances occur in the child's ability to think. However, there are still limitations to the child's thinking. As Piaget has shown, the child who is in the preoperational period of cognitive development (ages 2–7) cannot reason, so he makes mistakes on seemingly simple cognitive tasks. For example, it is not until the age of 6 that the child can classify objects according to their shape, color, or size consistently. The explanation for children's failure on such tasks is that children can only center, or focus, on one aspect of the problem, and they neglect other aspects. In addition, children's thinking is governed by irreversibility, meaning that they do not have the flexibility to go back and forth in their reasoning. Since they cannot visualize what an object looked like initially, they reason on the basis of what they visualize for the moment.

Children are also egocentric in their thinking—they understand life only as it revolves around them. If their parents divorce, they think it is their fault. They are also egocentric in their language, despite the fact that they acquire impressive language skills during the preschool years and evidence the ability to learn and apply complex grammatical rules of language. Egocentrism begins to decline during the preschool years.

Since children are egocentric in their thinking and also in their language, researchers ask: Is language related to thought? That is, do we think first and act later, or does language facilitate thinking? Psychologists disagree on this question. Piaget believed that language is possible only given the development of cognition and that language does not structure thought, it is simply the vehicle for communicating it. However, Bruner and Vygotzky, among others, disagree, noting that language expands the mind and regulates behavior.

Although, as Piaget has shown, the child learns by acting on the environment and through his manipulations of objects and interactions with others, there are ways in which parents can facilitate optimal cognitive development in their children. Studies have shown that parents who are responsive to their children, who encourage children to complete tasks independently, and who provide them with intellectually stimulating experiences enhance their children's cognitive growth. In the same way that parental behavior enhances the child's mental development, so does the behavior of the caregiver in a day care center.

Children learn not only in context of their home and the day care center, they also learn from television, and some of them also acquire cognitive skills in context of their nursery school experiences. Since nursery school is seen as an important transition between learning as it occurs at home and learning as it occurs within the more formal setting of the school, researchers, policy makers, and educators have developed early childhood education programs for economically disadvantaged children. These programs, the most notable example of which is Project Head Start, have had a positive impact on the lives of children and families. They also facilitated a turning point in the field of developmental psychology, and enhanced researchers' understanding of cognitive development and their appreciation of the fact that children's ability and motivation to learn is influenced not only by their intellectual capacities but also by their health and how they feel about themselves.

REVIEW POINTS

1. Between the ages of approximately 2 and 6 or 7 years, children are in what Piaget termed the preoperational period of cognitive development. During this period children refine their ability for representational thinking—they can mentally represent objects and events and can think about the past, the future, and what is going on right now somewhere else.

2. During the preschool years children also acquire a symbolic mode of thinking, and they can use symbols and signs, such as words, to represent objects and events in their lives. The symbolic mode of functioning is noted in three behaviors which emerge during the preschool years: deferred imitation, or the imitation of a behavior some time after that behavior was observed; pretend, or make-believe play; and the rapid development of language skills.

3. Although children make significant progress in their cognitive growth during the preschool years, they are unable to think logically. According to Piaget, children respond incorrectly to some questions because of the cognitive limitations inherent in preoperational thought. However, recent studies reveal that preschoolers are more capable than Piaget has given them credit for being.

4. During the preschool years children acquire language skills at a rapid rate. They learn new words each day, and with age, they use increasingly longer sentences.

5. Children also learn the use of grammar during the preschool years, progressing from simple rules to more complex rules. As they learn, they generalize the rules to other words as well, sometimes overgeneralizing to the extent that they render a uniqueness and charm to their speech.

6. Preschoolers also become more skilled in conversations with others. Piaget maintained that children are egocentric in their thinking as well as in their language and that they do not pay attention to what others are saying or to whether or not they are being understood by the people they are talking to. More recent studies have shown that children are not as egocentric in their language as Piaget thought them to be. When they address themselves to babies, for example, the children speak differently than they do to older children and adults, evidencing the fact that they do take into account the characteristics of those they are talking to and that they do make an effort to be understood.

7. Piaget also noted that language development is an extension of children's cognitive development and that cognitive skills must be acquired before language can be acquired, emphasizing that thinking occurs first and is then expressed in words. Other researchers such as Vygotzky note that language skills actually facilitate thinking and also that once the child learns language, language then functions to facilitate learning.

8. Given the more sophisticated cognitive and language skills of preschoolers, parents often attempt to teach their children academic skills to prepare them for success in school. Researchers note that an emphasis on academic skills is not warranted during the preschool years, but that parents can enhance the child's cognitive and language skills. Parents who interact with their preschoolers foster intellectual growth in their children.

9. Although the parents' interaction with the child is an important aspect of the child's cognitive growth, many parents do not have the time to devote to their children and place them in day care facilities. As is the case with parents, caretakers in day care centers or other settings who play with the children, read to them, and provide them with ample individual attention and playthings serve to enhance the children's cognitive and language skills.

10. Children learn not only from their parents and caretakers, but also from television. Mediating the child's television watching and offering the child explanations of what is on television are important, as children do not always know how to interpret what they see on television.

11. Preschool is yet another aspect of the children's learning environment. Some pre-schools, or nursery schools, have expanded to day care centers, offering care for the entire day. However, a nursery school is distinct from day care in that the child is in nursery school for a 2- to 3-hour period during the day. In nursery school the child learns to get along with other children in a formal setting and also some basic tasks such as recognizing the letters of the alphabet and naming colors.

12. Several preschool intervention programs, most notably the Head Start Project, have been developed as the means by which to reverse the cycle of poverty and give children from low-socioeconomic backgrounds some experiences which can help them when they later attend formal schooling. These programs have been evaluated as successful and have shown that they serve to enhance the quality of life of the children and families involved. Individuals who as children attended these programs are more likely than those who have not to succeed in school, obtain employment, or go on for further college or vocational training.

CHILD DEVELOPMENT AND
THE LIFE CYCLE

The study of child development is a fascinating enterprise that reveals the many transformations of the human organism from embryo to adult. The goal of researchers in this field is not only to describe the characteristics of children at different ages, but also to explain how children change as they develop and to identify those factors that influence their growth and development.

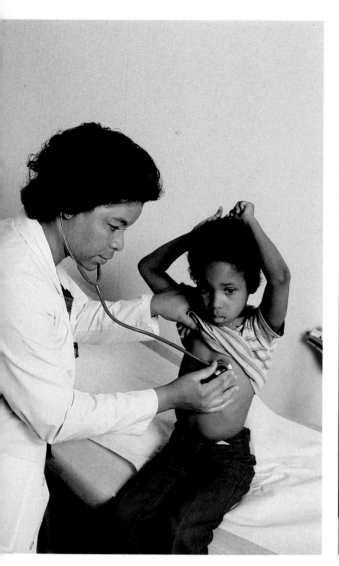

Researchers have yet to unravel all the mysteries of human development. However, they are making tremendous strides in their research, gaining insights into the processes that underlie development and uncovering new information about the competencies and vulnerabilities of children. They have learned that even newborns can see and hear and that they are prepared to interact with the people in their social surroundings.

The knowledge gained from research is important because it enhances our understanding of children and helps us create a better environment for them, ensuring that they grow up to be happy, productive adults. Numerous people who live and work with children use the knowledge gleaned from child development research. Some are, or plan to be, parents. Others are teachers, day care providers, pediatricians and nurses, or social workers who work directly with children and must understand the changing needs of children and the factors that can enhance or impede their growth and development.

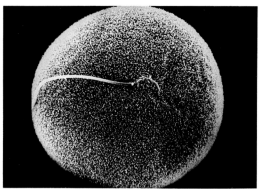

The ovum and the sperm at the moment of conception.

The fetus at 3 to 4 weeks.

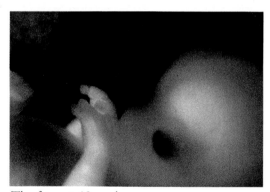

The fetus at 10 weeks.

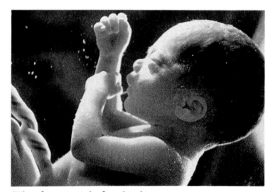

The fetus just before birth.

Mother and newborn.

Development is the product of a complex interaction between heredity and the environment. A child inherits a genetic blueprint, or potential, for development. Whether or not this potential is realized depends on factors in the environment. This is true even during prenatal life. Most people do not think of the womb as an environment. However, it is the first environmental setting of the human organism, and also a critically important one.

Development within the womb progresses along a precise and predetermined genetic path. The uterine environment is designed by nature to support the unborn baby in its development. Most of the time, development during this period of life is normal. But, the fetus is vulnerable to a host of harmful influences. Inadequate nutrition during pregnancy, diseases contracted by the mother, certain medications, drugs, alcohol, and even smoking can interfere with normal growth.

The extent to which the fetus is influenced by harmful environmental factors depends on the point in the prenatal period at which these influences occur and also on the genetic predisposition of the mother and the unborn child. Researchers cannot predict who is vulnerable, so they urge all expectant mothers to protect their babies by eating properly, abstaining from harmful substances, and avoiding other hazards that interfere with normal development.

Environmental factors can influence children after birth as well. Even a healthy child can grow up to be unhappy and developmentally vulnerable if she is not nurtured and if she is continuously neglected. On the other hand, a child who is born with developmental problems will eventually overcome them or compensate for the handicap, if given appropriate care.

Each child is a competent and unique individual. This is apparent even among very young infants who are found to possess a wide range of physical, cognitive, and social capabilities. Researchers have only recently begun to appreciate this fact, because in the past, infants and young children were thought to have very limited capabilities.

Although children have an intrinsic motivation to learn and profit from their experiences, each child develops at his or her own pace, so that individual differences among children are always apparent not only in the way they look or behave, but also in the rate at which they acquire skills.

The nature of family interactions makes an important contribution to individual differences among children. Parental behavior toward children is an important determinant in children's development. Parents who are authoritative in their interactions with their children but at the same time warm toward and supportive of them have children who are likely to be socially outgoing and intellectually competent. Such children enjoy life and are eager to learn from it.

The warmth and support of parents is also important in children's academic achievement. Researchers emphasize the central role of parents' involvement in their children's education, and they note that children whose parents spend time listening to and encouraging them are likely to feel competent and to succeed in their endeavors. This is true not only of younger children, but of adolescents as well.

Children not only influence and are influenced by people, they are also influenced by institutions, such as the school and the government, and by other environmental factors such as cultural values of their particular society, the economic conditions that prevail, as well as by policies and practices in the work place that affect family life. For example, researchers have found that child abuse and neglect are related to poverty and that they may increase in times of high unemployment. There are numerous examples of societal factors that can adversely affect children. However, there are positive influences as well. The creation and implementation of certain policies can help alleviate the stresses on family life and, therefore, enhance the conditions in which children grow.

Children and adolescents are also influenced by other people in their social world—siblings, peers, relatives, teachers, and others with whom they come into contact. In the past, researchers focused solely on the influence of people on children. They now realize, however, that children influence the people in their social world, thereby contributing to their own development and helping to shape the conditions in which they live.

Finally, although children undergo a series of striking developmental changes as they grow up to become adults, development does not stop at age 18. Individuals continue to grow and change throughout their lives, and they experience different needs and aspirations at different ages. The changes that occur in adulthood may not be as swift or as striking as the transformations that mark infancy, childhood, and adolescence. However, developmental psychologists are becoming increasingly cognizant of a lifespan view of development, noting that from early adulthood to old age, people continue to develop as individuals and contribute to the development of their own and others' children and grandchildren, often deriving many rewards from their efforts.

The fact is, human existence in any period of life is basically a social endeavor that does not occur in isolation, but rather, in the context of other people of many different ages. At all stages of development—from infancy to old age—there is the potential for change and for hope.

CHAPTER 9

SOCIAL AND EMOTIONAL DEVELOPMENT DURING THE PRESCHOOL YEARS

THE SOCIAL WORLD OF THE PRESCHOOL CHILD

The child's remarkable progress during the preschool years in physical development and in the acquisition of cognitive and language skills is paralleled by equally striking changes in social and emotional development. Whereas the two-year-old child begins the early childhood period as an individual who is primarily concerned with her own needs and desires and is still dependent on her parents' care, by the time she is five the child shows evidence of her growing independence and mastery of the environment and of her ability to recognize and accommodate the needs of others and to interact cooperatively with the people in her social world.

Through her interactions with those around her, the child develops a sense of her own identity and abilities. She discovers that the world holds endless opportunities for exploration and social interaction. As magical and as inviting as the world may appear, however, the child soon finds out that it is also fraught with frustrations, fears, jealousies, and angers that she must learn to deal with.

The child also learns that she is a member of a family and of the society and that as such she must abide by a set of rules, restrictions, and codes of social behavior appropriate to each. Although parents assume a major role in teaching the child to become a member of society, there are other influences on the child's development, as the child learns from her teachers, from television personalities, and from others she encounters in her daily life. Before we discuss the respective influences of parents and others in the child's socialization, we will take a look at the child's social world, which changes during the preschool years from one that is defined almost exclusively by the parents to one that involves extensive and influential relations with siblings and peers. It is in the context of these social relations that the child acquires socially appropriate ways of behaving and also evidences her emerging personality.

Expanding Family Relations

The changes in the child's social world occur against the background of the increased independence of the child and the developmental strides that characterize the preschool period. During the preschool years children progress from clumsy coordination to increasingly refined motor skills. They attain wider intellectual awareness and a deepening understanding of symbols; and they become increasingly able to talk and verbally communicate their feelings and desires. It is also during this period that many children, having established during infancy a warm and trusting relationship with their parents, feel secure in their explorations of the environment, meeting new people, and enjoying the company not only of their parents, but of grandparents, aunts and uncles, teachers, and playmates.

FIGURE 9.1 Enjoying her newly found independence, this little girl is not about to listen to her mother!

Emerging Characteristics of the Preschool Child

Always rushing and continuously on the move, preschool children are enthusiastically trying to find out as much as they can about the physical world. They wander off by themselves, touching and investigating every object in sight. Learning that they are quite capable of exploring the world by themselves, the children acquire a sense of their own independence. They begin to regard themselves as individuals who exist separately from their parents and who can assert their will and desires. A preschool child may become enraged at any suggestion that she stop playing to take a nap, and she seems to find pleasure in saying no many times a day. Frequently she chooses to do just the opposite of what her parents or other caretakers want her to do (see Figure 9.1).

The Preschool Child:
A Theoretical Perspective

*E*rik Erikson (1963) describes the emerging independence of the young preschooler as a function of the psychosocial crisis of *autonomy vs. shame and doubt,* which occurs at about age 2. He theorizes that if the child develops a healthy attitude toward being independent, she acquires a sense of autonomy and gradually becomes self-sufficient. If, on the other hand, the child is made to feel that her independent efforts are wrong, then shame and self-doubt develop instead of autonomy.

Children can be extremely obstinate when they are making their first bid for autonomy. They want to do things for themselves, and in their own way, often frustrating their parents and taxing their patience to the limit. Although the negativism of the young preschooler often results in difficult, rather stormy relations between the child and his parents, it is relatively short-lived, as the child eventually learns what he can and cannot do by himself, and his parents come to feel comfortable in letting him assume greater self-reliance. The tasks of the parents in this regard are by no means easy. They must recognize the child's innate motivation toward independence and foster in him a sense of pride in his independent accomplishments by letting him do as much for himself as he is capable of doing. At the same time, however, they must also monitor the child's activities and impose limits on his behavior so that he acquires an understanding of what he cannot do as well as of what he can. Erikson (1963) theorizes that once the child acquires a firm sense of what he is capable of doing and what he cannot do or is not allowed to do, he moves on to the next psychosocial crisis, *initiative vs. guilt.* During this stage, the child between the ages of 3 and 6 gains increasing confidence as he discovers ways to pursue activities on his own initiative. If such initiatives are successful, the child enjoys the accomplishments and acquires a sense of direction and purpose. However, parents are at times too demanding of a child this age, expecting her to be able to perform tasks well, and they sometimes belittle her when she tries to do something.

When parents are extremely demanding of the child or when they are too rigid, preventing the child from trying to learn to accomplish tasks on his own, the child is overwhelmed by feelings of guilt which may inhibit any further attempts on his part in pursuing activities on his own initiative.

Erikson's description of the preschool child is admittedly theoretical, but it provides a useful framework for understanding the emergence and development of personality and the potential influence of parents and others on the child's emerging personality.

Interactions with the Mother

Although the preschool child becomes increasingly independent, his relationship with his parents remains the primary focus of his interactions, and his attachment to his mother continues to be strong. The child enjoys spending time with his mother, talking to her, sharing his toys with her, and he draws emotional support from her presence. When playing, he frequently checks to see where she is, and he is more likely to play quietly for long periods of time as long as he can see or hear his mother, or when he knows where she is (Rheingold, 1973; Clarke-Stewart & Hevey, 1981). In one study researchers found that when three-year-olds are asked to stay in an unfamiliar place, they are more likely to feel relaxed and to play if they can hear their mother's voice or see her on a television screen than when either of these two conditions are not present (Adams & Passman, 1979).

The preschooler is also dependent on his mother's affection, often asking, especially after being scolded, "Do you love me, Mommy?" (Sears, Maccoby, & Levin, 1957). When he is under stress, or in a strange situation, such as the doctor's office or a new nursery school or day care center, he may have trouble separating from his mother. It is not unusual for a child who is eager to attend day care or nursery school to cry and refuse to let his mother go during the first few days. The older the child becomes, however, the more able he is to tolerate relatively long periods of separation from his mother (Rheingold & Eckerman, 1971; see Figure 9.2). Thus he is able to meet other people and form close relationships with them.

Interactions with the Father

The mother encourages independent behavior in the preschooler and becomes less tolerant of his demands for attention, often telling him that he is old enough to stay away from her for a while (Maccoby, 1980). Although mothers relax their involvement with their preschool child somewhat, in those households where the father is present, fathers come to play a more prominent role in the child's life at this age.

Most fathers enjoy their children from the moment of birth, and they interact with them throughout infancy (Lamb, 1977). However, during the preschool period fathers become increasingly involved in childrearing, and they are inclined to spend more time both playing with and disciplining the child. In addition, during the preschool years, children, especially boys, seem to prefer the father as a playmate, and they seek to play with him more often than with their mother (Lamb, 1981). The more time the father and child spend together, the stronger their relationship becomes, and the more the child recognizes that he has two parents to take care of his needs instead of just one. The child also learns quickly to differentiate

FIGURE 9.2   During the preschool years, the child is able to tolerate increasingly longer periods of separation from his mother. Also, the older he becomes, the more he is able to tolerate being a greater distance from her.

between his parents' characteristics and to direct some kinds of requests and concerns toward one and some toward the other. For example, if he wants cookies before dinner, he is more likely to ask that parent, mother or father, who is less concerned with his appetite at mealtime than the other.

FIGURE 9.3 Because their parents are divorced, many children see their fathers only a few hours a week or a month. Usually the time they spend with each other is away from a home setting.

Children of Divorce. Unfortunately, not all children have the opportunity to develop a close relationship with their father. One-fifth of children under five in the United States are in single-parent families, 90% of which are headed by women, in most cases as the result of divorce (Report of the Select Committee on Children, Youth and Families, 1983). Admittedly, there are instances where both parents are awarded custody of the children. Nevertheless, data show that custody determinations still award most children to their mothers and that about 9 out of 10 children live with their mothers following divorce (Spanier & Glick, 1981). Thus many children get to see their fathers for only a few hours every week or every two weeks and usually under strained circumstances. The limited experiences they have with their fathers are quite different from the interactions other children have with their fathers in the context of daily family life (see Figure 9.3).

The absence of a father in the household usually means less social, emotional, and financial support and less help for the mother in decision-making, childrearing, and household tasks (Hetherington & Camara,

Children's Fears

The emotional vulnerability of the preschool child and the fact that he is still dependent on his mother is also evident in his fears. Recall that infants are afraid of strange people and situations and that they sometimes cry when their mother leaves their sight. Preschoolers are better able than infants to tolerate long separations from their mother. However, they begin to be afraid of animals and imaginary creatures and of being left alone in the dark (Jersild & Holmes, 1935; Bauer, 1976). Thinking that they may be abandoned and harmed, many preschoolers are terrified of the dark and convinced that once the lights go out, a monster will gobble them up. They may refuse to go to sleep unless their mother stays with them to reassure them.

In an attempt to explain the fears of preschoolers, researchers note that separation anxiety is at the root of the fear of the dark, but that the rich fantasy life of the child and his limited cognitive capacity also play a role. A preschool child has trouble separating reality from fantasy, and he fails to understand that monsters, ghosts, or other creatures associated with the dark are actually figments of his imagination. That cognitive factors are important in determining the nature and intensity of children's fears is evident in the fact that as children mature, the number of both real and imagined stimuli capable of producing fear in them increases enormously.

At first the child tends to be fearful of physical events. Remembering a painful experience at the doctor's office, he will become fearful when he sees another person wearing a white lab coat. Later in the preschool period, the child will fear lions and other large animals, although he may not necessarily associate these with pain. As he grows older and is capable of thinking in the abstract, the child may fear such events as failure in school.

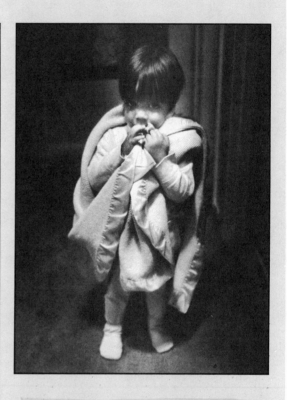

Researchers are also finding that the children's fears not only change with age, they are also brought on, in part, by social events. Many older children growing up today, for example, are afraid of nuclear war, a topic which was hardly known several years ago. Some preschool children growing up today are afraid of losing their parents. This is especially true of preschool children who have experience with the divorce of their parents, although it is not limited to them. Nadine Brozan (1983) cites the example of a four-year-old who insisted that his father, not mother, walk him to day care every day. After considerable questioning, the child explained that many of his friends at day care had no father living at home and he was afraid that this would happen to him.

1984). For children, the absence of a father may mean the loss of an effective disciplinarian and role model and also the loss of emotional support. Not only do children whose parents are divorced often have little opportunity to interact with their father, there are many cases where the father does not show any concern for or desire to be with the child. Mavis Hetherington and her colleagues (Hetherington, Cox, & Cox, 1976, 1978) found that during the first year after the divorce, fathers become emotionally detached from their children and that fewer than half the fathers see their children as frequently as once a week even though they live nearby. Similar findings are reported by Furstenberg et al. (1983), who notes that although immediately following the divorce noncustodial fathers may actually spend more time with their children than they did before the divorce, this close contact rapidly diminishes, and by the second year after the divorce many fathers rarely see their children.

The emotional detachment of the father from the child is also evident in problems that occur in the payment of child support. *Child support* is the monetary payment made by the parent who does not have custody of the child to the parent with custody (Espenshade, 1979). All states have some legal provisions binding the noncustodial parent to share in the expense of raising the child, the exact amount of money decided by the judge who presides over the divorce (Weitzman, 1981a). However, the amount of support awarded is often inadequate to meet the child's needs (Weitzman, 1981b). Close to two-thirds of noncustodial fathers refuse to make any payment at all (The Select Committee on Children, Youth and Families, 1983). The number of fathers who default on their obligation for child support has become so great that states have instituted a variety of measures to counteract the problem (Espenshade, 1979; Weitzman, 1981b) but have met with only modest success. Although failure to make child support payments often makes life very difficult for the mother and the children, its direct emotional effects on the child must also be considered. The preschooler may not be aware of the financial obligations of his father, but as he grows older he will realize that his father refuses to share in the cost of his care.

Besides the fact that children of divorce often do not have the opportunity to interact with and develop a close relationship with their father, the arguing and conflict between the parents that often precedes the divorce create a negative emotional climate that can undermine the child's psychological development (Kalter, 1977). Hetherington and her colleagues found that preschool children experience a great deal of stress at the divorce of their parents. They have difficulty understanding divorce, and they think that once the father leaves the house, he is no longer part of the family. The egocentrism of the preschool child also causes her to take the blame for the divorce and to feel rejected, abandoned, and unloved (Wallerstein & Kelly, 1980).

child support

The negative impact of divorce on the child is not inevitable, as the effects of divorce on the child and the extent that he is able to cope with and adjust to his new situation are often affected by the quality of the parents' post-divorce relationship. Several researchers have found that when ex-spouse relationships were harmonious, as revealed by high agreement on childrearing, positive attitudes toward the ex-mate, and low conflict following divorce, the child's functioning was less likely to be undermined (Hetherington, 1980; Wallerstein & Kelly, 1980; Raschke & Raschke, 1979). The resources available for supporting children in coping with divorce are also important. When children of divorce have a good relationship with a grandparent, uncle, or older brother, they are more likely to cope with the stress associated with the divorce of their parents and to evidence better social and personal functioning than the children who do not have such relationships (Hetherington, Cox, & Cox, 1981; Santrock, Warshak, Lindbergh, & Meadows, 1982; Zill, 1983).

Relations with Siblings

Beyond the changes that occur during the preschool years in the child's relations with his parents, in families where there are two or more children, the preschool child also has to learn to interact with and get along with younger or older brothers and sisters.

sibling rivalry

Researchers have tended to focus on the negative aspect of sibling relations, noting that *sibling rivalry,* the conflict between brothers and sisters, is common in families with children. A preschool child, if she has been the youngest child or an only child with exclusive claim on her parents' attention, views the arrival of a baby with negativity. She often expresses jealousy of the newborn in several direct ways. She may find it hard to resist to occasionally pinch, push, or otherwise harm the unwanted addition to the family. Making such remarks as "When are we going to bring the baby back to the hospital?", the preschooler also reveals the desire to see the baby gone. She may regress in some learned skills, symbolizing her longing to be a baby again and enjoy the attention her new sibling is receiving. She may lose bowel control even though toilet training has been well established, or she may ask to sleep in a crib or to be picked up and held in her mother's arms. This regressive behavior in reaction to the birth of a sibling is usually short-lived, especially if parents are sensitive to the child's feelings and bestow their attention and affection on her as well as on the newborn.

The relationship the preschool child has with older brothers and sisters also entails rivalry, as the child comes to resent the prerogatives of older children and to compete with them for parental affection and approval. However, researchers are increasingly cognizant of the fact that although there are frequent confrontations and acts of aggression between siblings,

FIGURE 9.4 In the preschool period, the child's interest in and involvement with other children is continually expanding.

brothers and sisters also show positive behaviors in their interactions with one another (Lamb & Sutton-Smith, 1982). In a recent study of the interaction of preschoolers with their older brothers and sisters, Abramovitch, Pepler, and Corter (1982) found that siblings treat each other in aggressive ways, but that they also cooperate with, help, and act affectionately toward one another (see Figure 9.4). Dunn and Kendrick (1979), having observed children in a home setting following the birth of a sibling, also found evidence of prosocial behaviors in sibling interactions, noting that often the older siblings offer toys or otherwise initiate social contact with younger siblings. In observations of children in a playroom, Lamb (1978) found evidence of prosocial behaviors among siblings and also that the younger siblings imitate the behaviors of their older brothers and sisters. Sutton-Smith and Rosenberg (1970) further note that some siblings also influence one another with regard to interests and skills. Thus, although sibling rivalry may be evident, especially during the preschool years, children also enjoy the company of their brothers and sisters, often exerting a positive influence on one another.

Peer Relations

Friends and Friendships. During the preschool years, the child also begins to spend more time with other children, playing with them and enjoying their company. Peer interactions do not necessarily begin in the early childhood period, as even infants are often given the opportunity to play with others their own age (Lewis, Young, Brooks, & Michalson, 1975). During the preschool years, however, the child's interest in and involvement with other children are continually expanding and changing. The child actively seeks out his peers, he has a preference for playing with children who are the same age and sex as he is and who have the same energy level (Jacklin & Maccoby, 1978). With age he becomes increasingly sociable in his interactions with children (Lougee, Grueneich, & Hartup, 1977), making friends with some of them.

Having a friend and being someone's friend are very important to preschool children. They frequently initiate social contact with one another by asking "Can I be your friend?" and they attempt to persuade one another to share toys by saying "I'll be your friend." However, they do not, until the school-age years, have a clear conception of friendship as an enduring relationship. Whereas the older child views friendship as a relationship that takes shape over a period of time and regards friends as providers of intimacy and support, the preschool child characteristically views his friends simply as momentary playmates (Rubin, 1980). That is, whomever he may be playing with at a particular time is considered a friend. Unlike the older child, the preschool child focuses on the physical attributes of his playmates rather than on their psychological attributes such as interests or personality traits. When asked what sort of person makes a good friend, preschoolers are likely to provide such answers as "Someone who plays a lot" or "Someone who lives in Watertown" (Selman & Jaquette, 1977).

The Value of Peer Relations. Although they are unable to conceive of friendship as an enduring relationship, children's interactions with one another do, in many cases, endure over a long period of time and they are of vital importance. Researchers have shown that the opportunity to interact with children of the same age is not only desirable but necessary for normal social development. Children who do not play with agemates miss out on important social learning experiences and are at considerable risk of becoming socially inept and uncertain of themselves in interpersonal situations later in life. These findings are derived from studies of children who have trouble establishing social relationships with other children and who are unable to initiate and maintain interactions with other children they encounter (Hartup, 1983). It is not known whether these children became socially incompetent because they lacked contact with other children or if they became socially isolated because of prior social incompetence. We do know from the research with animals that when the young of other species are raised without peers, they become socially inept, they are unable to mate successfully, and they may even subject themselves to serious danger by being aggressive toward or not knowing when to submit to dominant animals (Suomi & Harlow, 1975).

This is not to say that peer interaction should occur to the exclusion of adult interactions. Experimental and naturalistic studies have shown that when young animals (Harlow, 1961) and children (Freud with Dunn, 1951) grow up only in the company of their peers, they become extremely attached to one another, but they show disturbances in their development and are unable to effectively interact with others outside their group. When there is a balance between adult and peer interaction, however, peers can serve important functions in the child's life. One such function is providing emotional support. Four-year-old children in an unfamiliar situation, for example, are more likely to roam about and explore their surroundings when there are other children present than when they are alone (Schwartz, 1972).

Relationships with peers also provide preschool children with a way to compare themselves to others their own age. Researchers who observed preschool children at play note that in encounters between children, such utterances as "My picture is better than yours" and "Let's see who can run faster—me or you" are frequently heard (Rubin, 1980). At first, such utterances may suggest that the world of childhood is an extremely competitive one. Corsaro (1980), however, proposed that such encounters reflect not so much rivalry as the child's emerging sense of self and his need to define himself through comparisons with others.

Making a related point, Rubin (1980) gives an example of the opportunity for comparisons that peer relations provide:

Steven   You are bigger than me—right, Claudia?
          Claudia and Steven then stand back to back, measuring themselves.
          Claudia is in fact taller than Steven.
Claudia   We're growing up.
Steven   Yea. I'm almost as big as you, right? I'm gonna grow this big,
          right? [*He stretches his arms far apart.*]
Claudia   Me too.

Children are also valuable social resources for one another, and they learn a number of social skills through their interactions, including how to approach another child and initiate an interaction and how to maintain the interaction (Hartup, 1983; Asher & Hymel, 1981). Whereas children learn from their parents how to get along in one sort of social hierarchy, that of the family, it is from their interactions with peers that they learn how to survive among equals in a wide range of social situations. In fact, one unique role of peer group interactions is to provide children with egalitarian social relationships, something that is impossible in children's relations with adults, who are, obviously, bigger and more powerful (Hartup, 1978; Mueller & Vandell, 1979).

Play

Peers not only serve to expand the child's social horizons, making new behaviors possible, they also serve another important function: they are partners in play. Play was defined by one child as, "funstuff that kids do 'cause they like to do it" (quoted in Rubin, 1980). Many researchers agree with Garvey's (1977) definition of play as any pleasurable, spontaneous, and voluntary activity that is an end to itself and has no extrinsic goal.

Researchers have long been interested in children's play. In one of the earliest studies on the topic, Mildred Parten (1932) found that the play of children varies in the amount of social involvement, with children sometimes enjoying the role of observer (she called this onlooker play) and at other times playing alone or in groups. She observed 2- to 5-year-olds in nursery schools, and on the basis of her observation she has identified four different kinds of play behaviors the children engaged in.

Solitary Play.   In solitary play, the child is happily engrossed in playing alone with a toy or with another object, and he makes no attempt to initiate a conversation or otherwise interact with any of the other children in the room. Although children of all ages engage in solitary play some of the time, this type of play is characteristic of children aged 2 to 3 years.

Parallel Play.   Children 2 to 3 years of age also engage in parallel play. In this type of play, considered the first step toward playing with groups, the young preschool child still plays by herself, but she chooses to play close to another child and with a similar toy. However, the activities of the two children are unrelated; they are playing parallel to but not with each other.

Associative Play.   Slightly older children, aged 3 to 4, engage in associative play. In this type of play, the children may borrow and lend toys, talk about the same activity, or follow one another, but there is no attempt among any of the children to organize the group. Thus, although several children may be engaged in the same activity—playing with cars or with dolls, for example—each plays as he wishes, with none of the children attempting to change what the other children are doing.

Cooperative Play.   By the time they are 4 to 5 years of age, children spend most of their playtime in cooperative play. In this type of play, several children play in an activity that engages all those in the group and in which all the children have a shared goal.

FIGURE 9.5   Like most preschoolers, these two children enjoy playing with each other.

Influences on Play

More recent findings (Rubin, Watson, & Jambor, 1978) support Parten's observation that as they grow older, children become more sociable in their play, with the older preschooler engaging in more associative and cooperative play and in less solitary play. Although the age of the child is an important determinant of how children play, other factors influence the amount of time children spend playing alone or with other children. Experience is one such factor. When they are first introduced to a playgroup, even some older preschoolers may be shy and may avoid interacting with the other children. Although for a time they may engage in solitary or parallel play, usually after a few play sessions they overcome their shyness and become increasingly playful, deriving pleasure from their interactions with playmates (Mueller & Brenner, 1977; see Figure 9.5).

The *opportunity* for play is also important. Most children, when given the opportunity, automatically play, alone or with other children (Sutton-Smith, 1974), as play is, in effect, the "work" of childhood. However, in societies that require preschoolers to help with chores, children simply do not have the time to play (Whiting & Whiting, 1975) so they spend very little time playing (see Table 9.1). Children who are not given the *space* to

TABLE 9.1 The percentage of time children spend playing varies from culture to culture. In some societies, young children spend more time helping with chores than they do playing.

Activity	Nyansongo Kenya	Juxtlahuaca Mexico	Tarong Philippines	Taira Okinawa	Khalapur India	Orchard Town United States
Play	17	49	48	76	31	52
Casual social interaction	43	37	31	11	46	30
Work	41	8	14	9	11	2
Learning	0	6	7	4	9	16

Source: Whiting, B. B., & Whiting, J. W. M., (1975). *Children of Six Cultures: A Psycho-Cultural Analysis.* Cambridge, MA: Harvard Univ. Press; p. 48, table 11. Copyright © 1975 by the President and Fellows of Harvard College.

play in and *materials* to play with also do not play as much as children who do have the space and toys (Frost & Sunderlin, 1985). Toys need not be expensive, because children are very adept at finding any household items, such as a broom or a cooking pot, and using them as playthings. It is important, however, to have enough toys or other objects for the children to play with, as these are the focal point of the interactions between preschoolers. They are not only required for some social behaviors such as give and take, they also serve to attract a playmate (Mueller & Vandell, 1979), and they determine whether children will engage in positive or negative interactions with each other. In situations where there is only one or a very few toys, there are likely to be frequent confrontations among the children.

Dramatic Play

Play consists of any number of activities from which children derive pleasure: the manipulation of toys and other objects; physical games in which children run, jump, chase, or tickle one another; and language play in which children engage in verbal banter, enjoying the different rhythms and sounds of words. Children also engage in make believe play. Make believe, or pretend play begins at around age two when the child is capable of mental representation. Initially, the child plays by herself, pretending, for example, to feed a doll or brush her hair with an imaginary hairbrush. After age three, the child engages in make believe play in cooperation with another child, although on occasion a child who has no one to play with may play a sequence with an imaginary friend.

Sometimes called symbolic or dramatic play, make believe play becomes gradually more elaborate and complex (see Table 9.2). By the time children are 4 to 5 years old, they engage in *sociodramatic play*, which is

sociodramatic play

TABLE 9.2   Sequence of symbolic levels of play. With age, make believe play becomes more dramatic and complex.

		Examples
Sensorimotor Period Before Stage VI	1. Presymbolic scheme: The child shows understanding of object or meaning by brief gestures of recognition.	The child picks up a comb, touches it to his hair, drops it.
Stage VI	2. Autosymbolic scheme: The child pretends at self-related activities.	The child eats from an empty spoon.
Symbolic Stage 1	3. Single-scheme symbolic games: The child extends symbolism beyond his own actions:	
Type IA assimilative	A. Including other actors or receivers of action, like a doll or mother.	The child feeds mother or doll (A).
Type IB imitative	B. Pretending at activities of other people or objects like dogs, trucks, trains, and so on.	The child pretends to mop floor (B).
	4. Combinatorial symbolic games.	The child kisses doll, puts it to bed, puts spoon to its mouth. The child drinks from the bottle, feeds doll from bottle.
	5. Planned symbolic games: The child indicates verbally or nonverbally that pretend acts are planned before being executed:	The child picks up the play screwdriver, says "toothbrush," and makes the motions of brushing teeth.
Type IIA	A. Symbolic identification of one object with another.	The child picks up the bottle, says "baby," then feeds the doll and covers it with a cloth.
Type IIB	B. Symbolic identification of the child's body with some other person or object.	
Type IIIA	Combinations with planned elements, tending toward realistic scenes.	The child puts play foods in a pot, stirs them, then says "soup" before feeding the mother. She waits, then says "more?", offering the spoon to the mother.

Source: Fein, G. (1978). "Play Revisited." In M. E. Lamb (Ed.), *Social and Personality Development.* New York: Holt, Rinehart and Winston; p. 75, table 2. Copyright © by Holt, Rinehart and Winston.

make believe play about social situations. This type of play usually occurs in the context of a story or a specific plan of action that focuses on a role identity. Popular role identities among preschoolers are mother, father, baby, doctor, patient, fireman, and policeman. The sequence of make believe play begins with one of the children announcing, "Let's play house," and proceeding to assign different roles to those children who agree to play. "I'll be the mother. Lance, you be the father." It may also begin when a child has a plan and proposes, "Let's take a trip to the

FIGURE 9.6   These children are engaged in make believe play which gives them the opportunity to rehearse adult roles.

moon," in which case the children quickly improvise a spaceship and assign roles (see Figure 9.6).

Sociodramatic play is important for the child's development. It provides children with the opportunity to rehearse adult roles and acquire an understanding of these (Asher, 1978), and it helps them understand some of the events that they experience in real life. By repeatedly reenacting some of these events (for example, the birth of a baby in the family), the children are eventually able to assimilate and come to terms with them. Such play also provides children with the opportunity to try out activities which are usually forbidden by adults (Bruner, 1972). It also enhances their cognitive skills; those children who engage in dramatic play during the preschool years evidence creativity and imagination later in life (Vandenberg, 1980; Sutton Smith, 1974).

PERSONALITY AND EMOTIONAL DEVELOPMENT

Relating to Others

As children play together, it becomes apparent that there are striking differences between them in personality characteristics. Some are boisterous and outgoing, others are more passive. Some are cooperative, independent, and adventuresome; others are aggressive and disruptive. The child's personality, defined as his unique pattern of behavior, how he perceives things and reacts to them in his own way, is dependent upon a complex interplay between heredity and environment, as the child is born with certain personality characteristics. But, as you will see later in the chapter, parents and others help shape the child's personality through their attitudes toward and reactions to him.

Aggression

One personality characteristic that becomes evident during the preschool years is aggression. Preschool children often display hostility and aggression toward one another, just as adults do. Most children employ aggressive behaviors in an instrumental fashion, with the expectation of overcoming resistance. However, for some children, aggression becomes a dominant theme in all of their social interactions.

Theories of Aggression

Psychologists have long been interested in the study of the origin of aggression and have proposed various theories to explain it. They note that aggressive behavior is common to most species and thus has a biological component, but that aggression is also a method of problem solving and therefore subject to the influence of experience and learning.

Theories of aggression differ in the degree to which they emphasize biological or psychological determinants, and also in those biological or psychological determinants that they emphasize as important in the development of aggression and its expression in the social setting (Feshbach & Feshbach, 1976). For example, psychoanalytic theorists such as Freud (1930) believed that aggression is a biological instinct that is influenced by environmental factors. That is, the child is born with an aggressive drive, but the manner in which she expresses her aggression is learned. Ethologist Konrad Lorenz (1966) regarded aggression as an innate response to a particular stimulus. Learning theorists such as Bandura (1962, 1967) emphasize that early "training" in aggression is necessary, as aggression is a behavior that is learned through reinforcement and imitation. When the child sees his parents or others use physical force in their interactions with their children, with other people, or with each other, he too will use aggression as the primary means by which to resolve interpersonal problems.

Gerald Patterson (1982), on the basis of his clinical experience with aggressive children and their families, proposes a performance theory of childhood aggression, noting that aggressive and other maladaptive behaviors are learned, shaped, and maintained by forces that operate in the social setting. That is, aggression originates in the behavior modelled by the parents, among others, and is maintained by parental responses to the child (for example, parents' mode of punishment).

However, Linda Dowdney (1985) criticizes Patterson for failing to recognize the child's contributions to social interactions, noting that some children are more malleable in their behavior than others and thus less likely to provoke physical punishment and other aggressive responses on the part of the parents. Indeed, many researchers today stress the fact that both biological and environmental factors play a role in shaping the development of aggression and that several variables in the child, in the family, in the community, and in the culture contribute to aggressive behavior (Parke & Slaby, 1983; see Figure 9.7). Some children who are exposed to a great deal of violence at home or who are given little affection and attention (Feshbach, 1980; Feshbach and Feshbach, 1976) often use hostility in their interactions with people. This pattern of behavior is likely to endure later in life (Huesmann, Eron, Lefkowitz, & Walder, 1984).

Some researchers focus less on the long-range causes of aggression and more on its immediate precursors, saying that aggression is a reaction to frustration (Dollard et al., 1939; Berkowitz, 1962). As Parke and Slaby (1983) point out, although not all frustrating experiences produce aggressive acts, preschoolers have many occasions to feel frustrated. Several times a day, they may ask for something and are told they cannot have it; or they try to do something and fail, suffering both frustration and affronts to their dignity. It is not surprising, therefore, that displays of aggressive behavior are frequent among preschoolers, especially early in the preschool period. However, young children are rarely deliberately aggressive. They may strike someone who interferes with what they are doing, but only in order to get an object or to remove an obstacle. As they grow older, they resort to deliberate physical aggression. In one study of children between the ages of 4 and 7, Hartup (1974) found that *instrumental aggression* (which involves fighting over objects, for example) declines markedly with age but that *hostile aggression,* aggression that is an attack against someone rather than some thing, does not decline as rapidly. The researcher also found that the frequency of deliberate physical aggression reaches its peak late in the preschool years. But, as the children are reprimanded and told how they are expected to behave, they learn not only to control their anger, but also to use other means of attack, notably words and insults.

instrumental aggression

hostile aggression

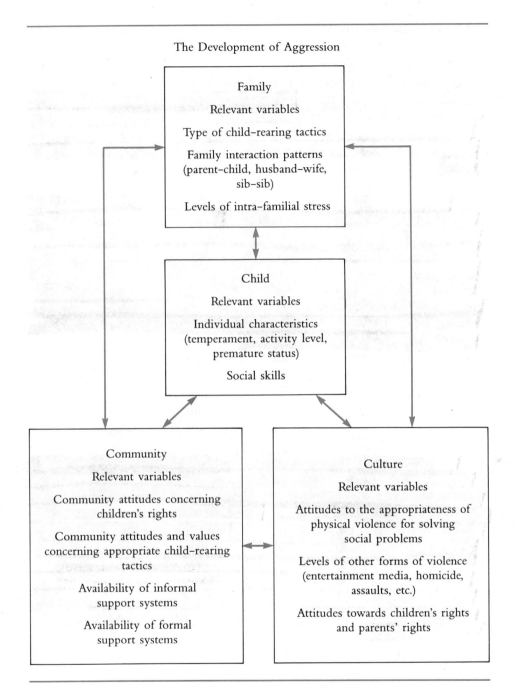

The Development of Aggression

Family

Relevant variables

Type of child–rearing tactics

Family interaction patterns
(parent–child, husband–wife,
sib–sib)

Levels of intra–familial stress

Child

Relevant variables

Individual characteristics
(temperament, activity level,
premature status)

Social skills

Community

Relevant variables

Community attitudes concerning
children's rights

Community attitudes and values
concerning appropriate child–rearing
tactics

Availability of informal
support systems

Availability of formal
support systems

Culture

Relevant variables

Attitudes to the appropriateness of
physical violence for solving
social problems

Levels of other forms of violence
(entertainment media, homicide,
assaults, etc.)

Attitudes towards children's rights
and parents' rights

FIGURE 9.7   An ecological view of aggression considers several variables in the child, in the family, in the community, and in the culture, all of which contribute to aggressive behavior. From Parke, R. D., and Slaby, R. G., "The Development of Aggression" from Mussen, P. H., editor *Handbook of Child Psychology,* Vol. 4, p. 559. Copyright © 1983, reprinted by permission of John Wiley & Sons, Inc.

Altruism and Empathy

altruistic
behavior

Although young children are sometimes aggressive toward one another, they also evidence positive behaviors in their interactions and are even capable of altruistic behavior. Altruism is an aspect of moral behavior that involves a concern for the welfare of others, with *altruistic behavior* defined as a voluntary and intentional action that benefits another and is not motivated by any desire to obtain external rewards (Eisenberg, 1982; Staub, 1975). A three-year-old who sees another child cry and goes over to offer him a toy to play with is evidencing altruistic behavior.

empathy

Such acts of kindness toward others require *empathy*, the ability to vicariously feel another person's emotions. According to Piaget, the egocentrism of young children prevents them from being able to see the perspective of others and therefore empathize with those around them. More recent research has shown, however, that although the ability to empathize increases with age, even two- to three-year-old children are capable of differentiating between such emotions as happy, sad, and mad (Harter, 1979). Also, they are aware of and are able to respond to other people's feelings (see Figure 9.8). As Borke (1971) maintains, "Observations of young children interacting suggest that preschool children are not only aware that other people have feelings but [that they] also actively try to understand the feeling they observe. A two-and-a-half-year-old who holds a toy to a crying child certainly appears to be demonstrating an awareness that the other youngster is experiencing unhappy feelings."

The origins of empathy are unclear. Psychoanalysts suggest that empathy develops in the context of the mother-infant relationship as the parent conveys her moods to the child by her tone of voice, facial expressions, and touch (Ekstein, 1978). Social learning theorists, on the other hand, contend that empathy is acquired through conditioning. The unpleasant feelings that accompanied one's painful past experiences are evoked by cries of distress from another person (Hoffman, 1976, 1978). For example, a child who cuts her finger feels pain and cries. At another time, when she sees another child cut himself, the sight of blood and the other child's cries evoke in her the feeling of distress she had experienced at an earlier time.

Although they disagree on the origins of empathy, researchers note that the way children respond to others' distress changes with age. These findings emerged from the research of Carolyn Zahn-Waxler and Marion Radke-Yarrow (1979), who observed children in laboratory and naturalistic settings to see how they reacted when their mother hurt her elbow and showed her distress. They found that the reaction by infants was emotional arousal, such as crying or agitation. Gradually this behavior lessened, and by age two, some of the children approached the mother, attempting to help or console her. They brought objects to the mother; they

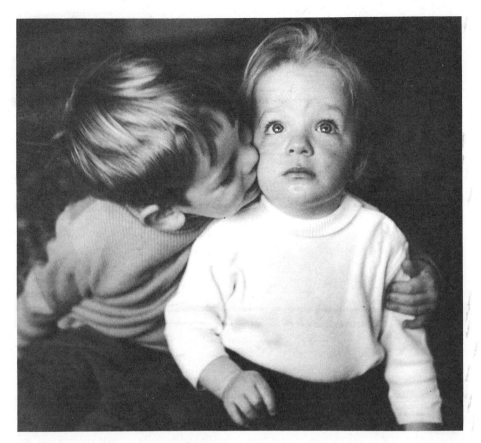

FIGURE 9.8   Even children as young as 2½ years of age are aware that others may be experiencing unhappy feelings.

made suggestions about what she could do; and they verbalized their sympathy. Not only did these young children attempt to help their mother while she was in distress, they also tried various ways of consoling the mother when one or more of their attempts failed. This suggests that they perceived the mother's distress as a problem to be solved. These and other (Dunn & Kendrick, 1979) observations of prosocial behaviors indicate that infants and young children are not only help-seeking creatures, they also "freely offer their own attention, affection, sympathy, help, and possessions to others" (Rheingold & Hay, 1976), and they can recognize when other people feel happy or sad.

The Emergence of the Self-Concept

With age, children learn not only about other people's feelings, they also learn about themselves, and they acquire a self-concept, which is a subjective understanding and evaluation of one's personality, qualities, and capabilities. The self-concept is a personal picture, made up of a whole range of impressions by which the individual distinguishes himself from others. These impressions depend on both the individual's own interpretation of his experiences in the social and physical environment and on the feedback he gets from other people (Harter, 1983).

The development of the self-concept is a gradual process that continues throughout the lifespan and changes with age. For example, preschoolers think of themselves in relatively specific and concrete terms, often defining themselves by name ("I am Sharon.") or in terms of frequent activities or behaviors ("I run fast," or "I watch television"). As they grow older and are more aware of their own thoughts and feelings, children think of themselves in terms of psychological traits, and they define themselves as "nice" or "friendly."

The self-concept includes not only the ability to define oneself, but also self-recognition, an awareness of oneself as a separate entity, as well as other components such as attitudes, motives, and values that together identify the individual as unique (Harter, 1983). Although many of these components of the self-concept do not emerge until the middle childhood years, even children as young as two years of age begin to acquire a sense of their identity and the realization that they are distinct from other people. Evidence of young children's emerging sense of self is found in their new ability to recognize themselves in the mirror or point to a picture of themselves and say "me" (Lewis & Brooks-Gunn, 1979) and in their excessive use of such linguistic terms as "me" and "mine" that refer specifically to themselves. In their strong desire to function autonomously and do things for themselves, they indicate that they have an awareness of themselves as separate individuals who can assert their own desires and wills (see Figure 9.9).

Gender Identity

Preschool children also evidence the development of a particularly important aspect of the self-concept, namely, *gender identity,* as they grow in their ability to label themselves according to sex.

gender identity

Gender identity refers to the child's awareness and acceptance of being either a boy or a girl. The awareness begins relatively early in life and is preceded by the child's ability to differentiate between the categories of male and female. Most children are able to differentiate between males and females by the time they are 2 years old, and by about age 2½, they also acquire the ability to identify their own gender and correctly answer the question, "Are you a boy or a girl?" (Huston, 1983; Thompson, 1975).

In an example of the research that has been done in this domain, Thompson (1975) showed children aged two, two-and-a-half, and three pictures that appeared on a screen. The pictures were of men, women, boys, and girls. The children were asked to indicate which of the pictures

FIGURE 9.9   Evidence of a young child's emerging sense of self is revealed in his new ability to recognize himself in a mirror.

were of "a man," "a lady," "a girl," or "a boy." They indicated their knowledge of gender by touching or pointing at the appropriate pictures. The children were also asked their own sex and to pick out the picture that was of the same gender as they. Thompson found that although children at age 2 could pick out the picture that was of the same gender as they, they could not always identify the picture as being of a boy or a girl. At age three, however, the children could correctly identify which pictures were of a boy or a girl.

Other researchers also note that it is not until the age of three that children can identify their own gender as well as that of others. Kohlberg (1966) describes a little boy named Tommy, aged 2½, who would go around the room saying, in reference to himself and his family, "I'm a boy, Daddy is a boy, Mommy is a boy, Joey is a boy." After being corrected, Tommy eliminated mother from his list, but he still had trouble labeling people outside the family correctly. Kohlberg points out further that although by age 2½ or 3 the child knows his own gender, he does not yet accept the *stability and constancy of gender*. That is, he doesn't realize that one's gender is an anatomical reality that cannot be altered. He thinks that by putting on a wig and wearing a dress he can become a girl (meaning that he has not yet accepted the constancy of gender). He also does not realize that he cannot grow up to be Mommy and that his sister cannot grow up to be Daddy (Kohlberg, 1966). That is, he has not acquired the notion of the stability of gender. It is not until the age of 5 to 7 that the child is able to completely and accurately identify the gender of other people as well as of himself and realize that it cannot be changed.

stability and constancy of gender

Gender Role

During the preschool years, children also acquire *gender (or sex) roles*. That is, they adopt socially defined behaviors and attitudes associated with being a male or a female. Gender role is also an important aspect of development, as it organizes one's behaviors and attitudes toward the self and others and influences the kinds of activities and occupations one will engage in as a child and later as an adult (Eccles & Hoffman, 1984).

It is important at the outset to distinguish between gender identity and gender role so as not to confuse the two concepts. The development of gender identity entails the ability to identify and accept one's gender and know that it will remain stable and constant throughout life. The development of gender role, on the other hand, involves the ability and willingness to engage in *sex-typed behaviors*. It is not merely the understanding of concepts related to gender, but the realization and acknowledgment that there are differences in the behaviors, abilities, and attitudes of males and females (Eisenberg, 1982).

sex-typed behaviors

sex-typed thinking

The development of gender identity does not invariably produce *sex-typed thinking* and behaviors among preschoolers (Marcus & Overton, 1978). A child may feel aware of and be satisfied with being a girl or a boy, but may not engage in sex stereotyped behaviors. Gender identity may lead, however, to knowledge of sex stereotypes. Although, as might be expected, children's knowledge of sex-stereotyped behaviors, values, and attitudes increases with age (Masters & Wilkinson, 1976; Thompson, 1975), children learn gender roles early in life. Children as young as 2 years of age have been shown to adopt sex-stereotyped behaviors (Smith & Daglish, 1977), and it has been found that preschoolers are very rigid in their adoption of such behaviors. They have been observed to prefer to play with objects that have been explicitly labeled as appropriate for their sex (Liebert, McCall, & Hanratty, 1971), or they prefer to engage only in activities that are deemed appropriate for their sex. This is true not only in our society, but in other cultures as well (Edward & Whiting, 1980). Boys tend to choose rough-and-tumble activities, and they play with trucks and airplanes more so than do girls, who often choose quieter activities—playing house or drawing and painting (see Figure 9.10).

Damon (1977) also found that children from age 4 to 7 are increasingly likely to believe that certain activities or tasks are restricted to one sex or the other, evidencing that they adopt not only sex-typed behaviors but sex-typed attitudes as well. Damon (1977) established this by telling a group of children aged 4 to 7 a story about a boy named George who liked to play with dolls even though his parents told him not to, since only little girls play with dolls. The children were asked if George was right or wrong. Children older than 6 revealed their flexible attitudes toward sex-stereotyped behaviors, indicating that George had a right to do what he pleased. Children younger than 6, however, thought it was wrong of George to play with dolls, many of them indicating that George should be punished for doing so. So rigid are preschoolers in their sex-typed behaviors and attitudes that it is as if they exaggerate their attitudes about what is appropriate for each sex in order to have a better understanding of their own identity (Maccoby, 1980). This may explain why, as they grow older and as their gender identity is stabilized, children are more flexible in their sex-typed behaviors and attitudes (Damon, 1977; Garrett, Ein, & Tremaine, 1977).

Explaining Sex Differences in Behavior

Sex differences in behavior continue to be evident throughout life. Of course, there are individual as well as sex differences among children and adults, and individuals may differ in the extent to which they evidence sex-stereotypic behaviors and attitudes. The question that has generated so much debate in recent years is whether the behavioral differences between the sexes are biologically determined or whether they are learned. Psychologists agree that biological factors contribute to sex differences in behavior, but they note that environmental factors account for most of the sex differences that are reported.

Biological Factors. Support for the view that biological factors are at play in sex differences in behavior is hard to come by because it is difficult to specify a behavior that is strictly biologically determined. However, there are studies which have shown that male infants at birth are more physically active than females (Phillips et al., 1978). Although this temperamental difference exists at birth, it is difficult to separate biological from environmental factors as studies have shown that soon after birth mothers respond to the temperament of their child and interact differently with daughters than they do with sons (Lewis, 1974). So, we cannot be sure that it is not the mothers' behavior that reinforces the increased levels

FIGURE 9.10 During the preschool period, children become aware of the fact that certain activities and tasks are restricted to one sex or the other, and they adopt not only sex-typed behaviors, but sex-typed attitudes as well.

of physical activity the boys were born with. However, studies indicate that there are some traits, most notably aggression, for which there may be a biological basis since not only boys but young male monkeys, too, are rougher in their play than their female counterparts (Harlow, 1962). Perhaps males' aggressiveness may be accounted for in part by high levels of testosterone, the male hormone, which is present in more quantities in males than in females (Davis, 1964; Money & Ehrhardt, 1972).

Environmental Factors.   Although hormonal factors may be important in establishing certain behavioral dispositions, experience and childrearing practices have an effect as well, and they account not only for the acquisition of sex roles but also for the child's awareness of gender. This point is made in a series of studies conducted by John Money and his colleagues. In a description of one of his studies, Money (1975) discusses a rare case of identical twin boys, one of whom lost his penis during circumcision at the age of 7 months. Growing up as a male without a penis would have given the individual psychological difficulties which might have been impossible to overcome, so the decision was made to reassign him as a girl. The parents thus changed the child's name, hairstyle, and clothes, and began treating him as a girl. During puberty, the child underwent a series of surgical procedures and hormone treatments that made the sex reassignment complete. Although these procedures and treatments did not take place until puberty, when the twins were preschoolers the mother reported how much more dainty the girl was than her brother. The girl was described as a tomboy and as bossy, but when asked whether she preferred to be a boy or a girl, she indicated her preference for being a girl.

In several other studies, Money, Hampson, and Hampson (1957) took advantage of similar naturally occurring experiments and studied children who were born with ambiguous genitals. In cases such as these, a decision is made by the family, with the support of the physician and other professionals, to assign a sex to the child and raise the child accordingly. Sometimes, as the child grows and the genitals develop normally, it becomes apparent that a mistake has been made, so the parents have to relabel the child consistent with his or her genetic sex. Money and his colleagues found that children who were raised from infancy as boys or as girls became aware of themselves and behaved as such, suggesting that rearing practices play an important role in the development of gender identity and gender roles. Furthermore, Money and his colleagues found that the first three years of life are a critical period for the development of gender identity. Those children who had been raised as the wrong sex and were relabeled before they were 2 or 3 years old developed a normal gender identity. Those who were relabeled after age 3 had trouble establishing a secure gender identity and adopting the gender role of their genetic sex.

Parents' Role.   The child learns about the behavioral differences between the sexes from the behavior of those around him, be they his siblings, peers, teachers (Fagot, 1977), or media personalities (Sternglanz & Serbin, 1974). He also learns about sex-typed behaviors from other sources, such as books (Wirtenberg, Murez, & Alepektor, 1980). However, parents play a vital role in the acquisition of sex-typed behavior, especially during the early childhood years (Huston, 1983).

The fact is that although sex-role attitudes and standards are changing, most adults continue to have traditional and stereotyped conceptions of sex-roles, and they behave accordingly (Eccles & Hoffman, 1984). Males in our society are regarded as and expected to be assertive, independent, and dominant. Females are regarded as submissive, warm, and sensitive to interpersonal situations and are expected to act accordingly. Not only do children learn from the differences in behavior between their parents (Rosen & Aneshensel, 1978), research evidence also shows that parents have different expectations of their sons and daughters (Rubin, Provenza, & Luria, 1974). They give boys and girls different types of toys to play with (Kacerguis & Adams, 1979), and they treat their children in ways that promote stereotypical functioning. A recent study by Block (1982), who studied more than 1,000 families, found that sons were encouraged more than daughters to be competitive, achievement-oriented, independent, and to control their emotions ("Boys don't cry"). On the other hand, daughters were encouraged to be warm, nurturant, and emotionally expressive.

Researchers have also found that the father plays an important role in sex-role development during the preschool years (see Figure 9.11). In particular, the father's degree of masculinity seems to promote traditional sex roles not only in sons but in daughters as well (Hetherington, Cox, & Cox, 1978). That fathers' masculinity and not necessarily the mothers' femininity is associated with the sex-role development of girls suggests that girls acquire sex roles through a process of *reciprocal role learning*. That is, they learn how to behave as females by complementing their father's masculinity (Lamb & Urberg, 1978). It is interesting to note, however, that the opposite is not true for boys. That is, boys tend to identify with and imitate their fathers' behavior, and those boys whose mothers are very feminine do not necessarily behave in a more masculine way.

The research on the role of fathers in the child's development also reveals that the preschool period may be critical for boys' sex-role development, although it is not so for girls'. This is revealed in studies on the effects of paternal absence. The studies document that boys whose fathers are absent due to divorce, desertion, or death before they are five years of age grow up to be less traditionally masculine than do boys whose fathers are at home and who attend to the children during this period of their lives, or whose fathers leave home after this period. Such boys tend to be less aggressive, more dependent, and to rely on greater use of verbal rather than physical aggression. Huston (1983) suggests that the fact that preschool boys whose fathers are absent evidence less traditionally mascu-

reciprocal role learning

FIGURE 9.11   Fathers play an important role in the development of sex roles.

line behaviors may be due to their lack of exposure to rough-and-tumble play and also to the fact that their mother is less likely to encourage independent behaviors in them than are mothers who have a male adult around to help them with childrearing. In cases where the children of absent fathers have some other adult male living in the household (for example, an older brother or the mother's boyfriend) the effects of paternal absence are lessened (Lamb & Urberg, 1978).

Theoretical Perspectives.   These findings on the role of the parents in children's acquisition and adoption of sex-typed behaviors are elicited from research which has been guided by several theoretical explanations of the processes by which children acquire gender identity and gender roles and other socially prescribed behaviors and attitudes. Although none of these theories offers an entirely satisfactory explanation (Katz, 1979), each is important in its contribution to our understanding that several mechanisms play a part in the acquisition of socially acceptable behaviors.

The Psychoanalytic Theory.   Psychoanalytic theorists contend that the adoption of sex-typed attitudes and behaviors is the result of identification with the same-sex parent. *Identification* is the process in which the child   *identification* responds to the attitudes and behaviors of another person by adopting them as her own. Unlike imitation, however, identification is largely an unconscious effort, meaning that the child is not aware of taking on the characteristics she sees in others.

Freud's explanation of how children come to identify with the same-sex parent is rather controversial and differs for boys and girls. He asserts that during infancy, the boy develops a unique attachment to his mother. He loves and wants to possess her, but sees his father as standing in his way. He grows to hate his father for this, but at the same time he also fears him. Because the child assumes that girls had their penises cut off, he becomes especially afraid that his father will find out his resentment for him and retaliate by castrating him. The boy attempts to relieve his anxieties by pushing out of his consciousness the desire to be with the mother and the resentment he has toward the father. At the same time he identifies with and adopts the attitudes and behaviors of his father. This enables him to feel safer, because his father is unlikely to hurt someone like himself. Freud referred to the boy's anxieties as the *Oedipus conflict,* as he saw an analogy here to the experiences of King Oedipus in Greek tragic drama.

Oedipus conflict

Electra conflict

He referred to girls' anxieties as the *Electra conflict,* also from an analogy to Greek drama. He explained that girls notice that boys have penises while they do not. They come to envy the boys' penises, and they devalue the mother for not having one. They also become angry at the mother for not allowing them to have a penis or for allowing them to be castrated. Therefore they renounce their love for the mother and come to desire to possess their father. At the same time, girls fear their resentment of their mothers, and to reduce the anxieties, they identify with the mother and adopt her behaviors and attitudes.

As we indicated in a previous chapter, the psychoanalytic theory falls short in many respects, one of its major problems being that it is difficult to test empirically (Zigler, Child & Lamb, 1982). Moreover, whereas the psychoanalytic theory places a great deal of importance on the parent-child relationship, emphasizing the child's identification with his parents, many other theorists note that children identify not only with their parents, they also identify with and imitate the behavior of others.

Learning Theory. This view is held by social learning theorists, who state that children acquire behaviors through the mechanisms of *reinforcement* and *punishment.* Socializers, such as parents, reinforce or reward the child for behaviors that are consistent with the child's gender role, and they punish the child for engaging in behaviors that are inappropriate. A young girl who is rewarded by affection, approval, and praise when she is engaged in stereotypically female activities, such as helping her mother prepare a meal or wash the dishes, is likely to repeat this or similar behaviors in the future. However, if she is scolded when she engages in rough-and-tumble play or gets dirty playing with parts of the car her father is working on, she will be unlikely to repeat the activity.

Observational learning theorists emphasize that children learn by observation and imitation as well and that they do not always need to be rewarded or punished to acquire or extinguish a behavior. Observational learning theorists further note that children observe and imitate not only their parents but other socializers as well. Siblings, peers, teachers, neighbors, sports heroes, and television personalities are some examples. Thus, when a girl sees in real life or on television that women usually stand about watching men fix a car when it breaks down, she learns that fixing the car is an activity that is inappropriate for her to engage in.

Cognitive-Developmental Theory.   Cognitive-developmental theorists further elaborate on the role of imitation in the acquisition of gender roles, emphasizing that an awareness of gender precedes any attempt by the child to imitate the behaviors of the same-sex people he encounters. Kohlberg (1966) proposes that the child's realization that he is a boy or that she is a girl (gender identity) stimulates the adoption of sex-typed gender role behaviors, so that the child is an active player in his own development. The reinforcement for imitating sex-typed behaviors comes from the child himself.

Explaining that the adoption of sex-typed behaviors occurs in stages, Kohlberg notes that at first, children observe anatomical and other differences in appearance between the sexes. Based on these observations, children come to label themselves according to gender and to regard themselves as boys or as girls. This label of "boy" or "girl" helps children organize their social behavior because children value others who are like themselves, and they begin to behave as such, reasoning, for instance: I am a girl; therefore I like to do girl things. The children then imitate the behaviors of the same-sex models.

The appeal of the cognitive-developmental theory is that it points out that the child does not simply imitate a behavior, he reasons before he does so. Although the development of gender identity and gender role is dependent, in part, on the cognitive status of the child, there are shortcomings to the cognitive theory. The theory fails to explain why children acquire gender identity at an early age and why those children who have had to undergo sex reassignment after age 3 have problems establishing a stable gender identity. The theory also does not account for the fact that children aged one and two years who have not attained gender identity nevertheless are found to exhibit sex-typed play activities (Etaugh, Collins, & Gerson, 1975).

In summary, although each of these theoretical perspectives on the adoption of sex-role behaviors provides only a partial explanation of the processes involved, taken together, the theories contribute to the understanding that parents and others in the preschool child's life play an important role in his development. Their influence operates in three ways: they are models for identification, providers of rewards and punishment, and models for imitation. The processes of identification, reward and punishment, and imitation function not only in children's acquisition of sex-role behaviors, but also in children's adoption of other expectations, standards, and values of their family and social group. Also, they serve to explain how children learn to behave in ways that are sanctioned by their family and society.

SOCIALIZATION

The process by which children come to behave in socially acceptable ways and by which members of one generation shape the behavior and personality of members of the younger generation is called *socialization*. One function of socialization is to ensure that there will be members of society capable of meeting the demands of people in that society. Thus, children are taught what is necessary in order to coexist with others and to survive. Although children in all societies are taught how to behave in socially approved ways, the precise behaviors one needs in order to survive differ from one society to another.

Socialization in the Family

There are many influences that contribute to the socialization of the child, as he is exposed not only to his parents' and siblings' demands, behaviors, values, and attitudes, he also learns from the behaviors of other children and adults within his expanding social world, and he acquires values from the religious institutions and the schools that he attends. The family, however, is the core socialization agency (Maccoby & Martin, 1983). Parents, depending on their socioeconomic status, culture, and religion, encourage children to adopt certain values, behaviors, and beliefs. Through their expectations of their children, parents influence the extent to which the children will pursue their education and attain occupational success. During the preschool years, however, the main attributes of socialization are *self-control* and *social judgment*. The young child has no innate sense of propriety and no knowledge of what is permissible and what is prohibited, so it is only with guidance that she learns to assess social situations and to form internal standards of conduct. She has to learn to regulate her behavior so as to minimize dangers to herself and others, and she must accept and adopt the restrictions placed upon her by her parents. She also must learn to be polite, wait her turn, to be patient when she wants something, inhibit excessive behavioral displays, and generally control her

self-control and social judgment

FIGURE 9.12 Having no innate sense of propriety, the preschool child learns to regulate her behavior with guidance from her parents.

impulses. Coupled with this need to regulate her behavior, the child needs to adopt positively valued behaviors (often referred to as *prosocial behaviors*), which in our society include sharing, cooperating, and helping (see Figure 9.12).

prosocial behaviors

Parental Caregiving Practices

Parents are continually teaching the preschool child how to behave in socially appropriate ways. They not only impose limits on his behavior, they also tell him when to say please, thank you, and goodbye. They also convey to him social amenities such as not to interrupt people while they are talking (Maccoby & Martin, 1983). Although all parents attempt to guide their children's behaviors, they differ greatly in how they go about raising their children, and they are not equally effective in their attempts to socialize the children. In a series of studies on parenting styles, Diana Baumrind (1967, 1968, 1971, 1975) has found not only that parents differ widely in their approach to childrearing, but also that parental caregiving practices are a major influence on the child's development (see Figure 9.13). Her findings are supported by studies conducted by Welsley Becker (1964) and Endsley et al. (1979). Baumrind has identified three broad types of parents and the characteristics of children that seemed to result from the childrearing practices they followed.

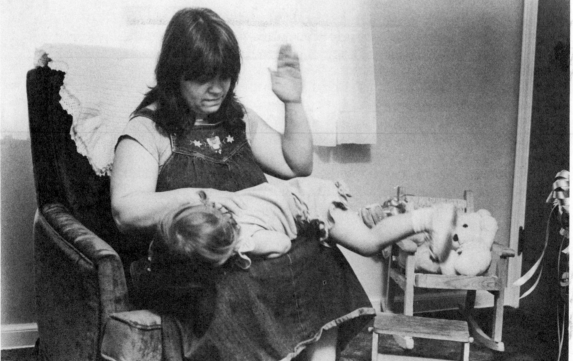

FIGURE 9.13 Parents differ widely in their approaches to childrearing, significantly influencing their childrens' development.

Authoritarian Parents.   One type of parent she identified is the authoritarian parent. This is the parent who tries to shape, control, and evaluate the behavior of the child in accordance with an absolute standard of behavior. Authoritarian parents, according to Baumrind, require the child to accept the word and authority of the adult, and they are likely to favor punitive and forceful disciplinary measures whenever the child's behaviors conflict with what the parent believes is correct. Parents such as these want to control their children, and they tend to be cold in their interactions with them. Children of authoritarian parents tend to be more moody than other children, as well as more apprehensive and unhappy. They are easily annoyed, sometimes hostile, and vulnerable to stress.

Permissive Parents.   The second type of parent is the permissive parent. Permissive parents attempt to interact with the child in a nonpunishing and accepting manner, and their relationship with the child tends to be warm and friendly. However, these parents allow the child to govern his own behavior and do not provide him with guidance and direction. Although permissive parents are well meaning, their approach to childrearing is inappropriate. Baumrind observed that although permissively reared children seem cheerful, perhaps as a result of the warmth these parents show toward them, they have no self-reliance, they are frequently out of control, and they have difficulty inhibiting their impulses.

Authoritative Parents.   The most nurturant and effective of the parents that Baumrind identified are the authoritative parents. These parents are warm in their interactions with their children, and they frequently use positive reinforcement to guide their children's behavior. However, they also use reprimand and punishment when the situation demands it. They are ready to exert direct control over the child and they are unwilling to yield to unpleasant behaviors such as nagging and whining. They also encourage mature and independent behavior in their children, and when they do punish their children, they explain the rationale behind their disciplinary actions. The children of authoritative parents are thus the most socially adept of all children. They are energetic and competent, cheerful and friendly in their relations with peers, and they approach any experience with interest and curiosity.

It is tempting to interpret Baumrind's findings to mean that children's personality styles are the direct result of childrearing practices and the characteristics of the parents. However, her findings are based on correlational data, so the direction of the cause-effect relationship is obscure. Although they are guided and shaped by their parents, children also influence their parents' behavior. It could well be that the reasonableness and effectiveness of authoritative parents are due, at least in part, to the fact

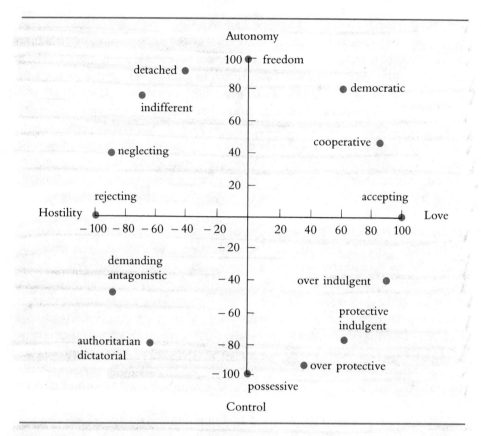

FIGURE 9.14   An analysis of several different studies on parental childrearing styles reveals that most parents' behavior toward their children can be described in terms of (a) how loving or hostile they are, and (b) how permissive or restrictive they are. From "A Circumplex Model for Maternal Behavior" by Earl S. Schaefer from *The Journal of Abnormal and Social Psychology, 59,* fig. 4, p. 232. Copyright © 1959 by the American Psychological Association. Reprinted by permission of the publisher and author.

that their children are by nature socially competent and easy to discipline. In other words, the parents' behavior may be as much a response to children's personality styles as the cause of them (Lamb, 1982).

Effective Punishment Techniques.   Although parents, for different reasons, differ in their effectivenes in disciplining their children and in the degree to which they are loving or hostile to the children (Schaeffer, 1959; see Figure 9.14), there is a great deal of information from the research that explains how parents can become effective disciplinarians.

Parents need to discipline the child, because failure to restrain and discipline him may deprive him of opportunities to regulate his behavior and learn self-control and appropriate ways of interaction with others. To be truly effective, however, the discipline of a preschool child should foster self-regulation and social judgment in the child without detracting from his initiative and self-confidence, and without generating excessive compliance or rebellion. To these ends, any punishment that is used to discipline the child should be instructive rather than merely punitive, and it should be directed toward the child's behavior rather than toward the child's essential worth as a person (Parke, 1977). In a review of the research on punishment as a technique for controlling behavior in young children, Ross Parke (1976) acknowledges some of the limitations of the studies in this area. But, he notes that despite these limitations, researchers have concluded that punishment is an effective means of suppressing undesirable behaviors and encouraging the child to behave appropriately. However, he emphasizes that in order to be effective, *timing* is crucial: "the longer the delay between the initiation of the act and the onset of punishment, the less effective the punishment." Also important is *consistency*. Parke cites a number of studies which have shown that parents of delinquent boys are more erratic in their disciplinary practices than parents of nondelinquent boys. At times they punish their children for certain behaviors and at other times they are lax in their approach to childrearing and ignore those same behaviors.

The nature of the *relationship* between the parent or other person administering the punishment and the child who is being punished is very important. When this relationship is close and affectionate, the punishment is more effective than when the relationship is cold or impersonal. Additionally, the punishment is likely to be effective when it is accompanied by a *reason* why the child is being punished. Taking these factors into account, Belsky, Lerner, and Spanier (1984) explain that when a child is being punished by an angry parent or told in an angry and hostile manner to stop doing something, the child walks away feeling demeaned at having been scolded. However, when the child is told in a controlled way to stop doing something and why, he gains an understanding of what he did and why it is unacceptable, and thus has insight that serves to guide his subsequent behavior.

Parents often feel that physical punishment is the most effective means of controlling the child's behavior. Although this mode of punishment may be somewhat effective when appropriately administered, that is when the timing of the punishment and other considerations are taken into account, Parke (1976, 1977) points out that this mode of punishment has undesirable consequences. Parents should consider employing other disciplinary techniques that have been found to be effective. As an example of an alternative to physical punishment, Parke suggests that parents reinforce desired behavior by rewards and encouragement, and ignore undesirable behavior. He further advises that "words, as well as deeds, can alter [the child's] physical behavior," hence there is no need for parents to resort to physical punishment as a means of controlling children's behavior. Feshbach and Feshbach (1976) offer similar advice, emphasizing the negative consequences of physical punishment and noting that when parents are hostile, coercive, and physically punitive they often fail to adequately discipline their children, and they also foster aggressive tendencies in children. Why? First, physically punitive disciplinary practices function as a model of aggression that the child is likely to imitate. Second, the frequent use of hostile disciplining techniques not only demeans the child, it also teaches her that physical action in the form of aggression is one viable way to solve interpersonal disputes (Feshbach, 1980).

DISCUSSION OF SOCIAL ISSUES: CHILD ABUSE

Despite the fact that punitive techniques are not the only effective methods by which to encourage children to behave, parents often use physical punishment to discipline their children. Most children are mildly spanked from time to time, and they suffer no harm as a result. It becomes a matter of child abuse, however, when parents continually resort to physical punishment in their interactions with children or when the punishment is so severe as to injure the child or pose a threat to his life. Although child abuse was once thought to be rare, now that there are laws that require the reporting of suspected cases of abuse, it has become all too apparent that many children are subjected to extreme forms of violence in their own homes (Gelles, 1978; Strauss, 1979; Strauss, Gelles, & Steinmetz, 1980; Gerbner, Ross, & Zigler, 1980). A surprisingly large number of parents assault, batter, or torture their children (see Figure 9.15). Over 2,000 children are killed each year by their parents or other caretakers, and another one-half to one-and-a-half million children are badly beaten or otherwise abused (Gil, 1976). As we have discussed in previous chapters, child abuse may include any number of transgressions against the child, from *acts of commission,* which refer to physical and sexual assault, to *acts of omission,* which include psychological abuse and neglect. Parents who fail to provide their children with emotional comfort, food, clothing, and shelter are as guilty of abuse as those parents who physically assault their children (Parke & Collmer, 1975).

Abusive treatment of children by their parents has attracted a great deal of attention from developmental psychologists and other concerned professionals who regard child abuse as one of the most difficult of all social problems to understand. How can a parent, who has come to know and love the child, inflict harm on that child even to the point of death?

Although it is difficult to understand how the loving relationship between parent and child can sometimes take such tragic turns, child abuse has been part of our history. In recent years, however, child abuse has come to be viewed as a problem that deserves society's concern, in part because of advancements in medical technology, most notably the devel-

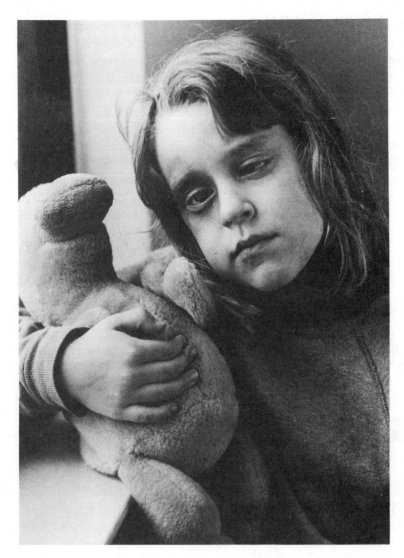

FIGURE 9.15   The widespread neglect and abuse of children by their parents has attracted a great deal of attention from child development professionals.

opment of x-rays. X-rays have enabled physicians (a) to discover and document the consequences of physical punishment, and (b) to identify those children who are repeatedly abused. The x-rays show not only recent injuries, but also previous injuries in various stages of healing (Caffey, 1946; Kempe et al., 1962), providing forceful evidence of the continued abuse of many children.

Causes of Child Abuse.   What causes parents to abuse their children? The answer to this question is important. Once we know the etiology of child abuse, steps can be taken to prevent it. Researchers are only just now beginning to understand some of the causes of abuse, noting that it is the result of many interrelated factors. In a review of the research on the etiology of child abuse, Belsky (1980), proposes that "child maltreatment is multiply determined by forces at work in the individual, in the family, in the community and in the culture in which the individual and family are embedded."

Although the abuse of children may be regarded as bizarre behavior, studies have shown that only about 10% of abusive parents suffer from mental disorders. On the basis of case studies and other research on child abuse, researchers note that parents who mistreat their children had been mistreated themselves by their parents or they are subject to abuse, neglect, or abandonment by their spouses (Belsky, 1978; Kempe & Kempe, 1978). This point is also made by Rutter (1979), who notes that adults who were subjected to abuse during their childhood years are more likely to be abusive of their children. However, more recent studies contradict these findings, noting that the cycle of abuse is found only in a limited number of families (Kaufman & Zigler, 1986).

Studies on abusive parents further reveal that adults who abuse their children lack effective child management techniques and other social skills, and that they have unrealistic expectations of what babies and young children can do. They regard ordinary infant behavior such as crying or dropping toys or other objects as intentional wrongdoing, and they attribute children's failure to obey instructions as willful disobedience or even malice. These parents become upset, for example, when their two-year-old child is unable to sit still for long periods of time or when, unable to drink from a glass of milk, she spills it.

Researchers have found that parents are more likely to abuse a particularly troublesome child. Low-birth-weight babies, who are hard to handle and to calm, are more likely to be abused than other infants (Egeland & Brunquell, 1979). Children who demand greater amounts of attention are also more likely to be the victims of abuse than are other children. A far greater incidence of abuse is reported among mentally retarded and tempermentally difficult children than among children who do not have these problems (Belsky, 1978).

Beyond the characteristics of the parent and the child that contribute to abuse, researchers have found that child abuse often occurs when the parent is overburdened with the responsibilities and the stresses of daily life. Parents who abuse their children are often unemployed and make frequent moves and they have trouble establishing community ties or getting to know their neighbors. Thus, they have no relatives or close friends to turn to for help in times of stress (Garbarino, 1977).

Other factors that increase the likelihood of abusive behavior on the part of the parent are alcohol abuse, legal problems, large family size, overcrowded and inadequate housing and marital discord (Green, 1976; Steinmetz, 1977). In fact, as Albee (1980) and Garbarino (1977) point out, the more stressful life conditions the family is experiencing, the more likely is the occurrence of abuse. Thus, it is not surprising that a great deal of child abuse is frequently reported among lower class families, as the stress of poverty does indeed create a climate for abuse. However, the mistreatment of children is not confined to poor families. Some parents in middle-class families also mistreat their children (Gil, 1970, 1976), although they are often better able than poor families to disguise the consequences of abuse.

Services That Prevent Child Abuse.   Given our knowledge of the factors that contribute to abuse, researchers propose that the solution to the problem requires multidisciplinary and coordinated efforts that focus not only on the treatment of abusive parents and their children but also on the prevention of abuse. Among the services that are offered to abusive parents and abused children are programs that include therapy to raise parents' low self-esteem and respite care programs where parents can leave their children at times of stress. Informal support groups and other services such as Parents Anonymous are also important because they provide parents with the nurturance and understanding of which they themselves have long been deprived. Beyond the provision of understanding to potentially abusive parents, researchers note that programs that support family life (for example, providing families with adequate day care services) would alleviate the stress many parents are feeling and would thereby serve to decrease the incidence of abuse (Zigler, 1980). In countries such as Sweden where social support programs are widespread, researchers report that the incidence of child abuse is significantly lower than it is in the United States (Tietjen, 1980).

Services that are geared toward the prevention of child abuse should also focus on parent education in which parents learn what to expect of their children at different ages and how they can effectively discipline the children without using physical force (Ross & Zigler, 1980). According to psychologists, parent education programs should be offered not only to parents who abuse their children but to all parents and prospective parents, since knowledge about children's needs and characteristics can help the parents to better understand their child and refrain from resorting to abuse (Bronfenbrenner, 1977).

To be successful on a large scale, however, efforts to prevent child abuse must be accompanied by changes in cultural attitudes toward violence. Ours is a violent society. The rate of violent crimes continues to rise and portrayals of violence on television are commonplace. Furthermore, we continue to condone the physical punishment of children, making it difficult for parents to subscribe wholeheartedly to other methods of discipline. As an example of society's sanction of abuse, Zigler (1978) points out that despite continued efforts by advocates for children to stem the abuse of children by their parents, the Supreme Court in the United States has upheld the right of school personnel to use physical punishment in the discipline of children. Although it does not appear to be directly related to child abuse, the message conveyed to parents is that the use of physical force against children is a preferred mode of punishment. If teachers and principals find this an effective mode of resolving problems with children, why shouldn't parents?

Consequences of Child Abuse.   You can see from even this brief discussion that the prevention of child abuse is a difficult and multifaceted task (Bakan, 1979). The importance of preventing it, however, cannot be overemphasized, because the physical and psychological consequences of abuse can be very serious. Child abuse can result not only in physical handicaps but also in severe neurological problems. Blows to the head can cause bleeding inside a child's skull, ultimately leading to brain damage. What is particularly surprising and disturbing is that infants, whose skull is much larger than their brain (which is still growing) can suffer hemorrhages throughout the brain simply by being shaken. Known as the *shaken baby syndrome,* this form of abuse can cause brain damage as well as visual problems and deficits in language and motor skills.

shaken baby syndrome

Besides the neurological consequences of abuse, abused children also suffer from disturbances in emotional and social development. They have learned from their home life that their involvement with other people carries with it a great deal of pain, and they tend to be inhibited and socially unresponsive, often backing away when a friendly caregiver or another child approaches them (George & Main, 1979; Gaensbauer & Sands, 1979). Such children have also been found to be overly compliant or to exhibit violent and aggressive behavior toward adults and peers (Herrenkohl & Herrenkohl, 1981). Some abused children are "hyper-vigilant" (Martin & Breezley, 1976), meaning that they are constantly on the lookout for danger, scanning the environment and ever-ready to attack. A variety of underlying processes may account for such behaviors among abused children. It may well be the case that because of the ill treatment they have received, these children failed to develop the social skills required to engage in harmonious social interactions (Aber, 1982). Or, they may be imitating the hostile interpersonal exchanges that they have experienced.

Television and Violence

Children imitate not only the behavior of their parents but the behavior of television personalities as well. As we have indicated in previous chapters, television has a great deal of influence on children. On the average, children spend 6,500 hours watching television before entering school (Gerbner, 1980). For children growing up today, television is a common and constant learning medium. Much of what the child sees on television can best be described as learning about people—how they behave, how they feel, and how they interact with one another. However, the world of television is not like the real world because television programs are produced to satisfy advertisers who are concerned with attracting those people who can spend money, namely, people in the middle years of life. Thus, there is relatively little attention paid on television to the portrayal of older people who are very much a part of real life. In recent years TV programs have featured the divorced, single-parent family and the dual-career family. Nevertheless, researchers emphasize that the overall picture that television presents is still far from the real world, and this may have consequences for the preschool child. Gerbner (1980) points out that crime is portrayed ten times more often on the screen than it occurs in real life.

In fact, much of the television programming is devoted to violence and aggression, so this is what children are exposed to. The report of the Surgeon General on Television Violence (Pearle et al., 1982) reveals that 80% of television programs surveyed contained at least one incident of overt physical aggression or a violent act. Despite continued efforts by advocates on behalf of children to reduce the amount of televised violence, it is becoming more intense and more widespread. It is evident not only in numerous programs but on music video channels as well. Often these depict popular rock groups and singers engaging in violence. In a study by the National Coalition on Television Violence (1984), it was found not only that a large number of music videos contained violence but also that they contained sadistic violence in which the attacker took pleasure in committing senseless acts such as choking people or knocking them unconscious.

Studies have shown that exposure to such violence on television increases children's aggression (Pearle et al., 1982). In one of the early studies that demonstrates that children can learn aggression from television, Bandura (1969) set up an experimental procedure in which a group of children watched a television program depicting violence. He found upon later observations of these children that they were more likely than children who did not watch the program to repeatedly hit a doll. In another study on the topic, Friedrich and Stein (1973) asked children to watch one of three types of programs: cartoons or other programs (such as Batman) depicting violence and aggression; programs depicting prosocial behaviors; and programs that depicted neither violence nor prosocial behaviors. The children were asked to watch one of the three types of programs daily for a period of four weeks. The children were observed three weeks prior to the time they were asked to watch the programs, and for two weeks after they watched the programs. The researchers found that after they watched programs depicting violence, children were more likely to be intolerant in their interpersonal interactions and to disobey rules than were the children who watched the other programs. The researchers found also that those children who were observed to be aggressive before they watched the aggression and violence on television became even more so afterwards, but that the children who were not aggressive did not.

In another study, Steuer, Applefield, and Smith (1971) selected pairs of preschoolers who were observed to exhibit about the same amount of aggressive behavior (kicking, hitting, etc.) while they were in a nursery school playground. One of the children in each pair was then shown violent TV programs each day for close to a two-week period, while the other child in each pair was shown programs that did not include violence and aggression. The researchers found that among all the pairs of children studied, the children who watched the violent TV programs became more aggressive in their play than the other children.

More recent studies (Singer & Singer, 1980) report similar findings with respect to preschool children. However, studies with older children (Feshbach & Singer, 1971) yield less clear-cut results, suggesting that it is preschoolers, particularly those who are aggressive, who are particularly prone to the negative effects of violent TV programs.

Television and Prosocial Behavior

The capacity of television as a socialization agency is not limited to violence and aggression. There are some television programs that attempt to teach prosocial behaviors. Notable among these is "Mr. Rogers' Neighborhood." Mr. Rogers is a soft-spoken man who is seen on public television stations addressing himself to preschool children across the country (see Figure 9.11). He discusses a number of different topics with the children, encouraging them in his quiet manner always to be polite and helpful. His show has been found to be effective in increasing sharing, helping, and cooperation among preschool children and in reducing the incidence of aggression they exhibit toward one another. In studies reviewed by Stein and Friedrich (1975), it was found that children who watched "Mr. Rogers' Neighborhood" become more self-controlled and more obedient than children who watched shows depicting aggression.

The Effects of Day Care on Socialization

Day care and nursery schools are another source of influence on the child's socialization. In such settings, children have the opportunity to interact with a number of children and adults and to learn to be cooperative and helpful in their interpersonal interactions, as well as to wait their turn and conform to rules. In reviews of studies that compared children who are being raised at home to children who are in day care, it was found that children in full-time day care centers are indeed more cooperative in their interactions with peers than are the children who are being raised at home (Clarke-Stewart, 1983). However, this is usually the case in high-quality day care centers and is generally dependent on the extent to which

FIGURE 9.16 Although the family is the primary socialization agent, day care centers and nursery schools are other sources of influence on children's socialization.

the day care providers discipline and provide direction for the children (Roupp et al., 1979). In such day care centers, children learn to obey rules and to interact effectively with adults and children in a group setting (see Figure 9.16).

It may appear that in day care centers the teacher is constantly disciplining the children, since there are so many children to supervise and keep in order. In reality, however, many day care providers actually do less disciplining than parents do (Cochran, 1977), perhaps because they are less emotionally invested in any one child than is the parent. Ambron (1980) also found that some day care staff are more permissive, more tolerant of disobedience and aggression, and less inclined to set standards and directions for children's behavior than are parents.

It is not surprising, therefore, that just as there are studies which point to the positive effects of day care, so there are some studies which suggest that there may be negative effects as well. Schwartz (1974), for example, found that preschoolers who have been in day care since infancy were more aggressive toward peers than children who enrolled in day care for the first time at age three or four. Ramey, MacPhee, and Yeats (1982) also found that children who had been enrolled in a day care program since infancy were noted as more hostile by their kindergarten teachers than were their counterparts who were reared since infancy at home. Robertson (1982) cites similar findings indicating not only that some day-care-reared children are aggressive toward their peers but also that they have problems interacting with adults. He found that boys with day care histories were rated by their first grade teachers as significantly more disobedient, quarrelsome, and uncooperative than children with no previous day care experience. We reiterate, however, that just as we cannot fully rely on the studies that have found no harmful effects of day care on children's development, so we cannot yet accept without question the findings that demonstrate the negative effects of day care. The point is that more studies on the effects of day care on children's social development need to be conducted. It appears that day care has both positive and negative effects depending on the particular practices of the day care providers.

SUMMARY

During the preschool years the child becomes increasingly independent and shows evidence of his mastery of the environment. He is more able than he was in the previous period to do things for himself and explore his surroundings, and he experiences changes in his interactions with his parents. He remains attached to his mother and enjoys being with her, but the father now assumes a more central role in his life. Although the relationship they have with their fathers becomes very important to preschoolers, children of divorced parents do not have the opportunity to develop a close relationship with their father.

Preschoolers interact not only with their immediate family but with peers as well. Peer relations provide the opportunity to develop social skills and also the opportunity to play. The play of children varies in the amount of social involvement, with younger preschoolers often playing alone and older preschoolers playing in groups. As they play together, it becomes apparent that there are striking differences between them in personality characteristics, as some children are cooperative and independent and other children are disruptive and aggressive. Aggression, which is in part a response to frustration, is common among young children, who eventually learn to contain their anger and become more cooperative in their interactions with others, often evidencing their ability not only to share but also to help others in distress.

Peer relations also provide children with the opportunity to learn about other people's needs and emotions. However, preschoolers learn not only about others but about themselves, and they develop a self-concept, which is an understanding and evaluation of one's personality, qualities, and capabilities. They evidence their emerging self-concept in their adoption of gender identity.

Psychologists note that although biological factors contribute to sex differences in behaviors, environmental factors account for most of the sex differences that are reported, as children learn from and imitate the behaviors of their siblings, peers, and others they interact with. Parents, however, play a vital role in this respect, and they not only influence the child's adoption of sex-typed behaviors, but other aspects of her personality as well. Researchers have found that when parents are reasonable and explain to them how they should behave and why, children are socially competent and happy. On the other hand, when parents are permissive in their interactions with children, children have difficulty controlling their behavior in social situations. When parents are hostile to their children, and when they resort to physical punishment of the children, the children are not only moody and unhappy, they also learn to behave aggressively themselves.

Although physical punishment is potentially harmful to the child, many parents employ this mode of discipline to the extent that they physically and/or emotionally abuse their children. Child abuse is one of the most difficult of all social problems to understand and prevent because it involves not only the behaviors and attitudes of individual parents, but of society as a whole since parents and children learn about violence from what they see on television. Violence is continually portrayed on television, and researchers have shown that by imitating the behaviors of television personalities, children come to behave aggressively as well. However, television has positive influences too. Those programs that provide models of prosocial behaviors help the children learn how to cooperate with one another and extend to others understanding and kindness.

REVIEW POINTS

1. During the early childhood years children attain more independence and their relationship with their parents changes. They become less dependent on the mothers than was true in infancy, and they spend more time with their fathers. Some children growing up today, however, are in single-parent families and do not have the opportunity to interact with their fathers on a daily basis.

2. During this period, children's social relations are expanding, and they have meaningful relationships with siblings. Although sibling rivalry is evident in most families, children have been observed to act compassionately toward their sisters and brothers and to imitate and learn from them.

3. Preschool children also develop meaningful relationships with peers. Peer relations are important. Children who do not play with other children miss out on important social experiences and are at risk for becoming socially inept and uncertain of themselves in interpersonal situations later in life.

4. Peers also serve as partners in play. There is a developmental component to children's play; the older the children are, the more likely they are to engage in associative and cooperative play with other children and less likely to engage in solitary play. Besides the age of the child, experience is also an important aspect of play, as are the opportunity to play and the availability of objects to play with.

5. As children play together, striking personality differences between them become apparent— as some are more aggressive than others and some are more cooperative and independent. The more time children spend with each other, the more they are likely to learn about others' feelings and to recognize that other people may feel and think differently than they do.

6. With age, children also learn more about themselves, and they acquire a self-concept, which is a subjective understanding and evaluation of one's personality, qualities, and capabilities. The development of the self-concept is a gradual process that continues and changes throughout the lifespan. During the preschool years children define themselves in concrete terms or in terms of what they do, whereas in later years children define themselves according to psychological traits.

7. An important aspect of the self-concept is gender identity, which refers to the child's awareness and acceptance of being either a boy or a girl. After the child has this awareness she acquires gender or sex roles and she realizes that there are differences between males and females in their behavior, attitudes, and abilities.

8. Researchers note that although there is a biological component that establishes certain behavioral dispositions, experience and childrearing practices for the most part account for the differences between the sexes. Parents' expectations of their children are especially important in children's acquisition of sex roles.

9. Three theoretical approaches serve to explain children's acquisition of sex roles—the psychoanalytic theory, the learning theory, and the cognitive theory. Each theory has its limitations, but together they help explain that children come to behave in a manner that is expected of their sex by the processes of identification, reward, and punishment.

10. These three processes also serve to explain socialization—how children come to behave in socially acceptable ways. Although there are many influences that contribute to the child's socialization, the family is the core socialization agency.

11. The manner by which parents attempt to socialize their children differs from parent to parent and influences the children. Some parents are authoritarian in their approach to childrearing; others are permissive or authoritative. Each of these parenting styles is associated with different personality characteristics in children. However, just as parents influence the personality of children, children, in turn, influence their parents' behavior.

12. Parents also differ in their disciplinary techniques. The most effective disciplinary techniques are those which occur when there is a warm relationship between parent and child and when the child is offered an explanation for the punishment. Physical punishment that is hostile and coercive is not effective and serves to foster aggressive tendencies in children. However, many parents resort to this type of punishment, some of them to the point of the physical abuse of their children. Child abuse is a pervasive social problem and its prevention requires multidisciplinary and coordinated efforts including social support programs and parent education.

13. Besides being socialized at home by their parents, children's behavior is also influenced by television and by their interactions with peers and caretakers in a day care center.

Atypical Development
in the Early Childhood Years

AUTISTIC CHILDREN

Although they may be present early in life, some severe developmental disorders are not diagnosed until late infancy or the early childhood years. During this period, normal children acquire increasingly sophisticated motor and language skills, and they begin to establish meaningful social relationships not only with their parents but with other adults and children as well. While most children seem to enjoy their expanded social world, some severely disabled children, notably those who suffer from autism, do not.

Characteristics

Autism is a disorder that was first identified over 40 years ago by Leo Kanner (1942). It occurs in about 1 out of every 2,500 children (Caparulo & Cohen, 1982). The disorder is characterized by a number of symptoms, one of which is the inability to establish emotional and social relationships. Autistic children are unresponsive to their social environment, they evidence a disinterest in being with other children or playing with them, and they may also actively avoid being with people, preferring instead to be by themselves. In a discussion of some of the symptoms of autism, Kanner (1942) presents a case study of a 6-year-old autistic boy, Frederick W., whose mother described him as

> . . . a child [who] has always been self-sufficient. I could leave him alone and he'd entertain himself very happily, walking around, singing. I have never known him to cry in demanding attention. . . . Until last year, he mostly ignored people. When we had guests, he just wouldn't pay attention to them. He looked curiously at small children and then go off alone. He acted as if people weren't there at all, even his grandparents. About a year ago, he began showing more interest in observing [people]. . . . But usually people are an interference. . . . If people come close to him, he'll push them away. He doesn't want me to touch him or to put my arms around him.

Besides being socially unresponsive and emotionally detached from people, autistic children fail to acquire normal language skills. Some autistic children are functionally mute. Others learn to speak, but they develop

444

bizarre speech patterns that are essentially noncommunicative, and they seem to be speaking to themselves whether or not there are other people present around them. For example, they may mechanically repeat a sentence or two they have heard, a condition called *echolalia,* or they repeat, over and over again, certain songs, television commercials, or slogans. Some autistic children also engage in the obsessive counting of numbers, or in repeatedly asking nonsensical questions such as, "Am I first, am I second, am I third?" without any apparent desire to hear an answer (Stewart & Gath, 1978).

In addition to such abnormal and noncommunicative use of language, clinicians note that autistic children usually do not evidence any prelinguistic skills such as babbling, and that some suddenly say a few words or a phrase but may not repeat these until several months or even several years later (Caparulo & Cohen, 1977).

Clinicians have also observed that in their behavior, autistic children are rigid and stereotypic (Tanguay, 1980). Whereas 2- or 3-year-old normal children engage in symbolic play and use their toys or other objects imaginatively, pretending these represent different things, autistic children invariably ignore their toys, or they bang and wave them around aimlessly. Normal preschool children spend much of their time playing, either alone or with other children. Autistic children engage in ritualistic behavior, spending an inordinate amount of time simply staring at or manipulating mechanical objects such as light switches, vacuum cleaners, or faucets. They may engage in unusual motor movements such as repeatedly moving their fingers in front of their eyes or repeatedly rocking back and forth. Some autistic children also bang their heads repeatedly against the wall, apparently impervious to any feeling of pain. They may also engage in other self-abusive behaviors such as biting themselves or digging their fingernails into their flesh.

These behavioral characteristics of autistic children—their unresponsiveness to people, their noncommunicative use of language, and their ritualistic and self-destructive behavior—point to the fact that such children are centered on their own bodies and are totally unaware of what is going on around them. However, autistic children may in fact be aware of the world around them. This becomes evident when we consider some other behavioral characteristics associated with autism. For example, autistic children are known to be resistant to any change in the environment. They become upset, frustrated, or afraid when the furniture in their room is rearranged, when they and their families move to another location, or go on vacation, or when a routine they have become used to is not followed (Cohen, Caparulo & Shaywitz, 1976). Although autistic children have a bizarre fascination with objects such as light switches, they have unrealistic fears of some other objects such as table lamps, believing that these will hurt them in some way.

Finally, it has been found that some autistic children are mentally retarded. Numerous studies indicate that over 50% of autistic children have IQ scores of less than 50 (Ando & Yoshimura, 1979; Barry & James, 1978; Schopler & Dalldorf, 1980). The fact that autism and mental retardation can and do coexist in some cases was not always known, however, because in the past these children were considered to be "untestable" so their mental status was never determined. In addition, many researchers observed that although autistic children exhibit bizarre behaviors, some also have unusual talents. This fact contributed to the general belief that in their mental functioning, autistic children are not necessarily impaired (Schopler & Mesibov, 1984). Although it is now known that some autistic children are mentally retarded, the remarkable talents of some autistic children should not be overlooked, for an appreciation of these can help our understanding of autistic children and may increase our ability to help them (Selfe, 1977). In discussing not only the handicaps but also the talents and unusual memory of some autistic children, Caparulo and Cohen (1977) describe a boy, James, who did not speak until he was 5 years old but was able, at an early age, to complete complicated puzzles designed for much older children. At age 5, James made his first statement.

> His mother reported that he had been looking at the sky and said "It looks like a flower." He did not speak again for 8 months, but then began speaking in full sentences. Most often the content was concerned with numbers—he read encyclopedias and reported, for example, to whoever would listen that a certain river was 1,000 miles long and had 200 tributaries.

Early Symptoms of Autism

Despite the abnormal behavioral characteristics associated with autism, autistic children are normal in their physical and motor development so that the disorder often remains undiagnosed until late infancy or the early childhood years. Recent research has shown that the behavioral and emotional disturbance of childhood autism are apparent as early as the first three or four months of life, especially to the parents of the autistic children. Whereas normal babies that age establish frequent eye contact with their parents and other caretakers, and they smile at them and seem happy and content to be in close physical contact with them, autistic infants do not evidence a similar interest in the social environment or the desire to be close to people. Instead, they seem content when they are alone, and they hold themselves rigidly when they are being held.

Caparulo and Cohen (1982) note that besides being socially unresponsive during infancy, infants who are eventually diagnosed as autistic tend to spend an inordinate amount of time staring at their fingers or repeatedly banging their heads against the crib. Some such infants are characterized as unusually good and compliant in their behavior, rarely crying or otherwise demanding attention. Other such infants, however, may cry excessively, and they are difficult to soothe, often evidencing unusual eating and sleeping patterns and difficulty modulating their activity level. That is, they tend to be underaroused or overaroused by environmental stimulation. Some parents become aware very early in infancy that there may be something wrong with their baby, and they bring their concerns to the attention of the child's pediatrician. However, because in their physical and motor development such infants are perfectly normal, physicians often adopt a wait-and-see attitude until the infant is about 18–24 months, when it becomes apparent not only to the parents but to the pediatrician as well that the baby is not following the normal course of development.

Causes of Autism

Researchers and clinicians have been intensely interested in autism in part because it is the most severe of emotional disturbances known to occur during the early childhood years. The cause of the disorder is not yet known, although some explanations have been put forward.

In one of the earlier explanations of the causes of autism, researchers considered the disorder to be a form of emotional or social withdrawal that stemmed from environmental factors. Adhering to such an explanation, child development professionals such as Bruno Bettelheim (1967) noted that autism is the child's response to negative interactions with parents, and it is a way of avoiding any further painful interpersonal experiences. Bettelheim noted that the child is likely to withdraw from affective contact with the environment if he experiences negative interactions during infancy when he becomes increasingly aware of and interested in people and cognizant of the fact that he can have an effect on them. Any negative interactions during this critical period of development (for example, if the child is ignored for lengthy periods of time) would force the child to simply turn inward and to be discouraged from any further attempts to establish social relations.

In support of the environmental explanation, Bettelheim (1967) and others (Eisenberg & Kanner, 1956) noted that parents of autistic children seem to be more emotionally detached and cold than do parents of children who suffer from other disturbances in development. Nevertheless, empirical studies have failed to establish a link between parental characteristics and childhood autism (Rutter, 1971; Reichter & Schopler, 1976), and researchers have since abandoned the environmental explanation in favor of a biological hypothesis. Researchers who adhere to the biological hypothesis explain that autism stems from one or several problems related to brain dysfunction. Such dysfunction, which may be caused by an assault to development experienced during the prenatal period, results in the inability of the child to comprehend sound or make any sense out of what is being said to him. Thus, the child's failure to establish social relationships is explained not in terms of parental pathology but as stemming from abnormalities in the central nervous system (Young & Cohen, 1979).

Although the biological explanation of autism is as yet far from complete, several recent findings associated with the disorder provide forceful evidence of possible organic damage as the cause of the disorder. For example, more than 25% of autistic children in some studies have been found to develop seizures during late infancy (Lotter, 1978). Autism has also been linked to maternal rubella during infancy (Chess, 1977) and to metabolic conditions such as Celiac's disease (Coleman, 1978). Some studies have also demonstrated a possible genetic factor (Folstein & Rutter, 1978), with some researchers also pointing out that the disorder is more likely to occur among boys than it is among girls. For every girl diagnosed as autistic, three to four boys are diagnosed with the disorder (Lord, Schopter, & Revicki, 1982). Finally, while it is unusual to find more than one autistic child in a family, there are families with autism, language disorders, and other developmental disabilities in siblings and relatives, a fact which suggests some genetic contribution to the disorder (Caparulo & Cohen, 1982). However, as Schopler and Mesibov (1984) point out, none of the mechanisms just identified are claimed to exist in all autistic children, but "the evidence indicates . . . that a number of biologic factors, acting singly or in combination are most likely to produce the autistic syndrome."

Treatment

Just as the exact causes of autism have yet to be identified, so treatment of the disorder is yet to be discovered. In the past, when autism was considered to be a form of emotional withdrawal, the treatment of autistic children consisted of play therapy. Through play, clinicians hoped to help the child acquire more confidence and trust in interpersonal interactions. At the same time that the child was in play therapy sessions, his parents were seen by another therapist who attempted to help the parents acquire better caretaking skills. At the present time, treatment efforts focus on helping autistic children acquire language skills and basic self-help skills by means of behavior modification techniques (Louaas, Young, & Newsom, 1978; Caparulo & Cohen, 1982). In many of the programs for autistic children, parents are trained as behavior therapists for their autistic children (Kolko, 1984). Although it is not yet known whether or not these techniques are successful and, if they are, to what extent, it is pointed out that advances have been made in the treatment of autistic children, with therapists now recognizing the need for developing comprehensive services for them and their families (Schopler, Mesibov, Shigley, & Bashford, 1984; Kozloff, 1984). However, any form of treatment or therapy that currently exists does not produce a cure for the disorder, although it may improve the autistic child's ability to function independently.

Although autistic children are socially withdrawn and often display bizarre behavior, some of them have remarkable talents. The drawing above was done by an autistic girl when she was 3½ years old. Psychologists do not yet understand how this child's extraordinary drawing ability developed. One hypothesis is that it emerged in compensation for her severe lack of language (Selfe, 1977).

THE
MIDDLE
CHILDHOOD
YEARS

Looking back over your own childhood, you may find that you regard with special fondness the middle childhood years (often referred to as the school-age years), the period of life that spans the ages from 6 to 12. Many adults would pick these years as the best years of their lives. Not only do they have vivid memories of this period, but life during the middle childhood years is generally characterized as happy and trouble-free. At this age the child does not have any major responsibilities, he acquires an impressive number of physical skills, and he attains a new level of psychological development as well as much greater independence from adult care. Not only does the child become increasingly self-sufficient in these ways, she also begins, during this period, the process of forming strong emotional ties with persons outside the family unit in preparation for the major task she will face in adolescence, namely, achieving independence and separation from the family.

CHAPTER **10**

PHYSICAL DEVELOPMENT
DURING MIDDLE CHILDHOOD

The self-sufficiency and interest of the school-age child in persons and activities outside of the family are evident in the fact that children of this age are everywhere. They are in the playground, at the local store, at the pizza shop, traveling on the school bus, in the movies, and many other places. This is especially true toward the latter part of the period, at the age of 11 or 12 years. Although children in the middle childhood years are perhaps the most visible of all age groups, adults pay surprisingly little attention to children that age, in part because school and friends take up much of children's time (Collins, 1984). Also, the physical and psychological changes that children undergo during the middle childhood period do not attract adult attention since they are not as obvious as the changes that occur during infancy, early childhood, and adolescence (Ryan & Applegate, 1976; Shonkoff, 1984). However, physical and psychological changes do not have to be obvious to be important. Although unobtrusive, developmental changes do indeed take place during the middle childhood years, they are accentuated by the fact that the child starts school during this period. He is thus exposed to many different people and he must also adapt to new social rules and expectations which inevitably affect his development. Between the time the child enters school and the time he reaches adolescence, there are marked changes in his ability to learn, think, and remember. In addition, during these years, the child grows in his capacity for knowledge of the self and of the social world, and for the first time he is able to establish intimate friendships.

PROGRESS IN PHYSICAL GROWTH AND MOTOR DEVELOPMENT

During the middle childhood years there are also subtle but important changes in physical growth. Physical development during this period is characterized by a steady and sustained growth and by the child's increased ability to execute motor skills and master more complex and elaborate motor tasks (Shonkoff, 1984). Swimming, skiing, and learning to dance or to play a musical instrument are among the skills the child is able to master if given the opportunity.

Whereas the principles that were important for early physical development continue to characterize later growth, an additional consideration becomes important during the middle childhood years: physical growth assumes great personal significance, and the child's attitude about himself becomes related to his conception about his body size and shape. This occurs because during the middle childhood years the child is no longer egocentric in his outlook, and he acquires the ability to think about what other people think; thus, others' reactions to him become important. You will see in this chapter that while for most children the middle childhood years can be happy and carefree, some children, those who are shorter, taller, or fatter than others, may be conscious of their differences and of what other people think of them and can develop low self-esteem as a result. In addition, variation in growth becomes very apparent during the middle childhood years, thus there are great differences among children of the same age in height and in rate of maturation. Not only do children of the same age grow at different rates, children today are taller than they were in previous generations, and they also mature at an earlier age—a phenomenon known as the secular trend. Several factors account for this phenomenon and there are also consequences associated with early maturation, especially for girls. Before we discuss these, however, let us examine in some detail the progress in physical growth and motor development that occurs during the middle childhood years, and the social significance during this period of life of the child's increased ability to perform a wide range of motor tasks.

Motor Skills

Physical development during the middle childhood years proceeds at a slow, even rate. What is significant during this period is the substantial progress in motor development. This progress can be observed in the child's play behavior. The school-age child seems to be forever racing around the neighborhood, climbing, jumping, hopping, or skipping. He is always in a hurry to get someplace so he tends to run more often than he walks, and he frequently takes to scooters, wagons, bicycles, or skates. So much energy does the child put into his motor activities at this age, it often seems that if he could fly, he would.

There is improvement during the middle childhood years in the child's control and coordination of fine motor skills. When she first enters school, the child's writing is quite clumsy, but with increased maturity, her writing of letters, numbers, and words becomes progressively neater and smaller. During this period, the child can also learn to play musical instruments, a feat which requires dexterity and control over the small muscles of the hands and fingers, and she can engage in such tasks as sewing and knitting, or drawing pictures in minute detail, all activities which require fine motor control.

During the middle childhood years there is also improvement in gross motor skills. The progress made in motor development during this period reflects increased speed, power, coordination, agility, and balance, which are the basic components of motor fitness (Gallahue, 1982). Thus, the school-age child is able to improve continuously upon gross motor skills he previously acquired, and he also learns many new skills. He is able to run faster during the middle childhood years, and he also evidences greater accuracy and distance in his ability to hop and jump, and he is better able to throw, catch, and kick a ball (Corbin, 1973). Improvements in these basic motor skills enable the child to participate in team sports

FIGURE 10.1 During the middle childhood years, children avidly explore new activities, to the point that sometimes their daily chores and responsibilities are neglected.

such as basketball, football, and baseball. In addition, the child becomes increasingly more able to learn and master rather complex tasks such as dancing, swimming, roller skating, and playing tennis (see Figure 10.1). Many children display an intense interest in acquiring and improving these skills. As McNassor (1975) observes, "This is a period when most children explore a new interest so intensely that daily chores or responsibilities are thoroughly neglected. Their need is to find out what they can do well and what they are really good at."

The extent of the child's ability to acquire new motor skills and become adept at motor activities depends in large part on opportunity for learning, encouragement, and practice (Tanner, 1970). Children who are not given the opportunity to learn to swim will not be able to do so. Having learned to swim, children need to practice swimming in order to become proficient at it. So it is with other motor skills. However, opportunity for learning and practice in and of themselves are necessary but not sufficient conditions for the acquisition of motor skills, as the ability to execute many such skills also depends on genetic and physiological factors such as body size, strength, and brain maturation (Tanner, 1970). In addition, the extent to which children develop their genetic potential for

Poor Physical Fitness: An Unhealthy Trend Among School-Age Children

Although many school-age children enjoy participating in sports and other physical activities, they are, in general, substantially less active than were children two or three decades ago. This is not surprising considering that children today favor watching television as a pastime. Moreover, many children whose mothers work have to stay home alone and are thus deprived of the opportunity to engage in physical activities. The result is that children are not physically fit. *Physical fitness* refers not to athletic ability but to the optimal functioning of the heart, lungs, muscles, and blood vessels.

To maintain physical fitness, one has to engage in exercises or sports which work four areas: muscle strength, muscle endurance, flexibility, and cardiovascular functioning. While activities such as tennis and swimming enhance physical fitness, other sports, such as baseball, which are popular among school children do not. In baseball, the child engages in relatively little physical activity because only one player moves at a time, and then only intermittently.

The fact that children today are less physically fit than were children in past decades is revealed in a report of a national survey of 8,800 children age 10 to 18 years (*National Children and Youth Fitness Study,* 1984). The survey was conducted over a three-year period, and its findings indicate that children today are not only less physically active than were children in the 1960s, they are also generally fatter than children were then. The findings further indicated that children's heart-lung fitness lags behind that of most middle-aged joggers; that more than half of the children do not engage in any physical activities during the winter months; and that most children do not learn at school about activities they can pursue to improve their physical fitness.

This study is only one of several other studies (for example, American Academy of Pediatrics, 1985; Reif, 1985), each revealing the startling facts about the health status of children. The findings from these studies raise concerns because evidence has shown that becoming a physically fit person is a habit that is learned in childhood and must be continued through the adult years (Select Panel for the Promotion of Child Health, 1981; Richmond, 1977). What is more startling is that studies have shown that the tendency toward such physical problems as cardiovascular disease can start as early as first grade (American Academy of Pediatrics, 1985). It appears that children today evidence a trend toward such health problems in adulthood. Reif (1985) found that among 7- to 12-year-olds, body fat levels are on the average 2% to 5% above what is considered normal for optimal health, that 41% of the children have high levels of cholesterol in their blood, and that 28% have higher than normal blood pressure. Furthermore, Reif found that 98% of the children in his study had at least one symptom which presented them at major risk for developing coronary heart disease later in life.

The poor physical fitness of school-age children is a problem that has national significance. Fortunately, the problem lends itself to easy solutions. In a model program tested in the Michigan school districts, researchers found that after participating in a well-designed physical education program which required children to exercise regularly and to take responsibility for choosing the type of foods they eat, the children's body fat measurements dropped an average of 16%, their blood cholesterol levels dropped 4%, and their blood pressure dropped 6% (Kuntzleman, 1983).

Developing such programs does not ensure their implementation in the schools. When there are fiscal constraints such as those that most schools are now experiencing, physical education courses are among the first courses to be eliminated from the curriculum. The fact that many schools have either eliminated or reduced physical education requirements during the past few years has been cited as one contributing reason for the poor physical fitness of children (*National Children and Youth Fitness Study,* 1984).

We mention several times throughout this book that in a climate of fiscal austerity, priorities must be established and on the basis of these, programs developed and implemented. Schools have numerous responsibilities and tasks and fewer dollars to carry these out. Some people maintain that schools should not be held accountable for the physical fitness of children—their primary responsibility is to teach children basic learning skills. Others argue that health is a fundamental aspect of children's development and that a sound body contributes to a sound mind. Providing children with the opportunities to improve their physical fitness *enhances* rather than detracts from their education. What is your position? Assume you were to appear before the Board of Education of a particular school district to present your views on the matter, either for more physical education courses in the schools or for less. What would your argument be? How would you attempt to convince Board members to agree with you?

motor skills depends on temperament and personality factors such as energy level, venturesomeness, aggressiveness, and persistence (Ausubel, Sullivan, & Ives, 1980) as well as on children's attitudes toward their body build and their eagerness to participate in group functions and competition. Shy children or children with low self-esteem will have difficulty competing with other children, and, since motor skills are developed primarily in the context of the peer group, these children will miss out on the opportunity to acquire and develop such skills. But, it is important for children to acquire and become better at motor activities, for progress in these enables them to become active members of society. Children can participate in many social and sports functions such as summer camp, scouts groups, or little league teams, and thereby learn to interact with other children and adults in a variety of settings. Or, they can round up a neighborhood game of football or baseball, and this provides for them a context within which to develop friendships and share interests. You should recognize, however, that although many school-age children are interested in sports activities, there are just as many children who prefer to read, watch television, or simply talk to one another.

Individual and Sex Differences and Similarities

A child who is good at some motor skill such as running or jumping is often good in other motor skills as well (Espenschade, 1960), and there are some children who eventually become good, all-around athletes. There is a wide range of individual differences among children in the execution of motor skills and in their ability to master complex motor tasks. However, in their ability to acquire and execute motor skills, boys and girls do not evidence many differences, in large part because during this period physical differences between the two sexes are minimal. But, as is true during the preschool years, boys tend to have greater strength than do girls, and girls tend to have better balance and coordination. Thus, the two groups have certain advantages in performing certain skills. Keogh (1965), in a study of children ages 5 through 12, found that boys ran faster and for greater distances than did the girls and that they were also better at target throwing and grip strength. On the other hand, girls, have an edge over some boys in gymnastics and specifically in such skills as beam walking, especially during the early part of the middle childhood years (Gallahue, 1982).

However, during this period it is not the sex of the child that is the determining factor in the mastery of skills. Rather, age is an important factor, as both boys and girls improve their ability to execute motor skills as they grow older (Keogh, 1965). Practice is very important in the mastery of skills. Therefore, now that more girls are participating in such sports as baseball, their ability to master these equals that of boys.

Physical Growth

Since physical growth during the school-age years proceeds at a slow but fairly even pace, the child has the opportunity to develop interests, skills, and knowledge without being hampered by exhausting physical changes. The child gains an average of 5 pounds a year during this period, and he grows approximately 2½ inches a year (see Figures 10.2 and 10.3). Other changes that occur include increased skeletal and muscular growth as well as an increase in the heart's strength and in the capacity of the lungs. These are changes that enable the child to become stronger and to go for longer periods of time without rest. They also facilitate the progress in motor development that occurs during this period.

Changes in body proportions are also evident during this period. By the time he enters school, the child has lost the squat, chubby appearance characteristic of the early preschool period, and during the school-age years, as he becomes even taller and more slender, his body proportions seem more graceful and adult-like. In addition, during the school-age years, the child loses his deciduous teeth, which are replaced with permanent ones. This is a gradual process which continues throughout the middle childhood years and results in changes in facial proportions as the child's jaw becomes increasingly larger.

Variations in Activity Level: Hyperactive and Hypoactive Children

It becomes apparent during this period that there is a wide range of individual differences among children in physical development. Some differences are related to activity level. These differences are present in infancy and the early childhood years, as some babies and young children seem more active than others, and some children are quiet and calm in their temperament (Thomas, Chess, & Birch, 1968). During the middle childhood years, however, these differences become accentuated, in part because the children are at school where they are required to sit still most of the time and to attend to specific tasks for increasingly long periods of time. Whereas most children can do so, in virtually every classroom there are two or three children, usually boys, who cannot sit still and whose behavior is described as hyperactive, distractible, impulsive, irritable, moody, slow learner, and inattentive (Cohen, 1977; see Figure 10.4). Until recently, children who exhibited these behaviors were said to suffer from the *hyperactive syndrome* or from *minimal brain dysfunction (MBD)*. Both terms were applied indiscriminately to any child who was inattentive, impulsive, or hyperactive. Within the last decade, significant advances have been made in the understanding of such children, and re-

hyperactivity

minimal brain dysfunction (MBD)

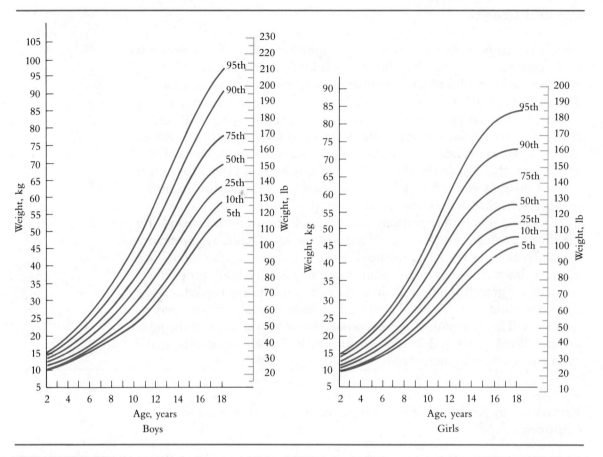

FIGURE 10.2 Weight gains during the middle childhood years. From the National Center for Health Statistics, 1976.

attention deficit disorder (ADD)

searchers have coined the term *attention deficit disorder* (*ADD*) to help explain the symptoms (Shaywitz & Shaywitz, 1984).

ADD is a relatively common disorder which occurs more frequently among boys than among girls; for every 4 boys who are characterized by hyperactivity and inattentiveness, there is only one girl who exhibits such behaviors (Cohen, 1977). These children tend to move from one site to another, they are unable to inhibit action, and they are constantly diverted by sounds and objects. Not only are the children chaotic in their behavior, they also tend to forget what they are told to do, and they seem at a loss when asked to engage in sequentially ordered behaviors (for example, when they are asked to go outside and fetch something). Thus, the children evoke a great deal of anger and frustration in their parents and teachers so that they are often scolded and punished (Cantwell, 1975). Their chaotic behavior annoys other children as much as it annoys adults, so such children are not popular among their peers.

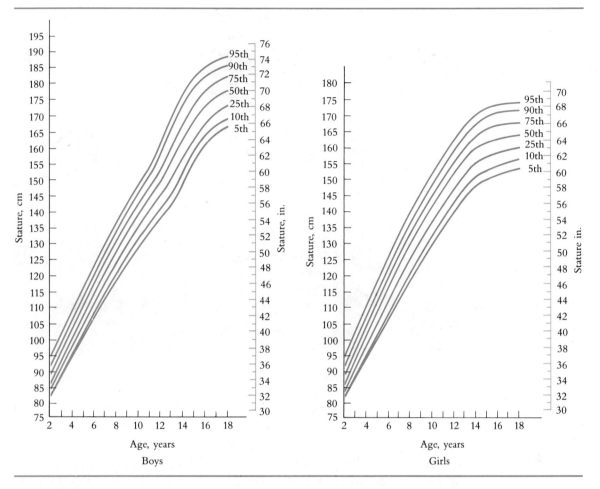

FIGURE 10.3   Height gains during the middle childhood years. From the National Center for Health Statistics, 1976.

Children with attentional problems may have a learning disability as well. They may seem normal when they are on the playground, because it is only when they are required to sit still that the disorder is evident. Whereas most people are annoyed by the ADD child who evidences hyperactivity because such a child is considerably more active and distracting than other children, there are some ADD children who are *hypoactive*.   *hypoactivity*
This form of attentional behavior disturbance is more common in girls than in boys, and is characterized by less than normal activity levels and excessive daydreaming. Hypoactive children may be quiet and undistracting in their behavior, but like the hyperactive children, they too are unable to attend to specific tasks. In the case of hypoactive children, however, their attentional deficits may go unnoticed for many years simply because they tend to be good and compliant in their behavior (Cohen, 1977).

FIGURE 10.4 Differences in activity levels among children are present even in early infancy. However, these differences become accentuated once the children are in school, where they are required to sit still for relatively long periods of time.

In the past, children with attentional problems were severely punished and even expelled from school (Ross & Ross, 1982). Although there are still ADD children who are scolded for their behavior, especially in the case of those who are hyperactive, during the past three decades there has been increased recognition that these children need help and that they cannot control their behavior because they have problems in cognitive processing, attentional regulation, and motor control (Cohen, 1977; Shaywitz & Shaywitz, 1984). The etiology of these problems is not entirely understood or agreed upon. Some researchers provide a biological explanation, arguing that prenatal and perinatal events (excessive radiation and smoking by the mother during pregnancy, lack of oxygen and head trauma during birth) are to blame (Shaywitz & Shaywitz, 1984). There are also those who note that there may be a genetic component to ADD since children who evidence the disorder often have siblings or parents who experienced similar problems (Pauls, Shaywitz, Kramer, Shaywitz, & Cohen, 1983). Food additives and allergies to certain foods have also been implicated as possible causes of ADD, most notably hyperactivity (Feingold, 1975).

Other researchers provide a social explanation for ADD, stressing the fact that the hyperactive behavior evidenced by some ADD children is defined by the child's social environment (Conrad, 1976). Thus, when a child's behavior is socially deviant, it is the family or the school that "creates" such a behavior by labeling the child as such. Lambert and Hartsough (1984) provide yet an additional explanation, noting that the problem may stem from an interaction between biological status and the child's social environment. Children who are unable to modulate their activity and regulate their attention (a biological factor) tend to evoke anger in those around them (an environmental factor) and so their difficulties are exacerbated.

Not only are there disagreements regarding the causes of ADD, there are also controversies surrounding the treatment of the disorder. These controversies stem largely from the fact that the children are given stimulant drugs. These drugs paradoxically have a calming effect on the children and are said to result in improved attentiveness, school work, and social performance (Fish, 1971; Cohen, 1977). However, there are some sides effects as well, as often the drugs may interfere with physical growth. This side effect can be prevented, however, if the children are taken off the drugs for a period of time when growth can resume. Other side effects include diminished appetite and loss of weight.

Besides concerns about the side effects of the drugs, there are also concerns that the drugs do not enhance children's ability to learn, that they dull the children's minds, and that they are addictive (Safer, 1971). Critics of drug use as a treatment for ADD contend that drugs are prescribed not because they are beneficial but as a means of avoiding real school reform (Safer, 1971; Whalen & Henker, 1976). It is difficult to establish the effectiveness of drug treatment; more longitudinal research is necessary. It could well be that whereas drug treatment is effective for some children, it is ineffective for others (Fish, 1971). Given the wide range of individual differences in temperament and activity levels among all children, not only those who are considered hyperactive, care must be taken to carefully evaluate the children before they are labeled hyperactive or hypoactive and before any medication is prescribed. Professionals further note that even when drugs are considered appropriate, they should not be prescribed indiscriminately. Careful evaluation of each child is needed, as is the monitoring of the child once the drug is prescribed (Fish, 1971; Cohen, 1977).

Besides drug treatment, there are other treatment possibilities that are advocated either instead of or in conjunction with drugs. These include behavior modification techniques, psychotherapy, and physical education, which helps children acquire more coordination and mastery over their bodies and movements (Cohen, 1977; Shaywitz & Shaywitz, 1984). Other treatment suggestions include changing the child's school and

FIGURE 10.5   Surprisingly, these girls are the same age!

home environment so that these have as few distractions as possible, as ADD children can learn better in such environments (Cruikshank, 1977), or eliminating certain foods from the child's diet (Feingold, 1975). Unfortunately, there is no evidence that these suggestions are effective.

Variations in Growth

Also apparent during the middle childhood years are variations in children's growth, alerting us to the fact that children, just like adults, differ. Some are naturally tall and slender, some short and chubby, and others skinny or muscular. Children not only differ in their body builds, they also grow at different rates. How fast they grow depends on genetic inheritance, nutrition, and physical and emotional health (Tanner, 1970; Roberts, 1969). Thus, even among children who are well fed and healthy, there are individual differences in rates of growth, and some children are fast, slow, or average growers. The variations in rates of growth are especially noticeable in children's height and result in great differences among age mates. Thus, if you enter a fourth-grade classroom and pick out the shortest 10-year-old and the tallest 10-year-old, the difference between them may be so striking that it will be hard for you to believe they are the same age (see Figure 10.5). Variations in height among children of the

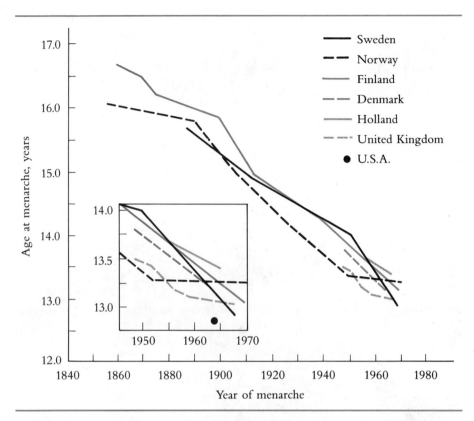

FIGURE 10.6   The secular trend in age at menarche, 1860–1970. From Tanner, J. M. (1978). *Foetus into man*. Cambridge, MA: Harvard Univ. Press, p. 152, fig. 49.

same age are especially evident when children from different countries are compared. Meredith (1969, 1971) found that among 8-year-old children from different countries, there is as much as a nine- to eighteen-inch difference in height, with the shortest children being from Southeast Asia and South America and the tallest from the United States and Europe.

The Secular Trend

An even more astounding aspect of physical growth is the difference among children of different generations, a phenomenon referred to as the secular trend, a term which describes the changes in physical growth over time as found in large samples of populations (Roche, 1979). Secular change is measured for different aspects of growth, including the rate of maturation and height. As you can see in Figure 10.6, the age of maturation of girls has decreased notably in the past few decades, showing that girls mature earlier today than they ever did before.

FIGURE 10.7 Improved health and nutrition are two of the causes cited for earlier maturation of both boys and girls.

menarche

    The age of maturation used for the purposes of measuring the secular trend is determined for girls by the onset of *menarche,* the first menstrual period. The secular trend for girls' maturation means that girls are becoming sexually mature at increasingly younger ages, and that more girls are capable of sexual reproduction during their childhood years. Boys also reach sexual maturity at an earlier age, but for boys the physiological and social implications of early maturation are not as significant as they are in girls (see Figure 10.7).

DISCUSSION OF SOCIAL ISSUES:
WHEN CHILDREN BEAR CHILDREN

In addition to the trend for early maturation, our society has also experienced changes which have contributed to sexual experimentation among children. The sexual revolution, spawned as a social protest on college campuses in the 1960s, has filtered down to high schools, junior high schools, and even elementary schools. Children are engaging in sex at a younger age than ever before, and much more frequently (Zelnik & Kantner, 1978).

One disturbing consequence of both early maturation and the trend for advanced sexuality is that about 1.2 million young girls become pregnant each year. Many of these girls are 10 to 14 years of age (U.S. Department of HHS, 1983). Of the 1.2 million preteen and teen pregnancies, about 100,000 end in miscarriage or stillbirth. About 449,000 preteen and teenage girls choose abortion. Over half of the girls (560,000) give birth each year (Alan Guttmacher Institute, 1981). Of these, 97 percent decide to keep the baby (Zelnik & Kantner, 1978).

Many problems are associated with the phenomenon of children bearing children, both for the young mother and for the baby. The mother is at risk for health complications as well as other problems that may stem from her emotional immaturity and the fact that she is young and without the financial resources necessary to be able to take care of herself and her child. The child born to the young mother is also at risk. Studies suggest that infants born to preteen and teenage mothers show deficits in physical health and in socioemotional and cognitive development (Center for Disease Control, 1980). These deficits may be related to the fact that young mothers are emotionally immature and therefore unable to provide nurturance for their babies. There are also other factors that affect the development of babies born to preteen and teen mothers that are related to the economic and educational disadvantages of the mother (Mednick, Baker, & Sutton-Smith, 1979). Studies reveal that when other adults are present in the home of the young mother and baby, the negative outcomes on the baby's socio-emotional and cognitive development and physical health are significantly lessened (Baldwin & Cain, 1980). In addition, when young mothers are provided with some emotional support and/or counseling after the birth of the baby, they are often able to continue their education, and they exhibit fewer problems and fewer repeat pregnancies than do mothers who do not receive such support (Badger, 1980).

Numerous programs have been developed in schools, hospitals, and community health centers to address the needs of pregnant girls and young mothers and to facilitate the development of their infants. There are also programs that address the needs of teen fathers (Klinman & Kohl, 1984).

While supportive programs for preteen and teenage parents are important, professionals and parents are advocating that attention be paid to the prevention of pregnancies as well. Whereas there is agreement that pregnancies among young girls should be prevented, there is some controversy as to the best method of prevention. This controversy stems in part from disagreements about the underlying causes of increased sexual activity and pregnancies among children (see Figure 10.8).

Some researchers note that the phenomenon of children bearing children is an outcome of a biological revolution associated with the secular trend for early sexual maturation. The average age at which American girls begin menstruating has been dropping about six months each decade (Tanner, 1970). Thus, one third of American girls are experiencing menarche before or during their twelfth year. Menarche is, for some girls, followed by a period of sterility, since it does not always occur in conjunction with ovulation, but for the most part menarche is taken to mean that the girl has become physiologically capable of reproduction. In addition, menarche is associated with the onset of sexual urges (Tanner, 1978). Researchers note that sexual feelings, along with the current trend for children to engage in sexual activity and the fact that during their preadolescent and early adolescent years children are likely to conform to the peer group are creating pressures for many girls that did not exist in prior generations. In 1840, for example, the average age at which the American girl experienced menarche was 17. Shortly after that she was married and became pregnant. Today, not only do girls reach sexual maturity earlier, they also tend to marry later.

Some experts note that to expect girls to abstain from sexual relations until they marry is physiologically unreasonable and also unrealistic, thus efforts should be made to attempt to reverse the trend for early maturation. Frisch (1974 & 1978) contends that this can be achieved in part through programs of strenuous exercise during the middle childhood years, since girls are experiencing menarche at an earlier age largely because of changes in dietary habits and a decrease in physical exercise which result in an increase in fat tissue. Frisch notes that 2 or 3 years before menarche, fat tissue increases 125 percent, with the critical weight for menarche being around 98 to 125 pounds. However, Frisch's suggestion is only theoretical. In addition, you should note that while early maturation is a factor in the phenomenon of children bearing children, it is only part of the problem since many girls have sexual relations and become pregnant during adolescence.

Others who agree that it is unrealistic to expect children to abstain from sexual relations suggest that the problem of preteen and teenage pregnancies can be prevented by providing and teaching the use of contraceptives (Freeman, 1980; Bran, 1979). In addition, many experts call for sex education as a preventive measure. These recommendations are made in light of evidence which suggests that children who are sexually active

WHEN CHILDREN BEAR CHILDREN

FIGURE 10.8   Every year about 1.2 million girls between the ages of 10 and 14 become pregnant; 97% of them decide to keep their babies. The school dropout rate for these young mothers is 5 times greater than for girls the same age who do not have babies. With limited education and poor prospects for employment, both the mothers and their children face lives of hardship and deprivation.

are ignorant of the hazards and consequences of sexual activity (Furstenberg, 1976). However, the use of contraceptives and sex education are controversial political issues. They are opposed by some people on the basis of moral and religious beliefs, and also on the grounds that they would promote sexual activity and result in more pregnancies rather than in their prevention (Dryfoos & Heisler, 1981). These objections are made despite the fact that there are numerous studies which indicate otherwise and which document the fact that sex education in particular can help young people avoid engaging in irresponsible sexual behavior (Scales & Gordon, 1978; Scales, 1976).

Sex education programs have not been available to all children, especially during the middle childhood years (Alan Guttmacher Institute,

1981). Our failure to implement sex education programs stems from other factors besides outright objections to these as a method of preventing pregnancies among young girls. Furstenberg (1976) notes that our failure to implement sex education stems from our society's emphasis on cure rather than on prevention.

> The general approach to social problems in American society is reactive rather than preventive. This posture might be understandable if preventive strategies were difficult to devise, but this excuse hardly seems to apply in the case of adolescent parenthood. We possess both the knowledge and the knowhow and the techniques to reduce the incidence of early pregnancy and limit the number of adolescent mothers. . . . Despite the fact that a clear majority of Americans favor birth control services for the sexually active teenager, and can endorse sex education in the schools, some institutional resistance and a great deal of inertia have blocked the development of widespread and intensive sex education and family planning service programs for teenagers. Few populations are as potentially accessible to these services as are school-age youth. Yet school systems have been avoided, by-passed, and ignored as sites for pregnancy prevention programs.

Even among those who believe that knowledge about sexuality and reproduction is a fundamental aspect of every child's education and that it should begin early, there are disagreements about whether sex education should be taught in schools or in the home. Some contend that parents should be the ones to teach children about sex. Yet, studies show that most parents fail to give their children sex education and that most children are either afraid to or are uncomfortable about approaching their parents regarding sexual matters (General Mills, 1977). As a result, most children obtain their sex education from their equally misinformed friends or they get distorted information about sex from television (Scales, 1976). Gordon and Scales (1979) note that the problem of preteen and teenage pregnancies stems from just this lack of closeness between parents and their children and from the fact that children are more likely to be influenced by their friends than they are by their parents. So, you can see that just as there are multiple factors underlying the phenomenon of children bearing children, there are also multiple factors that inhibit our prevention of the problem. This is tragic, for young girls who engage in sexual relations and who become pregnant do not realize the changes in lifestyle that having a baby entails. Most young mothers tend to drop out of school once they have a baby, even though the majority of them say they want to finish their education (Alan Guttmacher Institute, 1981) and despite the fact that many schools now have special provisions for the education of preteen and teen mothers. The dropout rate for young mothers is five times greater than it is for other girls their age who do not have a baby (Furstenberg, 1976). As a result of their limited education, these young mothers are less likely to find employment, and they begin a cycle of dependence on welfare.

The Secular Trend for Stature

The secular trend also reveals that children are growing taller. The secular trend for stature (height) evidences the fact that for the last several generations, the average height of children has been increasing. This is especially evident during the middle childhood years. In a study of British children it is noted that children between the ages of 6 and 12 are significantly taller now than were the children in previous generations (Tanner, 1978.) This phenomenon is also noted in a study of American children, for whom there has been an increase of about 1 inch per decade between the ages of 6 and 15 years. After that age, the secular trend is not quite so noticeable. Much of the trend in children's height is due to their reaching their adult height sooner (Meredith, 1976). This means that on the average, school-age children today are 4 inches taller than were school-age children 40 years ago (Roche, 1979).

There are several possible causes for the secular changes in reproductive maturation and in stature. According to Tanner (1978), better nutrition is a major factor. That children are not subjected to as many illnesses as in the past is another factor. An additional explanation, especially with regard to increases in height, is genetic. Researchers note that some degree of dominance occurs in some genes governing stature (Damon, 1968). This means that when a person who carries mostly genes for short stature marries a person who carries genes for tallness, the height of their offspring would not lie on the average exactly halfway between, but a little on the tall side (Garn, 1966). Since genetic dominance does exist in relation to stature, then outbreeding (breeding outside of one's genetic background) results in increasingly taller offspring over successive generations. Such social factors as immigration laws, which significantly contribute to changes in the ethnic makeup of nations, and marriage patterns are likely to be reflected in secular trends. Although secular changes have been rather dramatic since the turn of the century due to improved health and nutrition and societal changes that have resulted in genetically homogeneous nations, there is speculation that the secular trend for early sexual maturation and for height does have a ceiling and will eventually level off (Roche, 1979).

Variations in Height

Although school-age children are taller now than were children of previous generations, the gains in height during this period are not so significant when compared to gains in height during infancy or adolescence. In fact, as you can see in Figure 10.9, which depicts the average heights of children at different ages as well as the increments in height from one age to the next, growth in height proceeds on a fairly even course throughout

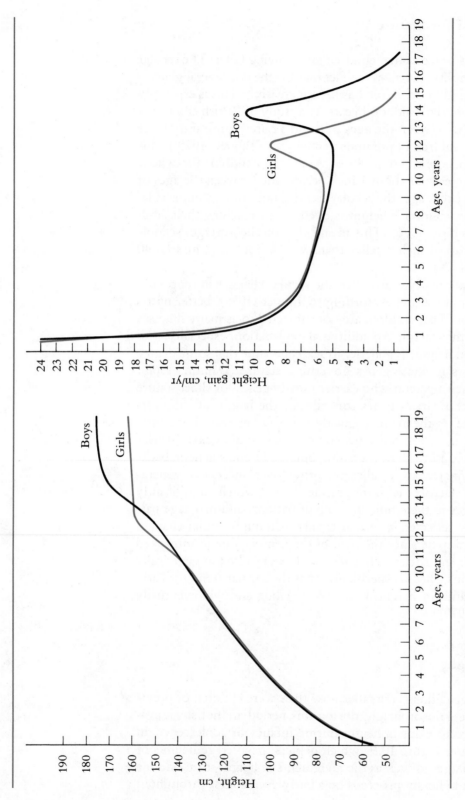

FIGURE 10.9 Typical height (left graph) and velocity (right graph) growth curves. The velocity of growth decreases from birth until puberty and then increases when the adolescent growth spurt occurs. At all ages until adolescence, the average girl is slightly shorter than the average boy. Then, because the adolescent growth spurt starts usually two years earlier for girls than for boys, girls become taller than boys during early puberty. The average boy then surpasses the average girl in height following his growth spurt. During the growth spurts of both sexes, the boys' peak height velocity is greater than the girls'. From Tanner, J. M. (1978). *Foetus into man*. Cambridge, MA: Harvard Univ. Press, p. 13, fig. 4 and p. 14, fig. 5.

FIGURE 10.10   During adolescence, it is not unusual for boys to be very different in height from their age-mates. However, during the middle childhood years
parents become concerned if their child is shorter than his peers.

the childhood years. It is not until adolescence that the individual undergoes a growth spurt. However, during this period the fact that there are
variations in height from child to child is significant. Parents often become concerned about their child's height, and they tend to use height
(probably because it is the most obvious aspect of growth) as the criterion
against which to evaluate the child's progress in physical development
(Tanner, 1978). They worry if one of their sons is shorter than the other
(Goldstein & Peckham, 1976) or when their child is either much taller or
much shorter than his or her age-mates (see Figure 10.10).

FIGURE 10.11 (above and on facing page) Like adults, children have various body types.

PHYSICAL GROWTH: IMPLICATIONS FOR PSYCHOLOGICAL DEVELOPMENT

Variations in height are not a source of concern from a medical point of view since even very tall children or very short children can be given hormone treatment to correct the disorder. Even if the disorder is not corrected, being too tall or too short is not a life-threatening or a particularly serious medical condition. In our society, however, deviating from the norm is not only a source of concern to parents, it can be emotionally traumatic for the children involved. In fact, being too small, too tall, or too fat is a source of embarrassment for many children during the middle childhood years, for during this period relationships with peers become important, and being regarded as different, or feeling different, tends to detract from a child's status in the peer group (Ausubel, Sullivan, & Ives, 1980). Children who are somewhat different from their peers in physical appearance, maybe because they are fat, for example, tend to be teased, picked on, and even rejected; they come to realize that they are different and may hate themselves as a result (Eveleth & Tanner, 1976).

Body Type and Personality

You can see that physical development has many implications for the child's social and emotional development. Physical development is associated with psychological development in other ways, too, as some researchers note that many aspects of an individual's physique, or body type, may be associated with a particular personality type. However, even if an individual's physique and personality are to a degree related, it is not easy to determine a cause and effect pattern between these two factors. That is, does one's body type cause one to have a particular type of personality or does one's personality type contribute to one's physique?

A well-known researcher who studied body type and personality is Sheldon (1940). His work has been criticized on methodological grounds and thus cannot be taken as valid. However, his studies are useful in that they suggest that there are three basic body types: endomorphous, mesomorphous, and ectomorphous, which are defined, respectively, by a predominance of fat, amount of muscle, and length of bone (see Figure 10.11). An *endomorphic* person is soft and round. A *mesomorphic* person is broad-shouldered, lean, and muscular. An *ectomorphic* person is tall and

endomorphous
mesomorphous
ectomorphous

very thin, tending to be stoop-shouldered. While most people have elements of all three body types, in many cases it is possible to identify a dominant theme in each individual. To test the hypothesis that a particular body type is associated with a particular temperament, Sheldon examined the degree of relationship between the two variables. Because of methodological difficulties associated with his research, some researchers contend that Sheldon's findings are invalid. Nevertheless, other studies suggest that there is some truth to his hypothesis. For example, teachers and parents rate endomorphic, or plump, girls as highly cooperative and ectomorphic, or thin, boys and girls as uncooperative, emotionally restrained, and aloof. Mesomorphic, or muscular, boys are rated as leaders and as having a great deal of confidence (Walker, 1962).

Cause or Effect?   It is important to remember that discovering a relationship between two variables such as body type and personality traits does not clarify the direction of causality. A number of environmental factors do impinge upon physical development, and there is no question that environmental factors also influence personality traits such as temperament. Thus, the relationship between body type and personality may be due to a series of complex interactions between individuals and their environments.

One explanation is that temperament results in part from the fact that individuals of different body types engage in different types of activities, which, in turn, affect the reaction of others. For example, the mesomorphic boy, who is strong and muscular, is much more likely to try to hang off a tree limb by his knees, and succeed at it, than is a boy of another body type. Other children admire and praise this feat, thus making the boy the center of attention and giving him a sense of being effective. Such a boy is chosen first when athletic games are played, and, because he has the admiration of his peers, he often assumes leadership roles. Thus the reaction of others affects the self-image of the child and enables him to become a leader. A lifetime of such psychological conditioning could well explain the relationship sometimes observed between body type and temperament, so it is not surprising that the lean, muscular type is often associated with the successful executive type as an adult (Cortes & Gatti, 1965).

Social Expectations.   Another explanation for the relationship found between body type and personality is the existence of societal stereotypes concerning ways in which people with particular body types are supposed to behave. How an individual acts is in large measure determined by how others react to him. Some strong stereotypes exist for various physiques. In several studies, people have been asked to describe the psychological characteristics of people with a particular body type. A clear finding is that the preferred body type is the mesomorph. In a study with adults, Brodsky (1954) found that the mesomorph was viewed as the individual who would make the best athlete, best soldier, and most successful leader. People also expected the mesomorph to be able to endure pain the best and was the individual they would most prefer as a friend. Having nothing to guide them other than the silhouette, people also noted that the mesomorph would not smoke at all, would drink the least, would be self-sufficient, and would never have a nervous breakdown! In studies using children, the mesomorphic body type was also the most preferred. Children expected this type of person to be brave, good looking, happy, strong, helpful, and intelligent (Lerner, 1969).

The least favorable stereotype among both adults and children was that of the endomorph, who was described by adults as the person who would make the worse athlete, soldier, and leader; who would be the least aggressive; and who would be least preferred as a friend. Staffieri (1967) found that mesomorphs were picked by children as "one of 5 best friends" more often than were endomorphs and ectomorphs and that the endomorphs were the least popular of the three body types. These findings suggest that the stereotypes about body build are developed early in the lives of children and could cause some children to be unhappy with and to reject their body type. If this dissatisfaction becomes great enough, it alone can produce the negative behavior attributed to the endomorphic and ectomorphic physique.

You should note, however, that while in some cases we can see a link between body type and personality, there are individual differences among all children. Just as there are some plump girls who feel shy and self-conscious and embarrassed by their figures, so there are other girls of the same body build who are socially outgoing and happy and who consider themselves good looking just the way they are.

SUMMARY

We have seen in this chapter that whereas physical growth during the middle childhood years proceeds at a slow, steady pace, the progress in motor development during this period is significant. This includes increased control over fine motor skills, as reflected by increases in speed, power, coordination, agility, and balance, which are the basic components of gross motor fitness. The school-age child is able to improve upon skills he previously acquired, and he can also learn many new skills such as playing a musical instrument, swimming, skiing, ballet dancing, or playing a variety of sports. The ability to learn these skills depends on opportunity for learning, practice, and encouragement. Children who are not given the opportunity to learn to swim, for example, will not be able to do so. Acquiring the ability to execute many motor skills is of great interest to school-age children. It is also important to their social development, for it enables them to participate in different social and sports functions and thereby to interact with other children and adults in a variety of settings.

There are wide differences among children in the extent to which they can execute motor skills. There are also variations in children's physical growth and development. These variations become especially apparent during the middle childhood years, in part because children grow at different rates. Some are slow growers, others are average or fast growers. Not only are there variations in growth among children, but children today seem to grow at a faster rate than did children of previous generations, a phenomenon known as the secular trend. The secular trend also reveals that children attain sexual maturity at an earlier age. As a result, some children are capable of sexual reproduction during the middle childhood years. One consequence of this trend is the increase in the number of children bearing children. Studies indicate that over one million preteen and teenage girls become pregnant each year and that the largest increase is occurring among girls who are age 10 to 14 years. The phenomenon of children bearing children is tragic, and it is associated with several physiological and social consequences for the young mothers and their babies. Young mothers are 5 times more likely to drop out of school than are other girls their age, and, with limited education, they are less likely to find and keep a job. Yet, the problem of preteen and teen pregnancies continues to be pervasive, in large part because we do not yet know all the factors that underlie the problem, and there are also disagreements about the best method for its prevention.

Children are also growing taller. School-age children today are about 4 inches taller than were school-age children 40 years ago. Growth in height is an important aspect of physical development during the school-age years even though there are no rapid increments in height during this period. However, because of great variations in children's height at this time, the child's height is often a source of concern for many parents who often focus on growth disorders. For most children there are no growth problems. However, some growth disorders such as extreme tallness for girls or an extreme short stature for either boys or girls do exist and can be treated.

Being too tall or too short is not a particularly serious physiological condition. However, it can have consequences for the child's socioemotional development. Being different can detract from children's status in the peer group, alerting us to the fact that physical development has implications for social and emotional development. Indeed, physical development is related to other aspects of psychological development, as one's physique, or body type, is associated with a particular personality type. While researchers know that physique and personality are related to a degree, it is not easy to determine whether the child's body type causes her to have a particular type of personality or vice versa. However, researchers note that children who are lean, muscular, and broad-shouldered tend to be popular among their peers and with adults, and they also exhibit personality traits associated with leadership and success. Children who are thin and tall, or who are plump, however, are not well liked, and many of them exhibit negative personality traits. In large part, the relationship found between body type and personality is related to social expectations and strong stereotypes that exist for various physiques which can cause children to develop different conceptions about themselves. In addition, school-age children become very aware of their body type and tend to have an awareness of the self in relation to what others think, an aspect of development that also extends to other areas.

REVIEW POINTS

1. Physical development during the middle childhood years proceeds at a slow, even rate. However, there are significant advances during this period in motor development. The child improves in both gross and fine motor skills, and she can engage in numerous sports and other activities that require speed, power, coordination, agility, and balance. Included among these activities are dancing, swimming, and playing basketball, football, and baseball. To perform well at such skills the child needs the opportunity to engage in and also practice them.

2. Because physical growth during the middle childhood years is relatively slow, the child has the opportunity to acquire interests and social skills without being hampered by exhausting physical changes.

3. There are individual differences among children, and these become especially noticeable during the middle childhood years. Some of the variations are related to activity level, with some children being hyperactive and some hypoactive. Hyperactivity and hypoactivity are related to attention deficit disorders.

4. There are also variations in children's growth—some children are tall and slender, others are short and chubby. Furthermore, children differ in their rate of growth. During the past few decades there have also been changes in the secular trend, meaning that today, children are taller than were children of previous generations, and they also mature faster.

5. The secular trend for maturation of girls is determined by the onset of menarche, the first menstrual period. The secular trend reveals that girls are becoming sexually mature at a younger age. This fact, coupled with society's more liberal views on sexual activities, is said to have contributed, in part, to the phenomenon of children bearing children. About 1.2 million preteen and teenage girls become pregnant each year. Many of the girls choose to keep their babies. Preteen and teenage mothers and their babies are at risk for a variety of social, emotional, and health problems. Thus far prevention of the phenomenon of increased pregnancies among teens and preteens has been hampered by disagreements and controversies and by limited knowledge of some of the causes of the problem.

6. Physical growth has important implications for psychological development, especially during the middle childhood years. During this period the child becomes aware of how other people react to and think of him. Some children who feel that they are physically different from others, either because they are too tall, too short, or perhaps fat, may feel self-conscious and may come to have a low self-image.

CHAPTER 11

COGNITIVE DEVELOPMENT DURING MIDDLE CHILDHOOD

The beginning of the middle childhood period marks a transition in the child's life. At this time, the child is enrolled in school and begins formal schooling for the first time. Admittedly, many children who attend day-care centers, nursery schools, and kindergarten are exposed to educational experiences during their preschool years. Yet, even these children and their parents regard being in the first grade as a turning point in the child's life—a time when the child is expected to engage in intellectual pursuits and a time when education is to be taken seriously. Not only in our society but in other cultures as well, children around the age of 6 or 7 experience a change in adults' expectations of their abilities. Whereas in our culture, children around this age begin school, in other cultures children this age begin to assume the roles and responsibilities required of the adults in their society. Recall that even during the Middle Ages, at the age of 7 children were no longer regarded as dependent. They were accepted as part of the community of men and women and were expected to share in adults' pastimes and responsibilities. The fact that adults in almost all societies expect more of the child when she reaches the school-age period is not coincidental, however. Significant changes in development occur at this time which make the child amenable to the demands of the school and of increased responsibility. These changes include the ability to give sustained attention to the task at hand, in addition to a range of other physical and physiological changes. Most importantly, as you will see in this chapter, the child shifts to a higher level of cognitive development so that she acquires mental abilities that enable her to engage in academic tasks and to profit from formal instruction.

COGNITIVE DEVELOPMENT

The Concrete Operations Period

During the middle childhood years, between the ages of approximately 7 and 12 years, the child is in the concrete operations period of cognitive development. During this period the child exhibits greater flexibility of thought than in the preoperational period, as well as the ability to think logically. She is capable of organizing her ideas in a systematic fashion, and her thinking is no longer dominated by immediate visual impressions, as was true during the preoperational period of cognitive development. In addition, the child is now able to perform *mental operations*. This means *mental* that she can mentally transform, modify, or otherwise manipulate what *operations* she sees or hears according to logical rules. For example, she is able not only to verbalize numbers but also to mentally manipulate numbers. Reversibility is the key here. As the child learns to add, subtract, multiply, and divide, she is also aware that one mental activity such as adding, as in $2 + 2 = 4$, is related to another activity such as subtracting. By *reversing*

FIGURE 11.1a   A child in the concrete operations period no longer relies on immediate perceptions, as was true in the previous period of cognitive growth. When the liquid from a short, wide container is poured into a tall, narrow container, the child knows that the amount of liquid has not changed.

the process, she is able to figure out that $4 - 2 = 2$. When the child is able to mentally manipulate information in this way, her thinking is said to become *operational*. However, the child is capable of performing mental operations only on concrete and tangible objects or on signs of these objects (as in word problems) but not on hypothetical ideas. Hence, Piaget called this the concrete operations period. It is not until the subsequent stage of cognitive development, the formal operations period, that the child will be able to apply her mental abilities to events and ideas that are abstract.

Impressed with the growth of thinking that occurs during the concrete operations period, Piaget noted that one of the most important aspects of operational thought is *reversibility*, which is the ability to perform mental inversions, or to mentally undo a sequence of actions. This new ability not only enhances the child's ability to figure out mathematical problems, but also, the child can draw conclusions about observed outcomes not on the basis of how things appear to be, as is the case with a child in the preoperational period of cognitive development, but on the basis of prior

reversibility

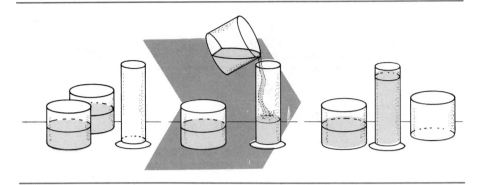

FIGURE 11.1b   Conservation of liquid.

relationships. This evidences her sensitivity to distinctions between what seems to be and what really is (Flavell, 1985). For example, if you take two short wide glasses of milk and pour the milk from one of the glasses into a tall narrow glass (see Figure 11.1a and b), the preoperational child, relying on her immediate perception of a single feature, say the height of the glass, arrives at the conclusion that the tall narrow glass contains more milk than the short wide glass. The child in the concrete operations period, however, does not have to rely on immediate perceptions. Rather, she is able to reverse the action, and, mentally pouring the milk from the tall glass into its original container, she recognizes that the amount of milk has not changed.

A related aspect of concrete operational thought is the ability to *decenter*. This means that the child can focus on multiple features of an object at the same time. The preoperational child can concentrate on only a single feature at a time, say the *height* of the glass of milk. The concrete operations child takes into account all relevant perceptual data and can focus on both the height and the width of the glass at the same time. She also realizes that one feature, such as the narrowness of the glass, makes up or compensates for its other feature, height, so that a shorter but wider glass holds the same amount of milk as the tall but narrow glass. This ability to recognize that a change in one feature is balanced by an equal and opposite change in another is known as *reciprocity*.

decenter

reciprocity

Conservation

Having acquired these mental abilities, the concrete operational child is able to approach problem solving in a more precise and logical manner than she was able to in the previous period of cognitive development. Piaget demonstrated this in his investigation of *conservation,* which, you recall, refers to the ability to recognize that two equal quantities remain equal even if one is changed in some way, as long as nothing has been

Various types of conservation

	Start With	Then	Ask The Child	Preoperational Children usually Answer
Conservation of Liquids	Two equal glasses of liquid. 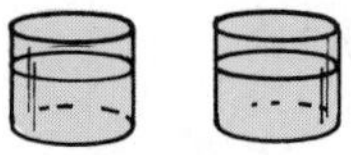	Pour one into a taller, thinner glass. 	Which glass contains more?	The taller one.
Conservation of Number	Two equal lines of checkers. 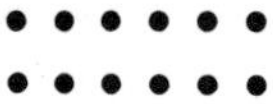	Lengthen the spaces between one line. 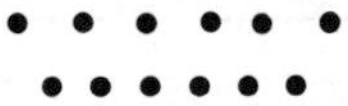	Which line has more checkers?	The longer one.
Conservation of Matter	Two equal balls of clay. 	Squeeze one ball into a long, thin shape. 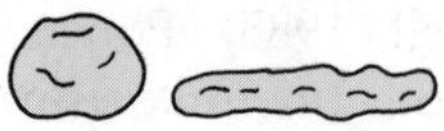	Which piece has more clay?	The long one.
Conservation of Length	Two sticks of equal length. 	Move one stick. 	Which stick is longer?	The one that is farther to the right.
Conservation of Volume	Two glasses of water with equal balls of clay inside. 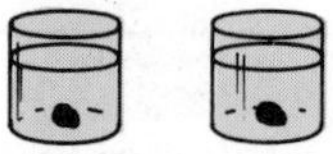	Change the shape of one ball. 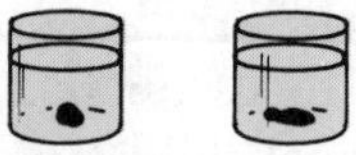	Which piece of clay will displace more water?	The long one.
Conservation of Area	Two identical pieces of cardboard on which are placed the same number of equally sized blocks. 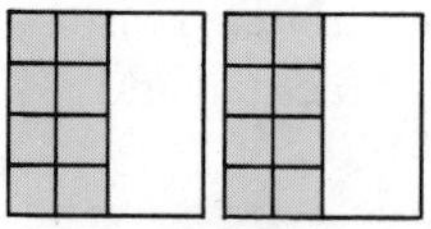	Rearrange blocks on one piece of cardboard. 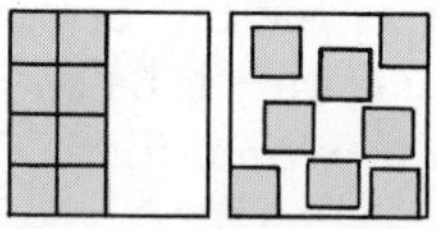	Which has more cardboard covered up?	The one with the blocks not touching.

FIGURE 11.2 The concrete operational child knows that two equal quantities remain the same even if one of them is changed in some way. As you can see from the answers, preoperational children do not have this ability.

added or taken away. As we have shown in the example of the two glasses, the concrete operational child has the ability to conserve liquid quantity. She recognizes that when milk is poured from one container into one that is differently shaped, the quantity of milk is not changed. Besides the ability to conserve liquid quantity, the concrete operational

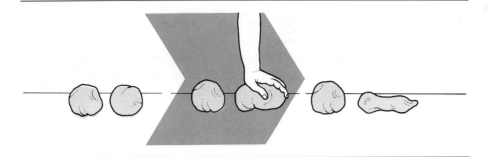

FIGURE 11.3 Conservation of substance. During the preschool years, children are swayed by immediate perceptions and they may say that a piece of clay rolled into a sausage shape is larger than a round piece of clay "because" it is longer. During the middle childhood years, children know that both pieces have the same amount of clay. Simply rolling one into a different shape does not increase or decrease the amount of clay.

child gradually acquires the ability to conserve number, length, mass, area, weight, and volume of objects and substances (see Figure 11.2), although not all at one time, because these abilities emerge in sequence.

Conservation, which is considered one of the most dramatic achievements of the concrete operations period, is not evident all at once, but emerges gradually over three stages. This is demonstrated by the classic experiment devised by Piaget to investigate the child's ability to conserve the amount of substance (conservation of mass). In this experiment the child is shown two balls made up of equal amounts of clay. After the child agrees that both balls have the same amount of clay, one of the balls is rolled into a thin, long sausage-shape (see Figure 11.3). The child is then asked if both pieces have the same amount of clay. Initially, at about the age of 4 or 5 years, the child may state that the sausage-shaped piece has more clay because it is longer.

At around the age of 6, the child vacillates in her answer and is not quite sure about which piece has more clay. Or, when asked to predict what would happen if one of the balls is rolled into a sausage shape, the child may guess correctly that the amount of clay in each would remain the same. Yet, she cannot give an accurate reason for her answer, or when one of the balls is actually rolled out into a sausage shape, she changes her mind and is swayed by seeing the longer length into thinking that the sausage shape has more clay. In this stage the child still relies on immediate perceptions and, not having the ability to reverse her mental images, she cannot take into account the fact that the sausage-shaped piece may be rolled back into its original ball shape. Not having this ability, the child cannot make mental reference to the initial state the clay was in, nor to the transformation that had taken place.

Finally, at approximately age 7, the child is able to follow and remember the transformations the ball of clay has undergone, and she realizes that despite the change in shape, both pieces still have the same amount of clay. When asked why she thinks the two pieces have the same amount of clay, the child may say, for example, "If you roll the piece back into a ball you will see that they are the same," evidencing the reversibility in her thinking. When the child is able to give the correct answer and also the correct reason why the two pieces have the same amount of clay, she can be said to be able to conserve substance.

Unevenness in Development

horizontal décalage

1. number
2. length
3. liquid quantity
4. mass
5. area
6. weight
7. volume

Children do not acquire conservation of all the properties of objects and substances at one time even though the principles and reasoning required in each case are the same. Rather, they first conserve number, then length, liquid quantity, mass, area, weight, and volume, in that order. Piaget referred to this phenomenon as *horizontal décalage*. *Décalage* is the French word for a gap, and he explained that since concepts vary in difficulty, the child masters some of these earlier than others. At the age of 7 the child may realize that the sausage-shaped piece of clay still has the same amount of clay as the ball of clay, but she does not realize that these two differently shaped pieces of clay also weigh the same. Whereas Piaget acknowledges that there is a décalage, or unevenness in the child's understanding of conservation and other concepts, he did not think this to be of great importance (Broughton, 1981).

Other researchers, however, have wondered why, since the same kind of reasoning is required in all conservation tasks, the child is first able to conserve number, length, and liquid, and then the other properties of objects. Some have explained that this unevenness in children's ability to reason may arise from environmental influence (Pulos & Linn, 1981). For example, the child has more experience with liquids (for instance, pouring milk and juice from a pitcher) than she does with other substances. Other researchers explain that when children learn to conserve one of the properties of objects, say liquid, they do not generalize this knowledge to other properties, so they have to go through the process of learning to conserve each property (Pinard, 1981).

Some of the researchers who have elaborated on Piaget's theory in this way, offering alternate explanations for the unevenness in development, are known as neo-Piagetian researchers. These researchers incorporate much of Piaget's theory in their work. However, although Piaget described the child as being in a particular stage of cognitive development, neo-Piagetians focus on specific behaviors, noting that during each stage of cognitive development the child exhibits some behaviors which are characteristic of that stage and some which are characteristic of the previous or next period of development. In other words, some researchers claim that cognitive growth does not occur in stages all at once, as each individual possesses a number of abilities, each at different levels of development (Fischer, 1983; Flavell, 1982). You should note, however, that the notion of whether cognitive development may be described in stages or not is a controversial one. Some researchers find the stage description useful. Others note that it is not useful for it fails to reveal the fact that within each stage there are gradual and transitional changes which occur at different times depending on the particular abilities (Flavell, 1985).

The Concept of Number

Although children do not attain conservation of all properties of objects all at once, they acquire conservation of these properties in much the same way as we described earlier, and the ability to conserve enhances their understanding of other concepts. For example, it is not until the concrete operations period that children can conserve number and have a full understanding of the concept of number. Many parents erroneously believe that their preschool child understands the concept of number, since she can count from 1 to 10 in the correct order. However, to find out that this capability is learned by rote and does not indicate a true understanding of the concept of number, they can conduct a simple experiment in which the child is given 6 glasses and 12 bottles and is asked to match an equal number of bottles with the glasses (see Figure 11.4). They will find out that instead of placing one bottle in front of each glass, a preschool child merely lengthens the row of glasses by increasing the space between each glass; she does not have the understanding that each bottle has to correspond to each glass (one-to-one correspondence) in order for there to be an equal number of each.

By the time they are in the concrete operations period, however, children exhibit an understanding of one-to-one correspondence, and they are also able to conserve number. Conservation of number is illustrated by an experiment in which the child is shown two rows of checkers, one row of five black checkers and one row of five red checkers. When the checkers in each row are placed one directly below the other so that both rows are of equal length (see Figure 11.5), the child, whether she is in the preoperations or concrete operations period, will agree that both rows have the same number of checkers. However, if the black checkers are spread out so that the row appears to be longer than the other, a 4-year-old child will reason, when she is asked if there are the same number of black checkers as red checkers, that there are now more black checkers, "because the black row is longer," or "because the red row is all bunched up." At about age 5 or 6, the child may answer correctly that there are the same number of checkers in both rows, but she justifies this correct answer by faulty reasoning.

By age 7 the child can be said to conserve number. She not only replies correctly that both rows have the same number of checkers, she also supports her answer by reasoning that nothing has been taken away or added—

FIGURE 11.4   When asked to match an equal number of bottles with glasses, a preschool child may simply lengthen the row of glasses, but the school-age child understands that each bottle has to correspond to a glass if there is to be an equal number of each.

reciprocal relationship

the checkers in one row were simply spread out a bit. In giving this reason, the child demonstrates that she realizes that certain properties of objects remain constant even when their outward appearance changes. The child may also reason that one of the rows is longer, but the checkers in that row are more spread out than the checkers in the other row, thus demonstrating her understanding that there is a *reciprocal relationship* between the two rows. That is, the length in one row is compensated for by the density of the other row, resulting in no net change to the number of objects. Or, the child may explain that if the checkers are moved back to the way they were before, this would demonstrate that the number of checkers in each row is the same, revealing the reversibility in her thinking, meaning that she can retrace the steps of the problem and think back to the original state the object was in.

FIGURE 11.5   Conservation of number.

Reversibility of thought is important not only in the child's mastery of conservation, but also in the academic activities the child engages in while in school. Its importance is demonstrated in arithmetic problems in which the child is required to find the solution to the question $6 \times 2 = ?$, for example, and also to perform the opposite operation, $12 \div 2 = ?$.

Classification

To be able to understand and solve numerical problems, the child needs to have not only an understanding of one-to-one correspondence and conservation of number, but also an understanding of "more than" and "less than" and of the fact that one number is included in another. That is, the number 2 is part of the number 3, which, in turn, is included in the

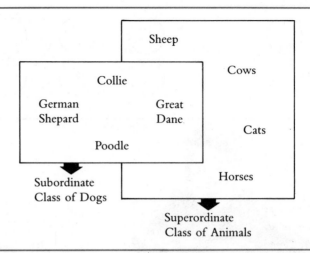

FIGURE 11.6   During the middle childhood years, children begin to have an understanding that there is a hierarchical relationship between subordinate and superordinate classes—German Shepards, Collies, and Great Danes belong to a subordinate class of dogs and a superordinate class of animals.

class inclusion

number 4. This is part of the concept of classification, and it refers to *class inclusion,* or the ability to understand that there is a hierarchical relationship between subordinate and superordinate classes. This understanding extends beyond numbers and includes all other objects the child encounters: the wooden object with four legs and a top belongs to a subordinate class of tables and also a superordinate class of furniture; German Shepherds, Great Danes, and Collies belong to a subordinate class of dogs and also to a superordinate class of animals. Similarly, daisies and tulips, although they are different in type, still belong to one superordinate class of flowers (see Figure 11.6).

The ability to understand the hierarchical structure inherent in classification has far-reaching implications. It aids the child's understanding of the social world and the multiple roles people play, and it also enhances her ability to learn such subjects as geography, which entails an awareness that a large area such as a continent contains several smaller areas, known as countries, which in turn contain even smaller areas—states, counties, cities, and towns.

Seriation

Another cognitive operation which emerges during the concrete operations period is *seriation,* which refers to the ability to arrange objects in an orderly series. This ability is important, as it demonstrates systematic, planful thinking on the part of the child.

In seriation experiments the child is given a pile of sticks of various lengths and is asked to arrange these in ascending order from the shortest

FIGURE 11.7   The ability to arrange objects in an orderly series demonstrates systematic, planful thinking on the part of the school-age child.

to the longest. During the preoperational period the child cannot accomplish this task. At first, at about age 4, the child picks out two sticks, puts the shorter of the two on one side and the longer one on the other side, and she repeats this process, comparing only two sticks at a time, so she ends up with two groups of sticks of various lengths (see Figure 11.7). She may be able to arrange some of the sticks in order of short, medium, and long, but she cannot arrange the whole pile of sticks into one series. At about age 5 or 6, when the child is shown that the sticks have to be arranged in one ascending order in a staircase effect, she is able to arrange the sticks with their tops in ascending order like stairs, but she overlooks the irregular pattern at the bottom. However, by the time she is in the concrete operations period, at around age 7, the child approaches the task systematically: she searches through the pile of sticks and picks out the shortest or longest one; then she picks out the next shortest or longest in the series, and so on, and she arranges these in ascending order without error.

The ability to seriate helps the child construct a logical view of reality. Since seriation problems require the understanding that A is greater than B, B is greater than C, and C is greater than D, the child can apply this knowledge to other tasks, and she is able to engage in *transitive reasoning,* which refers to the ability to recognize a relationship between two objects by knowing their relationship to a third. Thus, if A is greater than B and B is greater than C, then A is greater than C, even though that relationship has not been described. At times, it may be difficult for the concrete operations child to figure out relationships when such abstractions as the letters A, B, and C are used. However, in cases where concrete examples are used, the child does not need to be told, for example, that Amy is smaller than Carol. Being told only that Amy is smaller than Barbara and that Barbara is smaller than Carol, she can *reason* that Amy is smaller than Carol. Piaget attributed the concrete operational child's ability to engage in transitive thinking to the changes in cognitive structures that occur during this period. Other researchers propose that children's ability to remember may be the key here (Trabasso, 1975); when preoperational children are taught to memorize that Amy is smaller than Carol and so on, they are able to make the inference as well.

Challenging Piaget.   In numerous other challenges to Piaget's theory, researchers are finding that the manner in which Piaget presented the problems to the children can account for their erroneous answers. Consider the class inclusion problem in which it is not until the concrete operational period, according to Piaget, that children who are shown tulips and daisies are able to correctly answer if there are more tulips than there are flowers. Linda Siegel (1978) contends that language may be a problem here. When she showed preoperational children some M & Ms and other candies and asked the children, "Are there more M & Ms or more of *all* candies?" the children answered the question correctly. Siegel notes that in Piaget's presentation of the problem, "Are there more tulips than there are flowers?" an emphasis is placed on tulips, leading the children to make a distinction between tulips and flowers and thus to arrive at the erroneous conclusion.

Environmental Influences on the Attainment of Concrete Operational Thought

Although some researchers contend that language may be a problem in the ability of children to succeed on Piagetian tasks, Piaget himself did not consider language to be an issue. He believed that as children acquire such operations as conservation, classification, and seriation, they develop new mental structures which provide the foundation for the next period of cognitive development. This is true of previous periods of development as well. The child has to undergo the sensorimotor and preoperational periods before she can progress to the concrete operations stage; none of the periods is ever skipped, and each period lays the groundwork for the next.

Although Piaget formulated his theory on the basis of observations and data that he accumulated by testing middle-class children of culturally homogeneous Western backgrounds, other researchers have conducted crosscultural studies confirming the fact that children all over the world follow the same sequence of development, proceeding from the sensorimotor period to the preoperational, and then to the concrete operations

FIGURE 11.8 Mexican children from pottery-making families are found to conserve substance earlier than children from non-pottery-making families. This is not surprising, because cognitive development depends on the child's experiences and interactions with the environment.

period (Dasen, 1972, 1977). However, the rate at which children progress through one period and into the next differs among the different cultures and within cultures. This is shown, for example, in studies using conservation tasks. In Mexico, where pottery-making is a widespread skill, children from pottery-making families were found to conserve substance much earlier than children from non-pottery-making families. This is not surprising given the fact that these children have extensive experience working with clay (Price-Williams, Gordon, & Ramirez, 1969, see Figure 11.8). Recall from previous discussions that Piaget regarded intelligence as the process of adapting to the environment and that cognitive development depends on the child's experiences and interaction with the environment. Depending on their experiences, therefore, children from different backgrounds will vary in the rate that they acquire various cognitive concepts. You should note, however, that although there are variations in the rate at which children acquire cognitive skills, children of all backgrounds and cultures have been found to achieve concrete operations. The variations in the rate of development do not reflect differences in competence, but rather differences in the types of skills that are valued by the different cultural groups (Cole & Scribner, 1974).

The Role of Training.   Since experience and cultural background are known to influence the rate of cognitive development, researchers have sought to find out whether children can be trained to achieve concrete operations. Several training studies have been conducted to see if, through intensive training, children's acquisition of classification or transitive reasoning can be accelerated. Most of the training studies, however, have focused on teaching conservation to children. In one such study, Gelman (1969) hypothesized that children cannot conserve because they are distracted by irrelevant cues, and she set out to find out if this hypothesis is correct, reasoning that if it is, then children who are trained to attend to relevant aspects of the objects would be able to conserve. Her study is important for it attempts to ascertain the role of training in conservation and also to find out if there are other possible alternatives to Piaget's explanation of children's ability to conserve during the school-age years. Could it be that they can conserve because they have better attention skills during this period of their lives and not because of changes in cognitive structures?

Choosing a group of 5-year-old children whom Gelman determined through tests could not conserve, Gelman then gave them one of three types of training. In one type of training, children in a control group were given two sets of objects, and they were rewarded when they correctly identified the objects that were the same and the objects that were different. The purpose of the control group was to train the children to pick out two objects that are the same (for example, two dolls) and two objects that are different (for example, a doll and a toy car). In this way, the researchers could ensure that children do not fail conservation tasks simply because they do not know the meaning of *same* and *different*. The children in the second group were given two sets of objects, and they were rewarded when they appropriately differentiated between the objects along the dimensions required in the number and length conservation tasks. In other words, they were given training in conservation. The third group of children were given the same two sets of objects as the second group, but they were not rewarded for the correct answer, so they were given no idea if they had made the correct discrimination. Gelman found that the children in the second group did in fact do well on number and length conservation tasks when they were tested two weeks after the training procedure, whereas the children in the other two groups did not. This suggests that by receiving feedback, preoperational children can be helped to attend to relevant dimensions and can be trained to conserve.

Critics of Gelman's study note that since the children in her study were 5 years of age, they may have been close to attaining conservation anyway (Gardner, 1978). However, several other studies demonstrate that training (Brainerd, 1974) or other specific experiences such as observing others perform on similar tasks (Zimmerman & Lanaro, 1974; Murray, 1972) may accelerate children's acquisition of concepts. Despite demonstrations that children can be taught to answer conservation problems correctly, a number of issues should be considered. Some researchers argue that it is conceivable that accelerating mental growth, assuming it is possible, might interfere with normal cognitive development. Wohlwill (1970), for example, notes that the reasoning of preschool children is eventually outgrown, but it may remain useful later in life in the process of imaginative or creative acts. It may be that if children are hurried through the natural course of cognitive development, the early processes of cognition will not be fully incorporated into their cognitive apparatus and that as adults these children will not be as imaginative or creative as they would otherwise have been.

Piaget and Education.   Piaget himself saw no value in training procedures. He contended that these do not demonstrate learning but artificial, verbally acquired responses, since until about the age of 7 the child does not have the mental structures needed to grasp the notion of conservation. He argued that an important aspect of the progress in cognitive development that occurs during the concrete operations period is physiological maturation, since without refinement and differentiation of the central nervous system, thinking could not become more elaborate. Also important is the child's interaction with adults and peers. But, according to Piaget, at the core of the progress in cognitive growth is the child's self-initiated interaction with her physical surroundings. Thus, "each time one prematurely teaches a child something he could discover for himself, that child is kept from inventing it and consequently from understanding it completely" (Piaget, 1970).

Although Piaget was not particularly interested in applying his theory to classroom teaching, his notion that the child learns through discovery has been embraced by educators who developed the concept of the *open classroom*. In the open classroom, children do not sit at a desk facing the teacher as they do in the traditional classroom. Rather, they choose from a variety of activity centers that are placed around the room, and they progress from one center to another at their own pace (see Figure 11.9). In this way children of various abilities can learn together in the same classroom. Although widely encouraged during the late 1960s and the 1970s as a preferred mode of teaching (Silberman, 1970), researchers have found that

open classroom

FIGURE 11.9   Although at one time the open classroom (above) was being hailed as the preferred mode of teaching, educators now know that whereas this type of environment is suitable for some children, other children function better within the structured atmosphere of the traditional classroom (opposite page).

whereas the open classroom may promote certain skills such as creativity and social interaction, the traditional classroom is more effective for the transmission of academic tasks (Bennett, 1976). Moreover, since individual differences among children exist, one type of classroom may be more suitable for some children than for others. This is noted by several researchers who have shown that whereas some children, especially those who are anxious, function well within the structured atmosphere of the traditional classroom, others prefer and enjoy being in an open classroom (Horowitz, 1979). You should bear in mind that the same is applicable to teachers who may be more comfortable teaching in one setting than in another. For this reason, many large school systems have a mix of traditional and open classrooms.

Information Processing

The contributions that Jean Piaget has made to education and psychology are important. As we have just shown, much of his work provided insight into children's thinking, and it was also applied in practical settings such as the school. However, Piaget's view is not the only interpretation of children's cognitive development. The information processing view of cognitive development offers another way of describing children's thinking. This view holds that in order to understand their environment and

progress in their ability to solve problems, children must be able to acquire and process information. That is, they must register what they see or hear, store that information, and later retrieve it and apply it to new experiences.

During the past few years there has been an increase in the study of children's information processing abilities, with researchers offering interesting alternative explanations for conservation, classification, numerical understanding, and transitive thinking. They explain these in terms of children's ability to attend to, store, and retrieve information. However, the research in this area is characterized by numerous exemplary studies, but, as yet, no unifying theory. A major inspiration for this orientation to the study of cognitive development has been the invention of the computer (Kuhn, 1984). Information processing researchers view the human mind as analogous to a computer: in the same way that the output or final product of a computer is dependent upon its capacity, the kind of information that it is "fed" (the input), and the type of programming it has for organizing and retrieving this information, so the child's cognitive performance and her learning are based on her ability to receive, or encode, information, as well as to store it and later to retrieve it. According to information processing researchers, the child receives, stores, and retrieves information from her environment through basic cognitive processes such as perception and memory. These processes, although often described separately for the sake of clarity, function together to combine in the activity referred to as thinking. They are present at every age; however, they undergo incremental changes as the child grows older. Information processing theorists thus describe the changes in the child's cognitive development not in a qualitative way as does Piaget, but quantitatively. They explain that the school-age child's ability to approach problem solving in a logical manner is dependent upon her increased ability to process information.

Attention

selective attention

Essential in the ability to process information is the ability of the child to pay attention. The environment contains an array of different stimuli that we must attend to selectively, or else these will overwhelm us. *Selective attention* refers to the ability to focus on relevant aspects of the environment and to disregard irrelevant aspects. With age, children become increasingly able to selectively attend to stimuli (Pick, Frankel, & Hess, 1975) and also better able to control their attentional processes and concentrate on a specific task. That is, they are less easily distracted by irrelevant stimuli and more flexible in shifting their attention from one stimulus to another. To demonstrate this capability, Pick, Christy, and Frankel (1972) showed 8- and 12-year-old children colored wooden animals. The children were asked questions about the animals in such a way that they had to concentrate on one relevant aspect, such as the animals' color, or another aspect, such as their shape, while ignoring all other aspects about the animals. The older children responded more quickly than did the younger children, suggesting that they are better able than the younger children to attend to a relevant stimulus and shift their attention from one stimulus to another.

Older children are also able to attend to a particular task when they are specifically told to do so, for example, when they are told: "pay attention now" or "listen carefully" (Pick, Frankel, & Hess, 1975). Also, they can concentrate on a particular task for increasingly longer periods of time. Preschoolers can pay attention to a task for only a few minutes so that they frequently leave that task and move on to some other task that attracts their attention (Anderson & Levin, 1976). However, older children can spend more time with their attention focused on a particular task. This capability is reflected in the length of lessons children are taught in school. The lessons become longer as the children progress through the elementary grades.

Memory

The ability to pay attention to a task also enhances children's capacity for memory. Memory is an important aspect of learning. Having the ability to draw upon a store of memories from past experiences, the child can build upon what she already knows, and this aids her ability to solve problems and acquire new knowledge.

The process of storing information involves three kinds of storage systems: sensory memory, short-term memory, and long-term memory. In *sensory memory*, impressions are retained for less than a second and then transferred into short-term memory. In *short-term memory*, information is stored for a brief period of time—about 30 seconds. You would rely on short-term memory to remember a telephone number just long enough to take your eyes off the telephone directory and dial the number. However, if you encountered trouble locating a telephone and didn't have a pencil and paper, which means you would have to remember the number for a little longer period of time, you would have to resort to some mental technique which would facilitate your ability to remember longer. Most likely, you would repeat parts of the number over and over to yourself either mentally or verbally, a technique known as *rehearsal*. Using this technique, you would be able to remember the seven-digit telephone number. For the young child, however, this is a difficult task because at a younger age the child can remember fewer bits, or pieces, of information. At age 5, for example, she can remember only 4 bits of information (a bit, or piece, of information may be one digit in the telephone number). At a younger age, she can remember only 2 or 3 bits of information (Morrison et al., 1974). However, during the middle childhood years, the capacity for memory becomes greater, and the child cannot only remember more bits of information, each bit of information that she is able to place in memory is larger. For example, each bit of information she remembers may be a short sentence as opposed to a number or a word.

When an individual has to remember something for a longer period of time than 30 seconds, she relies on *long-term memory*. A vast number of childhood experiences (a vacation two summers ago or a movie seen last week) are stored in long-term memory. Just as is true with short-term memory, the capacity for long-term memory is dependent on the ability to use various techniques to facilitate memory. One such memory-aiding or *mnemonic device* is rehearsal, which, as we have noted earlier, entails repetition of items to be remembered. Another is *organization*, which refers to the grouping of items to be remembered into groups or clusters of information. The school-age child is better able to use this mnemonic strategy than the preschool child because she has acquired the ability to classify objects according to different categories (Mosley, 1977). When she is shown a list of different words such as *flute, hammer, bicycle, apple, violin, nail, boat,* and *orange,* she is able to remember more of these words than the preschool child because she can organize the words according to their different categories: musical instruments, tools, fruit, modes of transportation.

Unlike the preschool child, the school-age child also knows that by employing some memory-aiding device she will be better able to remember. This is because during the middle childhood years, children acquire *metamemory*, which refers to an intuitive understanding of how memory works (Flavell, 1977). Having this understanding, the school-age child

sensory memory

short-term memory

rehearsal

long-term memory

mnemonic device

organization

metamemory

realizes that there are some situations which require that she employ a planned strategy for remembering, and she not only knows what techniques will facilitate her ability to remember, she also knows when the information she is committing to memory is sufficiently memorized (Kail, 1979). To demonstrate that younger children do not employ any strategies for remembering and also that if older children are told to try to remember they do employ some such strategy whereas younger children do not, Appel, Cooper, McCarrell, Sims-Knight, Yussen, and Flavell (1972) studied children of different ages. Half the children were told to "look at the pictures"; the other half were told to "try to remember the pictures." Preschool children simply stared at the pictures even when told to try to remember the pictures, as did children in the first grade. By the fifth grade, however, the children responded differently to the two conditions. When they were told to remember, they employed a memory-aiding strategy and therefore remembered substantially more under this condition than when they were asked simply to look at the pictures.

LANGUAGE DEVELOPMENT

Metalinguistic Awareness

metalinguistic awareness

School-age children also have an intuitive awareness of how language works. This ability is known as *metalinguistic awareness*. It emerges at about age 5 and is enhanced during the middle childhood years, which suggests that although by the end of the preschool period children have acquired a substantial amount of knowledge about many aspects of language, further expansions in language development continue to occur between the ages of 6 and 12.

Communicative Competence

Metalinguistic awareness enables the child to think about language and is evident in two basic changes that occur during the middle childhood years in the child's understanding and use of language. One, having the ability to think about language, the child's communicative competence increases. Communicative competence is reflected in the school-age child's ability to think about what she is being told and to judge whether the message being conveyed to her is clear. The fact that it is not until the school-age years that children are able to think about what they are being told is demonstrated in studies in which children were given instructions for a game. The instructions left out a critical piece of information which made it impossible to play the game. Children in the first grade were not aware of the inadequacy of the instructions, nor of the fact that they did not understand them, so they proceeded to attempt to play the game, only later finding out that they could not do so. Third-grade children, on the other hand, noticed the problem with the instructions and did not have to attempt to play the game before finding out that they did not understand what was said to them (Markman, 1977).

The school-age child's communicative competence is further illustrated in her ability to understand complex grammatical sentences. Most of the simple grammatical rules are mastered during the preschool years. However, knowledge of *syntax,* the underlying grammatical rules that specify the order and function of words in a sentence, develops throughout the middle childhood years as the child becomes better able to understand the connections between words. For example, a 6-year-old child who hears the sentence, "John promised Mary to shovel the driveway," is likely to think that Mary is going to do the shoveling because she is thinking that the subject of a sentence is usually the noun that precedes the verb (C. Chomsky, 1969). An 8-year-old child, however, understands that it is John who is going to be shoveling.

syntax

In addition, school-age children acquire a more precise meaning of words, and, unlike preschool children, they do not confuse words. Preschool children, for example, often take the words *ask* and *promise* to mean "tell," so they misinterpret the sentence, "John asked Bill what to do," as meaning "John told Bill what to do" (C. Chomsky, 1969). Preschool children also confuse such words as *heavy, big,* and *strong.* When asked to judge objects that look alike but which have different weights, the preschool child may describe the heavier object as "bigger" or "stronger" because she confuses concepts that are similar. The school-age child, on the other hand, is unlikely to confuse such concepts; she is capable of understanding the precise meanings of words and of using such words correctly.

Understanding Metaphors

The second way in which language use changes during the middle childhood years is that it becomes increasingly nonliteral. That is, during this period children acquire the ability to understand that some words have a literal as well as a nonliteral meaning. This ability enables them to appreciate metaphors. A metaphor relies on the use of a word or a phrase out of context to suggest an unexpected similarity. Preschool children may know the meaning of the words *sweet* and *bright,* and they are able to use these words in their literal context: The chocolate is sweet; the light is bright. However, they have trouble comprehending the metaphors, "He is a sweet child," or "She is a bright student." Asch and Nerlove (1960) found that preschool children who correctly used the words *sweet* and *bright* to describe objects said that the same words could not be used to describe a person. Children aged 7 or 8 acknowledged that such words can be applied to both objects and people, but it was not until the children were age 10 or 11 that they were able to understand the figures of speech and explain the relationship between the literal and nonliteral meanings of the words.

Other researchers found that although preschool children are inventive in their own speech, often producing metaphors such as, "The bald man has a barefoot head," they are not able to comprehend metaphors. Gardner and Winner (1979) explain that in a figure of speech such as, "After many years of working in jail, *the guard had become a hard rock that could not be moved,*" a link is made between the physical universe (hard rocks) and the universe of psychological traits (stubborn lack of feeling). To make sense of the statement, one must perceive the similarity between physical and psychological inflexibility. Preschool children do not have this capacity. Most 5-year-olds, for example, instead of linking the two elements, misinterpret the meaning of the metaphor and explain that the guard piled rocks all day long. By the time they are 8 years old, children have made significant progress: they recognize the basic intent behind the figure of speech. However, they still do not appreciate the psychological trait at issue. They explain the metaphor as meaning that the guard had become angry or stupid, descriptions which allude to the intended negative connotation of the metaphor, but they fail to provide the precise psychological condition being described.

It is not until the latter part of the middle childhood period that children offer accurate explanations of metaphors and can be credited with genuine metaphoric comprehension. At that time, at around the age of 10 or 11, children are capable of thinking of psychological traits in nonliteral as well as literal terms and of understanding how a hard rock might bear a resemblance to the psychological condition, such as being stubborn. They are also capable of thinking about the two meanings of the terms at the same time. By using their cognitive capacity for reversibility, they mentally move back and forth between the two meanings, so they are able to discover the link between the literal meaning of the word or sentence and the idea conveyed by its use in a nonliteral context. In this example you can see evidence of the fact that there is a relationship between language development and cognitive growth.

Humor

The relationship between language and concrete operational thought is further evident in the school-age child's appreciation of jokes and riddles. In order to learn about children's comprehension of riddles, McGhee (1974) asked children to indicate which of two answers is funnier, a joking answer or a factual answer. In the question, "Why did the old man tiptoe past the medicine cabinet?" the joking answer would be, "So that he wouldn't wake up the sleeping pills," whereas a factual answer would be, "Because he dropped a glass and didn't want to cut his foot." McGhee found that children in the first grade chose the factual answer as the funny

I couldn't possibly eat 8 slices; please cut the pizza into 6 slices.

one as often as they chose the joking answer, indicating that they had no comprehension of what made the riddle funny; they were only guessing. Children in the second grade, however, showed a significant preference for the joking answer.

During the school-age years, children not only appreciate such riddles, they also love to engage in play on words and to tell jokes that involve double meanings. They can understand and appreciate these types of jokes because in order to understand these, some kind of a reclassification of a key word is required, a feat which children are not capable of until the concrete operations period. For example, the riddle, "What has an ear but cannot hear?" requires an understanding of the two meanings of the word *ear* and a reclassification of the word according to another context to find the answer—corn. That is, when the child first hears the riddle, she focuses on concepts associating ears with hearing, but the surprising answer, if it is to be funny, requires that she quickly shift her attention to another meaning of the word *ear*. The speed of reclassification is important because in order to appreciate the humor in the riddle, the child must keep both meanings of the word in mind at the same time and shift her attention back and forth between meanings, using her ability for reversibility of thought.

Other cognitive achievements of the concrete operations period such as conservation enable the school-age child to appreciate such jokes as

Waitress Should I cut the pizza into eight slices for you?
Fat Woman No, make it six. I could never eat eight.
(McGhee, 1979.)

School-age children also laugh at absurd jokes such as "Call me a cab. You're a cab," or "Order, Order in the court! Ham and cheese on rye, your Honor." To an adult, these jokes are not really humorous, but for the school-age child, they are hilarious. Why? Studies by Zigler and his colleagues (Pinderhughes & Zigler, 1985; Zigler, Levine, & Gould, 1967) and by McGhee (1976) indicate that humor is appreciated only when it offers a moderate amount of intellectual challenge. Many riddles and jokes that are based on incongruities of words and relations are not very funny to most adults because they are easy to understand, but they are amusing to school-age children because they are understandable but sufficiently difficult and challenging to surprise them.

Bilingualism and Black English

The increased sophistication of the school-age child in his understanding and use of language enhances his ability to profit from formal instruction in school. However, for many children, language presents not an opportunity for learning, but a barrier. For example, bilingual children often begin school unable to speak English. This presents a problem of how to teach them—in English or in their native language.

This is a controversial issue. There are those who recommend that the children be put into classes wherein only the English language is spoken. Others advocate bilingual education, contending that the children should be taught in their native language for the first few years of school and gradually eased into English. These recommendations stem from political and philosophical beliefs as well as from educational concerns. Those who oppose bilingual education contend that students who are taught in their native language are prevented from making progress in English, and they argue that bilingual education is a disservice to children because valuable classroom time is being spent supporting their native language when the criterion for success in the educational system is the strength of their English. Supporters of bilingual programs argue that by being taught in their native language, children are made to feel that their cultural background is important, and they note that if the children first have to wait to acquire proficiency in the English language before they are taught basic skills, their academic abilities would remain behind English-speaking children their age. Although research in this area could be an important basis upon which decisions on the education of bilingual children may be made, not much research is being done to document which approach is more effective in the teaching of bilingual children (Hakuta, 1986).

Children who are from a bilingual background grow up hearing and eventually speaking two languages. Generally, their primary or native language is learned in the home, and the English language is learned from playmates in the neighborhood or at school. The task of acquiring language is a challenging one for the bilingual child who must learn two systems of grammatical rules and two vocabularies instead of one. Initially, the bilingual child speaks two languages at one time, especially when she attempts to speak English but does not yet know all the words, in which case she borrows from her primary language (Voltera & Taeschner, 1978), including in one sentence words from both languages. Eventually, she is able to speak fluently in English, and she may even become more proficient in the English language than she is in her native language.

Although schools have always had bilingual students, teaching the bilingual child has recently become a policy issue that educators have to confront given the large influx of immigrants from Cuba, Puerto Rico, Latin America, and Asia. Their learning of English is hampered because, even in school, these children can find many playmates who speak in their native language. In cases where these children are placed in the same class with English-speaking children, they do not perform well on academic tasks or on IQ tests which require proficiency in the English language. But, if these children are given lessons in their native language, will they ever have the opportunity to learn English and function within our society as adults? You can appreciate the complexity of the issues regarding bilingual education. It is a problem not only for schools but for society at large. Already, in response to the increasing numbers of non-English-speaking adults in many communities, some states require that social and public services utilize English and one other language such as Spanish.

The problems that bilingual children face are shared by some black children from low-income families. These children speak English. However, they come to school having learned the language comfortably and informally in their homes and neighborhoods, only to find that in school they cannot use their language.

For a long period of time, researchers and educators held that black children from low socioeconomic homes have deficient language skills because the language environment of these children is impoverished. Summarizing some of the dogmatic views researchers held regarding black children's language development, Dale (1976) notes that researchers argued that black children "hear very little language, much of it ill formed. [They] cannot formulate complete sentences, and they do not know the names of common objects. They lack crucial concepts and they cannot produce or comprehend logical statements." These conclusions were made on the basis of tests which are based on standard English as spoken by white, middle-class individuals. However, researchers have since found that black children from low socioeconomic families speak a nonstandard dialect of English. One such nonstandard dialect is Black English. Although not all blacks use the Black English vernacular (Labov, 1972), this term is useful, for it highlights not the deficits in black children's language, but rather the fact that their language is different. Indeed, once researchers began to focus on the characteristics of lower-class black children's language, they found not only that these children are extremely verbal, but that verbal games and the ability to use language flexibly and creatively are important status symbols among black children and adolescents. Still, Black English is different from the English black children are likely to encounter in schools, in textbooks, and on tests, and as such, it may be a handicap unless teachers and others are sensitive to these differences. Black English is not only different from standard English in its intonation patterns and vocabulary (DeStefano & Rentel, 1975), it is also different in grammar and pronunciation. These differences do not reflect a sloppy use of standard English. Rather, Black English is governed by its own set of grammatical rules (Labov, 1970), so black children have to learn not one but two sets of rules, those of Black English and those that govern standard English.

Since standard English is the primary means of communication and instruction in schools, black children who use the Black English vernacular and bilingual children are at a disadvantage academically until they acquire proficiency in standard English. However, differences among children in their school performance are related to other aspects of development besides language.

THE CHILD IN SCHOOL

The School as a Learning Environment

The school environment plays an important role in the child's development. Throughout much of the middle childhood and adolescent years, children spend a large portion of their time either attending school or performing school-related tasks, so the school inevitably influences a child's values, her self-esteem, her achievements and aspirations, and her learning. Of course, learning occurs all the time, not only in school, and it begins well before the child enters school. However, the informal learning that occurs outside of school is different from the formal learning that occurs in school. Before she enters school, the child acquires concepts through her experiences with many concrete instances, whereas in school she is required to learn concepts that are set apart from their concrete referents. For example, she learns to add numbers, which are abstract, rather than to number items. Also, in school the child learns not necessarily by observing others and by trying out an activity for herself as is true of learning during the preschool years, but by following specific verbal instructions about how to carry out certain tasks. The verbal exchange the child experiences in school is also unique (see Figure 11.10). Outside of school the child engages in conversations in which there is a relatively free give and take among participants. In school the teacher dominates the exchange of information. For the most part, the child is limited in what she can say. She is generally expected to respond solely to the teacher and,

FIGURE 11.10 During the middle childhood years, children become capable of giving sustained attention to tasks, and they shift to a higher level of cognitive development. Thus, they are able to profit from formal instruction.

preferably, to respond correctly. This type of verbal exchange is an accepted characteristic of school life. The specific content may vary, but the basic format for the exchange of information remains constant no matter what subject matter is being taught or the age of the children in the class (Litwak & Meyer, 1974).

Although teaching children in schools is a relatively new phenomenon (Cremin, 1976), throughout the centuries adult members of society regarded it as their right and responsibility to modify the thinking of the young and to transmit to them knowledge and values, and they did so informally in the context of children's everyday experiences. As society became more complex, the education of children became more structured and was delegated to teachers within the formal setting of the school. For a time, formal schooling was reserved for the children of the very rich. About a century ago, schooling in America became not only universally available, but also compulsory, and schools have since grown to serve more children for a greater number of years.

In most countries in which formal schooling is compulsory, children begin school some time between the ages of 5 and 7. This is because during this period, the child experiences a number of significant changes in development which make her amenable to the demands of the school milieu (Sheldon White, 1965; 1970). Not only does the child become better able to follow instructions, as we have shown, and also better able to apply reasoning and memory skills to problem solving, she also becomes capable of paying attention for increasingly longer periods of time so she is better able to concentrate on learning specific tasks. Beyond these and other changes in mental development, the school-age child also experiences changes in social development which further enable her to profit from schooling. For example, the child at that age has the capacity to learn and operate according to rules, which is an ability that is basic for all lasting social exchange. The ability to learn rules makes formal education possible because most of what children learn as they acquire academic skills are rules. In learning to read, for example, they learn phonetic rules (the letter *e* at the end of a word is sometimes silent); in learning to write, they learn spelling rules (*i* comes before *e* except after *c*).

Cross-Cultural Studies.   Although it has been recognized that the child's ability to profit from formal instruction is dependent upon her attainment of a certain level of cognitive and social maturity, researchers in recent years have also wondered whether the school experience can enhance the child's cognitive functioning. To this end, they have taken advantage of a naturally occurring experiment made possible by the fact that although most societies have some form of schooling, it is neither compulsory nor universally available in many nontechnological societies. Hence, researchers have been able to compare the cognitive abilities of samples of children who vary in their amount of school experience. There are some limitations to these cross-cultural studies (Rogoff, 1981; Super, 1980). Nevertheless, the results of these studies have shown that children who attend school do better on some cognitive skills such as memory and classification (Stevenson, 1982; Sharp, Cole, & Lave, 1979), suggesting that to an extent, school experience does influence cognitive ability. Researchers have also found that school experience enhances language development. Children who attend school are more proficient in their use of language than are children from the same cultural background who do not attend school. They use a greater number of words to recount an experience and they are more verbally explicit (Scribner, 1977). This finding is not surprising since language is the primary means of interaction and exchange of information in school.

Learning Problems

Schools also enable children to acquire a considerable amount of knowledge so that through their school experiences, children's understanding of their world is enhanced. Even more importantly, in school, children learn such basic skills as reading, writing, and arithmetic, which, in our society at least, are essential to functioning in adult life. Once they acquire such skills, children can apply them in all kinds of situations in school and later in life. Although by the time they enter first grade most children have the ability to learn to read, write, and solve numerical problems, not all children actually learn these skills. A recent report of the National Commission on Excellence in Education (1983) documents the failure of many children in our country to acquire basic skills. Several other studies offer an equally negative description of the scholastic achievements of American children, indicating that children's average levels of achievement are low not only in relation to their peers of previous years, but, perhaps even more disturbingly, in relation to their present-day counterparts in other countries (Stevenson, 1983; Lynn, 1982). These findings are of major concern. Children who do not succeed in school and who fail to acquire basic skills will be unable to successfully negotiate life as adults. The findings are also of concern regarding the nation's future advances in technology, science, and industry. Without a well-educated workforce, it will be exceedingly difficult for the United States to maintain a leadership role among advanced technological societies and to compete economically with other nations, factors which will undoubtedly affect the well-being of our future generations.

The rising anxiety about the deterioration in school performance among children has produced a number of recommendations for educational reform, a discussion of which is beyond the scope of this book. From the perspective of developmental psychology, however, it is important to note that there are many reasons why some children fail to achieve their potential for learning. Recall from our previous discussions that prenatal factors and the child's health and nutritional status affect her ability to learn. In addition, you will see in this and the next chapter that the influences of the family, the peer group, and society can aid or impede the child's school achievement, as can various school practices. For example, children's school performance is measured on the basis of achievement tests. These tests are devised to measure how much knowledge a child has acquired in specific content areas such as reading or mathematics in relation to other children of the same age. Although the use of such tests is considered important by educators and may be regarded as helpful in assessing how well children are doing in school, the use of the tests brings to focus the differences among children and makes it inevitable that some children will be categorized as good learners, others as average learners, and still others as poor learners. Children who do not score well on such tests are regarded and come to regard themselves as failures, and they may lose their motivation to succeed in school.

Motivation for Learning.   Motivation is a basic ingredient of the child's learning. Children are born with an intrinsic motivation to learn and to understand the world around them, an aspect of development which Robert White (1959) refers to as *competence motivation*. Competence motivation

competence motivation

helps explain individuals' interest in their environment and their ability to persist in learning even difficult things such as how to read and write, how to ride a bicycle, or how to swim.

A child's motivation for learning can increase or diminish over time, depending, in part, on other people's reactions to her efforts. Harter and Zigler (1974) and Harter (1983) note that from birth the child is motivated to learn, and she makes an independent effort to do so. Her efforts in turn produce either positive or negative reinforcement both from the child's own perceptions of her performance and from important adults in her life such as her parents and teachers. When the reinforcement is positive and the child feels she succeeded, she is motivated to continue to learn and enjoy learning. When the reinforcement is negative, the child comes to regard herself as a failure, and her motivation to learn decreases, so she avoids challenges, comes to depend on adults more, and continues to fail as the cycle feeds on itself. Reinforcement does not have to be tangible, however. It may be verbal approval or disapproval of what the child is doing, but it may also occur in other instances, such as when the child feels pleasure in what she is doing. The approval of important people in their life—parents, relatives, and teachers—is usually a strong positive reinforcer for children. Indifference to the children's effort serves as a negative reinforcer, sometimes resulting in the children giving up on learning the task at hand. Some children, after repeated failures, come to believe that they cannot overcome failure. This attitude, referred to as *learned*

learned
helplessness

helplessness, inhibits the child in her learning. Children who feel helpless believe that they have no control over how well or badly they do in school, so they do not even try. They tend to attribute their failure to achieve not to their lack of effort, but to their bad luck, a bad teacher, or other factors which are beyond their control (Seligman, 1975).

Competence motivation varies depending on the skill being learned. A child who may not be motivated to learn to read may be motivated to acquire proficiency in some other skill, such as dancing, from which she derives a sense of competence and pleasure. Various aspects of development and events in the child's life influence her motivation and determine which types of skills she will be motivated to acquire. For example, although many 7- and 8-year-old children have the cognitive skills necessary for them to succeed in their learning to add, subtract, or otherwise manipulate numbers, some children are slower in their rate of development. Although these children may be able to learn arithmetic at a later age, they may become frustrated by their initial failures, and their motivation to study the subject matter may diminish.

Family Influences. Parents and other adults also determine what the child will be motivated to learn, as observational learning is an important aspect of motivation (see Figure 11.11). When a child sees her parents read, she too wants to read, so she is motivated to learn to read (Hess et

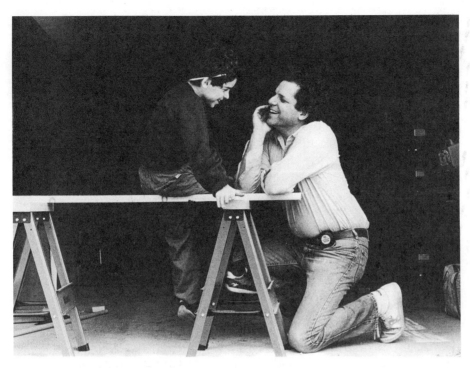

FIGURE 11.11 Parental approval reinforces motivation, but parents' indifference to a child can produce feelings of inadequacy.

al., 1982). The approval the child receives from parents or teachers when she attempts to learn a skill reinforces her motivation. Just as parental approval reinforces motivation, however, parents' indifference to the child can produce in her a feeling of inadequacy. In this case, the child may not only give up her efforts to learn the task, she may also be less willing to take up another task. Hence, researchers point out that the extent to which a child is motivated to succeed in school is often dependent on a warm and encouraging family atmosphere during the school-age years (Laosa & Sigel, 1982). Researchers also point out that such an atmosphere is important earlier in the child's life as well. Parents' involvement in their preschool child's activities, their tendency to respond to her questions and read to her have been linked to the child's later success in school (Rich, 1985; Gottfried & Gottfried, 1984).

Evidence of the family's influence on academic achievement is also available from a recent study by Harold Stevenson (1983) who found that the academic achievement of American school children in reading and arithmetic lags behind that of children in Japan and Taiwan. Of significance in Stevenson's findings is the fact that the American children lag behind their age-mates in other countries not only in the upper elementary grades, but also in the first grade. This suggests that achievement problems may indeed lie not only in American schools but in American homes as well. Stevenson looked at various factors which could have contributed to the differences in achievement, asking: "Are American children less bright than the other children? Are their parents less educated? Are their teachers less experienced?" He found that none of these factors—intelligence, parental educational status, or teachers' experience and training—could be said to account for the lower levels of achievement among American school children. However, he found some differences between American parents and parents in Taiwan and Japan in the way they interacted with their children and in the expectations that they have of their children. He found, for example, that mothers in Japan and Taiwan place more value on homework, that they are more eager to help their children perform academic tasks, and that they realize more than American mothers do that they can help their children succeed in school (see Figure 11.12).

Parent Involvement.   The policy implications of these findings point to the need for educators not only to educate children, but to instill in parents the awareness that they are partners in their children's education and that as such they should participate in school activities. This is not an easy task. Historically, schools and families are seen as having separate and distinct roles. The schools are charged with teaching children academic tasks while parents are charged with facilitating the children's moral and social development (Cremin, 1976). Nevertheless, efforts to bring parents and schools together date back to the beginning of the century (Hammer & Turner, 1985) and were intensified two decades ago when educators recognized that parent participation was a significant factor in the success of early intervention programs such as Head Start.

Since the inception of Project Head Start, the federal government mandated that any federally funded program serving children must include a parent involvement component. In addition, a number of programs have been developed that specifically encourage the participation of parents in the school. One such program is Follow Through, which was designed to provide services to low-income, elementary school children and their parents in order to maintain and extend the academic gains these children made as a result of their participation in Head Start programs. Follow Through included a variety of ways in which parents were encouraged to participate in their children's education. In some instances, parents joined the school system as volunteers or professionals, or they were taught how to encourage their children to study and how they could help children with homework. In other cases, parents became involved in a policy advisory council through which they were able to influence the formulation of school policies and decisions. Educators found that through the parents' participation in the school, children's academic achievement increased (Rhine, 1981).

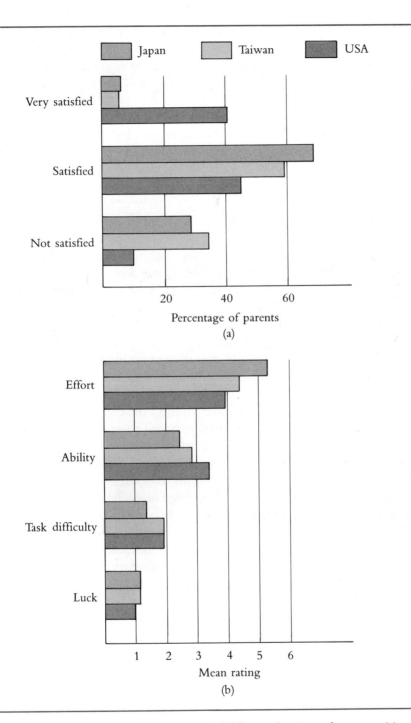

FIGURE 11.12 Mothers' attitude toward child's academic performance (a) and mothers' ratings of factors that contribute to academic success (b). From the *Annual Report* of the Center for Advanced Study in Behavioral Sciences, p. 49 (Stanford University, Stanford, CA).

Although parent involvement began as an aspect of programs for economically disadvantaged children, educators are reporting that throughout the nation, parents of all socio-economic levels are increasingly taking an active role in their children's education, serving as volunteers in the schools and enhancing school-home relations with the purpose of improving children's achievement. Williams (1985) reports that membership in parent-teacher organizations is at its highest level since the 1970s, and that the number of parents working as volunteers in schools has doubled between 1980 and 1984. Parents are finding that when they participate in a wide variety of school activities, their children improve in their attitudes toward learning (see Figure 11.13). Researchers are finding that there is a correlation between parents' involvement and improved pupil attendance in the school, as well as a reduction in suspension rates for disciplinary reasons (Thomas, 1980), although they acknowledge that more research on the effects of parent involvement needs to be done.

The increase in the numbers of parents who participate in school activities is encouraging. Yet, many educators feel that not enough parents are being included in the education process. A number of social factors impede parent involvement in schools, including the increase in the numbers of working mothers and in single-parent families—parents simply do not have the time to devote to school activities.

Anxiety. Another factor which may inhibit the child's ability to succeed in school is anxiety. That is, a child may fail to learn because she is too anxious or emotionally upset to pay attention to what is going on in the classroom. Some learning problems of this kind are due to a severe emotional disorder. Such emotional problems may also stem from the difficulties some children encounter in learning, in which case the school becomes a negative experience for the child (Gaudry & Spielberger, 1971). Although such negative experiences may be school-related, in many cases the problem is related to a stressful situation in the child's life. Researchers are finding that among elementary and secondary school students who have poor achievement records or who are often truant or suspended from school, a large percentage are from single-parent families (National Association of Elementary School Principals, 1980). In some single-parent families, both the parent and the children experience high levels of stress due to the divorce of the parents and other conditions such as poverty which characterize many such families.

Learning Disabilities. Learning problems are not always the result of the child's lack of motivation to learn or of some disruption in family life. They can have many other causes, one of which may be a learning disability. Learning-disabled children are at times mistaken as mentally retarded, emotionally disturbed, or simply lazy. Their difficulties at school do not stem from poor intelligence or laziness, however. In fact, learning-

FIGURE 11.13 The increase in the number of parents who participate in school activities is encouraging. Researchers have found that a correlation exists between parents' involvement in school activities and improved pupil attendance and performance in school.

disabled children usually have an average or above-average intellectual potential. Their difficulties do not stem from disturbances in feelings or from their lack of motivation. Rather, their performance on relatively simple academic tasks such as reading and writing is severely inhibited by specific disorders in the way they process information.

One type of learning disability is *dyslexia,* which is an impairment in the ability to read. Dyslexics often see letters upside down or reversed. Although young children make similar errors, they eventually outgrow them; dyslexics do not. Therefore, they have difficulty with spelling and other reading-related tasks they are required to engage in in school. The word *dyslexia* may be seen by the dyslexic child as "lybexia." In addition to seeing letters and words in this confused way, some dyslexic children also have impaired auditory perception—they cannot hear the sounds of language correctly. Others have frequent memory lapses so they cannot remember what words sound like. Needless to say, these children may have speech problems besides their difficulties in learning to read and write. Learning-disabled children may also have trouble telling their left

dyslexia

from their right, determining where they are in a room, organizing their work, and following multiple directions.

Although dyslexia is the best known of learning disabilities, it is only one of dozens of specific, education-related problems that have come to be recognized over the past few years. Others include *childhood aphasia,* which is the inability to speak or comprehend what is being said; *dyscalculia,* the inability to calculate numbers; and *hyperactivity,* the inability to settle down. Hyperactivity occurs in children with or without other learning disabilities. Hyperactive children are extremely restless and unable to sit still in the classroom. However, it is only in structured situations which require that they keep their attention on the tasks at hand that hyperactive children show restlessness (Whalen & Henker, 1976). In unstructured situations where attention to a particular task is not required, hyperactive children behave the same way as do other children. Chapter 10 contains a full explanation of hyperactivity.

Learning disabilities, which affect at least 1.8 million out of 40 million school children (Foundation for Children with Learning Disabilities, 1986), have become a major educational concern during the past several years. Government officials, private organizations, and parents are advocating that schools provide the necessary services to identify and help these children. Researchers point out that whereas learning disabilities present problems in school, their effect is not confined to the classroom. Learning disabled children may not be able to read street signs or house and telephone numbers. It is also becoming increasingly evident that beyond having such difficulties, learning-disabled children experience social and behavioral problems as well. They are often rejected by their peers (Bryan, 1974). They are not liked by most people (Bryan & Bryan, 1978). They are rated by their teachers as less cooperative, less attentive, and less able to cope with new situations, as well as less tactful and less sensitive than other children (Bryan & McCrady, 1972).

Although in part these problems may grow out of the frustrations these students encounter in school and the lowered self-esteem they experience from knowing they cannot accomplish certain tasks, they are also directly related to the learning disability. A learning-disabled child who cannot perceive words or numbers accurately on a page is also likely to misunderstand nonverbal communications. Therefore, in a social situation he is likely to say inappropriate things and thus to be regarded as insensitive. In addition, the learning disabled child's inability to hear some words correctly makes him vulnerable to being seen as stubborn and as unable to follow directions (Osman & Blinder, 1986), as he may do something different than the words indicate. Or, being confused, he may not act at all.

Researchers are not in agreement as to the cause of learning disabilities. Some contend that anxiety plays a large role in the problem. Hart-Johns and Johns (1982) note that some children have a mild learning disa-

childhood aphasia

dyscalculia

hyperactivity

bility which in time they would be able to overcome or compensate for. However, because of the stresses and frustrations they experience either in their initial failures to learn a task or due to some other stressful life event such as parental divorce, they are unable to overcome the disability, so the problem becomes increasingly severe. However, other researchers point to prenatal and perinatal factors relevant to learning disabilities (Brown, 1983) and to the biological mechanisms that underlie learning disorders. Shelley Smith (1981) notes that when one twin of a set of identical twins has a learning disability, in 90% of the cases the other twin has the same learning disability. She also notes that researchers have identified chromosome 15 as one that may carry a gene or genes related to a learning disorder. There is further evidence for the hereditary aspect of learning disabilities in the fact that several individuals in the same family often have similar learning disabilities.

Although researchers disagree on what causes learning disabilities, they are in agreement that a learning disability is not something a child outgrows or completely overcomes. With appropriate tutoring by teachers who are skilled at teaching learning-disabled children, such children can learn to compensate for the problem. Various strategies are utilized to help the learning-disabled child compensate for his disability. The most successful educational approaches are those which focus on the manifestation of the problem rather than its causes. This is an important change in the way researchers and clinicians now approach developmental problems: they attempt to treat symptoms as opposed to attempting to eliminate or figure out what caused the symptoms. Thus, educators have devised a broad educational therapy for learning disabled children, including remediation of social skills, help with academic tasks, and individualized instruction. Parents are also advised that when children's learning disabilities are identified early in life, even before the child enters school, his ability to profit from therapy is enhanced. It is important, however, that the child be given professional help that is appropriate to his particular disability. Not all teachers or parents are able to guide the learning disabled child in his effort to find and rely upon different means of processing information.

DISCUSSION OF SOCIAL ISSUES: MAINSTREAMING

Learning-disabled children, along with other children who have difficulty learning or who are deaf, blind, mentally retarded, or otherwise physically or mentally handicapped, were at one time isolated from other children and taught in special classes. Recent concerns for these children resulted in a law entitled the Education for All Handicapped Children Act (Public Law 94-142), passed in 1975, which guarantees every handicapped

Cognitive Style

Some children do not perform well in school because of their cognitive style. Cognitive style refers to the manner in which the individual perceives and responds to information in the environment. Recognizing that intellectual and verbal skills do not always account for academic problems some children encounter, Jerome Kagan (1965) noted that children's cognitive style plays a role in academic performance—some children are reflective in their approach to tasks, others are impulsive.

Kagan devised the *Matching Familiar Figures Test* to find out which children are reflective and which are impulsive in their approach to problem solving. The test includes pictures of a common object such as a bear sitting on a chair. The pictures are identical, but one of them differs from the other in a minute detail. To find out which of the pictures is different from the others, the child has to pay close attention to the details in the picture. Kagan found out that reflective children carefully look at each of the pictures, comparing them and making relatively few errors in their response. Impulsive children quickly glance at the pictures and without paying attention to the details, they give an answer, which is usually wrong.

Impulsivity declines somewhat with age, so the older the child, the more likely he is to be reflective in his thinking. In each classroom there are a number of children who are impulsive. Since academic tasks require careful consideration of the problem as well as accuracy, the impulsive child is at a disadvantage in school. Through training, it is possible to modify the behavioral and cognitive patterns of impulsive children. Giving the child verbal descriptions of appropriate ways to respond to cognitive tasks, and reinforcing and modeling appropriate response styles, can help the child modify his approach to problems (Debus, 1970).

Researchers note also that the characteristic of thinking impulsively or reflectively is present not only in children's approach to cognitive tasks, but in other situations as well. In their play behavior, for example, impulsive children tend to be those who run around the room playing with different toys for only a few minutes at a time and then diverting their attention to other toys. Reflective children, on the other hand, take time to choose a toy to play with, and they play with the same toy for longer periods. If children are asked a question in a social setting such as, "What is your favorite game?" impulsive children are quick to answer, whereas reflective children think a few minutes before they answer (Kagan & Kagan, 1970). Egeland (1974) also found that impulsive children can be taught to wait before they respond to questions and to consider all the details involved.

child an appropriate public education that is individually tailored to meet the child's specific needs. The law mandates that each handicapped child will have an individualized plan for educational goals that is formulated in cooperation with parents and teachers and that the child will be educated in "the least restrictive environment," which is interpreted to mean that she will be *mainstreamed* into the regular classroom. That is, that she will be taught alongside her normal peers. Although some children are so severely handicapped that they cannot be placed in a regular classroom, the majority of children who in the past were in special education classes are now being mainstreamed for at least part of their school day.

Public Law 94–142 represents a major landmark in educational legislation. With the passage of the act, handicapped children have gained access to a major public school system, whereas previously they had none. Their parents have also gained a tool to hold the state and local education authorities accountable for providing some of the services necessary to raise and educate a handicapped child. Another important aspect of the legislation is its mandate for parents' participation in the development of an individualized educational program for their handicapped child, which some experts see as a possible encouragement to the parents of normal children to become involved in their children's education (Zigler & Muenchow, 1979). Most importantly, PL 94–142 is laudable in its intent, which is to benefit handicapped children and expand the educational options available to them. By socializing with normal children and adults within the regular classroom setting, handicapped children are expected to have the same opportunities for education that normal children do and to learn more social and academic skills than they would if they were educated in special education classes with other handicapped children (Birch, 1976; Salend, 1980). Advocates of mainstreaming contend that the practice will not only benefit handicapped children directly in these ways, it will also result in a reduction of the stigma of being educated in segregated special education settings (see Figure 11.14). It may also force our society to change its negative attitudes toward the handicapped. Normal children and adults, through their interactions with handicapped children, will be better able to understand the needs, limitations, and strengths of handicapped individuals.

Although the intent of PL 94–142 is clearly to benefit handicapped children, the wisdom of the act has been vigorously debated (Sarason, 1983; Zigler & Muenchow, 1979). Experts are about equally divided in their opinions as to whether the law will prove beneficial or detrimental to learning disabled and handicapped children. Some experts contend that mainstreaming will result not in the expansion of educational opportunities for the handicapped, but in the reduction of such opportunities. A learning-disabled child, a blind child, a deaf or otherwise handicapped child needs not only the opportunity to interact with normal children, but also the opportunity to learn specific skills which will help her live and

FIGURE 11.14 In 1975, Public Law 94-142 was passed, guaranteeing every handicapped child an appropriate education and mandating that handicapped children will be taught alongside their normal peers. Although laudable in its intent, the law could have negative consequences for handicapped children.

work in the mainstream of society as an adult. One deaf teacher explains that the special education he received in a school for the deaf was not restrictive in any way but enabled him to acquire important skills without which he would have been hopelessly lost in the hearing world (Greenberg & Doolittle, 1977).

Those who question the benefits inherent in mainstreaming wonder if regular classroom teachers are qualified for and capable of teaching handicapped children. They argue that unless handicapped children are taught by teachers who are trained to teach the handicapped, the individualized education program mandated by PL 94-142 will be impossible to attain (Turnbull, Strickland, & Hammer, 1978). The fact is, most teachers in regular classrooms are not trained to meet the specific needs of handicapped children, and often they do not have adequate support personnel to assist them in their attempts to respond to the individual needs of all the children in the class (Sarason, 1983). In some school districts sufficient money is available to provide teachers with support personnel and with educational consultants who help them teach the handicapped, but in many schools such financing is not available. Even those who regard PL 94-142 as an important breakthrough in the education of the handicapped and who consider an integrated educational program as potentially superior to a segregated special education program acknowledge that there are problems in the translation of the law into practice. They note that there is considerable variation not only in the amount of money made available in schools to facilitate mainstreaming, but also in the way school districts define mainstreaming. Some schools do not provide handicapped children with the opportunity to be educated in the regular classroom; they simply count the time these children spend with normal children in the cafeteria or in the halls or on the playground during recess as time they spent being mainstreamed (Meyers, MacMillan, & Yoshida, 1980).

These and other problems associated with PL 94-142 are not unique. In the implementation of any social policy, obstacles are often encountered and unintended consequences surface, resulting in a discrepancy between the original intent of the policy and its subsequent outcome. This is because a policy, by definition, is a general guide for action. A policy specifies some general guidelines relevant to the achievement of a goal (Kahn, 1969), but these guidelines are subject to various interpretations which are not always congruent with the intent or goal of the policy. For this reason, any social policy, even one that appears to be beneficial to children and families, must be analyzed in terms of its possible advantages and disadvantages, and it must also be evaluated to ensure that it is implemented in keeping with its original intent. This type of evaluation is called *process evaluation,* and it is used to verify whether the services mandated by the policy are delivered and how. Another type of evaluation, *outcome evaluation,* is used to assess the impact of the policy, and to determine whether the services mandated by the policy are indeed beneficial. The use of both types of evaluation can yield valuable lessons about the program or policy so that the discrepancy between the original intent of the policy and its subsequent outcome may be minimized. *process evaluation*

outcome evaluation

Another way to minimize this discrepancy is to ensure that the policy is formulated on the basis of what we know from the research about the type of programs and experiences that enhance children's development and education. One problem with PL 94-142 is that it was conceived during the civil rights movement and in reaction to the mislabeling of many minority children as retarded (see Chapter 14). As such, it was based more on political and philosophical considerations than on any scientific evidence concerning the merits of any particular educational placement for children with handicaps (Zigler & Muenchow, 1979). The evidence that points to the advantages of educating handicapped children with nonhandicapped children is inconclusive. In many cases, researchers are finding that academically mainstreamed handicapped children fare no better or worse than handicapped children who are taught in special education classes (Budoff & Gottlieb, 1976; Gottlieb, 1980). In addition, whereas some note that mainstreamed handicapped children have a good self-image as a result of being in the regular classroom (Gleidman & Roth, 1980), others note that mainstreamed handicapped children feel just as stigmatized by their normal peers as do handicapped children who are educated in self-contained classes (Meyers, MacMillan, & Yoshida, 1980). Caparulo and Zigler (1983) found that in some schools, some handicapped children's self-image and academic performance seemed to improve as a result of mainstreaming, but that other handicapped children in other schools experienced an inordinate amount of failure in the context of the regular classroom and developed a sense of inadequacy which inhibited their ability to learn.

The mixed results reported by investigators may be related to variations in implementing PL 94-142. This variation is attributed in part to the lack of sufficient funds available to appropriately implement mainstreaming (Sarason & Doris, 1983), as well as to the lack of precise guidelines for implementing the procedure (Salend, 1984). Now that PL 94-142 has been legislated and put into practice, a key issue facing educators is to determine the ways in which the everyday experiences of handicapped children in integrated educational settings affect not only their academic achievement but also their self-esteem and their motivation to learn and succeed. You can see how the need for research is paramount in the social policy process. All policies, although they may present opportunities for children, carry with them not only the possibility of making things better but also the risk of making things worse.

SUMMARY

During the middle childhood years the child acquires a number of cognitive skills which facilitate her ability to profit from formal instruction in school. According to Piaget, the school-age child, who is in the concrete operations period of cognitive development, is able to perform mental inversions (reversibility of thought) so she draws conclusions about observed outcomes not on the basis of how things appear but on the basis of prior relationships. She is also capable of decentering, which means she is able to focus on multiple dimensions of an object at the same time. Having these mental abilities, the child can understand conservation, which refers to the ability to recognize that two equal quantities remain the same even if one of them has changed in one way, as long as nothing has been added or taken away.

The child also acquires the ability to classify and to seriate, which demonstrate that she is capable of systematic and planful thinking. In seriation experiments, the child is required to arrange a pile of sticks in ascending order according to their length, an achievement which requires the understanding that Object A is bigger than Object B, which is bigger than Object C. Once the child has this understanding, she can engage in transitive reasoning, which refers to the ability to recognize a relationship between two objects by knowing their relationship to a third: If A is greater than B and B is greater than C, then A must be greater than C. The child also acquires enhanced memory skills during the middle childhood years, as noted by information processing researchers. Those researchers who adhere to this view of cognitive development describe the progress in cognitive growth quantitatively, rather than qualitatively as Piaget does. They note that as she grows older, the child is better able to perceive, attend to, and remember aspects of her environment, and thus she can profit from formal instruction.

However, although most school-age children have the ability to learn such basic skills as reading, writing, and arithmetic, not all of them do. In fact, current studies show that there are increasing numbers of children who fail to acquire basic skills in school. Although the educational system is often blamed for the low levels of achievement among school children, children may fail to learn because they lack the motivation for learning, because of an emotional problem or conditions in their family life and the extent to which their parents encourage them to learn, or because they are unable to learn due to some learning disability. About 1.8 million school children are learning disabled, meaning that they have trouble learning to read and write. Many reasons may account for this inability, one of which may be that they are learning-disabled and cannot accurately process information. Some learning-disabled children have difficulty with words, others with calculating numbers or concentrating on a task.

Although in the past learning-disabled and other handicapped children were taught in special classrooms, a recent law (PL 94-142) requires school systems to mainstream the children into the regular classroom so they can be taught along with normal children. The intent of the law is to provide handicapped children with equal educational opportunity. However, since there is at times a discrepancy between the intent of the law and its subsequent outcome, it remains to be seen whether all mainstreamed handicapped children actually learn more than do handicapped children who are not mainstreamed. Now that PL 94-142 has been put into practice, researchers and educators have to determine the ways in which the everyday experiences of handicapped children affect not only their academic achievement, but also their self-esteem.

REVIEW POINTS

1. During the middle childhood years the child is in what Piaget termed the concrete operations period. This period is characterized by the child's greater flexibility of thought and ability to organize her ideas in a systematic fashion so that her thinking is no longer dominated by immediate visual impressions.

2. Two important aspects of concrete operational thought are reversibility and decentering. Reversibility refers to the ability to perform mental inversions, or to mentally undo a sequence of actions. Decentering refers to the ability to focus not only on one, but on several features of an object at one time so that all perceptual data are taken into account. With these two abilities, the concrete operational child can correctly answer questions related to conservation, classification, and seriation.

3. Although Piaget believed that the changes in children's abilities are the result of changes in mental structures, his is only one interpretation of cognitive development. Other researchers offer an alternative explanation, noting that as they grow older, children become better able to process information.

4. Essential in the ability to process information is the ability to pay attention to select stimuli in the environment. The child's ability for selective attention (the ability to focus on relevant aspects of the environment) increases with age, thus the child can concentrate on tasks for increasingly longer periods of time.

5. Also important in the ability to process information is the child's ability to remember and retrieve information. The capacity for memory increases during the middle childhood years as children are better able to employ memory-aiding devices. They also acquire an intuitive understanding of how memory works, which is referred to as metamemory.

6. During the middle childhood years children also acquire metalinguistic skills, or an intuitive understanding of how language works. This is reflected in their increased ability to communicate effectively and to acquire a more precise meaning of words. During this period children are also able to understand that words have literal and nonliteral meanings, so they can understand metaphors.

7. Increased cognitive and language skills enable the child to engage in academic tasks required in school. The extent to which the child will be able to do well on these tasks is also dependent on her motivation to succeed and the extent that her parents encourage her to succeed and become involved in her school activities.

8. Some children are unable to profit from instruction at school because of emotional problems or because they have a learning disability and are unable to process information. Children do not outgrow learning disabilities, but with special and individualized instruction, they can be taught to compensate for them.

9. At one time learning-disabled and physically or mentally handicapped children were taught in separate classrooms. In 1975, the Education for All Handicapped Children Act (PL 94-142) was passed, mandating that these children will be mainstreamed into the regular classroom and spend at least some part of the day with their peers. This law is important and may benefit learning-disabled and handicapped children. However, problems have arisen in its implementation.

CHAPTER 12

SOCIAL AND EMOTIONAL DEVELOPMENT DURING MIDDLE CHILDHOOD

The period of middle childhood is an exciting and happy time for most children. During this period, the 6- to 12-year-old child, although she still needs the protection and supervision of adults, acquires the freedom of an individual who can take care of herself in many ways. She becomes increasingly self-reliant, and she revels in her newly found independence, seeking to find out more about herself. She tests her skill at any number of activities, and she often channels her energies into constructive hobbies or becomes engrossed in elaborate school projects, in the process learning what she can and cannot do and acquiring a picture of herself as unique.

Just as the child learns more about herself, so she learns more about others in her world, and she experiences changes in social and emotional development that propel her toward greater social involvement and responsibility. She comes to know and is influenced by an increasing number of children and adults she meets at school or in the neighborhood, and the nature of her social relationships changes significantly. This is particularly evident in her relationships with peers. You will see in this chapter that as the child progresses through the middle childhood period, she becomes more independent of family life, and also more dependent on and selective of her peers. Whereas at the beginning of the period the child is tied to the family and views friends simply as occasional playmates, by the end of the period the child spends most of her time with "best" friends whom she considers as essential and trusted confidants. Not only does the child spend an increasingly greater portion of her time with age-mates, she also becomes part of a peer group. As she grows older, she is more inclined to yield to peer pressure, choosing to do what her friends do.

PROGRESS IN SOCIAL AND EMOTIONAL DEVELOPMENT

Advances in Social Cognition

Before we discuss the changes in the nature of the child's relationships with others, it is important to understand the impetus behind these changes. During the school-age years, the child makes enormous advances in social cognition—the ability to understand people and to think about social relations. She evidences her ability to infer accurately other people's thoughts and feelings, and she also realizes that since other people can do the same, her thoughts and feelings are the object of other people's thinking (Selman, 1976), so she begins to think about how other people will react to her actions and ideas.

Role-Taking

role-taking

The child's ability to make inferences about others' psychological experiences and states is enhanced by advances that occur in *role-taking*. Also

perspective-taking

called *perspective-taking,* role-taking is a cognitive skill which refers to the child's comprehension of information about another person's internal experiences. There are several types of role-taking abilities, including the capacity to understand what another person sees (perceptual role-taking), how another person feels (affective role-taking), and what another person thinks (cognitive role-taking).

Piaget was one of the first to investigate the development of children's role-taking abilities. He and Inhelder (Piaget & Inhelder, 1965) conducted the famous three mountain experiment (discussed in Chapter 8) to determine the age at which children can comprehend another's perceptual perspective when it differs from their own. Using this test, they found that because they are egocentric, children younger than age 7 were unable to take the perspective of others. Using different types of tests, researchers found that although preschoolers are not as entirely ignorant of others' feelings and thoughts as Piaget suggests (Shantz, 1975; Borke, 1975), role-taking is acquired gradually and becomes more refined with age. Selman (1976) and his colleagues (Selman & Bryne, 1974) suggest that children go through a developmental sequence of levels in acquiring role-taking ability. By asking children of different ages a series of questions, they tested the children's understanding of people's personalities—their desires, feelings, expectations, and probable reactions—and distinguished four levels of role-taking that occur between the ages of 4 and 12 years.

Level 0, Egocentric Role-Taking. At this level, children do not yet distinguish between their own perspective and that of others, and they assume that other people have feelings and thoughts that are more or less identical to their own.

Level 1, Subjective Role-Taking. At this level children realize that other people think or feel differently because they are in a different situation or because they have in their possession different kinds of information. They also realize that people may have different interpretations of the same event. However, the children have difficulty thinking about their own and others' perspectives at the same time, and they cannot put themselves in the position of the other person in judging what the other person thinks or feels.

Level 2, Self-Reflective Role-Taking. At this level, children become aware that people think or feel differently not just because they may be in a different situation or have different information, but also because each person may have her or his own particular values and interests. At this stage, children realize that their perspective is not necessarily the only right or valid one, and they can put themselves in the other person's place, realizing that the other person can do the same thing with regard to them. Thus, children begin to think about how others view them and to anticipate how others will react to their own actions and ideas.

TABLE 12.1   Between the ages of 4 and 10 years, children become less ego-centric and more adept at role-taking.

| | Percentage of Subjects Reaching a Given Role-Taking Level at Each Level of Chronological Age. | | | |
Stage	Age 4	Age 6	Age 8	Age 10
0	80	10	0	0
1	20	90	40	20
2	0	0	50	60
3	0	0	10	20
Total	100	100	100	100

Source: From article by Robert L. Selman and Diane F. Byrne from *Child Development*, 45, p. 806, Table 1. Copyright © 1974 by The Society for Research in Child Development, Inc.

(8 - 10 yrs.)

Level 3, Mutual Role-Taking.   At this level, children are able not only to differentiate their own perspective from that of other people, they can also think about their own point of view and that of another person simultaneously.

On the basis of their analysis of children's answers to questions about other people, Selman and his colleagues found that egocentrism begins to decline at about age four. By age six, children become aware that others view things differently than they do, and by age ten they are beginning to be able to consider simultaneously both their own and another person's point of view (see Table 12.1). You should note, however, that although researchers agree with Selman and his colleagues that there are developmental changes in role-taking ability, some disagree with the age levels they attached to these. They note that children younger than age 6 have the ability to take the perspectives of others, although this becomes evident not necessarily when the children are questioned about other people, as Selman did, but when they are observed in their play interactions (Hoffman, 1976; Rubin & Pepler, 1980). Other researchers point out that an exact age cannot be associated with each level, as a given child's role-taking ability may fluctuate from one occasion to another (Maccoby, 1980). Some children may be able to take another's perspective for a moment, but they may fail to do so if the task requires maintaining that perspective for longer periods of time. Also, a child who understands the perspective of familiar people in familiar situations may be much less skillful when the person or situation is unfamiliar (Flapan, 1968).

Finally, researchers point out that an important aspect of role-taking ability is social experience. No matter how old they are, children who lack the opportunity to interact with other children are less skilled at taking the

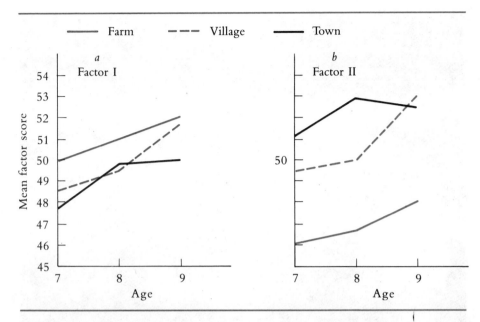

FIGURE 12.1   (a) Children who live on isolated farms are ahead of children who live in villages and towns when they are tested on cognitive tasks; (b) however, not having the opportunity to interact with children their own age, they lag behind in role-taking ability. From article by Marida Hollos from *Child Development,* 46, p. 645, fig. 1. Copyright © 1975 by The Society for Research in Child Development.

perspective of others than children who do have extensive social experiences (Hollos, 1975; see Figure 12.1). Apparently peer interactions provide the opportunity children need to become acquainted with how others behave, think, and feel in different situations. This point is demonstrated by Marida Hollos (1975) who tested children in Norway and Hungary, choosing children who lived on farms, in villages, and in towns. The children were tested on their cognitive skills, using some of the Piagetian tasks (for conservation and classification) described in Chapter 11, and also on their ability to take the perspective of others. The children were of similar socio-economic backgrounds, but they differed in the extent that they spent time with peers. The children from the farms spent most of their time helping their parents or playing alone, whereas children from villages spent more time with other children, and the children living in towns spent even more time with peers.

Hollos found that farm children outperform village and town children on Piagetian tasks, which measure the ability to think logically, but they are not as good as the village or town children in taking another person's perspective. This study is important for it clearly illustrates that while the ability to think logically and acquire cognitive maturity may not be influenced by the individual's interactions with other people, social interac-

FIGURE 12.2   Because of their enhanced role-taking skills, these two girls can communicate with one another effectively and each one can understand how the other is feeling.

tions are indeed important to the individual's ability to understand others and recognize that other people think and feel differently.

Just as social interactions enhance the child's role-taking skills, so the child's progress in role-taking enhances her interactions with other children and adults. Having the ability to take the perspective of others, the child becomes better able to communicate, since effective communication depends on an assessment of what other people already know and what they need to know (see Figure 12.2). The ability to understand how peo-

FIGURE 12.3   The Interpersonal Perception Test tests children's capacity to understand how others feel. In this test, children are told a story, and they are asked to pick out the face that best describes how the person in the story is feeling. Although four-year-old children can pick the correct face when they are told a simple story, it is not until the middle childhood years that children can do so when told complex stories.

ple think and feel also enhances empathy, the ability to understand and vicariously feel what another person is feeling. Empathy not only enables the child to help others who may be in distress, it also enhances her ability to think about the effects of her own behavior on others.

The child's capacity for empathy becomes gradually more refined during the school-age years. Recall from Chapter 9 that preschoolers are able to empathize with others in some situations. When they are told a simple story and then asked to pick out from a group of pictures the one that reflects how the person in the story feels (see Figure 12.3), 4-year-olds can accurately identify a happy face picture for happy stories (Borke, 1971). However, when the stories are more complex or when children are required not only to identify emotions, but also to infer how people may think about other people's feelings, it is not until the children are approximately 12 years of age that they can do so. Consider a study conducted by Dorothy Flapan (1968) which included children ages 6, 9, and 12 years. The children were shown movie scenes portraying feelings and motives within the context of family interactions and other social situations. In one scene, for example, a girl is being punished by her father who later takes her out to the circus to make up for the punishment. All children in the study understood the feelings being portrayed in the scene, but when the 6-year-olds were asked about the motives of the father, they could not answer, whereas the 9- and 12-year-olds responded accurately. In other words, they were able at this age to infer thoughts and intentions, they were also able to understand what the adults in the movie scene were thinking about the other actors' feelings.

Moral Development

The progress in social cognition that occurs during the middle childhood years also enhances the child's ability to evaluate her own behavior in relation to what other people think as well as to how they feel. Hence, the child grows in her ability to behave and reason about moral problems.

Every society has an unwritten moral code and explicit rules that specify people's moral behavior in the social setting. Examples of such rules include that a person should try to help others in distress or that he should be honest at all times even when he is not likely to get caught. If a clerk at the supermarket checkout counter gives you change for $20.00 instead of for the $10.00 bill you handed him, you are expected to point out the mistake that was made. If you don't, your conscience may bother you and you may feel guilty for having taken advantage of the situation. The *conscience* is a byproduct of moral development, which is the process of learning to accept standards of right and wrong as guides to behavior.

conscience

The Development of Moral Knowledge.   Children are not born with a moral code or a conscience; they acquire these gradually. Child psychologists have long been interested in the nature and course of moral development, asking: How do children learn the difference between right and wrong? How do they learn to be honest even when no one is looking? How do they learn to overcome the temptation to cheat? (See Figure 12.4.) Answers to these questions differ depending on one's theoretical orientation. Psychoanalysts focus on the emotional aspect of moral development, noting that guilt is a major component of morality. Moral growth, according to psychoanalytic theorists, is fostered by identification with the same-sex parent, which leads to the formation of a conscience. This occurs through the resolution of the Oedipus and Electra conflicts (Freud, 1965), which leave boys and girls with fear and anxiety at the thought of losing a parent's love and guilt over incestuous fantasies about the opposite-sex parent. From that point on, the fear, anxiety, and guilt generate moral sanctions which emanate from within, that is, from the conscience. Social learning theorists contend that moral behavior and values are shaped by cultural experience through modeling and reinforce-

Changes in Understanding Social Interactions

Studying changes in social cognition that occur during the middle childhood years, Dorothy Flapan (1968) selected a group of children aged 6, 9, and 12. She showed them movie scenes of adults and children portraying different feelings and motives, and later she analyzed the children's interpretation of what they had seen. She found that the older they were, the better the children could explain what had taken place and infer what the actors were feeling and intending. To appreciate the different ways children described what they had seen, compare the first description, by a 6-year-old, with the second description, which is by a 12-year-old.

6-Year-Old Child. ". . . Daddy was sitting in the chair . . . looking at the paper. And the little girl got out of her bed and said 'Pa, will you kiss me goodnight?' And the daddy said 'Go to bed,' and the little girl went to bed crying. And he tore up the paper and threw it down on the floor. Then he went into the kitchen and was ready to go out to the barn."

12-Year-Old "The father was reading the newspaper, but he was thinking about something else. He really couldn't read it. And the little girl was looking down and asked if her father didn't want to kiss her good night. The father wanted to say good night, but then he thought she did something bad, so he said 'No. Go back to bed.' And the little girl was crying. . . . The father tried to read the newspaper again, but couldn't read so he threw it away. He wanted to go up [to the girl] and say it wasn't so bad. But he decided he better not. So he went to the kitchen and said to his wife he was going out."

ment. From either of these points of view, the child becomes moral through the influences of external forces such as the parents.

The Cognitive-Developmental Approach. These ideas of the development of morality through external influences are contrary to the cognitive-developmental position that moral reasoning develops progressively along with cognitive abilities. Jean Piaget (1932) and Lawrence Kohlberg (1969) are the two best-known theorists who describe moral development from the perspective of cognition, both believing that the development of morality is a function of cognitive growth.

FIGURE 12.4   Gradually children come to accept standards of right and wrong as guides to behavior. Because children are not born with a moral code, researchers have long been interested in how moral development occurs.

Piaget was particularly interested in children's notions about rules. By studying how children thought about and followed the rules of a game, he noted that one could gain insight into their perceptions of morality. In playing marbles, for instance, children not only cooperate, they also have to deal with a number of moral issues such as fairness (who goes first), reciprocity (taking turns), and justice (yielding a marble if they lose). Analyzing his observations of children playing marbles, Piaget found that it is not until the middle childhood years, during the concrete operations period, that children begin to play by rules. During the previous period of development, preschoolers perceive rules as sacred and unalterable and they believe that rules are absolute extensions of authority figures such as God or Daddy. However, preschool children are still egocentric and essentially asocial, according to Piaget, so they have little regard for rules. They may think of rules as absolute and unchangeable, but when they are playing they change the rules to suit themselves, and they improvise new rules as the game progresses.

During the middle childhood years, children are very strict about following rules, especially during the early part of the period, at about the age of 7 or 8. They not only play games by following the rules, they also expect all other "rules" such as getting an allowance every Friday or being allowed to stay up late on Saturday to be followed. They often claim that it isn't fair when some of these precedents cannot be followed. They also have a rather rigid understanding of the concept of rules. This is illustrated by Piaget (1932) who asked 10-year-old Ben to invent a new rule for the game of marbles. After refusing to do so, Ben did invent a rule, but claimed that to adhere to the new rule would be cheating. Why? "Because I invented it," replied Ben. "It isn't a rule! It's a wrong rule because it's outside of the rules. A fair rule is one that is in the game." Gradually, however, children acquire a more realistic notion of rules, and by the end of the elementary school years they reject the idea that rules are absolute and believe instead that since the purpose of rules is to benefit all those involved, rules can be changed and reformulated through reasoning, discussions, and agreement among participants.

In another way of studying moral development, Piaget asked children questions about moral stories. He found that with age, children change in their moral judgment. For example, Piaget presented children with two different stories. One was about a boy who is called to dinner. As he goes to the dining room, he accidentally breaks 15 cups. Another story was about a different boy who climbs up on a chair to get some jam out of the cupboard. While he is trying to get the jam, he knocks over a cup and breaks it. In a variation of these stories, Piaget asked children to compare two children, one of whom accidentally broke 15 cups while helping his mother and one of whom broke one cup by throwing it across the room in anger. The children were asked who was the naughtier boy in the stories and who should be punished more—the one who accidentally broke a greater number of cups or the one who broke only one cup while doing something wrong. Piaget found that children aged 5 to 10 said the boy who broke more cups is naughtier since he broke a greater number of cups. That is, children based their judgment of the act on the *consequences*. By age 11, however, children based their judgments on the *intentions* of the individuals involved and said that the boy who broke one cup was naughtier, because he was intentionally engaged in an activity that led to breaking the cup.

Kohlberg's Stages of Moral Development. Building upon Piaget's observations, Kohlberg has formulated a more comprehensive theory of moral development and has found through his research that as children grow older, their way of understanding the social world and, consequently, their way of making moral judgments changes. He proposed six (later revised to five) stages of moral development, each one building upon the other and each associated with changes in cognitive structure. These stages are grouped within three levels of moral thought—preconventional, conventional, and postconventional—which correspond, roughly, to the preoperational (2–7 years), concrete operations (7–12), and formal operations (12–adulthood) periods of cognitive growth.

The Preconventional Level. At the lowest level of moral judgment, the preconventional level, children's emphasis is on avoiding punishment and getting a reward.

Stage 1. In Stage 1, which could be described as *might makes right,* children value obedience to authority, and they make moral decisions on the basis of the possible physical consequences, such as punishment, that may be associated with an act. They follow rules in order to avoid being punished.

Stage 2. In Stage 2, *the instrumental relativist stage,* children try to take care of their own needs, and they are motivated by the hedonistic consequences of an act, believing, for instance, that the reason one should be nice to people is so they will be nice to you. A child in this stage might share her candy bar with another child, but only if that child will let her have something in return.

The Conventional Level. At this level, the emphasis is on social rules and on maintaining the expectations of the individual's family, group, or nation.

Stage 3. This stage can be characterized by *the good girl and nice boy orientation.* In Stage 3, the child considers a behavior to be right if it meets with the approval of other people. Approval is more important at this stage than any specific reward.

Stage 4. This stage can be characterized by *the law and order orientation.* In Stage 4, the child emphasizes the maintenance of social order and regards right behavior as consisting of doing one's duty and showing respect for authority.

The Postconventional or Autonomous Level. At this level there is clear effort on the part of the individual to define moral values and principles that have validity and application.

Stage 5. This stage can be characterized by *the social contract or legalistic orientation.* In Stage 5, the individual has a sense of obligation to law because of the social contract existing between people and society for the common good. Right actions are defined in terms of individual rights and also in terms of standards that have been critically examined and agreed upon by the whole society. There is an awareness during this stage that these standards, or rules of society, exist for the benefit of all and that they are established by mutual agreement.

Stage 6.   This stage can be characterized by *the universal ethical principles orientation*. In Stage 6, the individual acquires a sense of personal commitment to moral principles because of the rational recognition of universal concepts. Right is defined by decisions of the conscience in accord with self-chosen ethical principles. Since so few people ever reach this highest stage of moral development, Kohlberg (1978) in his later writing combined this stage with Stage 5.

Kohlberg developed his theory of moral development on the basis of interviews he conducted with children and adults. In these interviews, the individual is presented with stories featuring a number of hypothetical moral dilemmas and is asked what the characters in the story should do and why. One example of such a dilemma is a story about Heinz, a man who broke into a druggist's store to steal medications for his sick wife. Was the stealing an immoral or a moral act? (see Figure 12.5). Kohlberg was not interested in the children's answers as much as he was interested in the kind of justification or reasoning they gave along with the answers. For example, a child who is at Stage 3 might say that the husband should steal the drug *because people will blame him for not saving his wife* or he might say that the husband shouldn't steal the drug *because he had already done everything he could legally and people would call him a thief if he stole*. In both answers, the child's justification shows that he considers moral behavior in terms of what other people might think. Presenting this and other moral dilemmas to children in various cultures, Kohlberg and others (Edwards, 1982) found that the developmental sequence of the stages of moral development is universal. Children in diverse cultures and with different experiences generally progress through the stages in much the same way. There are those, however, who question the universality of moral development, suggesting that more research is needed to establish whether children in all cultures do indeed progress through the same stages of moral development.

Kohlberg's theory has been useful in highlighting the developmental changes in moral judgment, and it has had extensive influence among educators in particular. For example, his theory forms the basis for a procedure known as *value clarification* in which children are encouraged to think about their values through discussions of hypothetical dilemmas (Beyer, 1978). However, not all researchers agree with Kohlberg. Some argue with his contention that children construct a moral code in keeping with cognitive capabilities, noting instead that children construct a moral code socially, through discussion and debate with others (Youniss, 1980). A number of researchers have criticized Kohlberg's use of moral dilemmas. Damon (1977), for example, argues that the dilemmas are too abstract. He suggests that if children were presented with more realistic moral stories that are relevant to their day-to-day experiences, they might employ more mature reasoning. In another instance, Carol Gilligan (1982)

value clarification

FIGURE 12.5   The Heinz Dilemma. To illustrate the characteristics of each of the levels of moral thought and the developmental changes in the child's reasoning about moral conflicts, Kohlberg presented children with stories featuring a number of hypothetical moral dilemmas, and he asked the children what the characters in the stories should do and why. The famous moral dilemma devised by Kohlberg follows. Children's reasons for why Heinz should or should not have stolen the drug reflect their level of moral reasoning. Source: Kohlberg, L. (1969). *Stages in the development of moral thought and action.* New York: Holt.

In Europe, a woman was near death from a special kind of cancer. There was one drug that the doctors thought might save her. It was in the form of radium that a druggist in town had recently discovered. The drug was very expensive to make, but, even so, the druggist was charging 10 times what the drug cost him to make; he paid $200 for the radium and charged $2,000 for a small dose of the drug. The sick woman's husband, Heinz, went to everyone he knew to raise money for the drug, but could only raise $1,000, which is half of what the drug cost. He explained to the druggist that his wife was deathly ill and asked if he could sell the drug cheaper or let him pay for it later. The druggist refused, claiming that he discovered the drug and expects to make money from it. Desperate, Heinz broke into the druggist's store and stole the drug for his wife. Should Heinz have done that? Why?

Stages	Pro	Con
Stage 1 Children are motivated to behave in order to avoid punishment.	Heinz should have stolen the drug. If he didn't and let his wife die, he would have been blamed for her death.	Heinz should not have stolen the drug because he could be caught and sent to jail and even if he gets away with it, his conscience would bother him and he would worry that the police would catch up with him.
Stage 2 Children are motivated to behave by the desire for benefit and reward.	If Heinz gets caught, he could give the drug back and wouldn't be punished much. Anyway, it wouldn't bother him to serve a sentence in jail since his wife is alive and will be there when he gets out of jail.	Heinz may not get much of a jail sentence for stealing the drug, but his wife may die anyway while he is in prison, so it wouldn't have helped him to steal the drug. If his wife dies, he shouldn't blame himself.
Stage 3 Right is defined according to what pleases other people and wins their praise.	No one will think that Heinz is bad for stealing the drug, but if he hadn't stolen the drug and let his wife die instead, his family would think of him as an inhuman husband.	Not only the druggist but everyone else will think that Heinz is a criminal and that he dishonored his family.
Stage 4 Right is regarded in terms of doing one's duty and showing respect for authority.	Heinz should not have been afraid to do anything that might save his wife because it's his duty to do so. If he didn't steal the drug and save her, he would have felt guilty.	When he was stealing the drug, Heinz was desperate and may not have realized that he was doing anything wrong. But after he is punished and jailed for his crime, he will feel guilty for his dishonesty and lawbreaking.
Stage 5 Right is defined in terms of standards that are agreed upon by the whole society.	If Heinz hadn't stolen the drug to save his wife, he would have lost other people's respect for him and his own self-respect.	By stealing the drug, Heinz lost the respect of everyone in the community and his own self-respect because he got carried away with emotion and forgot the long-term consequences of his action.
Stage 6 Right is defined by decisions of the conscience in accord with self-chosen ethical principles.	If he hadn't stolen the drug, Heinz would always have condemned himself afterward for not having lived up to his own standards of conscience.	Other people might not blame Heinz for having stolen the drug, but he would now condemn himself for not living up to his own conscience and standards of honesty.

also criticized Kohlberg, stressing his failure to look for possible sex differences in children's answers to moral dilemmas. In her own research Gilligan found that women base their moral decisions on different types of reasoning than do men. For example, women are concerned with relationships and social responsibilities and use these in their moral reasoning; men are concerned with legal issues and with rules. Since Kohlberg's levels of moral development focus on rules, Gilligan contends that they are not valid when used with women. Gilligan's research has also been criticized (Walker, 1984), but it nonetheless provides an important perspective on the issues involved in the study of moral development.

Moral Behavior

Researchers have further observed that children in the middle childhood period and some older children and adults as well, often endorse moral standards which they do not necessarily follow (Alston, 1971) and that both children and adults do not always behave in ways that they think best (Hoffman, 1984). The fact is, how a person decides to behave in any given situation is influenced not only by moral reasoning but also by the behavior of others, by one's personality characteristics, and by the standards of society. For example, most school-age children know that cheating is wrong, and they can usually explain why it is, evidencing an intellectual awareness of the issues involved. Nevertheless, when their peers put pressure on them to cheat or when they do not think that they will be caught, some of them do cheat (Harthorne & May, 1928).

Noting that there is a distinction between moral knowledge and moral behavior and that the two do not necessarily coincide, researchers have been interested in how children come to accept standards of right and wrong as guides to behavior and to behave accordingly. They found that the ability to take another's perspective is an important influence on moral behavior (Selman, 1980). Realizing how another child may feel if she had her watch stolen, a child may resist the temptation to steal. The child's ability to take the perspective of others increases during the school-age years, as we indicated in the previous section, and this ability is enhanced in the course of the child's social interactions, which offer children the exposure to how other people feel and think in numerous situations.

Perspective-taking ability is an important but not sufficient influence on moral behavior. Observational learning, reinforcements, and punishments also play a role. Social learning theorists such as Aronfreed (1968), for example, contend that children imitate the behavior of powerful and significant people and that through observational learning they learn specific moral behaviors such as sharing. Aronfreed also notes that social approval, by the people who are important in the child's life, such as the parents, is one of the most powerful reinforcers of moral behavior. As children learn that certain behaviors are approved or disapproved by their parents, they begin to think about their own behavior according to the expected consequences.

Aronfreed has outlined behavioral controls ranging from external to internal, noting that initially, the child's behavior is governed by external control. The child behaves morally only because she expects to be rewarded for doing so and she expects to be punished for behaving otherwise. With age, she learns about the different rules that govern good behavior, and she develops internal controls, or a conscience, and is motivated to behave morally in order to avoid feeling guilty; she punishes or rewards herself when she deviates from or conforms to appropriate norms of behavior. According to Aronfreed, children are likely to develop strong internal controls when parents, in the course of their attempts to socialize the child, specify the behavior that she is being punished or rewarded for and they explain why.

punitive techniques

inductive techniques

This view is supported by Hoffman (1970), whose theory of the development of moral behavior focuses on the type of disciplinary strategies parents adopt. Hoffman (1970) has distinguished two such strategies, punitive and inductive. *Punitive techniques* emphasize the personal consequences of breaking rules, in which parents may say, for example, "If you hit your little brother, you will not be allowed to watch TV." *Inductive techniques* stress the effects of misbehavior on the victims of moral transgressions, with parents explaining to the child that her actions are likely to have consequences: "If you hit your little brother, he will be hurt." Inductive techniques have proved to be more effective than the punitive techniques for teaching children to behave morally (Hoffman, 1970). The reason for this may be that by providing an explanation for the consequences of their behavior, children are encouraged to think about other people's feelings and to empathize with others (Hoffman, 1970, 1984).

Advances in the Self-Concept

It appears, then, that parents, through their actions and childrearing techniques, have a strong influence on the child's morality and her adoption of standards of right and wrong as guides to behavior. The parents' influence on the child extends beyond the development of morality, however. Parents also influence the child's self-concept and her self-esteem—her attitude toward herself (Maccoby, 1984). Although the parents' influence on the child's self-concept begins early in life, the middle childhood years are particularly crucial in this regard. It is during these years that the child becomes increasingly aware of herself as a unique individual (see Figure 12.6). It is also during these years that the child is more able than she was in previous periods of development to consider the views of others and take these into her consideration of what she herself is like.

FIGURE 12.6   Through extensive interactions with peers, children acquire an awareness of themselves as unique individuals.

Who Am I?   Young children have only a rudimentary notion of the self. Early in the preschool period, they come to regard themselves as separate individuals who can exert their own will and desires, and they also acquire an awareness of their gender identities and roles, recognizing themselves and behaving as boys or as girls. During the middle childhood years, children gain an even more refined sense of their gender identities and gender roles, and they continue the process of differentiating themselves from others in their surroundings (Harter, 1983). Gradually they discover more about themselves and they acquire a picture of the self that is unique and multifaceted (Markus & Nurius, 1984; Damon & Hart, 1982). Whereas at the beginning of this period children may still define themselves in terms of age and physical characteristics, by age 11 they give a more complex description of themselves that includes their inner thoughts and feelings. Asking children to answer the question, "Who am I?", Montemayor and Eisen (1977) found that a 9-year-old may say, for example, "My name is Bruce, I have brown eyes, I am nine years old, and I have 7 people in my family," and that an 11-year-old may reply:

> I'm a human being. I'm a girl. I'm a truthful person. I'm not pretty. I do so-so in my studies. . . . I am a very good swimmer. I try to be helpful. I'm always ready to be friends with anybody. Mostly I'm good, but I lose my temper . . . (Montemayor & Eisen, 1977).

How Do I Feel about Myself?   Children not only develop a more specific and multifaceted picture of themselves during the school-age years, they also begin to judge how worthy they are. The child's opinion of her own worth is a vital part of the child's personality, affecting all aspects of her behavior. The child with good self-esteem believes that she is a worthy individual who can achieve the goals she sets for herself and that she likes and is liked by the people around her. The child with little self-esteem, on the other hand, is convinced that she is not worthy of anyone's affection and that she is inadequate in comparison to others.

evaluative component of the self-concept

industry vs. inferiority

The self-esteem develops gradually during the middle childhood years and becomes part of the complex network of attitudes and beliefs that make up the self-concept. It is often referred to as the *evaluative component of the self-concept,* since it is formed on the basis of the child's perceptions of other people's reactions to her (Harter, 1983). Erik Erikson (1963) underscores the importance of the development of the self-esteem during this period of the child's life, noting that during the middle childhood years the child undergoes the psychological crisis of *industry vs. inferiority.* Erikson theorizes that the child who finds and concentrates on areas that she is good at and things that she can accomplish gains a sense that she can make and do things, a sense of industry, and she is ready and eager to move into the world of adulthood. The child who cannot find anything in which she can be competent soon develops a sense of inferiority and regards herself as insignificant in comparison to others.

Influences on Self-Esteem

Family Influences.   How the child comes to regard himself is largely, although not entirely, a function of his interactions with his parents. In a study of the influences on the self-esteem, Stanley Coopersmith (1967) found that parents' attitudes and childrearing practices tend to predict high or low self-esteem in children. In this study, Coopersmith measured the self-esteem of 10- to 12-year-old boys using the Self-Esteem Inventory he developed. He also tested their parents' attitudes, using the Parent Attitudes Research Instrument and in-depth interviews. He found that parents of boys with high self-esteem more often had the following attitudes and behavioral practices:

1. They were accepting, affectionate, and involved in their child's life, treating his interests and problems as meaningful, and showing genuine concern for him.
2. They enforced rules carefully and consistently, and they set clear limits to what the child could and could not do, encouraging him to uphold high standards of behavior.
3. They used noncoercive kinds of discipline, such as denial of privileges, and they typically explained to the child what he was being punished for and why his behavior was inappropriate.

4. They were democratic in their interactions with the child, often considering his opinions and allowing him to participate in making family plans when appropriate.

Explaining these findings, Coopersmith notes that when parents consider the child's opinions and allow him to express himself, they convey to the child that they think he is an important and worthy individual, so the child comes to regard himself as such. In addition, Coopersmith emphasizes that setting clear and realistic limits for the child and being consistent in what is expected of him are important because they lessen the chance of failure to meet parental standards for behavior. When the parents' standards for behavior are ambiguous, children are unclear about how they should behave and, thus, they have trouble monitoring, evaluating, and regulating their own behavior. Although there are some methodological shortcomings to Coopersmith's study in that his sample is small in size and restricted to boys (Wylie, 1979), his findings that parental childrearing practices are associated with high self-esteem are supported by the findings cited in Chapter 9 that authoritative parents have socially competent children. Recall that authoritative parents, as defined by Baumrind (1971), evidence characteristics that are similar to those emphasized by Coopersmith. They are warm, rational, and receptive to their children's opinions and concerns, but they also firmly enforce rules when the situation calls for it. They demand high standards of behavior and achievement from their children, and they employ noncoercive disciplining techniques, explaining to their children what they are being punished for and why. More recent studies by Loeb, Horst, and Horton (1980) also show that parental warmth is associated with children's high self-esteem, whereas physical punishment, or psychological punishment (withdrawal of love) are associated with low self-esteem.

Although parental attitudes toward the child and child-rearing practices are important influences on the self-esteem, others in the child's life exert their influence as well. You will see in the next section that teachers and peers can also help the child achieve success. If teachers praise the child for her work or her behavior in school, or if friends admire her for some specific skill or for her sociability, the child is likely to feel good about herself and to accept herself as a worthy person.

THE SOCIAL WORLD OF THE SCHOOL-AGE CHILD

The fact that the child is influenced by others besides her parents is documented in other chapters. Recall that during the preschool years children adopt certain modes of behavior by watching television and by observing other children and adults in day care and nursery school. However, during the preschool years, the family is still the major socializing agent. The

FIGURE 12.7   In school, as a result of increased contact with new adult models and with peers, children learn to behave in ways that are valued by teachers and friends.

child spends most of her time with family members, and it is in the context of family life that she learns how she is expected to behave. It is not until the middle childhood period that the child's sphere of social contacts widens considerably and that others besides parents assume a major role in shaping the child's behavior (Maccoby, 1984). Now in school, the child is exposed to new information and important, new adult models, as well as increased contact with peers. She learns that she is expected to behave not only in ways that are approved of by her parents, but also in ways that are valued and approved by her teachers and friends. Thus, schools and peers become powerful agents of socialization (see Figure 12.7).

Having the family, the school, and peers as socialization agents, the child often encounters conflicting messages about how he is expected to behave. He learns, for example, that behaving in class and getting good grades may be approved of by the teacher but not by his friends who may come to regard him as the teacher's pet. He also learns that while at home he may be encouraged to offer his opinion, at school he may not always be able to do so. Although he is exposed to these and other often conflicting expectations, the child's experiences in the school and with peers are important. These experiences promote the child's social development, enabling him to learn to express himself appropriately in different social settings (Epps & Smith, 1984). Furthermore, the child learns about different standards, values, and roles.

The School

The child's experiences at school are extremely important in this regard because schools have norms of behavior that define the children's and teachers' roles. These norms come from the *academic curriculum,* which includes tasks the child is expected to master, and from the *hidden curriculum* (Jackson, 1968), which refers to the mechanisms that maintain order and control in the classroom. These curricula define the teacher's role as an instructor, evaluator, and manager of the classroom, and they define the child's role as a pupil who is expected not only to learn what is presented to her but also to behave in an orderly and obedient manner, to respect authority, and to conform to rules (Hess & Holloway, 1985).

academic and hidden curricula

As we noted in Chapter 11, classroom structure (Schmuck & Schmuck, 1975) as well as other factors such as parent involvement (Stevenson, 1983) influence children's experiences in school. However, the extent to which the child will succeed in school and have positive interactions with her teachers also depend on how quickly she learns the roles that are defined by both the academic and the hidden curriculum. Teachers, for example, prefer students who learn well, who obey instructions, and who are quiet in class. Some teachers have difficulty relating positively to students who are bright but nonconforming in their behavior (Helton & Oakland, 1977). When asked to indicate their preference for children in the classroom, most student teachers in one study (Feshbach, 1969) said that they prefer rigid, conforming, and orderly children the most; dependent and acquiescent children the next; flexible but untidy and nonconforming children third; and independent, assertive, and active children last. In this study it was also revealed that those would-be teachers equate the children's behavior with their intellectual abilities. When asked which child in their class is likely to get the highest grade and which they considered to be the brightest, most of them indicated that the conforming child is the one whom they consider to be the highest-achieving and most intelligent.

The Influence of Teachers

The teachers' attitudes toward the characteristics of the children in their classes are important, as teachers assume a central role in the child's life, often determining to a large extent how she feels about being in school and about herself. This is especially true during the first year or two of school, when the child is still getting used to being subjected to the constant evaluation of her performance (Entwisle & Hayduk, 1978). Stipek

FIGURE 12.8   (*above and opposite*) When their teachers are friendly and encouraging, children often feel good about themselves and their school.

(1977), who studied the changes in children's social and motivational development that occurred during first grade, found that children's experiences of success or failure are defined more by their interactions with their teachers than by the children's actual academic performance; as long as the children had a friendly and positively reinforcing teacher, they felt successful and good about themselves in school.

The powerful influence of teachers on the lives of the children is hardly surprising. Most of us have fond memories of a teacher whom we consider to have had a significant role in shaping our lives—the teacher who responded to our particular needs, who acknowledged our feelings and ideas, and who inspired us toward greater academic involvement. Although teachers have always affected students' academic skills, behavior, and values, how some teachers encourage students is not entirely understood by researchers, in part because the research on the influences of teachers on children is riddled with a number of methodological flaws (Anderson, 1982). Nevertheless, some studies suggest that teachers who have a positive influence on their students are the teachers who rely heavily on praise and reasoning, and who create a warm and nurturant environment in the classroom (Gage, 1978; Brophy, 1983; see Figure 12.8).

Teachers' Expectations.   The teacher's belief that children are capable is also an important factor in the teacher's ability to positively influence

children. In a series of studies, Rosenthal and his colleagues found that teachers' expectations of children's capabilities affect their interactions with the children, and subsequently, the children's performance on academic tasks. In the original study in the series, Rosenthal and Jacobson (1966, 1968) gave a battery of intelligence tests to elementary school children who were told that the results of the tests would be communicated to their teachers. The researchers selected a number of students' names at random and told the teachers that these were, according to test results, the brightest of the children in the class. Some of the teachers were amazed, since the majority of these "bright" students had so far shown themselves to be, at best, average students. Nevertheless, the teachers accepted the test results and changed their attitudes toward the children, expecting them to do extremely well in their studies. A follow-up study revealed that the IQ of these randomly selected children, formerly considered to be average, was now higher than that of their fellow students. The researchers suggested that the change in the children's performance probably resulted from the altered attitudes of the teachers, who paid more attention to the children when they believed they were highly capable.

The universality of these findings for all schools and all children has yet to be established. Since they have conducted their landmark study, Rosenthal and his colleagues have been criticized on several methodological grounds (Cooper, 1979). However, after rigorous reanalysis of the data of this study and support from several other studies as well, researchers have concluded that although the interactions teachers have with children are influenced by many other factors, many teachers do indeed trans-

Corporal Punishment

Although the effects of the teacher on the child are known, many do not realize that teachers influence parents as well. Having examined teacher, student, and parent expectations in three elementary schools, Entwisle and Hayduk (1982) found that middle-class parents in particular are likely to change their expectations of their children on the basis of how teachers graded the children's work. Some parents, perceiving teachers as knowledgeable in matters pertaining to children, strive to adopt techniques similar to those the teachers use, especially when it comes to disciplining and managing children. Teachers can be a positive influence in this regard. When they are warm and nurturant in their interactions with children and when they employ noncoercive modes of punishment, they model for the parents appropriate ways of interacting with children, and they provide parents with alternatives to physical punishment.

Some teachers, however, have a negative influence and they serve to sustain inappropriate parental behaviors. These are behaviors that psychologists, policymakers, and other concerned individuals are trying to modify. Consider the matter of corporal punishment. Corporal punishment refers to spanking children or to other methods of physical punishment. It is often employed by parents and educators with the intent of teaching children to behave. Is physical punishment effective? Research with animals has shown that if physical punishment is intense, it may suppress an undesired behavior, but only temporarily (Solomon, 1964). Even if it were effective, however, physical punishment is associated with negative side effects, so its extensive use is not recommended. In Chapter 9 we discussed some of the negative effects of physical

punishment, including the fact that it serves to heighten children's anger and aggression (Feshbach, 1980), and it provides children with inappropriate models for resolving interpersonal problems (Parke, 1976, 1977). Researchers have come to the conclusion that although parents have to discipline children, they do not necessarily have to resort to physical punishment. Indeed, as we have seen in this and other chapters, the research has shown that parents who refrain from extensive use of coercive punishment techniques are more likely than other parents to have children who are well-behaved and socially competent (Baumrind, 1971).

Still there are many parents who believe that to spare the rod would result in spoiling the child. There are also many educators who feel that physical punishment is a necessary mode of punishment. Although it is difficult to assess the incidence of corporal punishment in the schools, experts on the topic estimate that 2 to 3 million incidents of physical punishment take place in public schools each year (Hyman, 1984). It is further indicated that thousands of children from kindergarten through twelfth grade are spanked every school day, sometimes for such trivial offenses as forgetting school supplies and being late for school. These reports also reveal that a large percentage of the children who are subjected to physical punishment are mentally or physically handicapped; they are punished because they have difficulty learning and mastering the material as quickly as other children or because they are too loud or perhaps too slow (Hyman, 1984; Rose, 1984).

Not only is corporal punishment common in many schools in America, it is socially and legally sanctioned. It is allowed in 43 states (several states, however, now explicitly ban corporal punishment by teachers and other school personnel), and it is reinforced by the nation's legal system. In 1977 the United States Supreme Court upheld a lower court decision that under circumscribed conditions—the presence of a witness, a preliminary warning, and an explanation to parents on request—teachers may use physical punishment (Zigler & Hunsinger, 1977). Furthermore, while there are parents who are opposed to having their children spanked in school, many parents are in favor of it, often asking school personnel to use corporal punishment as deemed necessary (Segal & Yahraes, 1978).

Educators who utilize or support the use of physical punishment contend that it is not only a valuable tool, but a necessary method of discipline without which teachers would not command respect. However, in a review of the research on corporal punishment in the schools, Norma Feshbach (1980) points out that the opposite is true. Children respect the teachers who are positive and noncoercive in their interactions with them. She, and others (Zigler & Hunsinger, 1977; Wessel, 1981), also point out that when educators resort to the use of physical punishment, they convey the message to parents that physical punishment is a preferred mode of punishment.

How do you feel about physical punishment, in general, and its use in the schools? Do you believe that educators should uphold this as a preferred method of discipline or would you suggest that they refrain from its use and adopt other methods of punishment? As you discuss your views with other students in your class, it will become clear to you that attitudes about physical punishment vary a great deal and that the topic is likely to engender emotionally laden arguments. Some people are totally against any type of physical punishment; others note that they have been spanked on numerous occasions and have probably benefited as a result.

mit their expectations to the children, some of whom, like the students in Rosenthal's study, begin to behave in ways that validate those expectations, setting into motion a self-fulfilling prophecy (Brophy, 1983). This is especially true of children in the first and second grades. The actual mechanics by which the teachers' expectations are communicated are not entirely known (Epps & Smith, 1984). However, it appears that words are not essential in this regard, as teachers subtly convey their attitudes and expectations by their tone of voice, facial expression, and posture. Chaikin, Sigler, and Derlega (1974) found that when teachers are interacting with children from whom they anticipate a superior academic performance, they engage in more positive nonverbal behaviors—smiling, leaning forward toward the student, making eye contact, and nodding their heads—than they do when they are interacting with students from whom they have no expectations or only expectations of inferior performance.

Teachers' expectations of children's performance are often not related to the children's actual abilities. Teachers have been found to base their expectations on such irrelevant characteristics as race and social class, expecting less in the way of achievement from lower-class students (Minuchin & Shapiro, 1983). They also base their expectations on the child's gender, expecting boys but not girls to succeed in such subject areas such as math (Meece et al., 1982). Some teachers also form expectations of a child's ability on the basis of the child's name. Harari and McDavid (1973) randomly assigned attractive names such as *Lisa* and *David* or unattractive names such as *Herbert* and *Gertrude* to a group of essays of similar quality and asked teachers to grade the essays. They found that teachers gave higher grades to essays that carried the attractive names.

A Society of Children

Besides being influenced by their teachers, during the middle childhood years children are also influenced by their peers. During these years the child spends an increasingly greater amount of time with peers, and she seeks to be with them not only when she is in school but at other times as well. As she interacts with age-mates, talking to them, telling secrets, squabbling, and engaging in a number of other social activities (Medrich et al., 1982), she prepares herself for her eventual independence from family life, learning at the same time about other people's perspectives, opinions, and values and about herself and how others view her (Fine, 1980; Asher, 1978).

Not only does the child spend more time with age-mates than ever before, she also becomes increasingly absorbed in her relations with peers and a part of what social scientists refer to as a *society of children*. The society of children is a social world that has its own rituals, traditions, activities, and social rules and its own songs and games that are handed down from one generation of children to another. It is theorized that school-age children through the ages have shared with each other a world all their own. It has also been found that children in a variety of different countries play very similar games (Opie & Opie, 1969) and that children this age develop their own vocabulary and have their own rules and codes of behavior, many of which involve independence from adults (Opie & Opie, 1959). Any child who violates any of these codes and is seen, for example, being kissed by her parents, is laughed at, teased, and called a baby.

Adults play no role in this social world of children. They rarely take notice of it and may not even realize that it exists. For their part, the children are reluctant to reveal what goes on in their world. They do not talk about what they do, and they tend to keep much of what goes on between them and their friends to themselves. As every parent of a school-age child knows, the older the child gets, the harder it becomes to obtain any information from her about her interactions with her friends. Asked, "Where did you go today?" or "What did you do with your friends?", the child is likely to reply, "Nowhere," and "Nothing."

FIGURE 12.9   Like many other children their age, these five boys enjoy spending time together in small groups.

Forming Groups

The social world of children is particularly evident in the formation of groups. These groups, which have common goals, aims, and rules of social conduct, include a hierarchical structure that identifies each member's relationship to the other members in the group, with one member usually designated as the leader (Rubin, 1980; Sherif & Sherif, 1964).

In a review of the research on peer groups, Hartup (1984) states that knowledge about peer groups is limited to relatively few studies. However, on the basis of these studies Rubin (1980) points out that the nature of peer groups changes as the children progress through the middle childhood period. He describes these changes, noting that in the early part of the period when the children are 6 or 7 years of age, peer groups are nothing more than play groups with few if any rules and no structure or hierarchy to define roles in the group and facilitate the interaction among members. Groups at this age form spontaneously and may include whoever happens to be nearby at the time they are formed (see Figure 12.9).

At a slightly older age, when the children are about 9, groups increase in their formality. The children now gather around shared interests and planned events, and they form nature clubs, fan clubs, and secret societies with special rules, observations, passwords, and initiation rites. These groups include a core of membership, with each member obligated to participate in activities, while nonmembers are excluded. Rubin points out that children's participation in such groups does not always last long, as often the groups are disbanded shortly after the selection of officers and other rituals for the formation of clubs.

Toward the latter part of the middle childhood period, peer groups become not so much official clubs as informal cliques of about 2 or 3 individuals (Hallinan, 1980), and these cliques play an important role in the child's development. It is during these years that the child begins the gradual process of leaving the safety of the family, so friends provide her with an invaluable support. It is also during these years that the child may begin to have a romantic interest in the opposite sex, and in the context of a group of friends she can exchange sexual information and get the reassurance and support she needs as she begins to deal with some of the concerns of growing up (Hartup, 1983, 1984). So taken are children with what they can learn from one another that they generally spend hours together discussing any number of issues and at the same time constantly laughing and giggling.

Close Friends

At this age children also have strong affection for a few of their close friends who are in the group, and they develop intense friendships. Such friendships are not evident early in the middle childhood period. When they first start school, children are still somewhat lacking in their ability to understand and empathize with other children and adults. They describe their friends in terms of superficial qualities such as appearance or possessions, and they interact with one another as buddies, companions, or playmates, but not necessarily as close friends. By age 10 or 11, however, children evidence their maturing notion of friendship, and they come to regard a friend as someone who will stick up for them and whom they will stick up for in times of need (Jacobson, 1975). They understand that friendships do not develop between people simply because they live nearby, and they consider friendship to be the sharing of inner thoughts and feelings (Youniss & Volpe, 1978; see Figure 12.10). As they grow older, children also begin to make a distinction between a "friend" and a "best friend," and they become concerned with clearly defining who is and who is not their friend. Gary Fine (1980) asked an 11-year-old boy who his best friends were and notes that the boy "made a big production of the answer, thinking very carefully and then explaining why his best friends should be ranked in [a] particular order." Having questioned chil-

FIGURE 12.10 Intense friendships are formed during the middle childhood years when it becomes important for the child to have a best friend with whom she can share some of the concerns of growing up.

dren on their notion of friendship, Fine found that among older school-age children, an important criterion for friendship is the sharing of personal information—facts and feelings that are not known to other people. Knowing so much about one another, their fears and failings, hopes and aspirations, children become close friends, providing one another with emotional support and the opportunity to understand some of the obligations of friendship. The children not only reveal their innermost feelings and thoughts to their friends, they also expect their friends to do the same, and failure to do so is viewed by children this age as a violation of the obligations inherent in friendship (Youniss, 1980; Bigelow, 1977). Children also view trust as a basic tenet of friendship, and they consider the betrayal of a secret as a serious breach in the relationship (Hinde, 1976). As one 12-year-old boy noted: "Trust is everything in a friendship. You tell each other things that you don't tell anyone else, how you really feel about personal things" (Selman & Selman, 1979).

Peer Acceptance

Children who are the same age, who live in the same neighborhood, or who attend the same school or summer camp are likely to become friends and to cluster into groups of friends (Hartup, 1984). Although the groups are informal, status hierarchies are evident as leaders usually come to the fore, and they dominate much of what goes on within the groups. Leaders are usually the children who are outgoing and energetic, who are witty and sociable, or who have some specific skill—they may be good basket-ball players, for example (Hartup, 1970, 1983).

Group membership comes about in several different ways. Sometimes the leader will make a decision of who will become a member of "his" or "her" group. At other times, a group begins with an existing pair of friends, both of whom decide whether or not to include others in their activities. In a review of the research, Hartup (1983) points out that usually children tend to exclude from their groups a child who may seem to them to be odd or different in appearance, skills, or temperament and to accept children who are sociable, fun, and who get along with others.

Popular Children.   Psychologists have long been interested in peer group formation and in status ranking within groups, and they have sought to find out which children tend to be popular. They have done so using observational studies that determine which children are often alone and which are sought out by others. They have also utilized a technique called *sociometry* (Hallinan, 1981). In this technique, children within an organized setting (for example, a classroom) are typically asked to name the child or children who fit categories such as "best friend," "best liked by other children," or "least liked." On the basis of the children's answers, a *sociogram* is drawn up (see Figure 12.11), with the children's choices tabulated to determine which children are accepted by other children and which by few or no children. With this information as a base, researchers have gone on to identify the attributes of popular and unpopular children.

sociometry

sociogram

They note that although there is no one quality that makes a child popular, there are a number of qualities which may contribute to an individual's popularity in various ways. Hartup (1970) notes that popular children are more outgoing, sociable, and friendly than other children and that they are also more socially sensitive and accepting of others, and more likely to cooperate with others than are less-liked children. Popularity is also related to IQ and academic achievement. Children prefer to be with moderately achieving children, and they often stay away from those who are very intelligent and who aspire to do well in school and those who do not do well academically. As we indicated in Chapter 10, body build and other physical attributes are also related to popularity, as are such factors as a child's name. Children who have names which other children rate as desirable are likely to be popular, even when the names are ranked by a separate group of children who do not know the children personally (McDavid & Harari, 1966).

Although popularity is one factor upon which children decide who to become friends with or who to accept into their groups, other factors such

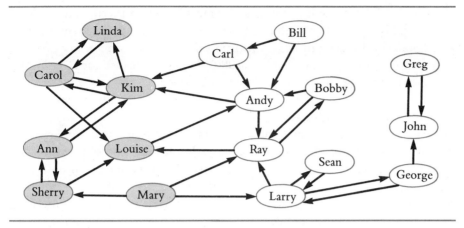

FIGURE 12.11   A sociogram shows the child who is most liked and the child who is least liked in a small group of children.

as ethnic background and sex also come into play. Researchers have observed that children of particular ethnic backgrounds tend to stick together and that they reject any child who has friends outside her own ethnic group. Janet Schofield (1980) reports a schoolgirl as saying: "They [the other black girls] get mad because you've made a white friend. . . . They say that blacks are supposed to have black friends and whites are supposed to have white friends."

There is also a tendency among children during this period to separate themselves into groups of boys and girls, resulting in what researchers have labeled a *sex cleavage* in the peer relationships of children. Recall that even preschool children choose to play with age-mates of their own sex. However, this tendency intensifies as children grow older, peaking when the children are about 10 years of age so that girls play only with girls and boys play only with boys, except perhaps during some activities. Boys and girls also evidence sex differences in their patterns of interactions. Boys form relatively large groups, whereas girls are happy functioning in groups of about two, a tendency that persists in both sexes through adolescence (Elder & Hallinan, 1978).

sex cleavage

Conformity.   Another characteristic of children during the middle childhood years is their inclination to imitate one another and to conform to the behaviors of other children. In an early study on peer conformity, Ruth Berenda (1950) found that 93% of children between 7 and 10 in her study conformed to the judgment of the majority of their classmates rather than to that of their teacher. Other researchers have demonstrated similar results, noting that during the school-age years children become increasingly likely to yield to peer pressure (Bixenstine et al., 1976;

Berndt, 1979). Also, when children are faced with conflicting advice, that of their parents or other adults and that of their peers, they side with their peers not only because of the assumption that "if everyone in my group is doing it, it must be right" (Rubin, 1980), but also because they are highly concerned with being accepted by their friends.

The pressure to conform to the behavior of other children is especially evident when the children are in groups. Peer groups tend to develop norms and expectations of their members, and the pressure toward conformity is exerted on the children involved. Although these pressures are sometimes helpful, as they prepare the children for cooperation with each other and independence from family life, subservience to the group also has dangers, as the group may force the children into doing something against their better judgment.

The pressure that group members exert on one another to conform to the beliefs and norms held by the group is demonstrated in a classic study by Muzafer and Carolyn Sherif (1964), who observed the ways in which social norms were established and enforced among two groups of 11- to 12-year-old boys at summer camp. They found that each of the groups developed its own unique set of standards. For example, in one of the groups, the children came to value "being tough," a norm which apparently originated when the group leader accidentally hurt himself. He did not complain to any adult or any of the group members, but endured the pain and continued on with whatever tasks he had on hand. Perceiving his behavior as courageous, other group members began to act tough by cursing and bearing pain, characteristics which all the group members had to have. Members of the other group, on the other hand, came to value consideration of others, and this was even reflected in their insistence on the use of good language. In both groups, any member who did not uphold the group's standards for behavior and who did not do things "right" was either reprimanded or shunned by his peers, so it did not take anyone long to bring himself to behave in line with group standards.

THE FAMILY: CHANGES IN PARENT-CHILD INTERACTIONS

Although children become increasingly susceptible to peer pressure during the middle childhood years, they are still very close to their parents and subject to their care and influence (Berndt, 1979). This is not to imply that there are no changes during the middle childhood years in the way parents and children interact. Indeed, researchers have found that parents spend about half as much time in caretaking, reading, talking to, and playing with children ages 5–12 years as they do with children younger than 5 years of age (Hill & Stafford, 1982). There are also different concerns that arise as parents interact with school-age children. With preschoolers, parent-child interactions often focus on bedtime routines, control of temper, and fighting with siblings or peers. During the middle childhood years, however, new issues emerge, including children's responsibilities for several household chores and whether or not they should be paid for such chores (Newson & Newson, 1976).

Although changes in parent-child relationships are evident in the middle childhood years, parents continue to play an important role in the child's life. They exert an enormous influence on her emerging self-esteem, as we have seen, and they provide her with guidance and support while allowing her to do things on her own and to think for herself (Hartup, 1979). Moreover, for her part, the child enjoys the company of her parents as much as she enjoys the company of peers. She may sometimes resent some of the demands they place on her, but she recognizes that she should obey her parents (Maccoby, 1980). In addition, the child is responsive to her parents' involvement in her activities and is encouraged by it. Recall from the previous chapter that the parents' active involvement in the child's school life is an important determinant of academic achievement. Parents who provide their children with help and encouragement to do homework and who themselves participate in school activities such as parent-teacher conferences have children who enjoy school more than other children do and who also score higher on achievement tests.

A warm and nurturant relationship between the child and the parents is similarly important and helps the child achieve independence and social competence (see Figure 12.12). Researchers have found that when parents are warm and accepting of their children and when they are able to appropriately discipline them and direct their behavior and activities but at the same time recognize the children's need for independence, the children are secure and sociable in their relations with other adults and children (Armentrout & Burger, 1972). Children who have a cool or hostile relationship with their parents, or whose parents are inattentive or hostile toward them are more likely than other children to be lacking in social skills and to evidence delinquent behavior (Rohner, 1975).

Realities of Family Life

So crucial is the impact of the parents on the child's development that it is important to consider some realities of contemporary life which may interfere with effective parenting.

Work and Family Life. One such reality that interferes with effective parenting is that in a large proportion of families both the mother and the father work. As we have indicated in previous chapters, this is the result of the progressive influx of married women into the labor force, with the greatest increase in recent years occurring among married women with children. Whereas in 1975 about 45% of married women with children

FIGURE 12.12   How children come to regard themselves is, in part, a function of their interactions with their parents. Warm, nurturant relationships between parents and children help the children achieve independence and social competence.

under 18 were in the labor force, by 1980 this figure rose to 54%, and in 1985 it was over 63% (U.S. Department of Labor, 1986). These women are working not only because of the personal satisfaction some of them derive from being employed, but principally because they have to earn money to meet their family's financial needs (Moen, 1982).

The research on the two-provider family has focused on the effects of the mother's employment on their children's development as well as on the family's well-being. Researchers have been conducting studies to determine the potential benefits and drawbacks of having two earners in the family. They found that although both the wife and husband may enjoy working and that the whole family benefits from the money earned, the strains of having to meet the obligations of the job and the family are often too difficult for many individuals to handle (Piotrkowski, 1979). The Rapoports (1976), who outline several problems faced by two-provider families, note that working spouses experience *mental overload,* which can occur when the demands of the job and the family are contradictory and excessive, leading to psychological strain. They also found that often the spouses in two-provider families have difficulty meeting the expectations of and their obligations to family and friends. They have little if any time in the evenings and on weekends for socializing and for relaxed and entertaining family activities, and they have to attempt to integrate and schedule child rearing in such a way that it is in harmony with the demands and expectations of their work. This is especially true of women. In families where both spouses work, husbands may share in household chores and child rearing (Holmstrom, 1973). However, these domestic tasks usually remain the principal responsibility of the wife (Pleck, 1979; Slocum & Nye, 1976; Hill & Stafford, 1980). It is the woman who has to remember what groceries the family is out of and which of the children needs new shoes or certain school supplies. It is also the woman who has to determine what to do when she has to work and one of the children is sick.

mental overload

The Effects on Children.

The effects on the children of being in a two-provider family vary according to the age of the child, which is one reason why we discuss these in several chapters of this book. Although during infancy the child is totally dependent on the mother's care and vulnerable to being separated from her during the day, during the middle childhood years, children become more self-reliant. They still need the love, guidance, and support from their parents, but because their school and social activities take up a considerable percentage of their time (Hill & Stafford, 1980), their parents' absence during the day does not necessarily have a negative influence on them. Furthermore, at this age the children can understand that their mother has to work. However, many express their dissatisfaction at their mother for not being able to give them attention, and often their mothers feel the same way. In a national survey it was found that mothers reported that their most precious commodity was time and that they felt they had too little time to spend with their children. In the same survey it was further found that school-age children complained that their parents do not spend enough time with them (General Mills American Family Report, 1977).

Although some children may feel deprived of their parents' attention when both parents are working, studies on school-age children whose mothers are working reveal that maternal employment is generally associated with positive consequences for the children. Several researchers have found that girls of working mothers show less stereotyped attitudes and

Corporate Support of Family Life

As we have indicated in various chapters, family functioning is related to the cultural and ecological niche in which the family is located (Bronfenbrenner, 1979; Weisner, 1982). Many aspects of family life, for example, whether or not the family lives near relatives and even the degree to which they must endure crowded housing conditions—can affect the child directly or indirectly through their impact on the parents and, consequently, parents' child-rearing techniques (Maccoby, 1984).

In part, parents determine some of the factors that serve to impinge on family life. However, parents themselves are constrained by social and economic conditions over which they have no control. In many families, both parents have to work. To the extent that there are adequate social support systems to meet the needs of families in which both parents are working, children and their parents will not be negatively influenced by this trend.

However, adequate social support systems, such as day care facilities for children when their parents are working, are seriously lacking in the United States. Federal and state governments, which in the past have taken the major responsibility for the support of social programs, are financially unable to do so to the extent that is necessary. Therefore, a new body of the research is focusing policy attention on the work-family link, attempting to ascertain how work systems can make it possible for women in particular to maintain effective participation in both worlds, work and family life.

American business and industry have been slow to respond to the needs of families in their employ (Zigler & Finn, 1982) in part because a dichotomy has existed between the workplace and the home. Leaders of business and industry fail to recognize that people come to work not just as individuals, but also as members of families that are themselves affected by the policies and practices of the workplace (Kanter, 1977). However, the numerous changes our society has been experiencing in the past decade (most notably the increase of married women in the paid labor force) are forcing both businesses and families to respond to the changes and to investigate ways in which the workplace can support family life (Menninger Perspective, 1980). Thus, questions about day care centers, part-time work, maternity and paternity leaves, executive transfers, spousal involvement in career planning, as well as the prevention and treatment of family dysfunctioning are becoming primary considerations among those who are in charge of businesses and corporations (Kanter, 1977).

The world of work has yet to help families on the scale that is required (Menninger Perspective, 1980). However, several corporations have taken the lead and have either instituted on-site corporate day care centers for their employees' children or they have in other ways supported their employees in this regard by helping them locate day care centers and family day care homes, or by paying for some of the costs of such care (Zigler & Finn, 1982). There have also been several innovations in the workplace, with many companies implementing changes in work schedules that should help facilitate family life. One such change is the greater use of flexible time, which allows workers to determine their starting and quitting times in a given work day (Steriel, 1979). For example, whereas traditional work hours are 8 to 4 or 9 to 5, with flexible hours an employee may start work at 7:00 A.M. and leave at 3:00 P.M. According to some surveys, many employees like flexible time, because they are better able to schedule their time so as to minimize frictions between personal and family needs on the one hand, and the demands and expectations of the job on the other (Kuhne & Blair, 1978). However, there are limitations to flexible hours. With personnel working at different hours, it is difficult to schedule meetings and to communicate with or supervise employees (Walton, 1979).

You can see that efforts to redesign workplace policies so that they meet the needs of families are by no means simple. By recognizing that work currently operates as a dominant constraint on family life, as well as a source of economic and personal sustenance, perhaps we can look forward to the time when the family and the workplace are institutions that are linked in many ways, to the benefit of both.

expectations about appropriate behaviors for men and women than girls whose mothers do not work (Lamb, 1982; Gold & Andres, 1978a). It is also noted that maternal employment contributes to girls' academic and occupational competence later in life. Girls whose mothers work get good grades in school, and they often aspire to careers outside the home (L. Hoffman, 1974).

However, Eleanor Maccoby (1984), among others, points out that there are limitations to the research on the effects of maternal employment in part because only a small percentage of the studies are related to school-age children (most of the studies focus on younger children). In many of the studies which have been conducted, no mention is made about whether the mother is working full- or part-time.

Although girls seem to benefit from having a mother who works, the same is not always the case for boys, especially boys from working-class homes whose relationship with the father seems to be undermined by the mother's working (Lamb, 1982). Working-class families tend to hold the traditional view that men are responsible for providing economic support for their families. When the mothers in these families do work, it is usually because the father has a low-paying job or no job at all, so it could well be that the father in these cases is looked down upon by the son not because the mother is working but because the father fails in meeting his obligation to the family. However, in a Canadian study of 223 ten-year-olds, Gold and Andres (1978b) found that within working-class families, boys not only evidenced disturbed relationships with their father, they were also nervous and were disliked in school, and they had low math and language achievement scores.

In middle-class homes, the mother's employment is not associated with particular strains on the father-son relationship. Some studies have found no negative consequences at all for middle-class boys associated with the mother's employment. But, other studies have found that boys from middle-class homes whose mothers are working have poor school achievement records (Gold & Andres, 1978a; Hoffman, 1979). This discrepancy in the research does not necessarily mean that either one or the other set of findings is correct or incorrect. As Lamb (1982) points out, how maternal employment affects any child—boy or girl, from a working-class or a middle-class home—depends on many factors that vary from family to family. One such important factor is how the mother herself feels about her work. Those children whose mothers feel good about their work and who enjoy working are likely to benefit from the fact that their mothers work more than the children whose mothers are dissatisfied with their roles in life. Indeed, satisfied mothers, whether they work or not, seem to have happy and well-adjusted children (Etaugh, 1974), whereas dissatisfied mothers, even if they do not work, seem to influence their children negatively (Hoffman, 1963).

DISCUSSION OF SOCIAL ISSUES: LATCHKEY CHILDREN

The extent to which mothers are satisfied with their dual role as mothers and workers is dependent in part on the availability of adequate child care and on how the child fares while her parents are working. In a review of the research, Pilling and Pringle (1978) found that mothers become concerned and experience a great deal of stress when their children are unsupervised while they are at work. Unfortunately, because of lack of adequate day care facilities for school-age children, this is a reality for many mothers who may have to leave their children unattended for several hours each day before and after school. In recent testimony submitted before a hearing held by the Select Committee on Children, Youth and Families (*Families and Child Care: Improving the Options,* 1984), it was indicated that between 2 and 4 million children aged 6 to 13 years come home *latchkey children* from school each day to an empty house. Known as *latchkey children,* because they often carry their house key on a string around their neck, these children are left to their own resources and suffer neglect during critical hours of the day. They return from school at around three o'clock in the afternoon, but their parents do not get home until five or six o'clock, or even later in some cases. Not only do these children stay home alone after school, they are also alone for an hour or two each morning, if their parents leave for work early.

FIGURE 12.13 Maternal employment per se does not have a negative influence on children. However, it presents difficulties to the family because often the children are left alone during critical hours of the day when they have to care for themselves.

There are disagreements on the possible effects of being left alone before and after school. Some researchers contend that children who are left to their own resources acquire a sense of independence and an earlier maturity, and they regard the phenomenon of the latchkey child as potentially beneficial (Korchin, 1981). Other researchers, however, contend that although school-age children are capable of taking care of their physical needs, they are still in need of adult supervision, suggesting, at the very least, that more research needs to be done in this area (Zigler, 1983; see Figure 12.13). There are a number of studies, for example, which have shown that unattended children are vulnerable to many kinds of harm. Over 6,000 children aged 5 to 14 die from injuries each year, including over 1,000 children who die in fires (National Safety Council, 1981). In a recent study in Newark, New Jersey, an investigator found that as many as 1 out of 6 fires in that city involved an unattended school-age child

(Smock, 1977). Children who are left alone are also victims of sexual assaults and other types of crimes, and they frequently encounter burglars (Finkelhor, 1979). Garbarino (1980) further notes that while children left alone in urban areas are vulnerable to high crime rates associated with urban areas, unattended children in rural areas also face problems due to the isolation of the country.

Besides being vulnerable to physical dangers, unattended children are confronted with emotional problems, and many of them often feel isolated, lonely, and afraid. In a study on children who are now or have been latchkey children, Lynette and Thomas Long (1983) found that because their parents are concerned for their safety, many children have to stay alone inside their homes and are not allowed to have other children with them, so they are not able to play with their peers. The Longs also found that most children are very much afraid of being left alone. This finding is documented in other studies as well (Whitbread, 1982) and was evident in an informal study conducted by the editors of *Sprint,* a language arts magazine for children aged 10 to 12 years. The editors of the magazine asked the children to respond to the question: "Think of a situation that is scary to you. How do you handle your fear?" Expecting to hear from the children that they are afraid of snakes or of getting a poor report card, the editors were surprised when 70% of the children answered that they are most afraid of being left alone at home. How do the children handle their fear? Some venture into the streets; others, also afraid of leaving their house or not allowed to go out, entertain themselves by watching television or playing a musical instrument or video games (School Age Child Care Project Newsletter, Vol. 2, No. 2, 1984).

School-Age Day Care.   Many parents are well aware of their children's fears of being left alone at home, and they themselves are concerned when they have to leave their children alone. Their concern is compounded on days when the children are on vacation or sick at home, because then the children are left alone for the entire day. However, for many parents it is simply not possible to take time off from work so they can be at home with their children.

Unlike many of the other social problems discussed in this book, the problem of latchkey children is one with an affordable solution. One alternative to leaving children alone at home is to provide them with before- and after-school care programs. No massive investment of public funds is needed in this case. No large-scale construction of new facilities is required because a logical place for before- and after-school day care is the school building. As Levine (1978) has demonstrated, it is possible to develop a partnership model in which schools provide the space and the parents pay for the personnel. Shared by the parents of the children enrolled, the cost of adult supervision of the children is thus relatively low. Numerous such programs are already in existence in about 100 school systems as well as in YMCAs, boys' clubs, and churches (Cook, 1985). With federal funding to help train personnel, many more such programs can be implemented to ensure that all children receive appropriate care and recreation while their parents are working (Zigler, 1983).

Single-Parent Families.   The need for after-school care is especially felt by single-parent families, in which the one parent is almost always working. Currently, 1 out of every 5 children is living in a single-parent family (among blacks, it is 1 child out of every 2). By 1990, the population of children age 10 and under in single-parent families is expected to reach unprecedented numbers. It is estimated that by that year, 3 out of every 5 children will spend at least part of their childhood living in a single-parent household (The Bureau of the Census, 1986; Norton & Glick, 1986).

Single-parent families are not a homogeneous group. Such families exist in all social classes, among all racial and ethnic groups, and in age groups ranging from 15 to over 50 (Mendes, 1979). They become single-parent households through divorce, separation, desertion, death, out-of-state employment, through single-parent adoption, or because the mother chose to give birth to a child without being married (Eiduson et al., 1982). These families differ not only in their reason for having one parent but also in their resources, motivations, and opportunities to function as a viable unit. In many such families, some of the children's and parent's needs may go unmet; in other such families, this is not the case.

Although single-parent families differ widely, they share some common characteristics. About 90% of all such families are headed by women, and most are the outcome of divorce (Schlesinger & Todres, 1975). As such, the families are in a state of transition during which the parents and the children have to adjust to changes in family relationships and responsibilities and they must learn to cope with the stress and pain of divorce (see Figure 12.14).

During the school-age years, children are better able to cope with divorce than younger children because they have a better understanding of the fact that they are not to blame for the family breakup. They are also more aware of their own feelings and more open about admitting their sadness (Hetherington, Cox, & Cox, 1982). Nevertheless, children this age are affected by the divorce. They feel abandoned by their parents and angry at their parents' decision to break up the family (Wallerstein & Kelly, 1980). They also evidence behavioral problems in school, often performing less well academically than they did prior to the divorce (Guidubaldi et al., 1983). The children may also exhibit behavioral problems at home. This is especially true of boys, who tend to compete with

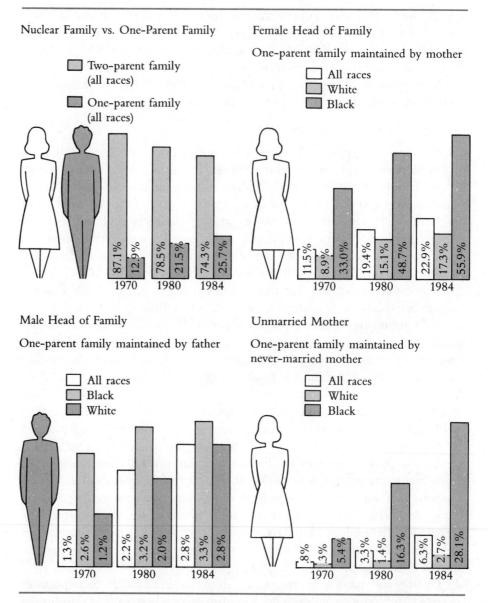

FIGURE 12.14   The family in transition. Since 1970, the number of single parent households has more than doubled. The majority of them are maintained by women, but fathers are taking up the role in increasing numbers as well. From *Newsweek*. July 15, 1985, pp. 46–47. Copyright © 1985, by Newsweek Inc. All rights reserved. Reprinted by permission.

the mother for the leadership role in the family, often challenging her authority over them and their siblings (Hetherington, Cox, & Cox, 1979). Although many of these problems persist for some time after the divorce (Guidubaldi et al., 1983), when the parents maintain a good relationship with each other after the divorce and the father remains involved in the

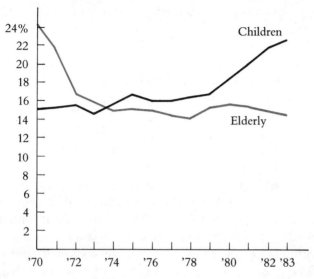

Percentage of children under 18 years and adults 65 years or older who are below the poverty level.

FIGURE 12.15 The percentage of children living in poverty has increased in recent years. From the *New York Times,* May 23, 1985, p. D26. Copyright © 1985 by The New York Times Company. Reprinted by permission.

day-to-day lives of the children, the negative effects of divorce on the children are diminished (Hess & Camara, 1979).

Poverty. Another characteristic of many single-parent families is poverty. In a recent report on the extent of poverty in the United States (U.S. Congress, 1985), it is documented that, due in part to the increases in single-parent households, there are now more poor children than there were since the mid-1960s and that the problem of poverty among families with children has grown deeper and more widespread in the 20 years since then. About 13.8 million children, representing 22.2% of Americans under age 18, are from poor families, and there are indications that the numbers of children in poverty are likely to grow (see Figure 12.15).

Besides the increase in the number of single-parent families, there are other factors that have contributed to the growing numbers of poor children. One of these is the change in federal policy in assistance to the poor, which has resulted in the reduction of the number of needy families that are eligible to receive food stamps and other government support. In addition, economic growth appears to have become less effective in reducing poverty, as more families with children have fallen further below the official poverty level. Whereas in 1968, the poorest of all families had an average of 91% of the income they needed for basic needs, in 1983 they had only 60% of the income they needed. This means that the children and adults in these families often go without food, health care, and other basic necessities.

Who are the poor children in America? According to the report cited earlier, the poor child tends to come from a single-parent family, and she is likely to be Hispanic or black. Over one-third (38.2%) of all Hispanic children and close to one-half (46.7%) of all black children are poor and likely to remain so for a long period of time. Whereas for most white children poverty is short-lived (about 10 months) and associated with changes in their parents' marital status or family earnings, for the Hispanic or black child this can be a condition that lasts throughout childhood.

The effects of poverty on the child are widespread and include not only malnutrition and poor health care, discussed in previous chapters, but also assaults on the child's emerging self-esteem. This is especially true during the school-age years when the child continually compares herself to others in terms of looks, skills, achievement, and activities engaged in. The poor child not only has fewer possessions than other children do, she often does not engage in such activities as tennis or dancing lessons, and has less opportunity to develop her skills and abilities, so she comes to regard herself as inferior to others, a feeling which may hinder her later in life (Keniston, 1977).

It is not surprising, therefore, that research studies have shown that poor children are more likely than their economically better off age-mates to fail in school and to believe that they have little control over their future. They often blame their poor performance in school on external factors such as a bad teacher (Bryant, 1974). Their parents, too, feel that they have no control over their own or their children's future, and they are often unable to effectively rear their children. It is not that parents who are poor care less for their children than other parents do. It is simply that they are so overburdened by their life conditions that they are severely limited in their ability to provide the warmth, caring, and nurturance that children need.

Helping Children Cope with Stress

All the disruptions and difficult conditions that characterize the lives of many children—being alone at home after school, living in a single-parent family that is often characterized by changes in family relationships and responsibilities due to divorce, living in poverty—mean that many children are subjected to severe life stresses. Most children manage to survive these stresses. They find ways of compensating for the problems they

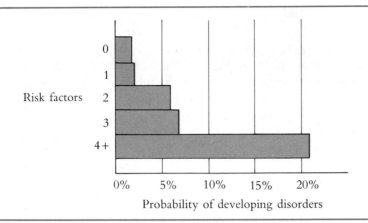

FIGURE 12.16 Multiplicity of risk factors and child psychiatric disorders. The more risk factors (for example, poverty and divorce) that children are subjected to, the higher is the probability that they will develop psychiatric disorders. From Rutter, M. (1979). Protective factors in children's responses to stress and disadvantage. In M. W. Kent & J. E. Rolf (eds.), *Primary prevention of psychopathology: Vol. 3. Social competence in children* (pp. 49–74). Hanover, NH: published for the University of Vermont by the University Press of New England. © by Vermont Conference on the Primary Prevention of Psychopathology.

experience and they seem to be happy in spite of their hardships (Murphy & Moriarty, 1976). Nevertheless, there are many children who are unable to cope or for whom the stresses are so numerous that they result in depression and behavioral problems at home and in school. That there are many such children is demonstrated in studies which reveal the prevalence of childhood depression and the fact that there are increasing numbers of children who are sad and unhappy and who exhibit withdrawal symptoms such as boredom and difficulty in their interactions with other children and adults (French & Berlin, 1979; Poznaski, 1979). These symptoms often stem from chronic, stress-producing difficulties in their families such as unemployment, marital discord, and divorce (Garrison, 1984).

Rutter (1979), who studied the effects of stress on children's emotional stability and mental health, identified several family variables which are strongly associated with behavioral and psychiatric disorders. Among these variables are severe marital discord, low social status, overcrowding or large family size, and maternal psychiatric disorders. He found that children who were exposed to one of these risk factors were no more likely to develop psychiatric disorders than children not exposed to any of the risks. However, when the children experienced two or more risk factors simultaneously, for example, a bitter divorce battle as well as poverty after the divorce, their chances of developing a psychiatric problem more than doubled (see Figure 12.16).

Since many children experience multiple stresses, it is important to ask why some children evidence behavioral problems in the face of life stresses while others do not. Garmezy and Rutter (1983), who studied children considered to be at high risk for the development of psychiatric problems and who seemed to be invulnerable to the effects of the stress they were living with, note that psychologists do not yet understand the sources of invulnerable children's strengths. However, it is becoming apparent that although the children's personality no doubt has much to do with their ability to withstand stress, other factors such as the influence of a caring adult, whether this be a parent, other relative, teacher, or neighbor, can help offset the negative effects of stress, as can the children's ability to understand some of the problems that they and their parents are facing. Rutter (1979) also notes that many children have the inner strengths to fight the psychological problems that can result from stress. What they often need in order to utilize and rely upon these strengths is the help and support of even one close and understanding adult. It is apparent, therefore, that just as support services can help facilitate the lives of many parents (Albee, 1980), so can such services help children cope with some of the difficult realities of contemporary life.

SUMMARY

During the middle childhood years the child experiences tremendous advances in social cognition, the ability to understand people and think about social relations. She becomes less egocentric than she was in the previous period of development, and she shows her increasing ability to take another person's point of view. She thus becomes better able to infer another person's feelings and thoughts and also better able to recognize that other people are evaluating her behavior.

These advances in social cognition enable children to develop in their interactions with other children and adults and to reason about moral problems. Moral development, which refers to the process of learning to accept standards of right and wrong as guides to behavior, occurs gradually and is influenced, according to one theory, by the child's cognitive growth. This view is held by Piaget, who found that as children grow they develop an enhanced understanding of rules, and they begin to obey rules, realizing that rules are created to benefit all those involved.

Kohlberg elaborated upon Piaget's work and found that there are six (later revised to five) stages in moral development that correspond to the cognitive level of the child. Kohlberg identified the levels of moral development by presenting children with moral dilemmas and studying their responses. Kohlberg was not interested in whether the children thought a particular action was right or wrong, but only in the reasoning they gave for their answers. Their justifications revealed how children think about right and wrong at different ages. Although Kohlberg's theory is highly regarded and is considered useful, many criticize it, noting, in part, that how a child or an adult thinks about a moral dilemma is not necessarily related to how the person actually behaves. In making a distinction between moral knowledge and moral behavior, researchers on moral behavior note that children learn how to behave by watching their parents and that they acquire a conscience and begin to monitor their own behavior when they are punished for doing wrong and reinforced for doing right.

During the middle childhood years, children also make advances in the development of the self-concept. They construct a more refined and complex picture of themselves as unique individuals, and they also develop self-esteem, which is a judgment about how worthy they are. The child with good self-esteem believes she is a capable individual, and she therefore attempts to learn and to try to do many things. The child with low self-esteem believes she is inadequate and develops a sense of inferiority. How the child feels about herself is related to her parents' reactions to her. However, during the middle childhood years, the child is not only influenced by her parents but by her teachers and peers as well. Peer interactions in particular are important during this period, and they enable the child to gradually acquire independence from family life.

Although the child is increasingly influenced by his peers, his relationship with his parents is still important to him, and he is responsive to their care and encouragement. However, in many families, parents are unable to provide their children with appropriate care, as they themselves are overwhelmed with responsibilities and stresses. This can occur in families where both parents are working and in single-parent families. One of the problems stems from the lack of suitable before- and after-school care facilities for children, which means that many children are left alone for several hours each day. Known as latchkey children because they carry their house key on a string around their necks, these children are subjected to many dangers and are often afraid of being left alone. Unlike many other social problems, however, the problem of latchkey children can be solved inexpensively by creating programs for them.

REVIEW POINTS

1. During the middle childhood years enormous advances occur in social cognition, which refers to the ability of children to understand people and think about social relations. This is evident in children's ability for role-taking, also referred to as perspective-taking.

2. There are developmental changes in role-taking as children become increasingly able to take the perspective of others and understand how other people may think and feel. Social experience is important in this regard; the more time children spend with peers, the more skilled they are in perspective-taking.

3. Just as social experience enhances children's role-taking skills, so children's progress in role-taking enhances their interactions with people. Having acquired this ability to understand how other people think and feel, children become better able to communicate and empathize with others. Empathy refers to the ability to vicariously feel what another person is feeling, and the capacity for empathy becomes more refined with age.

4. During the middle childhood years children not only acquire the ability to think about how others think and feel, they also begin to realize that their behavior has consequences for others. They also grow in their ability to behave morally and reason about moral problems.

5. Researchers differ in their explanation of how children learn to behave morally. Whereas psychoanalytic and social learning theorists emphasize external influences on children's moral development, cognitive-developmental theorists emphasize that moral reasoning develops progressively along with cognitive abilities. Lawrence Kohlberg is one of the most influential researchers who adheres to this view. On the basis of children's answers to questions about stories featuring moral dilemmas, he contends that there are three stages of moral development—preconventional, conventional, and postconventional, which correspond to the individual's stage of cognitive development.

6. Researchers note that although children may be able to reason about moral dilemmas, they do not necessarily behave in ways that are moral. How an individual decides to behave in any given situation is influenced not only by moral reasoning, but also by one's personality characteristics, standards of society, and also the behavior of others. Parents are especially influential in this regard. When in the course of their disciplining children parents explain to them what they did wrong and when they highlight the consequences of their behavior on other people, children acquire the ability to think about other people's feelings and refrain from doing something that may hurt them.

7. Parents also influence children's self-concept and how they feel about themselves. During the middle childhood years, children acquire a more specific and multifaceted picture of the self, and they begin to judge how worthy they are. The child's opinion of her own worth is known as self-esteem. Children with high self-esteem believe that they are capable of achieving goals and that other people consider them worthy. Children with low self-esteem are convinced that they are inadequate in comparison to others.

8. Although how the child comes to regard herself is largely a function of her interactions with her parents, teachers also influence the child, especially during the early elementary grades when the child is getting used to being subjected to the constant evaluation of her behavior. When teachers are friendly and positively reinforcing of children, children feel good about themselves.

9. Children are also influenced by peers. During the middle childhood years, children spend an increasing amount of time with peers, developing close friendships and interacting with friends in the context of a group. Initially, during the early part of the middle childhood years, children's group formation is rather formal. As children grow, groups become informal cliques made up of two or three close friends. These cliques serve important functions in the children's development as the children can exchange information about some of the concerns of growing up and they learn from one another.

10. Although children spend an increasing amount of their time with peers during the middle childhood years, they are still close to their parents and subject to their parents' influence. They are also responsive to their parents' involvement in their activities, and they are encouraged by it.

11. Given some of the contemporary realities of family life, many children whose mothers and fathers work feel that their parents don't pay enough attention to them. In cases of dual-worker families, parents do indeed suffer from mental overload, and they are under stress when the demands of the job and of family life are contradictory and excessive. Generally, however, the fact that both their mothers and the fathers work has no negative influences on children, but whether or not this is the case depends on many factors which vary from family to family.

12. When parents feel secure in the knowledge that their children are adequately supervised during the day, they are less likely to feel dissatisfied about working and to convey the dissatisfaction to their children. However, because of lack of adequate day care facilities for school-age children, many children remain alone during critical hours of the day. These children are known as latchkey children.

13. Many families, most notably single-parent families, live in poverty. The problem of poverty among families with children has grown deeper and more widespread during the past 20 years. Children who are poor suffer not only malnutrition and poor health care, they also feel inadequate in relation to other people, and many of them acquire a feeling of helplessness.

14. Although many children overcome the problems associated with poverty and with other life stresses, there are some children who are unable to cope or for whom the stresses are so numerous that they may result in depression and behavioral problems at home and in school. The more stresses children are subjected to, the more likely they are to develop behavioral and psychiatric disorders. However, when the children have the support of even one close and understanding adult, they are better able to understand and cope with the realities of their lives.

Atypical Development in the Middle Childhood Years

By far the most studied and most discussed group of children considered to be atypical in their development is the group of children who differ from others in intellectual functioning. Research interest in such children is usually focused, as we do here, on those who are mentally retarded. In recent years, however, increased recognition has also been awarded to those children who are gifted and considered to be intellectually superior, with some experts noting commonalities in the study of children at both intellectual extremes (Zigler & Farber, 1985). This may seem odd, since the two groups appear to be complete opposites. It is noted, however, that just as mentally retarded children are considered atypical because they differ from average children in intellectual ability, gifted children exhibit extreme deviations in intelligence, although at the opposite end of the scale, and they, too, differ significantly from the rest of the population of children and are therefore deserving of special attention and education (Miller & Price, 1981). Although not only scientific but also social interest in gifted children has soared in recent years, as yet, not as much is known about these children as about children who are mentally retarded.

Mentally Retarded Children

Interest in mentally retarded children has existed for centuries. The topic has been the subject of discussions throughout history, with numerous thinkers writing about the prevailing societal attitudes toward the retarded and dispensing their advice on the care of retarded individuals and their role in society (Zigler & Hodapp, 1986). However, the scientific study of the mentally retarded is relatively recent, as is the understanding of mental retardation. For example, it was not until the end of the 18th century that it was understood that mental retardation is distinct from emotional disorder (Szymanski & Tanguay, 1980). At that time, John Locke observed that "madmen put wrong ideas together and reason from them, but idiots make very few propositions and reason scarce at all" (quoted in Zigler & Hodapp, 1986).

Identifying the Mentally Retarded

Since Locke's days, our understanding and knowledge of mental retardation have become substantially more sophisticated. Researchers now note that mental retardation is more common and considerably easier to identify than other kinds of developmental psychopathology (Zigler, Lamb, & Child, 1982).

Mental retardation is characterized by significantly subaverage levels of general intellectual functioning. In some children, mental retardation is diagnosed at birth or shortly after. In many cases, however, the handicap is not diagnosed until the child enters school or sometime during his school-age years. This is indicated in studies where it is shown that the number of individuals who are identified as retarded before age 5 is low and increases significantly upon school entrance and throughout the school years (MacMillan, 1982). This finding is hardly surprising considering the fact that at school children are expected to perform a variety of intellectual tasks and their performance is judged against the performance of other children their age.

Children are diagnosed as mentally retarded largely on the basis of their performance on intelligence tests. As indicated in Chapter 14, there are numerous problems associated with such tests. Furthermore, just which children will be identified as retarded is often an arbitrary decision that is subject to change. For example, for many years, there was general agreement that mentally retarded individuals are those whose IQ scores were in the lowest 3% of the population. In 1959, this was changed, and the American Association on Mental Deficiency (AAMD) established a new definition of mental retardation to include individuals whose IQ score was more than one standard deviation below the mean (that is, individuals whose IQ score was 84 or less). Thus, the number of individuals in the United States who were considered to be retarded increased (just because the definition was changed) from approximately 5 million to over 30 million. In 1973, the AAMD changed the IQ criterion of mental retardation once again, this time to include people whose IQ score is more than two standard deviations below the mean, that is, individuals whose IQ score is less than 70. Given this new definition, a child with an IQ of 79 who prior to 1973 would have been labeled as mentally retarded is now considered normal. This fact alerts us to the error in rigidly adhering to such arbitrary cutoff points that draw the defining line between mental retardation and normal intellectual functioning.

The IQ score is not the only criterion used to define mental retardation. Consideration is also given to the individual's deficits in adaptive behavior and the extent that the individual is able to meet the standards of personal independence and social responsibility expected of his age and cultural group. Furthermore, within the segment of the population of individuals identified as mentally retarded, a differentiation is made on the basis of the severity of retardation. Thus, there are individuals who are considered to be mildly, moderately, severely, or profoundly retarded. This differentiation is useful, for it highlights the fact that mentally retarded individuals are not as totally incapacitated and socially incompetent as is sometimes believed. Rather, the great majority of them are only mildly retarded and are able to meet their own needs, hold jobs, and run a household with minimal aid. For example, depending on his abilities in such a category as economic activity, a 15-year-old mentally retarded boy would be classified in one of the following categories:

Mildly retarded *(IQ 55–69).* The mildly retarded person can go to some stores and purchase several items. He can make change correctly. He may be able to earn a living, although he may need help in managing his income.

Moderately retarded *(IQ 40–54).* The moderately retarded person can go on a shopping errand for several items and make minor purchases and he can handle bills and coins fairly accurately.

Severely retarded *(IQ 25–39).* The severely retarded person can go on simple errands with a note to the store clerk. He may be able to use a coin-operated machine. He may realize that money has value, although he does not understand how to use money.

Profoundly retarded *(IQ below 25).* The profoundly retarded person is not capable of economic activities.

Causes of Mental Retardation

organic disorder

cultural-familial retardation

Generally, individuals who are severely or profoundly retarded are those who are identified as being organically retarded. There are two types of mental retardation: (1) retardation with a known *organic disorder,* and (2) retardation with an *unknown organic disorder.* Often, the second type is referred to as *cultural-familial retardation.*

Approximately 30% of retarded individuals are identified as organically retarded. In most of these cases, the retardation is diagnosed shortly after birth or during infancy and is associated with a specific cause. It may be due, for example, to one of a very large group of genetic or chromosomal anomalies discussed in Chapter 2. The most common of these disorders is Down's syndrome. It can also be caused by one of several diseases inherited genetically, as in PKU. In addition, the causes of mental retardation may be related to brain damage that can occur prenatally (due, for example, to maternal rubella, lead poisoning, or nutritional deficiencies) or perinatally (due to oxygen deprivation or cerebral trauma). To date, over 200 causes of organic mental retardation have been identified, and new ones are discovered every year as more research on the topic is conducted (Grossman, 1982). The causes may be diverse, but they have one common factor: they result in impaired physiological development.

The cultural-familial group of retarded children accounts for as many as 70% of those who are identified as mentally retarded. These children are not diagnosed as mentally retarded until they are in school because many of them do not manifest noticeably slow development as infants and preschoolers. They evidence no abnormal genetic disorder or any brain damage. In other words, there appears to be nothing wrong with these children, except that they perform at a mentally retarded level: they learn slowly, they show little interest in their school surroundings, and they are poor in language and communication skills (Philips, 1980). These children are also immature in their behavior, inattentive to school tasks, and each year that they are in school they fall farther behind their peers in academic achievement. Cultural-familial retarded children are classified, almost invariably, as mildly retarded; their IQ scores are generally above 50 (Zigler & Cascione, 1984).

Why such children are retarded remains a mystery. However, it is generally agreed that cultural-familial retardation results from a combination of environmental (cultural) and hereditary (familial) factors. As you will see in Chapter 14, the relative contribution of each of these two factors is subject to controversy that remains unresolved.

Differing Theoretical Perspectives

In yet another unresolved controversy in the area of mental retardation, there are disagreements on whether cultural-familial retarded individuals should be regarded as different from other children or as essentially normal in their development, but with low intelligence.

Those who adhere to the difference or defect perspective stress the fact that just as organically retarded children suffer from some physiological impairment, so do cultural-familial retarded children suffer from one or another of a small set of defects such as impaired memory (Ellis, 1970) or deficiencies in attention (Fisher & Zeaman, 1973) which are inherent in the mentally retarded. By contrast, those who adhere to a developmental perspective make a distinction between organic and familial retarded groups. They believe that those who have organic problems should be viewed as different because of their faulty intellectual apparatus. However, they note that cultural-familial retarded children should not be viewed as such because they develop in the same sequence of stages as do children of average or high intelligence; they differ from "normal" children only in the rate at which they progress and the ultimate intellectual ceiling that they achieve (Zigler & Balla, 1982).

Theorists who adhere to the developmental perspective also believe that cultural-familial retarded children react to environmental influences in the same way as do normal children. Thus, such personality characteristics usually associated with the retarded—rigidity, overdependency, and low expectations of success—are attributable to the experiences these children encounter rather than to any inherent defect associated with mental retardation (Zigler, Lamb, & Child, 1982).

For example, a cultural-familial retarded child, because he is slower and substantially less capable than other children, is likely to experience a great amount of failure, especially once he enters school. Such a history of failure engenders certain behavior patterns not only among the retarded but among normal children as well. Thus, it is theorized that due to their repeated experiences with failure, retarded children characteristically expect to fail, more so than do other children who do not experience as much failure, and they settle for low degrees of success (Cromwell, 1963). In addition to expecting failure, the retarded are more likely to blame themselves as inadequate when they fail. This is demonstrated in experiments in which groups of retarded and normal children were asked to complete a task but were prevented from doing so. When asked why the task had not been completed, retarded children, in contrast to normal children, consistently attributed the failure to their own inadequacies (MacMillan, 1969; MacMillan & Keogh, 1971).

Care and Education of the Mentally Retarded

Another area of disagreement among experts regards the care and education of retarded children. Children who are severely or profoundly retarded are often institutionalized as soon as the handicap is diagnosed or later in life when caring for them becomes an insurmountably difficult task for the family. Children who are mildly or moderately retarded are rarely institutionalized. Rather, they remain with their families and they receive educational training, with 50 to 80% of them eventually becoming self-supporting.

However, this was not always the case. In the past, most retarded children were either denied schooling or they were offered special education in separate schools that served not only the mentally retarded, but children suffering from a variety of other handicaps as well. These schools were generally ineffective and did not prepare the child for self-sufficiency and integration into society, instead they concentrated on teaching basic self-help skills.

Aside from the educational ineffectualness of most such schools, these schools were usually residential institutions, which meant that the child was separated from the family and from society. Eventually, education of the mentally retarded became the responsibility of public schools, but the children remained isolated in special classrooms. However, parents and advocates for the mentally retarded became increasingly aware of the rights of these children, and educators and mental retardation experts began to identify the educational needs of the children (Chess & Gordon, 1984) to the extent that in the past two decades the practice of isolating the retarded has decreased substantially. Current educational approaches to the care and education of the retarded stress normalization, that is, allowing the retarded child to develop in as "normal" an environment as possible. Some retarded children must still attend special education classes, but at least for part of the day they are also placed in regular classes with normal children their age.

The fact that being in regular classes may not benefit retarded children academically or socially is noted in the previous chapter, so that the future direction of education for retarded children remains uncertain. You should also note that although some positive changes have occurred in societal attitudes toward the retarded, the school experience may still be very difficult for the retarded child who is especially vulnerable to the negative behaviors of some of his peers. As Philips (1980) notes, in the school setting, the retarded child tends to "consider himself different and unwanted. Thus he may be shunned and teased by his peers, called names, and taunted, be the 'fall guy' for the class bully, and the victim of jokes. . . . In reaction to his inability to solve this [problem], he may develop a variety of symptoms of emotional disorder. These run the gamut from simple transient behavior problems, to severe neurotic, delinquent, and behavioral disorders."

You can see that much more remains to be discovered about mental retardation, especially with regard to the care and education of the retarded. At the same time, there are many who consider the field of mental retardation to be in a period characterized by cautious optimism, an optimism born of research advances that shed increasingly more light on the handicap. Indeed, over the past three decades, the study of mental retardation has become a relatively sophisticated discipline (Zigler & Hodapp, 1986). We can expect, therefore, that the future will bring more progress and knowledge of the ways the lives of mentally retarded children may be enhanced.

UNIT VI

ADOLESCENCE

A dolescence is perhaps the most challenging and complicated of all periods of life. It is a time during which many developmental changes take place: the individual experiences changes in the way he thinks, looks, and behaves. It is also a period of transition from the secure and dependent life of a child to the insecure and independent life of an adult. In preparation for life as an adult, the adolescent begins to establish his own identity, and, in the process, he is faced with many questions that only he can answer and many decisions that only he can make. These questions and decisions are part of the adolescent experience. They are not resolved all at once, but rather, over a period of years that sometimes extends well beyond adolescence.

CHAPTER 13

PHYSICAL DEVELOPMENT DURING ADOLESCENCE

WHAT IS ADOLESCENCE?

During the first few years of adolescence, the individual experiences the dramatic changes brought on by *puberty,* the physiological event that culminates in sexual maturity. As the result of puberty, the adolescent undergoes major and rapid bodily changes that include a growth in height and changes in body proportions, as well as sexual differentiation, which involves the appearance of secondary sex characteristics and the growth of the sex organs, so that the individual becomes capable of reproduction. These changes are important in and of themselves, and they are also significant in their potential impact on psychological development, for the attainment of sexual maturity is a source of concern for many adolescents.

puberty

It is easy to see, given the social and physiological changes of adolescence, why the period is said to be not only challenging but also difficult to experience. This is true for the adolescent and also for his parents. At times, adolescents may experience difficulties getting along with their parents, and some adolescents may be prone to emotional outbursts, drastic changes in mood, and acute depression. What causes the rebelliousness and moodiness that some adolescents experience? Are they the outcome of societal factors, or are they caused by the biological changes of adolescence? Researchers do not agree on the answers to these questions. In fact, there are some who note that for many individuals, adolescence is no more or less stressful than other transition periods in the life cycle. Before we examine the physical and physiological changes of adolescence, let us take a close look at the different views psychologists have regarding this period of life and the emotional problems of adolescents. You will see that not only are there conflicting views regarding adolescents, there is also no consensus as to what adolescence is and when adolescence ends and adulthood begins.

Adolescence as a Cultural Invention

Adolescence is a difficult period to define. The difficulty is related not to when the period begins, since for the most part puberty can mark this point, but rather, when it ends. That is, when does the adolescent become an adult? Our difficulty in defining adolescence and determining when the period ends stems from several factors. One is the fact that adolescence, as such, is a cultural invention, and only recently did it come to be regarded as a separate period of life, a period that is different from both childhood and adulthood (see Figure 13.1).

Recall that before the 17th century the concept of adolescence and, for that matter, the concept of childhood did not exist (Aries, 1962). Society portrayed and treated children as miniature adults. It not only expected children to assume full adult responsibilities at an early age, it also gave them the rights and freedoms adults enjoyed. Thus, many children started

FIGURE 13.1 The idea of adolescence as a special period of life did not become a reality until the late nineteenth century when compulsory education, child labor legislation, and special legal procedures developed for youth served to highlight the separation of youths from adults.

to work at the age of seven, and they freely participated in adult games and pastimes as well.

The concept of childhood became increasingly more meaningful beginning in the 17th century. However, the idea of adolescence as a special period of life did not become a reality until the late 19th century (Bakan, 1972). Several societal conditions can be linked to the emergence of adolescence as a period of life. Among these were the increased need for specialized skills and education to satisfy the job requirements of an industrialized society and the expansion of high school education in order to meet these requirements (Elder, 1975). On a more formal level, the concept of adolescence received support from three major social movements: compulsory education, child labor legislation, and the special legal procedures developed for youth (Bakan, 1972). These social movements served to highlight the separation of youth from adults, and to emphasize the dependence of adolescents on adult care and guidance.

In recent years, adolescence has become an even longer period of life than it had been in the past (Coleman, 1973; Elder, 1980). Children mature earlier physically, and therefore, they enter adolescence sooner. Some argue, too, that not only in the physical sense but in the socio-cultural sense as well, children mature earlier, as they are exposed to adult aspects of life much earlier than was true even twenty years ago (Winn, 1983). At the same time, because our society requires more and more education and schooling, adolescents remain dependent on parental care longer, and they do not assume adult roles and responsibility as early as did individuals of previous generations. Hence the difficulty in determining when adolescence ends. For purposes of discussion, we define adolescence as the period that spans the years between 12 and 18. However, many individuals go on to college and remain dependent on their parents' care beyond the age of 18, so for them adolescence may last well into their twenties.

The Passage to Adulthood

The fact that our increasingly complex society requires that adolescence be a rather lengthy period causes problems for many adolescents because they have to live with the discrepancy of having a mature body but social and psychological characteristics that are deemed immature. In addition, in our society adolescents do not receive the psychological support they need to begin assuming adult roles. In primitive societies, there is no such period of life as adolescence. Adulthood is bestowed upon the child at a certain age, usually in conjunction with some type of *puberty rites,* which are ceremonies that mark the individual's assumption of new, more adult roles. Such ceremonies typically exist for boys as well as for girls, although they are frequently more complex for boys, often entailing painful tests of endurance and courage. For girls, on the other hand, the ceremonies are related to matters pertaining to sex and marriage, and they center around the onset of menstruation (Conger, 1973).

puberty rites

Puberty rites serve an important psychological function for the individual: they provide the child with some notion of what is expected of him at the new stage of his life. In our society, however, the passage from childhood to adulthood is not only longer, but the point at which the individual may be regarded as an adult is different for different purposes and in different places.

> All our own society has in a way of institutionalized patterns of recognizing the adolescent's increasing independence is a variety of laws, and these are often internally inconsistent. . . . For example, there are significant variations from state to state in the age at which a young person can drink alcohol, drive a car, marry, and own property. One of the ironies of our time is that until 1971, young people who were considered old enough to do most of the fighting for their elders . . . were not considered mature enough to vote. (Conger, 1973).

Storm and Stress or Cultural Expectations?

Our inability as a society to arrive at a consensus about when adulthood begins means that the adolescent, while he is undergoing changes that render him an adult physically, must face the problem of assuming independence "not with the solidarity of the expectations of adult society, but with their apparent confusion and divisiveness" (Conger, 1973). This, coupled with our society's failure to provide the individual with psychological support in the transition from childhood to adulthood, could well result in emotional difficulties for some adolescents. Thus adolescence has been characterized by deviation, rebelliousness (Eichorn, 1975), and emotional turmoil (Hall, 1904).

The behavioral difficulties of adolescents, the fact that some are rebellious, unruly, and overly emotional, have been the subject of theories and research for many years and have been thought to affect all adolescents. There is evidence that for some individuals adolescence is indeed an emotionally distressing period. However, some questions remain: Do all adolescents experience emotional turmoil? Even among those who do, are these emotional problems related to cultural factors or, are they the outcome of biological changes that occur during adolescence?

G. Stanley Hall (1904), who first named the phenomenon of "adolescence" and saw it as a period that signaled life beyond childhood but before the adoption of adult responsibilities, regarded the adolescent's behavior as the outcome of biological determinants. He described adolescence as a time of storm and stress during which the adolescent experiences vacillating and contradictory emotions. Hall's view is shared by psychoanalytic theorists, many of whom believe that the adolescent who does not have emotional problems and who is good and considerate toward his parents should be considered abnormal (A. Freud, 1968). However, Margaret Mead (1961; original publication was 1928) challenged this view, and, using evidence from her anthropological studies of adolescents in Samoa, she argued that adolescence does not have to be a time of stress. Indeed, since Mead's finding was that in Samoa adolescence is a relatively trouble-free period, it was her assertion that the storm and stress associated with adolescence in our society has its roots in cultural rather than biological determinants.

The validity of Mead's contentions have been questioned recently in view of methodological concerns with her research (Freeman, 1983). However, other researchers also challenged the view that adolescence is an especially turbulent period due to biological forces. Kurt Lewin (1939) described the behavior of the adolescent as being similar to that of any person in a minority group, as he noted that "to some extent behavior symptomatic for the marginal man [which he defines as underprivileged] can be found in the adolescent. He, too, is oversensitive, easily shifted from one extreme to the other . . . he knows he is not fully accepted by the adult." Bandura (1964) argues that if society labels adolescents as "teenagers" and expects them to be rebellious, unpredictable, sloppy, and wild in their behavior, and if this picture is repeatedly reinforced by the mass media, such cultural expectations may well force adolescents into the role of rebel.

It is clear that there is no consensus about what causes the emotional difficulties of adolescence. In addition, recent research indicates that too much has been made of the stress of adolescence, with researchers noting that some adolescents are emotional, erratic, and rebellious in their behavior, while many others are calm and predictable, the point being that this period may not be any more or less stressful than other periods of development (Adams, 1980). Offer and Offer (1975), who studied a group of adolescent boys, found that less than a third of them experienced a turbulent, crisis-filled adolescence, whereas for the rest, adolescence was characterized either by self-assurance and mutual respect between them and their parents or by periods of relative calm coupled with periods of anger and frequent mood changes. However, the fact that the emotional turmoil of adolescence is not universal should not be taken to mean that it is not related to the physiological events of adolescence. You will see in the following pages that for some individuals, the impact of physical growth and puberty is indeed significant and can influence psychological development. Therefore, the question may not be whether physiological events contribute to emotional problems, but rather, what kind of physiological changes produce problems among some adolescents, and under what circumstances? As you read the following discussion of the physical changes and the psychological impact of puberty, keep in mind that during adolescence the individual experiences many other cognitive and social changes as well. It may be the cumulative effect of all these changes that causes emotional difficulties for many adolescents.

PHYSICAL CHANGES DURING ADOLESCENCE

Puberty

The beginning of adolescence is marked by changes in physical development that are part of the transformation of the individual from child to adult. These changes occur in the context of *puberty*, which is the period of rapid growth that culminates in sexual maturity and reproductive capability (Roche, 1976). The changes of puberty may be grouped into two categories, those that are related to physical growth and the physique of the individual and those that are related to the development of sexual characteristics.

These physical and physiological changes of puberty are caused by hormone secretions. Hormones are chemical agents which are secreted into the bloodstream by the pituitary gland, often referred to as the master gland, which lies at the base of the skull. A portion of the brain called the

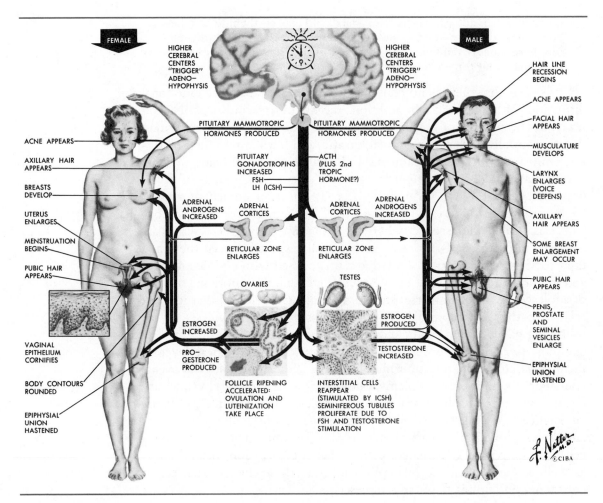

FIGURE 13.2   The production of hormones at puberty stimulates a number of physical changes and they affect many body organs and functions. Copyright © 1965, CIBA Pharmaceutical Company, Division of CIBA-GEIGY Corporation. Reprinted with permission from THE CIBA COLLECTION OF MEDICAL ILLUSTRATIONS illustrated by Frank H. Netter, M.D. All rights reserved.

hypothalamus signals the pituitary gland to produce hormones, and these hormones in turn stimulate other endocrine glands (the adrenal glands, the ovaries, in females, and the testes, in males) to produce and secrete sex hormones (see Figure 13.2). As the sex hormones enter the bloodstream, changes in physical growth and sexual development occur. Hormones, then, may be regarded as a means of communication within the body in that they carry messages from place to place that trigger changes in body function and structure (Petersen & Taylor, 1980).

androgen
testosterone
estrogen

There are several types of hormones. *Androgens,* from the Greek word for man, are the male sex hormones of which *testosterone* is one type. *Estrogen* is the female sex hormone. Although these hormones are designated as male or female, they are actually present in both males and fe-

FIGURE 13.3   Young adolescents experience a series of striking physical changes. These are triggered by the biological events of puberty and include a growth spurt and changes in body dimensions and in the proportion of muscle to fat.

males, but in differing amounts. During puberty, increased levels of androgens and estrogen in the bloodstream stimulate the events leading to sexual maturation and the development of male and female secondary sex characteristics. Whereas the effect of hormones is particularly noticeable during puberty, hormones actually control growth throughout the prenatal period and childhood, even though their effect may not always be apparent. In fact, high levels of sex hormones during the prenatal period cause sexual differentiation very early in prenatal development. During the first 6 weeks after conception, male and female embryos are identical. By about 6 weeks after conception, testosterone is produced in the male embryo, stimulating the development of male genitalia. Throughout the prenatal period, both male and female fetuses have high levels of sex hormones, but at the end of this period, the production of hormones is suppressed and does not resume until about age 7. At that time, hormone levels begin to rise gradually. By age 10 to 12 years, hormone levels become very high and puberty begins. Once the hormones have triggered the biological events of puberty, the process is very rapid, with most of the major changes occurring within a span of three years (see Figure 13.3).

The Growth Spurt

growth spurt

During puberty, boys and girls undergo a period of rapid physical growth, called the *growth spurt*. During this period, the individual's whole body seems to shoot up, and there are also changes in body proportions and dimensions. The growth spurt begins with a weight gain, about 26 pounds in boys and 20 pounds in girls. This gain in weight is largely due to the accumulation of fat around the legs, arms, abdomen, and buttocks (Tanner, 1978). After the initial weight gain, a spurt in height occurs, and some of the fat is redistributed.

The increase in height that occurs during the growth spurt is striking, especially for boys. As you can see in Figure 13.4, which shows the typical growth curves for boys and girls from birth to age 18, the velocity of growth in height progressively declines after infancy, and just before puberty it reaches its lowest point. When the growth spurt is at its peak, a boy typically grows 3½ inches during a 12-month period, and in some boys growth in height is even more striking, as they gain as much as 4 inches in 6 months (Tanner, 1978). Contrast this with growth prior to the growth spurt, which is less than two inches a year on the average, and you get an idea of how striking the change in height is. For girls, the gain in height is also significant in relation to their height increases in previous years, but it is not usually as pronounced as it is in boys. Girls, however, begin their growth spurt two years ahead of boys. For girls, rapid growth typically begins at age 11, whereas for boys, it begins around the age of 13 (Thissen, Bock, Wainer, & Roche, 1976). Thus, girls who are 11 and boys who are 13 are at a similar stage of physical development, and between the ages of 11 and 13, girls are usually several inches taller than boys their age.

Besides the differences between boys and girls, there are huge individual differences in the age at which the growth spurt begins. As you can see in Figure 13.5, which shows the growth spurt in height of 5 children of the same sex, there can be as much as a four-year difference in the age at which children begin their growth spurt. This individual difference holds true not only for height, but also for the other changes of puberty.

Changes in Body Dimensions and in the Proportion of Muscle and Fat

During the adolescent growth spurt, there are also changes in body parts and body proportions. Most noticeable of these changes is the growth of the hands, feet, and legs, which may take place not only at exaggerated rates but also according to different timetables. Thus at different times during puberty, the adolescent may feel awkward and clumsy, and he becomes concerned that his body will never catch up to his hands and feet, or that he is all legs (Tanner, 1978).

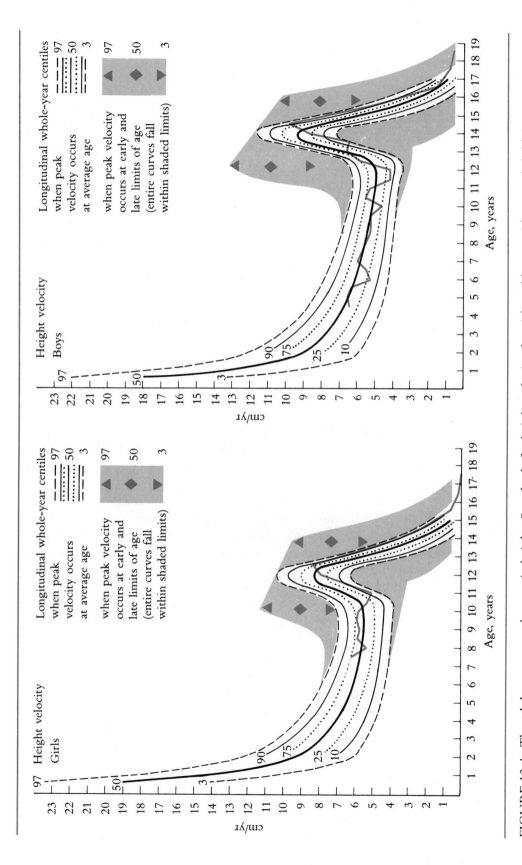

FIGURE 13.4 The adolescent growth spurt in height. Standards for height velocity for girls and boys, with normal children measured over a whole-year period, with a new period begun every 6 months. The average for peak velocity is 12.0 years in girls and 14.0 years in boys. The shaded portions represent the situation for early and late maturers. From Tanner, J. M. (1978). *Foetus into man: Physical growth from conception to maturity.* Cambridge, MA: Harvard Univ. Press; fig. 59, p. 177 (boys), fig. 60, p. 178 (girls). Copyright © 1978 by J. M. Tanner.

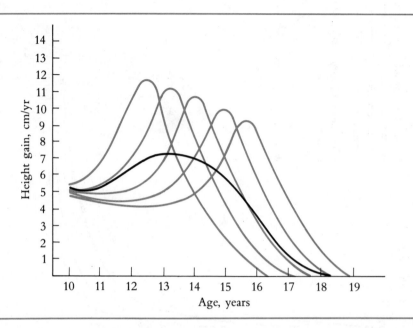

FIGURE 13.5   Age of maturation in five boys. You can see that some boys may begin puberty before age 12, whereas others do not begin puberty until they are close to age 16. From Rutter, Michael (1980). *Changing youth in a changing society: Patterns of adolescent development and disorder.* Cambridge, Mass.: Harvard University Press; p. 9, fig. 1.2. Copyright © by the Nuffield Provincial Hospitals Trust.

There are also subtle changes during this period that, collectively, contribute to the transformation of the individual from a child into an adult. The facial features that characterize the childhood years disappear as the low forehead becomes wider, the mouth widens, and the lips become fuller. In addition, head growth diminishes while other skeletal parts continue to grow. Thus the large head characteristic of the childhood years becomes smaller in proportion to total body size.

In addition to the changes in skeletal structure, there is a spurt of muscle growth during this period and, as a result, a decrease in the amount of fat (Tanner, 1962). In both boys and girls, muscular development occurs rapidly at the same time as their height increases. For boys, however, muscular development is more rapid than it is in girls, and they gain more muscle tissue. Both boys and girls also experience decreases in the amount of fat. In boys, the decrease can be so significant as to result in actual weight loss. In girls, the decrease in fat is less significant, and they retain a greater proportion of fat to muscle than do boys (Tanner, 1962), a characteristic that remains throughout the adult years. The acceleration in muscle development is accompanied by increases in strength. Because the differences between boys and girls in the proportion of fat to muscle are significant, after adolescence boys become, and remain, much stronger than girls.

Other, much less apparent aspects of the growth spurt include changes in the growth of the heart and in the capacity of the lungs. Boys develop larger hearts and greater lung capacity relative to their size than do girls. In addition, there is a gradual decrease in the rate of the heart beat during the growth spurt. This decrease is more pronounced in boys. Thus, beginning toward the latter part of puberty and from then on, the heart rate for boys is slower than it is for girls (Eichorn, 1975). These changes, together with increased skeletal and muscular maturity, enable adolescents to engage in physical activities that require endurance and to perfect the motor skills they developed during the early and middle childhood years. Many adolescents become involved in a variety of sports, and some go on to become skilled athletes.

At this point in the discussion it becomes apparent that there are striking differences in growth between adolescent boys and girls. In previous chapters on physical development during infancy and the childhood years, it was reasonable to generalize about the growth of children without regard to sex, since physical development for the two sexes is essentially similar during these years. During adolescence, however, sex differences in physical growth become pronounced. These differences extend in varying degrees to most aspects of growth. Men are larger than women, on the average, because they grow for an additional two years and because their growth is more vigorous; men differ from women in build because the rates of growth in different segments of the body differ for the two sexes (Stuart and Prugh, 1974). These sex differences in physical development may contribute in part, to differences in behavior and motivation to pursue certain careers and activities. However, they should not be overemphasized, for sex-typed behavior and motives are influenced by a complex interaction between biological, cognitive, and socio-cultural factors.

Nutrition

The increased rate of growth during puberty is coupled with a natural increase in appetite, so adolescents often seem to consume enormous quantities of food. Apparently, metabolic changes alter the appetite to take care of growth needs (Stuart and Prugh, 1974). However, while the inherent adaptive mechanism of the human body can be relied upon to accommodate increased nutritional needs, the adolescent cannot be relied upon to eat foods of the right quality. During puberty, the adolescent needs not only more calories, but also additional amounts of protein and additional amounts of specific minerals and vitamins, including calcium, iron, and vitamins A, B_2, C, and D (U.S. Dept. of Agriculture, 1980).

However, although adolescents eat more during puberty, they are deficient in these minerals and vitamins (*Report of the Select Panel for the Promotion of Child Health*, 1981). The nutrient most commonly deficient in the adolescent's diet is iron, and among girls who have started menstruating, iron deficiency anemia is very common. It is obvious that the adolescent needs help in following a proper diet. There are social and emotional factors which often interfere with the ability of the adolescent to eat properly. These include misinformation about food values, interest in group activities which often occur during mealtimes, and the increased frequency during adolescence of eating at fast food restaurants (National Academy of Sciences, 1978). There are additional problems that interfere with good nutrition, particularly in girls, for their high food needs occur at a time when they are increasingly aware of their physical appearance, and they tend to aspire to the slender figures that fashion models have.

anorexia nervosa

Eating Disorders.   The concern girls have over achieving the figure of a fashion model has an extreme form of expression in the problem of *anorexia nervosa*. Anorexia nervosa is an eating disorder which occurs largely among young adolescent girls, although it is also found among some young women, and, in some cases, among boys (see Figure 13.6). It is characterized by self-induced starvation, bizarre attitudes toward food, and distorted body image (Rollins & Piazza, 1978). Although they are often severely emaciated, anorexic girls believe they are fat and become preoccupied with dieting. So distorted are their perceptions of their own bodies that they do not see themselves as emaciated but, rather, as fat. Most victims of anorexia lose 25 percent or more of their normal body fat. Anorexia also causes its victims to stop menstruating, they become weak and they suffer muscle deterioration. From 5 to 15 percent of anorexics literally die of starvation (Goetz, Succop, Reinhart, & Miller, 1977).

Anorexia, which means "without food," seems to be an epidemic among young girls, although it was hardly a problem two decades ago. The cause of anorexia is not known, but researchers are investigating the possibility that it is related to a psychological need. One theory is that the need is to avoid becoming an adult, since starvation can impede physical growth and the onset of puberty. Another theory is that anorexia is related to a rejection of the mother figure or to the experience of being the daughter of an overly protective and controlling mother. It is theorized that by being anorexic, the girl demonstrates her ability to control at least one aspect of her own life (Landau, 1983; MacLeod, 1981). In addition, researchers note that the problem may stem from a faulty body image, which many adolescents have, given the societal ideal of feminine beauty of being very thin (Bruch, 1978). Since so much exposure is given to the tall, thin, almost emaciated female body in magazine ads and on television, it can be difficult for adolescents to accept their own body type.

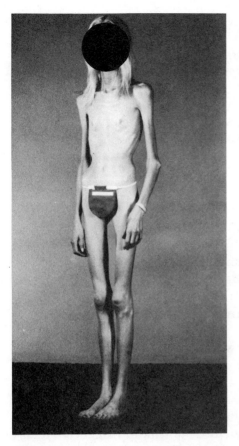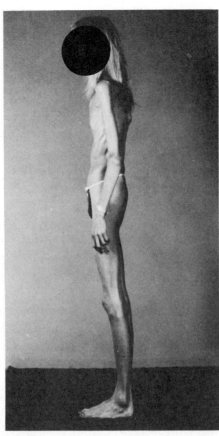

FIGURE 13.6   A young woman suffering from advanced stages of anorexia nervosa. The literal meaning of *anorexia* is "without food."

Another problem that affects teenage girls and young women is *bulimia,* which is characterized by enormous eating binges followed by self-induced vomiting (Johnson et al., 1981). Both anorexia nervosa and bulimia are difficult to treat, although some strides have been made with psychotherapy as well as with behavior modification procedures (Goetz, Succop, Reinhart, & Miller, 1977; Geller, Kelley, Traxler, & Marone, 1978). Without treatment of any kind, only half of anorexics and bulimics improve (Minuchin & Fishman, 1981; Minuchin, Rosman, & Baker, 1978), and the others suffer many severe health problems that can culminate in death.

bulimia

Sexual Maturation

The physiological event that is most often associated with puberty is sexual maturation. This includes a series of changes in the reproductive organs and the appearance of secondary sex characteristics. These changes usually follow an invariant sequence (see Figure 13.2); however, there are individual differences in the age at which these changes occur. The first event associated with sexual maturation in puberty is an increased secretion of hormones by the pituitary gland. As noted earlier, this causes the ovaries and testes to mature and to secrete sex hormones. Estrogen production also rises in adolescent boys, but for them it is not cyclic, and there is also a very sharp increase in testosterone. In both boys and girls, the production of androgens from the adrenal gland also increases greatly during puberty, and these are responsible for the development of some of the secondary sex characteristics we will discuss (Petersen & Taylor, 1980).

Reproductive Organs.   The increased levels of hormones stimulate certain internal changes. In girls, the uterus grows larger and the vaginal lining thickens. In boys, the penis grows and thickens, and, about a year later, the scrotal sac enlarges. As these organs grow, the individual becomes capable of reproduction. For girls, the physiological event that signals fertility is *menarche,* the first menstrual period. For boys, reproductive potential is said to exist when they achieve *ejaculation,* the discharge of seminal fluid containing sperm. However, menarche and ejaculation do not necessarily indicate reproductive capability, as they are simply one of a series of events leading toward full sexual maturity. In fact, girls may not become fertile for about 6 months to a year after menarche, since ovulation does not usually occur in the first several menstrual periods. In the same way, the ability to ejaculate does not mean that there are any sperm, or a sufficient concentration of live and motile sperm in the seminal fluid for the boy to be considered fertile. However, as you read in Chapter 10, it is not safe to take into account the relative infertility of individuals in puberty, as many young girls before the age of twelve do in fact become pregnant.

menarche
ejaculation

Secondary Sex Characteristics.   Hormonal secretion initiates several other changes in different parts of the body that further contribute to sex differentiation. One of these is the change in physique. By the end of puberty, boys have wide shoulders and relatively narrow, slim hips. Girls develop wider, more rounded hips and narrow shoulders.

Breasts.   Another change that contributes to obvious differences between boys and girls is the development of the breasts. In girls, the growth of the breast "bud," which occurs when a small concentration of fat causes a slight rise of the breast, is one of the first signs that puberty has begun. From then on, the breasts develop gradually for several years, and by the time most of the changes of puberty are over, full breast growth is attained. The gradual growth of the breasts is quite difficult for girls to accept, for once the breast bud appears, girls cannot wait for their breasts to be large enough for them to wear a bra. Also, in our society breast development is a symbol of femininity, so girls whose breasts are not as developed as those of other girls tend to feel embarrassed and also worried that their breasts will remain small.

Breast changes occur in boys, too, as the *areolla,* the pigmented area around the nipple, grows in diameter, and their breasts become slightly larger. Many boys also experience what they consider to be abnormal breast enlargement. However, this enlargement is usually temporary and subsides within a year or two (Roche, French, & Davilla, 1971).

areolla

Hair Growth.   During puberty, both boys and girls also experience changes in hair growth. First, head and body hair becomes darker and coarser. Second, hair growth occurs in regions of the body that were previously smooth as pubic, axillary (underarm), facial, and, in boys, chest hair appears. This hair is usually very sparse and of a light color when it first appears. As puberty continues, the hair growth becomes more substantial and also darker.

Voice.   The voices of boys and girls also change during puberty and become lower as the larynx enlarges and the length of the vocal cords increases. In boys, this change is quite pronounced and is referred to as the breaking of the voice. Until it actually occurs, boys tend to feel embarrassed and conscious of their high-pitched voice. Many adolescent boys, in anticipation of the change in their voice, tend to "practice" speaking in a lower voice when they are in the presence of their parents or others they feel comfortable with. Although boys expect the change of voice to occur suddenly, and also relatively early in puberty, it is often a gradual process that occurs rather late, after several of the other biological changes take place.

Other Hormonal Effects

Acne.   The increased production of androgens that stimulates sexual maturation during adolescence leads to other conditions, one of which is the skin problem acne. Acne occurs when glands in the skin, stimulated by androgens, produce a fatty substance called *sebum* which, when mixed with skin cells, can plug up pores and cause blackheads or whiteheads to form. If bacteria begin to grow in a sealed-off pore, infection may cause painful boils, the acne, which can leave permanent scars.

sebum

Acne is very common, affecting, according to some estimates, over two thirds of adolescents at some point (Stuart and Prugh, 1974). There is no evidence that poor eating habits or poor hygiene cause acne, although these may aggravate the condition once it is present (Stuart and Prugh, 1974). The genes, however, do play a role in acne, as children of parents who were acne sufferers are likely to be similarly affected (Sommer, 1978). Acne is often made light of, as "part of growing up" that most

FIGURE 13.7 Acne is often made light of as part of growing up, and it usually clears up with time. However, to the adolescent who is painfully aware of his or her inflamed face, acne can be the source of embarrassment and shame. © Norcliff Thayer, Inc.

everyone goes through, and it does usually clear up with time. However, for the adolescent, who is painfully aware of his or her inflamed face, acne can cause significant psychological trauma (see Figure 13.7). Embarrassed by pimples and marks, adolescents may be afraid to date or become involved in social situations, sure their peers will reject them. In severe cases, medical treatment can relieve acne symptoms, and treatment is very important for minimizing the lasting psychological and physical effects of the condition (Stuart and Prugh, 1974).

Hormonal Effects on Behavior.   There is also some indication that hormones affect emotions and behavior, although the evidence for this is not conclusive. In girls, the hormonal changes of puberty, which include cyclic increases in the levels of estrogen, may contribute to temporary changes in mood. Researchers report, for example, that in the few days preceding menstruation, some girls are likely to be depressed (Kessel and Coppen, 1963). This condition, referred to as the premenstrual syndrome, is known to persist beyond adolescence as some women suffer a variety of emotional disturbances as well as fatigue during the premenstrual phase (Dalton, 1977). However, it is not known if hormones are the only cause of premenstrual syndrome or if vitamin deficiencies are also part of the problem, as vitamin supplements and changes in dietary habits are said to alleviate the problem in many women (Lauersen & Stukan, 1983).

In boys, high levels of androgen secretion in puberty is said to increase the *sex drive* (Money and Ehrhardt, 1972), which refers to the basic biological need to achieve sexual stimulation and satisfaction. Since androgens are secreted in both boys and girls, it is likely that they affect the sex drive in girls as well (Rutter, 1980). Until recently, however, it was generally believed that the sex drive is much stronger in males than it is in females. Psychoanalysts in particular held the view that since the sex drive in males is stronger, males are destined to be dominant and sexually aggressive and that females are destined to be passive (Deutsch, 1945).

sex drive

The prevalence of such beliefs led to the idea of *the double standard,* which refers to a different set of rules for sexual behavior for men and women. That is, since their sex drive was considered strong, men were until recently expected to be sexually aggressive and to pursue as much sexual experience and gratification as possible. Women, on the other hand, whose sex drive was considered less strong, were expected to have no interest in sex and to ward off any sexual advances by men. Until the mid-1960s, most adolescents believed in the double standard and acted accordingly (Schwartz & Merten, 1967). Recent surveys indicate, however, that such attitudes and behaviors are changing. Most teenage girls believe that women have as much desire for sex as do men, and that they enjoy sex as much as men. In addition, as indicated in Chapter 10, the number of girls who experience sexual intercourse during adolescence has increased in recent years.

the double standard

Some interesting perspectives regarding the effects of hormones on behavior and the sex drive may be gained from animal studies which point to the fact that high levels of androgen secretions influence assertiveness, dominance, and the sex drive in both sexes, not just in males. Joslyn (1973) reports that when female rhesus monkeys were injected with androgens, they became increasingly more aggressive and replaced males in the top position in the social hierarchy. However, while this study shows the effects of androgens on behavior, Rutter (1980) points out that the association between hormone levels and behavior is a two-way street. A study by Rose, Gordon, and Bernstein (1972) underscores this point. This study shows that when adult male monkeys were in the company of receptive female monkeys, they displayed dominance and assertiveness and their hormone levels increased dramatically. When these male monkeys were subjected to a sudden defeat by an all-male group of monkeys, their hormone levels fell. Whether these changes occur in humans is not known, but in animals, at least, it appears that it is not only that hormones influence behavior, but that social experience can influence hormone level.

The Tensions and Problems of Adolescence

Having examined the physical and physiological changes of adolescence, let us now look at the problems some individuals experience during this period, and the possible relationship these problems have to psychological growth and development.

Early and Late Maturers.   First, let us examine the psychological impact of the timing of puberty. As we have shown earlier, individual variation in the rate of physical growth and development is most dramatic during adolescence. At the ages of 11, 12, and 13 in girls and 13, 14, and 15 in boys, the variations in development are enormous, ranging from complete preadolescence to complete maturity. Thus two children of the same age and sex may look and feel totally different, one resembling a child, the other looking very much like a young adult (see Figure 13.8).

You are perhaps young enough to remember how acutely aware you were of your growth during adolescence. Most adults, however, tend to forget that during adolescence, feelings about sexuality and personal appearance are very important. In fact, adolescents of both sexes are egocentric, and they become more concerned about their sexual maturation and physical growth than anything else (Jersild, 1952). It is not surprising, therefore, to discover that whether the individual matures early or late has an important and, for boys, long lasting, impact on behavior. That this is indeed the case has been confirmed by a series of investigations emanating from the *California Growth Study* (reviewed by Eichorn, 1963), a longitudinal study in which the physical and psychological characteristics of a large group of individuals were studied over a long period of their lives.

In this study, researchers found that for girls, maturing either early or late can be a source of great embarrassment and concern which can affect the development of the self-concept. Early maturing girls tend to feel embarrassed and isolated because none of their peers are at the same stage of development, and they are often teased by other children, and regarded as freaks. However, these feelings are only temporary, for once other girls begin puberty, early maturing girls experience a great deal of popularity among girls as well as boys. Studies show that in the 8th grade when most

FIGURE 13.8   These three boys are the same age but they are at different stages of development.

other girls are in puberty, early maturing girls are likely to be well respected and liked (Faust, 1960). Girls who mature late, on the other hand, tend to be more tense and more active in attention-seeking than other girls, and they also tend to have low self-esteem. However, once these late maturing girls start menarche, these feelings of low self-esteem diminish.

Boys who mature late also evidence negative feelings about themselves, but to a greater degree than do girls. Early maturing boys, however, tend to have positive self-esteem. As Jones and Bayley (1950) note

> [Adolescent boys] who are physically accelerated are usually accepted and treated by adults and other children as more mature. They appear to have relatively little need to strive for status. From their ranks come the outstanding student body leaders in senior high school. In contrast, the physically retarded boys exhibit many forms of relatively immature behaviors. This may be in part because others tend to treat them as the little boys they appear to be. Furthermore, a fair proportion of these boys give evidence of needing to counteract their physical disadvantage in some way—usually by greater activity in striving for attention, although in some cases by withdrawing.

While the physical events of puberty can, and often do, significantly influence important personality traits such as self-confidence and self-esteem, you should be aware that the psychological impact of early and late maturing is largely determined by cultural forces (Clausen, 1975). In the United States, where physical strength and size are associated with masculinity, these physical traits are highly valued by boys. It is not surprising, therefore, that early maturers are found to be more self-assured and independent than late maturers, who are found to be lacking in self-confidence. However, this is not necessarily the case in other countries. In Italy, for example, where family membership rather than physical size is emphasized as a source of prestige, there are no differences due to early or late maturation in the attitudes and behaviors of boys (Mussen & Bouterline-Young, 1964).

Long-Term Effects. In addition to the cultural differences associated with the psychological consequences of early and late maturing, there is the question of how long these effects last. As noted earlier, the psychological consequences of early maturation are temporary for girls. In addition, no striking differences are found among women who had matured early rather than late. In boys, however, the psychological impact of the timing of puberty tends to be more long lasting. When early and late maturing males of the *California Growth Study* were tested in their thirties, there were no longer any differences between the two groups in size and physical attractiveness, but some differences in their personality characteristics, social behavior, and occupational level were discovered. Descriptions of the early and late maturers at maturity were suprisingly similar to the descriptions of them during adolescence. The early maturers made a good impression and were cooperative, enterprising, sociable, and conforming. They were also more likely to be in occupational positions requiring the supervision of others. Late maturers were more rebellious, touchy, self-assertive, and more frequently sought the aid and encouragement of others.

Depression During Adolescence

Besides the psychological problems associated with the timing of puberty, the experience of puberty itself is difficult for many individuals, since it entails having to adjust to so many physiological changes: the changes in hormonal levels and physical growth, and the first experience with such physiological events as menarche and ejaculation.

Any period of adjustment to change is associated with stress, and early adolescence, the time when puberty occurs, is a time of a great deal of stress not only for the adolescent, but for parents as well. The stress young people experience during adolescence is manifested in a variety of behavioral and psychological problems. Offer (1969) notes that during early adolescence quarrels between adolescents and their parents are very common. These quarrels tend to diminish, in many cases, toward late adolescence. In another study (Simmons, Rosenberg, & Rosenberg, 1973), researchers found that between the ages of 11 and 14, adolescents

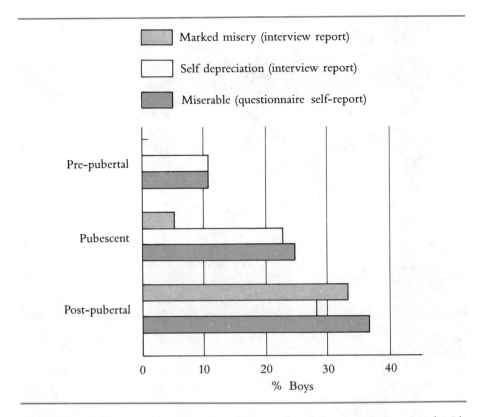

FIGURE 13.9   Researchers have found that early adolescence is associated with marked increase in the incidence of depression, especially among boys.

evidence a poor self-concept, whereas by age 16 to 18 there is a marked improvement in the way adolescents think of themselves. In addition, Rutter (1980) notes that early adolescence is associated with a marked rise in the incidence of depression, especially among boys. This depression is associated more closely with puberty than with chronological age. As you can see in Figure 13.9, prepubescent boys rarely show depressive feelings, whereas the percentage of boys who are rated depressed or who report feeling miserable rises significantly during puberty and remains high for some time after puberty. You should be aware, however, that besides the physiological changes of puberty, many other profound changes occur during adolescence which may contribute to stress and behavioral changes among adolescents. These include the acquisition of self-identity and in- dependence, and the formation of close social and sexual relationships outside the family. In addition, at this point in life, the adolescent often has to make important career and other choices, so you can see that there are many factors which can affect the relationship between the adolescent and his parents and bring on feelings of doubt about the self and depres- sion.

FIGURE 13.10 For many adolescents, depression is so severe that it becomes a psychological as well as a health hazard. Depression can alienate the teenager from family and friends and it inhibits the attainment of self–identity.

Depression, which is broadly defined as a state of feeling extremely sad, is marked by a pervasive sense of loss, inactivity, fatigue, and difficulty in thinking and concentrating (Weiner, 1980). Many things can bring on depression, including the divorce of parents, the death of grandparents, or even rejection by peers and failure in school or in sports. Illness or physical injury can also bring on depression. Thus, many individuals experience depression at various times during their adolescence and also later in life (see Figure 13.10). During the past two decades, however, there has been a significant increase in the incidence of depression not only among adolescents, but also among younger children (*Report of the Select Panel for the Promotion of Child Health,* 1981). Also, for many adolescents and children, depression is so severe that it becomes a psychological and a health hazard. One of the dangers of depression among adolescents is alienation from the family and friends. Depression inhibits the individual from striving toward the attainment of self-identity and from making important career and other choices, since the tendency among the depressed is to give up trying and to think "What's the use of going on?"

DISCUSSION OF SOCIAL ISSUES: ADOLESCENT SUICIDE

Depressed adolescents are emotionally vulnerable and they often think of committing suicide. Adolescent suicide is not new. Terman (1914) wrote about the problem as it existed in the early part of the century, and statistics on adolescent suicide indicate that it was also a problem in the 1950s (U.S. Vital Statistics, 1949–1973). Today, however, self-destruction among youth not only continues to be a problem, it has been increasing at a rapid rate. It is now the third leading cause of death among adolescents, after accidents and homicide (*Report of the Select Panel for the Promotion of Child Health,* 1981). In fact, accidents, homicides, and suicides account for three quarters of adolescent deaths. The death rate for males, by accidents, poisoning, and violence, takes a sharp rise at about age 15, peaking at about age 21 (see Figure 13.11).

The adolescent suicide rate is twice as high as it was 10 years ago, and three times as high as it was 20 years ago (Hollinger, 1978). These statistics alone do not give a complete picture of the extent of the problem. For every successful suicide there are fifty to one hundred adolescent suicide attempts (Finch & Poznanski, 1971; Mishara, 1975). Researchers also note that, because of the social stigma associated with suicide, many deaths that are said to be due to accidents are actually due to suicide (Tishler, McKenry, & Morgan, 1981). In addition, there is the related phenomenon of suicide epidemics, in which one successful suicide triggers several other suicide attempts or successful suicides by the victim's friends or other adolescents in the community.

No single factor sufficiently explains adolescent suicide or its increase during the past two decades. Researchers have not yet isolated the causes of adolescent suicide, since studies that have been done thus far have produced conflicting results (Tishler, 1983). Although researchers do not yet know the causes of adolescent suicide, they do know that there are multiple factors associated with the problem. For example, there is an indication of a relationship between suicide and the advent of puberty (Garfinkel & Golombek, 1974). Poor school performance is also found to be related to adolescent suicide. In one study, researchers found that 75 percent of those who attempted suicide had exceptionally low academic ratings, learning disabilities, or a history of behavioral problems in school,

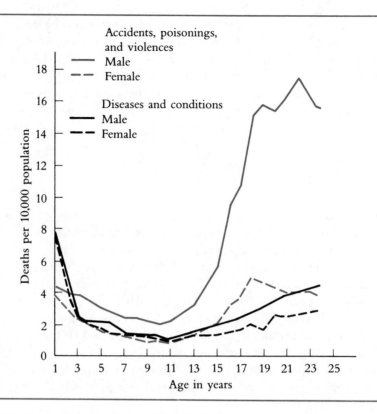

FIGURE 13.11   The death rate for individuals between the ages of 15 and 24 years.

and also stressful home situations such as a divorce or an alcoholic parent (Rohn, Sarles, Kenny, Reynolds, & Heald, 1977). However, in another study, Marks and Haller (1977) found that many of the adolescents who attempted to commit suicide have a history of successful school experiences.

Some personality traits are found to be related to suicide. Cantor (1976) found that young women who attempted suicide had a low level of frustration tolerance and were likely to be in conflict with their parents. In other studies, poor communication between the parents and the adolescents in conjunction with disruption in family life are cited as factors related to suicide (Garfinkel et al., 1982). In addition, researchers note that individuals who suffer from depression during their childhood years as well as during adolescence are more likely than others to commit suicide (Garfinkel & Golombek, 1974). Researchers also note that the sex of the individual may be a factor in the number of deaths due to suicide. More girls than boys (a ratio of 4 to 1) attempt suicide, but more boys than girls succeed in killing themselves because of their tendency to use more violent methods (Weissman, 1974).

These findings cannot be interpreted to mean that any of these factors cause the suicide, but it is easy to see that during the emotionally vulnerable period of adolescence, the individual who experiences emotional difficulties and a great deal of stress can be at risk of attempting a suicide. Suicide usually comes as a surprise to family and friends of the victim. However, researchers note that it rarely occurs without some warning signals, so that sensitive and observant individuals can often help prevent a suicide. Tishler (1983) notes that in order to prevent a suicide, physicians, teachers, parents, relatives, and friends of adolescents should recognize that there are certain precipitating events that occur that could lead to suicide. Among these events are the divorce or remarriage of parents, the anniversary of the divorce or remarriage, death in the family, or the suicide or death of a close friend. Besides watching out for the adolescent who experiences such events, Tishler also advises monitoring any changes in behavior as a possible clue to the suicidal intentions of the adolescent. A drastic change in personal appearance, frequent or continual complaints about aches and pains, changes in school work and daily routines, emotional outbursts, excessive use of alcohol and drugs, an overwhelming sense of guilt or shame, or talking about death are all possible warning signals.

Of course, many adolescents do exhibit any or all of these behaviors and they do not necessarily commit suicide. But the family, friends, and others who come in contact with adolescents should nonetheless be alert to the possibility of a suicide so that they can help prevent the tragic and needless waste of human life by extending an offer to help, by talking to the adolescent, or in some other ways alleviating the stress the young person may be experiencing.

SUMMARY

Adolescence is a difficult period of life to define, in large part because it is a recent social invention engendered by the need for extensive schooling in preparation for life in a complex society. While the adolescent in our society is not psychologically ready for adult life, he is physiologically ready to function as an adult. This discrepancy between the cultural and physiological aspects of adolescence causes a great deal of emotional turmoil for the adolescent. At one time psychologists believed that all adolescents had emotional difficulties and that emotional turbulence was an inevitable, biologically caused characteristic of adolescence, which was described as a time of storm and stress. Recent research reveals, however, that not all adolescents are emotionally troubled, although some are, due in part to the physical changes brought on by puberty and also to social and emotional changes associated with adolescence.

Puberty is the physiological event which culminates in sexual maturity, and it includes a series of physical and physiological changes such as a spurt in body growth and changes in body dimensions, maturation of the sex organs, and the appearance of secondary sex characteristics. These changes are triggered by the increased levels of hormone secretion which occur during puberty. Hormones not only cause physiological changes, they can also cause the skin problem acne, and they affect mood and behavior, most notably the sex drive.

The impact of puberty extends beyond bodily changes. During adolescence, the individual is preoccupied with the process of sexual maturation and with his physical appearance. In addition, there is great variation in the age during which individuals begin puberty. Individuals who mature late or early are likely to be distressed by their physical development or lack of it, and in boys the effects of such distress on personality can last well into adulthood.

In addition to the psychological problems associated with early and late maturation, the physical changes of puberty cause a great deal of stress for the individual, who has to adjust to internal and external bodily changes. Thus, many adolescents evidence behavioral difficulties, especially during early adolescence when puberty occurs. They may also experience a negative self-concept and depression. Associated with depression is the phenomenon of adolescent suicide. During the past 20 years, there has been a dramatic increase in youth suicides, now the third leading cause of death among adolescents, after accidents and homicide.

REVIEW POINTS

1. Adolescence is a cultural invention which did not come to be considered a period of life until the late 19th century. Several social conditions are linked to the emergence of adolescence as a special period of life, including industrialized society's increased need for education and specialized job skills and the expansion of high school education to help meet this need.

2. At one time adolescence was thought to be a period of storm and stress, which refers to the emotional turmoil and rebelliousness some adolescents experience. Researchers now believe that adolescence is no more stressful than other transitional periods in the life cycle.

3. The physical and physiological changes associated with adolescence occur in the context of puberty. Puberty culminates in sexual maturity and sexual capability, and it is also associated with a growth spurt.

4. Puberty in girls occurs 2 years earlier than it does in boys. Additionally, there are individual differences among girls and among boys, in the age at which puberty begins. Thus, some adolescents who are the same age may look and feel very different. Some may look more like young adults, others may still retain their childish looks. For many adolescents, this variation in the age at which puberty and its associated physical and physiological changes occur is a source of embarrassment.

5. Puberty is associated with other changes as well. These changes stem from hormone secretion and include acne and depression. Boys in particular are vulnerable to depression during puberty.

6. For some adolescents, depression may lead to suicide. Although adolescent suicide is not new, but was in fact recorded early this century, during the last 10 to 20 years there has been a significant increase in the incidence of adolescent suicide. No single factor sufficiently explains adolescent suicide or its increase in recent years. Researchers note, however, that it rarely occurs without warning signals. Researchers further note that there are some life events that could lead to suicide. Among these are the divorce or remarriage of parents, a death in the family, or the death or suicide of a close friend.

CHAPTER 14

COGNITIVE DEVELOPMENT DURING ADOLESCENCE

The biological changes of puberty transform the child by giving her the physique and sexuality of an adult. Important as these changes are, they represent only one aspect of the transformation of the individual from child to adult. During the adolescent period, the individual also attains an intellectual maturity which enables her to think logically about ideas and events that are abstract. Unlike the younger child who thinks largely about the present and the concrete and who can discuss logically how the world is, the adolescent speculates about the future and her role in life, and she can discuss logically how the world might be.

As adolescents attain a more sophisticated level of cognitive functioning, the type of education with which they are provided changes too. However, not all adolescents are given the same opportunities for education. Some who are considered bright are placed in accelerated educational programs. Others are placed in slow-paced or vocational programs. The decisions of which students are bright and which are average or slow are based in part on intelligence tests. Do intelligence tests actually measure how intelligent an individual is? What is intelligence, anyway, and what factors determine individual differences in intellectual performance? We answer these questions in this chapter after we discuss the progress that occurs in intellectual growth during adolescence and the implications of such growth for the type of educational experiences the adolescent receives.

COGNITIVE DEVELOPMENT

The Formal Operations Period and Characteristics of Formal Operations Thought

During the adolescent years, the individual is in the fourth and final stage of cognitive development. Piaget termed this stage the *formal operations period*. During this period the individual's capacity to acquire and utilize knowledge reaches its peak efficiency. Although not all adolescents attain this final level of cognitive development, many do, and as a result they experience a change in their mode of thinking from that of a child to that of an adult. No longer tied to a rigid way of looking at things, adolescents in the formal operations period can deal with problems from a variety of perspectives, systematically applying complex logical operations as they do so.

The Development of Abstract Thinking

Drawing upon Piaget's theory and the research of others, Keating (1980) suggests that there are five ways in which the thinking of the adolescent differs from that of the child in the previous period of cognitive development. First, whereas during the concrete operations period the child's thinking is tied to concrete reality (that is, she can think logically only about real things in the immediate physical world), the adolescent who attains formal operations is capable of thinking in the abstract. With this ability to think abstractly, the formal operations individual can think logically not only about things but about statements and ideas. This is illustrated in an experiment in which an experimenter at times conceals and reveals a poker chip, telling the individual: "The chip is either green *or* not green," and "The chip is green *and* it is not green." The individual, a child or an adolescent, is asked whether each of the two statements is true, false, or impossible to judge. A concrete operations child answers the question on the basis of what she sees. When the chip is concealed, she says it is impossible to judge; when it is revealed, she answers on the basis of what the color of the chip actually is. However, the adolescent focuses not on the chip but on the *statements*. She can discern, for example, that there is the possibility that the statement "The chip is either green *or* not green" is true, whereas the statement, "The chip is green *and* it is not green" can never be true. She needs no physical evidence to arrive at the answers (Osherson, 1975).

Second, having this capacity to think in the abstract, that is, to separate the real from the possible, the adolescent is capable of thinking about hypotheses. A concrete operations child who is asked the hypothetical question, "If all dogs were pink and you had a dog, would your dog be pink, too?" laughs at the question, rejecting the suggestion that all dogs are pink, saying that this is not possible. She knows from her experience that this is not true, and she stops there and never makes an attempt to go a step further and consider the hypothetical question. In contrast, the adolescent who has attained formal operations can make a logical connection between the two statements in the question. She recognizes that if all dogs were pink, then her dog would have to be pink, too. In other words, the formal operations adolescent realizes that the same logical rules that are applied to the solutions of concrete problems are applicable to the solution of hypothetical problems as well. Piaget refers to this as *interpropositional logic,* or the ability to evaluate the logical relationship between propositions, which he sees as the basis for mature reasoning. He notes that whereas the concrete operations child tests the truth of each proposition in isolation and her thinking is limited by what she knows to be true from her experience, the formal operations individual can manipulate the logic of the propositions without regard to their content. Therefore, her thinking is not only more flexible, it also allows her to consider all the actual and *possible* solutions to a problem.

interpropositional logic

Third, the formal operations individual is capable of thinking ahead and planning. This enables the individual to approach problem solving in a systematic and efficient manner, integrating what she has learned in the past and considering all the possible combinations of relevant factors. To

FIGURE 14.1   The chemistry problem requires the individual to find the correct combination of liquids that will yield a yellow mixture.

demonstrate this in an experimental setting, Inhelder and Piaget (1958) devised an experiment, called the chemistry problem, in which the child or adolescent is shown five colorless, odorless liquids in test tubes. Four of the test tubes are labeled 1, 2, 3, and 4, and another is labeled *g*. The individual is told that by adding a few drops of *g* to some combination of the other liquids, a yellow mixture will be obtained. The individual's task is to find out the correct combination (see Figure 14.1). The concrete operations child attempts to solve the problem through trial and error. She adds a few drops of *g* to each of the other test tubes and then gives up. When prompted by the experimenter to continue, she haphazardly combines the liquids, forgetting which she has already mixed and which she has not. The formal operations adolescent, however, proceeds to solve the problem along a preconceived plan of action. She anticipates the kind of information that she will require to solve the problem, and, knowing that she must try out all the possible combinations, she systematically adds *g* to the four liquids. Then, she picks up the test tube labeled 1 and combines it, along with *g*, with the test tube labeled 2, then with the test tube labeled 3, and then with 4, often keeping a log of what she has tried, so that when she is asked by the experimenter what she had to do to obtain the yellow mixture, she can explain in detail what worked and what did not.

Fourth, unlike the concrete operations child, the formal operations individual acquires the capability of *reflective thinking,* or thinking about the processes of thinking and how these may be made more efficient. This ability is referred to by Piaget as performing *operations on operations.* Information processing theorists refer to it as *metacognition,* noting that just as at

reflective thinking

metacognition

a younger age the individual acquires metalinguistics (an intuitive aware-ness of how language works) and metamemory (which enables her to use memory-aiding devices to improve her capacity for memory), so the ado-lescent becomes capable of thinking about her own cognitive processes, making these more efficient. Given this new ability, the formal operations adolescent can analyze her own thoughts and judge whether they are ap-propriate for the task at hand, and she can decide, for example, whether an argument she is formulating is strong or weak. Related to this ability is the characteristic of the adolescent to probe her own ideas about the nature of things. Not only ideas but the thinking process itself becomes a subject to be thought about. Mussen and his colleagues (1974) quote an adolescent as saying, "I found myself thinking about my future and then I began to think about why I was thinking about my future, and then I began to think about why I was thinking about why I was thinking about my future."

Finally, the content of adolescent thought is broadened. The adoles-cent thinks about a number of topics she has never considered before. Enhanced by her ability to think in the abstract and to separate reality from possibility, she not only thinks about the world as it is, she thinks about what it might become, and she does so without restraint. At times she even constructs her own elaborate political and economic theories or complex plans for the reorganization of society, often thinking that she can accomplish everything by thought alone. In addition, anything that the adolescent thinks about takes on an enlarged significance and meaning:

> Topics of identity, society, existence, religion, morality, friendship, and so on are examined in detail and are contemplated with high emotion as well as increased cognitive capability. The spark for such consideration is not purely cognitive, of course; there are many lines of development converging with special significance for the adolescent. But . . . the cog-nitive skills applied to the task are much sharper, which makes the enter-prise all the more exciting (Keating, 1980).

Testing for Formal Operations

In testing for formal operations, Inhelder and Piaget (1958) developed a number of classic experiments, some of which we have already noted. The experiments illustrate the gradual development of logic in children and their ability during the formal operations period to engage in what is often referred to as the scientific method of problem solving. This ap-proach involves a planned course of action to the solution of the problem, and the variables of the problem are systematically controlled and ob-served in order to test for specific hypotheses.

In one such experiment, known as the pendulum problem, the indi-vidual is given a pendulum created by suspending a weight from a string and allowing the weight to swing freely back and forth (see Figure 14.2).

Adolescent Egocentrism

In spite of the fact that during the adolescent years the individual attains the capacity for formal operational thought, there is some limit to the cognitive capacities and logic of the adolescent because he is susceptible to *adolescent egocentrism*. Adolescent egocentrism is not the same as the egocentrism which characterizes the thinking of the preschool child. Unlike the preschool child, the adolescent knows that other people have their own thoughts which may be different from his, but he has the tendency to believe that he alone experiences such intense feelings as love, anger, and hate, hence he often feels misunderstood. Elkind (1978) explains that adolescent egocentrism occurs because adolescents fail to differentiate between the unique and the universal:

> A young woman who falls in love for the first time is enraptured with the experience, which is entirely new and thrilling. But she fails to differentiate between what is new and thrilling to herself and what is new and thrilling to humankind. It is not surprising, therefore, that this young woman says to her mother, "But Mother, you don't know how it feels to be in love" (Elkind, 1978).

Egocentrism is also evident in the adolescent's preoccupation with physical appearance. Fantasizing that everyone else is as interested in what he looks like or what he wears as he is, the adolescent often creates an *imaginary audience* for himself. He thinks when he walks into a room that everyone's attention is focused on him and that everyone is either admiring or criticizing him. This helps explain the self-consciousness of early adolescence and why every tiny pimple or strand of hair out of place assumes such great importance. Related to this characteristic is the *personal fable* (Elkind, 1967), which refers to the adolescent's belief that since everyone is interested in him, he must be unique and special. Elkind (1978) believes that the personal fable can have positive consequences: "The young person who feels that he or she is unique may strive to excel in music, literature, sports or other areas of endeavor. The sense of specialness can also be a source of personal strength and comfort in the face of many inevitable social, academic, and familial trials and tribulations of adolescence." However, it can have negative consequences as well. The adolescent who regards himself as heroic or destined to great fame also tends to have a *sense of indestructibility,* believing that he is magically protected from the things that happen to other people. These beliefs form the basis for many of the problems of adolescence and reinforce the excessive risk-taking which characterizes the behavior of some adolescents who are convinced that they can never become addicted to drugs or alcohol, that they can't get pregnant, that they won't get killed even though they are driving dangerously.

Although egocentrism does not disappear entirely and it may even be present during adulthood to some degree, eventually, at about the age of 15 or 16, the adolescent realizes that others are not preoccupied with him and that they have their own concerns about themselves. He also understands that he is not as unique and indestructible as he imagined. Other people are more like himself than he ever thought possible. With this realization,

the adolescent overcomes his egocentrism, and his thinking becomes more realistic.

Researchers explain that adolescent egocentrism begins to decline when the individual becomes more interested in thinking about the future and determining his place in society. They note further that the more time the adolescent spends talking about his beliefs and ideas as well as listening to other people, learning about their values, feelings, and thoughts about different issues, the sooner he overcomes his egocentrism (Youniss, 1980).

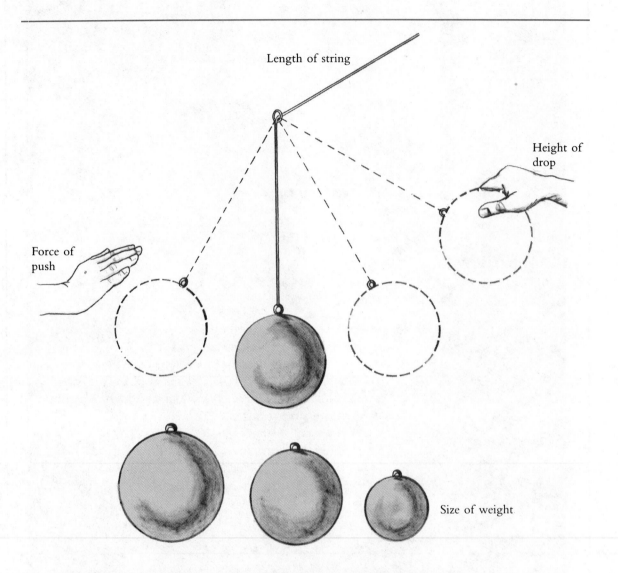

Length of string

Height of drop

Force of push

Size of weight

What causes the pendulum to swing faster or slower?

FIGURE 14.2 In the pendulum problem, the individual is asked what causes the pendulum to swing faster or slower. Adolescents in the formal operations period of cognitive development consider all possible factors involved: the size of the weight, the force of the push, the height of the drop, and the length of the string.

The individual is asked which of the four variables affect the rate at which the weight will swing: the force with which it is pushed; the amount of weight suspended from the string; the height from which the weight is released; or the length of the string. The individual is then given a set of different weights, and she is shown how to change the weight and manipulate the other three variables so she can experiment with all the possible ways that might affect the rate that the pendulum swings.

In order to arrive at the answer to the problem, the concrete operations child often pushes the weight at different speeds and says that it is only the force with which the weight is pushed that causes the weight to swing faster or slower. If she does try to manipulate the other variables, she does so haphazardly. The formal operations adolescent, however, is capable of systematically trying out all the possible manipulations. Exhibiting a planned approach to the solution of the problem, she proceeds along a number of steps. First, she sets standards for each of the variables. Then she holds constant three of the variables and varies a fourth so she can see whether there is a change in the rate at which the weight swings. In successive steps she continues to hold three variables constant while varying the standard of another of the variables. In doing so, she evidences not only the ability to follow a planned strategy of problem solving, but also her inclination to test all the possible hypotheses or combinations of these.

Formal Operations—Not a Universal Stage

Using this and other experiments which are designed to test the formal operations individual's logic and her systematic approach to problem solving, researchers have found that unlike previous periods of cognitive development, the formal operations period is not universally attained. Cross-cultural studies have shown that individuals in nontechnological societies where schooling is not available to everyone do not attain formal operations (Dasen, 1977). Other studies have shown that even in such cultures as ours where schooling is compulsory, not everyone attains this final level of cognitive functioning (Keating, 1980; Niemark, 1975).

However, researchers who have critiqued or elaborated on Piaget's theory note that in testing for formal operations, Piaget focused on scientific problems, but that the ability to think abstractly is applied to other tasks as well, not only to scientific tasks. Thus, there is a question regarding these findings: Do some individuals fail to attain formal operations or are the findings reflective of the inadequacy of the tests used to measure formal operations? For example, anthropological evidence suggests that whereas individuals in nontechnological societies do not demonstrate the ability to think abstractly when they are tested on Piagetian experiments, they do think abstractly on tasks that are relevant to their way of life and they are able to make and follow systematic plans and consider all of the various possible solutions to problems that they confront in their daily living. The work of Cole (1981; 1983), who has done extensive research on cognitive development as viewed in the cultural context, provides support for these findings. In addition, Kenny (1983) notes that some adolescents and adults are capable of formal operations thought when performing some tasks but not when performing others. This may be the result of motivational and environmental factors, as the more knowledge the individual has, the more his abstract reasoning capacity increases.

As Fischer and Lazerson (1984) note, an adolescent who has recently purchased a new car and who does not have much money to spend on car repairs will make every effort to learn as much as he can about the functions of the different parts of his car. When his car breaks down, he is able to put his knowledge to use, and he applies abstract mental skills as he considers all the possible reasons why the car does not start, systematically testing each one of these. This same adolescent, however, depending on the extent of his interest and the depth of his knowledge in other areas, say, psychology or physics, may or may not be able to think abstractly when engaged in tasks related to these subjects.

The fact that both interest and the accumulation of knowledge can affect the individual's attainment of formal operations has led Piaget to change his original assertion that the process of cognitive development is invariant and universal. Whereas this holds true for the previous periods of development, Piaget in his later writing noted that the formal operations period is not a universal stage. He acknowledged that the attainment of formal operations is made possible by the physiological maturation of adolescence (or puberty, to be exact). But, he noted that in the absence of interactions with individuals who practice abstract and logical thinking or of school experience, which encourages abstract thinking skills through the in-depth study of a variety of subjects, the individual will remain in the concrete operations stage (Piaget, 1972).

THE HIGH SCHOOL EXPERIENCE

Given the fact that the adolescent has the potential to attain a more sophisticated level of cognitive functioning, the kind of education that schools, teachers, and parents provide her changes. Whereas in the elementary grades the child's education is based upon the acquisition of basic skills with some emphasis also on such subjects as social studies and science, in high school the adolescent not only studies a greater number of subjects, she also studies these in more depth. In addition, hypotheses and the consideration of abstract notions now form part of the adolescent's schooling. The study of history, for example, includes not only consideration of what happened in the past, but also class discussions of what might have happened had certain different conditions prevailed. Similarly, science and mathematics lessons no longer focus on visible experiments and problems that are suited to the concrete operational mode of thinking characteristic of middle childhood. Instead, they involve explanations and discussions of theoretical issues such as the laws of physics or the principles of algebra and geometry. Since the majority of high school students are only in the process of attaining formal operational thought, most teachers do not altogether abandon the use of concrete examples in favor of an instruc-

FIGURE 14.3 Once they have reached the formal operations period, adolescents in high school formulate hypotheses and consider abstract ideas. In history, they can discuss not only what the world is, but also what it might have been and what it will become. Studying the sciences, the formal operations individual can focus on complex theoretical issues as well as concrete examples.

tional mode that emphasizes the logical and the hypothetical. Rather, some of the best teachers provide students with a variety of academic experiences, recognizing that even though many adolescents have not reached formal operational thinking, they have the potential for doing so. An instructional mode that takes advantage of this fact is more challenging and stimulating than one that does not (Elkind, 1983; see Figure 14.3).

However, not all schools or all teachers provide these kinds of high quality intellectual stimulation and training, and the education that some adolescents receive is not necessarily conducive to the attainment of formal operations. Dale (1970) points out that even among students who are taught science in high school (science being an area which requires abstract thinking), there are those who may not attain formal operational thought, since some science teachers often emphasize learning by rote rather than the active problem solving that is essential for cognitive growth.

Individual Differences in Intellectual Performance

Since there are variations among students in their school performance and in their potential to excel academically, not all students pursue the same course of academic training. Some students are considered brighter than others and are placed in an accelerated educational program where they are challenged to study increasingly complex subjects that will prepare them for further education in college. Others are placed in a slower-paced academic program or in a vocational program which prepares them for the world of work. Although the conventional rationale underlying this almost universal practice of "tracking" students into fast, slow, and vocational classes is to allow students to study at a pace that is realistic for them or to acquire training that will be useful to them in adult life, some educators criticize the practice, arguing that it results in inequalities in the type of educational experiences students are given. In a comprehensive study of public schools, Goodlad (1983) found that in the high track classes more time was spent on instruction and more homework was assigned to students than in the middle and low track classes. He also found that whereas teachers in the high track classes focused on the teaching of higher level skills, teachers in the middle and low track classes encouraged passivity in the students and did not expect the students to make full use of their abilities.

achievement vs. aptitude

The decision as to which students are brighter than others and are therefore eligible to participate in high track classes is made on the basis of students' scores on a battery of tests. Some of these tests measure student *achievement,* which refers to how much has been learned. Others measure student *aptitude* or potential for learning. The test scores reflect the norms, that is, how much a student has learned or her potential for learning in relation to other students her age. Although such tests are given throughout the child's school experience, they become especially important in high school. Whether students are considered bright or slow can determine not only the type of courses they take in high school, but their future direction in life, as well as how they feel about themselves and how others regard them.

There is a great deal of controversy surrounding the use of such tests to evaluate students. On the one hand, when the test scores accurately reflect the student's intellectual ability, they can be useful to schools and teachers who strive to help all children reach their potential for learning. Placing a child with a limited potential for intellectual growth in a high track class where she would be expected to work far beyond her potential is unfair and means that the child will be doomed to certain failure. Similarly, it is a shame to place a student with high intellectual potential in a class that presents him with few, if any, opportunities to develop this potential. However, critics of the use of tests in the evaluation of students wonder if the tests results are used to *provide* educational opportunities for children, or to *exclude* such opportunities, especially for children in the middle and low or vocational tracks. Also, they question the practice of making important decisions that determine the future course of the student's life on the basis of test scores. Do such scores really indicate the individual's ability to succeed in school? If a student gets poor scores on such tests during her freshman year in high school, does that mean that she is not likely to succeed in college?

At the crux of the controversy surrounding student evaluation practices is the use of intelligence test scores as evidence for the intellectual inferiority of students from some racial and ethnic groups and the prediction, made on the basis of test scores, that such students are not likely to succeed in school. On the basis of such scores, students are not only placed in fast or slow classes, some, who are considered to be intellectually retarded, are placed in special education classes. There are many reasons why a student may not do well academically, including his motivation to succeed, the extent that his parents encourage him to succeed, and his emotional status. Obviously, a student who is under stress and who is emotionally upset is not likely to pay attention to what is going on in the classroom nor will he do well on a test (see Figure 14.4). In addition, a specific learning disability, an individual's way of responding to learning, or the extent of his proficiency in the English language could hinder his ability to perform successfully on academic tasks. Nevertheless, educators often do not examine these factors but point to the students' scores on tests of intelligence as the reason for their poor levels of achievement in school.

The focus on individual differences in intellectual performance embodies the psychometric approach to the study of cognitive development which is a tradition within developmental psychology that emphasizes not how children's thinking changes over time (Piaget's approach), but on how children of the same age differ in their intelligence. The most common way of measuring differences in intelligence is through the administration of standardized intelligence tests which yield a score. This score, known as the *intelligence quotient,* or *IQ,* is the basis for comparing the student's intellectual performance to the performance of other students. Individual differences in intellectual performance as measured by intelligence tests are impressively large. Those who obtain very low IQ scores are considered mentally retarded; those who obtain very high scores are

intelligence quotient or *IQ*

FIGURE 14.4   A great deal of controversy surrounds the use of intelligence test scores to evaluate students, who may not do well academically for many reasons, including lack of parental encouragement, emotional upset due to stress, and lack of proficiency in the English language. Even the physical setting within which the test is administered can affect the outcome. Unfortunately, educators do not always take such factors into consideration when evaluating students' performances.

considered gifted. Even within both groups there are significant individual variations, as individuals with the same IQ may be very different in the way they behave and in what they accomplish. To understand the meaning of individual differences in intelligence, therefore, we must first consider the nature of intelligence.

What Is Intelligence?

intellectual potential intellectual behavior

intelligence A and intelligence B

Over the years, psychologists have proposed numerous, different definitions of intelligence. Although there appears to be no consensus among psychologists on a precise definition of intelligence, most agree that intelligence has two aspects. One aspect of intelligence is *intellectual potential;* the other is *intellectual behavior,* or performance, which, unlike intellectual potential, can be observed and measured. Hebb (1972) calls the two aspects of intelligence *intelligence A* and *intelligence B*. Intelligence A refers to the child's innate potential to develop intellectual capacities, whereas intelligence B refers to the level of the child's intellectual functioning. Cattell (1963) and Horn (1970) also illustrate the distinction between the two aspects of intelligence. They advance the theory that there is fluid intelligence and crystalized intelligence. *Fluid intelligence* refers to basic mental abilities such as analytic ability, memory, and speed of thinking. These innate mental abilities are relatively uninfluenced by prior learning. *Crystalized intelligence* refers to what the individual knows and it is influenced by the individual's experience, her cultural background, and her education. Crystalized intelligence reflects the kinds of skills and knowledge acquired in school such as mathematical ability, vocabulary, and knowledge of history. Thus, two children who have equal fluid intelligence may differ in their crystalized intelligence depending on the kind of schools they attend and other experiences they have had.

fluid intelligence

crystalized intelligence

Although most people, including psychologists, do not fully understand the true nature of intelligence, they have some ideas about what intelligence is. In his attempt to compare popular ideas of intelligence with notions of intelligence offered by psychologists, Sternberg (1982) found that the two groups describe intelligence similarly as consisting of three basic components: *verbal intelligence,* which refers to good vocabulary, verbal fluency, and comprehension; *problem-solving ability,* which refers to abstract thinking, reasoning skills, and the ability to see connections between ideas; and *practical intelligence,* which refers to the ability to identify and to accomplish goals, and to display an interest in the world at large. However, the question remains: How do we define an intelligent person? Is a person intelligent if she is found to be intelligent in all three components of intelligence? In this case we may conclude that these intellectual components stem from a general intellectual source. Or, is a person considered intelligent on the basis of any one of the intellectual components, in which case we may conclude that the three types of intelligence are separate and distinct from one another.

Historically, psychologists have argued about this point. Early theorists regarded intelligence as a global or all-encompassing factor that influences the individual's abilities. Spearman (1904) proposed that intelligence is composed of two factors: general intelligence, or the *g factor,* which represents the general intellectual ability applied in all intellectual tasks, and the *s factor,* which refers to specific abilities required for particular tasks. It is the *s* factor which accounts for the fact that some individuals are better at some skills than they are at others. For example, a student may perform well on verbal problems but not on problems which measure mathematical ability. Spearman claimed that in designing intelligence tests, the goal should be to design tests which measure as much of *g* as possible.

g factor

s factor

However, other psychologists challenged the view that there is a general intelligence that contributes to overall intellectual functioning, and for a time there was some enthusiasm for the view that intelligence is made up of a number of independent mental abilities, which psychologists argued should be measured separately. Thurstone (1938) suggested that the intellect is made up of seven primary mental abilities: spatial perception, perceptual speed, verbal comprehension, numerical ability, memory, word fluency, and reasoning. He developed separate tests for each of these primary mental abilities, but he found that an individual's scores on these tests were often interrelated, again pointing to a general factor for intelligence. Thus, the initial enthusiasm for differential aptitudes as measures of intelligence has waned, since these have not demonstrated greater utility than the single measure of intelligence proposed by earlier theorists.

Measuring Intelligence

Validity, Reliability, and Standardization.

Psychologists develop different tests to measure intelligence, incorporating into the tests the assessment of those skills or abilities which they propose make up intelligence. Although intelligence tests may differ depending on the definition of intelligence, there is a common set of principles which guides the construction of such tests.

validity

First, the test must have *validity*. That is, it must measure what it proposes to measure. This is not as simple as it sounds. Since intelligence is difficult to define, how do we know that the test actually measures intelligence? This presents problems, as you will soon see.

reliability

Second, the test must have *reliability,* meaning that the test is a consistent measuring device, yielding about the same results when the individual is retested on it a short while afterward. Thus, using a test-retest method in which a group of individuals is tested twice, researchers can establish the reliability of the test. There are other methods by which reliability is determined. Also, both validity and reliability are determined through field testing, which means that before each test is considered suitable, it is tried out with many children of different ages. The children are tested and retested a number of times, and on the basis of these field tests, some questions are eliminated and others are rewritten until the test is considered both valid and reliable.

standardization

Finally, the test must be standardized. *Standardization* is an arduous process that involves administering the test to a group of children typical of the children who will eventually take the test. Again, the questions on the test are rewritten or eliminated in cases where it appears that there are differences in children's responses that are related to a particular characteristic. For example, if boys consistently fail to answer a particular question which most girls get right, then this question is rewritten or eliminated since it may reflect overall differences between boys and girls that are not attributable to IQ. Two important principles in standardization should be emphasized. One, the larger the sample group of children used to standardize the test, the more applicable the test is to all other children of similar characteristics. Two, it is imperative that the characteristics of the children in the standardization sample be as similar as possible to the characteristics of the total population for which the test will be used. That is, there should be the correct proportion of males to females, of urban dwellers to rural dwellers, of people residing in different parts of the country, and of persons of various socioeconomic classes and ethnic backgrounds. In 1972, the Stanford-Binet was standardized with samples of American individuals from various backgrounds (Terman & Merrill, 1972). You should note, however, that various problems arose in the use of the test, in part because it was at one time standardized only with samples of white, middle-class, English-speaking Americans, and thus it was considered inapplicable to Americans of other ethnic and socioeconomic backgrounds.

There is also a question regarding the validity of the IQ test. Does the IQ test actually measure intelligence? The fact is, since intelligence is a comprehensive term which includes different attributes, the IQ test may not be a good measure of intelligence. Although the IQ test cannot be said to be a valid measure of an individual's intelligence, it is, however, the most relied upon measure of *intellectual performance,* and it is extensively used in the evaluation of students because the IQ score has proven, over the years, to be a good predictor of how well a child will succeed in school.

intellectual performance

The History of Intelligence Tests

The reason that the score on the IQ test is a good predictor of school success is not due to chance. The early versions of the test were developed expressly for that purpose by two Frenchmen, Alfred Binet and Théophile Simon. At the turn of the century, Binet was asked by the French government to develop a test that would identify mentally retarded or "dull" students so they could be given special instruction. At that time, intelligence tests measured such abilities as sensory acuity, eye-hand coordination, and reaction time, since intelligence was thought to have a physiological basis. These tests did not have any useful function, for it was found that performance on such tests was not related to how well children did in school, or to how intelligent their teachers thought them to be. Thus, Binet contended that a more useful measure of intelligence would incorporate the assessment of mental skills typically used in school, so he included in his test items which were intended to measure such mental functions as memory, imagery, imagination, attention, and comprehension. Binet (see Figure 14.5) viewed these and several other specific abilities as related to each other and as reflective of some more basic general intellectual ability.

He was joined by Simon and together they constructed a test consisting of thirty items which were presented in ascending order of difficulty.

FIGURE 14.5   At the turn of the century, two Frenchmen, Alfred Binet (shown here) and Théophile Simon, were asked by
the French government to develop a test to identify mentally
retarded children so they could be provided with special instruction. The test they constructed became the forerunner of the IQ
tests now used in schools.

mental age

Eventually, they devised a larger test, and they also included in the test
different tasks for each different age group, since they found that older
children could pass more items than the younger children. This allowed
them to determine the children's *mental age*. That is, if a 5-year-old child
can do the problem usually assigned to 7-year-old children, then that
child, although his chronological (actual) age is 5, has a mental age of 7.
They found that one problem with mental age, or MA, is that it does not
facilitate the comparison of children of different ages. That is, a 10-year-

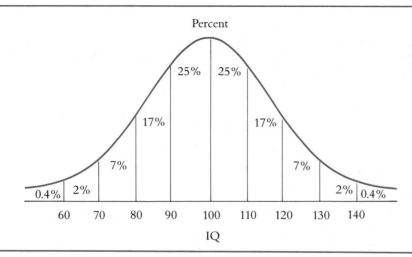

FIGURE 14.6   Distribution of IQ scores.

old child with an MA of 13 may know more than a 5-year-old with an MA of 7, but does that mean that he is more intelligent than the 5-year-old? Subsequent revision of the tests, incorporating the views of William Stern (1911), resolved this problem. Stern developed the concept of the intelligence quotient, or IQ. The IQ, which is, essentially, a comparison of the child's chronological age with his mental age, was developed so that it would remain relatively constant with age. It is derived on the basis of the following formula:

$$\frac{\text{Mental age (MA)}}{\text{Chronological age (CA)}} \times 100 = \text{IQ}$$

The use of this formula allows us to compare the mental abilities of children at different ages: the 10-year-old with an MA of 13 has an IQ of 130 (13/10 × 100). The 5-year-old with an MA of 7 has an IQ of 140 (7/5 × 100). Thus the 10-year-old may know more than the 5-year-old, but he has a lower IQ than the 5-year-old. Most children, of course, have the same mental age as their chronological age, so their IQ is average, or 100. Intelligence tests are no longer based on this formula because now more advanced statistical methods are used to calculate the IQ score, and the score is also statistically adjusted with a standard deviation of 15 points so that two-thirds of all people fall within the average or "normal" range of IQ between 85 and 115 (see Figure 14.6).

The test developed by Binet and Simon was revised in the United States by Lewis Terman and his colleagues at Stanford University. Known as the Stanford-Binet test, this test was standardized for use with American children. Like its French version, it relies heavily on the measurement of verbal abilities. Since this can be a problem with individuals

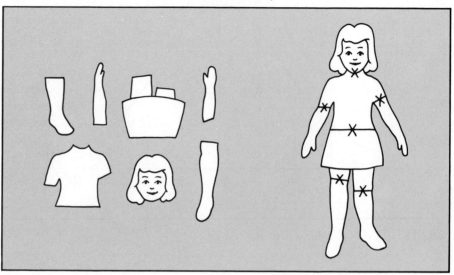

Information

Test Questions	Acceptable Responses
1. **What do you call this finger?** (Show thumb.)	Thumb.
2. **How many ears do you have?**	Two. (If the child's response suggests that he heard "How many *years* do you have?" repeat the question, emphasizing the word "ears.")
3. **How many legs does a dog have?**	Four.
4. **What must you do to make water boil?**	Heat it . . . Put it on the stove . . . Put a fire under it . . . Turn the stove on . . . Cook it (or any such response indicating that the water must be heated).

FIGURE 14.7 Examples of performance and verbal test items from the Wechsler Intelligence Scale for Children—Revised (WISC-R), with the correct responses. This Object Assembly item is given to all children taking the test. The Information items are for 6- and 7-year-olds. The WISC-R is administered individually. Reproduced by permission from the WECHSLER INTELLIGENCE SCALE FOR CHILDREN—REVISED. Copyright © 1974 by The Psychological Corporation. All rights reserved.

verbal IQ and *performance IQ*

who do not have verbal skills, David Wechsler (1958, 1974) developed other tests—the Wechsler Adult Intelligence Scale, WAIS; the Wechsler Intelligence Scale for Children, WISC; and the Wechsler Preschool and Primary Scale of Intelligence, WPPI. All these tests yield not one, but two scores: the *verbal IQ,* which is based on verbal abilities; and the *performance*

IQ, which is based on performance. In an example of a performance problem, the child is shown a picture of a car with a wheel missing, and she is
asked to complete the picture. Or, the child is shown a maze, and she is
asked to trace the route from start to home. As a general rule, the performance part of the tests is considered to be a valid indicator of the
individual's intellectual aptitude, especially in cases of individuals who are
not native speakers of the English language. However, the verbal part of
the tests is a better predictor of school success since much of the work the
child is expected to do in school is based on language skills (see Figure 14.7).

What Do IQ Tests Measure?

Although IQ tests are the most relied upon measure of intellectual performance, unresolved problems remain in their use. First, although intelligence test scores are useful in predicting school achievement, they are
less useful in predicting everyday adult functioning. Intelligence cannot be
defined solely on the basis of school performance, since other cognitive
abilities are important in other situations. Intelligence tests do not measure
these other abilities. We have seen previously that Piaget regarded intelligence as the process of adapting to the environment. Do intelligence tests
measure an individual's capacity to adapt to life circumstances? The answer is no. A child may have an IQ of 80, which is below normal. That
child may not do well in school, but he may be quite adept at holding his
own among his friends and in his neighborhood. Likewise, an adult with
an IQ of 80 is quite capable of working and supporting a family. In both
these cases, the individuals evidence that they are good at adapting to life
circumstances.

In addition, when it is said that the IQ score is a good predictor of
school success, this statement is based on correlational studies which indicate that IQ scores and academic success are correlated at about .60. Recall
from the introductory chapter to this book that correlation coefficients
range from 0.0 to 1.0, so a correlation of .60 is quite good. The IQ score
also correlates well (.50) with later occupational success (McCall, 1977),
meaning that individuals with a high IQ tend to succeed in their careers.
However, whereas a correlation of .60 or .50 is good, it also shows that
there are other factors that are important in educational attainment and
career success that are not reflected in the IQ score. Otherwise there
would be a perfect correlation (1.0) between the IQ and academic and
occupational achievement.

In fact, the IQ test measures not intellectual *ability,* but intellectual
performance. Intellectual performance in general is determined by a complex interaction between aptitude, achievement, and motivation (Zigler &
Butterfield, 1968) and is influenced by a number of factors, including
intellectual potential, amount of information or knowledge acquired, the
ability to read, and skill at taking tests. Even a seemingly simple factor

cognitive style

impulsive style vs. reflective style

such as whether the student feels comfortable in the test-taking situation can have a significant effect on his performance (Zigler, Abelson, & Seitz, 1973). In addition, the individual's *cognitive style,* that is, her way of responding to a task, may influence her ability to score well on an IQ test. Jerome Kagan (1965) among others (Kogan, 1983) notes that one of the most important differences in cognitive style is the tendency to respond either immediately, in a hurried manner—an *impulsive style*—or slowly and deliberately, that is, in a *reflective style*. Reflectivity or impulsivity are characteristics of many children and adults. When children who are reflective in their approach to tasks are asked, for example, "What do you like to do after school?" or "What are your favorite games?", they tend to think for a minute or two before they respond. Children who are impulsive in their approach to tasks would answer the questions immediately, not stopping to think. The same is true when the individuals are confronted with a test: reflective individuals tend to approach the task slowly and carefully, making sure that they get as many answers right as they can. Some impulsive individuals, on the other hand, tend to make more mistakes on a test, not because they are unable to answer correctly, but because they scan the test questions hurriedly and are careless in their responses.

Finally, performance on the test is also influenced by the experiences of the child. Many critics of IQ tests argue that IQ tests are culturally biased and that they give an unfair advantage to middle-class, white children. Kagan (1972) notes that the tests usually include words and concepts that are common in middle-class homes, but not necessarily in the homes of children from low socioeconomic backgrounds. For example, a question on the test may be "What is the advantage of keeping money in the bank?" The low-income student whose family does not have enough money to meet its basic daily needs may not know the answer to this question since in her home this issue is never discussed. Another question might be "What would you do if you were sent to a store to buy a loaf of bread and the grocer said he didn't have any more?" The correct answer is, "Go to another store." However, a child in a rural area or in a neighborhood where there is only one store would have to answer "Go home." Despite the fact that this is a reasonable answer for the child, given her circumstances and prior experiences, she would not get credit for such an answer.

The consequences of using culturally biased tests are very serious. Students from minority groups and from lower socioeconomic levels tend to score low on such tests and are, therefore, labeled as slow learners or as mentally retarded and placed in slow-paced educational programs or in special education classes. In studies conducted in California, Jane Mercer (1971, 1972) discovered that a disproportionate number of blacks and Mexican-Americans were being placed in special education classes because of the low IQ scores they had obtained. However, when Mercer tested these children on tests which measured their ability to adapt to life circumstances, she found that 90% of the blacks and 60% of the Mexican-Americans passed the test, indicating that they are not retarded, but simply unfamiliar with words, objects, and strategies presented on the IQ test. Because of these and similar findings from other studies, schools are now required to use several criteria, not only the IQ score, as the basis on which to decide that a child needs to be in a special education class. The point to remember is this: A child who scores low on an IQ test may indeed be mentally retarded, but we cannot take it for granted that she is only on the basis of her IQ score. Further investigations are needed to determine why the child's score is low.

In an effort to reduce the influence of culture on test results, a number of *culture-fair tests* have been devised. These tests include fewer verbal items, and they assess children's intellectual performance by asking them to complete drawings, or fit irregularly shaped blocks into holes, or copy designs with multicolored cubes. However, such tests still tend to favor some cultural experiences, since a completely culture-fair test has proven to be difficult to develop. Even if a perfectly culture-fair test is devised, researchers point out that it will never be predictive of school performance, inasmuch as successful school performance is also culturally biased. Schools, after all, encourage achievements and ways of performing that are considered valuable in the white, middle-class community.

culture-fair tests

The IQ Test Controversy: Socioeconomic Status and IQ

The controversy surrounding the use of the IQ test in the evaluation of students is related to this problem of cultural bias inherent in the test. In numerous studies it has been found that children from low-income homes tend to score, on the average, 10 to 15 points lower on IQ tests than children from middle-class families. In general, the higher a family's socioeconomic status, the higher the IQs of both parents and children. You should keep in mind, however, that the IQ differences are average differences for groups of people and have nothing to do with the intelligence of any one individual in any socioeconomic class. Furthermore, you should also bear in mind that the socioeconomic status refers to income and not to cultural and ethnic background.

Several hypotheses have been forwarded to explain differences in IQ among different socioeconomic levels. That there is a cultural bias inherent in the IQ test is one of these hypotheses which we have already covered. Another explanation is related to motivational-emotional factors of persons in different social classes. For example, a student from a low-income family may not be motivated to do well on a test or he may not even want to take the test in the first place. A low IQ score obtained by that student is not necessarily indicative of low intelligence. Rather, it may be indicative of a lack of motivation to do well on a test (Zigler &

Butterfield, 1968). Usually children who are not motivated in test taking are also not motivated to succeed in school, so again, there will be a correlation between their IQ score and their school performance.

The third hypothesis is that social class differences in intellectual performance are related to genetic differences. Since representation in a low socioeconomic class is higher among some ethnic groups, most notably blacks, than among whites, Jensen (1969), contended that the lower average IQ scores of blacks from low socioeconomic status families are evidence of a genetic factor in intelligence and that these blacks are intellectually inferior. However, most investigators consider the strong relationship between IQ and social class to be primarily environmental rather than hereditary in nature. They point out, for example, that children from various ethnic backgrounds excel in different mental abilities. When the groups are separated along socioeconomic dimensions, the profiles of abilities for lower-class ethnic groups parallel the profiles of the middle-class ethnic groups. However, the lower-class ethnic groups score lower on all abilities, suggesting a relatively greater socioeconomic disadvantage for the lower-class ethnic groups (Lesser, Fifer, & Clark, 1965).

Heredity and Environment

The notion that social class differences in IQ stem from genetic differences in intelligence is controversial not only because of the erroneous label it attaches to some ethnic groups, but also because of its many social and political implications. For instance, if we believe that intelligence is an inherited trait, then we would not argue for the implementation of programs which would try to improve the educational achievement of economically disadvantaged children. However, if we believe that intelligence is affected by environmental factors, then we would contend that such programs are important.

In their attempts to find out the relative contributions of the genes and the environment to intelligence, researchers have focused on studies using identical and fraternal twins and studies using adopted children. Recall from Chapter 3 that these studies showed that both heredity and the environment affect intelligence. The conclusion arrived at on the basis of these studies was that although a child's genetic makeup determines her intellectual potential, the extent that this potential will be realized is dependent on environmental factors. Even within the same family, environmental factors are known to affect children's IQs. For example, the IQs of children in the same family may differ according to the birth order, family size, and the number of years between the births of the children (Zajonc & Bargh, 1980; Zajonc, 1983). As you can see in Figure 14.8, later-born children, not in all families but in some, tend to have, on the average, a lower IQ than earlier-born children. One widely accepted explanation for these differences in IQ scores is the observation that parents spend more

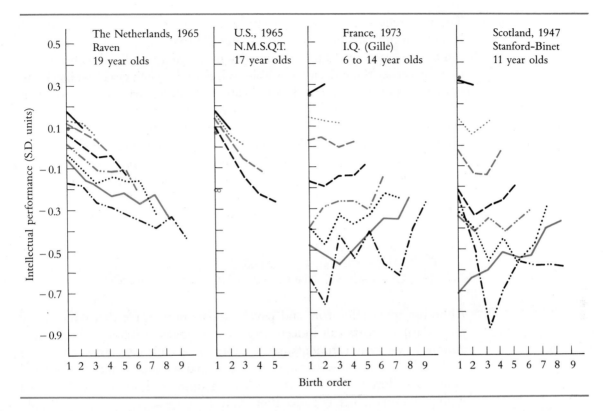

FIGURE 14.8 Intellectual performance of four large populations, plotted as function of birth order and family size. Separate curves in each graph represent different family sizes, which can be read from the last birth order on each curve. Solid circles represent only children. The double open circle in the U.S. data represents twins. The years show when data were collected. The means of the Dutch, American, French, and Scottish data sets are 2.82, 102.5, 99.2, and 36.74, respectively. The corresponding standard deviations are 1.43, 21.25, 14.53, and 16.10. From "Family Configuration and Intelligence," Zajonc, R. B., in *Science,* vol. 192, fig. 1, p. 228, 16 April 1976. Copyright © 1976 by the American Association for the Advancement of Science.

time with their first-born than with their later-born children. Researchers note, however, that birth order does not stand alone as an influence on intellectual performance. Rather, the influence of birth order is likely to be subtle and less consequential by far than the impact of parental attitudes, values, and behaviors that are evident to the child in the family environment no matter what the child's place in the hierarchy of siblings (McCall et al., 1973).

The fact that environmental factors account for some of the differences in intellectual performance among children from economically disadvantaged ethnic backgrounds is clearly demonstrated by Sandra Scarr and Richard Weinberg (1976, 1977), who studied the IQ scores of black children who were adopted and raised by white middle-class families. They found that the younger the children were at the time of adoption, the closer they came to the average IQs of white, middle-class children.

The researchers note that their study does not refute the importance of heredity in intelligence, but it does indicate that an individual's IQ score can be increased by 10 to 20 points by living in a middle-class home and that the earlier the individual is able to live under such circumstances, the better. In addition, recent data indicate that young black children generally have better achievement records than their counterparts of earlier generations. Researchers note that this may be due to the compensatory educational programs the children receive during their preschool years, as well as to their improved schooling and other social programs that have been made available to them since the late 1960s (Berrueta-Clement, 1984). This suggests that through intervention efforts the educational achievement of economically disadvantaged children may be improved.

DISCUSSION OF SOCIAL ISSUES: HIGH SCHOOL COMPENSATORY EDUCATION

Although most educators and psychologists now agree that educational intervention efforts can indeed improve the level of school achievement among low-income students (see Chapter 9), public concern with regard to the education of low-income children usually focuses on preschool and younger children. In cases where low-income adolescents are provided with programs which enhance their education, these programs are usually provided not to the most educationally deficient students, those who have low IQs, but to the economically disadvantaged capable students for whom a number of educational programs such as Upward Bound offer a variety of challenging educational opportunities (Stipek, 1979).

critical period

In part, efforts to help adolescents who have low IQ scores have been thwarted by the widely held belief that adolescence is too late to overcome educational handicaps. This belief is based on the idea of the *critical period* which has dominated educational policy during the past two decades. This belief holds that unless learning deficits are identified and ameliorated at an early age, the individual is foredoomed to continued educational failure. This emphasis (not only among educators but among social scientists as well) on the importance of the infant and preschool years as the critical period for intervention has left unexplored the possibilities of intervening during the adolescent years.

However, direct evidence is available which points to the fact that intervention programs can be successful, even when they are provided during adolescence, suggesting that there are possible benefits inherent in high school compensatory education programs. This evidence comes from the work of Reuven Feuerstein (1980), who demonstrates that even adolescents with an IQ of 60 to 80 (which would place them in the category of mentally retarded) are capable of significant increases in mental abilities, as long as they do not suffer from some organic damage to the

FIGURE 14.9 The belief that adolescence is too late to help educationally defi-cient students is widespread. However, there is now direct evidence which clearly demonstrates that intervention programs, such as high school compensatory edu-cation programs, can be beneficial even when provided during adolescence.

brain or central nervous system. Feuerstein believes that before an indi-vidual can benefit from formal schooling, she needs to master certain underlying cognitive skills. She needs to be able to regulate her attention and observe the stimuli she encounters, and she needs to be able to figure out and express the relationship between various aspects of her environ-ment. Feuerstein's strategy is to guide adolescents' experiences so that they acquire these skills. To this end, he developed a program of mediated learning experiences in which adolescents are not actually taught basic cognitive skills but work closely with their teachers who guide them in their interactions with the environment so that they gradually adapt to new ways of perceiving the world and processing information. Eventu-ally, these adolescents, who would have been unable to master basic read-ing and writing skills and who would have been dependent on public assistance for the rest of their lives, are able to be trained for economically useful roles in society (see Figure 14.9).

Illiteracy in the United States.   Feuerstein's program, which has been implemented in Israel and in selected schools in the United States and other countries, is expensive because of its emphasis on intensive and individualized instruction. But, it is worthy of consideration because of its potential savings in later costs to society. Its implementation in high schools in the United States would be especially valuable given the fact that a significant number of high school students either drop out of school without ever having acquired basic reading and writing skills or they graduate from high school without having attained these skills, so they are functionally illiterate (Fisher, 1976). According to a recent report (Bennett, 1985; National Commission on Excellence in Education, 1983), 17 to 21 million English-speaking Americans are functionally illiterate—unable to write a check, address an envelope, or read a sign in a store. Another 46 million people cannot read proficiently, meaning they cannot read beyond the level of 9- or 10-year-old children. In many cases, these people are high school graduates (Irwin, 1986). These individuals are not mentally retarded and their failure to acquire basic skills is deep rooted and traceable to their inability to succeed in elementary school. Nevertheless, the need to help these students is paramount, for without the ability to read and write their chances for employment are minimized, and their ability to assume an independent way of life is jeopardized.

Recent national attention on illiterate high school graduates has resulted in highly publicized lawsuits such as *Peter W. Doe vs. The San Francisco Unified School District* in which individuals have sued the school systems for educational malfeasance, claiming that the schools have failed to provide them with adequate education. Changes in educational standards have been made as a result of this attention. Some states now require that an individual demonstrate an adequate grasp of basic skills before being allowed to graduate. In other states, laws which abolish "social promotions" have been passed, and students who are below grade level in reading and other basic skills are not allowed to pass onto the next grade (Larson, 1977). The value of these measures is questionable, however. They may result in there being no more illiterate high school graduates, but not necessarily in the decrease in the number of illiterate youths.

Preventing Truancy and School Dropout.   Illiteracy stems from a number of problems. One of these problems may be related to the fact that although schooling is free and mandatory in this country, many children simply do not attend school. In reports on the issue (U.S. Bureau of the Census, 1983; National Education Association, 1984–85), it is indicated that over 3 million children between the ages of 7 and 17 do not attend school and that one million of these children are between the ages of 7 and 15. In addition, the reports note that these figures may be conservative because they are based only upon the U.S. Bureau of the Census data on nonenrollment. Interviews with school officials and community leaders reveal that the census data reflect only a partial count of how many children do not attend school, as often the parents of those children who do not attend school do not speak English and therefore do not correctly answer the census school enrollment questionnaire, or they are afraid to admit that their children do not go to school.

Those children who do not attend school are likely to be poor, non-white and non-English-speaking. Failure to go to school is becoming especially prevalent among Hispanic children. In a report of the National Commission on Secondary Schooling for Hispanics (National Commission, 1984), it is stated that among Hispanic youths, 45% never complete high school and that 4 out of 10 of those who drop out of school do so before reaching the tenth grade. The significance of these findings lies not only in their implications for the Hispanic-American community, but also for society at large, since Hispanic Americans are becoming the majority of the school population in major cities and will be the country's largest minority group by the end of the century. Nonenrollment is also a problem for black youths, among whom 40% do not graduate from high school.

Nonenrollment in the school includes not only the number of children who drop out of school, but also the number of children and adolescents who are truant. A truant is a child or adolescent who stays away from school without parental or school permission. Those students who are truant often drop out of school eventually. That is, they formally terminate their relationship with the school. School officials have encountered problems in their attempts to stem the increase in the number of students who are truant, so the average daily student absence rate for secondary schools across the nation has increased and is now about 12%, with some urban high schools reporting daily absenteeism rates as high as 30% and 40% (Kaeser, 1979; Rogus, 1983).

Several studies identified some of the characteristics of truants, indicating that students who are truant tend to have underdeveloped reading and academic skills, a negative self-concept, a negative attitude toward school subjects, stressful family situations, anxiety because of economic need, lack of personally satisfying experiences with other students or teachers, as well as intense personal problems which are unrelated to the school experience (Kohler, 1976). Despite these findings from the research, which clearly point to the need to respond to the needs of the students, to alleviate some of the pressures they are experiencing, and to make the learning experiences relevant for them, most school officials take a punitive approach and view truancy as a crime to be punished. Although punitive approaches are understandable, they yield no positive effect and may result, in fact, in further rebellion on the part of the student and, eventually, in her dropping out of school (Rogus, 1983).

Do Schools Make a Difference?   Not all schools take the punitive approach. Several recent studies have shown that some secondary schools have been effective not only in reducing truancy and dropout rates, but also in increasing student achievement. Rogus (1983) analyzed several of

TABLE 14.1　Characteristics of effective schools

1. Central Office	a.	Central office staff are supportive of efforts to build a strong school program.
2. Principal	a.	School goals for the year are clearly stated.
	b.	Teachers and community representatives provide input during goal-setting process.
	c.	Progress toward school goals is closely monitored.
	d.	Expectation of high-level teacher and student performance.
	e.	Teacher performance is frequently monitored and feedback to teachers is provided regularly.
	f.	The building environment is orderly and quiet.
	g.	The principal is strongly involved with the instructional program.
	h.	The principal's power, as perceived by staff, derives from his expertness in managing the school.
	i.	The principal knows what is happening in the classroom.
	j.	The principal assumes responsibility for achieving the school's objectives.
	k.	The principal places equal emphasis upon program development and management of day-to-day activity.
3. Teachers	a.	High expectations are set for students.
	b.	Classes are characterized by a high emphasis upon cognitive outcomes.
	c.	Direct instruction is the most common teaching strategy employed.
	d.	Faculty perceive that they are free of administrative intervention in determining their teaching strategies.
	e.	Faculty believe that students can achieve.
	f.	Clear instructional goals are set for students.
	g.	Class time lost during transition, periods of confusion, and disruptions requiring disciplinary action are minimal.
	h.	Student time on task is closely monitored in each class.
	i.	Homework assignments are regularly collected.
	j.	Classroom testing for diagnostic purposes is common.
	k.	Students are aware of the objectives of a given class lesson.
	l.	Students experience a high success rate in their daily work.
	m.	Faculty assume responsibility for teaching skills.
	n.	School standards are enforced in classrooms, in hallways, and on school grounds.
	o.	Students are held accountable for their work.
4. Parent-Aide Involvement	a.	Parent-initiated involvement in the school is encouraged.
	b.	Aides work heavily with small groups of students with academic needs.
	c.	Aides have extensive involvement with teaching staff and other aides.
5. Program: Elementary Schools	a.	Youngsters indicate a positive self-image and a feeling of controlling their own identity as early as grade two.
	b.	Emphasis is placed on the importance of achieving mathematics and reading-program objectives.
6. Program: Middle and High Schools	a.	Departments are vital subgroups with clearly stated goals.
	b.	Students experiencing difficulties are identified and provided help.
	c.	An extensive, prosocial cocurricular program exists.
	d.	Rewards for program excellence are equally distributed.
	e.	School identification is emphasized through a variety of activities.

Source: Rogus, Joseph F., "Education as a Response to Developmental Needs," in L. Eugene Arnold (ed), *Preventing Adolescent Alienation* (Lexington: Heath, 1983).

these studies, noting that those schools that are effective in these ways are those schools in which parent involvement is encouraged and in which homework assignments are regularly collected. Table 14.1 is a list of characteristics of effective schools.

Similar points are made by Michael Rutter and his colleagues (Rutter, Maughan, Mortimore, & Ouston, 1979) who carried out an extensive study in Great Britain on the effects of secondary schools on student achievement. In examining the effects of secondary school experience, Rutter and his colleagues rejected standardized intelligence tests as indicators of academic progress, contending that such tests are indicators of general functioning but do not directly test what the school has attempted to teach. Instead, they assessed adolescents on five measures: examinations specifically constructed to test the acquisition of knowledge in the subjects taught; behavior in school (e.g., violence); attendance; employment; and delinquency. They conducted their study in schools serving lower- and lower-middle-class populations in a large section of London. Lower-class children were specifically chosen because they represented the population researchers often claim cannot be positively affected by school. They found that individual differences among students that existed at the beginning of the secondary school period correlated with achievement levels at the end of the period. That is, high-achieving students tended to maintain their advantage. However, students in some schools, although they were judged to be truant, violent, or delinquent at the beginning of the secondary school period, significantly improved in their behavior and were able to succeed academically, more so than the students in other schools. The schools which were able to foster good behavior and academic achievement in the students were those in which there was academic emphasis, as indicated by such factors as homework assignments; those in which teachers spent more time in interacting with the whole class rather than in individualized instruction; those in which there were good conditions for the students, as indicated by such factors as freedom to use the school facilities, availability of hot drinks, access to a telephone, and so on; those in which students were given opportunities for taking responsibility and participating in various activities; and those in which there was a continuity of the school population, as indicated by factors such as the number of years teachers had been in the school and the extent to which the same group of children remained together in the school. These findings are impressive; they indicate that some schools can and do make a difference in enhancing student achievement.

SUMMARY

During the adolescent years, the individual attains a higher level of cognitive maturity, termed by Piaget formal operations thought. He is able to think abstractly not only about concrete things, but also about ideas and hypothetical statements as well. He approaches problem solving in a scientific manner, systematically considering all the possible solutions.

Piaget developed a number of scientific experiments which are used to measure the attainment of formal operations. Using such experiments, researchers have found that unlike the previous period of cognitive development, the formal operations period is not universally attained. Even in such cultures as ours where schooling is compulsory, not everyone attains this higher level of cognitive functioning. In addition, some people are able to think abstractly and systematically in some subjects but not in others, since the ability to think abstractly depends in part on the amount of education the individual receives and the extent of his interest in and knowledge of different topics.

As the adolescent attains a more sophisticated level of cognitive functioning, the type of education he is provided changes as well. The adolescent studies not only more subjects, he studies these subjects in more depth. In addition, whereas in elementary school the child's education centers on the acquisition of basic skills through concrete examples, in high school the adolescent is encouraged to consider abstract notions. However, not all students have the same opportunity to study subjects in depth, or to use high-level cognitive skills, because some are considered brighter than others and are placed in accelerated educational programs, whereas others are placed in slower paced or vocational programs. The decision as to which students are brighter than others is made on the basis of achievement and aptitude tests, which measure what the individuals have learned and their potential for learning.

The use of such tests in the evaluation of students is controversial. At the center of the controversy is the IQ test which is said to measure the individual's intellectual potential. Although the IQ test is a good predictor of school achievement, it should not be used to indicate an individual's intellectual ability, since it measures not intellectual potential but intellectual performance. Intellectual performance is influenced by an interaction between a number of factors, including innate intellectual ability, the ability to read, the ability to take tests, as well as emotional and motivational factors. For example, a student who is anxious in the test situation is likely to get a low score even though he may be intellectually capable.

In addition, IQ tests are culturally biased. Low-income and minority students are unfamiliar with many of the words and concepts on the test, therefore, they tend to obtain lower scores. This fact has led some researchers to state that these students are intellectually inferior. However, these researchers have been proven wrong by studies which document that intelligence is influenced both by genetic and environmental factors and that children who are adopted by middle-class families obtain IQ scores that are close to the scores obtained by middle-class individuals. Other studies have shown that young children from low socioeconomic backgrounds obtain higher IQ scores than their older siblings because they have the benefit of compensatory education programs and other intervention efforts implemented to increase the level of school achievement among low-income children. Although many educators and psychologists believe that such intervention efforts are successful only during the early childhood years, evidence is available which shows that even adolescents with IQs as low as 60 or 80 (which places them in the category of mentally retarded) can be helped to learn cognitive skills and to increase their levels of school achievement. Enhancing the abilities of such adolescents is important given the fact that many adolescents today either drop out of high school or they are allowed to graduate from high school unable to read or write; they are, in fact, illiterate.

REVIEW POINTS

1. During adolescence the individual enters what Piaget termed the formal operations period of cognitive development. This period is characterized by the ability of the individual to think in the abstract and test hypotheses, by the ability to think ahead and approach problem solving in a systematic manner, and by the ability to think about the process of thinking and how he can make it more efficient. Unlike other, previous periods of cognition, the formal operations period is not universally attained.

2. Although the individual attains these capabilities, there are limitations to the cognitive abilities of the adolescent, who is susceptible to adolescent egocentrism, thinking that everyone is interested in how he or she looks. Adolescent egocentrism is also characterized by the individual's sense of indestructibility, causing him to think that nothing bad will ever happen to him even if he engages in excessive risk-taking behaviors.

3. Piaget's approach to the study of cognition emphasizes how children's thinking changes as they grow older. Another approach is the psychometric approach, which focuses on individual differences in intelligence and on how children the same age differ in their intellectual abilities. In this approach there is emphasis on the measurement of intelligence using IQ tests.

4. IQ tests have been useful because they predict school performance and occupational success later in life. However, they do not necessarily measure intelligence because there are numerous reasons why a child may fail on IQ tests and also in school-related tasks.

5. IQ tests are further problematic because they reflect the language, values, and attitudes of middle-class individuals. Hence, those from low socioeconomic backgrounds are likely to fail such tests. In recent years, several culture-fair tests have been developed, but these cannot be predictive of school performance because school performance in and of itself is culturally biased, requiring all children to perform in ways that are valued in the middle-class community.

6. Because IQ tests are culturally biased, children from low socioeconomic backgrounds fail to do well on these. This has led to speculations that these children are intellectually inferior. This argument is based on the notion that intelligence is primarily influenced by heredity. However, researchers have shown that intelligence is influenced both by heredity and the environment.

7. Young children from low socioeconomic backgrounds can improve their chances of succeeding in school if they attend educational programs in their early childhood years. Because of the focus on this period of life, however, many do not realize that there is no one magic period for educational intervention and that intervention programs can and should be implemented in high schools as well. It has been shown that when high school students receive help in attending to environmental stimuli and in processing information, they can often make significant increases in mental ability.

8. Intervention programs for high school students are important given the fact that so many students either drop out of school or they complete schooling without having learned to read and write. There are several reasons for illiteracy among adolescents, including high rates of truancy and school dropout.

CHAPTER 15

SOCIAL AND EMOTIONAL DEVELOPMENT DURING ADOLESCENCE

Adolescence is a time of challenge and risk. A time when the individual, thinking about the possibilities that he has before him, and also about his limitations and skills, begins the slow transition from secure family life to the unknown world of life as an adult. In the face of numerous demands and choices, the adolescent's task is to establish a personal identity and decide who his friends will be, what kind of lifestyle he should adopt, and what kind of worker he will be.

The task of establishing an identity is by no means new. As an infant, the individual began to define himself as a person separate from the physical environment. From that time on his ideas and attitudes about himself became increasingly refined and elaborate, so that by the end of the middle childhood period he had a complex and multifaceted picture of himself as a unique individual with many positive attributes, skills, thoughts, and feelings, as well as some failings. During adolescence, however, when the individual moves from childhood to adulthood, many changes occur in physical and intellectual development and the individual has to redefine himself not only in terms of who he is but also in terms of what he will become. He struggles with such questions as: Who am I, really? What do I want to do with my life? and What do I believe in? He is not at all certain of the answers. This is evident in a 17-year-old girl's answer to the question: Who am I? She answers, "I am a human being. I am an individual. I don't know who I am . . . I am a confused person" (Montemayor & Eisen, 1977).

THE SEARCH FOR A PERSONAL IDENTITY

In the course of this chapter you will see that this confusion, characteristic of many adolescents, stems in part from the fact that in our pluralistic society young people have numerous values and beliefs to choose from and many possible lifestyles that they can adopt. The task of having to make decisions about their existence and future is all the more difficult because they are in a transitional phase in their lives. Especially early in the period, the adolescent finds the prospect of life as an independent adult inviting but also frightening, and she vacillates between her need for independence and her need for dependence. Sometimes she thinks of herself and expects others to think of her as an autonomous individual. At other times she is in need of security and she yearns for support and guidance. She is also in the throes of becoming acquainted with herself as a changing person. Her body is changing, and she experiences intellectual challenges brought on by newly acquired cognitive skills. At times she feels superior and capable of an infinite number of tasks, often exaggerating the degree of her emancipation and becoming derisive and rebellious toward her parents. At other times she feels helpless and is vulnerable to the criticisms of those around her. Having to make major choices and decisions is difficult at any age. However, given all the other developmental factors that converge during the teenage years, you can appreciate how confusing the task is to the adolescent. For some, the transition from childhood to adulthood is a smooth process that is facilitated by nurturant and understanding parents and friends. For others, the journey to adult life is more difficult because they lack the security, guidance, and support they need as they attempt to establish a personal identity.

Theoretical Perspective

Erik Erikson (1963, 1968) has had extensive influence on current views on adolescence. He explains the adolescent's quest for a personal identity and answers to the questions of who she is and what she believes in as functions of the psychosocial crisis of *identity versus role confusion*. According to Erikson, having a sense of identity is as important and fundamental to existence as food, security, and sexual satisfaction. The individual, whether an adolescent or an adult, must have a sense of herself—what her strengths and weaknesses are, what she believes in, and what she wants to do in life. In Erikson's words, " . . . in the jungle of human existence, there is no feeling of being alive without a sense of identity" (1968).

The individual gradually develops some sense of herself as a unique being throughout childhood. However, it is not until adolescence that the quest for a personal identity becomes an all-consuming task. During that period, the individual's identity is influenced by the experiences she has had in the past and the kinds of identifications she formed during infancy and childhood. However, the identity "includes but is more than the sum of successive identifications of those earlier years when the child wanted to be, and was often forced to become, like the people [s]he depended on" (Erikson, 1959). Now capable of thinking in the abstract and preparing for life as an adult, the adolescent thinks about her past as well as her future. She makes a commitment to an ideology, a lifestyle, and a vocation as she establishes a personal identity that is relatively stable and integrated into a coherent, consistent, and unique whole. With this identity, she will have a sense of the continuity of the self. She will have the sense that no matter what she chooses to do in life or what role she may assume, whether as worker, spouse, or parent, she remains a unique person with strengths and weaknesses and a set of values, beliefs, and principles to guide her through life.

Crisis and Commitment

The formation of such a personal identity is not completed during the adolescent years. As with most aspects of growth and development, identity formation occurs gradually through countless experiences and numerous decisions. Many decisions, whether they seem important or trivial, can have implications for the formation of a personal identity, and they determine, in part, what one's adult life will be like. However, none of these and other decisions made during adolescence is irrevocable. There are opportunities for growth beyond the adolescent period, and a redefinition of one's lifestyle, vocation, and ideology often occurs. Nevertheless, Erikson emphasizes the fact that the decisions made during adolescence profoundly affect the way the individual deals with young adulthood, middle age, and old age, and the options that will be available to her in the future.

Erikson further points out that the task of forming a personal identity is not easy. The adolescent, who is undergoing an identity crisis at the same time that she experiences rapid physical growth and sexual maturation, wrestles with the questions of who she is and who she will become. Eventually and over the course of several years that may extend beyond adolescence, she either resolves the crisis by committing herself to some decisions about her being and her future (*identity achievement*), or she feels anxious and confused and becomes incapable of making decisions and choosing roles (*role confusion*). The individual who eventually achieves an identity feels secure in herself and aware of the kind of life she would like to lead. But, the individual who fails to establish an identity remains confused about her future or she may become committed not to her own ideals but to the ideals of a close friend or someone she admires. *identity achievement*

role confusion

James Marcia (1980), elaborating upon Erikson's theory, also underscores the fact that the process of identity formation is difficult and fraught with pitfalls. For example, some adolescents, bewildered and pressured by demands from their family and friends, and confused by the sheer number of possible avenues available to choose from, instead of experiencing an increasing cohesion of their identity, experience *identity diffusion*. They withdraw from efforts to shape their identity, or they feel ambivalent or unconcerned about making decisions. *Foreclosure,* or premature identity formation, can also occur when adolescents accept and incorporate the values of their family and society without ever questioning them. Finally, instead of finding an identity and making commitments to what they believe in and what they want to do, some adolescents declare a *moratorium.* They wrestle with questions of who they are and what their future holds, but they defer a resolution of the crisis. For some, a short moratorium is constructive as it gives them the opportunity to find out and examine the possibilities that exist for them. For others, however, the moratorium is long-lasting and therefore destructive, because they fail to make decisions about what they want to do and what it is they believe in. They may remain undecided and without commitments throughout much of their adult life. *identity diffusion*

foreclosure

FIGURE 15.1   In simpler societies (above), the transition from being a child to assuming an identity as an adult is relatively easy, since the individual does not have many choices to make. In our society (right), becoming an adult is more difficult given the numerous social roles from which the individual must choose.

The Social Context

The ease with which the individual establishes an identity for herself and decides on her eventual role as an adult is in part dependent on the society within which she lives. In primitive cultures, the transition from being a child to assuming an identity as an adult, although it entails tests of skill and endurance of pain, is a relatively simple task that is quickly accomplished (see Chapter 13). In such societies, the individual does not have many choices to make. These societies do not change much, if at all, from generation to generation, and all members of society hold essentially the same values and notions about what is expected of one as an adult. Therefore, societal demands on the individual are relatively few and straightforward, so the individual simply has to learn the skills and values of her elders and incorporate these as her own (see Figure 15.1).

In contemporary and complex societies such as ours, identity formation is not as simple a task. The individual in our society is faced with various identifications she must synthesize and with a variety of values

and social roles from which she must choose. In addition, social change in our society occurs at an incredibly fast pace. With communication, transportation, and scientific techniques becoming increasingly more sophisticated, the individual is faced with the prospect of a future that is substantially different from the life her parents had when they became adults. Moreover, in the face of an uncertain future she has to make numerous, major decisions that will affect all aspects of life as an adult. All the decisions that have to be made some time during adolescence and young adulthood will have consequences for later life and thus they must be carefully considered.

Not only does the adolescent have to give careful thought to decisions regarding what she wants and thinks she would like to do in the future, she also has to make the decisions in light of her own talents and capabilities, her family's economic resources, and the choices open to her. She may want to go to college, but does she have the qualifications and skills to do so and can she or her parents afford the cost? In addition, although our society prides itself on the great variety of choices that are available to individuals, the range of choices varies according to the individual's social class, ethnic background, and sex. Consider, for example, vocational choices. Some jobs are open only to those with certain knowledge and skills, and although women in our society have many more opportunities open to them than ever before, they still face the prospect of sex discrimination in the workplace.

Vocational Identity

Decisions about vocational roles and the question of what to do for one's life work are essential aspects of every individual's identity. A job not only provides the means to an independent life, it also defines one's place in society, determines what kinds of people one associates with, and it can also offer the personal satisfaction of being productive. It is hardly surprising, therefore, that adolescents spend much of their time thinking not only about what they would like to do when they grow up, but also about what they are capable of doing.

The decision of what to do for one's life's work is influenced in part by past and present academic achievements and also by parental aspirations for the child. In informal discussions with parents, children grow up expecting and knowing that it is expected of them to go to college, for example, to aspire to a career, and to value the security and respectability of a job (Kohn, 1977). It is during adolescence, however, that the individual is capable of generating possibilities and of reasoning about what he would like to do. For some, arriving at a decision of what to do for a life's work may take several years, and they may remain undecided even after an education in college. Even though adolescents may be undecided about what they want to do, early in their high school experience they have to make a major decision that will affect the options they have later on— whether to pursue an academic course of study which will lead to college or to pursue a vocational course. Not all individuals choose the academic course; only half of middle-class adolescents and one-quarter of black adolescents will attend college. This means that many teens not only have to decide what they want to do, they also have to look for and find a job when they are between 16 and 19 years of age (National Commission on Youth, 1980).

Youth Unemployment

For those individuals who are looking for permanent work during their adolescent years, the question: What do I want to do with my life as an adult? poses a dilemma that is not easily resolved by simply making a choice of occupation. The national economic crisis and continually high rates of unemployment have had a devastating impact on youths who are seeking employment, especially black youths. According to recent statistics compiled by the U.S. Department of Labor, unemployment among whites age 16 to 19 is 15%, and for blacks in the same age range it is 43% (Bureau of Labor, 1985). What is more, these figures take into account only those teens who had already entered the job market and had a job at one time. Half the white teenagers and three-quarters of black teenagers are not in school or in the labor force and, thus, they are not counted among the unemployed even though they are not working and may be looking for a job.

The bleak picture of youth unemployment is due in part to economic difficulties and shifts in the labor market. During the past two decades, many jobs for unskilled laborers have vanished and members of the baby boom generation have entered the labor force, thus displacing the teens who are the least skilled workers. In addition, federal minimum wage laws have priced teens out of the market. As long as employers have to pay a minimum wage that is substantially higher than in the past, they choose to employ individuals with experience. These factors, however, are only part of the picture. Another reason for youth unemployment is the high rate of illiteracy among youth and the fact that many of them leave school unprepared for the world of work (Gueron, 1984).

The solution to the teen unemployment problem is not an easy one as youths are competing for decreasing numbers of unskilled jobs with older individuals who have families to support. Any measure that would help provide jobs for youths might result in the unemployment of others. However, in an effort to stimulate business to hire unskilled and inexperienced youths, various programs have been proposed. One of these is the establishment of a low "youth unemployment opportunity" wage for teens aged 19 or under. This low wage for teens, to be in effect only during the summer months, is proposed as an experiment to see if it would in fact create the expected opportunities for youths. The rationale is that even short-term employment would give youths some paid work experience. However, there are many who question its effects. Citing as an example a previous effort to help alleviate teen unemployment, a *New York Times* editorial (March 21, 1985) claims that in 1978 employers were allowed to write off 85% of the salary paid to low-income youths. Although the tax credit is of even bigger benefit to employers than the savings on the proposed youth unemployment opportunity wage for teens, the program had no impact on overall youth unemployment. What teens need (and what have proved in the past to be successful and cost-effective) are education and training programs that will teach them basic skills and prepare them for the types of jobs that are now available and will be available in the future (Gueron, 1984). That such programs' benefits far outweigh their costs is demonstrated in a number of evaluations of these programs (Opportunities for Success, 1985; Farkas, 1984).

Many youths either drop out of school or they graduate from high school unable to read or write beyond a fourth-grade level. Thus, they are severely limited in the kinds of jobs that they can hold. Although further education and vocational training for these youths is important and might alleviate some of the problems of youth unemployment, the economic crisis our nation is undergoing resulted not only in shifts in the labor market and in a decrease in the number of unskilled jobs, but also in the

FIGURE 15.2   Numerous factors account for the high unemployment rate we are experiencing today: many jobs for unskilled laborers have vanished, and federal laws have priced teens out of the market. As long as employers have to pay a minimum wage that is higher than in the past, they choose to employ individuals with experience.

elimination of these programs. Furthermore, there seems to be little likelihood that public funds will be made available for such programs in the near future. The result for many teens is the inability to establish a positive vocational identity, a feeling of hopelessness and despair, and the realization that they are, as indicated by the title of David Elkind's book on teens, "all grown up [with] no place to go" (Elkind, 1984; see Figure 15.2).

It is not only the youths who are seeking employment during their adolescence who are forced into dilemmas about what to do for their life's work. With economic changes and shifts in labor market trends, many teens and young adults are making their decisions about whether or not to go on to college and what career to choose, not necessarily on the basis of their interests and aptitudes, but on the basis of available job openings. Many who are unable to find employment and are unprepared for the job market even though they have college degrees continue on with their education as long as they or their parents can afford it. Although for some individuals a higher degree or a change in field of study may turn out to be a good choice in the end, for a large number of young adults, the tasks of establishing a place for themselves in the workplace and earning an independent living are simply postponed further into the future.

The Depression Era.   In previous generations adolescents have had to face the reality of social problems during the critical period of identity formation and have had to adapt to major social changes. This point is made by Glen Elder (1980), who has shown that the larger social context in which people grow up has a significant impact on the course of human development, including the identity formed during adolescence. According to Elder and others (Feather, 1980), the kinds of choices adolescents make and the values they adopt differ in times of war, peace, and social unrest, and in times of prosperity and economic depression. Elder gives an example of adolescents who grew up and became young adults in America during the 1920s and 1930s. He notes that during the 1920s, the nation was experiencing a social revolution in which there was a drastic shift from strict Victorian standards of behavior to far more liberal social norms. The whole society enjoyed an unleashing of new possibilities. Young women especially were affected, as they were for the first time encouraged to think of their future in terms of education and a career. This prosperous and exuberant period in history was followed by the Depression of the 1930s during which many people lost their jobs after the stock market crashed, and thousands of families became poor. Many men, having been raised to believe that their primary task in life is to support a family, suffered loss of face as a result and had trouble later regaining their self-esteem and going back to work. Traditional family roles were thus thrown into disarray. By necessity, women often assumed a more powerful role in their family than was true when the men were the breadwinners, and they went out to work. Girls, because their mothers were working, played a major role in household operations, and boys went out to work to help support the family.

Information on how the Depression affected some adolescents is available from the Oakland Growth Study, which was a longitudinal study conducted by the Berkeley Institute of Human Development. The study began in 1931 and included a series of studies and interviews of a group of children from the time they were 10 to the time they were 19 years of age. Follow-up surveys were also conducted of these individuals through the 1960s, by which time they had become adults. The teens included in the study were old enough to play important roles in the household economy and to confront future prospects within the context of Depression realities. Elder (1974) analyzed the data from the Oakland Growth Study, seeking to find out how the social change associated with the Depression affected the individuals involved. He found that although in the 1920s many girls expected to pursue an education, the Depression of the following decade and the kinds of roles they had to assume within their family resulted in their marrying early and assuming traditional identities as

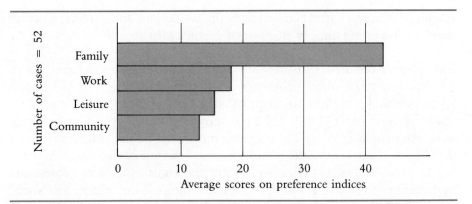

FIGURE 15.3 Although in the 1920s many girls expected to pursue an education, the depression of the following decade and the kinds of roles they had to assume within the family resulted in their marrying earlier and preferring, as this figure illustrates, family activities. From *Children of the Great Depression: Social Change in Life Experience* by Glen H. Elder, Jr., p. 224. Copyright © 1974 by The Society for Research in Child Development, Inc.

homemakers. This was especially so among adolescent girls whose families were hardest hit by the Depression (see Figure 15.3).

Boys in these families were also influenced by the Depression. They had to go out to work and their early experiences in the adult world seem to have benefited them. Those who came from the poorest families showed higher motivation to succeed than the adolescents whose families were not as hard hit by the Depression. As adults the boys and girls who lived through the Depression were family centered, and they considered children to be the most important aspect of a marriage. They not only emphasized the responsibilities of parenthood, they also stressed the value of dependability in children. As Elder (1980) notes, "personal aspects of Depression life are reflected in these preferences—the role of children in helping out [and] the importance of family support in times of need."

How does the present economic instability affect the identity and values of our youths? Those teens who are unemployed have a sense of hopelessness about their future, and they wander aimlessly in the streets, some of them resorting to crime (Gueron, 1984). Other teens, however, are generally satisfied with life, and, according to a Gallup Youth survey, they are becoming increasingly conservative. During the 1960s and early 1970s—a period characterized by social and political unrest brought on by the Vietnam War and civil rights demonstrations—young people sought to change the world. Many of them seriously questioned and even repudiated the values of their parents and attempted to create new values. Youth in the 1980s, however, have no difficulty accepting the kind of life society has to offer, and a large majority of them say they adhere to such traditional values as hard work and close family ties (Gallup, 1986a). Although

FIGURE 15.4 The sexual revolution our society has undergone has had many consequences for teens and adults alike, changing their conceptions of traditional sex roles.

many factors account for the conservatism of today's young people, the economy is one important factor. With jobs harder to find, especially for youth, hard work and parental support are all the more valuable.

Sex Roles and Sexual Behavior

The economy is only one aspect of social change that significantly influences identity formation in adolescence. Our society has also witnessed a sexual revolution that has had many consequences for teens and adults alike, changing their conceptions of traditional sex roles as well as their sexual behavior. In the past, boys were taught that as adults their responsibility would be to support a family and girls were taught that their roles in life would be as wives and mothers. However, these traditional sex roles are eroding rapidly. Adolescents are realizing that although differences in anatomy and physiology exist, as men and women they have equal potential to assume any role in life that they want, as long as they have the aptitude and the opportunity (see Figure 15.4). Although the changes in attitudes toward sex roles have had an influence on adolescent boys as well as girls, they have had the most impact on girls who as a result feel differently about themselves, their prospects in life, the value of their performance in school, and the kinds of jobs they aspire to (Rossi, 1977). Many young women are no longer satisfied with simply completing basic educational requirements and shortly afterwards getting married. They want to savor life and the opportunities it holds for them, and many of them are now deferring marriage and parenthood until they have established themselves in a career.

Whereas in some ways the sexual revolution has opened up opportunities for girls, in other ways it has had the opposite effect, resulting in an interruption or premature end to their education and a subsequent life of poverty and despair. This is the course of events for many teenage girls who become pregnant and decide to keep their babies. One aspect of the sexual revolution has been a trend toward increased sexual activity by adolescents (see Figure 15.5). In 1948 only 25% of males were sexually active as adolescents and in 1953 only 10% of females admitted having intercourse by age 18 (Kinsey et al., 1948, 1953). By 1981, 80% of males and 70% of females were sexually active (Alan Guttmacher Institute, 1981). Not only are more teens sexually active than ever before, they are also having sexual intercourse at an earlier age, and many girls become pregnant, with the result that there is now an epidemic of teenage pregnancies. Many young women, ignorant of or uncomfortable with the use of contraceptives, and often thinking that they are too young to become pregnant (Furstenberg, 1976), do in fact become pregnant (see Table 15.1). Most of these young women carry the baby to term and keep the baby (Zelnik & Kantner, 1978). Whether they marry the baby's father, or another man, or remain single, many of these young women are unprepared for the responsibilities of parenthood and are unable to care for their babies.

The consequences associated with teenage parenthood are discussed in depth in Chapter 10. Suffice it to note here that besides the poor health and the poverty that characterize the lives of the teenage mother and her baby, teenage parenthood has a devastating impact on the years of education a woman receives. In general, girls who bear children during adolescence tend to complete fewer years of schooling than their peers who become mothers later in life (Card & Wise, 1978; Furstenberg, 1976). Also, they are more likely to leave school before graduating. Moreover, these girls are much less likely to achieve their previously anticipated educational goals such as receiving a high school diploma or going to college (Moore & Waite, 1977).

This brings to light a point made previously in the chapter and attributed to Erikson: There is no finality to some of the decisions and choices made during adolescence, and redefinition of one's identity often occurs. Nevertheless, some of the choices and decisions made during adolescence

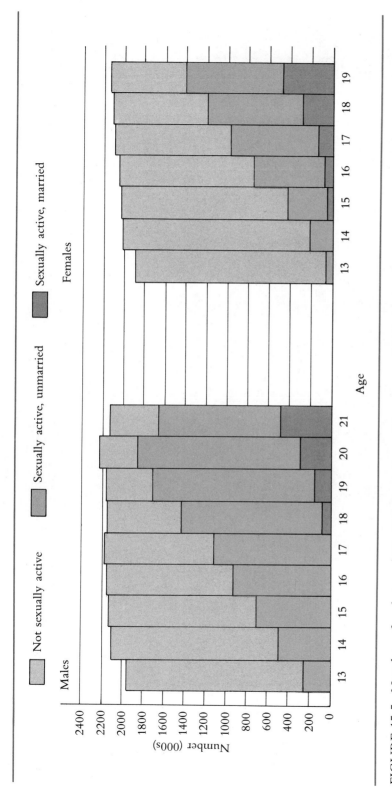

FIGURE 15.5 Number of males aged 13–21 and number of females aged 13–19 who are sexually active, by age and marital status, United States, 1978. Reprinted with permission from *Teenage Pregnancy: The Problem That Hasn't Gone Away*, published by The Alan Guttmacher Institute, New York, 1981.

TABLE 15.1 Current statistics on adolescents who become pregnant. Numbers, rates, and ratios of births to unmarried women, by age of mother and race of child: United States, 1980. [Based on 100 percent of births in selected states and on a 50-percent sample of births in all other states. For 41 states and the District of Columbia, marital status of mother is reported on the birth certificate, and for 9 states, mother's marital status is inferred. Populations estimated as of July 1]

Age of mother	Number				Rate per 1,000 unmarried women in specified group				Ratio per 1,000 live births			
	All races	White	All other		All races	White	All other		All races	White	All other	
			Total	Black			Total	Black			Total	Black
Under 15 years	9,024	3,144	5,880	5,707	---	---	---	---	887.4	753.8	980.3	985.2
15–19 years	262,777	127,984	134,793	128,022	27.6	16.2	81.7	89.2	475.9	329.8	821.4	851.5
15 years	21,908	9,223	12,685	12,223					777.5	615.7	961.1	971.6
16 years	41,386	19,653	21,733	20,786	20.6	11.8	63.1	69.6	654.9	495.2	924.3	940.7
17 years	58,606	28,885	29,721	28,195					548.5	395.7	877.9	901.1
18 years	69,173	34,427	34,746	32,929	39.0	23.6	111.6	120.2	451.1	312.5	805.1	838.2
19 years	71,704	35,796	35,908	33,889					357.4	238.3	712.7	751.4

Source: *Monthly Vital Statistics Report*, National Center for Health Statistics.

serve to determine what one's future will be. Fortunately, numerous schools and hospitals now have programs for teenage mothers which provide support services such as day care and enable many young mothers to complete their education (Badger, 1977). Thus, social policies, such as those that facilitate the development and implementation of programs for teen mothers, can make a difference in the lives of adolescents.

Peers

Although broad social changes and social policies have important effects on the development of adolescents and their eventual course in life, the family and friends also exert a great deal of influence. The choice of friends in particular is one of the major factors in the search for identity, as friends not only help determine one's lifestyle and values, they also provide emotional support to the adolescent, who is undergoing the slow process of disengaging himself from the family and establishing an independent life (Ausubel et al., 1977). This process is never an easy task. Most adolescents are embarrassed at one time or another at some of their own real or imagined social mistakes. They also experience times of joy and excitement as well as apprehension about a special date, for instance. Discussing such experiences with understanding friends who are themselves experiencing similar emotions can make the difficulties associated with adolescence much easier to handle and the happy moments all the more exciting. It is not surprising, therefore, that studies reveal that a popular social activity among adolescents is talking to peers (Berndt, 1982).

Friendships. Friends, of course, have been important in the life of the individual at an earlier age and have become valuable and trusted confidants in the latter part of the middle childhood period. During the adolescent period, however, friends serve different functions. Douvan and Adelson (1966), whose research is supported by more recent findings (e.g., Bigelow & La Gaipa, 1975; Coleman, 1974), studied changes in girls' friendships in early, middle, and late adolescence. They note that between the ages of 11 and 13, friendships tend to focus on *shared activities,* things that the adolescents can do together. Friends are defined by adolescents this age as "people with whom things can be done." In middle adolescence, between the ages of 14 and 16, adolescents stress the *security* that friendships provide, noting that friends should be loyal and trustworthy. At this stage, adolescents describe friends as people who are understanding and sensitive to their needs, and they express concern at losing a friend or about finding a friend.

Why such emphasis on the security that friendships provide? According to Douvan and Adelson (1966), who discuss the importance of friendships among girls at this age:

> . . . the girl is seeking in the other some response to or mirroring of herself, [and] she is in need of someone who is going through the same problems at the same time. In some sense, it could be argued that the middle adolescent girl is dealing with her problems by [identifying with her friend]. . . . With so much invested in the friendship, it is no wonder that the girl is so dependent on it.

Coleman (1980) further points out that during mid-adolescence, girls are becoming used to the physiological and physical changes they have undergone and are seeking the confidence of a friend who has undergone the same changes. In addition, although by mid-adolescence many girls are sexually active, others are only beginning to date at this age, and for them a friend provides much-needed emotional support in this new and exciting but also, for some, somewhat frightening experience.

By late adolescence, physical maturation is complete, and the adolescents are more at ease with themselves, and they have a better sense of their personal identity. During this stage, friendships become more relaxed experiences. Needing friends less, the adolescents are not anxious about being abandoned or betrayed by friends, and they value the *individuality* of their friends, choosing friends because of their personality and interests and what they can contribute to the relationship.

Boys, who are about two years behind girls in physiological and emotional maturity, have a different timetable for the changes in the quality of friendships. At age 13 or 14, for example, they exhibit the same attitudes toward friends that are characteristic of girls aged 11 or 12. Are friendships as meaningful to boys as they are to girls? In a review of the studies on friendships of adolescent boys as well as girls, Coleman (1980) notes that for adolescent boys, friends are as important as they are for girls. However, some findings of the research reveal that girls and boys differ somewhat in the expectations they have of friendship. Whereas girls generally say that they value in a friend such characteristics as sensitivity and empathy, these are usually not mentioned by boys, who tend instead to discuss the value of friends in terms of common pursuits. Not only do adolescent girls and boys have slightly differing notions about the importance of friends, a few studies have shown that boys also seem to be slightly less dependent on friends than girls are and less anxious about having a friend (e.g., Coleman, 1974). The evidence that this is the case for most adolescent boys is still rather sparse. Nevertheless, if there are indeed differences between the sexes in the adolescent's conceptions of and dependence on friendship, this would not be surprising since, according to Coleman (1980), "for girls in our society, a stronger interpersonal orientation is expected; the capacity for intimacy and dependency are not only acceptable, they are highly valued, and there is no doubt that the processes of socialization all tend in this direction. For boys, however, the stress is placed on skills, achievement, and self-sufficiency."

FIGURE 15.6   By mid- to late adolescence, teens spend most of their time in a crowd of as many as 20 members that includes both sexes.

Cliques and Crowds.   Adolescents enjoy spending time not only with one or two close friends but with a number of friends, and they often form groups of 5 to 20 members (Coleman, 1980). These groups, which tend to be closed to outsiders, are usually formed on the basis of shared interests, and they change in size and other qualities depending on the age of the adolescents involved (see Figure 15.6).

The change in the nature of peer groups is documented in a classic study by an Australian researcher (Dunphy, 1963) who studied peer groups that adolescents and young adults aged 13 to 21 belonged to. He found that early in adolescence, peer groups are single-sex *cliques* of about 5 members, all of whom are of the same socioeconomic background and age. Typically the members of a clique have the same values and interests, and they tend to be intolerant of anyone who is different than they are. Slightly later, at about age 14, members of different cliques begin to interact, and boys and girls in separate cliques tend to tease and embarrass members of the opposite-sex groups. While the adolescents are in high school, they belong to a clique of two or three friends of the same sex, but may also be friendly with a clique of two or three teens of the opposite sex. Gradually, the cliques merge and by mid to late adolescence teens spend most of their time in a *crowd* that includes as many as 20 members of both sexes. They congregate wherever they can, on street corners, in the park, in shopping malls, and at school, spending as much time as they can with the group. Eventually, in their early years as young adults, they are

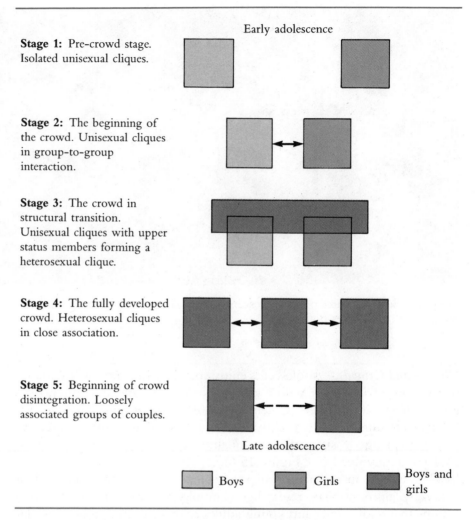

Stage 1: Pre-crowd stage. Isolated unisexual cliques.

Stage 2: The beginning of the crowd. Unisexual cliques in group-to-group interaction.

Stage 3: The crowd in structural transition. Unisexual cliques with upper status members forming a heterosexual clique.

Stage 4: The fully developed crowd. Heterosexual cliques in close association.

Stage 5: Beginning of crowd disintegration. Loosely associated groups of couples.

Early adolescence

Late adolescence

Boys   Girls   Boys and girls

FIGURE 15.7   Stages of peer group development during adolescence.

no longer comfortable in a crowd and function instead in groups of couples (see Figure 15.7).

Popularity and Rejection.   Within cliques and crowds there is usually one or several adolescents who stand out as leaders because they are admired by others in the group and considered by them to be the most popular. Generally, boys and girls define popularity differently, with boys admiring other boys for their athletic ability or good looks and girls admiring other girls who have nice clothes and who are also good looking (Coleman, 1961). For both boys and girls, however, popularity is mostly affected by personality factors such as cheerfulness, friendliness, and a sense

FIGURE 15.8 Despite the fact that adolescents admire some of their peers, there are some adolescents who do not belong to a group.

of humor. Adolescents, like younger children and adults, like to be near those who are friendly, enthusiastic, and who are capable of initiating games and activities that the entire group can enjoy.

Just as they admire some of their peers, however, adolescents can also be rejecting, often refusing to accept as their friends or as part of a group individuals whom they consider to be socially awkward or unattractive. Thus, there are some adolescents who do not belong to a group and who have no friends (see Figure 15.8).

In a study on adolescents who have no friends, Rosenberg (1975) found that in many cases, these adolescents have low self-esteem. Thinking of themselves as unworthy, they are afraid to approach their peers because they are certain that their peers would reject them. The reasons for adolescents' low self-esteem are numerous. For example, a boy who is much shorter than his classmates or who does not perform well in school can feel inadequate (Rosenberg, 1965). Other adolescents, by rejecting someone whom they perceive as different from themselves, can also contribute to that individual's poor self-esteem (Harter, 1983), as can parents. Recall from Chapter 12 that children whose parents are unresponsive to their needs and who fail to take an interest in their activities grow up

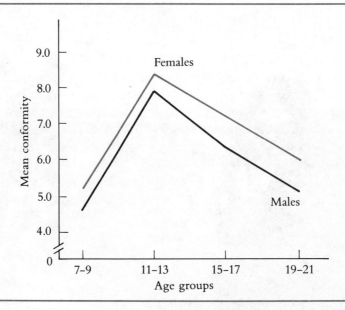

FIGURE 15.9 From middle to late adolescence there is a marked decrease in adolescents' need to conform to peers. Figure from J. Adelson, editor, *Handbook of Adolescent Psychology*, p. 422, figure 7. Reprinted by permission of John Wiley & Sons, Inc.

feeling inadequate and not worthy of anyone's attention. However, low self-esteem is not the only reason why some adolescents are isolated from others. Often, intellectually or creatively gifted adolescents who think highly of themselves are nonetheless rejected by their peers because they are so different from the rest of the crowd. Thus, they spend much of their time alone or with adults unless they can find others like themselves with whom they can establish friendships.

Conformity. Since most adolescents are so intimately associated with close friends or a group of friends, it is usually thought that they are under pressure to conform, as was true in previous periods of development. Furthermore, the fact that adolescents tend not only to spend as much time as they can with their friends, but also to dress and to talk alike, and to prefer the same music as their friends, further reinforces the stereotype of "slavish conformity" (Coleman, 1980) as characteristic of adolescents. However, studies reveal that the need to conform is not uniformly high during adolescence but is related to age and status in the peer group. As you can see in Figure 15.9, during early adolescence there is a marked increase in adolescents' need to conform, peaking at age 11 to 13. During the course of adolescence, however, there is a marked decrease in conformity, and teens aged 15 and over are not as likely as they were at a younger age to be susceptible to peer pressure (Constanzo & Shaw, 1966).

Adolescents do not depend entirely on a group of peers to the exclusion of their dependence on their parents. Rather, they tend to seek and depend on the advice of their peers when it refers to such dilemmas as how to dress for a particular occasion and what courses to take in school. When it comes to other issues, such as whether or not to take a part-time job and which college to attend, they tend to seek and rely on the advice of their parents rather than that of their peers. These findings are derived from early studies on the topic conducted by Brittain (1963, 1969) who analyzed adolescents' answers to hypothetical dilemmas concerning their relationships with parents and peers. More recent studies support Brittain's findings. Smith (1976), for instance, in a study of over 1,000 12- to 18-year-old urban and suburban adolescents, found that although peers influence the adolescent's choice of clothes and music, it is the family rather than the peer group that influences the adolescent's decisions on a variety of other and substantially more important issues regarding future goals and educational and vocational plans. In another study, this one of adolescents and their parents in the United States and Denmark, researchers found that in both countries, most adolescents are influenced by their parents in their thinking about life goals rather than by their age-mates (Kandel & Lesser, 1972). Thus, although the adolescent does indeed spend more time with his peers than with his parents, this shift in time commitments does not necessarily indicate a change from parental to peer influence (Lerner & Spanier, 1980). Is there, then, a generation gap between adolescents and their parents? Apparently not; adolescents, as we have shown not only in this but in previous chapters as well, are understanding of and are understood by their parents despite media projections to the contrary. However, there are some adolescents who do conform to the behaviors of their peers and fail to seek parental advice. This is especially the case among adolescents whose parents are punitive or permissive to the point of neglect or whose parents are themselves troubled and concerned about their marriage and the family's finances (Devereux, 1970; Hartup, 1983). In such families the adolescent does not feel that her parents are supportive toward and nurturant of her, so it is not surprising that she turns to her peers.

The Family

For most adolescents, the family is not only an important source of influence regarding future goals and educational and vocational plans, it also facilitates the adolescent's transition from childhood to adulthood. Parents support their growing child by offering her advice and guidance as she attempts to find her place in life and by imparting to her their values and traditions. Most adolescents believe that their parents are supportive of them (Offer, Ostrov, & Howard, 1981), and they tend to be responsive to their parents in this regard, accepting many of their parents' values and

Drug and Alcohol Abuse

Whether they are in the company of their friends or alone, an increasing number of adolescents are using a variety of illegal drugs such as marijuana, cocaine, and heroin. They become addicted to these drugs as well as to alcohol. Not only has drug and alcohol abuse become a pervasive factor in the lives of many adolescents, drugs are available and in large supply in virtually every high school in the country and also in an increasing number of elementary schools. All this suggests that it is not only adolescents, but younger children as well, who have the opportunity to use and become addicted to drugs.

Alcohol is a legal drug which is freely available in our society and found in many homes. It is the most popular drug among adolescents, many of whom become problem drinkers at an early age. As you can see in the graph, over 60% of seventh-grade boys and over 75% of seventh-grade girls regularly drink alcohol, and 5% of boys and 4.4% of girls are problem drinkers, meaning that they become drunk at least 6 times during the course of one year (Matarazzo, 1982; Califano, 1978). Alcohol abuse becomes more pervasive with age. Close to 90% of twelfth-grade boys and 83% of twelfth-grade girls drink alcohol regularly, and 33.9% of these boys and 19.9% of these girls are problem drinkers. Marijuana is also a popular drug among teens, with over 40% of teens reporting that they have tried it, and about 10% to 25% of them also using a variety of other illegal drugs including cocaine (Miller et al., 1983).

The widespread use of alcohol, marijuana, and other illicit drugs not only among adolescents but among adults as well (see Table 15.a) represents one of the most striking instances of social change in the last decade. Drug and alcohol abuse among adolescents, however, is of particular concern not only because the use of drugs can have devastating emotional and physical consequences for a developing mind and body, but also because among adolescents, the use of one drug, marijuana, for instance, is associated with extensive use of other drugs as well. In studies on drug and alcohol abuse, researchers found that there are stages in drug involvement. At first, children and adolescents drink beer and wine. At a slightly older age they supplement these with cigarette smoking and/or hard liquor, followed by marijuana. Eventually they use not only these combinations of drugs and alcohol but other illicit drugs as well (Kandel, 1981).

Drug and alcohol abuse takes its toll on the physical and emotional health of adolescents and subjects them to other dangers as well. It is the leading cause of automobile accidents, which account for the deaths of many adolescents and other people; it interferes with school work; and it creates social problems with family and friends (Albas et al., 1978; Brunswick, 1977). Although the research on drug and alcohol abuse has thus far yielded only partial answers regarding the possible effects of drug use, researchers do know that the effects of drugs and alcohol differ among individuals depending on their biological makeup, personality, and extent of drug abuse. For some adolescents, the use of some drugs for short periods of time may not be associated with any devastating consequences. For others, however, drug use results not only

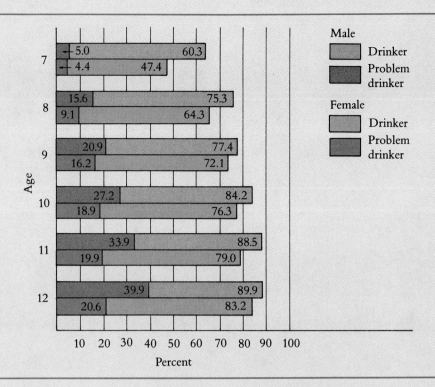

Percentage of adolescent boys and girls who drink and are problem drinkers. From Califano, J. A., Jr. (1979). *Healthy people: Surgeon General's report on health promotion and disease prevention, Background papers 1979*. Washington, D.C.: U.S. Government Printing Office; p. 353, Fig. 2.

in changes in physiological and biochemical functioning (Cohen, 1981), but also in psychosocial consequences. Many young people who are regular drug and alcohol users experience loss of interest in virtually all social and educational activities, often dropping out of school and experiencing conflict in the home (Miller, 1981; Scarpitti & Datesman, 1980; Albas et al., 1978). Their parents are also affected by their changed behavior. They feel anger, shame, and guilt at the toll the drugs are taking on their child. At the same time they feel helpless because they are unable to help the adolescent and worried about their child's future prospects in life.

Indeed, not only parents but educators, physicians, social workers, and policymakers are not sure of what measures to take to stem the increase in the number of children and adolescents who become regular and addicted drug users. Some states have tried to raise the legal age of drinking from 18 to 21 in an effort to prevent teens from becoming problem drinkers. Noting that increasing the legal age of drinking is of little consequence since alcoholism is becoming a pervasive problem among children aged 18 and under, other states have instituted educational programs, hoping that knowledge of the consequences of drug and alcohol abuse might serve to deter youngsters from the use of drugs and liquor. There have also been other changes in some states which have liberalized laws regarding possession and use of marijuana because leniency is considered to be important in an effort to reduce the problems associated with drug abuse (Hanson, 1980). At the same time, however, schools persist in taking punitive

TABLE 15.a Patterns of drug use in 1977 by age and sex.

Age	Used during past month		
	Cigarettes	Alcohol	Marijuana
12–13	10	13	4
14–15	22	28	15
16–17	35	52	29
18–21	51	71	31
22–25	45	70	24
26–34	47	70	12
35–49	45	61	2
50 +	34	44	1
Youth (12–17 years, N = 1,272)			
Male	23	37	19
Female	22	25	13
Adult (18 years and over, N = 3,322)			
Male	47	67	30
Female	35	50	19

Age	Used during past year					
	Psychoactive nonmedical			Psychoactive medically prescribed		
	Stimulants	Sedatives	Tranquilizers	Stimulants	Sedatives	Tranquilizers
12–13	—	—	—	1	3	3
14–15	3	2	2	1	5	8
16–17	8	4	7	1	6	5
18–21	11	10	10	3	4	10
22–25	11	6	6	4	8	12
26–34	3	2	4	6	7	18
35–49	—	—	1	3	8	19
50 +	—	—	—	2	11	20
Youth (12–17 years, N = 1,272)						
Male	5	3	4	2	4	5
Female	3	2	2	1	6	6
Adult (18 years and over, N = 3,322)						
Male	4	3	4	2	8	12
Female	1	1	2	5	10	23

Source: Lettieri, Dan J., & Ludford, Jacqueline P. (Eds.). (1981). *Drug abuse and the American adolescent* (NIDA Research Monograph 38, A RAUS Review Report), p. 3, Table 1. (U.S. Dept. of Health and Human Services, Public Health Service, Alcohol, Drug Abuse, and Mental Health Administration, National Institute on Drug Abuse.)

measures and consider drug and alcohol abuse as a serious offense. In a study of drug discipline policies in secondary schools across the nation, Schwartz (1984) found that educators expel or suspend from school not only those teens who are found to use or possess drugs, but also those who voluntarily admit to drug use, thus preempting any help that the teens may have been asking for.

Whichever method is used in the fight against drug and alcohol abuse among adolescents, it is agreed that preventing extended use of the drug is imperative and that educators and parents should intervene and offer help to teens as soon as they start taking drugs. This is not always easy, however, since drug users become experienced con artists and are often able to hide their drug use (Rees & Wilborn, 1983). Nevertheless, there are some symptoms to look for which indicate drug use, including: changing attitudes toward parents, decline in academic performance, missing money or expensive items, severe mood swings, changes in friends, dropping out of extracurricular activities, decreased interest in leisure time activities, and spending an increasing amount of time alone. Looking for these symptoms and identifying the youths who may be using drugs may not be helpful in every case, but it can at least identify some teens who are taking drugs so they can be given help before they become addicted.

following in their footsteps. They tend to choose friends from the same social class as their parents. They are as interested or disinterested in politics and religion as their parents are, often favoring the same candidate for presidential elections as their parents do and attending the same church. Also, they often choose occupational paths that reflect their parents' aspirations for them (Conger, 1973; Feature, 1980).

Changes in Family Interactions. This is not to say that there are no disagreements between teens and their parents. On the contrary, in their attempts to establish their identity, adolescents question their parents' ideologies, and the teens' views at times seem to be worlds apart from the views of their parents. Most adolescents, however, have respect for and get along with their parents (see Figure 15.10). Sorenson (1973) found that 88% of the teens he surveyed respected their parents, and in a Gallup Poll survey (1986b) almost all adolescents said that they get along well with their parents. These findings reinforce a point made earlier in the chapter, that in most families, the generation gap is a myth and evident only with respect to differences in dress and hairstyle, music, and manners of speech (Offer & Offer, 1975). When parents and teens get past these superficial differences and listen to each other's concerns, thoughts, and values, they find that they have much in common and that they can be a source of information for and influence on one another (Hartup, 1983).

However, during the course of adolescence and especially at the beginning of the period, the parents and teens have to adjust to the developmental changes the adolescent is going through, in the process establishing new patterns of authority and interaction. In a review of the research on the interactions between parents and adolescents, John Hill (1980)

667

FIGURE 15.10   Despite media attention to the rift between parents and their adolescents, researchers have found that the "generation gap" is a myth and evident only with respect to the differences in dress, hairstyle, music, and manner of speech. When parents and teens get past these superficial differences, they find that they have much in common.

notes that during this period, parents are adjusting to having a "new" person in the household, " . . . [a person] 'new' in stature, 'new' in approaching reproductive capability, 'new' in cognitive competence." Garbarino and Gilliam (1980) also note that at the same time that adolescents have to adjust to physical, intellectual, and emotional changes that they are experiencing, their parents have to make adjustments to living with an adolescent. They contend that the task of being the parent to an adolescent is substantially different from the task of being the parent to a child. Adolescents have far greater physical power than they did in previous periods. They can stimulate and influence family conflict, they can also leave the family, harm themselves and others, and embarrass their parents. This enhanced power, according to the researchers, is often a destabilizing force unless the parents and the teens are flexible and willing to compromise.

Besides enhanced physical power and capability, adolescents become increasingly able to reason like an adult, and they have a broader field of significant individuals in their life, most notably friends of the same and the opposite sex, that parents must come to terms with. Another important consideration is that the cost of raising children increases substantially during the adolescent years. According to U.S. Department of Agriculture (1982) figures, the yearly cost of maintaining a teenager is about 140% that of maintaining a young child. Garbarino (1986) notes that this drastically increased cost is stressful for many parents and can be the source of family conflict, "particularly in families where the increased financial demands of adolescence are not matched by increased family income."

Given these changes of adolescence, it is not surprising that surveys indicate that a majority of parents report that the adolescent years are the most difficult ones for childrearing (Pasley & Gecas, 1984). Not only do parents have to adjust to an individual—the adolescent—who is substantially different than she was in the past, they also have to adjust to the fact that their child will one day leave the family and pursue an independent life. Their task is to guide the adolescent and offer her the support and advice she needs, and at the same time nurture her quest for independence. This task is by no means easy, however, and it is exacerbated by the fact that in many families, it is not only the adolescent who is changing and seeking to establish an identity but the parents as well. Now that their child is ready to embark on an independent path in life, the parents may be contemplating their past and their future and redefining their existence in terms of the possibilities and limits they are faced with (Levinson, 1978).

Parenting Styles.   The extent that parents are able to adjust to their parenting tasks, and the approaches that they employ in their interactions with the adolescent, have important effects on the adolescent's development. Diana Baumrind, who identified three distinct parenting styles and the effects these have on preschoolers (see Chapter 9), also reviewed the literature on parent-adolescent relationships. She found that although the adolescent brings to the relationship with her parents her own temperament and personality, how the parents react to the adolescent and the approaches to childrearing that the parents adopt are reflected in the adolescent's personality and behavior (Baumrind, 1975).

Authoritative parents, according to Baumrind, evidence their interest in their adolescent's activities and are warm and supportive toward her. They give the teen consistent standards to abide by, but they are at the same time willing to grant her sufficient autonomy. They are flexible, often even willing to learn from the adolescent. Adolescents whose parents are authoritative are socially active and responsible, they have high self-esteem, and they evaluate their life possibilities, committing themselves to certain values and goals.

authoritative parents

Authoritarian parents are controlling in their interactions with the adolescent. They expect the adolescent to abide by numerous rules, and they are unwilling to adjust to the adolescent's need for independence. The interactions between authoritarian parents and the adolescent are likely to be conflict-ridden. Adolescents of authoritarian parents have problems developing their own identity, often prematurely withdrawing from attempts to evaluate their life choices and make commitments.

authoritarian parents

permissive
parents

Permissive parents are undemanding of their adolescent. They expect the adolescent to be sufficiently mature to make major life decisions on his own, and they provide her with inconsistent or no rules, standards, and expectations. Permissive parents often attempt to interact with the adolescent as though they were friends, and they resent the adolescent's attempts to form attachments with peers. Adolescents of permissive parents feel rejected and confused from the lack of direction in the home and resentful of their parents' attempts to be friendly. They often develop emotional and behavioral problems as a result of the inadequate guidance they receive and the inconsistencies and lenience in their parents' stand toward them. Generally, girls of permissive parents evidence emotional problems, including alienation and an attitude of helplessness, whereas boys of such parents evidence behavioral problems (Duke, 1978).

Adolescent Abuse

Inappropriate parenting styles sometimes lead to the abuse and neglect of adolescents. In the past, concern for the problems of abuse has been limited to infants and young children, perhaps because it was assumed that by adolescence youngsters are no longer helpless and vulnerable to abuse by adults. Recent studies reveal, however, that although adolescents are old enough to counteract the abuse in certain respects, physical and emotional abuse of adolescents is prevalent and related to inappropriate parenting styles and conflict between the parents and teens.

Research on the incidence of adolescent abuse is limited to several studies and surveys due in part to public and professional emphasis on the abuse and neglect of children. Although the data from the available research is, as yet, inconclusive, it is estimated that 650,000 adolescents are subjected to abuse each year and that these figures account for about 47% of the known cases of maltreatment of children aged 18 and under (Burgdorff, 1980). Considering that adolescents account for only 38% of the population of individuals under the age of 18, the fact that close to half the cases of abuse are of adolescents gains in significance.

Garbarino (1986), in a review of the research on the dynamics of adolescent maltreatment, draws a distinction between child and adolescent abuse, noting that unlike young children, teenagers are imperfect victims for abuse since they are able to strike back and do, which often creates potentially dangerous domestic quarrels involving mutual assault. He further points out that while many cases of the abuse of children are reported among low-income families, there are indications that the maltreatment of adolescents, although it does occur in families which experience financial difficulties, occurs most frequently among middle- and upper-middle-class families. Among other characteristics of families in which the abuse of adolescents occurs, Garbarino cites the following: The family is likely to contain a stepparent. Abused adolescents are less socially competent and they are likely to exhibit more developmental problems than their nonabused peers. Families in which abuse occurs are characterized by divorce, and abusive parents are authoritarian parents. These parents are harsh and rigid in their interactions with the adolescent. They are unable to understand adolescents' need for independence, and they cannot adjust to the fact that adolescents are physically and mentally capable of challenging parental authority.

In addition to the above findings, it is noted that adolescents are subjected to both physical and psychological abuse, which includes being terrorized, rejected, and isolated by their parents (Garbarino & Vondra, 1983), often to a greater degree than is true of young children. This is documented in a national survey on the severity of child abuse and neglect (Burgdorff, 1980) which found that children are more frequently physically abused than adolescents, whereas adolescents are more frequently psychologically abused.

DISCUSSION OF SOCIAL ISSUES: RUNAWAY, HOMELESS, AND DELINQUENT YOUTH

Adolescents who are subjected to abuse and neglect sometimes run away from home, only to find themselves in desperate situations and homeless. Some adopt a life of violence and crime. Researchers acknowledge the need for more research in this area, but at the same time they are becoming increasingly cognizant of the fact that maltreatment of adolescents is at the root of many adolescent problems including prostitution (Garbarino, 1986), and that in 60 to 65% of the cases, it leads to the problems of runaway, homeless, and delinquent youths (Report to the Committee of the Judiciary, 1980).

Runaway Youths. The problem of runaway youths has become a major national concern. About 500,000 adolescents run away from home each year. They are ill-equipped to fend for themselves adequately, and in many cases they are only 12 to 14 years old, which means they cannot legally hold a job. Even if they were capable of holding their own in the world, their opportunity to do so is slim since pimps and hustlers await them in the bus stations of cities they are running to (see Figure 15.11). They lure the unsuspecting teens by promising them food, shelter, and money, but they then torture them physically and emotionally, forcing them into submission and putting them to work as prostitutes or in pornographic movies. This is true for both girls and boys, but it is especially prevalent among boys, who become prostitutes for homosexuals. These adolescents suffer untold damage to their minds and bodies and cannot escape the terrible situation they are in as they are constantly watched and, in effect, held hostage by those who took them off the streets.

FIGURE 15.11   Approximately 500,000 adolescents run away each year, often finding themselves in situations they cannot easily get out of.

Who are runaway youths? Why do they leave home? In a survey on runaways, D'Angelo (1974), notes that teens who run away from home felt isolated and degraded while they were home. The typical runaway episode stems from conflict or frustration in the parent-teen relationship, including disagreements over appearance, friends, house rules, curfews, or level of expectation about school performance. Running away often reflects the adolescent's feeling of assumed parental rejection and anger at the parents' unwillingness to relax restrictions and enable her to assume some independence. Usually, the runaway episode is a spontaneous, impulsive act which may dramatically bring to a head the youth's desperate need for a flexible and responsive dialogue with the parents. Some of the parents of runaways also feel angered, concerned, and rejected by the teen's behavior, but many are at the same time overjoyed when she contacts them and they are willing to do anything just to get their child to return. Other parents, however, refuse to accept the youth back in their home, leaving her homeless.

Homeless Youths.   The family situation of youths who become homeless is substantially different from that of youths who run away and eventually return. Whereas runaways who return home have experienced family conflict that emanates from their behavior and their parents' inability to exert their authority appropriately, homeless youths are rejected by their family and sometimes have even been flatly told to leave home. According to reports submitted to the Committee of the Judiciary (1980) at a hearing on homeless youths, families of such youths are overburdened with financial responsibilities, and they are characterized by divorce and by parents whose self-esteem is low. In many cases the divorced parent has taken a new partner into the household and subsequently becomes competitive with or jealous of their son's or daughter's more youthful sexuality, an emotional situation that leads to conflict in the family and often to reprisals against the teenager. In other cases the youth is subjected to sexual and physical assault by the parent's lover. Unable to withstand the abuse, the youth leaves home, knowing that her family is not eager to have her back.

Numerous federal and state funded programs are available in cities across the nation to help runaway and homeless youths. The National Runaway Switchboard helps teens get in touch with their parents in the hope that they can go home again. There are also youth shelters that provide a safe, albeit temporary, place where the teens can get some food, sleep, and counseling. Often, however, the temporary shelter and counseling are not effective. The teens are past the point where they are willing to listen to anyone, and they often have unrealistic expectations of their capabilities and future. At the same time that they are worried about a place to sleep and not knowing where their next meal will come from, they are thinking that they can make it on their own, get a job, and buy a car. Many of them, however, don't make it and instead "[end] up in the city workhouse or state penitentiary. . . . It's a bleak outlook for homeless kids who have no adult taking care of them and providing emotional support. They float around, latch onto someone, get married, are unemployed and continue the same cycle" (Report of the Committee of the Judiciary, 1980).

Delinquent Youths.   Similar situations characterize the lives of delinquent youths. Delinquency, which is sometimes confused with minor behavior problems that are typical of adolescents (for example, stealing items from a grocery store), refers to a pattern of destructive behavior. It covers a wide range of violations of the law, including murder, assault, vandalism, and theft, as well as promiscuity, truancy, and running away from home. The last three examples are considered crimes only when they are committed by a minor (Offer, Marhorn, & Ostrov, 1979).

When asked to report, confidentially, if they have broken any laws, most teens confess to one or more chargeable offenses, noting that they

Deinstitutionalization of Status Offenders

Runaway and homeless youths pose a problem to the judiciary system since being away from home for long periods of time is considered to be a criminal offense when children aged 16 and under are involved. In the past these teens were given the same consideration as criminals. Now adolescent offenders are distinguished either as *juvenile delinquents,* for offenses that would be considered a crime if they were adults (robbery, vandalism, shoplifting, and prostitution) or as *status offenders,* for misdeeds that would be ignored by the courts if engaged in by adults. Truancy, incorrigibility, promiscuity, and running away from home are included among the offenses.

These offenses represent not the breaking of any laws as such but affronts to the parents, the schools, and the community. So, the task of the police and the courts is not to punish the teens for their misdeeds, but to ascertain what kinds of problems they experience at home or in school, and to help them if they can. Unfortunately, neither the police nor the courts are set up in such a way that would facilitate their helping rather than punishing teens, so, often status offenders who could not be returned home were sent to detention centers or correctional facilities where they were treated as criminals. In 1974, the federal government enacted the Juvenile Justice and Delinquency Prevention Act (P.L. 93-415). This act, which was amended in 1977 (P.L. 95-115) and in 1980 (P.L. 96-509), was intended, in part, to bring about the deinstitutionalization of status offenders. That is, to remove status offenders from detention and correctional facilities and to provide them with alternative and appropriate services. Such alternative services include group homes, for example, where youths are provided not only with a safe and supervised place to live, but also with counseling and other help. Communities which lacked such services were expected to develop them.

Although not everyone is in agreement that the current trend in the juvenile justice system—the move away from institutionalization to community-based services—is appropriate for all status offenders (Ludman & Scarpitti, 1978; Erickson, 1978). Many contend that status offenders, many of whom are teens who are not wanted by their parents, deserve to be given support rather than to be treated as criminals (Handler & Zatz, 1982). The question is, however, now that there is a law governing the treatment of status offenders, is the law being implemented in all states?

This question is of great importance. Any social policy needs to be considered not only with regard to its goals and intended consequences, but also with regard to its implementation. Thus the Office of Juvenile Justice and Delinquency Prevention of the U.S. Department of Justice commissioned a three-year study to assess what has been happening to youth who commit status offenses in the aftermath of the legislation that calls for their being placed in community-based programs and for the development of such programs. The study, published in a report called *Neither Angels Nor Thieves: Studies in Deinstitutionalization of Status Offenders* (Handler & Zatz, 1982), found that in many ways, the needs of status offenders are being served. In all of the states that were included in the study, teens are no longer sent to correctional institutions, and in many states grants are provided to private agencies for the development of residential and nonresidential services for runaway and homeless youths. In some states, however, services are so lacking, especially for the most troubled youths, that the teens are often sent out of state to receive some type of treatment. Furthermore, although the study found that there are now fewer status offenders being processed by the courts than before 1974 when the legislation was enacted, it was not entirely clear whether teens are being sent directly to a community-based program by the police or another agency, or whether they are simply being ignored. Obviously, more research must be done to ascertain the effects of the policy aimed at the deinstitutionalization of status offenders. At the very least, however, it is a great step forward that these teens, whose lives in many cases are troubled, are not considered criminals but are given help instead.

are guilty of minor crimes such as smoking marijuana or sexual intercourse with an underage girl (Gold & Petronio, 1980; Jessor & Jessor, 1977; Gold, 1970). However, not all crimes committed by adolescents are minor. According to statistics compiled by the U.S. Department of Justice (1985), 54% of all serious crimes such as murder, assault, and robbery are committed by youths age 13 to 18, and 31% of all general arrests nationally involve individuals age 18 and under.

Developmental psychologists have shown an interest in the problem of delinquent youths, seeking to find out what causes an adolescent to progress from relatively minor delinquent acts to the adoption of delinquency and crime as a way of life. They note that delinquent youths have low self-esteem (Offer, Marhon, & Ostrov, 1979), that they are likely to have a history of school problems and that their lives are characterized by chronic unemployment (National Commission on Youth, 1980). Another characteristic of delinquent youth is a history of abuse and neglect (Garbarino, 1986). Having experienced abuse and disrepect from their parents, not only during their teens but for much of their childhood, these adolescents learn aggression and exploitation as a means of negotiating life, and they imitate the behavior of their parents, exerting their strength on those who are less powerful than they are. Not only do these teens terrorize women, the elderly, and defenseless men on the streets, they are also violent in school, with the result that an increasing number of teachers and students have become seriously concerned for their own safety in school.

Facilitating the Transition from Childhood to Adulthood

The serious problems that many of our young people face—the poverty and despair associated with unemployment and teen parenthood, the life of violence and crime, and lack of a supportive family life—have existed for a number of years and are becoming more prevalent each year. In an attempt to help teens and to find ways to prevent their problems from occurring in the first place, in 1980 policymakers created a National Commission on Youth. Members of the commission, who were experts in adolescent development and representatives from various public sectors and from education, industry, and labor, were charged with the tasks of studying the problems of youth, of appraising the social institutions that exist to assist youth, and of making recommendations for the creation of new environments that might better enable our young people to grow and to become useful members of society.

In their report, *The Transition from Youth to Adulthood* (National Commission on Youth, 1980), members of the commission noted that the bridge between youth and adulthood is difficult to cross "even in the best of times," but it is especially difficult for young people today because the traditional institutions that have assisted them in the past (the family and the school among them) are changing, crumbling, and even collapsing. "The decline of the family unit is well documented," it is written in the report, "[and] beleaguered school systems are attacked from all sides—by students, parents, and employers—for their failure to teach marketable skills to the young. In addition, governmental bodies are unresponsive to the serious plight of youth." The result, according to the commission's findings, is that unemployment is a way of life for many youths; that some teens are so turned off that they resort to alcohol and drugs and even to suicide; and that many youths are illiterate and unprepared for life as adults, so instead they commit violent and illegal acts, many of them terrorizing innocent people in the streets or "languishing" in jails and juvenile detention centers (National Commission on Youth, 1980).

Members of the commission made numerous recommendations for change that might alleviate some of these problems of adolescence, even suggesting that a National Youth Service be established to provide teens with the opportunity for at least one year of full-time service to their community or to the nation. They have also made suggestions regarding changes in educational, employment, and juvenile justice laws, stressing in particular that efforts should be made to foster connections between all institutions that serve adolescents—between the home and the school, and between the school and the workplace. These and other of the commission's recommendations, if implemented, may indeed benefit youth. Perhaps more importantly, however, we need to focus not only on the needs of adolescents but on the needs of families. The problems that teens are experiencing stem only in part from their adolescent experience; they are rooted also in their experiences as children. As Erikson (1963) so eloquently states, young people "find an identity consonant with [their] own childhood . . . [and] by their responses and actions [they] tell the old whether life as presented by the old and as presented to the young, has meaning; it is the young who carry in them the power to confirm those who confirm them, and, joining the issues, to renew and regenerate, or to reform and rebel."

SUMMARY

During the adolescent years the individual is faced with the task of establishing a personal identity and defining herself not only in terms of who she is but also in terms of what she wants to become. This is by no means an easy task, and the adolescent, who undergoes the psychosocial crisis of *identity versus role confusion,* wrestles with such questions as Who am I really? What do I want to do with my life? and What do I believe in? She either resolves the crisis by committing herself to some decisions about her being and her future, or she feels anxious and confused and becomes incapable of making decisions. Instead of resolving the crisis and achieving a sense of their personal identity, some adolescents withdraw from efforts to shape an identity. Others adopt the values of their family and society without questioning these. Some declare a moratorium—they defer resolution of the crisis and they do not make any decisions about what they believe in and what they want to do.

The ease with which the individual establishes an identity for himself and decides on his eventual role as an adult is in part dependent on the society within which he lives. In a contemporary and complex society such as ours, identity formation is a difficult process because the individual is faced with various identifications he must synthesize and a variety of values and social roles he must choose from. He has to make decisions about what he believes in and what he wants to do in life not only on the basis of his interests and skills, but also on the basis of what society has to offer. This is especially true with regard to vocational decisions. For some adolescents, the question, "What do I want to do when I grow up?" poses a dilemma that is not easily resolved by simply making a choice of occupation, since there are no jobs available for them. As a result, there are increasing numbers of youths age 16 to 19 who are unemployed and unable to ascertain what they will do in the future. However, it is not only these days that adolescents are faced with social problems in the course of their forming an identity. During the Depression era, for example, adolescents had to make decisions in the face of severe economic hardship and had to adapt to the prevailing social conditions. The social context is only one source of influence on identity formation as friends and the family also influence the individual's ideas about himself and the plans he makes for the future.

Friends, in particular, are important to the adolescent as they provide her with emotional support as she begins the slow process of disengaging herself from the family and establishing an independent life. Although the adolescent spends as much time as she can with her friends, her parents remain an important source of influence on her and are often supportive of her, imparting to her their values and helping her make decisions about the future. However, given the fact that the adolescent is becoming increasingly independent, parents have to adjust somewhat in their expectations of her and in the way they discipline her. Some parents, unable to do so, resort to abuse and neglect.

Until the past few years, researchers and policymakers were unaware of the extent of adolescent abuse. It is becoming increasingly clear, however, that adolescents are not only being subjected to physical abuse, they are also neglected and isolated by their parents. Some adolescents who are mistreated at home run away; many of them become homeless. Others adopt a life of delinquency and crime. Numerous solutions have been proposed to help resolve some of the problems of youths and help stem the increase in the number of runaways, homeless, and delinquent youths. The most important of these solutions may be the support of family life not only during the adolescent years but throughout childhood as well.

REVIEW POINTS

1. During the adolescent years the individual begins the tasks of forming a personal identity and making decisions about future roles in life. Erik Erikson, whose theory has had an extensive influence on current views on adolescents, notes that the task of establishing an identity is not easy and entails a crisis wherein the adolescent struggles with the question of who she is and what she would like to be later in life. Although many adolescents resolve the crisis and eventually make a commitment to the kind of life they would like to lead, others may withdraw from any attempts to make such a commitment or they defer a resolution of the crisis to a later time.

2. The ease with which the individual establishes an identity and decides on an eventual role as an adult depends in part on societal factors. In our society, this task is difficult because there are so many and varied values and social roles from which an individual can choose. The adolescent must not only choose from these in light of what she wants to do and is capable of doing, she must also consider what choices are open to her as these vary according to the individual's social class, ethnic background, and sex.

3. Many youths today are unable to define their place in society and acquire a vocational identity because of the continually high rates of unemployment which have had a devastating impact on youths who are seeking full-time work. Not only today but in the past as well, economic conditions have had an impact on youths during the critical period of identity formation. This is noted by Glen Elder who analyzed data available on individuals who as adolescents grew up in the Depression era. He found that because of the economic difficulties they and their families encountered, these adolescents came to value the responsibilities of parenthood and to consider children and family support as important in times of need.

4. Current economic conditions seem to account in part for the conservatism of young people today and the fact that unlike adolescents of the 1960s and early 1970s, they value education and family life. The economy, however, is only one aspect of social change that significantly influences identity formation during adolescence. Our society has also experienced a sexual revolution, with the result that teens and adults alike are changing their conceptions of traditional sex roles as well as their sexual behavior.

5. Besides societal factors, peers play an influential role in the individual's identity formation. During different phases of adolescence, peers serve different needs. At the beginning of the period, the adolescent values her friends because of the activities they can engage in together. Slightly later, she values friends for the security and emotional support they provide as she attempts to deal with some of the concerns of growing up. At the end of the adolescent period, the teen values the individuality of friends, and she chooses them on the basis of their personality. Boys as well as girls change during the three stages of adolescence in their conceptions of friendship and what they value in a friend, but boys do so at a different age than girls. Also, boys are not so dependent on the security of friendship as are girls.

6. Changes also occur in peer groups. At the beginning of the period adolescents spend their time in single-sex cliques of about 5 members. Over the course of the adolescent period, these cliques merge and adolescent boys and girls spend most of their time in a crowd of about 20. During early adulthood, however, they are no longer comfortable in a crowd and function instead in groups of couples.

7. Although adolescents spend an increasing amount of time with peers, they value the advice and guidance that their parents offer them. They are influenced by their parents to a greater degree than they are influenced by their peers, at least when they are considering important issues such as future goals and educational and vocational plans.

8. There are often disagreements between parents and teens, and parents in particular have to change in the way they interact with their adolescent. Some parents are unable to adjust to the changes of being the parents of an adolescent; at times they resort to physical and emotional abuse. Although in the past researchers paid attention only to the abuse and neglect of infants and young children, it is becoming apparent that the problem of adolescent abuse is more pervasive than was previously realized.

9. Adolescent maltreatment is at the root of many adolescent problems, and it often leads to the problems of runaway, homeless, and delinquent youths.

10. Having examined these and other problems of youths, including unemployment, drug and alcohol abuse, teenage pregnancy, and teenage suicide, policymakers, educators, and other experts have pointed to a need to foster connections between all institutions that serve adolescents— between the home and the school, and between the school and the workplace. While such recommendations may indeed benefit teens, it is recognized that many of the problems of youths do not begin in adolescence; they are rooted in their experiences as children. Thus, any efforts to help teens should also include a focus on the childhood years.

Atypical Development in Adolescence

SCHIZOPHRENIA

A disorder that does not emerge until adolescence or the early adult years is schizophrenia. Schizophrenia is a psychiatric illness characterized by serious loss of contact with reality and a marked deterioration in the individual's ability to function.

Symptoms of the Schizophrenic Adolescent

The term *schizophrenia* means, literally, "split mind." However, contrary to popular misconception, individuals who are diagnosed as schizophrenic do not have a "split personality," which is a psychiatric disorder that is distinct from schizophrenia. Rather, they suffer from delusions, hallucinations, or severe disordering of their thought processes so that they are unable to think straight and they evidence bizarre behaviors. There are several types of schizophrenia; all have similar features and symptoms; and each is diagnosed on the basis of which symptoms predominate. These symptoms include deep apathy and the inability to muster an interest in the social world, as well as paranoia, delusions of persecution or grandeur, and hallucinations. Typically, the hallucinations of the schizophrenic are auditory rather than visual—the individual hears voices of people whom he believes are attempting to control or harm him or who are divulging to him certain information to which no one else is privy.

In his discussion of some of the symptoms of schizophrenia, Maxmen (1985) describes schizophrenic adolescents who are convinced that a noted politician or well-known news reporter is conspiring to kill them, and those who believe that their thoughts are being monitored by a listening device inserted into their brain by the telephone company or the FBI. Some adolescent schizophrenics believe that messages are being relayed to them or that they are being controlled in some way via radio waves, television, or the print media. It is not unusual, therefore, for schizophrenic adolescents to destroy such communicating devices that they encounter, or to cover their television set with foil or order everyone in their home not to tune into radio or television or read the newspapers. At times schizophrenic individuals evidence their paranoia in these ways, but at other times they may evidence feelings of superiority, believing themselves to be talented in some way and destined to great fame. Ekstein (1973) describes such delusions of grandeur in one of his adolescent patients who was at times vulnerable to paranoia and at other times saw himself as a "famous musician ready for Carnegie Hall," or as a "political world leader ready for a rich and powerful life, and a great success."

Besides the auditory hallucinations and delusions associated with schizophrenia, the disorder is characterized by incoherent thought processes. This is evident in the senseless and illogical speech of schizophrenic individuals who at times speak in sentences which are meaningless and hard to follow, conveying nothing more than a series of disconnected thoughts. Some schizophrenics may also develop *abnormal affect*. For example, they may laugh or giggle continuously for no apparent reason or inappropriately for the occasion (say, at a funeral). Or, they may display no emotion at all but describe any event, whether sad, tragic, or joyous, without any expression in their voice, as if nothing had happened.

abnormal affect

The schizophrenic at times experiences brief episodes of relief from the symptoms of schizophrenia. During these periods the schizophrenic appears to be relatively normal. Still, most of the time the schizophrenic's behavior is so bizarre that he becomes increasingly distant and remote to outsiders. Thus, he gradually retreats into the self, dwelling on his own thoughts and becoming socially isolated and mistrustful of people. Often he believes that everyone is "out to get" him (Maxmen, 1985). However, the schizophrenic individual may be aware of his own bizarre behavior and may be desperately trying to change. That there may be an enormous inner struggle within the schizophrenic individual is evident in the writing of one schizophrenic young woman who wrote that

> the most wearing aspect of schizophrenia is the fierce battle that goes on inside the [schizophrenic's] head in which conflicts become irresolvable. . . . I feel like I am trapped inside my head, banging against its walls, trying desperately to escape while my lips can utter only nonsense (Sheehan, 1982).

This same young schizophrenic woman also described some of the hallucinations she experienced. "Recently," she writes, "my mind played tricks on me, creating people inside my head. . . . They surround me in rooms, hide behind trees, and haunt me and devise plans to break me." She goes on to describe some of the other symptoms of schizophrenia, as well as her desire, but total inability, to establish any level of trust even with the people with whom she is familiar. Her only sense of peace, and of feeling good, she confides, comes with the brief episodes of relief from these symptoms, "even if for just a short time."

Causes of Schizophrenia

What causes such disabling disturbances in thought and behavior? Researchers and clinicians are not sure of the answer to this question, noting that schizophrenia is perhaps the most baffling of all mental disorders. Although the etiology of schizophrenia remains a mystery, some advances have been made in our understanding of the disorder. For example, whereas in the past schizophrenia was thought to be the result of dysfunctions in the family and of pathological interactions between the individual and his parents, today this explanation has been dismissed as a myth, giving way to a biological explanation of the disorder. In their discussion of studies that point to biological factors implicated in the etiology of schizophrenia, Schowalter and Anyan (1979) note that there is strong evidence that the tendency to become schizophrenic is inherited. This is established on the basis of studies which reveal that although schizophrenia may occur in 1% of the general population, it occurs in 12% of children who have one schizophrenic parent and in 35 to 44% of the children whose parents are both schizophrenic. However, it is not so much the disease itself that is inherited as it is the vulnerability to the disease, since even in identical twins, schizophrenia may be present in one but not the other. For individuals who have inherited a great vulnerability to schizophrenia, then even mild environmental stress can trigger the disorder. For those who inherited only some vulnerability, much greater stress is required to produce the condition (Zubin & Spring, 1977).

Besides the genetic link associated with schizophrenia, it has been discovered that the brain chemistry of schizophrenic adolescents differs from that of normal adolescents, especially in how the brain handles dopamine. Dopamine, one of the chemicals that transmits signals in the brain, is present in excessive amounts among schizophrenics. Hence, schizophrenics who are treated with drugs that block the action of dopamine seem to respond to the treatment. In addition, recent studies that use scanning instruments have shown that schizophrenic individuals often have an enlarged cavity in the interior of the brain, as well as other abnormalities such as unusual electrical impulses or decreased blood flow in the brain (Shapiro, 1981). Although these findings clearly point to the biological nature of the disorder, at this writing, researchers do not know precisely what role biological factors play in causing schizophrenia.

Treatment and Diagnosis of Schizophrenia

At this time researchers have not found a cure for the disorder. However, a major breakthrough in the treatment of schizophrenia occurred about thirty years ago with the discovery of antipsychotic drugs. These drugs are useful in controlling some of the bizarre behaviors associated with schizophrenia, enabling patients to become somewhat receptive to other treatment approaches such as psychotherapy. Despite their apparent usefulness, there are several limitations to the drugs. First, they are associated with some side effects such as involuntary movements of the mouth and arms or other motor dysfunction, so that schizophrenic individuals often refuse to be treated with them. Second, the drugs are effective in controlling the symptoms of some but not all schizophrenics. Even in cases where they are effective, the drugs do not prevent the symptoms from occurring, they merely reduce their frequency. For this reason, drug therapy is recommended only as one aspect of an overall treatment plan which includes other therapeutic approaches, some of which hold the promise of being effective. In one such effective treatment approach, schizophrenic individuals participate in a residential program where they are provided with help in managing everyday problems and stresses and where they are taught basic social skills which will eventually enable them to establish friendships.

Although some treatments focus only on the adolescent schizophrenic, other approaches focus not only on the schizophrenic but on the family as well. The rationale for such approaches is that the parents and family members of the schizophrenic need support in their attempts to live with the schizophrenic and help in understanding some of the symptoms of schizophrenia and the nature and course of the disease (Torrey, 1983).

Indeed, living with a schizophrenic individual—one who is oblivious to his surroundings, who talks nonsense, or who may be relatively calm and normal one day and totally bizarre in his behavior the next day—can be a frightening ordeal. This is especially so in the cases of adolescents in whom a diagnosis of the disorder has not yet been made, so the family may not know what is happening to the individual. However, a diagnosis of schizophrenia is not easily made, in part because the psychotic behavior associated with it can occur among youths who are not schizophrenic but who use hallucinogenic drugs (Schowalter & Anyan, 1979). With so many teens using drugs, it is not surprising that any bizarre behavior among adolescents is thought at first to be the result of drugs.

Schizophrenia is difficult to diagnose also because it is first noticeable in individuals between the ages of 15 and 24. (In boys, the onset of the disease is likely to occur during adolescence; in girls, during the mid-twenties.) In the past, schizophrenia was known as *dementia praecox,* a Latin term meaning a mental deterioration occurring in youth. However, although the onset of the disorder is at times spontaneous, most often there is only a gradual deterioration in the individual's behavior, so that relatives and friends may notice that the individual is more aloof than he had been, but they will tend to assume that this is a transient behavior problem. Such rationalization continues until such time as the schizophre-

dementia praecox

683

nia becomes so pronounced that it is obvious that there is something seriously wrong.

Although the onset of schizophrenia does not occur until adolescence, researchers have tried to determine whether some children are more likely to be diagnosed as schizophrenic during their adolescence than are others. As yet, no specific conclusions in this regard can be drawn. However, some of the preliminary findings may eventually shed light on the disorder. These findings reveal that adolescents who become schizophrenic are more likely to have been reclusive and antisocial in their behavior as children (Watts et al., 1970; Woerner et al., 1972); to have had few if any friends with whom to share common activities and interests (Kreisman, 1970); and to have behaved more aggressively than other children who did not become schizophrenic during adolescence. Furthermore, some researchers have found sex differences in the kinds of behavior that may precede the onset of schizophrenia. These researchers note that schizophrenic males tend to be described as irritable, aggressive, and defiant during their childhood years. Schizophrenic females are described as emotionally immature and passive during their childhood years (Watts, 1978). However, more firm data are needed before any conclusions can be drawn in this regard.

What is the outlook for the schizophrenic adolescent? Currently, no cure has been found for schizophrenia. However, it is known that some schizophrenics may suddenly overcome the disorder and suffer no relapses (Harding et al., 1986). This is especially true for those who had a sudden rather than a gradual onset of the disease, those who have had a history of good social adjustment, and those who experienced an emotional shock or an illness just prior to the onset of the disease. For those who remain mentally ill, the outlook is somewhat better than it has been in the past. In previous years most schizophrenics were hospitalized for the rest of their lives. Today, however, most schizophrenics are treated on an outpatient basis, with clinicians noting that their chances of being helped are at least four times better today than they were at the turn of the century. They may not be totally cured of the disorder, but they may be assisted in their ability to function relatively normally. Schowalter and Anyan (1979) point out that the family and proper medication both play a major role in the schizophrenic adolescent's chances for rehabilitation: ". . . If the family is supportive and willing to follow up good professional advice, to look after the patient as much as possible, and to help make sure that he or she takes prescribed medication, the prospects are improved."

CONCLUSION

CHILD DEVELOPMENT
AND
THE LIFE CYCLE

In this book we have discussed some of what is currently known about the growth and development of children. We began with an overview of current and historical trends in the study of developmental psychology and we went on to trace the wondrous journey of life from the time of conception to the time the individual reaches the end of adolescence and is ready to live life as an adult.

Our focus has been on the study of the growth and development of children and adolescents. However, we do not want to leave you with the impression that psychological development stops at age 18. On the contrary, throughout their lives people not only experience the physiological changes associated with increasing age, they also undergo many changes as the result of the events they experience and problems they encounter. They change in their perceptions and expectations of themselves and of others and in their relationships with one another. The adult years of life are in fact dynamic and ever-changing. During adulthood, individuals often reappraise their past and plan their future, they make numerous decisions that affect their lives and the lives of other people, and they also ". . . control the political and economic power of society. They produce and reproduce, and they reach the apex of their abilities. They achieve success, they fail, and they grow old" (Kimmel, 1980).

In the limited space of this chapter, and because this book is about child development, we can present only a brief glimpse of what is known about the developmental changes associated with adulthood and aging. You will see, however, that the study of adult development and old age enhances our understanding of psychological development and the cycle of human life from conception to death, and it provides the opportunity to think about the growth and development of children in the context of their social reality. Children, after all, do not grow up in isolation. Rather, they are reared in the context of other developing people who influence them and who are influenced by them.

ADULTHOOD AND AGING

The study of adulthood and aging and the perception of its relevance to the field of developmental psychology are relatively recent (Baltes, 1979; Bronfenbrenner, 1977). With the exception of a few developmental psychologists (e.g., Hollingworth, 1927; Pressey, Janney, & Kuhlen, 1939), most researchers once considered psychological development to be complete by the end of adolescence. They believed that not much change occurs between early adulthood and old age, so they had little interest in the study of these years of the lifespan. As Zigler (1963) explains, even among researchers who recognized that developmental psychology is concerned with the study of change in behavior as this occurs at any age, there was more interest in the study of childhood and adolescence in part because these periods, more so than other periods of life, are "characterized by continuous and striking change."

The view that there is not much change during the adult years and the lack of interest in the study of adulthood may have existed, in part, because adult life in earlier generations was as a rule predictable. Most people did not deviate very much from the life course they had chosen for themselves in their late teens and early twenties. Since the 1960s, however, major changes in society such as the sexual revolution and the women's liberation movement, as well as changes in the economy, have opened up new possibilities for change during the adult years. Men and women now have different experiences as well as different expectations of themselves than did their counterparts of two or three decades ago. It is no longer uncommon for individuals to change careers, jobs, and/or marriage partners not only once, but, for some, several times during adulthood and even in old age. Nor is it unusual today for individuals to experiment with various lifestyles, to begin higher education during middle or old age, or to alter plans in pursuit of a changed life (Sheehy, 1981). Once adulthood became more open to these and other possibilities for change, developmental psychologists began to be interested in the study of the lives of adults, and they have become increasingly aware of the fact that people do indeed continue to grow, change, and develop beyond adolescence.

Research on Adulthood

Researchers have found, for instance, that seemingly ordinary events such as marriage and parenthood function to influence people's perceptions of themselves, and they are now seeking to understand some of the ways in which individuals cope with adult life and how adult behavior is culturally conditioned (Brim, 1976). Developmental psychologists who study the adult years of life face an exciting road ahead as they attempt to develop research and analytic procedures that will make the study of adulthood as common and productive as the study of childhood. Many of the researchers also recognize that although adulthood should not be conceived as simply a continuation of the growth and development that occur during childhood (Kimmel, 1980), there is a relevance between the two fields of study (Bronfenbrenner, 1977), and that, "indeed, the greatest need may be to relate the two" (Erikson, 1978). Researchers have not yet specified all of the possibilities inherent in linking the study of children and the study of adults. Some are suggesting that a lifespan perspective which takes into consideration not only the development of children but the development of adults as well, not only serves to enhance our understanding of human life (Baltes, Reese, & Lipsitt, 1980), it may also provide a framework within which to conceptualize the research on child development (Lerner & Spanier, 1978, 1980; Goldberg & Deutsch, 1977; Bronfenbrenner, 1977). As Belsky, Lerner, and Spanier (1984) point out, "one cannot adequately understand the key features of child development unless the child is studied in the context in which he or she develops," and that context includes adults.

There are some researchers, however, who disagree with the idea that the study of adulthood can enhance our understanding of human life and the growth and development of children. T. G. R. Bower (1979), for example, notes that the study of adults is of no relevance to developmental psychology, which is a discipline that is primarily concerned with the study of biological and age-related changes in human behavior. He acknowledges that people do change after age 20 or so, but argues that these changes are for the most part cultural and are not genuine developmental changes as they do not result "from gene expression, nor are they age-linked, nor indeed are they universal." Any changes that occur during adulthood, according to Bower, "are at the most differentiated end of psychological functioning. As such, they are a continuation of the abstract accomplishments of the growth end of development."

Although Bower is right in saying that the changes of adulthood do not always result from gene expression, his views on adulthood seem rather narrow in light of some of the recent findings from the research. These findings have dispelled some of our myths about adult development and have shown that there are indeed changes during adulthood not only in the kinds of events individuals experience but also in such functions as intelligence. The research in this area is as yet inconclusive. It does appear, however, that adult intelligence does not exhibit universal decline as was once believed. Although there may be some mental abilities that inevitably decline, particularly during old age, adults may undergo improvements in their intellectual functioning as their experiences expand significantly and they learn to manipulate their environment better with age (Horn, 1970, 1978; Arlin, 1975; Labouvie-Vief, 1977, 1980; Baltes, Reese, & Lipsitt, 1980).

Developmental Milestones

The research on adult development has also shown that there are several developmental milestones that are reached during adult life. These milestones, or life events, are different in kind from the milestones of the childhood years, but they suggest that there is an orderly developmental progression through the entire life cycle:

> Certainly there is a qualitative difference between the milestones in child development (such as weaning, walking, talking, and toilet training) and the milestones of adulthood (such as marriage and widowhood). Yet in both cases the milestones suggest a sequential order to the lifespan and

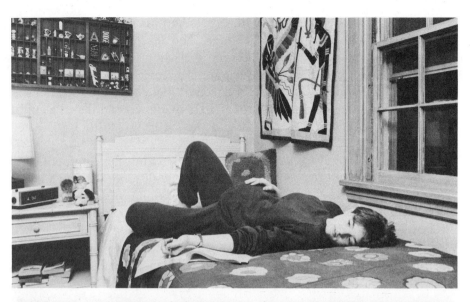

The timing of life events is critical to their impact on an individual. Obviously, the teenage girl will experience motherhood very differently than the more mature and financially secure 35-year-old woman.

[they] bring changes in a wide range of experiences that have effects on such important psychological characteristics as personality and the self-concept (Kimmel, 1974).

Researchers emphasize, however, that although there is an orderly progression through the life cycle, age in itself is not as important in understanding the development of adults as it is in understanding the development of children. This is because the developmental milestones of childhood, such as learning to walk and to talk, which have major effects on the individual's interactions with others and his or her perception of the self, occur within a specific age range. The developmental milestones of adulthood—getting married, becoming a parent or grandparent, and retiring, to name just a few—also trigger changes within the individual, but they are not all universally experienced or there are wide variations in the ages during which these milestones are experienced, so that the application of a chronological framework to the study of adulthood is often inappropriate.

While age is not always a good predictor of adult development, it is not entirely irrelevant to our understanding of adulthood. Having a baby, for example, is a significant life event, but the timing of that event in the individual's lifespan is critical to its impact on the person (Hultsch & Deutsch, 1981). A 15-year-old mother, for example, with no educational background and little, if any, means of support, will experience motherhood in a substantially different way than will a 35-year-old woman with a career behind her and supportive family life ahead of her.

The Social Clock

Many of the milestones that mark one's progress through the life cycle are expected to occur within a specific age range. Neugarten (1968) refers to this phenomenon as the *social clock,* noting that every culture has a sense of social timing or chronological standards for appropriate social behaviors. That is, individuals are expected to choose a vocation at a certain age, get married at another, and shortly afterwards have children. These expectations, according to Neugarten, operate as prods or brakes upon behavior. Individuals are very much aware of whether they are early, late, or on time with regard to many of their experiences so that they gauge their progress through life according to whether or not they have fulfilled the expectations of the society in which they live.

The social clock, or appropriate time for family and occupational events, varies from culture to culture and within cultures (Kuhlen, 1968), and it changes with time. Not long ago, for example, girls were expected to marry at an early age, and many of them felt painfully aware of their impending spinsterhood if they were not married by age 26. Today, many women regard even the mid- or late-twenties as too early for marriage, and there are many who choose to remain single or childless, feeling that for them, marriage or parenthood would present constraints (Faux, 1984). Similarly, two decades ago most men and women pursued college education or vocational training only during their early adulthood, often prior to marriage. Today, a "typical" college or vocational school student may be a mother who resumes her education when her children begin school or when they are in high school or college. There are older individuals, some in their eighties, who are beginning or continuing a formal education. You can see, then, that the social clock has been reset so to speak and

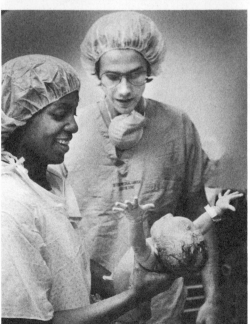

The research on lifespan developmental psychology has shown that there are several milestones, or life events, that are reached during adulthood, each of which has an impact on the individual's psychological characteristics, personality, and self-concept.

Although even two decades ago most people pursued college education or other preparation for a career only in their late teens and in early adulthood, today there are many who feel that they can attend college or begin a career at any time in life.

that people are no longer as preoccupied with experiencing life events "on time." This is true of older individuals, many of whom are healthy and feel they should not be forced into retirement (Sheppard, 1976), and it is true of those young people who choose to delay childbearing. Indeed, for many couples it is no longer the social clock that is ticking with regard to some major life decisions, but the biological clock. As women in particular approach the age of 35 or 40, they realize that they can no longer afford to remain undecided about whether or not to have children, because by waiting they may forego their option altogether. In spite of this, the age range within which women may look forward to having a first child has broadened considerably from what it has been previously.

THE LIFE COURSE

Erikson's Theory

Acknowledging that developmental milestones can be experienced at any time in life and that there are individual differences among adults, researchers nonetheless note that there is an underlying structure to adulthood and a sequence of periods—young adulthood, middle adulthood, and old age—during which individuals experience change. This point is made by Erik Erikson. Recall that Erikson (1963) describes psychosocial development in terms of eight "crises" or stages from birth through old age. The fifth stage, *identity versus role confusion*, occurs during adolescence (see Chapter 15) and if resolved, it is followed by three stages of psychosocial development that occur during the adult years: *intimacy versus isolation; generativity versus stagnation;* and *integrity versus despair.*

These stages, which correspond to young adulthood, the middle years of life, and old age, are built upon the earlier stages of childhood. They represent some of the new challenges and central issues or concerns that are faced by individuals during the adult years of their lives. Thus, the sixth stage of psychosocial development, intimacy versus isolation, occurs during early adulthood and is characterized by the individual's need to establish intimate relationships with others and acquire from these an awareness of the value of love. Such intimate relationships may include sexual intimacies, but these are only one facet of a relationship, which also includes friendship, deep caring for another individual, and the appreciation of that individual's uniqueness.

Young adults may feel isolated and lonely at times, but, according to Erikson, most eventually resolve the crisis of this stage. That is, they establish intimate relationships and find someone for whom they care and whose uniqueness they cherish. For individuals to be able to do so, however, they must have a stable sense of their own identity and uniqueness, for without this sense of self they will not be able to appreciate the unique identity of others or care deeply for them, and they will experience instead a sense of isolation and loneliness.

This stage is followed by the seventh and longest stage of psychological development, generativity versus stagnation, which encompasses the years between early adulthood and old age. This stage is characterized by individuals' need to create something which will outlive them. Individuals usually achieve this by bearing and raising children and/or by working toward occupational achievements. The resolution of this crisis results in a sense of productivity, a feeling of having created something that will have a positive effect on people, and the ability to have concern and to care for what one has created. Failure to resolve the crisis, however, results in a sense of stagnation, a feeling of boredom and dissatisfaction with life, and perhaps even preoccupation with oneself.

The final stage of psychosocial development, integrity versus despair, occurs late in life as individuals become aware of the finality of life and of their closeness to death. The task of individuals during this stage is to evaluate their life accomplishments and experiences and arrive at the conclusion that life has been meaningful and productive. Thus, the resolution of this crisis is dependent in part on the previous stages, or crises, of development. If the individual looks back upon and evaluates his or her past and concludes that life has been a meaningful adventure, the individual acquires a sense of integrity and satisfaction with life, and he or she is

Several researchers have become interested in recent years in charting the course of love and have shed some light on this relatively unexplored area. One of these researchers is Robert Sternberg. Having studied relationships that had lasted just one month and some which have lasted as long as 36 years, he was able to identify three elements—passion, intimacy, and commitment—which are the basic components of love, each of which becomes important to couples as time goes on. Passion, for example, is the quickest to develop and also the quickest to fade, while intimacy develops more slowly, and commitment more slowly still. According to Sternberg, couples cannot count on any of these elements because they need to continually work at the relationship. Sternberg, R. J. (1986). A triangular view of love. **Psychological Review, 93, 119–135.**

ready to accept inevitable death. If, on the other hand, the individual feels that life has been meaningless or disappointing, he or she acquires a sense of despair and faces death with a feeling of bitterness that life has been wasted and sorrow at not having another chance at life (see table).

Erikson points out that these three stages of psychosocial development are not brought about simply by becoming older, as developmental change is the outcome of individuals' adaptation to the varied circum-

Erikson's crises of adulthood and old age.

Stage 6	*Intimacy vs. Isolation—Young Adulthood* Once he develops a sense of personal identity and is comfortable with it, the individual can begin to establish intimate relationships with other people. Forming close relationships and committing himself to another person, the individual feels gratified. However, intimate relationships are also fraught with dangers. The individual can be rejected, or the relationship may fail through disagreement, disappointment, or hostility. Individuals who focus on the negative possibilities of intimate relationships may be tempted not to take a chance on becoming close to another person and instead withdraw from social contact, thereby becoming isolated, or establishing only superficial relationships.
Stage 7	*Generativity vs. Stagnation—Middle Age* Erikson regards generativity as emanating from marriage, parenthood, and a sense of working productively and creatively. Having a sense of accomplishment in adult life means giving loving care to others and regarding one's contributions to society as valuable. Working, getting married, and bearing and rearing children in and of themselves are not sufficient to give an individual a sense of generativity. The individual must also enjoy his work and his family. An individual who does not enjoy his work and who cares little for other people acquires a sense of stagnation, a sense that he is going nowhere and is doing nothing important.
Stage 8	*Integrity vs. Despair—Old Age* Toward the end of life, the individual reflects on his past accomplishments and the kind of person he has been. He looks back on life either with a sense of integrity and satisfaction or with despair. If earlier crises have been successfully met, the individual realizes that his life has had meaning, and he is ready to face death. If earlier crises have not been resolved successfully, the individual has a feeling of despair as he realizes that he has no time now to start another life and try out alternate roads to integrity. Individuals who have a sense of despair are not ready to face death, and they feel bitter about their life.

stances of their lives, and this occurs at different ages for different people. For many individuals the last stage of psychosocial development occurs during old age, toward life's end. However, this stage is triggered by the closeness of death rather than by age, so that it can occur at any time in life, as in the case of individuals who suffer from a terminal illness.

Other researchers who have studied adults have observed the stages described by Erikson (e.g., Vaillant, 1977). Some of them note that individuals may experience not only broad stages or periods in their adult lives, but transition stages as well. Levinson (1978), for example, studied a group of men from the middle and working classes and proposes that there are five eras within the lifespan: preadulthood (0–22); early adulthood (17–45); middle adulthood (40–65); late adulthood (60–85); and late late adulthood (80+). Within these five eras there is a series of developmental periods and transitions. During the stable periods of life, individu-

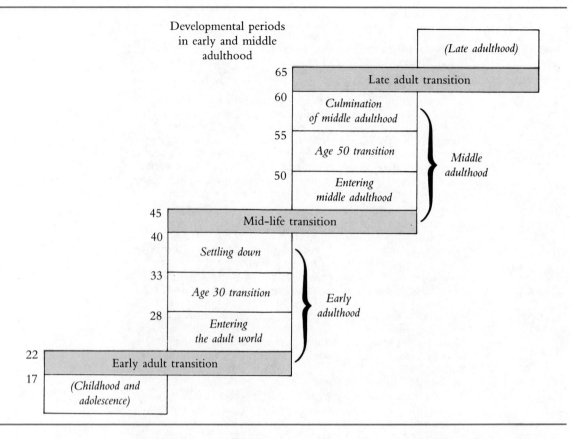

Levinson's stages of adulthood. Levinson, Daniel J. (1978). **The seasons of a man's life.** *New York: Knopf; p. 57. Copyright © 1978 by Daniel J. Levinson.*

als build a life structure by making certain choices and by striving toward the accomplishment of specific goals. During the transitions, individuals attempt to terminate their existing life structure and initiate a new one, so that they are engaged in reappraising previous choices and goals and moving toward making new ones. Within this sequence of periods and transitions, different life events tend to stand out at different points in the life cycle.

Early Adulthood

During early adulthood, which extends from the end of adolescence to age 40 to 45, individuals go through several different periods and transitions. In the earliest years of this period, from approximately age 18 to 23, individuals are in a transition, as their task is to forge an identity and the life structure of an adult. This involves modifying relationships with the family, with other people, and with major institutions of the preadult world such as the school, and exploring some of the choices that are available for adult life. Among the life events that individuals experience during this transition are graduation from high school, entrance into and graduation from college or beginning regular, full-time work, and moving out of the family home.

Between the ages of 22 and 30, individuals are in a relatively stable period, and they begin to make certain commitments to the kind of life they would like to lead. They decide on a job or a career path, they begin to date seriously, and some get married. However, the choices that people make during their twenties are provisional. Individuals often experience a certain amount of conflict. They are not entirely certain that they want to remain committed to the choices they have made, and feel that they should explore further.

Between the ages of about 28 to 33, individuals experience what Levinson terms the "age thirty transition." This transition gives individuals the opportunity to change the commitments to a life structure that they had made earlier. During this transition, individuals begin to realize that they must seriously reevaluate the choices they have made, as they may not be able to make a change at a later age. During this time, writes Levinson (1978) "[individuals realize that] life is becoming more serious, more 'for real.' A voice within the self says: If I am to change my life—if there are things in it I want to modify or exclude, or things missing I want to add—I must now make a start, for soon it will be too late." For some individuals, the age thirty transition is relatively smooth and entails adjusting to and building upon the life of the past. Some people, however, experience a crisis during this time in their lives, and they may divorce or make substantial occupational changes. Or, they may undertake further education as the means by which they seek to build a life which is more congruent with their dreams and desires.

Following this period, during their thirties, individuals settle down, making deeper commitments to their occupation and family life or to whatever else is of significance to them. There is a feeling among individuals during this period that they have to become successful. Such achievements as a promotion or a new job may be the goal for many. Moreover, individuals now become increasingly independent of their friends or mentors who influenced or guided them in their twenties, and they are concerned with what Levinson terms "becoming one's own man."

Levinson's theory thus focuses not so much on particular life events as on life as it evolves, highlighting the life structure and the major events (marriage, divorce, work, etc.) as part of this organized whole. As such, his theory is a provocative view of adult development that enhances our understanding of the individual's participation in the world, his various roles in life, and his concerns and aspirations (Hultsch & Deutsch, 1981). However, Levinson's theory is rather limited, in part because it portrays adulthood as a series of stages. According to Neugarten (1979), describing adult life as a series of "discrete and neatly bound stages" may be a distortion, as it serves to obscure the fact that there are many developmental events which cannot be predicted by age alone. Furthermore, Levinson's theory is based on a study of a small group of men at a certain time in their lives. It remains to be shown that there is a universal sequence of adult development for men and whether women experience a similar or a different sequence. Typically, however, young adulthood is considered, for both men and women, to be a time during which individuals embark upon a career, date, perhaps fall in love, make a commitment to a relationship with another person, and begin a family. Men and women, however, may have different concerns during early adulthood. Notman (1980), for example, found that although some women experience an age thirty transition "crisis" just as some men do, their conflict is centered primarily on work and family life. That is, they struggle between making a commitment to a career or to marriage and parenthood. This conflict, which is not experienced by men, most of whom have been socialized to expect to have a career as well as a family, is not necessarily over once a decision has been made, say, to have children. Rather, for several years after a child or children are born, some women struggle with how much time they should or want to devote to their work, how much time they have for their family, and where their priorities are—with the career or with family life. That most women of previous generations did not have these concerns alerts us to the fact that cultural experiences have an effect on people's attitudes, values, and expectations, as well as on the kinds of concerns that they may experience during their adult life (Elder, 1977, 1980).

Middle Adulthood

You should also note that another limitation, not only of Levinson's work but of other theories and research studies on adulthood, is that they offer only a general description of adult development. They fail to give an indication of the ways in which not only sex differences, but also cultural, ethnic, and social class differences interact with the general developmental progression of adulthood (Kimmel, 1980; Hultsch & Deutsch, 1981). Thus, much of what is known about adulthood can best be described as a general description of the lives of some middle-class adults.

The Midlife Crisis

Although there are several limitations inherent in the study of adulthood, the research that has been done thus far does provide us with a useful outline for understanding the sequential progression of the human life cycle. The research also provides a glimpse of some of the ways in which people in the second half of life might be expected to differ from people in

Children and adults continue to change and develop throughout their lives and to be influenced by the people and the environments around them. A perspective that takes both childhood and adulthood into account as times of growth may add to our understanding of both periods.

the early years of adulthood, and of some of the crises that they may experience.

As they approach their forties, for instance, individuals are in what Levinson (1978) terms a midlife transition period. They reappraise their past and think about what they want their future to be like. Unlike other transitions, however, the midlife transition is characterized by individuals' awareness of the fact that they are aging. This is noted not only by Levinson but by other researchers as well, who found that during their early forties, people begin to think of themselves not in terms of how many years they have lived but in terms of how many years they have left to live (Neugarten, 1968). This is a major reorientation for many people who at this age wonder if they have fulfilled their aspirations and if they want to continue with the kind of life they had chosen for themselves at a younger age (Mann, 1980). As they reappraise their lives, people do not simply think in terms of their past successes and failures, although this is an important element of the process. Rather, they judge their past and evaluate their future prospects in terms of whether these are congruent with how they perceive themselves. Thus, the men in Levinson's (1978) study, for example, began to ask themselves at around the age of 40 to 45, such questions as: What have I done with my life? What do I get out of and give to my wife, my children, my friends? What do I get out of and give to my work? Most of the men became emotionally upset as they evaluated their present in light of past events and future prospects, and they experienced a crisis. Some of them realized that they had not and might never achieve that culminating event that they had set as a goal for themselves. Others who had realized their goal in life found out that the anticipation of the dream was more rewarding than its attainment, and many of them felt that perhaps they had focused on the wrong choices in life.

Did men in previous generations experience such a midlife crisis? The answer to this question is not known. Some researchers speculate that the problems associated with the middle age period are indeed ancient and are reflected in the myths and folktales of Western civilization (Datan, 1980). Others, however, portray the midlife crisis as a new phenomenon, suggesting that it is the outcome of recent social changes (Borland, 1978). Some researchers have even found that the mid-life crisis is relatively rare (Brim, 1976; Costa & McCrae, 1980). For example, although most of the men in Levinson's study (8 out of 10) experienced emotional upset, or a crisis, during this midlife transition, Vaillant (1977) found that during their early forties the men in his study reassessed their life experiences and the relationships that they had established in the past. A few of them became dissatisfied with their lives, but many others experienced renewed vigor and excitement, and they felt that life was vibrant and interesting and that their future held much promise.

Thus, a valid conclusion that may be drawn about midlife is that it is but one of the periods of the life cycle and, as such, it is characterized by changes and transitions. For some individuals, such changes may precipitate a crisis. For others, however, they do not. As Hultsch and Deutsch (1981) maintain, "The question 'Is there a midlife crisis or not?' is not the right one to ask. . . . [Rather,] attention should be focused on how various events which tend to occur in the middle years affect the individuals and on what role mediating variables play." During middle age, for example, individuals may be at a point in their lives and in their family's life cycle that is associated with an inordinate amount of stress. This stress may come from a number of sources. One example is the stress associated with having to take care of one's aging parents, or having to arrange for such care (Sussman, 1976). This may entail an increased awareness of life's decline and the inevitability of death, and also heavy financial expenses.

Parents and Children

Not only do middle-aged individuals face the possibility of incurring the expenses associated with the care of their aging parents, they may also incur increased financial responsibilities associated with the growth of their children, so that many of them feel "sandwiched" in between their obligations to their parents and those to their children. The cost of raising a child increases dramatically with the child's age. By adolescence, parents have to spend 140% more than they did when the child was young (U.S. Department of Agriculture, 1982). There are also tremendous and ever-escalating expenses associated with college education, and many parents who may want to send their child to college have to take out substantial loans in order to pay for these costs.

Besides being pressured by obligations to both their parents and children, middle-aged individuals experience changes in their relationship with their children and with each other. The children are no longer dependent on constant parental care. The parents now have much more time to themselves than they did when their children were young, so that they have to adjust to this time alone together and establish new ways of being together. Middle-aged parents must also come to terms with the fact that their children will leave home, if they have not done so already, and that they themselves will one day assume new roles in relation to their children, as in-laws and grandparents.

It has also been noted that middle-aged mothers in particular may experience what is called the *empty nest syndrome*—the depression and sense of loss and boredom that are experienced for a period of time after the children are grown and have left home. Whether most mothers in past generations actually experienced this syndrome is not known. Most mothers today, however, probably do not (Glenn, 1975). In a study of 160 middle-aged women, most of whom were full-time homemakers while their children were young, Lillian Rubin (1979) found that the empty nest

*empty nest
syndrome*

syndrome is, today at least, a myth. Only one of the subjects in her study suffered from the classical symptoms of the empty nest syndrome, and the rest of the women, in fact, experienced a sense of relief when their children left home. Many of them took that opportunity in their lives to embark on a career or an education. Rubin found that whereas most mothers felt good about themselves when their children left home, many fathers became depressed, possibly because, as Rubin notes, ". . . often, the father never had a lot of time for the kids in previous years; he didn't share as much as the mother in their development, and suddenly, they're gone."

Old Age

As they get older, individuals continue to experience changes in their lives and in their relationships with others around them, and they have to adapt to such life events as grandparenting, retirement, and loss of a spouse. During previous periods of their lives, individuals exercised a certain amount of choice regarding the kind of life they would like to lead and the life events they wanted to experience. During old age, however, individuals have less and less control over their roles in life. Consider the role of a grandparent, which we discuss in more depth later in this chapter. Some older individuals may not care whether or not they have grandchildren, while others yearn to have them. However, the decision is hardly up to them, as it is their children who decide whether or not to have children and when. In a similar vein, there are many older people who feel that they can be contributing members of the workforce and who want to work until such time as they are unable to. However, older individuals often do not have the luxury of making a choice between retiring or continuing to work, as public and private sector policies are such that standards set by society and not the individual dictate when it is time to retire. Thus, the transition to life as retirees is difficult for many people who feel that they have a lot to offer but they are made to feel bored and useless instead (Chown, 1977; Haynes, McMichael, & Tyroler, 1978).

In addition to having to adjust to some life events over which they have no control, older people have to contend with a number of myths regarding old age (Butler, 1975; Neugarten, 1985). One such myth is that with age individuals inevitably become senile. Senility is often confused with a slight memory loss that may occur with age and is often attributed to older individuals who are quite healthy. However, senility is a devastating and dehumanizing disease. It is not part of the normal process of aging and indeed, the vast majority of older people are not senile. Although the victims of senility are often old people, the disease may strike individuals of any age. There is no consensus among researchers as to the causes of the disease. However, it is believed to be the result of an inherited susceptibility to certain viruses, to be related to the autoimmune system, with a person's own antibodies attacking the cells of the brain, or perhaps the result of a combination of these and other factors (Arehart-Treichel, 1977).

Other myths regarding old age abound, including the myth that all older people are rendered useless by poor health. This myth may have its roots in our history, because earlier in this century many old people were looked down upon as worn out and dependent. Indeed, many were in poor health and dependent on their family or on charity, as there were no provisions for public support of individuals who could no longer work. During the past half-century, however, Social Security and other social welfare programs for the aged have enabled many older individuals of all socioeconomic classes to lead more dignified lives than they could have otherwise. Another important consideration is the advances in medicine that have helped to improve the health of many older people and lengthen their life expectancy.

This is not to imply that the elderly in today's society have no problems or needs that have to be met. On the contrary, there are many elderly individuals who have poor health, who suffer from malnutrition, and who are poor and socially isolated. This is especially true among some older women and elderly persons of minority groups. However, people are now realizing that there are many old people who lead vigorous and active lives and who enjoy good health. Bernice Neugarten (1985) makes this point, noting that there are individual differences among the elderly. Some may be frail, ill, or suffering from "poverty and all its attendant deprivations and vulnerabilities," but others are vigorous, active people who lead useful and independent lives. Thus, the negative stereotypes of old age are beginning to give way to a more realistic view that the elderly do not necessarily share a common set of circumstances and that old age in and of itself is not necessarily debilitating. Researchers also note that the biological aspects of old age do not occur in a vacuum. Rather, the sum of a person's life experiences and the social resources that he or she has available do much to determine how that person ages and how he or she feels about being old (Riley, 1978; Neugarten, 1985).

In fact, a new view of the elderly is emerging in this country. As a society we are becoming cognizant of the elderly as a valuable national resource, since many elderly individuals have the vitality to contribute to our lives as well as have many years of experience to bring to activities they participate in. The population of those who are age 65 and over in the United States is one of the largest in the world, and, at 25 million, it is continually growing not only in absolute numbers but also in proportion to the general population (Kovar & Drury, 1980). With the number of older individuals increasing, old people are gaining a viable political voice in society, ensuring that the elderly get the services that they need (National Council on Aging, 1981) and that the aged are recognized for their important contributions to the family and to society.

Many old people today can look forward to a vigorous and interesting period of old age. For some, however, old age brings loneliness, poverty, and despair.

Grandparenthood

Some of the contributions that older individuals can make are inherent in their role as grandparents. This does not mean that all older individuals are or should be conceived of as grandparents, or that they all enjoy the role. Indeed, some grandparents, particularly those who are relatively young, contend that although they are close to their families (Shanas, 1979), their greatest gratifications in life are not necessarily related to their role as grandparents but come instead from experiences outside the family (Troll, 1980, 1971). Nevertheless, the role of grandparent is a prevalent one in our society. Grandparenting, however, is one of the least understood familial roles, and researchers are only now beginning to ask such questions as: What is the meaning of grandparenthood for various generations? How does the grandparent role vary for different individuals? How do grandparents influence their grandchildren?

The answers to these questions are not yet entirely known. Researchers suggest that not only among social scientists, but in our society in general, the role of a grandparent is not clearly defined and that this is so particularly among middle-class families (Clavan, 1978). That is, kinship status is associated with the role of a grandparent, but there are few normative and clearly delineated rights and responsibilities that would help define the relationship between grandparents, their children, and their grandchildren. Thus, many grandparents feel that they must earn a place in the family life (Troll, 1971), and they engage in giving and helping behaviors toward their children and grandchildren, in return for some affection and attention (Robertson, 1977).

Although most grandparents eventually establish a comfortable relationship with the younger members of the family, problems can arise as in the cases of families of divorce. Do grandparents have a right to continue their relationship with their grandchildren beyond the divorce or must they relinquish their role with the breakup of the family? There are no guidelines that specify what happens to grandparents when a child of theirs divorces, so some have looked to the courts to determine whether they have rights as grandparents and whether they can be granted visitation days so that their relationship with their grandchildren is not terminated. You should note, however, that although divorce may result in the breakup of the relationship between grandchildren and grandparents, this is not always the case. In a recent survey, Cherlin and Furstenberg (1986) found that in some cases, divorce enhances the relationship between grandchildren and grandparents. This can occur with maternal grandparents in particular because on many occasions a divorced woman and her children sometimes have to move in with the grandparents who thus have more of an opportunity to get to know, interact with, and even discipline the children.

Grandparents and Grandchildren

Aware of the diffuse nature of the role of grandparent in our society and the unclear expectations associated with grandparenthood, researchers have sought to determine the kinds of relationships that are forged between grandparents and grandchildren and the different meanings of the relationship for different people. Within this context, Neugarten and Weinstein (1964) found that for some older people grandparenthood provided a sense of biological renewal and/or continuity, and it evoked within them the feeling that there is an extension to the self. For others, grandparenthood was a source of emotional self-fulfillment, as it evoked within them feelings of companionship and satisfaction from the development of a strong bond and a special relationship between an adult and child—a bond that was often missing in their interactions with their own children. These findings have been noted in more current studies (e.g., Robertson, 1977) and are reflected in statements by some grandparents who explain grandparenthood as one of the most rewarding of the roles they have had in life. "As a parent," recalls one grandmother, "I was always hurried and there was so much to worry about, buying the children clothes, sending them off to school, making sure we had enough money. It is only now, as a grandparent, that I have the time and the objectivity to really get to know and enjoy the vitality of children and their precious nuances and their ability to enjoy life" (Finn, 1985). This point is also made by several other grandparents, who emphasize the fact that being a grandparent is different from being a parent: "In some ways," notes one grandfather, "it is my job to spoil the kids when they are young, listen to them when they are older and do things for them that their parents do not have the time to do" (in Kornhaber & Woodward, 1981).

This special relationship between an adult and a child is also recognized by grandchildren who, as teens and young adults, feel a sense of responsibility toward their grandparents. Most of them state that they would have missed much had they not had grandparents while they were growing up (Robertson, 1976). Unfortunately, however, not all children are so lucky as to develop a close relationship with their grandparents; they see them only on formal visits or on holidays, and sometimes not even as frequently as that (Kornhaber & Woodward, 1981). When they do see and interact with their grandparents, they derive from such interactions not only a sense of their family history, but also a sense of security in the knowledge that their grandparents understand and love them.

Foster Grandparents

The affinity between a grandparent and a grandchild and the positive reciprocal influences that are inherent in the relationship between children

Many grandparents thrive in their relationship with grandchildren, noting that their role is to spoil their grandchildren when they are young, listen to them when they are older, and do things for them that their parents don't have time to do.

and older individuals have been harnessed by government and private agencies who have made provisions for foster grandparent programs. These programs typically bring together older people who are lonely or who need part-time work and children and teens who need help. Some such programs include older women who are paid to spend at least eight hours a week with young mothers whose babies were born prematurely or who have been identified by pediatricians as potential targets of abuse. Other programs team an older woman and a teenage mother who needs support in her attempts to take care of her baby, whereas still other programs send old people to help with learning disabled, physically handicapped, or retarded children (Bingham, 1985). These types of programs which capitalize on older individuals as valuable resources are important not only in terms of the benefits that are realized by the children and teens who are helped, they are also important in terms of the benefits realized by the older people, many of whom would be otherwise lonely and without a sense of purpose or direction in life. Relating the experiences of her first day in one such program, a 75-year-old woman said, "They took me to see the little boy. He was so darling. They call him a mongoloid, but I couldn't tell. The first thing he did was hug me. He squeezed my legs so tight, I thought I'd fall over. I knew it would be okay. We didn't talk much that day. We just sat and hugged. I felt warm all over." She continued to describe her work, noting that she now has five foster grandchildren. "I buy and do things for [them] and they are growing up real well. I feel so good now. . . . I am not empty inside" (in Hultsch & Deutsch, 1981).

Toward Life's End

Any efforts to enrich the lives of the aged are valuable, for these ensure that people lead productive and satisfying lives even toward the end of life. Of course, life does come to an end with death. It may seem odd that we include a discussion of death in a book about growth and development. Death, however, marks the end of development as we know it, and consideration of it can enhance our understanding and appreciation of human life. "The finality [of death]," as one researcher wrote, and the loss, pain, and sorrow that go with it, "need not diminish life, but could give it a new quality of fulfillment" (Pincus, 1974).

Most people avoid the subject of death, and many are sometimes even afraid to be near an old or dying person, fearing that they might also die if they get too close. During the past few years, however, significant strides have been made in our understanding of how people experience the approach of death, and researchers have shown that as people confront their own mortality and as they become aware of their fears of death, they gradually come to feel at ease with the notion that they will die. One of the researchers who is noted for bringing the subject of death to the attention of the public is Elisabeth Kübler-Ross (1969). Reminding us that death is not something that happens just to the elderly, but that it can occur at any time, Kübler-Ross has noted that sometimes death occurs unexpectedly, even for older individuals. However, there are times when people are aware of their impending death, and she discovered that for them there appears to be an orderly progression even to this final part of life.

Kübler-Ross has made this point on the basis of her studies of over 200 patients who were dying from terminal illness and who seemed to experience five emotional stages in confronting their impending death. Her work has been followed by a number of other researchers who have not found the same five stages of dying (e.g., Pattison, 1977) or who have noted that Kübler-Ross's research does not take into account the particular disease the individual is dying from, the treatment he or she receives, or the individual's age. All of these factors may result in different emotional reactions to death (Kalish, 1976, 1981). Nevertheless, her research does provide us with an insight into the emotions of those who are dying and their possible reactions to death. According to Kübler-Ross, the first such reaction is *denial,* as individuals refuse to accept the fact that they are dying. *Anger* follows, with the dying person becoming angry at the unfairness of death, feeling that it is happening all too soon. This anger is felt by older people as well as younger ones, and is often directed at people who are not dying, in particular, those who are yet relatively young and full of the promise of life. Kübler-Ross also found that many dying individuals become depressed in part because they are aware that they no longer have a future:

> The patient [who is dying] is in the process of losing everything and everybody he loves. If allowed to express his sorrow he will find final acceptance much easier, and he will be grateful to those who can sit with him during this stage without constantly telling him not to be sad.

After feeling anger and sadness, individuals go through a *bargaining* stage in which they bargain with God for a little more time, promising to do something in return or explaining that there are important reasons why they need more time. Eventually, however, some people are able to accept death, or they are too weak and tired to deny that they are dying or to become angry and depressed, and they feel that they have to rest before the long and unknown journey that is ahead. Throughout all these stages of dying, there are many dying people who maintain their hopes. They hope for some miracle of recovery, or perhaps a new drug, and some simply hope that they will experience a good death—a death that is neither prolonged nor painful.

For many people, however, dying is an unnecessarily long and painful process, in part because of medical advances which allow us to use extraordinary measures to prolong life, so that people are deprived of the opportunity of dying with dignity. This results in the prolonged suffering of the dying person as well as of those around him or her, and it often ends with the death of the individual in impersonal hospitals and among strangers (Smyser, 1982).

Noting that many medical attempts to prolong life, especially in the case of the terminally ill, can simply be described as needless torture, there are those who advocate *passive euthanasia,* which means inaction on the part of physicians so that a person is allowed to die as his or her condition dictates. There have also been attempts to enable individuals to experience the support of their family and friends while they are waiting to die, as old people in particular often fear dying alone more than they fear death itself (Ross, 1977). To this end, there are *hospices,* which are communities dedicated to promoting the well-being of dying people and their families. In hospices, people spend their remaining days in a friendly atmosphere that is not at all like a hospital. There the terminally ill receive medical care and also psychological support and individual attention, and they are allowed to have visitors whenever they want them. There are many who are critical of the hospice concept, arguing that choosing to go to a hospice might

passive euthanasia

hospices

indicate that a person is giving in to death too soon (Klagsburn, 1982). However, there are also many who value the psychological support that they and their families receive in the hospice as they mourn and prepare for the end of life. Obviously, there are individual preferences, and there are also many moral and other issues surrounding the questions: Should we attempt to prolong the life of those who are terminally ill? Should we let nature take its course and let those who are ill die without any medical intervention? However, few would find argument with the notion that in the very least, it is important to attend to the wishes of those who are dying and to let those who so desire end their lives in comfortable surroundings. Unfortunately, there are limited numbers of hospices in the United States, and they are available only to the affluent as neither Medicare nor other insurance currently pays for hospice care.

EPILOGUE: CHILDREN AND ADULTS

So far in this chapter we have discussed some of the theories and research that govern the study of adulthood, and we have shown that just as children grow up and are influenced by the people around them and by the community and society in which they live, so adulthood and old age do not occur in a vacuum. Rather, people grow toward psychological maturity in the context of social reality, and whether they lead lives that are enjoyable and productive is often determined not only by the choices they make, but also by the social support that they have available to them.

Our intent in this concluding chapter was threefold. First, to demonstrate that psychological development is a continuous process that does not end in adolescence, but occurs throughout the lifespan. Second, to encourage students to think of child development in the context of social reality. Since children grow up alongside adults and, often, old people as well, it may be interesting to consider such questions as: How do the life events of adulthood and old age affect children?

Finally, we intended to illustrate in this chapter that not only during the childhood and adolescent years, but throughout the cycle of human life, from conception to death, there is potential for growth and enrichment. There are times when individuals need support and when some form of intervention can serve to enhance the quality of their lives. The recent advances we have made in the research in child and adult development have enabled us to translate some of what we know into programs that address the needs of children and families. We have discussed some of these social programs throughout the book, including those that are geared toward intervention during the prenatal period so as to prevent physical and mental handicaps in children. We have also discussed programs that provide preschoolers from lower socioeconomic classes with a good start in life, programs that support adults in their role as parents, and

Families in the Year 2000

Any decisions regarding programs that are geared to enhance child and family life must be made on the basis of and in response to the needs of children and adults. Obviously, these needs change. We have made this point throughout the book, as we have shown that societal changes in the past 30 years—including the introduction of television to our lives, divorce, the women's movement, and recent economic decline—have significantly affected the lives of children and adolescents and their parents.

In trying to ascertain the future direction of programs for children and families, it is important to ask, what would society be like in the year 2000? The U.S. Department of Health and Human Services attempted to answer this question in a symposium on *Social Services in the Year 2000* (Federal Register, vol. 50, no. 171, September 4, 1985). Findings from the symposium were in part positive, as they suggested that our society may experience a period of good, overall economic growth. If this is so, perhaps there will be fewer financial pitfalls in attempts to enhance child and family life.

In terms of demographics, the findings from the symposium indicated that there will continue to be dramatic changes in the age group configuration of the population.

The number of children will decrease by the mid-1990s, and the number of the young old (people 65 to 74) will begin to decline. But the number of people 75 and over will continue to increase at a rapid pace.

Black, Hispanic, and Native American population growth rates will be substantially higher than the rest of the population, increasing their proportion of the total.

The maturing of the baby-boom generation will usher in a new family-oriented era, but both family and household structures will be more diverse than in the past. Female family heads will continue to increase, and blended families will be widespread. Over 60% of children born in the 1980s are expected to live with one parent for at least a year during their childhood, and 35% will live with a stepparent at some time. More than half of all children in married couple families are expected to have two employed parents.

Finally, the income of two-person elderly households will outpace those of other age groups. However, the elderly of minority groups and aged women who live alone will continue to experience extreme financial difficulties and will warrant our concern.

These are only some possibilities for the future that the Department of Health and Human Services is taking into consideration as they think about human services and programs in the year 2000. Can you think of the role that developmental psychologists and others who are concerned with child and family life may play in ensuring that the needs of children are met? Can you think of program funding or other issues that might arise given the expected changes in the ethnic and age group configurations of the population?

programs that bring together the elderly and the young. Some of these programs have been evaluated, others have yet to be proven effective. The need for any of these programs may change or diminish with time. You should also be aware of the fact that whereas in the past most of these programs were funded by government grants, in the future we may need to find other means of support. As Campbell (1969) says, our task is to be

> [an] experimenting society . . . one which will rigorously try out proposed solutions to recurrent problems, which will make hard-headed and multi-dimensional evaluations of the outcomes, and which will move on to try other alternatives when evaluation shows one reform to have been ineffective or harmful.

That this book focuses on the application of knowledge from the research to the solution of social problems is an indication that we are beginning to take on the characteristics of the "experimenting society" that Campbell refers to. We hope that you, the student of today, will continue with the task we began and ensure that ours continues to be a society which recognizes and responds to the changing needs of children and adults.

GLOSSARY

Italic type has been used to designate cross-references—that is, terms appearing in the text of a definition that are themselves defined in a separate entry.

accommodation   In Piaget's theory, an aspect of adaptation involving a change or expansion of one's cognitive view in response to new information from the environment.

acne   A skin problem due to bacterial infection under the skin, which leads to painful boils and potential scarring of the facial tissue. Although common among adolescents, acne can strike older individuals as well.

Action for Children's Television (ACT)   A group of parents who monitor television and try to change its impact on children.

adaptation   Principle of functioning that refers to the inherent tendency to adjust to the environment through the processes of assimilation and accommodation.

adenine   One of the four nitrogenous bases comprising the chemical bonds that link together the pair of intertwined coils within the *DNA* molecule. Adenine links only with thymine.

age of viability   The age at which fetal development is sufficiently advanced so that, if birth occurs, the baby will survive. The age of viability is estimated to be at the end of twenty-eight weeks after conception, but with medical advances, the age is periodically revised downward.

albinism   A hereditary condition characterized by white hair, pink eyes, and the absence of skin pigmentation. Albinism is transmitted by a recessive allele; it is therefore an observable characteristic only if the individual is homozygous for that trait.

alleles   The component parts of a gene. For any given gene, there are two alleles, one from the father and one from the mother.

altruistic behavior   A voluntary and intentional action that benefits another and is not motivated by a desire to gain approval or reward.

amniocentesis   A procedure to test for genetic abnormalities during pregnancy that involves taking a sample of the amniotic fluid by inserting a needle through the abdomen into the amniotic sac in the uterus. This test can be done only during the sixteenth week of pregnancy. Results are obtained in approximately three weeks.

amnion   The inner of the two membranes of the amniotic sac, which contains the amniotic fluid.

amniotic fluid   A liquid substance found within the amniotic sac that protects the embryo against physical shock and temperature change.

amniotic sac   A bag containing amniotic fluid in which the embryonic baby develops. It is formed by two membranes (the *chorion* and the *amnion*) that develop from cells on the outside of the fertilized egg.

androgens   A global term for the male sex hormones.

animism   The belief that inanimate objects are alive and endowed with intentions and feelings.

anorexia nervosa   A severe eating disorder found most frequently among adolescent girls that is characterized by self-induced starvation and may be accompanied by frequent purging activities. People with this disorder have a distorted body image and a tremendous fear of being fat.

anoxia   A condition that results in the birth of children who suffer a severe lack of oxygen. Anoxia often leads to a variety of motor defects subsumed under the general term *cerebral palsy*.

Apgar Scoring System A rating system used immediately after birth to assess the condition of the newborn infant.

apnea Temporary cessation of breathing.

areola The pigmented area around the breast nipple.

artificialism The childhood myth that holds that everything is made by someone.

assimilation In Piaget's theory, a term that refers to the incorporation of new information into preexisting schemes.

attachment The loving and enduring bond between the infant and the caregiver. Ainsworth has classified infants' attachments to primary caregivers into three types: secure, anxious, and avoidant.

attention deficit disorder (ADD) A recently developed diagnostic category that applies to a relatively common disorder among children characterized by *hyperactivity* (or *hypoactivity*) and an inability to concentrate or attend to specified tasks in an orderly manner; supercedes the labels "hyperactive syndrome" and "minimal brain dysfunction" to describe such children.

autonomy versus shame and doubt Erikson's second psychosocial crisis, occurring around age two, through which the toddler will acquire either a basically healthy attitude toward independence, or fear and shame, which inhibit a healthy sense of self-sufficiency.

autosomes The twenty-two pairs of chromosomes in each cell nucleus, possessed equally by the male and female, which determine traits other than the sex of the individual; the twenty-third chromosome pair determines gender.

autostimulation theory A theory that suggests that the high degree of REM sleep during the newborn period stimulates the development of the central nervous system.

axon Wirelike extension of nerve-cell cytoplasm that transmits outgoing messages from the cell.

birthing rooms Comfortable, homelike rooms where both labor and delivery take place, often to the sounds of soothing music and under dim lights.

black English A nonstandard dialect of English spoken by black children whose families are at a low socioeconomic level. It is governed by its own grammatical rules and should not be regarded as a simplified form of the standard dialect.

bone age (or **skeletal age**) The rate of an individual's bone ossification as compared with norms for his or her particular age; can be used as an assessment tool in predicting a skeletal feature such as eventual height.

bulimia A severe eating disorder found most frequently among adolescent girls that is characterized by enormous eating binges followed by self-induced vomiting.

canalization The process by which some kinds of behaviors follow a prescribed genetic course. The less canalized the behavior, the easier it is to modify; highly canalized behaviors are difficult to alter.

capacitation A process undergone by sperm that reach the outer end of the fallopian tube. As a result of capacitation, the successful sperm is able to dissolve the outer membrane surrounding the egg cell and penetrate into its center.

cell The smallest unit of living matter that is capable of independent functioning, made up of a *cell wall* containing *cytoplasm* and a *nucleus*. The human body is comprised of billions of cells, which have specialized functions.

cell wall The outer membrane of the cell, which contains fluid called the *cytoplasm*.

(to) center In Piaget's preoperational period, the tendency to focus on one aspect of a problem or situation and neglect other properties that must be taken into account in order to arrive at the correct solution.

central nervous system The bodily system comprised of the brain, brainstem, and spinal cord.

cephalocaudal Moving from head to toe; a principle governing physical growth.

cerebral palsy A general term used to describe a variety of motor defects (such as paralysis of the limbs, tremors of the face or fingers, inability to use the vocal muscles) caused by brain damage due to a severe lack of oxygen before or during birth.

childhood aphasia A type of learning disability that involves the inability to speak or to comprehend what is being said.

childhood social indicators Measures of changes or constancies in the conditions of children's lives as well as in the health, achievement, behavior, and well-being of children themselves.

child support The monetary payment made by the parent without custody of the child to the parent with custody.

cholinesterase An enzyme crucial for the transmission of neural impulses that is synthesized in the nervous system of the organism.

chorion The outer of the two membranes of the amniotic sac, which encloses the inner membrane (the *amnion*).

chorion biopsy A recently developed screening test for genetic abnormalities that can be conducted during the first month of pregnancy; it involves taking a sample of the chorion cells outside the fertilized egg for examination and biopsy, with results yielded within one day.

chromatin Long, tiny fibers, located within the nucleus of a cell, on which the genes are found.

chromosomes Name given to chromatin—the long, tiny fibers located in the nucleus of the cell—after it was found that these fibers take up stain very well and become highly visible under a microscope; from the Greek words "chromo" and "soma," meaning "color-body." There are forty-six chromosomes in a normal human cell, each chromosome holding thousands of genes.

classical conditioning A type of learning, demonstrated by Pavlov, whereby an individual can be taught or conditioned to make a specific response to a neutral stimulus after repeated pairings of that neutral stimulus with another stimulus that naturally elicited that specific response.

class inclusion An aspect of the concept of classification that refers to the ability to understand that there is a hierarchical relationship between subordinate and superordinate classes.

cloning A form of genetic engineering that involves asexual reproduction in which all offspring are identical.

cochlea The main hearing organ of the ear.

competence motivation A term referring to the child's intrinsic motivation to learn and understand the world.

concrete operations period According to Piaget, the third stage of cognitive development, from approximately age seven to twelve years, characterized by the ability to mentally manipulate tangible and concrete information according to logical rules.

conservation A concept that refers to the fact that certain characteristics of an object remain the same despite superficial changes in appearance.

continuum of caretaking casualty Refers to the notion that the extent to which the effects of a teratogen will be manifested is often determined by experiences after birth.

continuum of reproductive casualty The range of variations in the degree to which the influence of a specific teratogen will culminate in abnormalities in the child.

conventional level Kohlberg's second level of moral judgment, wherein morality is based on social rules and on living up to the expectations of the individual's family, group, or nation.

cretinism A syndrome caused by iodine deficiency in the mother that is characterized by mental retardation and dwarfing in the offspring.

critical periods Specific periods of time in

development during which environmental influences can play a crucial role in the extent to which an individual's genotype is expressed in his or her phenotype; times in the process of development during which the organism is especially sensitive to a particular influence.

crossing over   The random exchange of corresponding segments between pairs of chromosomes that may occur during meiosis.

cross-modal transfer of information   Process involving the exchange of information among the senses.

cystic fibrosis   A disorder of the exocrine glands transmitted as a recessive trait; the most common severe genetic disease of childhood in the United States.

cytoplasm   The fluid contained within the cell wall and outside the nucleus; that part of the cell where the instructions originated by the *DNA* in the nucleus are ultimately carried out.

cytosine   One of the four nitrogenous bases comprising the chemical bonds that link together the pair of intertwined coils within the *DNA* molecule. Cytosine links only with guanine.

decidua   The thickened lining of the uterus into which the zygote, or fertilized egg, implants itself.

deep structure   According to Chomsky, one of the two levels of the structure of language. It refers to the basic syntactical relationship between words.

dendrite   Wirelike extension of nerve-cell cytoplasm that receives incoming impulses to the cell.

DES (or **diethylstibestrol**)   A synthetic hormone, prescribed between the late 1940s and early 1960s to women in the United States who were at risk of having a miscarriage. It was found to cause delayed effects in female offspring, some of whom developed vaginal abnormalities and cervical cancer during maturity.

dishabituation   An observable phenomenon wherein interest in a familiar object will be reactivated if a comparable but slightly different object appears with it.

dizygotic twins (or **fraternal twins**)   A pair of individuals who develop simultaneously in the womb from two separate eggs.

DNA (or **deoxyribonucleic acid**)   The component of the chromosome that controls the biological inheritance of all living things through a genetic code that directs the production of protein within the body and contains instructions about how the organism is to develop. It consists of a pair of intertwined coils of indefinite length comprised of sugar phosphate molecules, the cells being linked together by chemical bonds derived from the four bases—adenine, thymine, cytosine, and guanine.

dominance   Refers to the relationship between alleles within the heterozygous gene. One allele will dominate over the other in determining the phenotype, or observable characteristic, associated with a particular trait.

double standard   The two different sets of rules or expectations for sexual behavior for men and women.

Down's syndrome   A disorder that is caused by a mutation involving the twenty-first chromosome, which results in mental retardation, abnormalities affecting internal organs, and distinctive physical features.

dyscalculia   A type of learning disability involving the inability to calculate numbers.

dyslexia   A type of learning disability that involves an impairment in the ability to read.

ectoderm   One of the three layers into which the inner mass of the *zygote* differentiates during the *period of the embryo*. From the ectoderm develop the hair, nails, part of the teeth, the outer layers of the skin, and skin glands as well as the nervous system and sensory cells.

ectomorph   A basic body type in which the

individual is tall, very thin, and often stoop-shouldered.

egocentrism   The belief that the world centers on one's own life, which is characteristic of the child in the preoperational period.

ejaculation   The discharge of seminal fluid containing sperm.

empathy   The capacity to experience another person's emotions vicariously.

empty-nest syndrome   A depression associated with a sense of loss felt when one's children have left home.

endoderm   One of the three layers into which the inner mass of the *zygote* differentiates during the *period of the embryo*. From the endoderm develop the gastrointestinal tract, trachea, bronchi, eustachian tubes, glands, and other organs such as the lungs, pancreas, and liver.

endomorph   A basic body type characterized by softness and roundness.

estrogen   The female sex hormone.

evolution   The process of change in life forms over time that is guided in a particular direction through natural selection and the survival of organisms whose genetic characteristics foster constructive adaptations to the environment.

finalism   The childhood myth that holds that everything has a purpose and every event is meant to accomplish some end.

fine motor   See *motor*.

foreclosure   Premature identity formation during adolescence, characterized by an uncritical and unquestioning acceptance of the values of one's family and society as one's own.

gametes   See *germ cells*.

gender identity   An aspect of the self-concept that refers to an individual's awareness and acceptance of being either male or female.

gender (sex) roles   Socially defined behaviors and attitudes associated with being a male or a female.

gene   The unit of transmission of hereditary material, which is located on the chro-

mosomes. Each chromosome holds thousands of genes, which are typically in pairs, one member of the pair contributed by the male and the other by the female. A gene can also be described as a complete chain of a multiple protein (a section of code from a start signal to a stop signal) along a *DNA* coil. See also *alleles*.

gene locus   The specific location of a particular gene on a chromosome, which is repeated on every chromosome of that type.

genetic engineering   A research activity that involves the manipulation of genes.

genotype   The total genetic makeup of the individual, which, in interaction with the environment, can produce a wide range of possible *phenotypes*.

germ cells (or **gametes**)   The reproductive cells—that is, the sperm and the ovum. Germ cells contain twenty-three chromosomes each, versus somatic, or body, cells, which contain forty-six chromosomes (twenty-three pairs) each.

germinal mutations   Changes in a gene, in the arrangements of the genes, or in the quantity of chromosomal material that affect the gametes.

glial cells   See *neuralgia*.

gross motor   See *motor*.

growth spurt   A period of rapid physical growth that occurs in puberty.

guanine   One of the four nitrogenous bases comprising the chemical bonds that link together the pair of intertwined coils within the DNA molecule. Guanine links only with cytosine.

habituation   Refers to the individual's lack of interest in or reaction to a particular stimulus because it has become familiar through repeated exposure.

hemophilia   A sex-linked recessive disease often referred to as the "bleeding disease" because its victims lack a certain factor necessary for blood clotting and thus bleed excessively, either spontaneously or from cuts and bruises.

heritability ratio A mathematical estimate of the proportion of trait variance having genetic causes. It is used in determining the relative importance of both heredity and the environment.

heterozygous Having a gene-pair composition of two alleles that give different hereditary directions for the determination of a particular trait. In this case, one allele will dominate over the other. See also *dominance, recessiveness*.

homozygous Having a gene-pair composition of two alleles that give the same hereditary direction for the determination of a particular trait.

horizontal décalage Piagetian term referring to the unevenness in children's understanding of concepts. For example, in conservation tasks, the child is first able to conserve number, then length, liquid quantity, and finally other properties of objects.

hostile aggression Aggression that is an attack against someone rather than something.

hyperactive syndrome See *attention deficit disorder*.

hyperactivity A type of attentional disorder involving the inability to settle down within structured situations that require concentrated attention to tasks.

hypoactivity A form of attentional disturbance, found more frequently in girls, characterized by less-than-normal activity levels and excessive daydreaming.

identification An unconscious mental process that results in the adoption of attitudes, behaviors, or values of another person as one's own.

identity diffusion An experience of a lack of consolidation of identity during adolescence, characterized by ambivalence or indifference about making decisions and a withdrawal of efforts to shape one's personal identity.

identity versus role confusion According to Erikson, the psychosocial crisis of adolescence that involves the struggle for a personal sense of identity.

industry versus inferiority Erikson's psychosocial crisis of middle childhood, during which time the child either gains increasing confidence in his or her sense of competence and industry or, conversely, manifests shrinking confidence in his or her abilities in comparison to others.

initiative versus guilt Erikson's third psychosocial crisis, occurring between ages three and six, during which the child will develop either an increasing sense of confidence in, and mastery of, his or her pursuit of activities or increasing feelings of inadequacy and a lack of pleasure in, and motivation toward, accomplishing tasks on his or her own.

instrumental aggression Aggression that involves fighting over objects in order to attain a desired goal.

intervillus space In the uterine environment, the space occupied by the villi, the fingerlike projections of the placenta, in which the vital exchange of substances and nutrients between the mother and the unborn baby occurs.

intrapair concordance The similarity between twins.

irreversibility According to Piaget, a principle governing preoperational thinking that refers to the child's inability to go forward and then backward in thinking, thus inhibiting the application of logical rules to solve problems or understand change.

juvenile delinquents A statutory designation for children aged sixteen and under who commit offenses that would be considered criminal if they were adults.

karyotype A pictorial arrangement of chromosomes within a cell that have been grouped in pairs according to length and that can be studied to detect gross abnormalities.

Klinefelter's syndrome A sex-chromosome abnormality in males characterized by an extra X chromosome (XXY instead of XY), which results in sterility, the development of many female characteristics, and a tendency to be very tall and slim.

language-acquisition device   According to Chomsky, a mental structure that enables infants to process sounds and patterns of speech and later triggers milestones of speech, including the capacity to understand the structure of language and the fundamental relationship between words.

latchkey children   A term coined to describe the large population of children who carry their house key on a chain around their neck (because they return home each day after school to a house without adult supervision).

learned helplessness   The belief that failure is not the result of one's own actions but rather is due to forces outside one's control.

learning disability   A learning problem that is not due to mental retardation, emotional disturbance, or lack of motivation but to specific disorders in the processing of verbal and written information.

mainstreaming   The educational practice of placing children with special needs alongside their normal peers in regular classrooms.

maturation   The orderly physiological changes that occur in all species over time and that appear to unfold according to a genetic blueprint.

meiosis   A form of cell division involved in the production of the gametes, or germ cells. In meiosis, each part of the chromosome pair migrates to opposite sides of the dividing nucleus, and the resultant cells then contain twenty-three single chromosomes (versus the twenty-three pairs within the somatic cells).

menarche   The first menstrual period.

mental operations   Mental manipulation of information, characteristic of Piaget's *concrete operations period*.

mesoderm   One of the three layers into which the inner mass of the zygote differentiates during the *period of the embryo*. From this layer develop the muscles, skeleton, excretory and circulatory systems, and inner skin layer.

mesomorph   A basic body type characterized by well-developed muscles, broad shoulders, and little or no evidence of excess body fat.

metalinguistic awareness   An intuitive understanding of how language works.

metamemory   An intuitive understanding of how memory works.

minimal brain dysfunction (MBD)   See *attention deficit disorder*.

mitosis   The process by which somatic (body) cells divide. It involves duplication of each of the forty-six chromosomes within the cell nucleus, resulting in two identical sets of forty-six chromosomes. The two sets of chromosomes then move to opposite sides of the cell, and the cell divides, to form two cells with identical chromosomes.

modifier genes   Genes that influence the actions or observable characteristics of other genes.

monozygotic twins (or **identical twins**)   A pair of individuals who develop simultaneously in the womb from a single fertilized egg and have identical genes.

Moro reflex   A reflex of infancy wherein the baby will throw its arms upward and clench its fingers in response to being suddenly dropped about six inches in midair.

motor   Term used to denote muscular movement. Gross motor involves the use of the large muscles; fine motor involves the use of the small muscles of the hands and fingers.

mutant genes   Genes that increase the rate of mutations in individuals who carry them.

mutation   Change in a gene, in the arrangement of the genes, or in the quantity of chromosomal material.

myelination   A maturational process of the nervous system during which nerve fibers become coated with myelin, a protective fatty sheath that facilitates the transmission of neural signals.

myelogenetic cycles   Periods during which

myelination occurs to particular functional centers within the brain.

natural childbirth   Childbirth in which the mother takes no medication during labor or takes it sparingly only at the final phase of delivery.

neuralgia (or **glial cells**)   Cells of the nervous system that feed and support the neurons.

neurons   Nerve cells.

new morbidity   Term encompassing a wide range of behavioral and psychosocial factors that threaten the health of children.

nondisjunction   An anomaly involving the twenty-first chromosome that is characterized by the presence of an extra chromosome, or part of a third chromosome, which leads to Down's syndrome. In this case, the individual will have forty-seven instead of the normal forty-six chromosomes.

nucleus   A special compact structure within the cell that contains genetic material as well as other structures that direct the manufacture and transport of substances within the cell.

object permanence   The cognitive capacity to understand that objects continue to exist even when one cannot see, touch, or smell them directly.

operant conditioning   A type of learning whereby an individual is conditioned to make a specific response as a result of being rewarded whenever that response is initiated.

operator gene   A type of gene that regulates protein synthesis in adjacent structural genes.

organization   According to Piaget, a principle of functioning that refers to the inherent tendency to organize experience by integrating two or more schemes into a more complex, higher-order scheme.

ossification   The formation of solid bone.

outcome evaluation   A type of social-policy evaluation that is used to assess the impact of a particular policy or program and determine whether it is beneficial.

overregularization   The application of general rules of language to all words, including cases where the correct word form represents an exception to the rules.

ovum   The unfertilized egg cell of the female; also known as a germ cell or gamete.

parity   The number of births a woman has had.

perception   The interpretation of sensory experience into coherent signals.

period of the embryo   One of three periods that comprise the development of the organism in utero. This period lasts from the time of the zygote's attachment to the uterine wall (at about two weeks) until the first occurrence of the formation of solid bone *(ossification)* in the embryo (at about the eighth week). The period is marked by differentiation of important organs and can be a hazardous time for the embryo, since most miscarriages—involving an estimated 30 percent of embryos—occur during this time.

period of the fetus   One of three periods that comprise the development of the organism in utero. This period lasts from the beginning of the third month until birth and is marked by rapid muscular and central nervous system development.

period of the ovum   One of three periods that comprise the development of the organism in utero. This period lasts approximately two weeks from the moment of conception. During this time, the zygote establishes itself in the uterine wall and begins a physiologically dependent relationship with the mother that will continue throughout pregnancy.

phenocopy   An individual whose gene expression has been environmentally altered so that it mimics the observable characteristic, or phenotype, that is usually associated with another specific genotype.

phenotype   The observable characteristic of an individual or organism resulting from the interaction of the environment and the *genotype.*

phenylketonuria (PKU) A hereditary condition caused by a recessive gene that leads to the absence of a certain enzyme needed to convert the protein phenylalanine, found in milk, into tyrosine, resulting in mental retardation.

phocomelia The most unusual and characteristic deformity in the offspring associated with thalidomide ingestion by the mother during early pregnancy. It takes the form of the absence of limbs, with the feet and hands attached to the torso like flippers.

physical fitness Term that refers to the optimal functioning of the heart, lungs, muscles, and blood vessels.

placenta An auxillary structure that develops during the embryo period and allows for the passage of substances from the maternal bloodstream to that of the fetus, forming the vital link between the mother and the unborn baby on which the life of the fetus depends; also known as the "afterbirth."

play Any pleasurable, spontaneous, and voluntary activity that is an end in itself and has no extrinsic goal (Garvey, 1977). Several types of play have been distinguished: solitary, parallel, associative, cooperative, and sociodramatic.

pleiotropy A single gene influencing more than one characteristic.

polygenetic Refers to a trait that has as its source a constellation of genes acting together.

population gene pool The collection of similar genetic characteristics in a particular part of the world or population.

postconventional level (or **autonomous level**) Kohlberg's highest level of moral judgment, wherein morality is based on individually chosen moral values and ethical principles that have validity and application.

preconventional level According to Kohlberg, the lowest level of moral judgment, wherein emphasis is placed on avoiding punishment and getting a reward.

preoperational period According to Piaget, the period of cognitive growth beginning in the latter part of the second year of life and continuing to age six or seven, characterized by the acquisition of a prelogical symbolic mode of thinking that is dominated by egocentrism.

preparedness See *canalization.*

process evaluation A type of evaluation that is used to verify whether, and under what circumstances, the services mandated by a policy are delivered and the manner in which a particular policy or program was implemented.

productive memory The process of remembering an event or stimulus experienced previously, without the reappearance of that event or stimulus.

proximodistal Moving from near to far; a principle governing physical growth.

puberty The period of rapid growth that culminates in sexual maturity and reproductive capability.

puberty rites Ceremonies that mark the individual's assumption of new, more adult roles.

range of reaction The array of possible variations in responsiveness that an individual will exhibit under different life experiences.

recessiveness Referring to the relationship between alleles within the heterozygous gene. The recessive allele is subordinated to the dominant one and will not be expressed in the phenotype; however, it continues to be transmitted and thus may reappear as an observable characteristic in successive generations.

reciprocal role learning A theory of sex-role development in girls based on research suggesting that their femininity is associated more strongly with the degree of masculinity of their fathers than with their mothers' femininity.

reciprocity In mental operations, the ability to recognize that a change in one feature of an object is balanced by an equal and opposite change in another feature of that object.

reflexes Specific, involuntary responses to stimuli.

regulator gene A type of gene that produces molecules that tell all genes when to turn on and off, thereby modifying the basic biochemical processes of the genes and resulting in individual differences.

rehearsal A memory-aiding technique involving mental or verbal repetition.

reversibility The ability to go back and forth mentally, to perform mental inversions, or to mentally "undo" a sequence of actions, a hallmark of Piaget's *concrete operations period*.

RNA (or **ribonucleic acid**) That component of the chromosome which serves as a messenger to carry the directions, originated by the *DNA*, from the nucleus of the cell to its cytoplasm.

role-taking (or **perspective-taking**) A cognitive skill that refers to the individual's ability to understand how another person perceives or feels in a certain situation.

rooming in A practice many hospitals currently offer that allows the mother and baby to stay in one room together rather than separating them after birth.

rooting reflex An adaptive reflex of infancy in which the baby will attempt to suck a finger that is touched gently to its mouth or cheek.

schemes In Piaget's theory, the strategies by which the individual understands the environment and makes sense out of what he or she encounters. Schemes evolve from simple innate reflexes to complex mental representations.

sebum A fatty substance produced by skin glands when stimulated by androgens.

selective attention The ability to focus on relevant aspects of the environment and disregard irrelevant aspects.

selective breeding A technique used in animal studies that involves mating animals that are similar in the degree to which a trait is manifested or not manifested in order to determine what traits are inherited.

sensation Sensory detection of a certain stimulus in the environment.

sensorimotor period In Piaget's theory, the first period of cognitive development, which lasts from birth to age two. During this period, the infant's interactions with the environment are governed by overt sensory and motor abilities, and learning takes place in the context of perceiving and acting upon objects and people in the environment.

seriation A cognitive achievement of the concrete operations period that involves the ability to arrange objects in an orderly series.

separation anxiety A fear of separation, especially evident during the first year of life. It is characterized by the infant's distressed behavior when separated from a parent or other significant caregiver.

sex drive The basic biological need to achieve sexual satisfaction.

shaken-baby syndrome A form of infant physical abuse characterized by hemorrhages throughout the brain, as a result of simply being shaken. This can result in brain damage, visual problems, and deficits in language and motor skills.

sibling rivalry The conflict or competition existing between children within a family.

sickle-cell anemia A hereditary and ultimately fatal disease that attacks mostly the black population but also some Greeks and Italians, causing 100,000 deaths yearly. An individual who is homozygous for this gene produces abnormal hemoglobin that results in the distortion of the blood cells upon their exposure to low oxygen levels, usually causing death at an early age.

signs According to Piaget, means of communication (for example, words) that have public meanings shared and understood by society but that bear no resemblance to that which they represent.

social clock   A term used to explain the fact that, in each culture, there are chronological standards for appropriate behavior, so that individuals are "expected" to marry at a certain age, have children at another, and so on.

socialization   The process by which children come to behave in socially acceptable ways and by which members of one generation shape the behavior and personality of members of the younger generation.

social referencing   An ability or tendency for one's own reactions to be influenced by other people's emotional expressions.

society of children   Social science term referring to the social world of children, which has its own rituals, traditions, activities, and social rules, handed down from one generation of children to another.

sociometry   A research technique used to establish children's social status and acceptability among their peers.

somatic cells   Body cells that compose the muscles, bones, and various body systems. Somatic cells have twenty-three pairs of chromosomes, or forty-six chromosomes in all.

somatic mutations   Changes in a gene, in the arrangements of the genes, or in the quantity of chromosomal material that affect body cells after cell division has begun.

state   Term referring to a point along a continuum of consciousness ranging from sleep to arousal.

status offenders   A statutory designation for children aged sixteen or under whose misdeeds would be ignored by the courts if engaged in by adults.

stranger anxiety   A fear of strangers, especially evident during the first year of life, characterized by the infant's negative response to the approach of unfamiliar people.

structural gene   A type of gene that guides the manufacture of material (protein) that goes into the structural organization of the cell.

subcortex   Part of the brain consisting of the mid- and hindbrain, which make up the brainstem.

surface structure   According to Chomsky, one of the two levels of the structure of language. It refers to the grammatical rules of language.

symbolic functioning   A term referring to the ability to understand, create, and use symbols to represent something that is not present. The acquisition of a symbolic mode of thinking is a major distinction between the child in the preoperational period and the child in the sensorimotor period.

symbols   According to Piaget, representations or meanings that are personal and individualized, as distinguished from signs, which have shared public meanings.

syntax   The underlying grammatical rules that specify the order and function of words in a sentence.

Tay-Sachs disease   A genetic disorder transmitted as a recessive trait, found almost exclusively among Jews of Eastern European descent. It causes brain destruction, blindness, and eventually death at an early age.

temperament   Term that refers to the individual's pattern of responding to the environment.

teratogen   An environmental agent that can produce abnormalities in the developing fetus.

teratology   The scientific study of abnormalities caused by environmental influences during the prenatal period; from the Greek word "teras," meaning "monster."

testosterone   One of the male sex hormones.

thymine One of the four nitrogenous bases comprising the chemical bonds that link together the pair of intertwined coils within the *DNA* molecule. Thymine links only with adenine.

toxemia A common maternal disorder during pregnancy, caused by toxic substances in the mother's blood. It results in the swelling of limbs and dysfunction of the kidneys and circulatory system in the mother and can lead to brain damage in the offspring.

transductive reasoning Prelogical reasoning that links one particular event with another, often resulting in erroneous deductions regarding cause-and-effect relationships.

transitive reasoning The ability to recognize a relationship between two objects by knowing their relationship to a third.

translocation A process of mutation in which part of the twenty-first chromosome becomes attached to another chromosome—a misarrangement that results in Down's syndrome.

trust versus mistrust Erikson's first psychosocial stage, during which the infant acquires either a sense that the world is a safe place to be in and that his or her needs will be met or a sense of mistrust of the people in the environment.

Turner's syndrome A sex-chromosome abnormality in females characterized by the absence of the sex chromosome X (XO instead of XX). It results in short stature, incompletely developed breasts, sterility, and often short fingers and unusually shaped mouth and ears.

upper cortex The forebrain.

villi Fingerlike projections of the placenta that burrow into the lining of the uterus and come to lie in an area called the *intervillus space*.

visual acuity The ability to detect the separate parts of an object.

WIC The Supplemental Food Program for Women, Infants, and Children, a government-sponsored preventive health and nutrition program for pregnant women and young children.

zygote The fertilized egg cell of the female.

REFERENCES

Abel, Z. L. (1980). Fetal alcohol syndrome: Behavioral teratology. *Psychological Bulletin, 87*(1), 29–50.

Aber, J. L., III. (1982). The socio-emotional development of maltreated children. Unpublished doctoral dissertation. Yale University.

Abraham, S., Collins, G., & Nordsieck, M. (1971). Relationship of childhood weight status to morbidity in adults. *Public Health Reports, 86,* 273–84.

Abramovitch, R., Pepler, D., & Corter, C. (1982). Patterns of sibling interaction among preschool-age children. In M. Lamb & B. Sutton-Smith, (Eds.), *Sibling relationships: Their nature and significance across the life-span.* Hillsdale, N.J.: Erlbaum.

Acredolo, L. P., & Hake, J. L. (1982). Infant perception. In B. B. Wolman & G. Stricker, (Eds.), *Handbook of developmental psychology.* Englewood Cliffs, N.J.: Prentice-Hall.

Adams, F. F. (1980). *Understanding adolescence: Current developments in adolescent psychology.* Boston: Allyn & Bacon.

Adams, R. E., & Passman, R. H. (1979). Effects of visual and auditory aspects of mothers and strangers on the play and exploration of children. *Developmental Psychology, 15,* 269–74.

Adelson, E., & Fraiberg, S. (1974). Gross motor development in infants blind from birth. *Child Development, 45,* 114–26.

Ad Hoc Day Care Coalition. (1985). *The crisis in infant and toddler child care.* Washington, D.C.: Ad Hoc Day Care Coalition.

Advisory Committee on Infant Care Leave. (1985). *Infant care leave project: Summaries of research components.* Unpublished manuscript. Bush Center in Child Development and Social Policy, Yale University.

Ainsworth, M. D. S. (1973). The development of infant-mother attachment. In B. Caldwell & H. Ricciuti, (Eds.), *Review of child development research* (Vol. 3). Chicago: University of Chicago Press.

Ainsworth, M. D. S. (1980). Attachment and child abuse. In G. Gerbner, C. Ross, & E. Zigler, (Eds.), *Child abuse: An agenda for action.* New York: Oxford University Press.

Ainsworth, M. D. S., Bell, S. M., & Stayton, D. J. (1972). Individual differences in the development of some attachment behaviors. *Merrill-Palmer Quarterly, 18,* 123–43.

Ainsworth, M. D. S., Blehar, M., Waters, E., & Wall, S. (1978). *Patterns of attachment: Observations in the strange situation and at home.* Hillsdale, N.J.: Erlbaum.

Ainsworth, M. D. S., & Wittig, B. A. (1969). Attachment and exploratory behavior of one-year-olds in a strange situation. In B. M. Foss, (Ed.), *Determinants of infant behavior* (Vol. 4). London: Methuen.

Alan Guttmacher Institute. (1981). *Teenage pregnancy: The problem that hasn't gone away.* New York: Alan Guttmacher Institute.

Albas, D., Albas, C., & McClusky, K. (1978). Anomie, social class and drinking behavior of high school students. *Journal of Studies of Alcohol, 39,* 910–13.

Albee, G. W. (1980). Primary prevention and social problems. In G. Gerbner, C. J. Ross, & E. Zigler, (Eds.), *Child abuse: An agenda for action.* New York: Oxford University Press.

Allen, J. (1985, Summer). European parental leave policies. *The Networker, 6*(4), 5–6. (Available from the Bush Center in Child Development and Social Policy, Yale University.)

Als, H. (1981). Assessing infant individuality. In C. C. Brown, (Ed.), *Infants at risk: Assessment and intervention.* Skillman, N.J.: Johnson & Johnson.

Als, H., Tronick, E., Adamson, L., & Brazelton, T. (1976). The behavior of the full-term yet underweight newborn infant. *Developmental Medicine and Child Neurology, 18,* 590–602.

Alston, W. P. (1971). Comments on Kohlberg's "From is to ought." In T. Mischel, (Ed.), *Cognitive development and genetic epistemology.* New York: Academic Press.

Ambron, S. (1980). Causal models in early education research. In S. Kilmer, (Ed.), *Advances in early education and child care* (Vol. 2). Greenwich, Conn.: Jad Press.

American Academy of Pediatrics (1978). Breastfeeding: A commentary in celebration of the International Year of the Child. *Pediatrics, 62*(4), 591–601.

American Academy of Pediatrics. (1985). *Getting your child fit: Special report.* Grove Village, Ill.: American Academy of Pediatrics.

Anastasi, A. (1958). Heredity, environment and the question "How?" *Psychological Review, 65,* 197–208.

Anderson, C. S. (1982). The search for school climate: A review of the research. *Review of Educational Research, 52,* 368–420.

Anderson, D. R., & Levin, S. R. (1976). Young children's attention to Sesame Street. *Child Development, 47,* 806–11.

Ando, H., & Yoshimura, I. (1979). Effects of age on communication skill levels and prevalence of maladaptive behaviors in autistic and mentally retarded children. *Journal of Autism and Developmental Disorders, 9,* 83–94.

Annis, L. (1978). *The child before birth.* Ithaca, N.Y.: Cornell University Press.

Appel, L. F., Cooper, R. G., McCarrel, N., Sims-Knight, J., Yussen, S., & Flavell, J. H. (1972). The development of the distinction between perceiving and memorizing. *Child Development, 43,* 1365–81.

Arehart-Treichel, J. (1977, October). Senility: More than growing old. *Science News, 1,* 218–21.

Aries, P. (1962). *Centuries of childhood.* London: Jonathan Cape.

Arlin, P. (1975). Cognitive development in adulthood: A fifth stage? *Developmental Psychology, 11,* 602–6.

Armentrout, V. A., & Burger, G. K. (1972). Children's reports of parental child-rearing behaviors at five grade levels. *Developmental Psychology, 7,* 44–48.

Aronfreed, J. (1968). *Conduct and conscience: The socialization of internal controls over behavior.* New York: Academic Press.

Asch, S. E., & Nerlove, H. (1960). The development of double function terms in children: An exploratory investigation. In B. Kaplan & S. Wakner, (Eds.), *Perspectives in psychological theory: Essays in honor of Heinz Werner.* New York: International Universities Press.

Asher, S. R. (1978). Children's peer relations. In M. E. Lamb, (Ed.), *Social and personality development.* New York: Holt, Rinehart and Winston.

Asher, S. R., & Hymel, S. (1981). Children's social competence in peer relations: Sociometric and behavioral assessments. In J. D. Wine & M. D. Singe, (Eds.), *Social Competence.* New York: Guilford Press.

Ashmead, D. H., & Perlmutter, M. (1984). Infant memory in everyday life. In M. Perlmutter, (Ed.), *New directions in child development: Naturalistic approaches to children's memory.* San Francisco: Jossey-Bass.

Ault, R. L. (1977). *Children's cognitive development: Piaget's theory and the process approach.* New York: Oxford University Press.

Ausubel, D. P., Montemayor, R. R., & Svajian, P. N. (1977). *Theory and problems of adolescent development* (2d ed.). New York: Grune & Stratton.

Ausubel, D. P., Sullivan, E. V., & Ives, S. W. (1980). *Theory and problems of child development* (3d ed.). New York: Grune & Stratton.

Badger, E. (1977). The infant stimulation/mother training project. In B. Caldwell & D. Stedman, (Eds.), *Infant education: A guide for helping handicapped children in the first three years.* New York: Walker.

Badger, E. (1980). Effects of a parent education program on teenage mothers and their offspring. In K. G. Scott, T. Field, & E. Robertson, (Eds.), *Teenage mothers and their offspring.* New York: Grune & Stratton.

Badger, E. (1982). *The joy of learning.* New York: McGraw-Hill.

Baecher, C. M. (1983). *Children's consumerism: Implications for education.* Paper presented at the Bush Center in Child Development and Social Policy, Yale University.

Baer, A. S. (1977). *The genetic perspective.* Philadelphia: W. B. Saunders.

Bakan, D. (1972). Adolescence in America: From idea to social fact. In J. Kagan & R. Cole, (Eds.), *Twelve to sixteen: Early adolescence.* New York: W. W. Norton.

Bakan, D. (1979). *Slaughter of the innocents.* San Francisco: Jossey-Bass.

Baker, S. P. (1981). Childhood injuries: The community approach to prevention. *Journal of Public Health Policy, 2*(3), 235–46.

Baldwin, W., & Cain, U. S. (1980). The children of teenage parents. *Family Planning Perspectives, 12*(1), 34–43.

Baltes, P. B. (1979). Life-span developmental psychology: Some converging observations on history and theory. In P. B. Baltes & O. G. Brim, Jr., (Eds.), *Life-span development and behavior* (Vol. 2). New York: Academic Press.

Baltes, P. B., Reese, H. W., & Lipsitt, L. P. (1980). Life-span developmental psychology. *Annual Review of Psychology, 31,* 65–110.

Bandura, A. (1962). Social learning through imitation. In M. R. Jones, (Ed.), *Nebraska Symposium on Motivation*. Lincoln: University of Nebraska Press.

Bandura, A. (1964). The stormy decade: Fact or fiction? *Psychology in the School, 1,* 224–31.

Bandura, A. (1967). The role of modeling processes in personality development. In W. W. Hartup & N. L. Smothergill, (Eds.), *The young child: Reviews of research*. Washington, D.C.: N.A.E.Y.C.

Bandura, A. (1969). Social learning theory of identificatory processes. In D. A. Goslin, (Ed.), *Handbook of socialization theory and research*. Chicago: Rand McNally.

Bandura, A. (1977). *Social learning theory*. Englewood Cliffs, N.J.: Prentice-Hall.

Bane, M. J. (1976a, Summer). Paying for childhood. *Working Papers for a New Society, 4*(2), 74–81.

Bane, M. J. (1976b). Marital disruption in the lives of children. *Journal of Social Issues, 32,* 103–17.

Banks, M. S., & Salapatek, P. (1983). Infant visual perception. In Paul H. Mussen, (Ed.), *Handbook of child psychology*. Vol. 2, *Infancy and developmental psychobiology*. New York: Wiley.

Baraonkar, D. S., & Shah, S. A. (1974). The XYY male—or syndrome? *Progress in Medical Genetics, 10,* 135–222.

Barbero, G. (1975). Failure-to-thrive. In M. H. Klaus, T. Leger, & M. A. Trause, (Eds.), *Maternal attachment and mothering disorders: A roundtable*. Skillman, N.J.: Johnson & Johnson.

Barker, R. G., & Wright, H. F. (1951). *One boy's day*. New York: Harper & Row.

Barker, R. G., & Wright, H. F. (1955). *Midwest and its children*. New York: Harper & Row. Reprinted in 1971 by Archon Books, Hamden, Conn.

Barrett, D. E. (1982, May). An approach to the conceptualization and assessment of social-emotional functioning in studying nutrition-behavior relationships. *American Journal of Clinical Nutrition, 35*(5 Suppl.), 1220–27.

Barrett, D. E., Radke-Yarrow, M., & Klein, R. E. (1982). Chronic malnutrition and child behavior: Effects of early caloric supplementation on social and emotional functioning at school age. *Developmental Psychology, 18,* 541–56.

Barry, R. J., & James, A. L. (1978). Handedness in autistics, retardates, and normals of a wide range. *Journal of Autism and Childhood Schizophrenia, 8,* 315–23.

Bartoshuk, A. K. (1964). Human neonatal cardiac responses to sound: A power function. *Psychonomic Science, 1,* 151–52.

Bauer, D. H. (1976). An exploratory study of developmental changes in children's fears. *Journal of Child Psychology and Psychiatry, 17,* 69–74.

Baumrind, D. (1967). Child care practices anteceding three patterns of preschool behavior. *Genetic Psychology Monographs, 75,* 43–88.

Baumrind, D. (1968). Authoritarian vs. authoritative parental control. *Adolescence, 3,* 255–72.

Baumrind, D. (1971). Current patterns of parental authority. *Developmental Psychology Monographs, 41* (1, Pt. 2).

Baumrind, D. (1975). Early socialization and adolescent competence. In S. Dragastin & G. H. Elder, Jr., (Eds.), *Adolescence in the life cycle*. New York: Wiley.

Bayley, N. (1965). Comparisons of mental and motor test scores for age 1–15 months by sex, birth order, race, geographic location, and education of parents. *Child Development, 11,* 184–90.

Beal, C. R., & Flavell, J. H. (1983). Young speakers' evaluations of their listeners' comprehension in a referential communication task. *Child Development, 54*(1), 148–53.

Beck, J. (1975). *How to raise a brighter child*. New York: Pocket Books.

Beck, R. (1982). Beyond the stalemate in child care public policy. In E. Zigler & E. Gordon, (Eds.), *Day care: Scientific and social policy issues*. Boston: Auburn House.

Becker, W. C. (1964). Consequences of different kinds of parental discipline. In M. L. Hoffman & L. W. Hoffman, (Eds.), *Review of child development research* (Vol. 1). New York: Russell Sage.

Beckwith, J., & King, J. (1974). The XYY syndrome: A dangerous myth. *New Science, 64,* 474–76.

Belsky, J. (1978). Three theoretical models of child abuse: A critical review. *International Journal of Child Abuse and Neglect, 2,* 37–49.

Belsky, J. (1980). Child maltreatment: An ecological integration. *American Psychologist, 35,* 320–35.

Belsky, J. (1981). Early human experience: A family perspective. *Developmental Psychology, 17,* 3–23.

Belsky, J., Gilstrap, B., & Rovine, M. (1984). The Pennsylvania Infant and Family Development Project: 1. Stability and change in mother–infant and father–infant interaction in a family setting at 1, 3, and 9 months. *Child Development, 55*(3), 692–705.

Belsky, J., Lerner, R. M., & Spanier, G. B. (1984). *The child in the family*. Reading, Mass.: Addison-Wesley.

Belsky, J., & Steinberg, L. D. (1978). The effects of day care: A critical review. *Child Development, 49,* 929–49.

Bench, J. (1978). The auditory response. In V. Stave, (Ed.), *Perinatal physiology*. New York: Plenum.

Benedek, R. S., & Benedek, E. D. (1977). Postdivorce visitation: A child's right. *Journal of the American Academy of Child Psychiatry, 16,* 256–71.

Bennett, N. (1976). *Teaching styles and pupil progress*. Cambridge, Mass.: Harvard University Press.

Bennett, W. J. (1985, December 4). Statement of William J. Bennett, secretary of education, before the Task Force on Literacy, U.S. Senate.

Berenda, R. W. (1950). *The influence of the group on the judgments of children*. New York: King's Crown Press.

Berko, J. (1958). The child's learning of English morphology. *Word, 14,* 5–17.

Berkowitz, L. (1962). *Aggression: A social psychological analysis*. Englewood Cliffs, N.J.: Prentice-Hall.

Berndt, T., & Zigler, E. (1985). Developmental psychology. In G. Kimble & K. Schlesinger, (Eds.), *Topics in the history of psychology* (Vol. 2). Hillsdale, N.J.: Erlbaum.

Berndt, T. J. (1979). Developmental changes in conformity to peers and parents. *Developmental Psychology, 15,* 608–16.

Berndt, T. J. (1982). The features and effects of friendship in early adolescence. *Child Development, 53,* 1447–60.

Berrueta-Clement, J., Schweinhart, L. J., Barnett, W. S., Epstein, A. S., & Weikart, D. P. (1984). *Changed lives: Effects of the Perry Preschool Program on youths through age 19*. Ypsilanti, Mich.: High/Scope Press.

Bettelheim, B. (1967). *The empty fortress: Infantile autism and the birth of the self*. New York: Free Press.

Bettelheim, B. (1969). *Children of the dream*. New York: MacMillan.

Bevan, W. (1982). A sermon of sorts in three plus parts. *American Psychologist, 37*(12), 1303–22.

Beyer, B. (1978). Conducting moral discussions in the classroom. In P. Scharf, (Ed.), *Readings in moral education*. Minneapolis: Winston.

Bigelow, B. J. (1977). Children's friendship expectations: A cognitive developmental study. *Child Development, 48,* 246–53.

Bigelow, B. J., & LaGaipa, J. J. (1975). Children's written descriptions of friendship. *Developmental Psychology, 11,* 857–58.

Binet, A., & Simon, T. (1905). Methodes nouvelles pour le diagnostic du niveau intellectuel des anormaux. *L'année psychologique, 11,* 191–244.

Bingham, J. (1985, September 2). Old, young, and the labor of love. *New York Times*, p. 21.

Birch, H. G. (1972). Health and the education of socially disadvantaged children. In U. Bronfenbrenner, (Ed.), *Influences on human development*. Hinsdale, Ill.: Dryden Press.

Birch, H. G., & Gussow, J. D. (1970). Disadvantaged children: Health, nutrition, and school failure. New York: Harcourt Brace & World.

Birch, J. W. (1976). Mainstreaming: Definition, development and characteristics. In J. B. Jordan, (Ed.), *Teacher, please don't close the door*. Reston, Va.: The Council for Exceptional Children.

Bixenstine, V., DeCorte, M., & Bixenstine, B. (1976). Conformity to peer-sponsored misconduct at four age levels. *Developmental Psychology, 12,* 226–36.

Black, L. (1979, July 7). Developmental correlates of sleep apnea. Address delivered at the International Congress of Psychology of the Child, Paris.

Blau, A. (1963). The psychogenetic etiology of premature births. *Psychosomatic Medicine, 25,* 201–11.

Block, J. H. (1982). Another look at sex differentiation in the socialization behaviors of mothers and fathers. In J. Sherman & F. Denmark, (Eds.), *Psychology of women: Future of research*. New York: Psychological Dimensions.

Blom, G. E., Keith, J. G., & Tomber, I. (1984). Child and family advocacy: Addressing the rights and responsibilities of child, family and society. In R. P. Boger, G. E. Blom, & L. E. Lezotte, (Eds.), *Child nurturance*. Vol. 4, *Child nurturing in the 1980s*. New York: Plenum Press.

Bloom, B. S. (1964). *Stability and change in human characteristics*. New York: Wiley.

Bloom, L. (1973). *One word at a time*. The Hague: Mouton.

Bloom, L. (1975). Language development. In F. D. Horowitz, (Ed.), *Review of child development research* (Vol. 4). Chicago: University of Chicago Press.

Bodenheimer, B. M. (1974–75). The rights of children and the crises in custody litigation in and out of state. *University of Colorado Law Review, 46,* 495–508.

Boocock, S. S. (1977). A cross-cultural analysis of the child care system. In L. Katz, (Ed.), *Current topics in early childhood* (Vol. 1). Norwood, N.J.: Ablex.

Borke, H. (1971). Interpersonal perception of young children: Egocentrism or empathy? *Developmental Psychology, 5,* 263–69.

Borke, H. (1975). Piaget's mountain revisited: Changes in the egocentric landscape. *Developmental Psychology, 11,* 240–43.

Borland, D. C. (1978). Research on middle age: An assessment. *The Gerontologist, 18,* 379–86.

Boukydis, C. F. Z. (1985). Perception of infant crying as an interpersonal event. In B. M. Lester & C. F. Z. Boukydis, (Eds.), *Infant crying: Theoretical and research perspectives.* New York: Plenum.

Bower, T. G. R. (1971). The object in the world of the infant. *Scientific American, 225*(4), 30–38.

Bower, T. G. R. (1974). *Development in infancy.* San Francisco: W. H. Freeman.

Bower, T. G. R. (1977). *A primer of infant development.* San Francisco: W. H. Freeman.

Bower, T. G. R. (1979). *Human development.* San Francisco: Freeman.

Bowlby, J. (1951). *Maternal care and mental health.* Geneva: The World Health Organization.

Bowlby, J. (1953). Some pathological processes set in train by early mother-child separations. *Journal of Mental Sciences, 99,* 265–72.

Bowlby, J. (1969). *Attachment and loss.* Vol. 1, *Attachment.* New York: Basic Books.

Bowlby, J. (1980). *Attachment and loss.* Vol. 3, *Loss, sadness and depression.* New York: Basic Books.

Brackbill, Y. (1958). Extinction of the smiling responses in infants as a function of reinforcement schedule. *Child Development, 29,* 115–24.

Brackbill, Y. (1970). Continuous stimulation and arousal levels in infants: Additive effects. *Proceedings of the 78th Annual Convention, American Psychological Association, 5,* 271–72.

Brackbill, Y. (1971). Cumulative effects of continuous stimulation on arousal level in infants. *Child Development, 42,* 17–26.

Brackbill, Y. (1979). Obstetrical medication and infant behavior. In J. Osofsky, (Ed.), *Handbook of infant development.* New York: Wiley.

Bradley, R. H., & Caldwell, B. M. (1976). The relation of the infant's home environment to mental test performance at fifty-four months: A follow-up study. *Child Development, 47,* 1172–74.

Brainerd, C. J. (1974). Training and transfer of transitivity conservation and class inclusion. *Child Development, 27,* 114–16.

Bran, E. A. (1979). Strategies for the prevention of pregnancy in adolescents. *Advances in Planned Parenthood, 14,* 68–76.

Bray, A., (Ed.). (1979). *Obesity in America.* Washington, D.C.: U.S. Department of Health, Education and Welfare, NIH Pub. No. 79-359.

Brazelton, T. B. (1961). Effects of maternal medication on the neonate and his behavior. *Journal of Pediatrics, 58,* 513–18.

Brazelton, T. B. (1961). Psychophysiologic reactions in the neonate. Pt. I, The value of observation of the neonate. *Journal of Pediatrics, 58,* 508–12.

Brazelton, T. B. (1962). A child-oriented approach to toilet training. *Pediatrics, 29,* 121–27.

Brazelton, T. B. (1973). *Neonatal behavioral assessment scale.* Clinics in Developmental Medicine (No. 50). Philadelphia: Spastics International Medical Publications, J. B. Lippincott.

Brazelton, T. B. (1976). Early mother–infant reciprocity. In V. C. Vaughn III & T. B. Brazelton, (Eds.), *The family—Can it be saved?* Chicago: Yearbook Medical Publishers.

Brazelton, T. B., Als, H., Tronick, E., & Lester, B. M. (1979). Specific neonatal measures: The Brazelton neonatal behavior assessment scale. In J. D. Osofsky, (Ed.), *The handbook of infant development.* New York: Wiley.

Brazelton, T. B., Koslowski, B., & Main, M. (1974). The origins of reciprocity: The early mother–infant interactions. In M. Lewis & J. Rosenblum, (Eds.), *The Origins of Behavior.* New York: Wiley.

Brent, L. (1977). Radiations and other physical agents. In J. G. Wilson & F. C. Fraser, (Eds.), *Handbook of teratology.* New York: Plenum.

Bridges, K. (1932). Emotional development in early infancy. *Child Development, 3,* 324–41.

Brim, O. G., Jr. (1976). Theories of the male midlife crisis. *Counseling Psychologist, 6,* 2–9.

Brim, O. G., Jr., & Abeles, R. P. (1975). Work and personality in the middle years. *Social Science Research Council Items, 29,* 29–33.

Brittain, C. V. (1963). Adolescent choices and

parent–peer cross pressures. *American Sociological Review, 28,* 385–91.

Brittain, C. V. (1969). A comparison of rural and urban adolescents with respect to peer versus parent compliance. *Adolescence, 13,* 59–68.

Brodsky, C. M. (1954). *A study of norms for body form–behavior relationships.* Washington, D.C.: Catholic University Press.

Bronfenbrenner, U. (1970). Who cares for America's children? Paper presented at the annual meeting of the National Association for the Education of Young Children.

Bronfenbrenner, U. (1973). *Two worlds of childhood: U.S. and U.S.S.R.* New York: Pocket Books.

Bronfenbrenner, U. (1974). Developmental research, public policy, and the ecology of childhood. *Child Development, 45,* 1–5.

Bronfenbrenner, U. (1975). Is early intervention effective? In H. J. Leichter, (Ed.), *The family as educator.* New York: Teachers College Press.

Bronfenbrenner, U. (1977). Toward an experimental ecology of human development. *American Psychologist, 32,* 513–31.

Bronfenbrenner, U. (1979). Contexts of child rearing: Prospects and problems. *American Psychologist, 34*(10), 844–50.

Brooks, J., & Lewis, M. (1976). Infants' responses to strangers: Midget, adult, and child. *Child Development, 47,* 323–32.

Brophy, J. E. (1983). Research on the self-fulfilling prophecy and teacher expectations. *Journal of Educational Psychology, 75,* 631–61.

Broughton, J. M. (1981). Piaget's structural developmental psychology. Pt. III, Function and the problem of knowledge. *Human Development, 24,* 257–85.

Brown, A. L., Branford, J. D., Ferrara, R. A., & Campione, J. C. (1983). Learning, remembering, and understanding. In P. H. Mussen, (Ed.), *Handbook of child psychology* (4th ed.). Vol. 3, J. H. Flavell & E. M. Markman, (Eds.), *Cognitive development.* New York: Wiley.

Brown, B. F. (1980). A study of the school needs of children from one-parent families. *Phi Delta Kappan, 61,* 537–40.

Brown, C. C., (Ed.). (1983). *Childhood learning disabilities and prenatal risk.* Skillman, N.J.: Johnson & Johnson.

Brown, J. V., & Bakeman, R. (1978). The at-risk infant in an at-risk population: The effects of pre-

maturity on mother-infant interactions. Unpublished manuscript, Georgia State University.

Brown, R. (1973). *A first language.* Cambridge, Mass.: Harvard University Press.

Brown, R., & Hanlon, C. (1970). Derivational complexity and order acquisition. In J. R. Hayes, (Ed.), *Cognition and the development of language.* New York: Wiley.

Brozan, N. (1983, May 2). New look at fears of children. *New York Times,* p. B5.

Brozek, J., & Schurch, B., (Eds.). (1984). *Malnutrition and behavior: Critical assessment of key issues.* Lausanne, Switzerland: The Nestlé Foundation.

Bruch, H. (1978). *The golden cage: The enigma of anorexia nervosa.* Cambridge, Mass.: Harvard University Press.

Bruner, J. S. (1964). The course of cognitive growth. *American Psychologist, 19,* 1–15.

Bruner, J. S. (1965). Growth of mind. *American Psychologist, 20,* 1007–19.

Bruner, J. S. (1972). Nature and the uses of immaturity. *American Psychologist, 27,* 687–708.

Brunswick, A. F. (1977). Health and drug behavior: A study of urban black adolescents. *Addictive Diseases, 3,* 197–214.

Bryan, J. N., & Bryan, T. H. (1978). *Understanding learning disabilities.* Sherman Oaks, Calif.: Alfred Publishing.

Bryan, T. H. (1974). Peer popularity of learning disabled children. *Journal of Learning Disabilities, 7,* 261–68.

Bryan, T. H., & McCrady, H. J. (1972). Use of a teacher rating scale. *Journal of Learning Disabilities, 5,* 199–206.

Bryant, B. K. (1974). Locus of control related to teacher–child interpersonal relationships. *Child Development, 45,* 157–64.

Budoff, M., & Gottlieb, J. (1976). Special class EMR children mainstreamed: A study of an aptitude (learning potential) x treatment interaction. *American Journal of Mental Deficiency, 81,* 1–11.

Bureau of Business Practice. (1979). *Fair Employment Practice Guidelines, 170,* 9–29.

Bureau of Labor Statistics. (1985). U.S. Department of Labor. *Employment and earnings. January 1985.* Table 6. Annual Averages.

Burgdorff, K. (1980, December). *Recognition and reporting of child maltreatment: Findings from the National Incidence and Severity of Child Abuse and Ne-*

glect. Prepared for the National Center on Child Abuse and Neglect, Washington, D.C.

Burnham, S. (1972, January 9). The heroin babies are going cold turkey. *The New York Times Magazine,* pp. 21–22, 24, 26.

Butler, J. A., Starfield, B., & Stenmark, S. (1984). Child health policy. In H. W. Stevenson & A. E. Siegel, (Eds.), *Child development research and social policy* (Vol. 1). Chicago: University of Chicago Press.

Butler, N. R., Goldstein, H., & Ross, E. M. G. (1972). Cigarette smoking in pregnancy: Its influence on birth weight and perinatal mortality. *British Medical Journal, 4,* 573–75.

Butler, R. N. (1975). *Why survive? Being old in America.* New York: Harper & Row.

Caffey, J. (1946). Multiple fractures in the long bones of children suffering from chronic subdural hematoma. *American Journal of Roentgenology, Radium Therapy, and Nuclear Medicine, 56,* 163–73.

Caldwell, B. (1970). Infant day care and attachment. *American Journal of Orthopsychiatry, 40,* 397–412.

Califano, J. A., Jr. (1978). Keynote address. In *Summary of the Conference on Adolescent Behavior and Health.* Washington, D.C.: National Academy of Sciences.

Campbell, A. G. M. (1983). The right to be allowed to die. *Journal of Medical Ethics, 9,* 136–40.

Campbell, A. G. M., & Duff, R. S. (1979). Deciding the care of severely malformed or dying infants. *Journal of Medical Ethics, 5,* 65–67.

Campbell, D. T. (1969). Reforms as experiments. *American Psychologist, 24,* 409–29.

Campos, J. J., & Barrett, K. C. (1984). A new understanding of emotions and their development. In C. E. Izard, J. Kagan, & R. B. Zajonc, (Eds.), *Emotions, cognition, and behavior.* New York: Cambridge University Press.

Campos, J. J., Langer, A., & Krowitz, A. (1970). Cardiac responses on the visual cliff in prelocomotor human infants. *Science, 170,* 196–97.

Cantor, P. (1976). Personality characteristics found among youthful female suicide attempters. *Journal of Abnormal Psychology, 85,* 324–29.

Cantwell, D. (1975). *The hyperactive child: Diagnosis, management and research.* New York: Spectrum.

Caparulo, B., & Zigler, E. (1983). The effects of mainstreaming on success expectancy and imitation in mildly retarded children. *Peabody Journal of Education, 60*(3), 85–98.

Caparulo, B. K., & Cohen, D. J. (1977). Cognitive structures, language, and emerging social competence in autistic and aphasic children. *Journal of the American Academy of Child Psychiatry, 16,* 620–45.

Caparulo, B. K., & Cohen, D. J. (1982). The syndrome of early childhood autism: Natural history, etiology, and treatment. In E. F. Zigler, M. E. Lamb, & I. L. Child, (Eds.), *Socialization and personality development* (2d ed.). New York: Oxford University Press.

Card, J. J., & Wise, L. L. (1978). Teenage mothers and teenage fathers: The impact of early childbearing on the parents' personal and professional lives. *Family Planning Perspective, 10,* 199.

Carew, J. V. (1980). Experience and the development of intelligence in young children at home and in day care. *Monographs of the Society for Research in Child Development, 45* (Serial No. 187), 6–7.

Carey, S. (1977). The child as a word learner. In M. Halle, J. Bressman, & G. Miller, (Eds.), *Linguistic theory and psychological reality.* Cambridge, Mass.: MIT Press.

Casler, L. (1967). Perceptual deprivation in institutional settings. In G. Newton & S. Levine, (Eds.), *Early experience and behavior.* New York: Springer.

Cattell, R. B. (1963). Theory of fluid and crystalized intelligence: A critical experiment. *Journal of Educational Psychology, 54,* 1–22.

Center for Disease Control. (1980). *Teenage childbearing and abortion patterns—United States, 1977, 29,* 157–59.

Cerutti, G. B. (1969). In Ferreira, A. J. *Prenatal environment.* Springfield, Ill.: Charles C. Thomas.

Chaikin, A. L., Sigler, E., & Derlega, V. J. (1974). Nonverbal mediators of teacher expectancy effects. *Journal of Personality and Social Psychology, 30*(1), 144.

Chall, J. S. (1983). *Stages of reading development.* New York: McGraw-Hill.

Chase, H. C., & Byrnes, M. E. (1983). Trends in prematurity: United States, 1967–1983. *Journal of Public Health Policy, 60.*

Chen, E. (1979, December). Twins reared apart: A living lab. *The New York Times Magazine,* p. 110.

Cherlin, A. J. (1981). *Marriage, divorce, remarriage.* Cambridge, Mass.: Harvard University Press.

Cherlin, A. J., & Furstenberg, F. F., Jr. (1986). *The new American grandparent: A place in the family, a life apart.* New York: Basic Books.

Chess, S. (1977). Follow-up report on autism in congenital rubella. *Journal of Autism and Childhood Schizophrenia, 1,* 69–81.

Chess, S., & Gordon, S. G. (1984). Psychosocial development and human variance. In E. Gordon, (Ed.), *Review of research in education* (Vol. 11). Washington, D.C.: American Educational Research Association.

Children's Defense Fund (1978). *Children without homes: An examination of public responsibility to children in out-of-home care.* Study by J. Knitzer, M. Allen, and B. McGowan. Washington, D.C.: Children's Defense Fund.

Children's Defense Fund (1985). *A children's defense budget: An analysis of the president's FY 1986 budget and children.* Washington, D.C.: Children's Defense Fund.

Chinese Medical Journal (Peking) (1975, March). New Series Vol. 1, pp. 81–94. Child health care in new China, by Society of Pediatrics of the Chinese Medical Association.

Ching, C. C. (1982). Single-child families. *Studies in family planning* (United Nations), *6,* 115–18.

Chomsky, C. (1969). *The acquisition of syntax in children from 5 to 10.* Cambridge, Mass.: MIT Press.

Chomsky, N. (1968). *Language and mind.* New York: Harcourt Brace & World.

Chown, S. M. (1977). Morale, careers, and personal potentials. In J. E. Birren & K. W. Schaie, (Eds.), *Handbook of the psychology of aging.* New York: Van Nostrand Reinhold.

Christopherson, E. R., & Sullivan, M. A. (1982). Increasing the protection of newborn infants in cars. *Pediatrics, 70,* 21–25.

Clark, E. V. (1973). What's in a word? On the child's acquisition of semantics in his first language. In T. E. Moore, (Ed.), *Cognitive development and the acquisition of language.* New York: Academic.

Clark, H., & Clark, E. (1977). *Psychology and language: An introduction to psycholinguistics.* New York: Harcourt Brace Jovanovich.

Clarke, A. M., & Clarke, A. D. B., (Eds.). (1976). *Early experience: Myth and evidence.* New York: Free Press.

Clarke-Stewart, K. A. (1973). Interactions between mothers and their young children: Characteristics and consequences. *Monographs of the Society for Research in Child Development, 38* (Serial No. 153), 6–7.

Clarke-Stewart, K. A. (1977). *Child care in the family:*
A review of research and some propositions for policy. New York: Academic Press.

Clarke-Stewart, K. A. (1978). And daddy makes three: The father's impact on mother and young child. *Child Development, 49,* 466–78.

Clarke-Stewart, K. A. (1980). The father's contribution to child development. In F. A. Pedersen, (Ed.), *The father-infant relationship: Observational studies in a family context.* New York: Praeger Special Studies.

Clarke-Stewart, K. A. (1982). *Day care.* Cambridge, Mass.: Harvard University Press.

Clarke-Stewart, K. A., & Apfel, N. (1979). Evaluating parental effects on child development. In L. S. Shulman, (Ed.), *Review of research in education* (Vol. 6). Itasca, Ill.: Peacock.

Clarke-Stewart, K. A., & Hevey, C. M. (1981). Longitudinal relations in repeated observations of mother-child interactions from 1 to 2½ years. *Developmental Psychology, 17,* 127–49.

Clausen, J. A. (1975). The social meaning of differential physical and sexual maturation. In S. E. Dragastin & G. H. Elder, (Eds.), *Adolescence in the life cycle: Psychological change and social context.* London: Halsted Press.

Clavan, S. (1978). The impact of social class and social trends on the role of grandparent. *The Family Coordinator, 27,* 351–58.

Clifford, S. H. (1954). Postmaturity with placental dysfunction. *Journal of Pediatrics, 44,* 1–13.

Clifton, R., Sigueland, E. R., & Lipsitt, L. P. (1972). Conditioned head turning in human newborns as a function of conditioned response requirements and state of wakefulness. *Journal of Experimental Child Psychology, 13,* 43–57.

Cochran, M. M. (1977). A comparison of group care and family childrearing patterns in Sweden. *Child Development, 48,* 702–7.

Cohen, D. J. (1977). Minimal brain dysfunction: Diagnosis and therapy. In J. H. Masserman, (Ed.), *Current psychiatric therapies.* New York: Grune & Stratton.

Cohen, D. J., Caparulo, B. K., & Shaywitz, B. (1976). Primary childhood aphasia and childhood autism: Clinical, biological, and conceptual observations. *Journal of the American Academy of Child Psychiatry, 15*(4), 609–45.

Cohen, S. (1981). Adolescents and drug abuse: Biomedical consequences. In D. J. Lettier & J. P. Ludford, (Eds.), *Drug abuse and the American adolescent.*

Rockville, Md.: National Institute on Drug Abuse.

Cohen, S. E. (1978). Maternal employment and mother-child interaction. *Merrill-Palmer Quarterly, 24,* 189–97.

Cole, M. (1981). *The zone of proximal development: Where culture and cognition create each other.* Center for Human Information Processing, University of California at San Diego, Report No. 106.

Cole, M. (1983). Culture and cognitive development. In P. H. Mussen, (Ed.), *Handbook of child psychology* (4th ed.). Vol. 1, W. Kessen, (Ed.), *History, theory and methods.* New York: Wiley.

Cole, M., Gay, J., Glick, J. A., & Sharp, D. W. (1971). *The cultural context of learning and thinking.* New York: Basic Books.

Cole, M., & Scribner, S. (1974). *Culture and thought: A psychological introduction.* New York: Wiley.

Coleman, J. C. (1974). *Relationships in adolescence.* Boston: Routledge & Kegan Paul.

Coleman, J. C. (1980). Friendship and the peer group in adolescence. In J. Adelson, (Ed.), *Handbook of adolescent psychology.* New York: Wiley.

Coleman, J. S. (1961). *The adolescent society.* New York: Free Press.

Coleman, J. S., Campbell, E., Hobson, C., McPartland, J., Mood, A., Weinfield, F., & York, R. (1966). *Equality of educational opportunity.* Washington, D.C.: U.S. Government Printing Office.

Coleman, M. (1978). A report on the autistic syndrome. In M. Rutter & E. Schopler, (Eds.), *Autism: A reappraisal of concepts and treatment.* New York: Plenum.

Collins, W. A. (1984). Conclusion: The status of basic research on middle childhood. In W. A. Collins, (Ed.), *Development during middle childhood: The years from six to twelve.* Washington, D.C.: National Academy Press.

Condon, W. S., & Sander, L. W. (1974). Neonate movement is synchronized with adult speech: Interactional participation and language acquisition. *Science, 183,* 99–101.

Condry, J. C., & Siman, M. A. (1974). Characteristics of peer- and adult-oriented children. *Journal of Marriage and the Family, 36,* 543–44.

Condry, J. C., & Siman, M. A. (1976). *An experimental study of adult versus peer orientation.* Unpublished manuscript, Cornell University.

Conger, J. J. (1973). *Adolescence and youth: Psychological development in a changing world.* New York: Harper & Row.

Conger, J. J. (1977). *Adolescence and youth.* New York: Harper & Row.

Conrad, P. (1976). *Identifying hyperactive children and the medicalization of deviant behavior.* Lexington, Mass.: Lexington Books.

Constanzo, P. R., & Shaw, M. E. (1966). Conformity as a function of age level. *Child Development, 37,* 967–75.

Conway, E., & Brackbill, Y. (1970). Delivery medication and infant outcome: An empirical study. *Monographs of the Society for Research in Child Development, 35*(137), 24–34.

Cook, J. T. (1985). *Child day care.* Davis, Calif.: International Dialogue Press.

Cooper, H. M. (1979). Pygmalion grows up: A model for teacher expectation, communication and performance influence. *Review of Educational Research, 49,* 389–410.

Cooper, R. M., & Zubek, J. P. (1958). Effects of enriched and restricted early environment on the learning ability of bright and dull rats. *Canadian Journal of Psychology, 12,* 159–64.

Coopersmith, S. (1967). *The antecedents of self-esteem.* San Francisco: Freeman.

Corah, N. L., Anthony, E. J., Painter, P., Stern, J. A., & Thurston, D. L. (1965). Effects of perinatal anoxia after seven years. *Psychological Monographs, 79,* 3.

Corbin, C. B. (1973). *A textbook of motor development.* Dubuque, Iowa: W. C. Brown.

Corrigan, R. (1983). The development of representational skills. In K. Fischer, (Ed.), *Levels and transitions in children's development.* San Francisco: Jossey-Bass.

Corsaro, W. A. (1980). Friendship in the nursery school: Social organization in a peer environment. In S. R. Asher & J. M. Gottman, (Eds.), *The development of children's friendships.* New York: Cambridge University Press.

Cortes, J. B., & Gatti, F. M. (1965). Physique and self-description of temperament. *Journal of Consulting Psychology, 29,* 432–39.

Costa, P. T. Jr., & McCrae, R. R. (1980). Still stable after all these years: Personality as a key to some issues in aging. In P. B. Baltes & O. G. Brim, Jr., (Eds.), *Life-span development and behavior* (Vol. 3). New York: Academic Press.

Cox, M. J., & Cox, R. D. (1985). *Foster care: Current issues and practices.* Norwood, N.J.: Ablex.

Cranston, A. (1979). Testimony. U.S. Congress, Senate Committee on Finance, Subcommittee on Public Assistance and Foster Care, Ninety-sixth Congress.

Cravioto, J., DeLicardie, E. R., & Birch, H. G. (1966). Nutrition, growth and neurointegrative development: An experimental and ecologic study. *Pediatrics, 38*(2), Pt. II, Suppl.

Cremin, L. A. (1976). *Public education.* New York: Basic Books.

Crnic, K. A., Greenberg, M. T., Ragozin, A. S., Robinson, N. M., & Basham, R. B. (1983). Effects of stress and social support on mothers and premature and full-term infants. *Child Development, 54*(1), 209–17.

Crnic, K. A., Greenberg, M. T., Robinson, N. M., & Ragozin, A. S. (1984, April). Maternal stress and social support: Effects on the mother-infant relationship from birth to eighteen months. *American Journal of Orthopsychiatry, 54*(2), 224–35.

Crockenberg, S. (1981). Infant irritability, mother responsiveness, and social support influences on the security of infant-mother attachment. *Child Development, 52,* 857–65.

Cromwell, R. L. (1963). A social learning approach to mental retardation. In N. R. Ellis, (Ed.), *Handbook of mental deficiency.* New York: McGraw-Hill.

Cronbach, L. J. (1975). Five decades of public controversy over mental testing. *American Psychologist, 30,* 1–14.

Crook, C. K., & Lipsitt, L. P. (1976). Neonatal nutritive sucking: Effects of taste stimulation upon sucking rhythm and heart rate. *Child Development, 47,* 518–22.

Crosby, F. (1984). Relative deprivation in organizational settings. *Research in organizational Behavior: An Annual Series of Analytical Essays and Critical Reviews, 6,* 51–93.

Crowder, R. D. (1982). *The psychology of reading.* New York: Oxford University Press.

Cruikshank, W. M. (1977). *Learning disabilities in home, school, and community.* Syracuse, N.Y.: University Press.

Dale, L. (1970). The growth of systematic thinking: Replication and analysis of Piaget's first chemical experiment. *Australian Journal of Psychology, 22,* 227–86.

Dale, P. S. (1976). *Language development: Structure and function* (2d ed.). New York: Holt, Rinehart and Winston.

Dalton, K. (1977). *The premenstrual syndrome and progesterone therapy.* London: Heinemann Medical.

Damon, A. (1968). Secular trend in height and weight within old American families at Harvard 1870–1965. Pt. 1, Within twelve four-generation families. *American Journal of Physical Anthropology, 29,* 45–50.

Damon, W. (1977). *The social world of the child.* San Francisco: Jossey-Bass.

Damon, W., & Hart, W. (1982). The development of self-understanding from infancy through adolescence. *Child Development, 53,* 841–69.

D'Angelo, R. (1974). Families of sand: A report concerning the flight of adolescents from their families. Columbus, Ohio: Publication of the School of Social Work, Ohio State University.

Darwin, C. (1968). *On the origin of species.* New York: Penguin. (Original work published 1859.)

Dasen, P. R. (1972). Cross-cultural Piagetian research: A summary. *Journal of Cross-cultural Psychology, 3*(1), 29–39.

Dasen, P. R., (Ed.). (1977). *Piagetian psychology: Cross-cultural contributions.* New York: Gardner Press.

Datan, N. (1980). Midas and other midlife crises. In W. H. Norman & T. J. Scaramella, (Eds.), *Midlife: Developmental and clinical issues.* New York: Bruner/Mazel.

Davies, A., Devault, S., & Talmadge, M. (1971). Anxiety, pregnancy, and childbirth abnormalities. In H. Munsinger, (Ed.), *Readings in child development.* New York: Holt, Rinehart and Winston.

Davis, D. E. (1964). The physiological analysis of aggressive behavior. In E. Etkin, (Ed.), *Social behavior and organization among vertebrates.* Chicago: University of Chicago Press.

Davis, K., & Schoen, C. (1978). *Health and the war on poverty: A ten year appraisal.* Washington, D.C.: The Brookings Institution.

Debus, R. L. (1970). Effects of brief observation of model behavior on conceptual tempo of impulsive children. *Developmental Psychology, 2,* 22–32.

DeLone, R. H. (1982). Early childhood development as a policy goal: An overview of choices. In L. Bond & J. Joffe, (Eds.), *Facilitating infant and early childhood development.* Hanover, N.H.: University Press of New England.

Dement, W. C. (1960). The effects of dream deprivation. *Science, 131,* 1705–7.

DeMyer, W. (1975). Congenital anomalies of the central nervous system. In D. B. Tower, (Ed.), *The nervous system: The clinical neurosciences.* New York: Raven.

Denney, N. (1972). A developmental study of free classification in children. *Child Development, 43,* 1161–70.

Dennis, W. (1960). Causes of retardation among institutional children: Iran. *Journal of Genetic Psychology, 96,* 47–59.

Dennis, W. (1973). *Children of the crèche.* New York: Appleton-Century-Crofts.

Dennis, W., & Dennis, M. G. (1940). The effects of cradling practice upon the onset of walking in Hopi children. *Journal of Genetic Psychology, 56,* 77–86.

Dennis, W. A. (1936). A bibliography of baby biographies. *Child Development, 136,* 71–73.

Dershewitz, R. A. (1979). Will mothers use free household safety devices? *American Journal of Diseases of Children, 133,* 61–64.

Dershewitz, R. A., & Williamson, J. W. (1977). Prevention of childhood household injuries: A controlled clinical trial. *American Journal of Public Health, 67,* 1148–53.

DeStefano, J. S., & Rentel, V. M. (1975). Language variation: Perspectives for teachers. *Theory into Practice, 14*(5), 328–37.

Deutsch, H. (1945). *The psychology of women: A psychoanalytic interpretation* (Vol. 2). New York: Grune & Stratton.

Devereux, E. C. (1970). The role of peer group experience in moral development. In J. P. Hill, (Ed.), *Minnesota Symposium on Child Psychology* (Vol. 4). Minneapolis: University of Minneapolis Press.

deVilliers, J. G., & deVilliers, P. A. (1978). *Language acquisition.* Cambridge, Mass.: Harvard University Press.

deVries, M. W., & deVries, M. R. (1977, August). The cultural relativity of toilet training readiness: A perspective from East Africa. *Pediatrics, 60*(2), 170–77.

deVries, M. W., & Sameroff, A. J. (1984). Culture and temperament: Influences on infant temperament in three East-African societies. *American Journal of Orthopsychiatry, 54*(1), 83–96.

Dick-Read, G. (1972). *Childbirth without fear* (4th ed.). New York: Harper & Row.

Dobbin, J. (1974). The later development of the brain and its vulnerability. In T. A. Davis & J. Dobbin, (Eds.), *Scientific foundations of pediatrics.* Philadelphia: Saunders.

Dollard, J., Doob, L. W., Miller, N. E., Mowrer, O. H., & Sears, R. R. (1939). *Frustration and aggression.* New Haven, Conn.: Yale University Press.

Doman, G. (1975; 2d ed., 1983). *How to teach your baby to read.* Garden City, N.Y.: Doubleday.

Donovan, W. L., & Leavitt, L. A. (1985). Physiology and behavior: Parents' response to the infant cry. In B. M. Lester & C. F. Z. Boukydis, (Eds.), *Infant crying: Theoretical and research perspectives.* New York: Plenum.

Dore, J. (1978). Conditions for the acquisition of speech. In J. Markova, (Ed.), *The social context of language.* New York: Wiley.

Douvan, E., & Adelson, J. (1966). *The adolescent experience.* New York: Wiley.

Dowd, M. (1983, December 4). Many women in poll equate values of job and family life. *New York Times,* pp. 1, 66.

Dowdrey, L. (1985). Critical notice. (Review of *Coercive family process,* by Gerald R. Patterson.) *Journal of Child Psychology and Psychiatry, 26*(5), 829–33.

Dryfoos, J. G., & Heisler, T. (1981). Contraceptive services for adolescents: An overview. In F. Furstenberg, R. Lincoln, & J. Menken, (Eds.), *Teenage sexuality, pregnancy, and childbearing.* Philadelphia: University of Pennsylvania.

Duff, R. (1979, July). Guidelines for deciding care of critically ill or dying patients. *Pediatrics, 64*(1), 17–23.

Duff, R. (1981, March). Counseling families and deciding care of severely defective children: A way of coping with 'medical Vietnam.' *Pediatrics, 67*(3), 315–20.

Duke, D. L. (1978). Why don't girls misbehave more than boys in school? *Journal of Youth and Adolescence, 7,* 141–58.

Dunn, J., & Kendrick, C. (1979). Interactions between young siblings in the context of family relationships. In M. Lewis & L. Rosenblum, (Eds.), *The child and its family.* New York: Plenum.

Dunphy, D. C. (1963). The social structure of urban adolescent peer groups. *Sociometry, 26,* 230–46.

Dutton, D. B. (1981). Children's health care: The myth of equal access. In Select Panel for the Promotion of Child Health, *Better health for our chil-*

dren: A national strategy (Vol. IV). Washington, D.C.: U.S. Government Printing Office.

Easterbrooks, M., & Lamb, M. (1979). The relationship between quality of infant-mother attachment and infant competence in initial encounters with peers. *Child Development, 50,* 380–87.

Eccles, J. S., & Hoffman, L. W. (1984). Sex roles, socialization, and occupational behavior. In H. W. Stevenson & A. E. Siegel, (Eds.), *Child development research and social policy.* Chicago: University of Chicago Press.

Economic Policy Council. (1986). *Work and family life in the United States: A policy initiative.* Available from Publications Dept., United Nations Associations of the United States of America, 300 East 42d St., New York, N.Y. 10017.

Edna McConnell Clark Foundation. (1985). *Keeping families together: The case for family preservation.* New York: Edna McConnell Clark Foundation.

Edward, C. P., & Whiting, B. B. (1980). Differential socialization of girls and boys in the light of cross-cultural research. In C. M. Super & S. Harkness, (Eds.), *Anthropological perspectives on child development.* San Francisco: Jossey-Bass.

Edwards, C. P. (1982). Moral development in comparative cultural perspective. In D. A. Wagner & H. W. Stevenson, (Eds.), *Cultural perspectives on child development.* San Francisco: Freeman.

Egeland, B. (1974). Training impulsive children in the use of more efficient scanning techniques. *Child Development, 45,* 165–71.

Egeland, B., & Brunquette, D. (1979). An at-risk approach to the study of child abuse: Some preliminary findings. *Journal of the American Academy of Psychiatry, 18,* 219–35.

Eichorn, D. H. (1963). Biological correlates of behavior. *Yearbook of the National Society for the Study of Education, 62,* 4–61.

Eichorn, D. H. (1975). Asynchronizations in adolescent development. In S. E. Dragastin & G. H. Elder, (Eds.), *Adolescence in the life cycle: Psychological change and social context.* Washington, D.C.: Hemisphere Publishing.

Eichorn, D. H. (1979). Physical development: Current foci of research. In J. D. Osofsky, (Ed.), *Handbook of infant development.* New York: Wiley.

Eiduson, B., Kornfein, M., Zimmerman, I., & Weisner, T. (1982). Comparative socialization practices in traditional and alternative families. In M. E. Lamb, (Ed.), *Nontraditional families: Parenting and child development.* Hillsdale, N.J.: Erlbaum.

Eimas, P. D. (1982). Speech perception: A view of the initial state and perceptual mechanisms. In J. Mehler, M. Garrett, & E. Walker, (Eds.), *Perspectives on mental representation.* Hillsdale, N.J.: Erlbaum.

Eimas, P. D., Sigueland, E. R., Jusczyk, P., & Vigorito, H. (1971). Speech perception in infants. *Science, 171,* 303–6.

Eimas, P. D., & Tartter, V. C. (1979). On the development of speech perceptions: Mechanisms and analogies. In H. W. Reese & L. P. Lipsitt, (Eds.), *Advances in child development and behavior.* New York: Academic Press.

Eisenberg, L., & Kanner, L. (1956). Early infantile autism. *American Journal of Orthopsychiatry, 26,* 556–66.

Eisenberg, N. (1982). Social development. In C. B. Kopp & J. B. Krakow, (Eds.), *The child: Development in a social context.* Reading, Mass.: Addison-Wesley.

Eisenberg, R. B., Coursin, D. B., Griffin, E. J., & Hunter, M. A. (1964). Auditory behavior in the human neonate: A preliminary report. *Journal of Speech and Hearing Research, 7,* 245–69.

Ekstein, R. (1973). The schizophrenic adolescent's struggle toward separation and individuation. In S. C. Feinstein & D. L. Giovancchini, (Eds.), *Adolescent psychiatry* (Vol. 2). New York: Basic Books.

Ekstein, R. (1978). Psychoanalysis, sympathy, and altruism. In L. Wispe, (Ed.), *Altruism, sympathy, and helping: Psychological and sociological principles.* New York: Academic Press.

Elder, D., & Hallinan, M. T. (1978). Sex differences in children's friendships. *American Sociological Review, 43,* 237–50.

Elder, G. H., Jr. (1974). *Children of the Great Depression.* Chicago: University of Chicago Press.

Elder, G. H., Jr. (1975). Adolescence in the life cycle: An introduction. In S. E. Dragastin & G. H. Elder, (Eds.), *Adolescence in the life cycle: Psychological change and social context.* Washington, D.C.: Hemisphere Publishing.

Elder, G. H., Jr. (1977). Family history and the life course. *Annual Review of Sociology, 2,* 279–304.

Elder, G. H., Jr. (1980). Adolescence in historical perspective. In J. Adelson, (Ed.), *Handbook of adolescent psychology.* New York: Wiley.

Elkind, D. (1967). Egocentrism in adolescence. *Child Development, 38,* 1025–34.

Elkind, D. (1978). *The child's reality: Three developmental themes.* Hillsdale, N.J.: Erlbaum.

Elkind, D. (1981). *The hurried child: Growing up too fast too soon.* Reading, Mass.: Addison-Wesley.

Elkind, D. (1983). Teenage thinking and the curriculum. *Educational Horizons, 61*(4), 163–68.

Elkind, D. (1984). *All grown up and no place to go: Teenagers in crisis.* Reading, Mass.: Addison-Wesley.

Ellis, N. R. (1970). Memory processes in retardates and normals. In N. R. Ellis, (Ed.), *International review of research in mental retardation* (Vol. 4). New York: Academic Press.

Emde, R. N., Harmon, R. J., Metcalf, D., Koening, K. L., & Wagonfeld, S. (1971). Stress and neonatal sleep. *Psychosomatic Medicine, 33,* 491–97.

Endsley, R. C., Hutchers, M. A., Garner, A. P., & Martin, M. J. (1979). Interrelationships among selected maternal behaviors, authoritarianism, and preschool children's verbal and nonverbal curiosity. *Child Development, 50*(2), 331–39.

Entwisle, D. R., & Hayduk, L. A. (1978). *Too great expectations: The academic outlook of young children.* Baltimore: Johns Hopkins University Press.

Entwisle, D. R., & Hayduk, L. A. (1982). *Early schooling—Cognitive and affective outcomes.* Baltimore: Johns Hopkins University Press.

Epps, E. G., & Smith, S. F. (1984). School and children: The middle childhood years. In A. W. Collins, (Ed.), *Development during middle childhood: The years from six to twelve.* Washington, D.C.: National Academy Press.

Erickson, M. L. (1978). Schools for crime? *Journal of Research in Crime and Delinquency, 15,* 31–34.

Erikson, E. (1959). Identity and the life cycle. *Psychological Issues, I* (Monograph No. 1).

Erikson, E. (1963). *Childhood and society* (2d ed.). New York: Norton.

Erikson, E. (1968). *Identity: Youth and crisis.* New York: Norton.

Erikson, E. (Ed.). (1978). *Adulthood.* New York: Norton.

Erlenmeyer-Kimling, L., & Jarvik, L. F. (1963, December 13). Genetics and intelligence: A review. *Science, 142,* 1477–79.

Espenshade, T. J. (1979). The economic consequences of divorce. *Journal of Marriage and the Family, 41,* 615–25.

Etaugh, C. (1974). Effects of maternal employment on children: A review of recent research. *Merrill-Palmer Quarterly, 20,* 71–98.

Etaugh, C., Collins, G., & Gerson, A. (1975). Reinforcement of sex-typed behaviors of two-year-old children in a nursery school setting. *Developmental Psychology, 11,* 255.

Etzioni, A. (1977). Sex control, science, and society. In A. S. Baer, (Ed.), *Heredity and society: Readings in social genetics.* New York: Macmillan.

Eveleth, P. B., & Tanner, J. (1976). *Worldwide variations in human growth.* Cambridge, England: Cambridge University Press.

Fafouti-Milenković, M., & Uẑgiris, I. C. (1979). The mother-infant communication system. In I. C. Uẑgiris, (Ed.), *Social interaction and communication during infancy.* San Francisco: Jossey-Bass.

Fagan, J. F., III (1973). Infants' delayed recognition and forgetting. *Journal of Experimental Child Psychology, 16,* 425–50.

Fagot, B. (1977). Consequences of moderate cross-gender behavior in preschool children. *Child Development, 48,* 902–7.

Families and child care: Improving the options. (1984). Report by the Select Committee on Children, Youth, and Families (Ninety-eighth Congress). Washington, D.C.: U.S. Government Printing Office.

Fantz, R. L. (1961). The origin of form perception. *Scientific American, 204,* 66–72.

Fantz, R. L. (1963). Pattern vision in newborn infants. *Science, 140,* 296–97.

Fantz, R. L. (1966). Pattern discrimination and selective attention as determinants of perceptual development from birth. In A. H. Kidd & J. L. Rivoire, (Eds.), *Perceptual development in children.* New York: International Universities Press.

Farber, S. L. (1981). *Identical twins reared apart.* New York: Basic Books.

Farel, A. (1980). Effects of preferred maternal roles, parental employment and socio-demographic status on school adjustment and competence. *Child Development, 51,* 1179–86.

Farkas, G. (1984). *Post program impacts of the Youth Incentive Entitlement Pilot Project (YIEPP).* New York: Manpower Demonstration Research Corp.

Farran, D. C., & Ramey, C. (1977). Infant day care and attachment behaviors toward mothers and teachers. *Child Development, 48,* 1112–16.

Faust, M. S. (1960). Developmental maturity as a determinant in prestige of adolescent girls. *Child Development, 31,* 173–84.

Faux, M. (1984). *Childless by choice: Choosing childlessness in the 80's.* New York: Doubleday.

Feather, N. T. (1980). Values in adolescence. In J. Adelson, (Ed.), *Handbook of adolescent psychology*. New York: Wiley.

Federal Register (1985, September 4). Vol. 50, No. 171. *Social services in the year 2000*. Washington, D.C.: U.S. Dept. of Health and Human Services.

Feingold, B. (1975). *Why your child is hyperactive*. New York: Random House.

Feinman, S., & Lewis, M. (1983). Social referencing at ten months: A second-order effect on infants' responses to strangers. *Child Development, 54,* 878–87.

Ferreira, A. J. (1969). *The prenatal environment*. Springfield, Ill.: Charles C. Thomas.

Feshbach, N., & Feshbach, S. (1976). Children's aggression. In W. W. Hartup, (Ed.), *The young child: Reviews of research* (2d ed., Vol. 2). Washington, D.C.: National Association for the Education of Young Children.

Feshbach, N. D. (1969). Student teacher preferences for elementary school pupils varying in personality characteristics. *Journal of Educational Psychology, 60,* 126–32.

Feshbach, N. D. (1980). Corporal punishment in the schools: Some paradoxes, some facts, some possible directions. In G. Gerbner, C. J. Ross, & E. Zigler, (Eds.), *Child abuse: An agenda for action*. New York: Oxford University Press.

Feshbach, S. (1980). Child abuse and the dynamics of human aggression and violence. In G. Gerbner, C. J. Ross, & E. Zigler, (Eds.), *Child abuse: An agenda for action*. New York: Oxford University Press.

Feshbach, S., & Singer, R. D. (1971). *Television and aggression*. San Francisco: Jossey-Bass.

Feuerstein, R. (1980). *Instrumental enrichment: An intervention program for cognitive modifiability*. Baltimore, Md.: University Park Press.

Field, T. (1978). Interaction behaviors of primary versus secondary caretaker fathers. *Developmental Psychology, 14,* 183–84.

Field, T., Woodson, R., Greenberg, R., & Cohen, D. (1982). Discrimination and imitation of facial expressions by neonates. *Science, 218,* 179–81.

Field, T. M., Dabiri, C., Hallock, N., & Shuman, H. H. (1977). Developmental effects of prolonged pregnancy and the postmaturity syndrome. *Journal of Pediatrics, 90,* 836–39.

Finch, S. M., & Poznanski, E. D. (1971). *Adolescent suicide*. Springfield, Ill.: Charles C. Thomas.

Fine, G. A. (1980). The natural history of preadolescent friendship groups. In H. Foot, A. Chapman, & J. Smith, (Eds.), *Friendship and social relations in children*. New York: Wiley.

Finkelstein, N. W., & Ramey, C. T. (1977). Learning to control the environment in infancy. *Child Development, 48,* 806–19.

Finklehor, D. (1979). *Sexually victimized children*. New York: Free Press.

Finn, A. (1985). Personal communication.

Finn, M. (1977). *The politics of nutrition education*. Unpublished dissertation, Ohio State University, Columbus.

Finn, M. (1981). Surviving the budget cuts: Policy options. *Young Children, 37,* 62–64.

Fischer, K., & Lazerson, A. (1984). *Human development*. New York: Freeman.

Fischer, K. W. (1983). Developmental levels as periods of discontinuity. In K. W. Fischer, (Ed.), *Levels and transitions in children's development*. San Francisco: Jossey-Bass.

Fish, B. (1971). The one child, one drug myth of stimulants in hyperkinesis: Importance of diagnostic categories in evaluating treatment. *Archives of General Psychiatry, 25,* 193–203.

Fisher, D. L. (1976). *Functional illiteracy and the schools: A reanalysis of several large-scale surveys*. Report to the U.S. Department of Health, Education and Welfare, National Institute of Education.

Fisher, M. A., & Zeaman, D. (1973). An attention-retention theory of retardate discrimination learning. In N. R. Ellis, (Ed.), *International review of research in mental retardation* (Vol. 6). New York: Academic Press.

Fishman, B., & Hamel, B. (1981, May). From nuclear to stepfamily ideology: A stressful change. *Alternative Lifestyles, 4*(2), 181–204.

Fitzgerald, H. E., & Brackbill, Y. (1976). Classical conditioning in infancy: Development and constraints. *Psychological Bulletin, 83,* 353–75.

Fitzgerald, T. A. (1974, Fall). Exploring childhood. *Colorado Audio-Visual Advance*.

Fitzgerald, T. A. (1981, Spring). Exploring childhood in a private school. *Education for Parenthood Exchange, 7*(2)

Flapan, D. (1968). *Children's understanding of social interactions*. New York: Teachers College Press.

Flavell, J. (1977). *Cognitive development*. Englewood Cliffs, N.J.: Prentice-Hall.

Flavell, J. (1985). *Cognitive development* (2d ed.). Englewood Cliffs, N.J.: Prentice-Hall.

Flavell, J. H. (1963). *The developmental psychology of Jean Piaget*. Princeton, N.J.: Van Nostrand Reinhold.

Flavell, J. H. (1982). On cognitive development. *Child Development, 53,* 1–10.

Folstein, S., & Rutter, M. (1978). A twin study of individuals with infantile autism. In M. Rutter & E. Schopler, (Eds.), *Autism: A reappraisal of concepts and treatment*. New York: Plenum.

Foltz, A. (1980). *The politics of prevention: Child health under Medicaid*. New Haven, Conn.: Yale University Press.

Fontana, V. J. (1973). *Somewhere—A child is crying*. New York: Macmillan.

Formanek, R., & Gurian, A. (1980). *Why? Children's questions: What they mean and how to answer them*. Boston: Houghton Mifflin.

Fosburg, S. (1980). *National Day Care Home Study*. Cambridge, Mass.: Abt Associates.

Foundation for Children with Learning Disabilities (1986). Personal communication. 99 Park Avenue, New York, N.Y.

FRAC (Food Research and Action Center). (1983). *How to document hunger in your community*. Washington, D.C.: FRAC.

Fraiberg, S. (1968). Parallel and divergent patterns in blind and sighted infants. *Psychoanalytic Study of the Child, 19,* 5–7.

Fraiberg, S. (1971). Intervention in infancy: A program for blind infants. *Journal of the American Academy of Child Psychiatry, 10,* 381–405.

Fraiberg, S. (1974). Blind infants and their mothers. In M. Lewis & L. A. Rosenblum, (Eds.), *The effect of the infant on its caregiver*. New York: Wiley.

Fraiberg, S. (1977). *Insights from the blind: Comparative studies of blind and sighted infants*. New York: Basic Books.

Francis-Williams, J., & Davies, P. A. (1974). Very low birth weight and later intelligence. *Developmental Medicine and Child Neurology, 16,* 709–28.

Frankenburg, W. K. (1981). Early screening for developmental delays and potential school problems. In C. C. Brown, (Ed.), *Infants at risk: Assessment and intervention*. Skillman, N.J.: Johnson & Johnson.

Frasier, S. D., & Rallison, M. L. (1972). Growth retardation and emotional deprivation: Relative resistance to treatment with growth hormone. *Journal of Pediatrics, 80,* 603–05.

Frazier, T. M., Davis, G. H., Goldstein, H., & Goldberg, I. (1961). Cigarette smoking: A prospective study. *American Journal of Obstetrics and Gynecology, 81,* 988–96.

Freedman, D. G. (1964). Smiling in blind infants and the issue of innate versus acquired. *Journal of Child Psychology and Psychiatry, 5,* 171–84.

Freedman, D. G. (1965). Hereditary control of early social behavior. In B. M. Foss, (Ed.), *Determinants of infant behavior* (Vol. 3). New York: Wiley.

Freedman, D. G. (1971). Behavioral assessment in infancy. In G. A. B. Stoelinga & J. J. Van Der Werff Ten Bosch, (Eds.), *Normal and abnormal development of brain and behavior*. Leiden, The Netherlands: Leiden University Press.

Freedman, D. G., & Freedman, N. C. (1969). Behavioral differences between Chinese-American and European-American newborns. *Nature, 224,* 1227.

Freeman, D. (1983). *Margaret Mead and Samoa: The making and unmaking of an anthropological myth*. Cambridge, Mass.: Harvard University Press.

Freeman, E. W. (1980). Adolescent contraceptive use: Comparisons of male and female attitudes and information. *American Journal of Public Health, 70,* 790–97.

Freeman, J. (1983). *Clever children*. Middlesex, United Kingdom: Hamlyn.

French, A., & Berlin, I. (Eds.). (1979). *Depression in children and adolescents*. New York: Human Sciences Press.

Freud, A. (1968). Adolescence. In A. E. Winter & D. L. Angus, (Eds.), *Adolescence: Contemporary studies*. New York: American Books.

Freud, A., with Dunn, S. (1951). An experiment in group upbringing. *Psychoanalytic Study of the Child, 6,* 127–68.

Freud, S. (1930; 2d ed., 1957). *Civilization and its discontents*. London: Hogarth.

Freud, S. (1965). *The ego and the mechanism of defense*. C. Baines (Trans.). New York: International University Press. (Original work published 1933.)

Friedman, S. L., Jacobs, B. S., & Werthman, M. W. (1978, October 6–7). Information processing and temperament in preterm, full-term, and post-term infants at the neonatal period. Invited address, Workshop on Birth Not at Term: Constraints to

Optimal Psychological Development. Bethesda, Md.: National Institute of Mental Health.

Friedman, S. L., & Sigman, M. (Eds.). (1980). *Preterm birth and psychological development*. New York: Academic Press.

Friedrich, L. K., & Stein, A. H. (1973). Aggressive and prosocial television programs and the natural behavior of preschool children. *Monographs of the Society for Research in Child Development, 38*(4), (Serial No. 151).

Frisch, R. (1974). Body composition, hormones, and growth: Discussion. In M. M. Grumbach, G. D. Grave, & F. E. Mayer, (Eds.), *Control of the onset of puberty*. New York: Wiley.

Frisch, R. (1978). Population, food intake, and fertility: There is historical evidence for a direct effect of nutrition on reproductive ability. *Science, 199,* 22–30.

Frodi, A. (1985). When empathy fails: Aversive infant crying and child abuse. In B. M. Lester & C. F. Z. Boukydis, (Eds.), *Infant crying: Theoretical and research perspectives*. New York: Plenum.

Frost, J. L., & Sunderlin, S. (1985). *When children play*. Wheaton, Md.: Association for Children's Education International.

Frye, D. (1982). The problem of infant day care. In E. Zigler & E. Gordon, (Eds.), *Day care: Scientific and social policy issues*. Boston: Auburn House.

Fuchs, F. (1980). Genetic amniocentesis. *Scientific American, 242,* 47–53.

Fuller, J. L. (1967). Experimental deprivation and later behavior. *Science,* 1645–52.

Furstenberg, F. F., Peterson, J. L., Nord, C. W., & Zill, N. (1983). The life course of children of divorce: Marital disruption and parental contact. *American Sociological Review, 48*(5), 656–68.

Furstenberg, F. F., Jr. (1976). *Unplanned parenthood: The social consequences of teenage childbearing*. New York: Free Press.

Gabel, S., & Erickson, M. T. (Eds.). (1980). *Child development and developmental disabilities*. Boston: Little, Brown.

Gaensbauer, T. J., & Sands, K. (1979). Distorted affective communication in abused/neglected infants and their potential impact on caretakers. *Journal of The American Academy of Child Psychiatry, 18,* 236–50.

Gage, N. L. (1978). *The scientific basis of the art of teaching*. New York: Teachers College Press.

Gallahue, D. L. (1982). *Understanding motor development in children*. New York: Wiley.

Gallo, A., Connor, J., & Boehm, W. (1980, Winter). Mass media food advertising. *National Food Review,* pp. 10–12.

Gallup, G., Jr. (1986a). Gallup Youth Survey (May–June 1985). Princeton, N.J.: The Gallup Organization.

Gallup, G., Jr. (1986b). Gallup Youth Survey (August–October 1985). Princeton, N.J.: The Gallup Organization.

Gamble, T. J., & Zigler, E. (1986). Effects of infant day care: Another look at the evidence. *American Journal of Orthopsychiatry, 56,* 26–42.

Garbarino, J. (1977). The price of privacy: An analysis of the social dynamics of child abuse. *Child Welfare, 56,* 565–75.

Garbarino, J. (1980). Latchkey children. *Vital Issues, 30*(3), 1–4 (whole issue). Available from the Center for Information on America, Washington, CT 06793.

Garbarino, J. (1986). Troubled youth, troubled families: The dynamics of adolescent maltreatment. In D. Cicchetti & V. Carlson, (Eds.), *Research and theoretical advances on the topic of child maltreatment*. Hawthorne, N.Y.: Aldine DeGruyter.

Garbarino, J., & Gilliam, G. (1980). *Understanding abusive families*. Lexington, Mass.: Lexington Books.

Garbarino, J., & Sherman, D. (1980). High-risk families and high-risk neighborhoods: Studying the ecology of child maltreatment. *Child Development, 51,* 188–98.

Garbarino, J., & Vondra, J. (1983, August). The psychological maltreatment of children and youth. Keynote presentation of the First International Conference on Psychological Abuse and Neglect, Indianapolis, Ind.

Gardner, H. (1978). *Developmental psychology*. Boston: Little, Brown.

Gardner, H., & Winner, E. (1979, May). The child is father to the metaphor. *Psychology Today, 12,* 81–91.

Gardner, L. I. (1972). Deprivation dwarfism. *Scientific American, 227*(1), 76–82.

Gardner, R. A., & Gardner, B. T. (1980). Two comparative psychologists look at language acquisition. In K. E. Nelson, (Ed.), *Children's language* (Vol. 2). New York: Gardner.

Garfinkel, B. D., Froese, A., & Hood, J. (1982). Suicide attempts in children and adolescents. *American Journal of Psychiatry, 139*(10), 1257–61.

Garfinkel, B. D., & Golombek, H. (1974). Suicide

and depression in childhood and adolescence. *Canadian Medical Association Journal, 110,* 1278.

Garmezy, N., & Rutter, M. (Eds.). (1983). *Stress, coping, and development in children.* New York: McGraw-Hill.

Garn, S. M. (1966). Body size and its implications. In L. W. Hoffman & M. L. Hoffman, (Eds.), *Review of child development research* (Vol. 2). New York: Russell Sage.

Garrard, J. W. (1974). Breastfeeding: Second thoughts. *Pediatrics, 54,* 757.

Garrett, C. S., Ein, P. L., & Tremaine, L. (1977). The development of gender stereotyping of adult occupations in elementary school children. *Child Development, 48,* 507–12.

Garrison, W., & Earls, F. (1982). Preschool behavior problems and the multigenerational family: An island community study. *International Journal of Family Psychiatry, 2,* 195–207.

Garrison, W., & Earls, F. (1983). Life events and social supports in families with a two-year-old: Methods and preliminary findings. *Comprehensive Psychiatry, 24,* 439–52.

Garrison, W. T. (1984). Inpatient psychiatric treatment of the difficult child: Common practices and their ethical implications. *Children and Youth Services Review, 6(4),* 353–65.

Garvey, C. (1977). *Play.* Cambridge, Mass.: Harvard University Press.

Gaudry, E., & Spielberger, C. (1971). *Anxiety and educational achievement.* Sydney, Australia: Wiley.

Geber, M. (1962). Longitudinal study of psychomotor development among Baganda children. *Proceedings of the XIV International Congress of Applied Psychology, 3,* 50–60.

Geber, M., & Dean, R. F. A. (1957). The state of development of newborn African children. *Lancet, 1,* 1216–19.

Geller, M. I., Kelley, J. A., Traxler, W. T., & Marone, F. J., Jr. (1978). Behavioral treatment of an adolescent female's bulimic anorexia: Modification of immediate consequences and antecedent conditions. *Journal of Clinical Child Psychology, 7,* 138–42.

Gelles, R. (1978). Violence toward children in the United States. *American Journal of Orthopsychiatry, 48,* 580–92.

Gellis, S. S., & Hsia, D. Y. (1959). The infant of the diabetic mother. *American Journal of Diseases of Children, 97,* 1.

Gelman, R. (1969). Conservation acquisition: A problem of learning to attend to relevant attributes. *Journal of Experimental Child Psychology, 7,* 167–87.

General Mills American Family Report. (1977). *Raising children in a changing society.* Minneapolis: General Mills.

General Mills American Family Report. (1979). *Family health in an era of stress.* Minneapolis: General Mills.

General Mills American Family Report. (1981). *Families at work—Strengths and strains.* Minneapolis: General Mills.

George, C., & Main, M. (1979). Social interactions of young abused children: Approach, avoidance, and aggression. *Child Development, 50,* 306–18.

Gerbner, G. (1980). Children and power on television: The other side of the picture. In G. Gerbner, C. J. Ross, & E. Zigler, (Eds.), *Child abuse: An agenda for action.* New York: Oxford University Press.

Gerbner, G., Ross, C., & Zigler, E. (Eds.). (1980). *Child abuse: An agenda for action.* New York: Oxford University Press.

Gesell, A., & Ilg, F. L. (1942). *Infant and child in the culture of today.* New York: Harper.

Gewirtz, J. L. (1965). The course of infant smiling in four childrearing environments in Israel. In B. M. Foss, (Ed.), *Determinants of infant behavior* (Vol. 3). New York: Wiley.

Gibson, E. J. (1969). *Principles of perceptual learning and development.* New York: Appleton-Century-Crofts.

Gibson, E. J., & Walk, R. R. (1960). The "visual cliff." *Scientific American, 202,* 2–9.

Gil, D. (1976). Primary prevention of child abuse: A philosophical and political issue. *Journal of Pediatric Psychology, 1,* 54–57.

Gilligan, C. (1982). *In a different voice.* Cambridge, Mass.: Harvard University Press.

Gleidman, J., & Roth, W. (1980). *The unexpected minority: Handicapped children in America.* New York: Harcourt Brace Jovanovich.

Glenn, N. D. (1975). Psychological well-being in the post-parental stage: Some evidence from national surveys. *Journal of Marriage and the Family, 37,* 105–10.

Goetz, P. L., Succop, R. A., Reinhart, J. B., & Miller, A. (1977). Anorexia nervosa in children: A follow-up study. *American Journal of Psychiatry, 47,* 597–603.

Gold, D., & Andres, D. (1978a). Comparisons of

adolescent children with employed and non-employed mothers. *Merrill-Palmer Quarterly, 24,* 243–54.

Gold, D., & Andres, D. (1978b). Developmental comparisons between ten-year-old children with employed and nonemployed mothers. *Child Development, 49,* 75–84.

Gold, M., & Petronio, R. J. (1980). Delinquent behavior in adolescence. In J. Adelson, (Ed.), *Handbook of adolescent psychology.* New York: Wiley.

Goldberg, S. R., & Deutsch, F. (1977). *Life-span individual and family development.* Monterey, Calif.: Brooks-Cole.

Golden, G. S. (1984). The developmentally disabled child: Detection, assessment, referral, and treatment. *Child Care, 3*(1), 8–11.

Goldstein, H., & Peckham, C. (1976). Birth weight, gestation, neonatal mortality and child development. In D. F. Roberts & A. M. Thompson, (Eds.), The biology of fetal growth. *Human Biology, 15,* 81–108.

Goldstein, J., Freud, A., & Solnit, A. (1973). *Beyond the best interests of the child.* New York: Free Press.

Goldstein, J., Freud, A., & Solnit, A. (1979). *Before the best interests of the child.* New York: Free Press.

Goodlad, J. (1983). *A place called school.* New York: McGraw-Hill.

Gordon, E. W. (1979). Evaluation during the early years of Head Start. In E. Zigler & J. Valentine, (Eds.), *Project Head Start: A Legacy of the War on Poverty.* New York: Free Press.

Gordon, S., & Scales, P. (1979). Preparing today's youth for tomorrow's family. In M. W. Kent & J. E. Rolf, (Eds.), *Primary prevention of psychopathology.* Vol. 3, *Social competence in children.* Hanover, N.H.: University Press of New England.

Gorski, P. A. (1984). Infants at risk. In M. J. Hanson, (Ed.), *Atypical infant development.* Baltimore: University Park Press.

Gottesman, I. (1963). Genetic aspect of intelligent behavior. In N. Ellis, (Ed.), *Handbook of mental deficiency: Psychological theory and research.* New York: McGraw-Hill.

Gottfried, A. W., & Gottfried, A. E. (1984). Home environment and mental development in young children. In A. W. Gottfried, (Ed.), *Home environment and early mental development: Longitudinal research.* New York: Academic Press.

Gottlieb, G. (1976). The roles of experience in the development of behavior and the nervous system. In G. Gottlieb, (Ed.), *Studies on the development of behavior and the nervous system* (Vol. 3). New York: Academic Press.

Gottlieb, G. (1983). The psychobiological approach to developmental issues. In P. H. Mussen, (Ed.), *Handbook of child psychology* (4th ed.). Vol. 2, M. Haith & J. J. Campos, (Eds.), *Infancy and developmental psychobiology.* New York: Wiley.

Gottlieb, J. (Ed.). (1980). *Educating mentally retarded persons in the mainstream.* Baltimore: University Park Press.

Gottman, J. (1977). The effects of a modeling film on social isolation in preschool children: A methodological investigation. *Journal of Abnormal Psychology, 5,* 69–78.

Gratz, R. (1979). Accidental injury in childhood: A literature review of pediatric trauma. *Journal of Trauma, 19,* 551–55.

Green, A. A. (1976). A psychodynamic approach to the study and treatment of child abusing parents. *Journal of Child Psychiatry, 15,* 414.

Greenberg, J., & Doolittle, G. (1977, December 11). Can schools speak the language of the deaf? *New York Times Magazine,* 50–102.

Greenfield, P. M. (1984). *Mind and media: The effects of television, video games and computers.* Cambridge, Mass.: Harvard University Press.

Greenspan, S., & Greenspan, N. T. (1985). *First feelings: Milestones in the emotional development of your baby and child.* New York: Viking.

Grossman, H. J. (Ed.). (1982). *Manual on terminology and classification in mental retardation* (3d rev.). Washington, D.C.: American Association on Mental Deficiency.

Gueron, J. M. (1984). *Lessons from a job guarantee: The Youth Incentive Entitlement Pilot Project.* New York: Manpower Demonstration Research Corporation.

Guidubaldi, J., Perry, J. D., Cleminshaw, H. K., & McLoughlin, C. S. (1983). The impact of parental divorce on children: Report of the nationwide NASP study. *School Psychology Review, 12*(3), 300–23.

György, F. (1960). The late effects of early malnutrition. *American Journal of Clinical Nutrition, 8,* 344–45.

Haith, M. M. (1980). *Rules newborns look by.* Hillsdale, N.J.: Erlbaum.

Haith, M. M., Bergman, T., & Moore, M. J. (1977). Eye contact and scanning in early infancy. *Science, 199,* 853–54.

Hakuta, K. (1986). *Mirror of language: The debate on bilingualism*. New York: Basic Books.

Hall, G. S. (1904). *Adolescence: Its psychology and its relations to physiology, anthropology, sociology, sex, crime, religion, and education*. New York: Appleton.

Halliday, M. A. K. (1975). *Learning how to mean: Explorations in the development of language*. London: Arnold.

Hallinan, M. (1981). Recent advances in sociometry. In S. Asher & J. Gottman, (Eds.), *The development of children's friendships*. New York: Cambridge University Press.

Hallinan, M. T. (1980). Patterns of cliquing among youth. In H. C. Foot, A. J. Chapman, & J. R. Smith, (Eds.), *Friendship and peer relations in children*. New York: Wiley.

Hammer, T. J., & Turner, P. H. (1985). *Parenting in contemporary society*. Englewood Cliffs, N.J.: Prentice-Hall.

Handler, J. F., & Zatz, J. (Eds.). (1982). *Neither angels nor thieves: Studies in deinstitutionalization of status offenders*. Washington, D.C.: National Academy Press.

Hanson, D. (1980). Drug education: Does it work? In F. Scarpitti & S. Datesman, (Eds.), *Drugs and the youth culture*. Beverly Hills, Calif.: Sage Publications.

Hanson, M. J. (1984a). Early intervention: Models and practices. In M. J. Hanson, (Ed.), *Atypical infant development*. Baltimore: University Park Press.

Hanson, M. J. (1984b). The effects of early intervention. In M. J. Hanson, (Ed.), *Atypical infant development*. Baltimore: University Park Press.

Harari, H., & McDavid, J. (1973). Teachers' expectations and name stereotypes. *Journal of Educational Psychology, 65*, 222–25.

Harding, C. H., Brooks, G. W., Ashikaga, T., Strauss, J. S., & Breier, A. (1986). *The Vermont Longitudinal Study*. Pt. II, *Long-term outcome for DSM-III schizophrenia*. Manuscript submitted for publication.

Harlow, H. (1971). *Learning to love*. San Francisco: Albion.

Harlow, H., & Mears, C. (1979). *The human model: Primate perspectives*. New York: Wiley.

Harlow, H. F. (1961). The development of affectional patterns in infant monkeys. In B. M. Foss, (Ed.), *Determinants of infant behavior*. London: Methuen.

Harlow, H. F. (1962). The heterosexual affectional system in monkeys. *American Psychologist, 17*, 17–19.

Harlow, H. F. (1963). The maternal affectional system. In B. M. Foss, (Ed.), *Determinants of infant behavior* (Vol. 3). New York: Wiley.

Harlow, H. F., & Novak, M. A. (1973). A psychopathological perspective. *Perspectives in Biology and Medicine, 16*, 461–78.

Harlow, H. F., & Zimmerman, R. R. (1959). Affectional responses in the infant monkey. *Science, 130*, 431–32.

Harman, D., & Brim, O. G., Jr. (1980). *Learning to be parents: Principles, programs, and methods*. Beverly Hills: Sage.

Harper, L. V., & Sanders, K. M. (1975). Preschool children's use of space: Sex differences in outdoor play. *Developmental Psychology, 11*, 119–21.

Harper, R. M., Leake, B., Hoffman, H., Walker, D. V., Hoppenbrouwers, T., Hodgman, J., & Sternman, M. B. (1981). Periodicity of sleep states is altered in infants at risk for the sudden infant death syndrome. *Science, 213*, 1030–32.

Harter, S. (1979, May–June). Children's understanding of multiple emotions: A cognitive-developmental approach. Paper presented at the Ninth Annual Symposium of the Jean Piaget Society, Philadelphia.

Harter, S. (1983). Competence as a dimension of self-evaluation: Toward a comprehensive model of self-worth. In R. Leahy, (Ed.), *The development of the self*. New York: Academic Press.

Harter, S. (1983). Developmental perspectives on the self-system. In P. H. Mussen, (Ed.), *Handbook of child psychology* (4th ed.). Vol. 4, E. M. Hetherington, (Ed.), *Socialization, personality, and social development*. New York: Wiley.

Harter, S., & Zigler, E. (1974). The assessment of effectance motivation in normal and retarded children. *Developmental Psychology, 10*, 169–80.

Hart-Johns, M., & Johns, B. (1982). *Give your child a chance*. Reston, Va.: Reston Publishing Co.

Hartshorne, H., & May, M. (1928). *Studies in the nature of character*. Vol. 1, *Studies in deceit*. New York: Macmillan.

Hartup, W. W. (1970). Peer interaction and social organization. In P. H. Mussen, (Ed.), *Carmichael's manual of child psychology*. New York: Wiley.

Hartup, W. W. (1974). Aggression in childhood: Developmental perspectives. *American Psychologist, 29*, 336–41.

Hartup, W. W. (1978). Perspectives on child and family interaction: Past, present and future. In R. M. Lerner & G. B. Spanier, (Eds.), *Child influ-*

ences on marital and family interaction: A life-span perspective. New York: Academic Press.

Hartup, W. W. (1979). The social worlds of childhood. *American Psychologist, 34,* 944–50.

Hartup, W. W. (1983). Peer relations. In P. H. Mussen, (Ed.), *Handbook of child psychology* (4th ed.). Vol. 4, E. M. Hetherington, (Ed.), *Socialization, personality, and social development.* New York: Wiley.

Hartup, W. W. (1984). The peer context in middle childhood. In W. A. Collins, (Ed.), *Development during middle childhood: The years from six to twelve.* Washington, D.C.: National Academy Press.

Harvey, T. J. (1983, July 12). Statement of the Executive Director of the National Conference of Catholic Charities before the Select Committee on Children, Youth and Families, Ninety-eighth Congress (first session), Washington, D.C.

Harwood, R. (1985). Summary: Work, parenting, and stress in the early postpartum months. In *Infant Care Leave Project: Summaries of research components.* Unpublished manuscript, Bush Center in Child Development and Social Policy, Yale University.

Haynes, H., White, B. L., & Held, R. (1965). Visual accommodation in human infants. *Science, 148,* 528–30.

Head Start in the 1980s: Review and recommendations (1980, September). Washington, D.C.: Head Start Bureau, Administration for Children, Youth, and Families, U.S. Dept. of Health and Human Services.

Hebb, D. (1980). *Essay on mind.* Hillsdale, N.J.: Erlbaum.

Hebb, D. O. (1972). *Textbook of psychology.* Philadelphia: Saunders.

Helton, G. B., & Oakland, T. D. (1977). Teachers' attitudinal responses to differing characteristics of school students. *Journal of Educational Psychology, 69,* 261–66.

Hendershot, G. E., & Placek, P. (1981). *Predicting fertility.* Lexington, Mass.: D. C. Heath, Lexington Books.

Herrenkohl, R. C., & Herrenkohl, E. C. (1981). Some antecedents and developmental consequences of mild maltreatment. In R. Rigley & D. Cicchetti, (Eds.), *New directions for child development.* San Francisco: Jossey-Bass.

Hess, R. D., & Camara, K. A. (1979). Post-divorce relationships as mediating factors in the consequences of divorce for children. *Journal of Social Issues, 35,* 79–96.

Hess, R. D., & Holloway, S. D. (1984). Family and school in educational institutions. In R. D. Parke, (Ed.), *Review of child development research.* Vol. 7, *The family.* Chicago: University of Chicago Press.

Hess, R. D., Holloway, S. D., Price, G. G., & Dickson, W. P. (1982). Family environments and the acquisition of reading skills: Toward a more precise analysis. In L. M. Laosa & I. E. Sigel, (Eds.), *Families as learning environments for children.* New York: Plenum.

Hetherington, E. M. (1980). Children and divorce. In R. Henderson, (Ed.), *Parent-child interaction: Theory, research and prospect.* New York: Academic Press.

Hetherington, E. M., & Camara, K. A. (1984). Families in transition: The processes of dissolution and reconstitution. In R. D. Parke, (Ed.), *The family: Review of child development research* (Vol. 7). Chicago: University of Chicago Press.

Hetherington, E. M., Cox, M., & Cox, R. (1976). Divorced fathers. *The Family Coordinator, 25,* 417–28.

Hetherington, E. M., Cox, M., & Cox, R. (1978). The aftermath of divorce. In J. H. Stevens, Jr., & M. Mathews, (Eds.), *Mother-child father-child relations.* Washington, D.C.: National Association for the Education of Young Children.

Hetherington, E. M., Cox, M., & Cox, R. (1979). The development of children in mother-headed families. In H. Hoffman & D. Reiss, (Eds.), *The American family: Dying or developing?* New York: Plenum Press.

Hetherington, E. M., Cox, M., & Cox, R. (1981). Divorce and remarriage. Paper presented at the meeting of the Society for Research in Child Development, Boston.

Hetherington, E. M., Cox, M., & Cox, R. (1982). Effects of divorce on parents and children. In M. Lamb, (Ed.), *Nontraditional families: Parenting and child development.* Hillsdale, N.J.: Erlbaum.

Hicks, L. E., Langham, R. A., & Takenaka, J. (1982, October). Cognitive and health measures following early nutritional supplementation: A sibling study. *American Journal of Public Health, 72* (10), 1110–18.

Hill, C. R., & Stafford, F. P. (1980). Parental care of children: Time diary estimate of quantity, predictability and variety. *Journal of Human Resources, 15,* 219–39.

Hill, H. (1984). *WIC: A retrospective analysis of a success.* Unpublished ms. Bush Center in Child Development and Social Policy, Yale University.

Hill, J. P. (1980). The family. In M. Johnson, (Ed.), *Seventy-ninth yearbook of the National Society for the Study of Education.* Chicago: University of Chicago Press.

Hinde, R. A. (1976). On describing relationships. *Journal of Child Psychology and Psychiatry, 17,* 1–19.

Hock, E. (1980). Working and nonworking mothers and their infants: A comparative study of maternal caregiving characteristics and infant social behavior. *Merrill-Palmer Quarterly, 26*(2), 79–101.

Hodapp, R., & Mueller, E. (1982). Early social development. In B. Wolman, (Ed.), *The handbook of developmental psychology.* Englewood Cliffs, N.J.: Prentice-Hall.

Hodapp, T. (1977). Children's ability to learn problem-solving strategies from television. *Alberta Journal of Educational Research, 23,* 171–77.

Hofferth, S. C. (1979). Day care in the next decade: 1980–1990. *Journal of Marriage and the Family, 41,* 649–57.

Hoffman, E. (1983). Social policy and advocacy. In E. Zigler, S. L. Kagan, & E. Klugman, (Eds.), *Children, families and government: Perspectives on American social policy.* New York: Cambridge University Press.

Hoffman, L. W. (1963). Mother's enjoyment of work and effects on the child. In F. I. Nye & L. W. Hoffman, (Eds.), *The employed mother in America.* Chicago: Rand McNally.

Hoffman, L. W. (1974). Effects of maternal employment on the child: A review of the research. *Developmental Psychology, 10,* 204–28.

Hoffman, L. W. (1975). The employment of women, education, and fertility. *Merrill-Palmer Quarterly, 20,* 99–119.

Hoffman, L. W. (1975). The value of children to parents and the decrease in family size. *Proceedings of the American Philosophical Society, 119*(6), 430–38.

Hoffman, L. W. (1979). Maternal employment—1979. *American Psychologist, 34*(10), 859–65.

Hoffman, L. W., & Hoffman, M. L. (1963). The value of children to parents. In J. T. Fawcett, (Ed.), *Psychological perspectives on population.* New York: Basic Books.

Hoffman, M. L. (1970). Conscience, personality, and socialization techniques. *Human Development, 13,* 90–126.

Hoffman, M. L. (1976). Empathy, role-taking, guilt, and development of altruistic motives. In T. Lickona, (Ed.), *Moral development and behavior.* New York: Holt, Rinehart and Winston.

Hoffman, M. L. (1977). Moral internalization: Current theory and research. In L. Berkowitz, (Ed.), *Advances in experimental social psychology* (Vol. 10). New York: Academic Press.

Hoffman, M. L. (1978). Empathy: Its development and prosocial implications. In C. B. Keasey, (Ed.), *1977 Nebraska Symposium on Motivation.* Lincoln: University of Nebraska Press.

Hoffman, M. L. (1984). Moral development. In M. H. Bornstein & M. E. Lamb, (Eds.), *Developmental psychology: An advanced textbook.* Hillsdale, N.J.: Erlbaum.

Holden, C. (1980). Identical twins reared apart. *Science, 207,* 1323–25, 1327–28.

Hollenbeck, A., & Slaby, R. (1979). Infant visual and vocal responses to television. *Child Development, 50,* 41–45.

Hollinger, P. C. (1978). Adolescent suicide: An epidemiological study of recent trends. *American Journal of Psychiatry, 135,* 754–56.

Hollingworth, H. L. (1927). *Mental growth and decline: A survey of developmental psychology.* New York: Appleton.

Hollos, M. (1975). Logical operations and role-taking abilities in two cultures: Norway and Hungary. *Child Development, 46,* 638–49.

Holmstrom, L. L. (1973). *The two-career family.* Cambridge, Mass.: Schenkman.

Honzik, M. (1964). Personality consistency and change: Some comments on papers by Bayley, MacFarlane, Moss, Kagan and Murphy. *Vita Humana, 7,* 139–42.

Honzik, M. P. (1957). Developmental studies of parent-child resemblance in intelligence. *Child Development, 28,* 215–28.

Hook, E. B. (1973). Behavioral implications of the human XYY genotype. *Science, 179,* 139–50.

Horn, J. L. (1970). Organization of data on life-span development of human abilities. In L. R. Goulet and P. B. Baltes, (Eds.), *Life-span developmental psychology: Research and theory.* New York: Academic Press.

Horn, J. L. (1978). Human ability systems. In P. B. Baltes & O. G. Brim, Jr., (Eds.), *Life-span development and behavior* (Vol. 1). New York: Academic Press.

Horowitz, F. D., & Paden, L. Y. (1973). The effectiveness of environmental programs. In B. Caldwell & H. N. Ricciuti, (Eds.), *Review of child development research*. Vol. 3, *Child development and social policy*. Chicago: University of Chicago Press.

Horowitz, R. A. (1979). Psychological effects of the "open classroom." *Review of Educational Research, 49,* 71–86.

Huesmann, L. R., Eron, L. D., Lefkowitz, M. M., & Walder, L. O. (1984). Stability of aggression over time and generations. *Developmental psychology, 6,* 1120–34.

Hultsch, D. F., & Deutsch, F. (1981). *Adult development and aging: A life-span perspective.* New York: McGraw-Hill.

Hunt, J. McVicker (1961). *Intelligence and experience.* New York: Ronald Press.

Huston, A. C. (1983). Sex typing. In P. H. Mussen, (Ed.), *Handbook of child psychology* (4th ed.). Vol. 4, E. M. Hetherington, (Ed.), *Socialization, personality, and social development.* New York: Wiley.

Hutt, S. J., Hutt, C., Lenard, H., Bernuth, V., & Muntjewerff, W. (1968). Auditory responsivity in the human neonate. *Nature, 318,* 888–90.

Hutt, S. J., Lenard, H. G., & Prechtl, H. F. R. (1969). Psychophysiology of the newborn. In L. P. Lipsitt & H. W. Reese, (Eds.), *Advances in child development.* New York: Academic Press.

Huttenlocher, J., & Presson, C. B. (1973). Mental rotation and the perspective problem. *Cognitive Psychology, 4,* 277–99.

Huttenlocher, P. R. (1979). The nervous system. In V. Vaughan III, P. McKay, & R. Behrman, (Eds.), *Nelson: Textbook of pediatrics* (11th ed.). Philadelphia: Saunders.

Hyman, I. (1984, October 17). Testimony before the Subcommittee on Juvenile Justice, Committee on the Judiciary, United States Senate, Ninety-eighth Congress, Second Session. Oversight on corporal punishment in schools and what is an appropriate range of discipline by school officials. Serial No. J-98-146.

Inhelder, B., & Piaget, J. (1958). *The growth of logical thinking from childhood to adolescence.* New York: Basic Books.

Inhelder, B., & Piaget, J. (1959). *The early growth of logic in the child.* (Trans. G. A. Lunzer & D. Papert.) New York: Harper & Row.

Irwin, P. M. (1986). Adult literacy issues, programs, and options, updated 01/06/86. Washington, D.C.: Education and Public Welfare Division, Congressional Research Service. Unpublished manuscript.

Jacklin, C. N., & Maccoby, E. E. (1978). Social behavior at thirty-three months in same-sex and mixed-sex dyads. *Child Development, 49,* 557–69.

Jackson, P. (1968). *Life in the classroom.* New York: Holt, Rinehart and Winston.

Jackson, R. L. (1966). Effects of malnutrition on growth in the preschool child. In *Preschool child malnutrition: Primary deterrent to human progress.* Proceedings of the International Conference on Prevention of Malnutrition in the Preschool Child, Washington, D.C., December 7–11, 1964. National Academy of Sciences, National Research Council Publication No. 1282, Washington, D.C.

Jacobs, P. A. (1968). Chromosome studies on men in a maximum security hospital. *Annals of Human Genetics, 31,* 339.

Jacobson, D. (1975). Fair-weather friend: Label and context in middle-class friendship. *Journal of Anthropological Research, 31,* 225–34.

Jacobson, D. J. (1979, May). Stepfamilies: Myths and realities. *Social Work, 24*(3), 202–7.

James, W. (1890). *The principles of psychology.* New York: Holt.

Janis, J. (1983). Health policy for children. In E. Zigler, S. Kagan, & E. Klugman, (Eds.), *Children, families and government: A perspective on American social policy.* New York: Cambridge University Press.

Janis, J. M., & Bulow-Hube, S. (1986). *Healthy children.* Downey, Calif.: Los Angeles County Office of Education.

Jensen, A. R. (1969). How much can we boost IQ and scholastic achievement? *Harvard Educational Review, 39,* 1–123.

Jersild, A., & Holmes, F. B. (1935). *Children's fears.* Child Development Monograph 20. New York: Teachers College Press.

Jersild, A. T. (1952). *In search of self.* New York: Columbia University Press.

Jessor, R., & Jessor, S. L. (1977). *Problem behavior and psychological development.* New York: Academic Press.

Johnson, C., Stuckey, M., Lewis, L., & Schwartz, D. (1981). Bulimia: A descriptive survey of 509 cases. In P. Garfinkel, D. Gasner, & P. Darby, (Eds.), *Anorexia nervosa: A multidimensional perspective.* New York: Dorsey Press.

Jones, K. L., & Smith, D. W. (1973). Recognition of the fetal alcohol syndrome in early infancy. *Lancet, 2*, 999–1001.

Jones, L. (1985, Winter). Permanency and continuity: New issues in foster care planning. *The Networker, 6*(2), 4, 7. (Available from the Bush Center in Child Development and Social Policy, Yale University.)

Jones, M. C., & Bayley, N. (1950). Physical maturity among boys as related to behavior. *Journal of Educational Psychology, 41*, 129–48.

Joslyn, W. D. (1973). Androgen-induced social dominance in infant female rhesus monkeys. *Journal of Child Psychology and Psychiatry, 14*, 137–45.

Juel-Nielsen, N. (1965). *Individual and environment*. Copenhagen: Munksgaard.

Kacerguis, M. A., & Adams, G. R. (1979). Implications of sex-typed childrearing practices, toys, and mass media materials in restricting occupational choices of women. *Family Coordinator, 28*, 368–75.

Kaeser, S. C. (1979). *Orderly schools that serve all children*. Cleveland, Ohio: Citizens' Council for Ohio Schools.

Kagan, J. (1965). Impulsive and reflective children: Significance of conceptual tempo. In J. D. Krumholz, (Ed.), *Learning and the educational process*. Chicago: Rand McNally.

Kagan, J. (1972). Case against IQ tests: Concept of intelligence. *Humanist, 32*, 7.

Kagan, J. (1976). Emergent themes in human development. *American Scientist, 64*(21), 186–96.

Kagan, J. (1978). On emotion and its development: A working paper. In M. Lewis & L. A. Rosenblum, (Eds.), *The development of affect*. New York: Plenum.

Kagan, J. (1984). The idea of emotion in human development. In C. E. Izard, J. Kagan, & R. B. Zajonc, (Eds.), *Emotion, cognition, and behavior*. New York: Cambridge University Press.

Kagan, J. (1984). *The nature of the child*. New York: Basic Books.

Kagan, J., & Kagan, N. (1970). Individual variations in cognitive processes. In P. Mussen (Ed.), *Carmichael's manual of child psychology*. New York: Wiley.

Kagan, J., Kearsley, R., & Zelazo, P. (1978). *Infancy: Its place in human development*. Cambridge, MA: Harvard University Press.

Kahn, A. J. (1969). *Studies in social policy and planning*. New York: Russell Sage.

Kail, R. V., Jr. (1979). *The development of memory in children*. San Francisco: Freeman.

Kalish, R. A. (1976). Death and dying in the social context. In R. H. Binstock & E. Shanas (Eds.), *Handbook of aging and the social sciences*. New York: Van Nostrand Reinhold.

Kalish, R. (1981). *Death, grief, and caring relationships*. Monterey, CA: Brooks/Cole.

Kalter, N. (1977). Children of divorce in an outpatient psychiatric population. *American Journal of Orthopsychiatry, 51*, 85–100.

Kamerman, S., & Kahn, A. (1976). *European family policy currents: The question of families with very young children*. Unpublished manuscript, Columbia University, School of Social Work.

Kamerman, S. B., & Kahn, A. (1981). *Child care, family benefits, and working parents: A study in comparative policy*. New York: Columbia University Press.

Kamerman, S., & Kahn, A. (1983, September). Income transfers and mother-only families in eight countries. *Social Service Review*, 448–464.

Kamerman, S., Kahn, A., & Kingston, P. (1986). *Maternity policies and working women*. New York: Columbia University Press.

Kandel, D. B. (1981). Drug use by youth: An overview. In D. J. Lettieri & J. P. Ludford (Eds.), *Drug abuse and the American adolescent*. Rockville, MD: National Institute on Drug Abuse.

Kandel, D. B., & Lesser, G. S. (1972). *Youths in two worlds*. San Francisco: Jossey-Bass.

Kanner, L. (1942). Autistic disturbances of affective contact. *Nervous Child, 2*, 217.

Kanter, R. M. (1977). *Work and family life in the United States: A critical review and agenda for research and policy*. New York: Russell Sage Foundation.

Katz, A. J. (1979). Lone fathers: Perspectives and implications for family policy. *Family Coordinator, 28*, 521–528.

Kaufman, J., & Zigler, E. (1986). Do abused children become abusive parents? Unpublished manuscript, Yale University.

Kaye, K. (1980). Why we talk "baby talk" to babies. *Journal of Child Language, 7*, 489–507.

Keating, D. P. (1980). Thinking processes in adolescence. In J. Adelson, (Ed.), *Handbook of adolescent psychology*. New York: Wiley.

Kellogg, R. (1967, May). Understanding children's art. *Psychology Today, 1*(1), 16–25.

Kellogg, R. (1969). *Analyzing children's art*. Palo Alto, Calif.: National Press Books.

Kempe, C., Silverman, E., Steele, B., Droegemueller, W., & Silver, H. (1962). The battered child syndrome. *Journal of the American Medical Association, 181,* 17.

Kempe, H. C., & Helfer, R. E. (Eds.). (1972). *Helping the battered child and his family*. Philadelphia: Lippincott.

Kempe, R. S., & Kempe, H. C. (1978). *Child abuse*. Cambridge, Mass.: Harvard University Press.

Keniston, K. (1977). *All our children: The American family under pressure*. New York: Harcourt Brace Jovanovich.

Kenny, S. L. (1983). Developmental discontinuities in childhood and adolescence. In K. Fischer, (Ed.), *Levels and transitions in children's development*. San Francisco: Jossey-Bass.

Keogh, J. F. (1965). Motor performance in elementary school children. *Monographs*. Los Angeles, Calif.: College of Education, University of California at Los Angeles.

Kessel, N., & Coppen, A. (1963). The prevalence of common menstrual symptoms. *Lancet, ii,* 61–64.

Kessen, W. (1965). *The child*. New York: Basic Books.

Kessen, W. (1975). *Childhood in China*. New Haven, Conn.: Yale University Press.

Keyserling, M. D. (1972). *Windows on day care*. New York: National Council of Jewish Women.

Kimmel, D. (1974). *Adulthood and aging*. New York: Wiley.

Kimmel, D. (1980). *Adulthood and aging* (2d ed.). New York: Wiley.

Kinsey, A. C., Pomeroy, W. B., & Martin, C. E. (1948). *Sexual behavior in the human male*. Philadelphia: Saunders.

Kinsey, A. C., Pomeroy, W. B., Martin, C. E., & Gebhard, P. H. (1953). *Sexual behavior in the human female*. Philadelphia: Saunders.

Klagsburn, S. (1982). Ethics in hospice care. *American Psychologist, 37,* 1263–65.

Klaus, M. H., & Kennell, J. H. (1976). *Maternal-infant bonding*. St. Louis: Mosby.

Klinman, D. G., & Kohl, R. (1984). *Fatherhood USA: Services and resources for and about fathers*. New York: Garland.

Klinnert, M., Campos, J., Sorce, J., Emde, R., & Suejda, M. (1983). Emotions as behavior regulators: Social referencing in infancy. In R. Plutchik & H. Kellerman, (Eds.), *Emotions in early development*. Vol. 2, *The emotions*. New York: Academic Press.

Klinnert, M., Emde, R., Butterfield, P., & Campos, J. (1983). Emotional communication from familiarized adults influences infants' behavior. Paper presented at the meeting of the Society for Research in Child Development, Boston.

Kogan, N. (1983). Stylistic variation in childhood and adolescence: Creativity, metaphor, and cognitive style. In P. H. Mussen, (Ed.), *Handbook of child psychology*. Vol. 3, J. H. Flavell & E. M. Markman, (Eds.), *Cognitive development*. New York: Wiley.

Kohlberg, L. (1966). A cognitive developmental analysis of children's sex-role concepts and attitudes. In E. E. Maccoby, (Ed.), *The development of sex differences*. Stanford, Calif.: Stanford University Press.

Kohlberg, L. (1969). Stage and sequence: The cognitive-developmental approach to socialization. In D. A. Goslin, (Ed.), *Handbook of socialization theory and research*. Chicago: Rand McNally.

Kohlberg, L. (1978). Revisions in the theory and practice of moral development. In W. Damon, (Ed.), *New directions in child development: Moral development*. San Francisco: Jossey-Bass.

Kohler, L. (1976, February 23). The student absentee. Paper presented at the annual convention of the American Association of School Administrators, Atlantic City, N.J.

Kohn, M. L. (1977). *Class and conformity: A study in values* (2d ed.). Chicago: University of Chicago Press.

Kolata, G. (1984, July 20). Studying learning in the womb. *Science, 225,* 302–3.

Kolko, D. J. (1984). Parents as behavior therapists for their autistic children: Clinical and empirical considerations. In E. Schopler & G. B. Mesibov, (Eds.), *The effects of autism on the family*. New York: Plenum.

Kopp, C. B., & Parmelee, A. H. (1979). Prenatal and perinatal influences on infant behavior. In J. D. Osofsky, (Ed.), *Handbook of infant development*. New York: Wiley.

Korchin, S. (1981, February 16). Quoted in *Newsweek,* p. 97.

Korner, A. F. (1968). REM organization in neonates: Theoretical implications for development and the biological function of REM. *Archives of General Psychiatry, 19,* 330–40.

Korner, A. F. (1971). Individual differences at birth: Implications for early experience and later development. *American Journal of Orthopsychiatry, 41,* 608–19.

Korner, A. F. (1972). State as a variable, as obstacle and as mediator of stimulation in infant research. *Merrill-Palmer Quarterly, 18,* 77–94.

Korner, A. F., Kraemer, H. C., Hoffner, E., & Cosper, L. M. (1975). Effects of waterbed flotation on premature infants: A pilot study. *Pediatrics, 56*(3), 361–67.

Kornhaber, A., & Woodward, K. L. (1981). *Grandparents/grandchildren: The vital connection.* Garden City, N.Y.: Anchor Press.

Kotelchuck, M., et al. (1981). *Final Report: 1980 Massachusetts Special Supplemental Food Program for Women, Infants and Children Evaluation Project.* Submitted to Food and Nutrition Service, USDA, Washington, D.C.

Kotelchuck, M., et al. (1984, October). WIC participation and pregnancy outcomes: Massachusetts Statewide Evaluation Project. *American Journal of Public Health, 74,* 1084–92.

Kotelchuck, M., & Richmond, J. B. (1982, April 17). Advocacy for child health: Past, present and future. In Proceedings of the Conference on Better Health for Children: Action for the Eighties, held at Harvard University School of Public Health, Cambridge, Mass.

Kotz, N. (1979, April). *Hunger in America: The federal response.* New York: Field Foundation.

Kovas, M. D., & Drury, T. F. (1980). Elderly people: The population 65 and over. Tables prepared for the Annual Meeting of the American Public Health Association, Detroit.

Kozloff, M. A. (1984). A training program for families of children with autism: Responding to family needs. In E. Schopler & G. B. Mesibov, (Eds.), *The effects of autism on the family.* New York: Plenum.

Kreisman, D. (1970). Social interaction and intimacy in schizophrenic adolescents. In J. Zubin & A. M. Freedman, (Eds.), *The psychopathology of adolescence.* New York: Grune & Stratton.

Kübler-Ross, E. (1969). *On death and dying.* New York: Macmillan.

Kuhlen, R. G. (1968). Developmental changes in motivation during the adult years. In B. L. Neugarten, (Ed.), *Middle age and aging.* Chicago: University of Chicago Press.

Kuhn, D. (1984). Cognitive development. In M. H. Bornstein & M. E. Lamb, (Eds.), *Developmental psychology: An advanced textbook.* Hillsdale, N.J.: Erlbaum.

Kuhne, R., & Blair, C. (1978). Changing the workweek. *Business Horizons, 21,* 2–4.

Kuhne, R. J., & Blair, C. O. (1978, April). Flexitime. *Business Horizons,* p. 42.

Kuntzleman, C. T. (1983). *Feeling good.* Unpublished report of a three-year project funded by the W. K. Kellogg Foundation. Spring Arbor, Michigan: Department of Health Services, Spring Arbor College.

La Barbera, J. D., Izard, C. E., Vietze, P., & Parisi, S. A. (1976). Four- and six-month-old infants' visual responses to joy, anger, and neutral expressions. *Child Development, 47,* 535–38.

Labouvie-Vief, G. (1977). Adult cognitive development: In search of alternative interpretations. *Merrill-Palmer Quarterly, 23,* 227–63.

Labouvie-Vief, G. (1980). Beyond formal operations: Uses and limits of pure logic in life-span development. *Human Development, 23*(3), 141–61.

Labov, W. (1970). The logic of nonstandard English. In F. Williams, (Ed.), *Language and poverty.* Chicago: Markham.

Labov, W. (1972). *Language in the inner city: Studies in the black English vernacular.* Philadelphia: University of Pennsylvania Press.

Lamb, M. E. (1977). Father-infant and mother-infant interaction in the first year of life. *Child Development, 48,* 167–81.

Lamb, M. E. (1978a). Interactions between eighteen-month-olds and their preschool-aged siblings. *Child Development, 49,* 51–59.

Lamb, M. E. (1978a). Social interactions in infancy and the development of personality. In M. E. Lamb, (Ed.), *Social and personality development.* New York: Holt, Rinehart and Winston.

Lamb, M. E. (1978b). The father's role in the infant's social world. In J. H. Stevens, Jr., & M. Mathews, (Eds.), *Mother/child, father/child relationships.* Washington, D.C.: National Association for the Education of Young Children.

Lamb, M. E. (1981). The development of father-infant relationships. In M. E. Lamb, (Ed.), *The role of the father in child development* (2d ed.). New York: Wiley.

Lamb, M. E. (1982). Maternal employment and child development: A review. In M. E. Lamb, (Ed.), *Nontraditional families: Parenting and childrearing*. Hillsdale, N.J.: Erlbaum.

Lamb, M. E. (1982). Parent-infant interaction, attachment, and socioemotional development in infancy. In R. N. Emde & R. J. Harmon, (Eds.), *The development of attachment and affiliative systems*. New York: Plenum.

Lamb, M. E. (1982). What can "research experts" tell parents about effective socialization? In E. Zigler, M. E. Lamb, & I. L. Child, (Eds.), *Socialization and Personality Development*. New York: Oxford University Press.

Lamb, M. E. (1984). Social and emotional development in infancy. In M. H. Bornstein & M. E. Lamb, (Eds.), *Developmental psychology: An advanced textbook*. Hillsdale, N.J.: Erlbaum.

Lamb, M. E., & Sutton-Smith, B. (Eds.). (1982). *Sibling relationships: Their nature and significance across the life-span*. Hillsdale, N.J.: Erlbaum.

Lamb, M. E., & Urberg, K. A. (1978). The development of gender role and gender identity. In M. E. Lamb, (Ed.), *Social and personality development*. New York: Holt, Rinehart and Winston.

Lambert, N. M., & Hartsough, C. S. (1984). Contribution of predispositional factors to the diagnosis of hyperactivity. *American Journal of Orthopsychiatry, 54*(1), 97–109.

Lampl, M., & Emde, R. (1983). Episodic growth spurts in infancy: A preliminary report on length, head circumference and behavior. In K. Fischer, (Ed.), *Levels and transitions in children's development*. San Francisco: Jossey-Bass.

Landau, E. (1983). *Why are they starving themselves? Understanding anorexia nervosa and bulimia*. New York: Julian Messner.

Laosa, L. M., & Brophy, J. E. (1972). Effects of sex and birth order on sex role development and intelligence among kindergarten children. *Developmental Psychology, 6*, 409–15.

Laosa, L. M., & Sigel, I. E. (Eds.). (1982). *Families as learning environments for children*. New York: Plenum.

Larrabee, E. (1960). Childhood in twentieth-century America. In E. Ginsberg, (Ed.), *The nation's children* (Vol. 3). New York: Columbia University Press.

Larson, M. (1977). *Better skills for youth: Four proposals for federal policy*. Report to the National Institute of Education, Department of Health, Education and Welfare. Contract No. UEC-400-75-0078. Stanford Research Institute.

Lash, T. W., Sigal, H., & Dudzinski, D. (1980). *The state of the child: New York City II*. New York: Foundation for Child Development.

Lasswell, H. D. (1971). *A preview of policy sciences*. New York: American Elsevier.

Lauersen, N., & Stukan, E. (1983). *Premenstrual syndrome and you: What it is, how to recognize it, and how to overcome it*. New York: Simon & Schuster.

Lazar, I., & Darlington, R. (1982). Lasting effects of early education: A report from the Consortium for Longitudinal Studies. *Monographs of the Society for Research in Child Development, 47*(2–3), Serial No. 195.

Lazar, I., Hubbell, R., Murray, H., Rosche, M., & Royce, J. (1977, September). The persistence of preschool effects: A long-term follow-up of fourteen infant and preschool experiments. Final Report, Grant No. 18-76-07843. Washington, D.C.: Office of Human Development Services., Dept. of Health and Human Services.

Lazarus, W. (1982). *Paying for children's health bills: Do's and don'ts in tight fiscal times*. Washington, D.C.: Children's Defense Fund.

Leach, P. (1983). *Babyhood*. New York: Knopf.

Leboyer, F. (1975). *Birth without violence*. New York: Knopf.

Lecours, A. R. (1975). Myelogenetic correlates of the development of speech and language. In E. H. Lenneberg & E. Lenneberg, (Eds.), *Foundations of language development*. New York: Academic Press.

Lefkowitz, B., & Andrulis, D. (1981). The organization of primary health and health related preventive, psychosocial, and support services for children and pregnant women. In *Better health for our children: A national strategy* (Vol. IV). Washington, D.C.: U.S. Government Printing Office.

Leiderman, P. H. (1983). Social ecology and childbirth: The newborn nursery as environmental stressor. In N. Garmezy & M. Rutter, (Eds.), *Stress, coping and development in children*. New York: McGraw-Hill.

Lein, L., Durham, M., Pratt, M., Thomas, R., & Weiss, H. (1974). *Work and family life: Final report to the National Institute of Education*. Cambridge, Mass.: Center for the Study of Public Policy.

Lenke, R. R., & Levy, H. L. (1980). Maternal phenylketonuria and hyperphenylketonuria: An international survey of untreated and treated pregnancies. *New England Journal of Medicine, 303,* 1202–8.

Lenke, R. R., & Levy, H. L. (1982). Maternal phenylketonuria—Results of dietary therapy. *American Journal of Obstetrics and Gynecology, 142,* 548–53.

Lenneberg, E. (1967). *Biological foundations of language.* New York: Wiley.

Lerner, R. M. (1969). The development of stereotyped expectancies of body build relations. *Child Development, 40,* 137–41.

Lerner, R. M., & Spanier, G. B. (1980). *Adolescent development: A life-span perspective.* New York: McGraw-Hill.

Lesser, G. S., Fifer, G., & Clark, D. H. (1965). Mental abilities of children from different social class and cultural groups. *Monographs of the Society for Research in Child Development, 30,* Serial No. 102.

Leventhal, A. S., & Lipsitt, L. P. (1964). Adaptation, pitch discrimination, and sound localization in the neonate. *Child Development, 35,* 759–67.

Levine, J. A. (1978). Day-care and the public schools: Current models and future directions. *Urban Sociology, 12*(1), 17–21.

Levine, J. A. (1982). School-age child care: An overview. In E. Zigler & E. Gordon, (Eds.), *Day care: Scientific and social policy issues.* Boston: Auburn House.

Levinson, D. J. (1978). *The seasons of a man's life.* New York: Knopf.

Levitin, T. E. (1979). Children of divorce: An introduction. *Journal of Social Issues, 35,* 4–9.

Lewin, K. (1939). Field theory and experiment in social psychology: Concepts and methods. *American Journal of Sociology, 44,* 868–97.

Lewis, D. O., & Balla, D. A. (1976). *Delinquency and psychopathology.* New York: Grune & Stratton.

Lewis, M. (1974). State as an infant-environment interaction: An analysis of mother-infant interactions as a function of sex. *Merrill-Palmer Quarterly, 20,* 195–204.

Lewis, M. (1984). Developmental principles and their implications for at-risk and handicapped infants. In M. J. Hanson, (Ed.), *Atypical infant development.* Baltimore: University Park Press.

Lewis, M., & Brooks, J. (1974). Self, other and fear: Infants' reactions to people. In M. Lewis & L. A. Rosenblum, (Eds.), *Origins of fear.* New York: Wiley.

Lewis, M., & Brooks-Gunn, J. (1979). *Social cognition and the acquisition of self.* New York: Plenum.

Lewis, M., & Feiring, C. (1981). Direct and indirect interactions in social relationships. In L. Lipsitt, (Ed.), *Advances in infancy research* (Vol. 1). New York: Ablex.

Lewis, M., & Michalson, L. (1982). The socialization of emotions. In T. Field & A. Fogel, (Eds.), *Emotions and early interaction.* Hillsdale, N.J.: Erlbaum.

Lewis, M., & Michalson, L. (1983). *Children's emotions and moods: Developmental theory and measurement.* New York: Plenum.

Lewis, M., Young, G., Brooks, J., & Michalson, L. (1975). The beginning of friendship. In M. Lewis & L. A. Rosenblum, (Eds.), *Friendship and peer relations.* New York: Wiley.

Lewis, T. L. Maurer, D., & Kay, D. (1978). Newborns' central vision: Whole or hole? *Journal of Experimental Psychology, 26,* 193–203.

Lewontin, R. C. (1982). *Human diversity.* San Francisco: Freeman.

Lewontin, R. C., Rose, S., & Kamin, L. (1984). *Not in our genes: Biology, ideology and human nature.* New York: Pantheon.

Liebert, R. M., McCall, R. B., & Hanratty, M. A. (1971). Effects of sex-typed information on children's toy preferences. *Journal of Genetic Psychology, 119,* 133–36.

Liebert, R. M., & Poulos, R. W. (1975). Television and personality development: The socializing effects of an entertainment medium. In A. Davids, (Ed.), *Child personality and psychopathology: Current topics* (Vol. 2). New York: Wiley.

Lindblom, C., & Cohen, D. K. (1979). *Usable knowledge.* New Haven, Conn.: Yale University Press.

Lipsitt, L. B., Engen, T., & Kaye, H. (1963). Developmental changes in the olfactory threshold of the neonate. *Child Development, 34,* 371–76.

Lipsitt, L. P. (1977). Taste in human neonates: Its effects on sucking and the heart rate. In J. M. Weiffenbach, (Ed.), *Taste and development: The genesis of sweet preference.* Washington, D.C.: U.S. Government Printing Office.

Lipton, E. L., Steinschneider, A., & Richmond, J. B. (1965). Swaddling, a child care practice: Historical, cultural, and experimental observations. *Pediatrics, 35*(3), 519–67.

Littman, B., & Parmelee, A. H. (1978). Medical correlates of infant development. *Pediatrics, 61,* 470.

Litwak, E., & Meyer, H. J. (1974). *Schools, family, and neighborhood: The theory and practice of school-community relations.* New York: Columbia University Press.

Loeb, R. C., Horst, L., & Horton, P. J. (1980). Family interaction patterns associated with self-esteem in preadolescent boys and girls. *Merrill-Palmer Quarterly, 26,* 203–17.

Long, L., & Long, T. (1983). *The handbook for latchkey children and their parents.* New York: Arbor House.

Lord, C., Schopler, E., & Revicki, D. (1982). Sex differences in autism. *Journal of Autism and Developmental Disorders, 12,* 317–30.

Lorenz, K. (1966). *On aggression.* New York: Harcourt Brace & World.

Lotter, V. (1978). Follow-up studies. In M. Rutter & E. Schopler, (Eds.), *Autism: A reappraisal of concepts and treatment.* New York: Plenum.

Louaas, I., Young, D., & Newsom, C. (1978). Childhood psychosis: Behavioral treatment. In B. B. Wolman, (Ed.), *Handbook of treatment of mental disorders in childhood and adolescence.* Berkeley, Calif.: University of California Press.

Lougee, M. D., Grueneich, R., & Hartup, W. W. (1977). Social interaction in same- and mixed-aged dyads of preschool children. *Child Development, 48,* 1353–61.

Love, H. D., & Walthod, J. E. (1977). Cerebral palsy. In *A handbook of medical, educational and psychological information for teachers of physically handicapped children.* Springfield, Ill.: Thomas.

Lowery, G. H. (1978). *Growth and development of children* (7th ed.). Chicago: Year Book Medical Publishers.

Ludman, R. J., & Scarpitti, F. R. (1978). Delinquency prevention: Recommendations for future projects. *Crime and Delinquency, 24,* 207–20.

Lynn, R. (1982). IQ in Japan and the United States shows a growing disparity. *Nature, 297,* 223.

Lyons, R. D. (1983, July 18). Physical and mental disabilities doubled in twenty-five years. *New York Times,* pp. A1, A10.

Lytton, H. (1976). Do parents create or respond to differences in twins? *Developmental Psychology, 13*(5), 456–59.

McCall, R. B. (1977). Childhood IQ's as predictors of adult educational and occupational status. *Science, 197,* 482–93.

McCall, R. B. (1980). *Infants: The new knowledge about the years from birth to three.* New York: Vintage.

McCall, R. B., Applebaum, M. I., & Hogarty, P. S. (1973). Developmental changes in mental performance. *Monographs of the Society for Research in Child Development, 38*(3), Serial No. 150.

McCall, R. B., Lonnborg, B., Gregory, T. G., Murray, J. P., & Leavitt, S. (1981, Fall). Communicating developmental research to the public: The Boys Town experience. *Newsletter of the Society for Research in Child Development,* pp. 1–3.

McCarthy, D. (1954). Language development in children. In L. Carmichael, (Ed.), *Manual of child psychology* (2d ed.). New York: Wiley.

McCartney, M., Scarr, S., Phillips, D., Grajek, S., & Schwartz, J. C. (1982). Environmental differences among day care centers and their effects on children's development. In E. Zigler & E. Gordon, (Eds.), *Day care: Scientific and social policy issues.* Boston: Auburn House.

Maccoby, E. (1964). Effects of the mass media. In M. L. Hoffman & L. W. Hoffman, (Eds.), *Review of child development research* (Vol. 1). New York: Russell Sage.

Maccoby, E. (1980). *Social development: Psychological growth and the parent-child relationship.* New York: Harcourt Brace Jovanovich.

Maccoby, E. (1984). Middle childhood in the context of the family. In W. A. Collins, (Ed.), *Development during middle childhood—The years from six to twelve.* Washington, D.C.: National Academy Press.

Maccoby, E. E., & Martin, A. (1983). Socialization in the context of the family: Parent-child interaction. In P. H. Mussen, (Ed.), *Handbook of child psychology* (4th ed.). Vol. 4, E. M. Hetherington, (Ed.), *Socialization, personality and social behavior.* New York: Wiley.

McDavid, J. W., & Harari, H. (1966). Stereotyping in names and popularity in grade school children. *Child Development, 37,* 453–59.

MacFarlane, J. A. (1975). Olfaction in the development of social preferences in the human neonate. In M. A. Hofer, (Ed.), *Parent-infant interaction.* Amsterdam: Elsevier.

McGhee, P. E. (1974). Cognitive mastery and children's humor. *Psychological Bulletin, 81,* 721–30.

McGhee, P. E. (1976). Children's appreciation of humor—Test of cognitive congruency principle. *Child Development, 47*(2), 420–26.

McGhee, P. E. (1979). *Humor: Its origin and development.* New York: Freeman.

McGillicuddy-DeLisi, A. V., & Sigel, I. (1982). Effects of the atypical child on the family. In L. A. Bond & J. M. Joffe, (Eds.), *Facilitating infant and early childhood development*. Hanover, N.H.: University Press of New England.

McGraw, M. B. (1940). Neural maturation as exemplified in achievement of bladder control. *Journal of Pediatrics, 16,* 580–89.

McHaynes, S. G., McMichael, A. J., & Tyroter, H. A. (1978). Survival after early and normal retirement. *Journal of Gerontology, 33,* 269–78.

MacLeod, S. (1981). *The art of starvation: A story of anorexia and its survival*. New York: Schocken Books.

MacMillan, D. L. (1969). Motivational differences: Cultural-familial retardates vs. normal subjects on expectancy for failure. *American Journal of Mental Deficiency, 74,* 254–58.

MacMillan, D. L. (1982). *Mental retardation in school and society* (2d ed.). Boston: Little, Brown.

MacMillan, D. L., & Keogh, B. K. (1971). Normal and retarded children's expectancy for failure. *Developmental Psychology, 4,* 343–48.

McNassor, D. (1975, April). The world of the preadolescent. *Childhood Education, 5,* 312–18.

MacRae, D., Jr. (1981). Combining the roles of scholar and citizen. In R. Haskins & J. Gallagher, (Eds.), *Models for the analysis of social policy: An introduction*. Norwood, N.J.: Ablex.

Malina, R. M. (1982). Motor development in the early years. In S. G. Moore & C. R. Cooper, (Eds.), *The young child: Reviews of the research* (Vol. 3). Washington, D.C.: National Association for the Education of Young Children.

Mann, C. H. (1980). Midlife and the family: Strains, challenges, and options of the middle years. In W. H. Norman & T. J. Scaramella, (Eds.), *Midlife: developmental and clinical issues*. New York: Brunner/Mazel.

Marcia, J. E. (1980). Identity in adolescence. In J. Adelson, (Ed.), *Handbook of adolescent psychology*. New York: Wiley.

Marcus, D. E., & Overton, W. F. (1978). The development of cognitive gender constancy and sex-role preferences. *Child Development, 49,* 434–44.

Marcusson, H., & Oehmish, W. (1977). Accident mortality in selected countries of different continents, 1950–1971. *World health statistics report, 30,* 57–92.

Margolis, L., & Farran, D. (1983, Fall). Consequences of unemployment. *The Networker, 4*(1), 1.

(Available from the Bush Center in Child Development and Social Policy, Yale University.)

Margolis, L. H., & Runyan, C. W. (1983). Accidental policy: An analysis of the problem of unintended injuries of childhood. *American Journal of Orthopsychiatry, 53*(4), 629–44.

Markman, E. M. (1977). Realizing that you don't understand: A preliminary investigation. *Child Development, 48,* 986–92.

Marks, P. A., & Haller, D. L. (1977). Now I lay me down for keeps: A study of adolescent suicide attempts. *Journal of Clinical Psychology, 33,* 400–8.

Markus, H. J., & Nurius, P. S. (1984). Self-understanding and self-regulation in middle childhood. In A. W. Collins, (Ed.), *Development during middle childhood: The years from six to twelve*. Washington, D.C.: National Academy Press.

Martin, G. B., & Clark, R. D., III. (1982). Distress crying in neonates: Species and peer specificity. *Developmental Psychology, 18*(1), 3–9.

Martin, H. P., & Breezley, P. (1976). Personality of abused children. In H. P. Martin, (Ed.), *The abused child: A multidisciplinary approach to developmental issues and treatment*. Cambridge, Mass.: Ballinger.

Marvin, R. S., Greenberg, M., & Mossler, D. (1976). The early development of conceptual perspective-taking: Distinguishing among multiple perspectives. *Child Development, 47,* 511–14.

Marx, J. L. (1978). Botulism in infants: A cause of sudden death? *Science, 201,* 799–801.

Masters, J., & Wilkinson, A. (1976). Consensual and discriminative stereotype of sex-type judgments by parents and children. *Child Development, 47,* 208–17.

Masters, J. C. (1983). Models for training and research in child development and social policy. In G. Whitehurst, (Ed.), *Annals of child development* (Vol. 1). Greenwich, Conn.: JAI Press.

Matarazzo, J. D. (1982). Behavioral health's challenge to academic, scientific, and professional psychology. *American Psychologist, 37*(1), 1–14.

Maxmen, J. S. (1985). *The new psychiatry*. New York: Morrow.

Mayer, J. (1968). *Overweight: Causes, cost and control*. Englewood Cliffs, N.J.: Prentice-Hall.

Mead, M. (1928). *Coming of age in Samoa: A psychological study in primitive youth for Western civilization*. New York: Dell.

Mead, M. (1961). *Coming of age in Samoa*. New York: Morrow.

Meadow, K. P. (1975). The development of deaf children. In E. M. Hetherington, (Ed.), *Review of child development research* (Vol. 5). Chicago: University of Chicago Press.

Meadow, K. P. (1980). *Deafness and child development.* Berkeley, Calif.: University of California Press.

Mednick, B. R., Baker, R. L., & Sutton-Smith, B. (1979). Pregnancy and perinatal mortality. *Journal of Youth and Adolescence, 8*(3), 343–57.

Medrich, E., Ruizen, J., Rubin, V., & Buckley, S. (1982). *The serious business of growing up: A study of children's lives outside of school.* Berkeley: University of California Press.

Meece, J. L., Parsons, J. E., Kaczala, C. H., Goff, F. B., & Futterman, R. (1982). Sex differences in math achievement: Toward a model of academic choice. *Psychological Bulletin, 91,* 324–28.

Mehler, J., Bertoncini, J., Barrière, M., & Jassik-Gerschenfeld, D. (1978). Infant recognition of mother's voice. *Perception, 7,* 491–97.

Meltzoff, A. N., & Moore, M. K. (1977). Imitation of facial and manual gestures by human neonates. *Science, 198,* 75–78.

Mendes, H. A. (1979). Single-parent families: A typology of lifestyles. *Social Work, 24*(3), 193–200.

Menninger Perspective. (1980). Work and the family: An American dilemma. A special issue of the *Menninger Perspective, 2*(4), 6–13.

Menyuk, P. (1972). *Speech development.* Indianapolis, Ind.: Bobbs-Merrill.

Mercer, J. (1972, September). IQ: The lethal label. *Psychology Today,* pp. 44–47.

Mercer, J. R. (1971). Sociocultural factors in labeling mental retardates. *The Peabody Journal of Education, 48,* 188–203.

Meredith, A. V. (1963). Changes in the stature and body weight of North American boys during the last 80 years. In L. P. Lipsitt & C. C. Spiker, (Eds.), *Advances in child development and behavior* (Vol. 1). New York: Academic Press.

Meredith, A. V. (1969). Body size of contemporary groups of eight-year-old children studied in different parts of the world. *Monographs of the Society for Research in Child Development, 34,* Serial No. 1.

Meredith, A. V. (1971). Growth in body size: A compendium of findings on contemporary children living in different parts of the world. In H. W. Rees, (Ed.), *Advances in child development and behavior* (Vol. 6). New York: Academic Press.

Meredith, A. V. (1976). Findings from Asia, Australia, Europe, and North America on secular change in mean height of children, youth and young adults. *American Journal of Physical Anthropology, 44,* 315–26.

Meredith, A. V. (1978). Research between 1960 and 1970 on the standing height of young children in different parts of the world. In H. W. Reese & L. P. Lipsitt, (Eds.), *Advances in child development and behavior* (Vol. XII). New York: Academic Press.

Meyers, C. E., MacMillan, D. L., & Yoshida, R. K. (1980). Regular class placement of EMR students— From efficacy to mainstreaming: A review of issues and research. In J. Gottlieb, (Ed.), *Educating mentally retarded persons in the mainstream.* Baltimore: University Park Press.

Miles, M., & Meluish, E. (1974). Recognition of mother's voice in early infancy. *Nature* (London), *252,* 123–24.

Miller, B. S., & Price, M. (Eds.). (1981). *The gifted child: The family and the community.* New York: Walker.

Miller, F. J. W., Court, S. D. M., Walton, W. S., & Know, E. G. (1960). *Growing up in Newcastle-upon-Tyne: A continuing study of health and illness in young children within their families.* London: Oxford University Press.

Miller, G. (1983). Children and the Congress: A time to speak out. *American Psychologist, 38*(1), 70–76.

Miller, J. D. (1981). Epidemiology of drug use among adolescents. In D. J. Lettier & J. P. Ludford, (Eds.), *Drug abuse and the American adolescent.* Rockville, Md.: National Institute on Drug Abuse.

Miller, J. D., Cisin, I. A., Gardner-Keaton, H., Harrell, A. V., Wirtz, P. W., Abelson, H. I., & Fisburne, D. M. (1983). *National survey on drug abuse: Main findings.* U.S. Department of Health and Human Services, Public Health Service. Rockville, Md.: National Institute on Drug Abuse.

Milunsky, A. (1977). *Know your genes.* Boston: Houghton Mifflin.

Mindel, E. D. (1980). Auditory disorders. In H. J. Grossman & R. L. Stubblefield, (Eds.), *The physician and the mental health of the child.* Monroe, Wis.: American Medical Association.

Minuchin, J., Rosman, B. L., & Baker, L. (1978). *Psychosomatic families.* Cambridge, Mass.: Harvard University Press.

Minuchin, P. P., & Shapiro, E. K. (1983). The school as a context for social development. In

P. H. Mussen, (Ed.), *Handbook of child psychology* (Vol. 4). New York: Wiley.

Minuchin, S., & Fishman, H. C. (1981). *Family therapy techniques*. Cambridge, Mass.: Harvard University Press.

Mishara, B. L. (1975). The extent of adolescent suicide. *Psychiatric Opinion, 12,* 32–37.

Moely, B. E. (1977). Organizational factors in the development of memory. In R. B. Kail & J. W. Hagen, (Eds.), *Perspectives on the development of memory and cognition.* Hillsdale, N.J.: Erlbaum.

Moen, P. (1982). The two-provider family: Problems and potentials. In M. E. Lamb, (Ed.), *Nontraditional families: Parenting and child development.* Hillsdale, N.J.: Erlbaum.

Moerck, E. L. (1980). Relationships between parental input frequencies and children's language acquisition: A reanalysis of Brown's data. *Journal of Child Language, 7,* 105–18.

Molnar, G. E. (1979). Cerebral palsy: Prognosis and how to judge it. *Pediatric Annals, 8,* 596–605.

Mondale, W. F. (1983). Forward. In E. Zigler, S. L. Kagan, & E. Klugman, (Eds.), *Children, families and government: Perspectives on American social policy.* New York: Cambridge University Press.

Money, J. (1975). Ablatiopenis: Normal male infant sex-reassigned as a girl. *Archives of Sexual Behavior, 4,* 65–72.

Money, J., & Ehrhardt, A. A. (1972). *Man and woman: Boy and girl: The differentiation and dimorphism of gender identity from conception to maturity.* Baltimore: Johns Hopkins University Press.

Money, J., Hampson, J. G., & Hampson, J. L. (1957). Imprinting and the establishment of gender role. *AMA Archives of Neurological Psychiatry, 77,* 333–36.

Montague, A. (1962). *Prenatal influences.* Springfield, Ill.: Thomas.

Montemayor, R., & Eisen, M. (1977). The development of self-conceptions from childhood to adolescence. *Developmental Psychology, 13,* 314–19.

Moore, K. A., & Waite, L. J. (1977). Early childbearing and educational attainment. *Family Planning Perspective, 9,* 220.

Moore, S. G., & Cooper, C. R. (1982). Personal and scientific sources of knowledge about children. In S. G. Moore & C. R. Cooper, (Eds.), *The young child: Review of research* (Vol. 3). Washington, D.C.: National Association for the Education of Young Children.

Morgan, G., & Ricciuti, H. N. (1969). Infants' responses to strangers during the first year. In B. M. Foss, (Ed.), *Determinants of infant behavior* (Vol. 4). New York: Wiley.

Morrison, F., Holmes, D. L., & Haith, M. M. (1974). A developmental study of the effects of familiarity on short-term visual memory. *Journal of Experimental Child Psychology, 18,* 412–25.

Moss, H. S. (1967). Sex, age and state as determinants of mother-infant interaction. *Merrill-Palmer Quarterly, 13,* 19–36.

Motoyama, E. K. (1966). Adverse effect of maternal hyperventilation on the foetus. *Lancet, 1,* 1966.

Mueller, E., & Brenner, J. (1977). The origins of social skills and interaction among playgroup toddlers. *Child Development, 48,* 854–61.

Mueller, E., & Lucas, F. A. (1975). A developmental analysis of peer interaction among toddlers. In M. Lewis & L. A. Rosenblum, (Eds.), *Friendship and peer relations.* New York: Wiley-Interscience.

Mueller, E., & Vandell, D. (1979). Infant-infant interaction. In J. D. Osofsky, (Ed.), *Handbook of infant development.* New York: Wiley.

Muenchow, S., & Gilfillan, S. S. (1983). Social policy and the media. In E. Zigler, S. L. Kagan, & E. Klugman, (Eds.), *Children, families and government: Perspectives on American social policy.* New York: Cambridge University Press.

Muller, E., Hollien, H., & Murray, T. (1974). Perceptual responses to infant crying: Identification of cry types. *Journal of Child Language, 1,* 89–96.

Murphy, D. P. (1947). *Congenital malformations.* Philadelphia: University of Pennsylvania Press.

Murphy, L. B., & Moriarty, A. E. (1976). *Vulnerability, coping and growth: From infancy to adolescence.* New Haven, Conn.: Yale University Press.

Murray, F. B. (1972). Acquisition of conservation through social interaction. *Developmental Psychology, 6,* 1–6.

Murray, J. P. (1980). *Television and youth: 25 years of research and controversy.* Boys Town, Nebr.: The Boys Town Center for the Study of Youth Development.

Mussen, P. H., & Bouterline-Young, H. (1964). Relationship between rate of physical maturing and personality among boys of Italian descent. *Vita Humana, 7,* 186–200.

Mussen, P. H., Conger, J. J., & Kagan, J. (1974). *Child development and personality.* New York: Harper & Row.

NAESP (National Association of Elementary School Principals) Staff Report. (1980, September). One-parent families and their children: The school's most significant minority. *Principal, 60,* 31–37.

NAEYC (National Association for the Education of Young Children). (1980). *The significance of the young child's motor development* (3d ed.). Proceedings of the conference sponsored by the American Association for Health and Physical Education and Recreation and NAEYC. Washington, D.C.: NAEYC.

Naeye, R. L. (1982). Fetal hypoxia as cause of SIDS. In J. Tildon, R. Tyson, L. M. Roeder, & A. Steinschneider, (Eds.), *Sudden infant death syndrome.* New York: Academic Press.

National Academy of Sciences. (1978). *Adolescent behavior and health.* Washington, D.C.: National Academy of Sciences.

National Center for Health Statistics (1976). NCHS Growth Charts. *Vital Statistics, 1976, 253* (Supp.). U.S. Department of Health, Education, and Welfare.

National children and youth fitness study. (1984). Washington, D.C.: Office for Disease Prevention and Health Promotion, U.S. Public Health Service.

National Coalition on Television Violence (NCTV). (1984). *NCTV Musicvideo report.* (Available from National Coalition on Television Violence, 1530 P Street, NW, P. O. Box 12038, Washington, D.C. 20005.)

National Commission on Excellence in Education. (1983). *A nation at risk.* Washington, D.C.: U.S. Government Printing Office.

National Commission on Secondary Schooling for Hispanics. (1984). *Make something happen.* (Available from Hispanic Policy Development Project, 1001 Connecticut Avenue, NW, Suite 310, Washington, D.C. 20036.)

National Commission on Youth. (1980). *The transition of youth to adulthood: A bridge too long.* Boulder, Colo.: Westview Press.

National Council on Aging. (1981). *Aging in the 80's: America in transition.* Washington, D.C.: National Council on Aging.

National Education Association. (1984–85). *Estimates of School Statistics.* Washington, D.C.: National Education Association.

National Research Council. (1982). *Alternative dietary practices and nutritional abuses in pregnancy: Summary report.* Committee on Nutrition of the Mother and Preschool Child, Food and Nutrition Board, Commission on Life Sciences.

National Safety Council. (1981). *Accident facts.* Chicago: National Safety Council.

Nelson, J. R. (1982). The politics of federal day care regulations. In E. Zigler & E. W. Gordon, (Eds.), *Day care: Scientific and social policy issues.* Boston: Auburn House.

Nelson, K. (1973). Structure and strategy in learning to talk. *Monographs of the Society for Research in Child Development, 38*(1 & 2), Serial No. 149.

Nelson, K. (1981). Individual differences in language development: Implications for development and language. *Psychological Bulletin, 17,* 170–87.

Nelson, K., & Ellenberg, J. (1979). Neonatal signs as predictors of cerebral palsy. *Pediatrics, 64,* 225–32.

Neugarten, B. L. (1968). The awareness of middle age. In B. L. Neugarten, (Ed.), *Middle age and aging.* Chicago: University of Chicago Press.

Neugarten, B. L. (1979). Time, age, and the life cycle. *American Journal of Psychiatry, 136,* 887–894.

Neugarten, B. L. (1985). Aging in the 1980's: Agenda for psychologists and policymakers. In R. A. Kasschau, L. P. Rehm, & L. P. Ullman, (Eds.), *Psychology research, public policy and practice: Toward a productive partnership.* New York: Praeger.

Neugarten, B. L., & Weinstein, K. K. (1964). The changing American grandparent. *Journal of Marriage and the Family, 26,* 199–204.

Newaceck, P., Burdetti, P., & Halfon, N. (1986). Trends in activity limiting chronic conditions among children. *American Journal of Public Health, 76*(2), 178–84.

Newport, E. L. (1976). Motherese: The speech of mothers to young children. In N. J. Castellan, D. B. Pisoni, & G. R. Potts, (Eds.), *Cognitive theory* (Vol. II). Hillsdale, N.J.: Erlbaum.

Newson, J., & Newson, E. (1976). *Seven-year-olds in the home environment.* New York: Wiley.

Niemark, E. D. (1975). Intellectual development during adolescence. In F. D. Horowitz, (Ed.), *Review of child development research* (Vol. 4). Chicago: University of Chicago Press.

North, A. F. (1979). Health services in Head Start. In E. Zigler & J. Valentine, (Eds.), *Project Head Start: A legacy of the War on Poverty.* New York: Free Press.

Norton, H. A., & Glick, P. C. (1986, January). One-parent families: A social and economic profile. *Family Relations, 35,* 9–16.

Notman, M. (1980). Adult life cycle transitions: Longitudinal effects on family members. *Journal of Marriage and the Family, 43,* 703–14.

Novitski, E. (1977). *Human genetics.* New York: Macmillan.

O'Brien, T., & McManus, C. (1978). Drugs and the fetus: A consumer's guide by generic and brand name. *Birth and the Family Journal, 5,* 58–86.

Offer, D. (1969). *The psychological world of the teen-ager: A study of normal adolescent boys.* New York: Basic Books.

Offer, D., Marhorn, R. C., & Ostrov, E. (1979). *The psychological world of the juvenile delinquent.* New York: Basic Books.

Offer, D., & Offer, J. (1975). *From teenage to young manhood.* New York: Basic Books.

Offer, D., Ostrov, E., & Howard, K. I. (1981). *The adolescent: A psychological self portrait.* New York: Basic Books.

Oller, J. W., Wienman, L. A., Doyle, W. J., & Ross, C. (1976). Infant babbling and speech. *Journal of Child Language, 3,* 1–11.

Oller, K. (1980). The emergence of the sounds of speech in infancy. In G. Yeni-Komshian & C. Ferguson, (Eds.), *Child phonology* (Vol. 1). New York: Academic Press.

Olmsted, B. (1979). Job sharing: An emerging work-style. *International Labour Review, 118,* 3–12.

Opie, I., & Opie, P. (1959). *The lore and language of schoolchildren.* Oxford: Clarendon Press.

Opie, I., & Opie, P. (1969). *Children's games in the street and playground.* Oxford: Clarendon Press.

Oppel, W. C., Harper, P. A., & Rider, R. V. (1968). The age of attaining bladder control. *Pediatrics, 42*(4), 614–26.

Opportunities for Success. (1985, August). *Cost effective programs for children.* Staff report of the Select Committee on Children, Youth and Families. Ninety-ninth Congress, first session. Washington, D.C.: U.S. Government Printing Office.

Osherson, D. N. (1975). *Logical abilities in children.* Vol. 3, *Reasoning in adolescence: Deductive inference.* Hillsdale, N.J.: Erlbaum.

Osman, B. B., & Blinder, H. (1986). *No one to play with: The social side of learning disabilities.* New York: Random House.

Ostrea, E. M., & Chavez, C. J. (1979). Perinatal problems in maternal drug addiction: A study of 830 cases. *The Journal of Pediatrics, 94,* 292–95.

Packard, V. (1983). *Our endangered children: Growing up in a changing world.* Boston: Little, Brown.

Papousek, H. (1967). Conditioning during early postnatal development. In Y. Brackbill & G. G. Thompson, (Eds.), *Behavior in infancy and early childhood.* New York: Free Press.

Papousek, H., & Papousek, M. (1979). Early ontogeny of human social interaction: Its biological roots and social dimensions. In M. Cranbach, K. Foppa, W. Lepenies, & D. Ploog, (Eds.), *Human ethology.* London: Cambridge University Press.

Parke, R., O'Leary, S. E., & West, S. (1972). Mother-father-newborn interaction: Effects of maternal medication, labor, and sex of the infant. *Proceedings of the American Psychological Association, 7,* 85–88.

Parke, R., & Peterson, J. L. (1981). Indicators of social change: Developments in the United States. *Accounting Organization and Society, 6,* 323–29.

Parke, R. D. (1976). Some effects of punishment on children's behavior. In W. W. Hartup, (Ed.), *The young child: Reviews of the research* (2d ed., Vol. 2). Washington, D.C.: National Association for the Education of Young Children.

Parke, R. D. (1977). Punishment in children: Effects, side effects, and alternative strategies. In H. Horn & P. Robinson, (Eds.), *Psychological processes in early education.* New York: Academic Press.

Parke, R. D. (1978). Children's home environments: Social and cognitive effects. In I. Altman & J. F. Wohlwill, (Eds.), *Children and the environment.* New York: Plenum Press.

Parke, R. D. (1981). *Fathers.* Cambridge, Mass.: Harvard University Press.

Parke, R. D., & Collmer, C. W. (1975). Child abuse: An interdisciplinary analysis. In E. M. Hetherington, (Ed.), *Review of child development research* (Vol. 5). Chicago: University of Chicago Press.

Parke, R. D., & O'Leary, S. (1976). Family interaction in the newborn period: Some findings, some observations, and some unresolved issues. In K. Riegel and J. Meacham, (Eds.), *The developing individual in a changing world.* Vol. 2, *Social and environmental issues.* The Hague: Mouton.

Parke, R. D., & Sawin, D. B. (1976). The father's role in infancy: A re-evaluation. *The Family Coordinator, 25,* 365–71.

Parke, R. D., & Slaby, R. G. (1983). The development of aggression. In P. H. Mussen, (Ed.), *Handbook of child psychology* (4th ed.). Vol. 4, E. M. Hetherington, (Ed.), *Socialization, personality, and social development*. New York: Wiley.

Parkinson, C. E., Wallis, S., & Harvey, D. (1981). School achievement and behavior of children who were small-for-dates at birth. *Developmental Medicine and Child Neurology, 23*(1), 41–50.

Parmelee, A. H., & Schulte, F. (1970). Developmental testing of pre-term and small-for-dates infants. *Pediatrics, 45,* 21–28.

Parten, M. B. (1932). Social participation among preschool children. *Journal of Abnormal and Social Psychology, 27,* 243–69.

Pasley, K., & Gecas, V. (1984). Stresses and satisfactions of the parental role. *Personnel and Guidance Journal, 62,* 400–404.

Pastor, D. C. (1981). The quality of mother-infant attachment and its relationship to toddlers' initial sociability with peers. *Developmental Psychology, 17,* 326–35.

Patterson, F. G. (1980). Innovative uses of language by a gorilla: A case study. *Children's Language, 2,* 497–561.

Patterson, G. R. (1982). *Coercive family process.* Eugene, Oreg.: Castalia Publishing.

Pattison, E. (1977). *The experience of dying.* Englewood Cliffs, N.J.: Prentice-Hall.

Patton, R. G., & Gardner, L. I. (1963). *Growth failure in maternal deprivation.* Springfield, Ill.: Thomas.

Pauls, D. L., Shaywitz, S. E., Kramer, P. L., Shaywitz, B. A., & Cohen, D. J. (1983). Demonstration of vertical transmission of attention deficit disorders. *Annals of Neurology, 14,* 363–84.

Pearl, D., Bouthilet, L., & Lazar, S. J. (Eds.). (1982). Report by the Surgeon General on Television Violence. *Television and behavior: Ten years of scientific progress and implications for the eighties.* Washington, D.C.: U.S. Government Printing Office.

Pedersen, F. A., Anderson, B. J., & Cain, R. L., Jr. (1980). Parent-infant and husband-wife interactions observed at age 5 months. In F. A. Pedersen, (Ed.), *The father-infant relationship: Observational studies in the family setting.* New York: Praeger.

Peery, J. C., & Stern, D. (1976). Gaze duration frequency distributions during mother-infant interactions. *Journal of Genetic Psychology, 129,* 45–55.

Petersen, A. C., & Taylor, B. (1980). The biological approach to adolescence: Biological change and psychological adaptation. In J. Adelson, (Ed.), *Handbook of adolescent psychology.* New York: Wiley.

Philips, I. (1980). The primary care physician and mental retardation. In H. J. Grossman & R. L. Stubblefield, (Eds.), *The physician and the mental health of the child.* Monroe, Wis.: American Medical Association.

Phillips, J. R. (1973). Syntax and vocabulary of mothers' speech to young children: Age and sex comparisons. *Child Development, 44,* 182–85.

Phillips, S., King, S., & DuBois, L. (1978). Spontaneous activities of female versus male newborns. *Child Development, 49*(3), 590–97.

Piaget, J. (1932). *The moral judgment of the child.* New York: Harcourt Brace.

Piaget, J. (1952). *The origins of intelligence in children.* New York: International Universities Press.

Piaget, J. (1955). *The language and thought of the child.* New York: Meridian Books.

Piaget, J. (1962). *Play, dreams, and imitation.* New York: Harcourt Brace & World.

Piaget, J. (1965). *The child's conception of the world.* Totowa, N.J.: Littlefield, Adams. (Original work published in 1929.)

Piaget, J. (1970). Piaget's theory. In P. H. Mussen, (Ed.), *Carmichael's manual of child psychology.* New York: Wiley.

Piaget, J. (1971). *The construction of reality in the child.* New York: Ballantine. (Original work published in 1954.)

Piaget, J. (1972). Intellectual evolution from adolescence to adulthood. *Human Development, 15,* 1–12.

Piaget, J., & Inhelder, B. (1963). *The child's conception of space.* F. J. Langdom & J. L. Lanzer (Trans.). London: Routledge & Kegan Paul.

Pick, A. D., Christy, M. D., & Frankel, G. W. (1972). A developmental study of visual selective attention. *Journal of Experimental Child Psychology, 14,* 165–75.

Pick, A. D., Frankel, D. G., & Hess, V. (1975). Children's attention: The development of selectivity. In E. M. Hetherington, (Ed.), *Review of child development research* (Vol. 5). Chicago: University of Chicago Press.

Pilling, D., & Pringle, M. (1978). *Controversial issues in child development.* New York: Schocken.

Pinard, A. (1981). *The concept of conservation.* Chicago: University of Chicago Press.

Pincus, L. (1974). *Death and the family: The importance of mourning.* New York: Vintage.

Pinderhughes, E., & Zigler, E. (1985). Cognitive and motivational determinants of children's humor responses. *Journal of Research in Personality, 19,* 185–96.

Pines, M. (1982, February). Baby, you're incredible. *Psychology Today,* 48–53.

Pinneau, S. (1955). The infantile disorders of hospitalism and anaclitic depression. *Psychological Bulletin, 52,* 429–52.

Piotrkowski, C. S. (1979). *Work and the family system: A naturalistic study of working class and lower-middle class families.* New York: Free Press.

Pistrang, N. (1984, May). Women's work involvement and experience of new motherhood. *Journal of Marriage and the Family, 46*(2), 433–47.

Pleck, J. (1979). Men's family work: Three perspectives and some new data. *The Family Coordinator, 28,* 481–87.

Pollitt, E., & Gilmore, M. (1977). Early mother-infant interaction and somatic growth. Paper presented at the Symposium on Disturbances of Early Parent-Infant Interaction: Symptoms and Origins, biennial meeting of the Society for Research in Child Development, New Orleans.

Pollitt, E., & Thomson, C. (1977). Protein-calorie malnutrition and behavior: A view from psychology. In R. J. Wurtman & J. J. Wurtman, (Eds.), *Nutrition and the brain* (Vol. 2). New York: Raven.

Powell, D. (1977). The coordination of preschool socialization: Parent-caregiver relationships in day care settings. Paper presented at the biennial meeting of the Society for Research in Child Development, New Orleans.

Poznaski, E. O. (1979). Childhood depression: A psychodynamic approach to the etiology and treatment of depression in children. In A. P. French & I. N. Berlin, (Eds.), *Depression in children and adolescents.* New York: Human Sciences Press.

Prechtl, H. F. R. (1982). Assessment methods for the newborn infant: A critical evaluation. In P. Stratton, (Ed.), *Psychobiology of the human newborn.* New York: Wiley.

Prechtl, H. F. R., & Beintema, D. (1977). *The neurological examination of the full-term newborn infant* (2d ed.) (Clinics in developmental medicine, No. 63). Philadelphia: Lippincott.

Pressey, S. L., Janney, J. E., & Kuhlen, R. G. (1939). *Life: A psychological survey.* New York: Harper.

Price-Williams, D. R., Gordon, W., & Ramirez, M. (1969). Skill and conservation. *Developmental Psychology, 1,* 769.

Pritchard, J., & McDonald, P. (1976). *Obstetrics.* New York: Appleton-Century-Crofts.

Provence, S. (1982). Infant day care: Relationship between theory and practice. In E. Zigler & E. Gordon, (Eds.), *Day care: Scientific and social policy issues.* Boston: Auburn House.

Pulaski, M. A. S. (1980). *Understanding Piaget.* New York: Harper & Row.

Pulos, S., & Linn, M. C. (1981). Generality of the controlling variables scheme in early adolescence. *Journal of Early Adolescence, 1,* 26–37.

Quigly, M. E., Sheehan, K. L., Wilkes, M. M., & Yen, S. S. (1979, March 15). Effects of maternal smoking on circulating catecholamine levels and fetal heart rates. *American Journal of Obstetrics and Gynecology, 133*(6), 685–90.

Quinn, P. O., Sostek, A. M., & Davit, M. K. (1978). The high-risk infant and his family. In P. R. Magrab, (Ed.), *Psychological management of pediatric problems.* Vol. 1, *Early life conditions and chronic diseases.* Baltimore, Md.: Baltimore University Press.

Radin, N. (1971). Maternal warmth, achievement motivation and cognitive functioning in lower-class preschool children. *Child Development, 42,* 1560–65.

Radin, N. (1982). The unique contribution of parents to childrearing: The preschool years. In S. G. Moore & C. R. Cooper, (Eds.), *The young child: Reviews of research* (Vol. 3). Washington, D.C.: National Association for the Education of Young Children.

Ramey, C., & Campbell, F. (1977). The prevention of developmental retardation in high-risk children. In P. Mittler, (Ed.), *Research to practice in mental retardation.* Baltimore, Md.: University Park Press.

Ramey, C., MacPhee, D., & Yeats, K. O. (1982). Preventing developmental retardation: A general systems model. In L. Bond & J. Joffe, (Eds.), *Facilitating infant and early childhood development.* Hanover, N.H.: University Press of New England.

Rapoport, R., & Rapoport, R. (1976). *Dual career families re-examined: New generations of work and family.* New York: Hoper Colophon.

Raschke, H. J., & Raschke, V. J. (1979, May). Family conflict and children's self-concepts: A comparison of intact and single-parent families. *Journal of Marriage and the Family,* 367–74.

Rees, C. D., & Wilborn, B. L. (1983). Correlates of drug abuse in adolescents: A comparison of families of drug abusers with families of non-drug abusers. *Journal of Youth and Adolescence, 12*(1), 55–63.

Reese, H. W., & Lipsitt, L. P. (Eds.). (1970). *Experimental child psychology*. New York: Academic Press.

Reichter, R. J., & Schopler, E. (Eds.). (1976). *Psychopathology and child development: Research and treatment*. New York: Plenum.

Reif, G. (1985). Fitness for youth. Unpublished report. Ann Arbor, Mich.: Department of Physical Education, University of Michigan.

Report of the Committee on the Judiciary, Subcommittee on the Constitution, United States Senate, Ninety-Sixth Congress, second session. (1980). *Homeless youth: The saga of pushouts and throwaways in America*. Washington, D.C.: U.S. Government Printing Office.

Report of the Comptroller General of the United States. (1979). *Early childhood and family development programs improve the quality of life for low-income families*. Washington, D.C.: U.S. General Accounting Office.

Rheingold, H. (1973). Independent behavior of the human infant. In A. D. Pick, (Ed.), *Minnesota Symposia on Child Psychology* (Vol. 1). Minneapolis: University of Minnesota Press.

Rheingold, H., Gewirtz, J. L., & Ross, H. W. (1959). Social conditioning of vocalizations in the infant. *Journal of Comparative and Physiological Psychology, 52*, 68–73.

Rheingold, H. L., & Eckerman, C. (1971). Departures from the mother. In H. R. Schaffer, (Ed.), *The origins of human social relations*. London: Academic Press.

Rheingold, H. L., & Eckerman, C. O. (1973). Fear of the stranger: A critical examination. In H. W. Reese, (Ed.), *Advances in child development and behavior* (Vol. 8). New York: Academic Press.

Rheingold, H. L., & Hay, D. F. (1976). Sharing in the second year of life. *Child Development, 47*, 1148–58.

Rhine, W. R. (Ed.). (1981). *Making schools more effective: New directions from Follow Through*. New York: Academic Press.

Rice, R. D. (1977). Neurophysiological development in premature infants following stimulation. *Developmental Psychology, 13*(1), 69–76.

Rich, D. (1985). *The forgotten factor in school success: The family*. Washington, D.C.: Home and School Institute.

Richmond, J. (1980). *The surgeon general's report on the health of Americans: 1980*. Washington, D.C.: Department of Health and Human Services.

Richmond, J. B. (1977). The needs of children. In J. H. Knowles, (Ed.), *Doing better and feeling worse: Health in the United States*. New York: Norton.

Richmond, J. B., Stipek, D. J., & Zigler, E. (1979). A decade of Head Start. In E. Zigler & J. Valentine, (Eds.), *Project Head Start: A legacy of the War on Poverty*. New York: Free Press.

Ricks, M. (1982, March). The origins of individual differences in quality of attachment to the mother: Infant, maternal and familial variables. Paper presented at the International Conference on Infant Studies, Austin, Tex.

Riesen, A. H. (1947). The development of visual perception in man and chimpanzee. *Science, 106*, 107–8.

Riesen, A. H. (1958). Plasticity of behavior: Psychological aspects. In H. F. Harlow & C. N. Wolsey, (Eds.), *Biological and biochemical bases of behavior*. Madison: University of Wisconsin Press.

Rieser, J., Yonas, A., & Wilkner, K. (1976). Radical localization of odors by human newborns. *Child Development, 47*, 856–59.

Riley, M. W. (1978). Aging, social change and the power of ideas. *Daedalus, 107*(4), 39–52.

Ritson, E. B. (1966). An investigation of the psychological factors underlying prolonged labor. *Journal of Obstetrics and Gynaecology of the British Commonwealth, 73*, 215–21.

Roberts, D. F. (1969). Race, genetics and growth. *Journal of Biosocial Science, 1*, 43–67.

Robertson, A. (1982). Day care and children's responsiveness to adults. In E. Zigler & E. Gordon, (Eds.), *Day care: Scientific and social policy issues*. Boston: Auburn House.

Robertson, J. F. (1976). Significance of grandparents: Perceptions of young adult grandchildren. *The Gerontologist, 16*, 137–40.

Robertson, J. F. (1977). Grandmotherhood: A study of role conceptions. *Journal of Marriage and the Family, 39*, 165–74.

Robertson, L. S. (1981). Environmental hazards to children: Assessment and options for amelioration. In Select Panel for the Promotion of Child Health, *Better health for our children: A national strategy*. Washington, D.C.: U.S. Government Printing Office.

Roby, P. (Ed.). (1973). *Child care—Who cares? For-*

eign and domestic infant and early childhood development policies. New York: Basic Books.

Roche, A. F. (1976). Growth after puberty. In E. Fuchs, (Ed.), *Youth in a changing world: Cross-cultural perspective on adolescence.* The Hague: Mouton.

Roche, A. F. (1979). Secular trends in human growth, maturation, and development. *Monographs of the Society for Research in Child Development, 44,* 3–4.

Roche, A. F., French, N. Y., & Davilla, G. H. (1971). Areolar size during pubescence. *Human Biology, 43,* 210–23.

Roeske, N. C. A. (1980). The visually handicapped child. In J. H. Grossman, R. L. Stubblefield, (Eds.), *The physician and the mental health of the child.* Monroe, Wis.: American Medical Association.

Rofes, E. (Ed.). (1980). *The kids' book of divorce: By, for, and about kids.* New York: Vintage.

Roffwarg, H. P., Muzio, J. N., & Dement, W. C. (1966). Ontogenetic development of the human sleep-dream cycle. *Science, 152,* 604–19.

Rogoff, B. (1981). Schooling and the development of cognitive skills. In H. C. Triandis & A. Heron, (Eds.), *Handbook of cross-cultural psychology.* Vol. 4, *Developmental psychology.* Boston: Allyn & Bacon.

Rogoff, B., Gauvain, M., & Ellis, S. (1984). Development viewed in its cultural context. In M. Bornstein & M. Lamb, (Eds.), *Developmental psychology: An advanced textbook.* Hillsdale, N.J.: Erlbaum.

Rogus, J. F. (1983). Education as a response to developmental needs: Preventing truancy and school dropout. In L. E. Arnold, (Ed.), *Preventing adolescent alienation.* Lexington, Mass.: Lexington Books.

Rohn, R. D., Sarles, R. M., Kenny, T. J., Reynolds, B. J., & Heald, F. P. (1977). Adolescents who attempt suicide. *Journal of Pediatrics, 90,* 636–38.

Rohner, R. (1975). Parental acceptance-rejection and personality: A universalistic approach to behavioral science. In R. Brislin et al., (Eds.), *Cross-cultural perspective on learning.* New York: Halsted Press.

Rollins, N., & Piazza, E. (1978). Diagnosis of anorexia nervosa. *Journal of Child Psychiatry, 17,* 126–37.

Rosch, E. (1975). Cognitive representations of semantic categories. *Journal of Experimental Psychology, 104,* 192–233.

Rosch, E., Mervis, C., Gray, W. D., Johnson, D., & Boyes-Braem, P. (1976). Basic objects in natural categories. *Cognitive Psychology, 8,* 382–439.

Rose, R. M., Gordon, T. P., & Bernstein, I. S. (1972). Plasma testosterone levels in the male rhesus: Influences of sexual and social stimuli. *Science, 178,* 643–45.

Rose, S. A. (1981). Developmental changes in infants' retention of visual stimuli. *Child Development, 52,* 227–33.

Rose, T. L. (1984). Current uses of corporal punishment in American public schools. *Journal of Educational Psychology, 76(3),* 427–41.

Rosen, B. C., & Aneshensel, C. S. (1978). Sex differences in the educational-occupational expectation process. *Social Forces, 57,* 164–86.

Rosenberg, M. (1965). *Society and the adolescent self-image.* Princeton, N.J.: Princeton University Press.

Rosenberg, M. (1975). The dissonant context of the adolescent self-concept. In S. E. Dragastin & G. H. Elder, (Eds.), *Adolescence in the life cycle.* Washington, D.C.: Hemisphere.

Rosenthal, R., & Jacobson, L. (1966). Teachers' expectancies: Determinants of pupils' IQ gains. *Psychological Reports, 19,* 115–18.

Rosenthal, R., & Jacobsen, L. (1968). *Pygmalion in the classroom.* New York: Holt, Rinehart and Winston.

Rosett, H. L., & Weiner, L. (1985). *Alcohol and the fetus: A clinical perspective.* New York: Oxford University Press.

Ross, C. J. (1983). Advocacy movements in the century of the child. In E. Zigler, S. L. Kagan, & E. Klugman, (Eds.), *Children, families and government: Perspectives on American social policy.* New York: Cambridge University Press.

Ross, C. J., & Zigler, E. (1980). An agenda for action. In G. Gerbner, C. Ross, & E. Zigler, (Eds.), *Child abuse: An agenda for action.* New York: Oxford University Press.

Ross, D. M., & Ross, S. A. (1982). *Hyperactivity: Research, theory and action* (2d ed.). New York: Wiley.

Ross, H. L., & Sawhill, I. V. (1975). *Time of transition: Growth of families headed by women.* Washington, D.C.: Urban Institute.

Ross, J. (1977). *Old people, new lives: Community creations in a retirement residence.* Chicago: University of Chicago Press.

Rossi, A. (1977). Social trends in women's lives. In *Changing roles of women in industrial societies*. New York: The Rockefeller Foundation Working Papers.

Roupp, R., Travers, J., Glantz, F., & Coelen, C. (1979). *Children at the center*. Cambridge, Mass.: Abt Associates.

Rousseau, J. J. (1962). *The Émile of Jean Jacques Rousseau* (W. Boyd, Ed., & Trans.). New York: Columbia Teachers' College. (Original work published in 1762.)

Rubin, J. Z., Provenza, F. J., & Luria, Z. (1974). The eye of the beholder: Parents' views on sex of newborns. *American Journal of Orthopsychiatry, 44,* 512–19.

Rubin, K. H., & Pepler, D. J. (1980). The relationship of child's play to social-cognitive growth and development. In H. Foot, A. Chapman, & J. Smith, (Eds.), *Friendship and childhood relationships*. New York: Wiley.

Rubin, K. H., Watson, K. S., & Jambor, F. (1978). Free-play behaviors in preschool and kindergarten children. *Child Development, 49,* 534–36.

Rubin, L. (1979). *Women of a certain age: The midlife search for self*. New York: Harper & Row.

Rubin, N. (1984). *The mother mirror: How a generation of women is changing motherhood in America*. New York: Putnam.

Rubin, Z. (1980). *Children's friendships*. Cambridge, Mass.: Harvard University Press.

Ruke-Dravina, V. (1977). Modifications of speech addressed to young children in Latvian. In C. E. Snow & C. A. Ferguson, (Eds.), *Talking to children*. Cambridge, England: Cambridge University Press.

Rutter, M. (1971). *Infantile autism: Concepts, characteristics and treatment*. Edinburgh: Whitefriars Press.

Rutter, M. (1979). Maternal deprivation, 1972–1978: New findings, new concepts, new approaches. *Child Development, 50,* 283–305.

Rutter, M. (1979). Protective factors in children's responses to stress and disadvantage. In M. W. Kent & J. E. Rolf, (Eds.), *Primary prevention of psychopathology*. Vol. 3, *Promoting social competence and coping in children*. Hanover, N.H.: University Press of New England.

Rutter, M. (1980). *Changing youth in a changing society*. Cambridge, Mass.: Harvard University Press.

Rutter, M. (1982). Socio-emotional consequences of day care for preschool children. In E. Zigler & E. Gordon, (Eds.), *Day care: Scientific and social policy issues*. Boston: Auburn House.

Rutter, M., Maughan, B., Mortimore, J., & Ouston, J., with A. Smith. (1979). *Fifteen thousand hours: Secondary schools and their effects on children*. Cambridge, Mass.: Harvard University Press.

Ryan, K., & Applegate, J. (1976). The missed middle. *Ohio State University College of Education, Occasional Publications, 5,* 1.

Ryder, N. (1978). A model of fertility by planning status. *Demography, 15,* 433–58.

Sachs, J. (1977). The adaptive significance of linguistic input to prelinguistic infants. In C. E. Snow & C. A. Ferguson, (Eds.), *Talking to children*. Cambridge, England: Cambridge University Press.

Sackett, G. P., & Tripp, R. (1968, July). Innate mechanisms in primate behavior: Identification and causal significance. Paper presented at the U.S.-Japan Seminar on Regulatory Mechanisms, Emory University, Atlanta, Ga.

Safer, D. J. (1971). Drugs for problem schoolchildren. *Journal of School Health, 41,* 491–95.

Salapatek, P. (1969, December). The visual investigation of geometric pattern by the one- and two-month old infant. Paper presented at the Convention of the American Association for the Advancement of Science, Boston.

Salapatek, P., & Kessen, W. (1966). Visual scanning of triangles by the human newborn infant. *Journal of Experimental Child Psychology, 3,* 155–67.

Salend, S. J. (1984). Factors contributing to the development of successful mainsteaming programs. *Exceptional Children, 50*(5), 409–16.

Salkind, N. J. (1983). The effectiveness of early intervention. In E. M. Goetz & K. E. Allen, (Eds.), *Early childhood education: Special environmental, policy, and legal considerations*. Gaithersburg, Md.: Aspen Systems Corporation.

Salomon, G., & Cohen, A. A. (1977). Television formats, mastery of mental skills, and the acquisition of knowledge. *Journal of Educational Psychology, 69,* 612–19.

Sameroff, A. J. (1968). The components of sucking in the human newborn. *Journal of Experimental Child Psychology, 6,* 607–23.

Sameroff, A. J. (1975). Early influences on development: Fact or fancy? *Merrill-Palmer Quarterly, 21,* 275–301.

Sameroff, A. J., & Cavanaugh, P. J. (1979). Learning in infancy: A developmental perspective. In

J. Osofsky, (Ed.), *Handbook of infant development*. New York: Wiley.

Sameroff, A. J., & Chandler, M. J. (1975). Reproductive risk and the continuum of caretaking casualty. In F. D. Horowitz, (Ed.), *Review of child development research*. Chicago: University of Chicago Press.

Santrock, J. W., Warshak, R. A., & Elliott, G. L. (1982). Social development and parent–child interaction in father custody and stepmother families. In M. Lamb, (Ed.), *Nontraditional families: Parenting and child development*. Hillsdale, N.J.: Erlbaum.

Santrock, J. W., Warshak, R., Lindberg, C., & Meadows, L. (1982). Children's and parents' observed social behavior in stepfather families. *Child Development, 53,* 472–80.

Sarason, S. B. (1983). Public Law 94-142 and the formation of educational policy. In E. Zigler, S. L. Kagan, & E. Klugman, (Eds.), *Children, families, and government: Perspectives on American social policy*. New York: Cambridge University Press.

Scales, P. (1976). *A quasi-experimental evaluation of sex education programs for parents*. Unpublished doctoral dissertation, Syracuse University.

Scales, P., & Gordon, S. (1978). The effects of sex education. In S. Gordon & P. Scales, (Eds.), *The sexual adolescent*. North Scituate, Mass.: Duxbury.

Scarpitti, F. R., & Datesman, S. K. (1980). *Drugs and the youth culture*. Beverly Hills: Sage.

Scarr, S. (1968). Environmental bias in twin studies. *Eugenics Quarterly, 15,* 34–40.

Scarr, S. (1969). Social introversion-extraversion as a heritable response. *Child Development, 40,* 823–32.

Scarr, S. (1984). *Mother care/other care*. New York: Basic Books.

Scarr, S., & Weinberg, R. A. (1976). IQ test performance of black children adopted by white families. *American Psychologist, 31,* 726–91.

Scarr, S., & Weinberg, R. A. (1977). Intellectual similarities within families of both adopted and biological children. *Intelligence, 3,* 31–39.

Scarr-Salapatek, S. (1975). Genetics and the development of intelligence. In F. Horowitz, (Ed.), *Review of child development research* (Vol. 4). Chicago: University of Chicago Press.

Scarr-Salapatek, S., & Williams, M. L. (1973). The effects of early stimulation on low birth weight infants. *Child Development, 44,* 94–101.

Schaefer, E. S. (1959). A circumplex model for maternal behavior. *Journal of Abnormal and Social Psychology, 59,* 226–35.

Schaffer, H. R. (1977). *Mothering*. Cambridge, Mass.: Harvard University Press.

Schaffer, H. R., Collis, G. M., & Parsons, G. (1977). Vocal interchange and visual regard in verbal and preverbal children. In H. R. Schaffer, (Ed.), *Studies on mother-infant interactions*. New York: Academic Press.

Schaffer, H. R., & Emerson, P. E. (1964). Patterns of response to physical contact in early human development. *Journal of Child Psychology and Psychiatry, 5,* 1–13.

Schlesinger, B., & Todres, R. (1976). Motherless families: An increasing societal pattern. *Child Welfare, 55,* 443–58.

Schlesinger, H. S., & Meadow, K. P. (1972). *Sound and sign: Childhood deafness and mental health*. Berkeley: University of California Press.

Schmuck, R., & Schmuck, P. (1975). *Group processes in the classroom* (2d ed.). Dubuque, Iowa: Brown.

Schofield, J. W. (1980). Complementary and conflicting identities: Images and interaction in an interracial school. In S. R. Asher & J. M. Gottman, (Eds.), *The development of children's friendships*. New York: Cambridge University Press.

School-Age Child Care Project (1984). *SACC Newsletter, 2*(2). Wellesley College, Center for Research on Women, Wellesley, Mass. 02181.

Schopler, E., & Dalldorf, J. (1980). Autism: Definition, diagnosis, and management. *Hospital Practice, 15,* 64–73.

Schopler, E., & Mesibov, G. B. (1984). Professional attitudes toward parents: A forty-year progress report. In E. Schopler & G. B. Mesibov, (Eds.), *The effects of autism on the family*. New York: Plenum.

Schopler, E., Mesibov, G. B., Shigley, R. H., & Bashford, A. (1984). Helping autistic children through their parents: The TEACCH model. In E. Schopler & G. B. Mesibov, (Eds.), *The effects of autism on the family*. New York: Plenum.

Schorr, L. B. (1982, April 17). Improving child health policy: Now and in the future. In Proceedings of the Conference on Better Health for Children: Action for the Eighties, held at Harvard University School of Public Health, Cambridge, Mass.

Schowalter, J. E., & Anyan, W. R., Jr. (1979). *The family handbook of adolescence.* New York: Knopf.

Schwartz, F. N. (1974, May). New patterns for better use of womanpower. *Management Review,* 4–12.

Schwartz, G., & Merten, P. (1967). The language of adolescence: An anthropological approach to the youth culture. *The American Journal of Sociology, 72,* 453–68.

Schwartz, J. (1974). Infant day care: Behavioral effect at preschool age. *Developmental Psychology, 10,* 502–6.

Schwartz, J. C. (1972). Effects of peer familiarity on the behavior of preschoolers in a novel situation. *Journal of Personality and Social Psychology, 24,* 276–84.

Schwartz, S. (1984). A study of drug discipline policies in secondary schools. *Adolescence, 19*(4), 323–31.

Scribner, S. (1976). Situating the experiment in cross-cultural research. In K. F. Riegel & J. A. Meacham, (Eds.), *The developing individual in a changing world.* Chicago: Aldine.

Scribner, S. (1977). Modes of thinking and ways of speaking: Culture and logic reconsidered. In P. N. Johnson-Laird & P. C. Wason, (Eds.), *Thinking.* Cambridge, England: Cambridge University Press.

Scrimshaw, N. S., Taylor, C. E., & Gordon, J. E. (1968). Interaction of nutrition and infection. *W.H.O. Monograph Series,* No. 57.

Searle, L. V. (1949). The organization of hereditary maze brightness and maze dullness. *Genetic Psychology Monographs, 39,* 279–325.

Sears, R. R., Maccoby, E. E., & Levin, H. (1957). *Patterns of childrearing.* New York: Harper & Row.

Segal, J., & Yahraes, H. (1978). *A child's journey.* New York: McGraw-Hill.

Select Committee on Children, Youth, & Families (Ninety-eighth Congress, first session). (1983, May). *U.S. children and their families: Current conditions and recent trends.* Washington, D.C.: U.S. Government Printing Office.

Select Committee on Children, Youth, & Families (Ninety-eighth Congress, second session). (1984, April). *Child care: Beginning a national initiative.* Washington, D.C.: U.S. Government Printing Office.

Select Panel for the Promotion of Child Health. (1981). *Better health for our children: A national strategy.* Washington, D.C.: U.S. Government Printing Office.

Self, P. A., & Horowitz, F. D. (1979). The behavioral assessment of the newborn: An overview. In J. D. Osofsky, (Ed.), *Handbook of infant development.* New York: Wiley.

Selfe, L. (1977). *Nadia: A case of extraordinary drawing ability in an autistic child.* New York: Academic Press.

Seligman, M. E. P. (1975). *Helplessness: On depression, development, and death.* San Francisco: Freeman.

Selman, R. L. (1976). Social cognitive understanding: A guide to educational and clinical practice. In T. Lickona, (Ed.), *Theory, research, and social issues.* New York: Holt, Rinehart and Winston.

Selman, R. L. (1980). *The growth of interpersonal understanding.* New York: Academic Press.

Selman, R. L., & Byrne, D. F. (1974). A structural-developmental analysis of levels of roletaking in middle childhood. *Child Development, 45,* 803–6.

Selman, R. L., & Jaquette, D. (1977). Stability and oscillation in interpersonal awareness: A clinical-developmental analysis. In C. B. Keasey, (Ed.), *The Nebraska Symposium on Motivation* (Vol. 25). Lincoln: University of Nebraska Press.

Selman, R., & Selman, A. (1979, October). Children's ideas about friendship: A new theory. *Psychology Today, 13,* 70–80, 114.

Shanas, E. (1979). Social myth as hypothesis: The case of the family relations of old people. *The Gerontologist, 19*(1), 3–10.

Shantz, C. U. (1975). The development of social cognition. In E. M. Hetherington, J. W. Hagen, R. Kron, & A. H. Stein, (Eds.), *Review of child development research* (Vol. 4). Chicago: University of Chicago Press.

Shapiro, S. A. (1981). *Contemporary theories of schizophrenia: A review and synthesis.* New York: McGraw-Hill.

Sharp, D., Cole, M., & Lave, C. (1979). Education and cognitive development: The evidence from experimental research. *Monographs of the Society for Research in Child Development, 44*(1–2), Serial No. 178.

Shatz, M., & Gelman, R. (1973). The development of communication skills: Modifications in the speech of young children as a function of the listener. *Monographs of the Society for Research in Child Development, 38*(5), Serial No. 152.

Shaywitz, S. E., & Shaywitz, B. A. (1984). Evaluation and treatment of children with attention deficit disorders. *Pediatrics in Review, 6*(4), 99–109.

Sheehan, S. (1982). *Is there a place on earth for me?* Boston: Houghton Mifflin.

Sheehy, G. (1981). *Pathfinders*. New York: Morrow.

Sheldon, E. B., & Parke, R. (1975). Social science researchers are developing concepts and measures of change in society. *Science, 188,* 693–99.

Sheldon, W. H. (1940). *The varieties of human physique*. New York: Harper & Row.

Sheppard, H. (1976). Work and retirement. In R. H. Binstock & E. Shanas, (Eds.), *Handbook on aging and the social sciences*. New York: Van Nostrand Reinhold.

Sherif, M., & Sherif, C. (1964). *Reference groups*. New York: Harper & Row.

Sherlock, R. (1979). Debate: Selective non-treatment of newborns. *Journal of Medical Ethics, 5,* 139–42.

Shields, J. (1962). *Monozygotic twins: Brought up apart and brought up together*. London: Oxford University Press.

Shirley, A. (1982, April 17). Better health for children: What are the barriers? In *Proceedings of the Conference on Better Health for Children: Action for the Eighties,* held at Harvard University School of Public Health, Cambridge, Mass.

Shirley, M. M. (1933). *The first two years: A study of twenty-five babies*. Institute of Child Welfare Monograph No. 8. Minneapolis: University of Minnesota Press.

Shonkoff, J. P. (1984). The biological substrate and physical health in middle childhood. In W. A. Collins, (Ed.), *Development during middle childhood: The years from six to twelve*. Washington, D.C.: National Academy Press.

Shultz, T. R., & Zigler, E. (1970). Emotional concomitants of visual mastery in infants: The effects of stimulus movement on smiling and vocalizing. *Journal of Experimental Child Psychology, 10,* 390–402.

Siegel, A. W., & White, S. H. (1982). The child study movement: Early growth and development of the symbolized child. *Advances in Child Development and Behavior, 17,* 233–85.

Siegel, L. S. (1978). The relationship of language and thought in the preoperational child: A reconsideration of non-verbal alternatives to Piagetian tasks. In L. S. Siegel & C. J. Brainerd, (Eds.), *Alternatives to Piaget: Critical essays on the theory*. New York: Academic Press.

Silberman, C. (1970). *Crisis in the classroom: The remaking of American education*. New York: Random House.

Simmons, R., Rosenberg, F., & Rosenberg, M. (1973). Disturbance in the self-image at adolescence. *American Sociological Review, 38,* 553–68.

Sinclair, C. (1973). *Movement of the young child: Ages two to six*. Columbus, Ohio: Merrill.

Singer, D. G., & Singer, J. L. (1976). Family television viewing habits and the spontaneous play of preschool children. *American Journal of Orthopsychiatry, 46,* 496–502.

Singer, D. G., & Singer, J. L. (1980a). Television viewing and aggressive behavior in preschool children: A field study. *Forensic Pathology and Psychiatry, 347,* 289–303.

Singer, J. L. (1981). *Cognitive and affective implications of television for the developing child*. Introduction. Revised draft submitted to the Committee to Update the Surgeon General's Committee Report on Television. New Haven: Yale University.

Singer, J. L., & Singer, D. G. (1979, March). Come back, Mister Rogers, come back. *Psychology Today, 12*(10), 56–60.

Singer, J. L., & Singer, D. G. (1980b). Television viewing, family style and aggressive behavior in preschool children. In M. Green, (Ed.), *Violence and the family: Psychiatric, sociological, and historical implications*. American Association for the Advancement of Science Symposium 47. Boulder, Colo.: Westview Press.

Singer, J. L., & Singer, D. G. (1982). Cognitive and emotional characteristics of the format of American television. In W. K. Agee, P. H. Ault, & E. Emery, (Eds.), *Perspectives on mass communications*. New York: Harper & Row.

Skeels, H. (1966). Adult status of children with contrasting early life experience: A follow-up study. *Monographs of the Society for Research in Child Development, 31*(3).

Skeels, H. M. (1942). A study of the differential stimulation on mentally retarded children: A follow-up report. *American Journal of Mental Deficiency, 46,* 340–50.

Skinner, B. F. (1953). *Science and human behavior*. New York: Macmillan.

Skinner, B. F. (1957). *Verbal behavior*. New York: Appleton-Century-Crofts.

Skodak, M., & Skeels, H. M. (1949). A final follow-up study of one hundred adopted children. *Journal of Genetic Psychology, 75,* 85–125.

Slater, E., & Cowie, V. (1971). *Genetics of mental disorders.* London: Oxford University Press.

Slobin, D. I. (1970). Universals of grammatical development in children. In G. B. Flores d'Arcais & W. J. M. Levelt, (Eds.), *Advances in psycholinguistics.* New York: American Elsevier.

Slocum, W. L., & Nye, F. I. (1976). Provider and housekeeper roles. In F. I. Nye et al., (Eds.), *Role structure and analysis of the family.* Beverly Hills: Sage Foundation.

Smith, P. K., & Daglish, L. (1977). Sex differences in parent and infant behavior in the home. *Child Development, 48,* 1250–54.

Smith, S. L. (1981). *No easy answers. The learning disabled child at home and at school.* New York: Bantam.

Smith, T. E. (1976). Push versus pull: Intrafamily versus peer group variables as possible determinants of adolescent orientation toward parents. *Youth and Society, 8,* 5–26.

Smock, S. M. (1977). *The children: The shape of child care in Detroit.* Detroit: Wayne State University Press.

Smyser, A. (1982). Hospices: Their humanistic and economic value. *American Psychologist, 37,* 1260–62.

Snow, C. E. (1972, August). Young children's responses to adult sentences of varying complexity. Paper presented at the Third International Congress of Applied Linguistics, Copenhagen.

Solomon, R. L. (1964). Punishment. *American Psychologist, 19,* 239–53.

Sommer, B. B. (1978). *Puberty and adolescence.* New York: Oxford University Press.

Sorce, J., Emde, R., Campos, J., & Klinnert, M. (1981, April). Maternal emotional signaling: Its effect on the visual cliff behavior of one-year-olds. Paper presented at the meeting of the Society for Research in Child Development, Boston.

Sorenson, R. C. (1973). *Adolescent sexuality in contemporary America: Personal values and sexual behavior, ages thirteen to nineteen.* New York: World.

Spanier, G. B., & Glick, P. C. (1981). Marital instability in the United States: Some correlates and recent changes. *Family Relations, 31,* 329–38.

Spearman, C. (1904). General intelligence objectively determined and measured. *American Journal of Psychology, 15,* 201–93.

Spelke, E. (1976). Infants' intermodal perception of events. *Cognitive Psychology, 8,* 553–60.

Spelke, E. J. (1982). The concept of affordance in development: The renaissance of functionalism. In W. A. Collins, (Ed.), *Minnesota symposia on child psychology* (Vol. 15). Hillsdale, N.J.: Erlbaum.

Spitz, R. A. (1945). Hospitalism: An inquiry into the genesis of psychiatric conditions in early childhood. *Psychoanalytic Study of the Child, 1,* 53–74.

Spitz, R. A. (1965). *The first year of life.* New York: International Universities Press.

Spock, B. (1968). *Baby and child care.* New York: Hawthorn Books.

Spring, D. R. (1974). Effects of style of maternal speech on infants' selection of vocal reinforcements. Unpublished manuscript, University of Washington.

Sroufe, L. A. (1977). Wariness of strangers and the study of infant development. *Child Development, 48,* 731–46.

Sroufe, L. A. (1979). Socioemotional development. In J. D. Osofsky, (Ed.), *Handbook of infant development.* New York: Wiley.

Sroufe, L. A., Schork, E., Motti, F., Lawroski, N., & La Frenière, P. (1984). Role of affect in social competence. In C. E. Izard, J. Kagan, & R. B. Zajonc, (Eds.), *Emotions, cognition and behavior.* New York: Cambridge University Press.

Sroufe, L. A., & Waters, E. (1977). Attachment as an organizational construct. *Child Development, 48*(4), 1184–99.

Stadley, K., Soule, A., Copans, S., & Duchowny, M. (1974). Local regional anesthesia during childbirth: Effects on newborn behaviors. *Science, 186,* 634–35.

Staffieri, J. R. (1967). A study of social stereotype of body image of children. *Journal of Personality and Social Psychology, 7,* 101–4.

Starr, R. H., Jr. (1979). Child abuse. *American Psychologist, 34,* 872–78.

Staub, E. (1975). To rear a prosocial child. In D. J. DePalma & J. M. Foley, (Eds.), *Moral development: Current theory and research.* Hillsdale, N.J.: Erlbaum.

Stayton, D. J., Hogan, R., & Ainsworth, M. D. S. (1971). Infant obedience and maternal behavior: The origins of socialization reconsidered. *Child Development, 42,* 1057–69.

Stein, A. H., & Friedrich, L. K. (1975). The effects of television content on young children. In A. D.

Pick, (Ed.), *Minnesota symposia on child psychology* (Vol. 9). Minneapolis: University of Minnesota Press.

Steinmetz, M. (1977). The use of force for resolving family conflict: The training ground for abuse. *Family Coordinator, 26,* 19–26.

Steinschneider, A. (1975). Implications of the sudden infant death syndrome for the study of sleep in infancy. In A. D. Pick, (Ed.), *Minnesota symposia on child psychology* (Vol. 9). Minneapolis: University of Minnesota Press.

Steriel, S. (1979). America's changing work ethic. *Editorial Research Reports, 22,* 903–20.

Stern, C. (1975). High points in human genetics. *American Biology Teacher, 32,* 144–49.

Stern, D. (1977). *The first relationship: Infant and mother.* Cambridge, Mass.: Harvard University Press.

Stern, W. (1911). The psychological methods of testing intelligence. G. M. Whipple (Trans.). Baltimore, Md.: Warwick & York.

Sternberg, R. J. (1982, April). Who's intelligent? *Psychology Today,* 30–39.

Sternberg, R. J. (1984). *Mechanisms of cognitive development.* New York: Freeman.

Sternberg, R. J., & Grajek, S. (1983). *The nature of love.* Unpublished manuscript, Department of Psychology, Yale University, New Haven, Conn.

Sternglanz, S. H., & Serbin, L. A. (1974). Sex role stereotyping in children's television programs. *Developmental Psychology, 10,* 710–15.

Steuer, F. B., Applefield, J. M., & Smith, R. (1971). Televised aggression and the interpersonal aggression of preschool children. *Journal of Experimental Child Psychology, 11,* 442–47.

Stevenson, H. W. (1982). Influences of schooling on cognitive development. In D. A. Wagner & H. W. Stevenson, (Eds.), *Cultural perspectives on child development.* San Francisco: Freeman.

Stevenson, H. W. (1983). Making the grade: School achievement in Japan, Taiwan, and the United States. *Annual Report,* Center for Advanced Study in Behavioral Sciences, Stanford University, Stanford, Calif.

Stewart, M. A., & Gath, A. (1978). *Psychological disorders of children: A handbook for primary care physicians.* Baltimore, Md.: Williams and Wilkins.

Stinson, P., & Stinson, R. (1983). *The long dying of baby Andrew.* Boston: Atlantic Monthly Press (distributed by Little, Brown).

Stipek, D. (1979). *The effectiveness of high schools in promoting intellectual achievement.* Working paper. New Haven, Conn.: Compulsory Education Project, Yale University Law School.

Stipek, D. J. (1977). Changes during first grade in children's social-motivational development. Unpublished doctoral dissertation, Yale University.

Strauss, M., Gelles, R., & Steinmetz, S. (1980). *Behind closed doors.* Garden City, N.Y.: Doubleday.

Strauss, M. A. (1979). Family patterns and child abuse in a nationally representative American sample. *Child Abuse and Neglect, 3,* 213–25.

Strauss, M. E., Lessen-Firestone, J. K., Starr, R., & Ostrea, E. M. (1975). Behavior of narcotics-addicted newborns. *Child Development, 46,* 887–93.

Strauss, M. S., & Cohen, L. B. (1980). Infant immediate and delayed memory for perceptual dimensions. Presentation made at the Second International Conference on Infant Studies, New Haven, Conn.

Strean, L. P., & Peer, L. A. (1956). Stress as an etiological factor in the development of cleft palate. *Plastic and Reconstructive Surgery, 18,* 1–8.

Streissguth, A. P., Barr, H. M., Martin, D. C., & Herman, C. S. (1980a). Effects of maternal alcohol, nicotine, and caffeine use during pregnancy on infant mental and motor development at eight months. *Alcoholism: Clinical and experimental research, 4*(2), 152–64.

Streissguth, A. P., Landesman-Dwyer, S., Martin, J. C., & Smith, D. W. (1980b, July 18). Teratogenic effects of alcohol in humans and laboratory animals. *Science, 209,* 353–61.

Stuart, H. C., & Prugh, D. G. (1960). *The healthy child: His physical, psychological and social development.* Cambridge, Mass.: Harvard University Press.

Suomi, S. J. (1977). Adult male-infant interactions among monkeys living in nuclear families. *Child Development, 48,* 1255–70.

Suomi, S. J., & Harlow, H. F. (1975). The role and reason of peer friendships in rhesus monkeys. In M. Lewis & L. Rosenblum, (Eds.), *Friendship and peer relations.* New York: Wiley.

Suomi, S. J., Harlow, H. F., & McKinney, W. T. (1972). Monkey psychiatrists. *American Journal of Psychiatry, 128,* 41–46.

Super, C. M. (1980). Cognitive development: Looking across at growing up. In C. M. Super & S.

Harkness, (Eds.), *Anthropological perspectives on child development* (New Directions for Child Development No. 8). San Francisco: Jossey-Bass.

Sussman, M. B. (1976). Family life of old people. In R. H. Binstock & E. Shanas, (Eds.), *Handbook of aging and the social sciences*. New York: Van Nostrand Reinhold.

Sutton-Smith, B. (1974). The role of play in cognitive development. In R. E. Herron & B. Sutton-Smith, (Eds.), *Child's Play*. New York: Wiley.

Sutton-Smith, B., & Rosenberg, B. G. (1970). *The sibling*. New York: Holt, Rinehart and Winston.

Szymanski, L. S., & Tanguay, P. (1980). *Emotional disorder of mentally retarded persons*. Baltimore: University Park Press.

Taft, L. T. (1981). Intervention programs for infants with cerebral palsy: A clinician's view. In C. C. Brown, (Ed.), *Infants at risk: Assessment and intervention*. Skillman, N.J.: Johnson & Johnson.

Takanishi, R. (1981). Graduate education for roles in child development and social policy. *UCLA Educator, 23*, 33–37.

Tanguay, P. E. (1980). Early infantile autism. In H. J. Grossman & R. L. Stubblefield, (Eds.), *The physician and the mental health of the child*. Monroe, Wis.: American Medical Association.

Tanner, J. M. (1962). *Growth at adolescence* (2d ed.). Oxford, England: Blackwell Scientific Publications.

Tanner, J. M. (1970). *Education and physical growth*. New York: International Universities Press.

Tanner, J. M. (1974). Variability of growth and maturity in newborn infants. In M. Lewis & L. Rosenblum, (Eds.), *The effect of the infant on its caregiver*. New York: Wiley.

Tanner, J. M. (1978). *Foetus into man: Physical growth from conception to maturity*. Cambridge, Mass.: Harvard University Press.

Tanner, J. M., Whitehouse, R. H., Marshall, W. A., Healy, M. J. R., & Goldstein, H. (1975). *Assessment of skeletal maturity and prediction of adult height*. London: Academic Press.

Tennes, K. H., & Lampl, E. E. (1964). Stranger and separation anxiety in infancy. *Journal of Nervous and Mental Diseases, 139*, 247–54.

Terman, L. M. (1914). Recent literature on juvenile suicide. *Abnormal Psychology, 7*, 61.

Terman, L. M. (1916). *The measurement of intelligence*. Boston: Houghton Mifflin.

Terman, L. M., & Merrill, M. A. (1972). *Stanford-Binet intelligence scale: Manual for the third revision*. Boston: Houghton Mifflin.

Thelen, E., & Fisher, D. M. (1982). Newborn stepping: An explanation for a "disappearing" reflex. *Developmental Psychology, 18*(5), 760–75.

Thissen, D., Bock, R. D., Wainer, H., & Roche, A. F. (1976). Individual growth in stature: A comparison of four growth studies in the U.S.A. *Annals of Human Biology, 3*, 529–42.

Thoden, C. J., Jarvenpaa, A. L., & Michelsson, K. (1985). Sound spectrographic cry analysis of pain cry in prematures. In B. M. Lester and C. F. Z. Boukydis, (Eds.), *Infant crying: Theoretical and research perspectives*. New York: Plenum.

Thoman, E. B. (1978). Individuality in the interaction process. In E. B. Thoman & S. Trotter, (Eds.), *Social responsiveness of infants*. Skillman, N.J.: Johnson & Johnson.

Thoman, E. B., Korner, A. F., & Beason-Williams, L. (1977). Modification of responsiveness to maternal vocalization in the neonate. *Child Development, 48*, 563–69.

Thomas, A., & Chess, S. (1977). *Temperament and development*. New York: Brunner/Mazel.

Thomas, A., Chess, S., & Birch, H. G. (1963). *Behavioral individuality in early childhood*. New York: New York University Press.

Thomas, A., Chess, S., & Birch, H. G. (1968). *Temperament and behavior disorders in children*. New York: New York University Press.

Thomas, W. B. (1980). Parental and community involvement: RX for better school discipline. *Phi Delta Kappan, 62*, 203–4.

Thompson, J. R., & Chapman, R. S. (1977). Who is "Daddy" revisited: The status of two-year-olds' overextended words in use and comprehension. *Journal of Child Language, 4*, 359–79.

Thompson, S. K. (1975). Gender labels and early sex-role development. *Child Development, 46*, 339–47.

Thurstone, L. L. (1938). *Primary mental abilities*. Chicago: University of Chicago Press.

Tietjen, A. M. (1980). Integrating formal and informal support systems: The Swedish experience. In J. Garbarino & S. H. Stocking, (Eds.), *Protecting children from abuse and neglect*. San Francisco: Jossey-Bass.

Tishler, C. L. (1983). Making life meaningful for youth: Preventing suicide. In L. E. Arnold, (Ed.), *Preventing adolescent alienation*. Lexington, Mass.: Lexington Books.

Tishler, C. L., McKendry, P. C., & Morgan, K. C. (1981). Adolescent suicide attempts: Some significant factors. *Suicide and Life Threatening Behavior, 2,* 92.

Torrey, E. F. (1983). *Surviving schizophrenia: A family manual.* New York: Harper & Row.

Touwen, B. (1976). *Neurological development in infancy.* London: Spastics International Medical Publishers.

Tower, R., Singer, D., Singer, J., & Biggs, A. (1979). Differential effects of television programming on preschoolers' cognition, imagination, and social play. *American Journal of Orthopsychiatry, 49*(2), 265–81.

Trabasso, T. (1975). Representation, memory, and reasoning: How do we make transitive inferences? In A. D. Pick, (Ed.), *Minnesota symposium on child psychology* (Vol. 9). Minneapolis: University of Minnesota Press.

Travers, J. R., & Light, J. (Eds.). (1982). *Learning from experience: Evaluating early childhood demonstration programs.* Washington, D.C.: National Academy Press.

Troll, L. E. (1971). The family of later life: A decade review. *Journal of Marriage and the Family, 33,* 263–90.

Troll, L. E. (1980). Grandparenting. In L. W. Poon, (Ed.), *Aging in the 1980's: Psychological issues.* Washington, D.C.: American Psychological Association.

Tronick, E. Z., & Gianino, A. (1986). Interactive mismatch and repair: Challenges to the coping infant. *Zero to Three, 6*(3), 1–6.

Turnbull, A. P., Strickland, B., & Hammer, S. E. (1978). The individualized education program. Pt. 2, Translating law into practice. *Journal of Learning Disabilities, 11,* 18–23.

Turner, E. K. (1956). The syndrome in the infant resulting from maternal emotional tension during pregnancy. *Medical Journal of Australia, 1,* 221–22.

Turner, J. (1980). *Made for life: Coping, competence, and cognition.* New York: Methuen.

Tyler, T. J. (1974). *A primer of psychobiology: Brain and behavior.* San Francisco: Freeman.

Tyron, R. C. (1942). Individual differences. In F. A. Moss, (Ed.), *Comparative psychology.* Englewood Cliffs, N.J.: Prentice-Hall.

Ungerer, J., Brody, L. R., & Zelazo, P. R. (1978). Long-term memory for speech in 2 to 4-week-old infants. *Infant Behavior and Development, 1,* 127–40.

Upton, A. C. (1981). Health impact of the Three Mile Island accident. In T. H. Moss & D. L. Sills, (Eds.), *The Three Mile Island nuclear accident: Lessons and implications.* New York: New York Academy of Sciences.

U.S. Bureau of the Census. (1981a). *Statistical abstract of the United States 1981.* Washington, D.C.: U.S. Government Printing Office.

U.S. Bureau of the Census (1981b). *Marital status and living arrangements* (Series P-20, Nos. 212 [1961] and 365 [1981]). Washington, D.C.: U.S. Government Printing Office.

U.S. Bureau of the Census (1983, March). Current Population Reports (Series P-60, No. 137). *Money income of households, families, and persons in the United States: 1981.* Washington, D.C.: U.S. Government Printing Office.

U.S. Bureau of the Census. (1983). School enrollment—Social and economic characteristics of students: October 1983. *Current Population Reports,* Series P-20, No. 394.

U.S. Bureau of the Census. (1986). Marital status and living arrangements: March 1985. *Current Population Reports.*

U.S. Congress, Committee on Ways and Means. (1985). *Children in poverty,* by the Congressional Research Service. Washington, D.C.: U.S. Government Printing Office.

U.S. Department of Agriculture. (1982). *Costs of raising children.* Washington, D.C.: U.S. Government Printing Office.

U.S. Department of Agriculture, Science and Education Administration. (1980, September). *Food and nutrient intake of individuals in one day in the U.S.: 1977–1978.* Nationwide Food Consumption Survey, USDA, Preliminary Report No. 2.

U.S. Department of Commerce, Bureau of the Census. (1982). Current Population Reports. Special Studies Series P-23, No. 129: *Child care arrangements of working mothers.* Washington, D.C.: U.S. Government Printing Office.

U.S. Department of Health and Human Services. (1983). *Monthly Vital Statistics Report: Final Natality Statistics, 29*(1), Suppl.

U.S. Department of Health, Education, and Welfare. (1979). *Smoking and health: A report of the surgeon general.* Washington, D.C.: Public Health Service.

U.S. Department of Justice. (1985). *Uniform Crime Reports for the United States.* Washington, D.C.: U.S. Government Printing Office.

U.S. Department of Labor, Bureau of Labor Statistics. (1984, December). *Monthly Labor Review*.

U.S. Department of Labor, Bureau of Labor Statistics. (1986, February). Wives' and mothers' labor force activity includes those with infants. *Monthly Labor Review*.

U.S. Vital Statistics: 1949–1973. Vol. II, *Mortality*. (1974). Washington, D.C.: National Center for Health Statistics.

Vaillant, G. E. (1977). *Adaptation to life*. Boston: Little, Brown.

Valentine, J., & Zigler, E. (1983). Head Start: A case study in the development of social policy for children and families. In E. Zigler, S. L. Kagan, & E. Klugman, (Eds.), *Children, families, and government: Perspectives on American social policy*. New York: Cambridge University Press.

Vandenberg, B. (1980). Play, problem-solving, and creativity. In K. H. Rubin, (Ed.), *Children's play*. San Francisco: Jossey-Bass.

Vandenberg, S. G. (1971). What do we know today about the inheritance of intelligence and how do we know it? In R. Cancro, (Ed.), *Intelligence: Genetic and environmental influences*. New York: Grune & Stratton.

Vasta, R. (1979). *Studying children: An introduction to research methods*. San Francisco: Freeman.

Vaughn, B. E., Gove, F. L., & Egeland, B. (1980). The relationship between out-of-home care and the quality of infant-mother attachment in an economically disadvantaged population. *Child Development, 51*(4), 1203–14.

Volterra, V., & Taeschner, T. (1978). The acquisition and development of language by bilingual children. *Journal of Child Language, 5*, 311–26.

Vygotzky, L. (1962). *Thought and language*. Cambridge, Mass.: MIT Press. (Original work published in 1934.)

Walker, L. (1984). Sex differences in the development of moral reasoning: A critical review of the literature. *Child Development, 55*(3), 677–91.

Walker, R. N. (1962). Body build and behavior in young children. Pt. 1, Body build and nursery school teachers' rating. *Monograph of the Society for Research in Child Development, 27*(84) (entire No. 84).

Wallerstein, J. S., & Kelly, J. B. (1979). Children and divorce: A review. *Social Work, 24*, 468–75.

Wallerstein, J. S., & Kelly, J. B. (1980). *Surviving the breakup*. New York: Basic Books.

Wallis, D. (1983, September 26). The stormy legacy of Baby Doe. *Time*, p. 58.

Walton, R. E. (1979, July–August). Work innovations in the United States. *Harvard Business Review*, p. 91.

Ward, E. H. (1976). CDA: Credentialing for day care. *Voice for Children, 9*(5), 15.

Warner, J. S., & Wooten, B. R. (1979). Human infant color vision and color perception. *Infant Behavior and Development, 2*, 241–74.

Washburn, S. L., & Hamburg, D. (1965). The study of primate behavior. In I. DeVore, (Ed.), *Primate behavior: Field studies of monkeys and apes*. New York: Holt, Rinehart and Winston.

Waters, E., Vaughn, B. E., & Egeland, B. (1980). Individual differences in infant-mother attachment relationships at age one: Antecedents in neonatal behavior in an urban, economically disadvantaged sample. *Child Development, 51*, 208–16.

Waters, E., Wippman, J., & Sroufe, L. A. (1979). Attachment, positive affect and competence in the peer group: Two studies in construct validation. *Child Development, 50*(3), 821–29.

Watson, J. B. (1926). What the nursery has to say about instincts. In C. Murcheson, (Ed.), *Psychologies of 1925*. Worcester, Mass.: Clark University Press.

Watson, J. B. (1928). *The psychological care of infant and child*. New York: Norton.

Watson, J. S., & Ramey, C. T. (1972). Reactions to contingent stimulation in early infancy. *Merrill-Palmer Quarterly, 18*, 219–27.

Watson, K. (1982). A bold new model for foster care. *Public Welfare, 40*(2), 15.

Watts, N. F. (1978). Patterns of childhood social development in adult schizophrenics. *Archives of General Psychiatry, 35*, 160–65.

Watts, N. F., Stolorow, R. D., Lubensky, A. W., & McClelland, D. C. (1970). School adjustment and behavior of children hospitalized for schizophrenia. *American Journal of Orthopsychiatry, 40*, 637–57.

Webster, R. L., Steinhardt, M. H., & Senter, M. G. (1972). Changes in infants' vocalizations as a function of differential accoustic stimulation. *Developmental Psychology, 7*(1), 39.

Wechsler, D. (1958). *The measurement and appraisal of adult intelligence* (4th ed.). Baltimore, Md.: Williams & Williams.

Wechsler, D. (1974). *Manual for the Wechsler Intelli-*

gence Test for Children, revised. New York: Psychological Corp.

Weikart, D. P. (1982). Preschool education for disadvantaged children. In J. R. Travers & R. J. Light, (Eds.), *Learning from experience: Evaluating early childhood demonstration programs.* Washington, D.C.: National Academy Press.

Weiner, I. B. (1980). Psychopathology in adolescence. In J. Adelson, (Ed.), *Handbook of adolescent psychology.* New York: Wiley.

Weinraub, M., Brooks, J., & Lewis, M. (1977). The social network: A reconsideration of the concept of attachment. *Human Development, 20,* 31–47.

Weir, R. H. (1966). Some questions on the child's learning of phonology. In F. Smith & G. Miller, (Eds.), *The genesis of language: A psycholinguistic approach.* Cambridge, Mass.: MIT Press.

Weisbrod, J. A., Casale, S., & Faber, S. (1981). *Family court disposition study.* Published by the Vera Institute for Justice, 377 Broadway, New York, N.Y.

Weisenfeld, A. R., & Klorman, R. C. (1978). The mother's psychological reactions to contrasting affective expressions by her own and unfamiliar infants. *Developmental Psychology, 14,* 294–304.

Weisner, T. S. (1982). As we choose: Family life styles, social class, and compliances. In J. G. Kennedy & R. Edgerton, (Eds.), *Culture and ecology: Eclectic perspectives.* A special publication of the American Anthropological Association, No. 15.

Weiss, C. H. (1978). Improving the linkage between social research and public policy. In L. E. Lynn, Jr., (Ed.), *Knowledge and policy: The uncertain connection.* Washington, D.C.: The National Research Council.

Weiss, H. (1983). *Programs to strengthen families: A resource guide.* New Haven, Conn.: Bush Center in Child Development and Social Policy, Yale University.

Weiss, R. (1979). Growing up a little faster: The experience of growing up in a single-parent household. *Journal of Social Issues, 35,* 97–110.

Weissman, M. M. (1974). The epidemiology of suicide attempts, 1960–71. *Archives of General Psychology, 30,* 737–39.

Weisz, J. R. (1978). Transcontextual validity in developmental research. *Child Development, 49,* 1–12.

Weitzman, L. J. (1981a). *The marriage contract.* New York: Free Press.

Weitzman, L. J. (1981b). The economics of divorce: Social and economic consequences of property, alimony, and child support awards. *UCLA Law Review, 28,* 1181–1268.

Wellman, H. M., & Lempers, J. D. (1977). The naturalistic communicative capabilities of two-year-olds. *Child Development, 48,* 1052–57.

Werner, H. (1948). *Comparative psychology of mental development.* New York: International Universities Press.

Wertmann, M. W. (1980). Medical constraints to optimal development of the preterm infant. In S. L. Friedman, & M. Sigman, (Eds.), *Preterm birth and psychological development.* New York: Academic Press.

Wessel, M. A. (1981, Fall). A local perspective—Corporal punishment: What is the policy in your school system? *The Networker, 3*(1). (Available from the Bush Center in Child Development and Social Policy, Department of Psychology, Yale University, New Haven, Conn.)

Whalen, C., & Henker, B. (1976). Psychostimulants and children: A review and analysis. *Psychological Bulletin, 83,* 1113–30.

Whitbread, J. (1982, February). Who's taking care of the children? *Family Circle,* p. 88.

White, B. L. (1967). An experimental approach to the effects of environment on early human behavior. In J. P. Hill, (Ed.), *Minnesota symposium on child psychology* (Vol. 1). Minneapolis: University of Minnesota Press.

White, B. L., & Held, R. (1966). Plasticity of sensorimotor development in human infants. In J. Rosenblith & W. Allinsmith, (Eds.), *The causes of behavior: Readings in child development and educational psychology.* Boston: Allyn & Bacon.

White, R. W. (1959). Motivation reconsidered: The concept of competence. *Psychological Review, 66,* 297–333.

White, S. H. (1965). Evidence for a hierarchical arrangement of learning processes. In L. P. Lewis & C. C. Spiker, (Eds.), *Advances in child development and behavior* (Vol. 2). New York: Academic Press.

White, S. H. (1970). Some general outlines of the matrix of developmental change between five and seven years. *Bulletin of the Orton Society, 20,* 41–57.

White, S. H. (1982). The idea of development in developmental psychology. In R. M. Lerner, (Ed.), *Developmental psychology: Historical and philosophical perspectives.* Hillsdale, N.J.: Erlbaum.

Whiting, B. B., & Whiting, J. W. M. (1975). *Children of six cultures: A psycho-cultural analysis.* Cambridge, Mass.: Harvard University Press.

Whittaker, J. K., & Garbarino, J. (1983). *Social support networks: Informal helping in the human services.* New York: Aldine.

Whol, T. (1963). Correlation of anxiety and hostility with adrenocortical function. *Journal of the American Medical Association, 183,* 113–14.

Wickstrom, R. L. (1977). *Fundamental motor patterns* (2d ed.). Philadelphia: Lea & Febiger.

Widdowson, Z. M. (1951). Mental contentment and physical growth. *Lancet, 1,* 1316–18.

Williams, L. (1985, January 16). Schools encourage active parent role. *New York Times,* pp. C1, C10.

Wilson, J. G., & Fraser, F. C. (Eds.). (1977). *Handbook of teratology.* New York: Plenum.

Winick, M. (1974). Childhood obesity. *Nutrition Today, 9,* 6–12.

Winick, M. (1975). *Childhood obesity.* New York: Wiley.

Winick, M., Brasel, J. A., & Rosso, P. (1972). Nutrition and cell growth. In M. Winick, (Ed.), *Nutrition and development.* New York: Wiley.

Winn, M. (1983). *Children without childhood.* New York: Plenum.

Wirtenberg, J., Murez, R., & Alepektor, R. A. (1980). *Characters in textbooks: A review of the literature.* Washington, D.C.: U.S. Commission on Civil Rights.

Woerner, M. G., Pollack, M., Rogalski, C., Pollack, Y., & Klein, D. F. (1972). A comparison of the school records of personality disorders, schizophrenics, and their sibs. In M. Roff, L. Robbin, & M. Pollack, (Eds.), *Life history research in psychopathology* (Vol. 2). Minneapolis: University of Minnesota Press.

Wohlwill, J. F. (1970). The place of structured experience in early cognitive development. *Interchange, 1,* 13–27.

Wolff, P. H. (1963). Observations on the early development of smiling. In B. M. Foss, (Ed.), *Determinants of infant behavior* (Vol. 2). New York: Wiley.

Wolff, P. H. (1969). The natural history of crying and other vocalizations in early infancy. In B. Foss, (Ed.), *Determinants of infant behavior* (Vol. 4). London: Methuen.

Wolff, P. H. (1971). Mother-infant relations at birth. In J. G. Howels, (Ed.), *Modern perspectives in international child psychiatry.* New York: Brunner/Mazel.

Wolfson, R. J., Aghamohamadi, A. M., & Berman, S. E. (1980). Disorders of the hearing. In S. Gabel & M. T. Erickson, (Eds.), *Child development and developmental disabilities.* Boston: Little, Brown.

Wylie, R. (1979). *The self-concept.* Vol. 2, *Theory and research on selected topics.* Lincoln: University of Nebraska Press.

Yankelovich, D. (1974). *The new morality: A profile of American youth in the 70's.* New York: McGraw-Hill.

Yarrow, L. J. (1964). Separation from parents during early childhood. In M. L. Hoffman & L. W. Hoffman, (Eds.), *Review of child development research.* New York: Russell Sage.

Yarrow, L. J. (1979). Historical perspectives and future directions in infant development. In J. Osofsky, (Ed.), *Handbook of infant development.* New York: Wiley.

Yarrow, L. J., Rubenstein, J. L., & Pedersen, F. A. (1975). *Infant and environment.* New York: Halsted Press.

Yogman, M., Dixon, S., Tronick, E., Als, H., & Brazelton, T. B. (1977). *The goals and structure of face-to-face interaction between infants and fathers.* Paper presented at the biennial meeting of the Society for Research in Child Development, New Orleans.

Young, J. G., & Cohen, D. J. (1979). The molecular biology of development. In J. D. Noshpitz, (Ed.), *Basic handbook of child psychiatry.* New York: Basic Books.

Young, K. T., & Zigler, E. (1986). Infant and toddler day care: Regulations and policy implications. *American Journal of Orthopsychiatry, 56,* 43–55.

Youniss, J. (1980). *Parents and peers in social development: A Sullivan-Piaget perspective.* Chicago: University of Chicago Press.

Youniss, J., & Volpe, J. (1978). A relational analysis of children's friendships. In W. Damon, (Ed.), *Social cognition.* San Francisco: Jossey-Bass.

Zahn-Waxler, C., Cummings, R. J., & Radke-Yarrow, M. (1984). Young offspring in depressed parents: A population at risk for affective problems. In D. Cicchetti & K. Schneider-Rosen, (Eds.), *New directions for child development: Developmental approaches to childhood depression.* San Francisco: Jossey-Bass.

Zahn-Waxler, C. Z., Radke-Yarrow, M. R., & King, R. A. (1979). Childrearing and children's prosocial initiations toward victims of distress. *Child Development, 50,* 319–30.

Zajonc, R. B. (1983). Validating the confluence model. *Psychological Bulletin, 93,* 457–80.

Zajonc, R. B., & Bargh, J. (1980, July). Birth order, family size, and decline of SAT scores. *American Psychologist, 35*(7), 662–68.

Zelazo, P. R., Zelazo, N. A., & Kolb, S. (1972). "Walking" in the newborn. *Science, 176,* 314–15.

Zelnik, M., & Kantner, J. F. (1978). First pregnancies to women aged 15–19: 1971 and 1976. *Family Planning Perspectives, 10,* 11–20.

Zelnik, M., & Kantner, J. F. (1978). Sexual activity, contraceptive use, and pregnancy among metropolitan area teenagers: 1971–1979. *Family Planning Perspectives, 12,* 230–37.

Zeskind, P. S., & Ramey, C. T. (1978). Fetal malnutrition: An experimental study of its consequences on development in two caregiving environments. *Child Development, 49,* 1155–62.

Zigler, E. (1963). Metatheoretical issues in developmental psychology. In M. Marx, (Ed.), *Theories in contemporary psychology.* New York: Macmillan.

Zigler, E. (1973). Project Head Start: Success of failure? *Learning, 1,* 43–47.

Zigler, E. (1978). Controlling child abuse in America: An effort doomed to failure. In R. Bourne & E. Newberger, (Eds.), *Critical perspectives on child abuse.* Lexington, Mass.: Heath.

Zigler, E. (1980). Controlling child abuse: Do we have the knowledge and/or the will? In G. Gerbner, C. J. Ross, & E. Zigler, (Eds.), *Child abuse: An agenda for action.* New York: Oxford University Press.

Zigler, E. (1983, June). School-age day care. Testimony for Senate Children's Caucus Policy Forum. "Latchkey children: Risks and alternatives." *Congressional Record, 129.*

Zigler, E., Abelson, W., & Seitz, V. (1973). Motivational factors in the performance of economically disadvantaged children on the Peabody Picture Vocabulary Test. *Child Development, 44,* 294–303.

Zigler, E., & Balla, D. (Eds.). (1982). *Mental retardation: The developmental-difference controversy.* Hillsdale, N.J.: Erlbaum.

Zigler, E., & Berman, W. (1983). Discerning the future of early childhood intervention. *American Psychologist, 38,* 894–906.

Zigler, E., & Butterfield, E. C. (1968). Motivational aspects of changes in IQ test performance of culturally deprived nursery school children. *Child Development, 39,* 1–14.

Zigler, E., & Cascione, R. (1980). On being a par-

ent. In *Parenthood in a changing society.* Champaign, Ill.: ERIC Clearinghouse on Elementary and Early Childhood Education, University of Illinois.

Zigler, E., & Cascione, R. (1984). Mental retardation: An overview. In E. S. Gollin, (Ed.), *Malformations of development: Biological and psychological sources and consequences.* New York: Academic Press.

Zigler, E., & Farber, E. (1985). Commonalities between the intellectual extremes: Giftedness and mental retardation. In F. Horowitz & M. O'Brien, (Eds.), *The gifted and talented: Developmental perspectives.* Washington, D.C.: American Psychological Association.

Zigler, E., & Finn, M. (1981). From problem to solution: Changing public policy as it affects children and families. *Young Children, 36,* 31–36.

Zigler, E., & Finn, M. (1982). A vision of childcare in the 1980s. In L. A. Bond & J. M. Joffe, (Eds.), *Facilitating infant and early child development.* Hanover, N.H.: University Press of New England.

Zigler, E., & Finn, M. (1984). Applied developmental psychology. In M. Lamb & M. Bornstein, (Eds.), *Developmental psychology: An advanced textbook.* Hillsdale, N.J.: Erlbaum.

Zigler, E., & Hodapp, R. M. (1986). Mental retardation. In J. O. Cavenar, (Ed.), *Psychiatry.* Philadelphia: Lippincott.

Zigler, E., & Hunsinger, S. (1977). Supreme Court on spanking: Upholding discipline or abuse? *Young Children, 32,* 14–15.

Zigler, E., Kagan, S. L., & Klugman, E. (Eds.). (1983). *Children, families and government: Perspectives on American social policy.* New York: Cambridge University Press.

Zigler, E., Lamb, M., & Child, I. (1982). *Socialization and personality development* (2d ed.). New York: Oxford University Press.

Zigler, E. & Lang, M. E. (1985, September–October). The emergence of "superbaby": A good thing? *Pediatric Nursing, 11*(5), 337–41.

Zigler, E., Levine, J., & Gould, L. (1967). Cognitive challenge as a factor in children's humor appreciation. *Journal of Personality and Social Psychology, 6,* 332–36.

Zigler, E., & Muenchow, S. (1979). Mainstreaming: The proof is in the implementation. *American Psychologist, 34*(10), 993–96.

Zigler, E., & Muenchow, S. (1983). Infant day care versus infant care leaves: A policy vacuum. *American Psychologist, 38,* 91–94.

Zigler, E., & Trickett, P. E. (1978). IQ, social competence, and evaluation of early childhood intervention programs. *American Psychologist, 33,* 789–98.

Zigler, E., & Turner, P. (1982). Parents and day care workers: A failed partnership? In E. Zigler & E. Gordon, (Eds.), *Day care: Scientific and social policy issues.* Boston: Auburn House.

Zigler, E., & Weiss, H. (1985). Family support systems: An ecological approach to child development. In N. Rapoport, (Ed.), *Children, youth, and families: The action-research relationship.* New York: Cambridge University Press.

Zill, N. (1983). *Happy, healthy, and insecure.* New York: Doubleday.

Zill, N., Sigal, H., & Brim, O. G., Jr. (1983). Development of childhood social indicators. In E. Zigler, S. L. Kagan, & E. Klugman, (Eds.), *Children, families, and government: Perspectives on American social policy.* New York: Cambridge University Press.

Zimmerman, B. J., & Lanaro, P. (1974). Acquiring and retaining conservation of length through modeling and reversibility cues. *Merrill-Palmer Quarterly, 20,* 145–61.

Zubin, J., & Spring, B. (1977). Vulnerability—A new view of schizophrenia. *Journal of Abnormal Psychology, 86,* 103–26.

Zuckerman, D., Singer, D. G., & Singer, J. L. (1980). Television viewing, children's reading and related school behavior. *Journal of Communications, 30,* 166–74.

PHOTO CREDITS

Unit I Opener, Michael Hardy/Woodfin Camp; **Introduction Chapter Opener** page 2, Mary Stuart Lang; page 4 (top left), Randy Matusow/Monkmeyer; (top right), Jean Claude Lejeune/Stock, Boston; (bottom), Jeffrey Myers/Stock, Boston; page 7 (both), Bettmann Archive; page 9, American Museum of Natural History; page 10, Bettmann Archive; page 16, Photo Researchers; page 19, Ted Streshinsky/Time Magazine; page 23, Bill Anderson/Monkmeyer; page 26, Michal Heron/Woodfin Camp; page 29, Nina Leen, Life Magazine © Time, Inc.

Chapter 1 Opener page 45, Jean Claude Lejeune/ Stock, Boston; page 49, Culver Pictures; page 51, Bettmann Archive; page 52, Eric Kroll/Taurus; page 57, Georg Gerster/Photo Researchers; page 64, Donald Dietz/Stock, Boston; page 69, Renee Lynn/ Photo Researchers; page 71, James R. Holland/Stock, Boston; page 79, Richard Howard/Black Star.

Unit II Opener page 84, Martin M. Rotker/ Taurus; **Chapter 2 Opener** page 86, Alan Carey/ The Image Works; page 102, Courtesy Dr. M. Lita Alonso, New York Hospital, Cornell Medical Center; page 103 and page 104, Courtesy Dr. John Money; page 106, Meri Houtchens-Kitchens/Picture Cube; page 107 (both), Omikron/Photo Researchers; page 117, Ralph Barrera/TexaStock.

Chapter 3 Opener page 126, © Ray Ellis 1986; pages 131, 133, Lennart Nilsson photographs from *A Child Is Born*, Albert Bonniers Forlag AB, Stockholm, Delacorte Press, New York; page 135, Mimi Forsyth/ Monkmeyer; page 138, Döring/Black Star; page 140, From P. Streissguth et. al., Teratogenic effects of alcohol in humans and laboratory animals, *Science,* 209, 1980, 353–61; page 146, Rick Smolan/Stock, Boston; page 151, Ed Lettau/Photo Researchers; page 153, David Powers/Stock, Boston; page 158, Ed Lettau/ Photo Researchers; page 163, Katrina Thomas/Photo Researchers.

Unit III Opener page 166, © Joel Gordon/1978; **Chapter 4 Opener** page 168, Larry Kolvoord/ TexaStock; page 171, Mimi Forsyth/Monkmeyer;

page 180 (top), Ed Lettau/Photo Researchers; (bottom left), © Carol Palmer; (bottom right), Ellis Herwig/ Stock, Boston; page 181 (top), © Joel Gordon 1975; (middle), James R. Holland/Stock, Boston; (bottom), © Ray Ellis 1986; page 185, Alan Carey/The Image Works; page 199, © Susan Lapides 1981; page 212, Mary Stuart Lang; page 214 (left), © Ray Ellis 1986; (right), Erika Stone/Photo Researchers.

Chapter 5 Opener page 217, Martha Stewart/ Picture Cube; page 221, Elizabeth Crews/Stock, Boston; page 225 (left), Randy Matusow/Monkmeyer; (right), Frostie/Woodfin Camp; page 235 (both, top), George Zimbel/Monkmeyer; (all three, bottom), Hazel Hankin/Stock, Boston; page 236, B. Griffith/ Picture Cube; page 247, Mimi Forsyth/Monkmeyer; page 253, Peter Vandermark/Stock, Boston; page 257, Martha Stewart/Picture Cube.

Chapter 6 Opener page 262, David Witbeck/ Picture Cube; page 266, Doug Wilson/Black Star; page 267, Elizabeth Crews/Stock, Boston; page 276, Hufnagle/Monkmeyer; page 281, David A. Krathwohl/Stock, Boston; page 283, Phiz Mezey/Taurus; page 290, University of Wisconsin Primate Laboratory, Madison, Wisconsin; page 295, © Susan Lapides 1982; page 300, Phiz Mezey/Taurus; page 302, Richard Frieman/Photo Researchers.

Unit IV Opener page 316, Bob Daemmrich/ TexaStock; **Chapter 7 Opener** page 318, Jean-Marie Simon/Taurus; page 324, Fig. 29 from J. M. Tanner, M. D., *Foetus into Man,* Harvard University Press, 1978; page 330, Elizabeth Crews/Stock, Boston; page 332, © Joel Gordon 1979; page 333, © Susan Lapides 1983; page 335, Courtesy Dr. M. W. de Vries; page 342, James R. Holland/Stock, Boston; page 345, Larry Kolvoord/TexaStock.

Chapter 8 Opener page 349, Michael Sullivan/ TexaStock; page 353 (top), © Ray Ellis 1986; page 353 (bottom), Ruth Silverman/Stock, Boston; page 359, Mimi Forsyth/Monkmeyer; page 363, Jerry Howard/ Positive Images; page 373, Michael Hayman/Stock, Boston; page 377, Peter Vandermark/Stock, Boston;

page 381, Michael Sullivan/TexaStock; page 383, Family Communications, Inc.; page 388, Alan Carey/The Image Works.

Color Insert page I, Carol Palmer; page II (left) David Kennedy/TexaStock; (top right) Louis Fernandez/Black Star; (bottom right) Jerry Howard/Positive Images; page III (left top) D. W. Fawcett, D. Philips/Science Source/Photo Researchers; (next) Biophoto Associates/Science Source/Photo Researchers; (next) Petit Format/Nestle/Science Source/Photo Researchers; (bottom left) Petit Format/Nestle/Science Source/Photo Researchers; (right) Ray Ellis/Photo Researchers; page IV (clockwise from top left) Bob Krist/Black Star Bill Binzen/Photo Researchers; Elizabeth Crews; Ellis Herwig/Picture Cube; Larry Kovoord/TexaStock; Meyer Rangell/The Image Works; page V (clockwise from top) Michal Heron/Woodfin Camp; Michael Sullivan/TexaStock; Julie O'Neil/Picture Cube; Alan Carey/The Image Works; Ellis Herwig/Picture Cube; page VI (left) David Woo/Stock, Boston; (top right) Robert Knowles/Black Star; (bottom right) Alan Carey/The Image Works; page VII (top left) Dede Hatch/Picture Cube; (top right) Ken Rogers/Black Star; (bottom left) Michal Heron/Woodfin Camp; (bottom right) Andrew Brilliant; page VIII (top) Janet Owen; (bottom) Dave Schaefer/Picture Cube.

Chapter 9 Opener page 393, Christopher Morrow/Stock, Boston; page 395, Suzanne Szasz/Photo Researchers; page 398, Jerry Howard/Positive Images; page 399, Alan Carey/The Image Works; page 400, William Strode/Woodfin Camp; page 403, © Carol Palmer; page 407, James R. Holland/Stock, Boston; page 410, Alan Carey/The Image Works; page 415, David Strickler/Monkmeyer; page 417, Dave Schaefer/Picture Cube; page 420 (top), Janice Fullman/Picture Cube; (bottom), George Malave/Stock, Boston; page 423, Susie Fitzhugh/Stock, Boston; page 427, © Carol Palmer; page 428 (top), Alan Carey/The Image Works; (bottom), Lew Merrim/Monkmeyer; page 433, Robert Kalman/The Image Works; page 439, Carol Palmer/Picture Cube.

Unit V Opener page 450, © Joel Gordon 1982; **Chapter 10 Opener** page 452, Alan Carey/The Image Works; page 455, © Walter S. Silver 1985; page 463, Robert Kalman/The Image Works; page 464, Jeffrey W. Myers/Stock, Boston; page 466, Miro Vintoniv/Stock, Boston; page 469, Polly Brown/Picture Cube; page 473, Elizabeth Crews/Stock, Boston; page 474 and page 475, Alan Carey/The Image Works.

Chapter 11 Opener page 480, Laimute E. Druskis/Taurus; page 482, Mimi Forsyth/Monkmeyer;

page 493, Chuck O'Rear/Woodfin Camp; page 496, © Susan Lapides 1981; page 497, Frank Siteman/Stock, Boston; page 507, John Eastcott/Yva Momatiuk/The Image Works; page 511, Avis Kalman/The Image Works; page 515, © Joel Gordon 1985; page 520, Bob Daemmrich/TexaStock.

Chapter 12 Opener page 525, Jean-Claude Lejeune/Stock, Boston; page 530, © Joel Gordon 1983; page 534, Paolo Koch/Photo Researchers; page 541, Paul Conklin/Monkmeyer; page 544, Ed Lettau/Photo Researchers; page 546, © Susan Lapides 1984; page 547, Elizabeth Hamlin/Stock, Boston; page 551, © Walter S. Silver 1985; page 553, Ginger Chih/Peter Arnold; page 558, Michael Hayman/Black Star; page 563, Margaret Thompson/Picture Cube.

Unit VI Opener page 570, David E. Kennedy/TexaStock; **Chapter 13 Opener** page 572, Ellis Herwig/Stock, Boston; page 574, Bettmann Archive; page 578, © 1965. CIBA Pharmaceutical Company, a division of CIBA-GEIGY. Reproduced with permission from Clinical Symposia—by Frank H. Netter, MD. All rights reserved; page 579, Frank Siteman/Taurus; page 588, Courtesy Norcliff Thayer Inc.; page 591, © Carol Palmer; page 594, Paul Conklin.

Chapter 14 Opener page 599, Jean-Claude Lejeune/Stock, Boston; page 605, Olive R. Pierce/Black Star; page 609 (top), Sybil Shelton/Peter Arnold; page 609 (bottom), Andrew Brilliant; page 612, Arthur S. Grace/Stock, Boston; page 616, Culver Pictures, Inc.; page 625, Rick Friedman/Picture Cube.

Chapter 15 Opener page 632, Frank Siteman/Taurus; page 636, Peter Buckley/Photo Researchers; page 637, Richard Wood/Taurus; page 640, Paul Conklin; page 643, Marilyn Sanders/Peter Arnold; page 649, Jean-Claude Lejeune/Stock, Boston; page 651, Arthur Tress/Photo Researchers; page 658, Harriet Gans/The Image Works; page 662, Paul Conklin/Monkmeyer.

Conclusion Opener page 675, George Bellerose/Stock, Boston; page 679 (top), Patricia Agre/Photo Researchers; page 679 (bottom), Hazel Hankin/Stock, Boston; page 681 (top left), Jeffrey Myers/Stock, Boston; page 681 (top right), The Photo Works/Photo Researchers; page 681 (bottom left), Bob Daemmrich/TexaStock; page 681 (bottom right), J. D. Sloan/Picture Cube; page 682, Michael Hayman/Stock, Boston; page 684, Frank Siteman/Stock, Boston; page 689 (top left), Jerry Howard/Postive Images; (top right), Alan Carey/The Image Works; (bottom), Frank Siteman/Taurus; page 694 (top), Janice Fullman/Picture Cube; (bottom), David E. Kennedy/TexaStock; page 697, Linda Ferrer/Woodfin Camp.

NAME INDEX

SUBJECT INDEX